OXFORD MONOGRAPHS ON MUSIC

Roman Monody, Cantata, and Opera

Volume I

Bernini's bust of Cardinal Montalto, *c*.1623. Kunsthalle, Hamburg. From Irving Lavin, 'Bernini's Bust of Cardinal Montalto', *The Burlington Magazine*, 127 (1985), 35

Roman Monody, Cantata, and Opera from the Circles around Cardinal Montalto

Volume I

JOHN WALTER HILL

CLARENDON PRESS · OXFORD

1997

Oxford University Press, Great Clarendon Street, Oxford OX2 6DP

Oxford New York

Athens Auckland Bangkok Bogota Bombay
Buenos Aires Calcutta Cape Town Dar es Salaam
Delhi Florence Hong Kong Istanbul Karachi
Kuala Lumpur Madras Madrid Melbourne
Mexico City Nairobi Paris Singapore
Taipei Tokyo Toronto Warsaw

and associated companies in
Berlin Ibadan

Oxford is a trade mark of Oxford University Press

Published in the United States
by Oxford University Press Inc., New York

© John Walter Hill 1997

This publication has been supported by a subvention from the American Musicological Society

British Library Cataloguing in Publication Data
Data available

Library of Congress Cataloging-in-Publication Data
Hill, John Walter, 1942–
Roman monody, cantata, and opera from the circles around Cardinal
Montalto / John Walter Hill.
p. cm. — (Oxford monographs on music)
Includes bibliographical references and indexes.
1. Vocal music—Italy—Rome—17th century—History and criticism.
2. Vocal music—Italy—Rome—17th century. 3. Montalto, Cardinal,
1571–1623. I. Title. II. Series.
ML1733.8.R6H55   1997   782'.00945'63209032—dc21   97–2394
ISBN 0–19–816613–3

1 3 5 7 9 10 8 6 4 2

Typeset by Graphicraft Typesetters Ltd., Hong Kong
Printed in Great Britain
on acid-free paper by
Bookcraft Ltd., Midsomer Norton, Somerset

For Nino Pirrotta

and in memory of Howard Mayer Brown

PREFACE

'Il non s'impresta'—'Not to be lent' or 'It does not circulate'—is the curious motto written on two of four closely related manuscripts of early seventeenth-century Italian solo songs with basso continuo accompaniment (monody) prepared by 'Francesco Fucci, Romano' for commercial sale. The motto must have been a boast or sales promotion, advertising a repertoire of music that was not in general circulation. Fucci appears to have been correct. Virtually no music in his manuscripts was ever printed, and very little of it was copied into any manuscripts outside of a small group of sources that have remained unexplored until now. This is the reason why the repertoire contained in Fucci's manuscripts, while very important at that time, has remained unknown to modern scholarship. And this is why there are significant lessons to be learnt from these sources about the origins of Baroque vocal music, even though this topic has long been a *locus classicus* for musicology. For many years Fausto Torrefranca had been the only scholar to have commented about 'Il non s'impresta' and any of the manuscripts that carry this motto.

During the darkest period of the last world war, when very little that was printed in Italy found its way to the international market, the prolific and provocative Torrefranca initiated a music journal called *Inedito: Quaderno musicale*, for the second number of which (1944) he wrote an article about an early seventeenth-century music manuscript entitled 'Grilanda musicale di diversi eccel.mi hautori, scritta da Francesco Maria Fucci Romano', which was in his private collection. Torrefranca included a transcription of the anonymous work that he hypothetically named in the title of his article, 'Il lamento di Erminia di Claudio Monteverdi'. Although he ascribed the lament to Monteverdi on shaky stylistic grounds, reference to the article has been preserved in Monteverdi bibliographies, without which it, too, would have been forgotten.

Torrefranca was wrong about the authorship of the lament, as Irving Godt already suspected ('A Monteverdi Source Reappears: The "Grilanda" of F. M. Fucci', 1979), but he was right to link the manuscript to the patronage of Alessandro Peretti (1571–1623), who became known as Cardinal Montalto. It was the obscure name of 'Cavaliere Marotti', that is, Cesare Marotta, that led Torrefranca to his richest source of information about Montalto and his musicians, Alberto Cametti's article 'Chi era l' "Hippolita", cantatrice del cardinal di Montalto', published in 1914, a remarkably detailed documentary study initiated by the seemingly chance discovery of seventeenth-century legal documents relating to Ippolita's challenge to the testament of her late husband, Cesare Marotta. These two articles formed the slender thread of information with which my own curiosity became intertwined when two pieces in the 'Grilanda musicale' concorded with items in an entirely anonymous manuscript of early Italian monody in the library of the University of Pennsylvania (MS Ital. 57), which had resisted all my previous efforts at classification and placement. Subsequent research led to the identification of eight other early Roman monody manuscripts related in content to the 'Grilanda musicale', three of them in the very hand of Francesco Maria Fucci and all of them connected in some way with the circle around Cardinal Montalto. None of these ten monody manuscripts had been described in the fundamental surveys of monody sources, the dissertations by William Porter and Nigel Fortune, and virtually no concordances were found between them and the Florentine sources on which the earliest history of the genre had previously been based.

These ten newly identified sources of early Roman monody, then, form the core of the study that is about to unfold. In trying to explain their contents, we are led into the social, cultural, and political orbit of a remarkable patron, an orbit that connected Rome, Naples, Florence, and Ferrara. In assessing the significance of these manuscripts, we shall discover an unsuspected connection between improvised solo singing in the sixteenth century and the emergence of the Roman chamber cantata, a connection not entirely dependent on the intervening emergence of written monody and recitative styles in Florence. The manuscripts contain fragments of the earliest surviving recitative for a stage work, the first secular Roman opera, and the last stage work by the immortal poet Battista Guarini. And they hold a great deal of music that is beautiful and stirring and worthy of preservation for its own sake. The supporting documentation includes some 112 unpublished letters written by Cardinal Montalto's musicians or about their activities, a large quantity of documents such as payrolls, ecclesiastical benefice records, parish census reports, birth, death, and marriage records, diaries, treatises, orations, prefaces, manuscript and printed collections of poetry, and libretti relating to theatrical productions of several kinds.

Some of these supporting documents have been cited recently in an excellent article by James Chater, 'Musical Patronage in Rome at the Turn of the Seventeenth Century: The Case of Cardinal Montalto', which appeared in print while the present study was being written. I shall mention Chater's study in conjunction with the original source when referring to unpublished documents uncovered in both his research and mine; I cite his study alone for material seen only by him. The major categories of material for the present study not mentioned by Chater include all the musical manuscripts, everything regarding the emergence of monody in Naples and Rome, the treatise on improvised counterpoint by Giovanni Bernardino Nanino, 99 of the 112 letters transcribed in

Appendix A, all the notarial documents from the Archivio di Stato in Rome, the registers of Cardinal Montalto's payment orders (*mandati*) from the Cardelli family archive, the documents in the principal Peretti family inheritance contained within the Sforza-Cesarini family archive, all the material concerning the Peretti family estates and art patronage, the poetry manuscripts and prints relating to the musical repertoire, and nearly all the documents that concern music for *Il pastor fido* and Guarini's last stage work. Chapter 8, which concerns the latter, is adapted from my paper 'Guarini's Last Stage Work'. Chapter 4 is a major expansion of my article 'Training a Singer for *Musica Recitativa* in Early Seventeenth-Century Italy: The Case of Baldassare'.

For permission to reproduce photographs I am grateful to *The Burlington Magazine* (frontispiece and Fig. 1.12), the Archivio fotografico of the Biblioteca Apostolica Vaticana (Fig. 1.1), Princeton University Press (Figs. 1.7, 1.8, 1.10, 1.11), and Vallecchi Editore (Fig. 1.7). It has not proved possible to trace the copyright holders in the case of Figures 1.2, 1.3, 1.4, 1.5, and 1.9.

Many individuals and institutions have extended their assistance to this project. I gratefully acknowledge the support of the National Endowment for the Humanities, the American Council of Learned Societies, the University of Illinois Center for Advanced Study, School of Music, and Research Board, and the Arnold O. Beckman Foundation. I wish to thank the directors and staffs of the libraries and archives identified in the List of Abbreviations for their kind cooperation. Among the many colleagues who have helped me with specific aspects of my research and the preparation of this book, I wish to mention in particular John Baron, Donna Cardamone, Tim Carter, James Chater, Dinko Fabris, Irving Godt, Frederick Hammond, Margaret Murata, Mary Paquette-Abt, and Louise K. Stein. Andrew Kearns, as my Research Assistant, did the initial encoding of the music in Volume II, while my other Research Assistant, Kelley Harness, provided valuable bibliographical updates. Loving thanks go to my wife, Laura Callegari Hill, who helped me correct my transcriptions and translations of Italian and Latin texts and documents. Finally, I wish to acknowledge my teachers and mentors Howard Mayer Brown and Nino Pirrotta, who, over the years, directly and indirectly through the example of their own research and writing, provided me with a vast store of ideas and inspiration. I can aim at no higher goal than to follow in their footsteps.

J. W. H.

CONTENTS

VOLUME I: TEXT

VOLUME II: MUSIC

LIST OF ILLUSTRATIONS

LIST OF TABLES

LIST OF MUSICAL EXAMPLES

LIST OF ABBREVIATIONS

CS:Pnm	Prague, Národní Muzeum, Hudební Odd'lení
E:Mn	Madrid, Biblioteca Nacional
GB:Lbm	London, British Library
GB:Ob	Oxford, Bodleian Library
I:Baf	Bologna, Biblioteca dell'Accademia Filarmonica
I:Bc	Bologna, Civico Museo Bibliografico Musicale
I:Fas	Florence, Archivio di Stato
I:Fc	Florence, Biblioteca del Conservatorio di Musica 'Luigi Cherubini'
I:FEas	Ferrara, Archivio di Stato
I:FEc	Ferrara, Biblioteca Comunale Ariostea
I:Fl	Florence, Biblioteca Medicea Laurenziana
I:Fn	Florence, Biblioteca Nazionale Centrale
I:Las	Lucca, Archivio di Stato
I:MAas	Mantua, Archivio di Stato
I:MOas	Modena, Archivio di Stato
I:MOe	Modena, Biblioteca Estense
I:Ra	Rome, Biblioteca Angelica
I:Rac	Rome, Archivio Capitolino
I:Ras	Rome, Archivio di Stato
I:Rasv	Rome, Archivio Segreto Vaticano
I:Rav	Rome, Archivio Storico del Vicariato
I:Rcas	Rome, Biblioteca Casanatense
I:Rli	Rome, Biblioteca dell'Accademia Nazionale dei Lincei e Corsiniana
I:Rn	Rome, Biblioteca Nazionale Centrale 'Vittorio Emanuele II'
I:Rsc	Rome, Biblioteca Musicale Governativa del Conservatorio di Santa Cecilia
I:Ru	Rome, Biblioteca Universitaria Alessandrina
I:Rvat	Rome, Biblioteca Apostolica Vaticana
I:Vc	Venice, Biblioteca del Conservatorio 'Benedetto Marcello'
US:PHu	Philadelphia, University of Pennsylvania Libraries
New Grove	*The New Grove Dictionary of Music and Musicians*, ed. Stanley Sadie, 20 vols. (London, 1980)

ROMAN MONEY

IN the following chapters, salaries, pensions, and other income are reported in terms of Roman money of the period about 1600. The purpose of this introduction is to enable the reader to form a subjective impression of the amounts in question. It is based upon information taken from Jean Delumeau, *Vie économique et sociale de Rome dans la seconde moitié du XVIe siècle* (Paris, 1959), ii. 655–750, and three unpublished letters.

In this period, the principal denominations of Roman silver money were the scudo, which was worth ten giulii, which, in turn, was worth ten baiocchi. Although silver money was the norm for accounting purposes, some figures are given in terms of gold scudi. The value of the gold scudo in relation to the silver varied according to the rate of exchange between the two metals. In the year 1600, a gold scudo was worth on average about 1.1215 silver scudi, and this is the figure that will be used here and elsewhere in this study.

In the year 1600 the gold scudo contained 0.1084 ounces (3.074 grams) of gold. Given the price of gold at the beginning of 1996 (US $385 per ounce), the gold in a gold scudo would be worth US $41.73. At the rate of exchange between gold and silver then in effect in Rome, a silver scudo would be worth about US $37.21 in present-day (1996) terms. Readers in the future or in other countries may perform a parallel calculation. The current price of gold in any currency, if given in terms of a price per one US ounce, would be multiplied by 0.1084, yielding the number of units in that currency that equal one gold Roman scudo of 1600. If the price of gold is given in terms of currency units per gram, then the number of those currency units would be multiplied by 3.074, and the product will be the number of those currency units that equals the value of one gold Roman scudo of 1600. In all cases, the corresponding number of current local currency units that equals one silver scudo is obtained by dividing the modern 'price' of a gold Roman scudo by 1.1215.

Another, perhaps better, way to judge the value of Roman money of about 1600 is with reference to commodity prices. In the second column, below, the prices of various commodities are given in terms of silver baiocchi. In the third column, these prices are translated into US dollars using the rate 1 baiocco = US $0.3721 (1 silver scudo = US $37.21), the rate established in the preceding paragraph on the basis of the current price of gold. The fourth column shows the

prices for these same commodities current in the Midwestern United States
in 1996. The last column to the right contains a blank in which readers in the
future and in various parts of the world may write current commodity prices in
any local currency. At the bottom of the right-hand column, a divisor is given
that will yield an approximate rate of exchange between the chosen modern local
currency and Roman money of about 1600. Please note that a Roman pound
weighed 339 grams or 11.865 US ounces.

Item	Roman price in 1600	@ 1 scudo = US $37.21	US wholesale price in 1996	Reader's local price
Mutton	4.12 baiocchi per Roman pound	US $2.07 per pound	$2.09	_____ per kg.
Heifer (beef)	3 baiocchi per Roman pound	US $1.51 per pound	$1.32	_____ per kg.
Lamb	3.5 baiocchi per Roman pound	US $1.76 per pound	$2.09	_____ per kg.
Eggs	8 baiocchi per hundred	US $0.36 per dozen	$0.88	_____ per 10
Raisins	4.1 baiocchi per Roman pound	US $2.06 per pound	$1.39	_____ per kg.
			$7.77 total[a]	_____ = total[b]

[a] This total divided by 0.2081 = $37.33 = 1 silver scudo. That dollar amount multiplied by 1.1215 = $41.86 = 1 gold scudo.
[b] This total divided by 0.4422 = _____, which is the amount of the chosen monetary denomination that equals 1 silver scudo. The same figure multiplied by 1.1215 = _____, which is the amount of the chosen monetary denomination that equals 1 gold scudo.

As can be seen, the price of these commodities when calculated at the rate of
exchange suggested by the price of gold is almost exactly the same as the price
of the same commodities in the Midwestern United States in 1996.

Now, in column 2, below, we may see retail prices, in terms of silver scudi
and baiocchi, for goods and services purchased in Rome in 1595 by Giovanni
Battista Gardone, guardian of Giovanni Battista Masi, son of Count Cosimo
Masi of Parma, as reported in letters of 2.ii.1595, 2.iv.1595, and 3.v.1595 (Parma,
Archivio di Stato, Carteggio farnesiano 411). In column 3, we see the same
prices converted to US dollars at the rate of exchange based upon the 1996 price
of gold. Column 4 shows the 1996 prices for these items in the Midwestern United
States. Column 5, again, contains blank spaces in which the reader may write
current prices for these things in terms of local currency.

Item	Roman Price in 1600	@ 1 scudo = US $37.21	US price in 1996	Reader's local price
A pair of shoes	45 baiocchi	$16.74	$16.74 is low, but possible	____
Laundry for one month	48 baiocchi	$17.86	$32	____
Six sheets of music paper	9 baiocchi	$3.35	$20	____
Binding a book of villanelle	30 baiocchi	$11.16	$20	____
A quintern of paper	6 baiocchi	$2.23	$3 for 10 sheets of high-quality stationery	____
Barber	35 baiocchi	$13.02	$16	____
Shoelaces	4 baiocchi	$1.49	$1.49 is possible	____
Postage for a letter from Parma	2 baiocchi	$0.74	$0.32 for domestic letters	
A book of *canzonette musicali*	2.04 scudi	$75.90	$90	____
Veal per [Roman] pound	7 baiocchi	$3.51 per US pound	$4.35	____
Food for one gentleman, per month	24 scudi	$893.04	$250	____
Rent, one month, 3 gentlemen [plus servants]	32 scudi	$1,190.72	$1,000 is possible	____

Here, again, we see that Roman prices of about 1600, when converted to US dollars at the rate of exchange suggested by the current price of gold (1 scudo = $37.21), correspond rather closely to actual US prices in 1996. The one item far out of line is the price of food for one gentleman for one month. The figure given in column 4 assumes that the food is purchased at a grocery and prepared at home. The higher price mentioned in the letter of 1595, which comes to about $30 per day, may reflect restaurant dining, as it corresponds roughly to a typical per diem allowance given to American university professors for supported travel in 1996.

From all this, it appears reasonable to conclude that the current price of gold offers a reliable means of approximately translating Roman currency of about 1600 into 1996 US dollars. Readers at other times and places may need to use the prices of the various given commodities and everyday goods and services as a control on the rate of exchange based on the price of gold.

As a sample application of this method, we may examine some of the payments and incomes mentioned in the following chapters, first in terms of Roman money of about 1600, then in terms of US dollars in 1996, and finally the reader's currency on the basis of the rate of exchange calculated by the means given above.

Item	Amount in Roman money	@ $37.21 per siver scudo	In the reader's currency
Cardinal Montalto's annual income	100,000 scudi	$3,721,000.00	____
Paulo Cortesi's suggested income for cardinals	12,000 scudi	$446,520.00	____
Papal commission's suggested income for cardinals	6,000 scudi	$223,260.00	____
Standard daily food allowance given to members of cardinals' households	10 baiocchi	$3.72	____
Monthly income of singers in the papal chapel	25 scudi	$930.25	____
Monthly salary paid to Cesare Marotta and his wife, Ippolita Recupito, by Cardinal Montalto	25 scudi	$930.25	____
Monthly rent allowance given to Cesare Marotta by Cardinal Montalto	6.67 scudi	$240.19	____

1

Cardine della cardinalizia dignità

෴

'GLORY of the Church, hinge of the cardinalate, crown of the Sacred College, splendour of the purple, gem of priests, standard of prelates, form of the royal and ruling life, protector of the orders, zealous pastor, father of the poor and needy, defender of widows and orphans, liberator of slaves and prisoners, chariot and driver of Israel, delight of mankind, honour of our century, and the greatest glory of the universe':[1] the honorific epithets paraded in Giliberti's funeral oration like emblematic *trionfi* in a *cortège*—vague though they seem to us and inviting scepticism—must have represented to the author, to his audience, and to his subject the public goals and official values of Cardinal Montalto's ecclesiastical life.

Alessandro Peretti Damasceni (1571–1623) was just 14 years old when his maternal grandmother's brother, Felice Peretti (1520–90), emerged from the conclave of 1585 as Pope Sixtus V. Although without family wealth or noble title, Felice, through ability and ambition, had become a functionary in the curia with papal protection during the 1550s, a cardinal in 1570, and bishop of Fermo in 1571.[2] Beginning in 1576, he began to acquire land for his estate within the walls of Rome, and in 1578 he had his palace built near the church of Santa Maria Maggiore.[3] As pope, he left an indelible mark upon Rome through his vast urban renewal and planning projects, which resulted in a system of wide, straight roads,

---

[1] Vincenzio Giliberti, *Montalto: Orazione . . . nel funerale d'Alessandro Peretti Cardinal Montalto Vicecancelliero di S. Chiesa* (Rome: Mascardi, 1623): 'La gloria della Chiesa, il cardine della Cardinalizia dignità, la corona del sacro Collegio, lo splendor della porpora, la gemma de' Sacerdoti, la norma de' Prelati, la forma della reale, e regia vita, il protettore delle Religioni, il zelante Pastore, il padre de' poveri, e bisognosi, il difensor delle vedove, e de' pupilli, il liberatore degli schiavi, e de' prigionieri, il carro, e condottiere d'Israel, le delizie del genere umano, l'onore del nostro secolo, e la gloria maggiore dell'Universo.'

[2] For a summary of Peretti family history, see James Chater, 'Musical Patronage in Rome at the Turn of the Seventeenth Century: The Case of Cardinal Montalto', *Studi musicali*, 16 (1987), 179–227 at 182–7, and the sources cited there, esp. 181 n. 4.

[3] Camillo Vittorio Emanuele Massimo, *Notizie istoriche della Villa Massimo alle Terme Diocleziane* (Rome, 1836), 260.

public monuments, expansive piazzas, imposing villas, new palaces, and restora-
tions undertaken with the distinctly propagandistic intentions of making Rome
the symbol of the Catholic Church's triumph over heresy.[4]

Sixtus was also ambitious for his family, and he began to provide for its dynasty
with the customary creation of a cardinal-nephew, who would receive church
income beyond that available directly to the Holy See and would become the
'hinge of the cardinalate' through the system of power-broking at future conclaves, with the hope that he would emerge from one of them as pope in his
own right.

Accordingly, Sixtus V created young Alessandro cardinal 'of Montalto' (using
his own former title) on 13 May 1585, naming him Cardinal Legate of Bologna
in 1587[5] and Vice-Chancellor of the Church in 1589, with powers and respons-
ibilities that would soon afterward be associated with the office of Secretary
of State. In addition, the new Cardinal Montalto was named Protector of the
Benedictine, Capuchin, and Celestine orders and of the Polish nation. This
meant that, in addition to the income from the many benefices and pensions that
Pope Sixtus conferred on him, he probably received a *propina* from every suc-
cessful candidate for provision to any Benedictine, Capuchin, Celestine, or Polish church in consistory, amounting to 15 per cent of the annual taxable value of
the benefice.[6] Montalto's fixed sources of income were no less impressive. In 1587
Sixtus granted him an annual lifetime 'pension' of 3,000 gold scudi upon all the
revenues collected by the current bishop of Ferrara and all his successors.[7] By the
year of Pope Sixtus' death, Montalto held a large number of benefices scattered
throughout the Kingdom of Naples, in the monastery of San Francesco of Assisi,
and in the cathedrals of Ferrara, Perugia, and Fermo, as well as the title to the
ancient church of Santo Stefano in Bologna and an abbey in Reggio Emilia.[8] In
1620 he added to these the title of bishop of Alba.[9] The number of his benefices
was so great that in many cases he amalgamated their income into rental agreements with individuals who undertook to collect the actual money or goods due
the cardinal in exchange for a fixed annual payment.[10] Altogether his yearly

---

[4] Morton Colp Abromson, *Painting in Rome during the Papacy of Clement VIII (1592–1605): A Documented Study* (New York, 1981), 1–8.

[5] Montalto served as legate 1587–90, 1592–1600, and 1601–5 according to M. Ferretti and M. Pasquali, 'Cronostassi critica dei legati, vicelegati e govenatori di Bologna dal sec. XVI al XVII', *Atti e memorie della Deputazione di Storia Patria per le Provincie di Romagna*, NS 23 (1972), 117–301 at 139–41.

[6] See D. S. Chambers, 'The Economic Predicament of Renaissance Cardinals', *Studies in Medieval and Renaissance History*, iii, ed. William M. Bowsky (Lincoln, Nebr., 1966), 289–311 at 300–2.

[7] A copy of the papal letter of 15 July 1587 is in I:Ras, Archivio dei 30 Notari Capitolini, Officio n. 25, Busta 87, fos. 508–11.   [8] I:Rasv, Confalonieri 48–53, *passim*, and below, App. A, Letter 12.

[9] Lorenzo Cardella, *Memorie storiche de' cardinali della santa romana chiesa* (Rome, 1793), v. 228; and I:Ras, Archivio dei 30 Notari Capitolini, Officio n. 25, Busta 87, fo. 526.

[10] Two volumes of these rental agreements are in I:Ras, Archivio Sforza-Cesarini, I[a] parte (etichetta ret-tangolare), vols. 60–1.

income amounted to about 100,000 scudi.[11] For comparison, the cardinal-nephew of Pope Paul V, Scipione Borghese, had an annual income of between 80,000 and 90,000 scudi in 1609, which was increased to 140,000 scudi in 1612, an income that allowed him to buy up entire villages and estates, which became the vast Villa Borghese park of present-day Rome.[12] Paolo Cortesi,[13] who was an outspoken advocate of cardinals' princely life styles, suggested curial incomes of 12,000 scudi, whereas papal commissions during the early sixteenth century had recommended 6,000 scudi, even that a very substantial sum.[14] Cardinal Montalto's income was so disproportionately large that he conceded an annual stipend of 12,000 scudi to Pope Paul V when the papacy neared bankruptcy.[15]

From the start, Sixtus made sure that his grand-nephew would be able to use his vast church income and prerogatives to maximum advantage. In a bull of 7 November 1587, the pope granted to Cardinal Montalto the unique privilege of transferring all or any part of his pensions or other forms of ecclesiastical income to any person, whether or not a cleric and whether or not already in possession of one or more benefices, by means of a simple notarial document, without having recourse to the curia or to any future pope or other ecclesiastical or secular authority.[16] An anonymous familiar of Pope Sixtus V comments on the pope's motives:

> To each cardinal he gave an indulgence to confer benefices in individual churches under bishops' authority, which are usually reserved to the Holy See, and that in order that the members of their households might nourish some hopes and remain more willingly in the service of their patrons. However, he reserved to the pope the authority to impose pensions upon the benefices and to the Apostolic Chancellery the right of [their] transference.[17]

In the event, Montalto transferred his pension on the cathedral of Ferrara to his younger brother, Michele, and other incomes amounting to a total of 4,305 scudi per year to twenty other individuals in a single day (31 May 1623) in conjunction with his testament.[18] We shall see that several musicians in the cardinal's

---

[11] Ludwig von Pastor, *The History of the Popes from the Close of the Middle Ages*, trans. Ralph Francis Kerr (London, 1932), xxi. 67 n. 2.   [12] Ibid., xxv. 62.

[13] *De Cardinalatu* (Rome, 1510), p. xlvii.

[14] Chambers, 'The Economic Predicament of Renaissance Cardinals', 294.

[15] Cardella, *Memorie storiche*, v. 224–8.

[16] I:Ras, Archivio dei 30 Notari Capitolini, Officio n. 25, Busta 87, fos. 506–7, 512–13. Approximately the same privilege is repeated in a bull of 1588, ibid., fos. 504–5, 514–15.

[17] 'A ciascun cardinale diede indulto di conferire i benefici delle singole chiese Vescovili, che sogliono essere riservati alla S. Sede: e ciò perchè gli aulici dei Cardinali potessero nutrire delle speranze e più volentieri rimanessero al servizio dei loro padroni. Tuttavia reservò al Papa la facoltà d'imporre pensioni sui benefici e alla Cancelleria Apostolica il diritto di spedizione.' Francesco Pistolesi (ed.), *La prima biografia autentica di Papa Sisto V scritta dall'Anonimo della Biblioteca Ferraioli di Roma* (Montalto, 1925), 58.

[18] I:Ras, Archivio dei 30 Notari Capitolini, Officio n. 25, Busta 87, fos. 498–500, 519–21, 526–8, 545–7.

household held church benefices 'from him', and we may surmise that many other grants of ecclesiastical income lay hidden in the vast, unindexed notarial archives of Rome, Naples, and other centres of Montalto's holdings.

Cardinal Montalto used his vast wealth and power to accumulate the indebtedness that would insure his continuing survival and influence. According to three published eulogies, he contributed 1,000 scudi per month to the construction of S. Andrea della Valle and maintained a large household. Undoubtedly acting on the recommendation of fellow cardinals, he gave financial support to scholars of sacred literature and to jurists, philosophers, poets, painters, singers, instrumentalists, ecclesiastics, and translators, and kept a large number of the same at his court. In Rome he distributed one hundred portions of bread and wine per day to poor families of his parish, provided doctors and medicine for the sick, paid the debts of widows and virgins, founded a college for poor students in Bologna, and gave to secular and regular priests, students, pilgrims, foreigners, schools, colleges, churches, confraternities, hospitals, monasteries, and convents. His bookkeeper estimated that in this manner Montalto gave away one and a half million gold scudi during his lifetime.[19] The figure does not seem impossible. Someone in Montalto's household, perhaps this same bookkeeper, made a tally of the cardinal's expenditures for the month of December 1620 on a slip of paper, which was at some point inserted into the volume that recorded the cardinal's payment orders (*mandati*) for that year.[20] If we add together the 1,540.26 scudi recorded as paid to members of the household, the 1,465.80 scudi distributed as alms (*elemosina*), and the 715 scudi disbursed for pensions, multiply the sum by the twelve months of year, and then multiply this product by the thirty-eight years of his cardinalate, we would arrive at a figure somewhat more than one and a half million scudi. Expenditures on this scale would have yielded exactly the sort of network of indebtedness that produced power and influence in Roman society during the late Renaissance.[21]

Over the course of his thirty-eight years as cardinal, Montalto participated in seven papal conclaves.[22] During this period, the shifting alliances of curial parties revolved around the poles representing the two major opposing secular powers in Italy: the grand duke of Tuscany (increasingly allied with the king of

---

[19] Giovanni Briccio, *Il pianto, et la mestitia dell'alma città di Roma, per la morte dell'Illustriss. et Reverendiss. Sig. Alessandro Peretti Cardinal Montalto, Vescovo Albanense, Vicecancellario, Summator Papae, & Protettore di Polonia* (Rome: Grignani, 1623). A similar list of Montalto's contributions and patronage can be found in Placido Filingerio, *In funere Alexandri Peretti Card. Montalti oratio habita Romae in Templo S. Andreae Cleric. Regular. ab eodem Cardinali aedificato* (Rome: Mascardi, 1623), and in Giliberti, *Montalto*.

[20] I:Rac, Archivio Cardelli, Appendice, vol. 52, at fo. 21.

[21] Ronald Weissman, 'Taking Patronage Seriously: Mediterranean Values and Renaissance Society', in F. W. Kent and Patricia Simons (eds.), *Patronage, Art, and Society in Renaissance Italy* (Oxford, 1987), 25–45.

[22] The following information about Montalto's conclaves, except where otherwise cited, is summarized from Pastor, *History of the Popes*, xxii and xxiii.

France) and the king of Spain. Montalto's basic loyalty was with the grand duke, Ferdinando de' Medici, who, as cardinal, had been instrumental in electing Sixtus V and from whom Montalto received a secret pension, at least in his early years.[23] Furthermore, Montalto's closest ally in Rome—probably his closest friend—was Cardinal Francesco Maria Del Monte, Grand Duke Ferdinando's surrogate and agent in the curia.[24] However, Montalto usually preserved enough independence to position himself as the decisive factor when Spain and Tuscany became deadlocked.

Montalto's politics achieved uneven results at first. He could not hold his 'Sistine party' together at his first conclave. He managed, however, to defeat the Spanish party at his second, in 1590, abandoning Florence and Mantua at the last minute and backing Cardinal Sfondrato (Gregory XIV) in the end. In 1591, on the other hand, he was forced to concede to a candidate acceptable to the Spanish, Cardinal Facchinetti (Innocent IX).

With more experience, greater wealth, and a better developed base of power, Montalto began a notable series of successes with the conclave of 1592. Pretending at first to promote Cardinal Santori in alliance with the Spanish, the grand duke, and Venice against an ad hoc group of cardinals vehemently opposed this, Montalto eventually held out against the other Spanish candidates only to bring forward at the end Cardinal Aldobrandini, whom he had previously supported in 1590. Little wonder, then, that Cardinal Del Monte wrote Grand Duke Ferdinando soon after that election, 'The pope loves Montalto more than his own nephews', but, in a secret message in code, he adds, 'but with this business of state, he trusts no one'.[25] In fact, Cardinal Montalto maintained a close social and political relationship with Clement VIII's nephew Cardinal Pietro Aldobrandini throughout most of the 1590s, their exchanges of hospitality even assuming the aspect of a social rivalry,[26] until they had a series of fallings out, the first coinciding with the devolution of Ferrara to the papacy in 1597,[27] which made Cardinal

---

[23] Zygmunt Waźbiński, *Il cardinale Francesco Maria Del Monte, 1549–1626* (Florence, 1994), 133 cites correspondence between Grand Duke Ferdinando and Cardinal Del Monte, 1590–2, to this effect.

[24] Francesco Maria Del Monte (1549–1626) of Florence was created cardinal on 14 December 1588 at the behest of Ferdinando de' Medici, who renounced the purple in 1587 to succeed his brother Francesco as grand duke of Tuscany. The close friendship between Cardinals Montalto and Del Monte is a central, recurring theme in Waźbiński, *Il cardinale Francesco Maria Del Monte*.

[25] I:Fas, Mediceo del Principato, Filza 3759, fo. 477ᵛ (Del Monte to Grand Duke Ferdinando de' Medici, 16 Oct. 1592): 'Il Papa ama Mont' Alto piu de proprii Nipoti . . . [in code:] ma con tutto questo in materia di stato non si fida di nessuno.'

[26] Concerning the Montalto-Aldobrandini rivalry, see Claudio Annibaldi, 'Il mecenate "politico": Ancora sul patronato musicale del cardinale Pietro Aldobrandini (*ca.* 1570–1621)', *Studi musicali*, 16 (1987), 67–9. For further details, mentioning the musical entertainments offered at these rounds of banquets, see Chater, 'Musical Patronage', 206–7. Concerning the 'fraternity' of cardinals Del Monte, Montalto, and Aldobrandini, see Waźbiński, *Il cardinale Francesco Maria Del Monte*, 137–43.

[27] Chater, 'Musical Patronage', 211 n. 179, quotes a letter from Cardinal Del Monte to Ferdinando de' Medici of 23 May 1597, which reports the falling out; but he does not speculate as to the cause, concerning which,

Pietro Aldobrandini ruler of the city as Papal Legate; the second in 1599, when a promotion of cardinals abruptly shifted the balance of power in the Sacred College in favour of the Aldobrandini;[28] and the last in 1605 at the death of Clement VIII.[29]

The main issue between the Spanish and grand ducal parties, at this time, was the absolution of Henry IV of France, the survivor of the War of the Three Henrys, in which Spain had supported one of his opponents and Tuscany the other. Eventually, at the grand duke's urging and with Montalto's help, Clement VIII absolved Henry of heresy, accepted his conversion to Catholicism, recognized him as King of France, annulled his marriage to Margaret of Valois (1599), and approved his marriage to Maria de' Medici (1600), which was the high point in Ferdinando de' Medici's struggle for independence from Spanish hegemony in Tuscany.

The other crucial conclave for Cardinal Montalto took place in 1605, after the twenty-five-day papacy of Leo XI (Alessandro de' Medici). Once again, after splitting the Spanish from the Aldobrandini party, Montalto brought forward a late dark-horse candidate, Camillo Borghese (Paul V), who had been his Vice Legate to Bologna from 1588 to 1591, with some interruptions.[30] The French were displeased, because Borghese held a 2,000-scudo annual pension from the king of Spain. And Cardinal Del Monte wrote to Grand Duke Ferdinando, 'I forgot to tell you that from Spain has come to the Marquis [Michele] Peretti the title of Prince of Venafro and a letter to Cardinal Montalto full of thanks for the things done at the past conclave; whence I conclude that it is a beautiful world'.[31]

Prince Michele was Cardinal Montalto's younger brother, and his participation in the creation of the family dynasty had been foreseen. In his bull of 18 November 1587, Sixtus V granted 10-year-old Michele the right to receive pensions, benefices, and all sorts of other ecclesiastical incomes whether or not he took orders or monastic vows and whether or not he married, and the pope con-

see below, Ch. 8. In spite of this, Cardinal Montalto joined Pope Clement VIII and his nephew in the triumphal entrance into Ferrara in May of 1598. On the occasion of this visit, Cardinals Montalto and Del Monte were lodged at the monastery of San Benedetto, which they converted into a regular court, with more than 200 dependants between them and frequent entertaining. See Waźbiński, *Il cardinale Francesco Maria Del Monte*, 152–3.

[28] Annibaldi, 'Il mecenate "politico" ', 68 n. 146. Chater, 'Musical Patronage', 211 n. 179, cites a letter from Cardinal Del Monte to Ferdinando de' Medici (11.v.1599) concerning this quarrel.

[29] The last reported event shared by the two cardinals was on 11 Jan. 1605, when Cardinal Montalto gave a banquet for Cardinals Aldobrandini, Del Monte, and Peretti; Chater, 'Musical Patronage', 208 and n. 170. Clement VIII died on 5 Mar. 1605.   [30] Ferretti and Pasquali, 'Cronostassi critica', 139–41.

[31] I:Fas, Mediceo del Principato, Filza 3761, letter of 20 Aug. 1605: 'Mi scordavo dirle che è venuto di Spagna il titolo al Marchese Peretti di Principe di Venafro, et una lettera al Cardinal Mont'Alto piena di rengratiamenti delle cose delli Conclavi passati; onde io concludo che q.to è un bel Mondo.' The diploma from King Philip of Spain granting the title of principality to his city of Venafro, dated 27 Sept. 1605, is in I:Ras, Archivio Sforza-Cesarini Iᵃ parte (etichetta rettangolare), 72, no. 26(a).

ceded to Michele the same right to transfer these pensions and other incomes by simple notarial document that he had granted to his cardinal-nephew.[32] Already in 1586 the territory of Venafro (without the title) in the Vice Realm of Naples had been purchased for Michele from the king of Spain for 86,000 scudi.[33] To this were added the Marquisate of Incisa, County of Celano, and Barony of Piscina. The latter two feuds were risky investments, at least in the short term. Grandmother Camilla Peretti purchased them in 1591 at a cost that eventually amounted to 307,500 ducats. She ceded them to Michele in 1596 before they were entirely paid for. Payment was largely financed by the sale of bonds, securing of private loans, and ceding some income from abbeys and customs taxes to creditors for a number of years. At least during this early period, the income from the feuds did not cover half of the payments on the debts incurred.[34] A rather significant portion of the purchase was financed by Cardinal Montalto,[35] so that a large part of his 400,000 debt in 1598, mentioned by Pastor,[36] was due not to his 'extravagance', as Chater would have it,[37] but to his investments in his family's future wealth and power.

In the first of his two marriages, Michele produced the next link in the chain of nepotism: Francesco Peretti (1597–1655), who became the third Cardinal Montalto in 1641, even though his uncle had not become pope as was expected.[38] Fig. 1.1 portrays Michele at age 12, dressed as Captain of the Papal Guard, to the right of Pope Sixtus V, with Cardinal Montalto (age 18), in profile to the pope's immediate left, at the presentation of Domenico Fontana's architectural plans for the Vatican library in 1589.

In addition to titles, large incomes, and unique prerogatives, Sixtus provided his grand-nephews with impressive palaces: the Palace of the Chancellery (Figs. 1.2 and 1.3), the palaces of the Villa Peretti on the Esquiline, which was the largest private estate within the walls of Rome, and the vast Villa Lante at Bagnaia. Such estates and palaces had been considered necessary symbols of the princely power and dignity of cardinals since the early Renaissance,[39] and treatises meant

---

[32] I:Ras, Archivio dei 30 Notari Capitolini, Officio n. 25, Busta 87, fos. 501–3, 516–18.

[33] Giambattista Masciotta, *Il Molise dalle origini ai nostri giorni*, iii: *Il circondario d'Isernia* (Cava dei Tirreni, 1952), 553.

[34] Enrico Celani, *Una pagina di feudalismo: La signoria dei Peretti-Savelli-Sforza-Cesarini sulla contea di Celano e baronia di Pescina (1591–1806)* (Città di Castello, 1893).

[35] I:Rac, Archivio Cardelli, Appendice, vol. 31, 'Copie de mandati, 1591–1594', *sub die* 24 May 1594 records Cardinal Montalto's payment of 139,764.2 scudi into his grandmother's (Camilla Peretti's) account in Naples as his share of the 307,500 to be paid to Alfonso Piccolomini di Aragona for the *stati* of Celano and Piscina. The account entry gives extensive details of the transaction.

[36] *History of the Popes*, xxi. 67 n. 2.   [37] 'Musical Patronage', 186.

[38] Pastor, *History of the Popes*, xxix. 193–4.

[39] Chambers, 'The Economic Predicament of Renaissance Cardinals', 289–313, cites, as an early instance of a later commonplace, a dialogue written in 1438 by Lapo da Castiglionchio the Younger, secretary to Pope Eugene IV, that argues that the pope and cardinals were obliged to be rich.

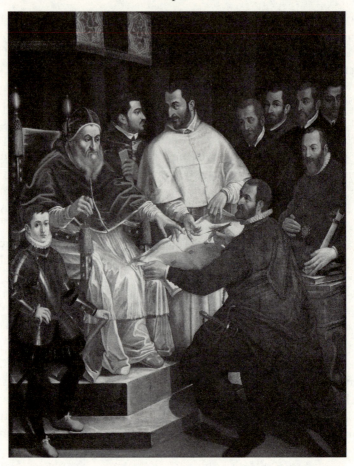

FIG. 1.1. Sixtus V, with Michele Peretti and Cardinal Montalto, receiving
Domenico Fontana's plans for the Vatican library, 1589. Biblioteca Apostolica
Vaticana, Archivio Fotografico

to be read by newly created cardinals included specific architectural details to be
observed in their construction or renovation.[40] The most relevant of these treatises for the present purpose is certainly the chapter entitled 'Istruzione necessaria
per fabbricare' in the 'Miscellanea di cose diverse per la Curia Romana &c. varj
discorsi e instruzioni &c.' by Vincenzo Giustiniani, marquis of Bassano, the banker,

[40] The earliest of these is apparently Paolo Cortesi, *De Cardinalatu* (1510), transcribed and translated in Kathleen
Weil-Garris and John F. D'Amico, 'The Renaissance Cardinal's Ideal Palace: A Chapter from Cortesi's De
Cardinalatu', *Memoirs of the American Academy in Rome*, 35: *Studies in Italian Art History*, 1: *Studies in Italian Art
and Architecture, 15th through 18th Centuries*, ed. Henry A. Millon (Rome, 1980), 45–123.

FIG. 1.2. Palazzo della Cancelleria. From Giorgio Torselli, *Palazzi di Roma*, photographs by Nicola Oscuro (Milan, 1965), 56–7

art collector, and friend of Cardinal Montalto.[41] Montalto's style of life, in fact, seems to have been Giustiniani's chief model of cardinal dignity, since he mentions Montalto in three of his chapters. His recommendations correspond very well with the designs of Montalto's villas: begin with a magnificent plan, build on a large, noble, elevated site, avoid attachment to other buildings, make square corners and symmetrical forms in order to demonstrate power and influence over the ambience. Use large, rough stones and strong windows and doors on lower levels facing public piazzas, but ornament richly on the upper levels and in private areas. Plan gardens for eventual expansion, and make long, straight roadways

[41] I:Las, Fondo G. B. Orsucci 48 (olim O.49). The chapters of the treatise are 'Dialogo tra Renzo et Aniello Napolitano sopra l'uso e costumanze di Roma e Napoli' (fos. 5–34), 'Avvertimenti per uno scalco' (fos. 35–48), 'Istruzione necessaria per fabbricare' (51–69), 'Istruzione per far viaggi' (72–104), 'Discorso sopra la pittura' (105–11ᵛ), 'Discorso sopra la musica' (fos. 113–135ᵛ), 'Discorso sopra la caccia' (137–71), and 'Istruzione per un maestro di camera' (fos. 173–200). This is a copy made in 1640 by Giovanni Battista Orsucci (1632–86): see fo. 5 and Salvator Bongi, *Inventario del R. Archivio di Stato in Lucca*, iv (Lucca, 1888), 289. The chapters on painting, sculpture, and architecture are published in M. Giovanni Bottari, *Raccolta di lettere sulla pittura, scultura ed architettura scritte da' più celebri personaggi dei secoli XV, XVI e XVII*, vi (Milan, 1822), 99–117. The chapter on music, to be discussed below, has been published by Salvatore Bongi as *Discorso sulla musica dei suoi tempi di Vincenzo Giustiniani Marchese di Bassano. MDCXXVIII* (Lucca, 1878), and by Angelo Solerti in *Le origini del melodramma: Testimonianze dei contemporanei* (Turin, 1903), 98–128. An English translation of the music chapter, 'Discorso sopra la musica', by Carol MacClintock is in American Institute of Musicology, Musicological Studies and Documents, 9 (Rome, 1962), 63–80.

FIG. 1.3. Palazzo della Cancelleria, main entrance. From Giorgio Torselli,
Palazzi di Roma, photographs by Nicola Oscuro (Milan, 1965), 55

that divide the ground into symmetrical areas. Everything should reveal a grand
spirit (*animo grande*) and avoid any suggestion of stinginess and ignorance.

The Villa Peretti on the Esquiline was begun in 1576 with the purchase by
Cardinal Felice Peretti (the first Cardinal Montalto), before he became pope,
of a vineyard contiguous to the north (right-hand) side of the basilica of Santa
Maria Maggiore.[42] It grew in size over the next fourteen years, until, at the
death of Sixtus V, its boundaries coincided with the strada di Porta San Lorenzo,
on the east, from the church of San Lorenzo (top centre on the map in Fig. 1.4;
present-day Piazzale Sisto V) to the head of the piazza Santa Maria Maggiore

---

[42] The most recent historical study of the early history of the Peretti villa is Matthias Quast, *Die Villa
Montalto in Rom: Entstehung und Gestalt im Cinquecento* (Tuduv-Studien, Reihe Kunstgeschichte, 45; Munich,
1991).

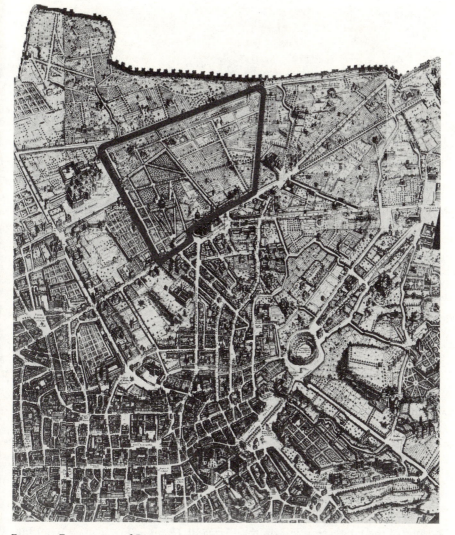

FIG. 1.4. From a map of Rome, *c*.1600. From Cesare d'Onofrio, 'Una grande scomparsa', *Capitolium*, 45/2–3 (1970), 59

(roughly at the present-day intersection of via Carlo Alberto and via Battazzi); on the south, along the piazza Santa Maria Maggiore, the north side of the church itself (just above the centre of Fig. 1.4), and along the strada Felice to the intersection with the via Panisperna (present-day via Viminale); on the west, up the via Panisperna and along the east side of the piazza di Termini (present-day Piazza dei Cinquecento); on the north along the present-day via Marsala. The

FIG. 1.5. The Palazzo di Termini shortly before its demolition in 1888. From Cesare d'Onofrio, 'Una grande scomparsa', *Capitolium*, 45/2–3 (1970), 62

entire Peretti estate, then, is the semi-trapezoid outlined in Fig. 1.4, touching the church of Santa Maria Maggiore and extending to the wall at its furthest point. Its total area was almost one square kilometre.

The Peretti estate included several palaces, towers, and villas, which were either purchased with various land acquisitions or built by the Peretti family itself. The most important of these were the following four:

1. The Palazzo Peretti, built between 1578 and 1581, at the south-east corner of the estate outlined in Fig. 1.4, on the Piazza di Santa Maria Maggiore.

2. The much larger Palazzo di Termini, built in 1586–8, at the north-west corner of the estate, fronting on the Piazza di Termini (Fig. 1.5). It would be located towards the upper left of Fig. 1.4. In the detail of the Peretti estate seen in Fig. 1.6, the Palazzo di Termini is in the lower right-hand area. Fig. 1.5 is a photograph taken shortly before its demolition in 1888 for the construction of the present-day principal railway station of Rome. The fountain in the foreground of Fig. 1.5 is now at the centre of the Piazza della Repubblica.

3. The Palazzo (or Torretta) della Vigna, the highest point in Rome, purchased in 1585 (at the middle-left in Fig. 1.6; seen in an engraving in Fig. 1.7).

4. The Palazzo or Palazzetto Felice (Palazzetto Peretti, Villa Negroni—right of centre in Fig. 1.6; in a period engraving in Fig. 1.8; in a photograph, Fig. 1.9,

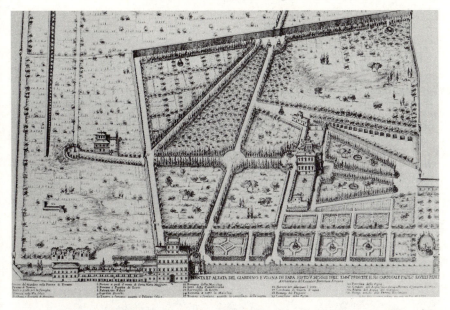

FIG. 1.6. A map detail showing the north-west corner of the Peretti estate. From David R. Coffin, *The Villa in Renaissance Rome* (Princeton, 1979), 367

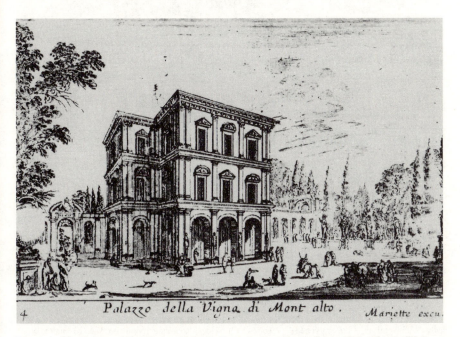

FIG. 1.7. The Palazzo della Vigna within the Peretti estate. From Cesare d'Onofrio (ed.), *Roma nel Seicento* (Florence, 1969), 327

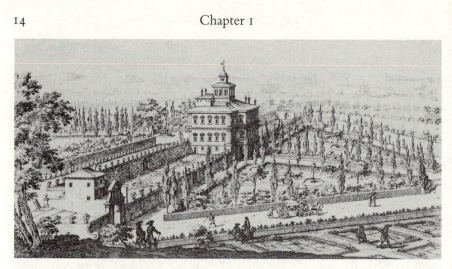

FIG. 1.8. The Palazzetto Felice in a period engraving. From David R. Coffin, *The Villa in Renaissance Rome* (Princeton, 1979), 366

FIG. 1.9. The Palazzetto Felice in a photograph taken just before its demolition in 1888. From Cesare d'Onofrio, 'Una grande scomparsa', *Capitolium*, 45/2–3 (1970), 62

taken just before its demolition in 1886), designed by Domenico Fontana (see Fig. 1.1).[43]

---

[43] Concerning the history of the Peretti (Montalto) estate and its palaces, see Massimo, *Notizie istoriche*, especially the chronological summary, 260–1; Cesare D'Onofrio, 'Una grande scomparsa: Villa Montalto, la più vasta esistita entro le mura', *Capitolium*, 45/2–3 (1970), 59–63; and Gaetano Moroni, *Dizionario di erudizione storico-ecclesiastica*, 100 (Venice, 1860), 241–63.

Because the Peretti estate incorporated many formerly separate villas, it also contained several gardens in various styles. The highly formal and symmetrical Giardini Segreti to the east and west of the Palazzo Felice stood at the centre of another walled garden, some of it formal, the rest in orchard; and this in turn was surrounded on two sides by the more rustic vineyard (see Fig. 1.6).[44] The concentric walls that surrounded the entire estate and its component gardens can be taken to symbolize the various levels of social hierarchy and concentric circles of friendship, patronage, alliance, and authority that were defined by law and custom. Similar levels and circles, already inherent in palace architecture, were also reflected in the decoration of the cardinal's palaces.

The gardens and most public spaces within the palaces of Cardinal Montalto's Roman estate were decorated with paintings whose subjects were the noble virtues of princes (secular and churchly) and the glories of the patron and his family, in conformity with the advice left by Paolo Cortesi and the common practice of the time.[45] For instance, the figure of Justice was depicted in a fresco by Giacomo Stella at the side of one entrance to the garden surrounding the Palazzo Felice, whose loggia was decorated with portraits of two ancient counsellors. At the head of the entrance stairway of the massive Palazzo di Termini was a large canvas depicting Alexander the Great, Cardinal Montalto's namesake and symbol of his majesty. In the grand entrance hall, the upper level of panels held frescos depicting the major rebuilding projects accomplished by Montalto's great-uncle, Pope Sixtus V. Around the lower level of the hall were the series of eleven large oval paintings depicting the princely virtues as illustrated in scenes from the life of Alexander the Great (once more), commissioned c.1609–16 from some of the leading, younger progressives in Rome at that time: Domenichino Zampieri (1581–1641), Antiveduto Grammatica (1571–1626), Francesco Albani (1578–1660), Antonio Tempesta (1555–1630), Giovanni Lanfranco (1582–1647), Giovanni Baglione (1571–1644), and Antonio Caracci (1583–1618).[46] Visitors to Montalto's palace could not escape the reflection that, just as Alexander the Great strove to unite all the Greek peoples and to bring the entire world as he knew it under dominion of Hellenic civilization, so Alexander Peretti, as pope, would unite the civilized world under the aegis of the true, universal, and Catholic Church, healing the rift caused by the Reformation and extending the Church's reach to

---

[44] The innovative character of the capricious and irregular parts of this estate are emphasized by Christian Norberg-Schulz, *Meaning in Western Architecture* (New York, 1980), 132.

[45] Cortesi, *De Cardinalatu*, in Weil-Garris and D'Amico, 'The Renaissance Cardinal's Ideal Palace', 91–7.

[46] See Erich Schleier, 'Domenichino, Lanfranco, Albani, and Cardinal Montalto's Alexander Cycle', *Art Bulletin*, 50 (1968), 188–93; Schleier, 'Le "storie di Alessandro Magno" del Cardinale Montalto', *Arte illustrata*, 5 (1972), 310–20; Carlo Volpe, 'Altre notizie per la storia di Alessandro del cardinal Montalto', *Paragone—Arte*, 28/333 (Nov. 1977), 3–7, pl. 1–3; Schleier, 'Ancora su Antonio Caracci e il ciclo di Alessandro Magno per il cardinal Montalto', *Paragone—Arte*, 32/381 (Nov. 1981), 10–25, pl. 7.

newly 'discovered' lands and peoples. This was, after all, the mission of Catholic triumphalism in Montalto's day. And, given the readiness with which popes and cardinals liken themselves to Roman emperors and senators, it would not be unexpected that Cardinal Montalto would also use the symbolism of ancient Greece in presenting himself to his colleagues and clients.

Paintings of biblical and mythological subjects of a far less hortative character were placed in the more private and intimate rooms of both palaces. A manuscript guide (c.1660) to the palaces of Rome lists eighty paintings or sculptures in Montalto's villa, including works by forty-two artists, most of them well-known Italians active in the second half of the sixteenth century or first two decades of the seventeenth.[47] Montalto has been credited with bringing several of these artists to Rome,[48] and he had two of them in his household at one time or another: Giuseppe Cesari (il Cavaliere d'Arpino), who was the most established painter in Rome at the turn of the century, superintendent for remodelling the transept of San Giovanni in Laterano and for decorating the dome of San Pietro under Pope Clement VIII and an Aldobrandini artist until joining Montalto's household sometime before 1611;[49] and Terenzio Terenzi, whom Giovanni Baglione accused of selling Montalto a forged Raphael (he was dismissed from service in 1619).[50] Towards the end of his life, Montalto commissioned from Gianlorenzo

[47] Fioravante Martinelli, 'Roma ornata dall'architettura, pittura e scultura [I:Rc, MS 4984]', transcribed in Cesare D'Onofrio, *Roma nel Seicento* (Florence, 1969), 323–28, lists works found in the Palazzo Felice by the following artists: Francesco Albani (1578–1660), Giovanni Baglione (1571–1644), Giacomo Barocchio (1507–73), Jacopo da Ponte Bassano (1510–92), Giovanni Lorenzo Bernini (1598–1680), Giovanni da Bologna (1524–1608), Paris Bordone (1495–1570), Paul Bril (1554–1626), Luca Cangiasi (1527–*c.*1585), Antonio Caracci (1583–1618), Giuseppe Cesari (1568–1640), Lodovico Cigoli (1559–1613), Henri Bres, 'il Civetta', Baldassarre Croce (*c.*1558–1628), Daniele Ricciarelli da Volterra (*c.*1509–66), Domenico Ferrerio (d. 1630), Lavinia Fontana (1512–97), Scipione Gaetano (before 1550–98), Antiveduto Grammatica (1571–1626), Giulio Romano (*c.*1492–1546), Giovanni Francesco Barbieri, 'il Guercino' (1591–1666), Giovanni Lanfranco (1582–1647), Girolamo Muziano (1528–92), Mutio Napolitano, Jacopo Palma (1544–1628), Girolamo Francesco Maria Mazzuoli, 'il Parmegianino' (1504–40), Niccolò Pomarancio (1517–after 1596), Raffaelle Sanzio (1483–1520), Guido Reni (1575–1642), Francesco Salviati (1510–63), Sebastiano del Piombo (1485–1547), Sofonisba Anguisciola (1530–1625), Giacomo Stella, Antonio Tanari, Antonio Tempesta (1555–1630), Terenzio Terenzi (1570–1620), Giorgio Vasari (1511–74), Alessandro Veronese (1578–1649), Marcello Venusti (*c.*1512–79), Giovanni Battista Viola (1576–1662), Domenichino Zampieri (1581–1641), and Federico Zuccaro (1543–1609). An inventory of the Peretti palaces made at the death of Montalto's nephew Francesco Peretti (who held the title Cardinal Montalto from 1641 to 1655) in 1655 lists a great many paintings and sculptures by content but none by artist: I:Ras, Notai Archivio Capitolino n. 6645 (J. Simoncellus), 13 May 1655, fos. 1190–1218. It would seem nearly impossible to match these descriptions with the foregoing list of artists.

[48] Waźbiński, *Il Cardinale Francesco Maria Del Monte*, 162–3, credits Montalto with bringing Francesco Albani, Domenichino, Guido Reni, and Annibale Caracci to Rome during the years around 1600.

[49] Concerning the historical position of Cesare, see Abromson, *Painting in Rome*; and Italo Faldi, Herwarth Röttgen, *et al.*, *Il cavalier d'Arpino: Roma—Palazzo Venezia, giugno—luglio, 1973* (Rome, 1973). The salary rolls of Cardinal Montalto, 1612–20, that include Cesare's name are in I:Ras, Archivio Giustiniani, 87; see Chater, 'Musical Patronage', 219–21.

[50] Giovanni Baglione, *Le vite de' pittori, scultori ed architetti dal Pontificato di Gregorio XIII. sino à tutto quello d'Urbano Ottavo* (2nd edn.; Rome: Manelsi, 1649), 157–8; see also Chater, 'Musical Patronage', 194, 218–21.

Fig. 1.10. The Villa Lante in Bagnaia. From David R. Coffin, *The Villa in Renaissance Rome* (Princeton, 1979), 342

Bernini a massive fish pond (1622–3), dominated by a figure of Neptune, which is now found in the Victoria and Albert Museum.[51] The date of the work, previously conjectural, can now be established by a payment on account to Bernini of 100 scudi on 20 March 1622.[52]

The same division of public and private art can be found in the vast Villa Lante at Bagnaia (see Figs. 1.10 and 1.11), which Cardinal Montalto was given by his great-uncle the pope in 1587 and which he used for his elaborate hunting parties.[53] For instance, to the original fountains and statues of the gardens, based on the theme of the Golden Age, commissioned by the original owner, Cardinal Giovan Francesco Gambara, Montalto made revisions and additions depicting

[51] Onofrio, *Roma nel Seicento*, 323–6.

[52] I:Rac, Archivio Cardelli, Appendice, vol. 38, 'Registro de mandati, quietanze, e mandati di franchitia, 1617–1622', under the date 20 Mar. 1622: 'A di d.to sc. 100 al cav.re Gio: Lorenzo Bernini quali si li paghiamo a bon conto d'una statua che lui fa per quistio del giard.no di S.ta M.a maggiore.'

[53] These are described by Vincenzo Giustiniani in his 'Discorso sopra la caccia', I:Las, Fondo G. B. Orsucci 48, fos. 137–71, who names Cardinal Montalto, Grand Duke Ferdinando de' Medici, and others of their circle as patrons of the hunts in which he participated during the years just prior to 1600. The *avvisi di Roma* that mention the devolution of the Villa Lante are transcribed in J. A. F. Orbaan, 'La Roma di Sisto V negli *avvisi*', *Archivio della R. Società Romana di storia patria*, 33 (1910), 296 and 300: '1587 giugno 3. Nostro Signore ha dato il governo di Bagnaja a Montalto' and '1587 settembre 26. Dicesi che'l Papa habbia donato a Montalto in vita di S. S. Ill.ma il giardino, vigna et palazzo di Bagnaia et che'l resto rimanga al vescovo di Viterbo.'

Fig. 1.11. The Villa Lante in Bagnaia. From David R. Coffin, *The Villa in Renaissance Rome* (Princeton, 1979), 349

elements of his coat of arms: the lion rampant and a two-tiered mound of small hills.[54]

Cardinal Montalto's patronage of painters and sculptors and his avid collection of art works was fostered, to a great extent, by his close friend, Cardinal Del Monte. It was Del Monte who had Caravaggio in his household from about 1595 to 1606, and the famous *Singer with Lute*, which was painted about 1596–8, evidently depicts a musician from the Montalto–Del Monte circle. When Caravaggio fled Rome in 1606, having committed homicide, he took refuge in Naples at the palace of Contestabile Marc'Antonio Colonna, the husband of Montalto's sister Orsina. Waźbiński hypothesizes that a visit to the exiled Caravaggio was the original motive for Montalto's and Del Monte's journey to Naples in 1607–8, a sojourn that extended to almost six months on account of Del Monte's illness.[55]

Towards the end of Montalto's life, or even shortly thereafter, Gianlorenzo

[54] Claudia Lazzaro-Bruno, 'The Villa Lante at Bagnaia' (Ph.D. diss., Princeton University, 1974); David R. Coffin, *The Villa in the Life of Renaissance Rome* (Princeton, 1979), 340–69; and Patrizia Cavazzini, 'New Documents for Cardinal Alessandro Peretti Montalto's Frescoes at Bagnaia', *Burlington Magazine*, 135 (1993), 316–27.   [55] Waźbiński, *Il Cardinale Francesco Maria Del Monte*, 192.

FIG. 1.12. Bernini's bust of Cardinal Montalto, *c*.1623. From Irving Lavin, 'Bernini's Bust of Cardinal Montalto', *The Burlington Magazine*, 127 (1985), 34

Bernini was commissioned to create the impressive marble bust of the cardinal shown in Fig. 1.12.[56] In the portrait, I think that we can see Cardinal Montalto's character as described by his friend Cardinal Guido Bentivoglio:

Montalto was barely 15 years old when his great-uncle promoted him to the cardinalate. Being of such a tender age, he took almost no part in the church government, and, as a result, also received none of the envy and hatred normally directed at those nephews who, either because of seniority or because of excessive ambition, have been in the uppermost position in the ministry of their uncles. Having inherited the office of Vice-Chancellor, vacated during Sixtus' time by the death of Cardinal Alessandro Farnese, along with other

---

[56] Concerning the recent rediscovery of this bust and its attribution to Bernini, see Irving Lavin, 'Bernini's Bust of Cardinal Montalto', *Burlington Magazine*, 127 (1985), 32–8.

very ample ecclesiastical incomes, Montalto, therefore, lived in the very large palace of the Vice-Chancellery, and there he maintained himself with one of the most numerous and splendid households that was seen in Rome at that time. His appearance was more rough than gracious; grave in personal comportment and hardly less in speaking and in habits, quite reticent in speaking and full of a certain external melancholy, which many judged to be concealed arrogance. And though in domestic conversations he showed himself to be very courteous and pliant, both his own reticence and his habit of almost entirely converting day into night and night into day made it extremely difficult to deal with him and made him even more distant from worldly affairs, towards which his nature little inclined him. But in any case he was a great cardinal, greatly esteemed at the court of Rome and, beyond it, by all princes, and by Grand Duke Ferdinando of Tuscany in particular, who gave up the cardinalate during the time of Sixtus V and always retained an affectionate and faithful friendship with the pope's nephew, Montalto. He was esteemed all the more because of his close relationships with all princes and with the heads of the Colonna and Orsini houses. Above all he loved music, and he maintained in his household truly excellent virtuosi of that profession. He was a great alms-giver. He built a church for the Theatines. He showed himself to be generous in all the noblest ways, and he uniquely possessed a quality that in Rome is often desired but rarely found, that is, he was truthful and always religiously fulfilled that which he promised. Certainly few other nephews than Cardinal Montalto who have obtained great fortunes have possessed that elusive personal greatness, which cannot be well described. And also the prince, his brother, no less than he. The Duchess of Sessa, a woman of rare intelligence and long experience of Rome, used to say that both of them seemed born rather than made great.[57]

---

[57] 'Era di quindeci anni Montalto appena quando il zio l'aveva promosso al cardinalato. Per essere di età così tenera egli non aveva quasi alcuna partecipazione del governo e per conseguenza neanco dell'invidia e dell'odio che resta per ordinario in quei nipoti, i quali o per lunghezza di tempo o per eccesso d'autorità sono stati nel supremo luogo del ministerio appresso i loro zii. Rimasto dunque Montalto con l'officio di vice-cancelliere vacato in tempo di Sisto per morte del cardinale Alessandro Farnese e con altre larghissime entrate ecclesiastiche, abitava egli nel palazzo amplissimo della vicecancelleria, e vi si tratteneva con una delle più numerose famiglie e più splendide che allora si vedessero in Roma. Aveva egli più del rozzo che dell'amabile nell'aspetto; grave di portamento nella persona e quasi non meno di communicazione eziandio ne' costumi, ritenuto assai di parole e pieno di certa esteriore malinconia che da molti era giudicata più tosto una sua interiore alterigia, e quantunque nelle conversazioni domestiche egli si mostrasse poi molto cortese e trattabile, nondimeno e la sua propria retiratezza e l'uso ch'egli aveva pigliato di convertire quasi intieramente i giorno in notte e la notte in giorno rendevano sopra modo difficile il trattar seco, e rendevano insieme lui stesso tanto alieno maggiormente dallo star sul negozio al quale per sua natura poco inclinava. Ma in ogni modo era gran cardinale, grandemente stimato nella corte di Roma e fuori di essa da tutti i prencipi, e dal granduca di Toscana Ferdinando in particolare, che aveva deposto il cardinalato in tempo di Sisto quinto e riteneva sempre un'affettuosa e costante amicizia col nepote Montalto. Facevanlo maggiormente stimare tanto più le sue parentele sì strette con tutti i prencipi, e con tutti due i capi delle due case Colonna e Orsina. Amava egli sommamente la musica, e manteneva in casa virtuosi in quella professione eccellentissimi. Era grand'elemosiniere; fabricava una religiosa chiesa alla religione de' teatini. Mostravasi liberale in ogni altra più nobil forma, e veniva commendato singolarmente in una qualità che spesso in Roma si desidera e di rado si trova, cioè ch'egli fosse verace e che sempre religiosamente osservasse quello che promettesse. E certo pochi altri nepoti che siano rimasti in elevata fortuna avranno avuto quel non so che di grande in se stesso che non si può bene esprimere come l'ebbe il cardinale Montalto, e non meno di lui anco il prencipe suo fratello. E soleva dire la duchessa di Sessa, donna di raro ingegno e longamente versata in Roma, che l'uno e l'altro di loro pareva nato grande e non divenuto.' Guido Bentivoglio, *Memorie e lettere*, ed. Costantino Panigada (Scrittori d'Italia, 150; Bari, 1934), 58–9.

2

Padrocinanza and *Clientela*

༄ঌ৵৵

THE acquisition of vast estates and the construction and decoration of magnificent palaces were obvious and customary ways to create a public front.[1] At
one side, the munificence and liberality for which Cardinal Montalto was praised
were even simpler and more direct expressions of the conspicuous consumption
of an *animo grande*.[2] On the other side, the more complex forms of personal presentation are those described in other chapters of Vincenzo Giustiniani's treatise
for new cardinals: table service, social grace and protocol, style of travel, hunt etiquette, and arts patronage. Of these, patronage is, perhaps, the most complex and
subtle, hence effective, mode of personal presentation, having symbolic meaning,[3] but also merging into the more concrete and practical web of *clientela* that
connected family ties, friendship, favour barter, political alliance, and exercise of
power with display of taste.[4]

The web of a cardinal's (or nobleman's) patronage in Montalto's Rome
resembled a series of concentric circles connected by strands of familial, personal,
and official relations. With the patron at the centre, the innermost ring was his
household, or *famiglia*, which itself was hierarchical in structure. Giustiniani
advises every Master of Ceremonies (*Mastro di Camera*) of a new cardinal to
make four lists: first, the *famiglia del padrone* in four categories: (1) gentlemen, (2)
chamber attendants (*aiutanti di camera*), (3) household staff (*staffieri*), and (4)
humble servants; second, cardinals, distinguishing between those (of the curia)

---

[1] See the discussion of 'front' in Erving Goffman, *The Presentation of Self in Everyday Life* (rev. edn., New
York, 1959), 22–3.
[2] See Peter Burke, 'Conspicuous Consumption in Early Modern Italy', in his *Historical Anthropology of Early
Modern Italy* (Cambridge, 1987).
[3] For a recent summary of theory concerning the semiotic component of cultural forms, see Stewart Hall,
'The Toad in the Garden: Thatcherism among the Theorists', in Cary Nelson and Lawrence Grossberg (eds.),
Marxism and the Interpretation of Culture (Urbana, Ill., 1988), 35–57.
[4] See E. Gellner, 'Patrons and Clients', in E. Gellner and J. Waterbury (eds.), *Patrons and Clients in
Mediterranean Societies* (London, 1977), 1–20; Werner L. Gundersheimer, 'Patronage in the Renaissance: An
Exploratory Approach', in G. F. Lytle and S. Orgel (eds.), *Patronage in the Renaissance* (Princeton, 1981), 3–23;
and Ronald Weissman, 'Taking Patronage Seriously', 25–45, and the additional bibliography cited there.

who stay at the court of Rome and who are *in governo* and those who are not; third, ambassadors of princes, realms, barons, major prelates, dukes, agents of princes, and principal friends or enemies of one's patron; fourth, other principal nobles and gentlemen (*signori*). He describes in minute detail where and by whom individuals of each class are greeted upon arrival at a cardinal's palace, where his coat is taken, where he is seated, and how far accompanied in departure.[5] In this very crucial activity of receiving and entertaining cardinals, princes, and their representatives, the gentlemen of the cardinal's *famiglia* became almost an extension of the patron himself, greeting and conversing with the guests with maximum professional expertise.

Cardinal Montalto's *famiglia*, in 1612 for instance, numbered 170, the largest known among the curia at that time.[6] The household list is, as usual, ordered according to social rank. It begins with *monsignori*, followed by *cavalieri*, *canonici*, and men dignified with the title *don*. There seem to be forty-three 'gentlemen' of the household. The *aiutanti di camera* seem to number fifteen, the group concluding with Giovanni Guerra, chief architect of Sixtus' urban renewal projects, and Terenzio Terenzi, whose paintings were found in many Roman churches. The sixtieth name is that of the *guardaroba*, who is followed by forty-seven other *staffieri*, mostly identified with service professions, including the captains of the guards and the kitchen staff. The sweeper, number 109, presumably begins the list of *servitù bassa*, which concludes with thirteen stable boys. The same document also contains lists of the separate *famiglie* of the obscure Cardinal Andrea Baroni Peretti, adopted and raised by Cardinal Montalto although only two years younger than he, and of Prince Michele Peretti. These households numbered twenty and nineteen, respectively, in 1612.

Each member of the *famiglia* received money from the cardinal's treasury each month.[7] This consisted of the traditional 10 baiocchi per day for *companatico* (literally, food to go with bread), received by each one regardless of rank, plus salary, provision, and/or rent allowance, if they did not live in the palace itself. Most of the members of the household received between 2.5 and 3 silver scudi per month. A few received considerably more: 23.75 for the salary and *companatico* of the physician and natural philosopher Pompeo Caimo and 20 or 23 for each

---

[5] Vincenzo Giustiniani, 'Istruzione per un Mastro di Cam.ra', I:Las, Fondo Orsucci 48, fos. 173–5.

[6] I:Ras, Archivio Giustiniani, Busta 87, '1612: Ruolo del Mese di Novembre dei giorni trenta—Ruolo dell'Ill.mo S.r Card.le Montalto', *passim*. Chater, 'Musical Patronage', 193, incorrectly reports this number to have been 146. Jean Delumeau, *Vie économique et sociale de Rome dans la seconde moitié du XVIᵉ siècle* (Paris, 1957), i. 434–5, argues that the wealth of cardinals declined during the course of the 16th c. and produces (p. 434) a list of curial cardinals in 1526–7 that shows households ranging in size from forty-five to 306 individuals, whereas in 1598 the cardinal-nephew of Clement VIII, Pietro Aldobrandini, supported a *famiglia* of 140, and in 1599 four newly created cardinals had households numbering only twenty.

[7] See the introductory essay on Roman money.

of the captains of the guard.[8] But there is no correlation between social rank and monthly payment. And in no case did any of these household members receive an amount equal to the cost of living in Rome at that time, at least not through the payroll. Some members received other payments, which were kept off the payroll, as we shall see presently. Only household members of the two lower orders should probably be considered salaried employees of the cardinal, and even in these cases the principal compensation was, in all likelihood, food and shelter. The rest of the *famiglia* were clients, and it was the cardinal's duty as their patron to use his influence to help them find other income or advantages, according to need.

The musicians in Cardinal Montalto's household are found in three of the four social categories. A parish census (*Stato d'anime*) of 1602, includes, as residing in the Palazzo della Cancelleria, a list of 125 of Montalto's household members that seems to have been copied from a role book. Fourteenth on the list, just before the dons, is the 'Cavalier del Leuto',[9] who was already in the cardinal's service in 1589, according to a letter of Giovanni de Macque.[10] This musician has recently been identified as the prolific lutenist-composer Lorenzino, born in Bologna, and trained in Parma by Fabrizio Dentice and Orazio Bassani at the expense of Duke Ottavio Farnese of Parma. Lorenzino remained in Duke Ottavio's service until 1586, except for a brief period (1570–1) in Tivoli and Rome, was made Knight of the Golden Spur before 1603, and was the recipient, after 1594, of an early archlute given originally to the madrigalist-prince Carlo Gesualdo by the Bolognese lutenist Alessandro Piccinini.[11] Giovanni de Macque, in April 1589, claimed that the Cavalier del Leuto was then about to leave the service of Cardinal Montalto, but in a dedication to his first book of five-voice madrigals, signed 10 May 1593, Sebastiano Raval (*c.*1550–1604) places the Cavaliere in Montalto's palace along with Scipione Dentice (1560–*c.*1635), Luca Marenzio

---

[8] Pompeo Caimo (1568–1634) was the author of *De calido innato libri tres* (Venice: Piutus, 1626); *Parallelo politico delle repubbliche antiche e moderne* (Padua: Tozzi, 1627); *Dell'ingegno humano, de' suoi segni, della sua differenza negli huomini, e nelle donne, e del suo buono indirizzo* (Venice: Brogrollo, 1629); and *De nobilitate* (Udine: Schiratti, 1634).

[9] I:Rav, S. Lorenzo in Damaso 61, fos. 77ʳ–78ᵛ, cited by Chater, 'Musical Patronage', 195.

[10] On 28 Apr. 1589 the composer Giovanni de Macque in Naples wrote to Camillo Norimberghi in Rome, 'La ringratio delle nove dattemi et la prego a continuare et di farmi intendere se il Cavaliero del liuto et messer Bartolomeo si sono retirati alli servitij del Cardinale Mont'alto come si è detto qua', transcribed by Ruth Irene DeFord, 'Ruggiero Giovannelli and the Madrigal in Rome, 1572–1599' (Ph.D. diss., Harvard University, 1975), i. 292. See also Friedrich Lippmann, 'Giovanni de Macque fra Roma e Napoli: Nuovi documenti', *Rivista italiana di musicologia*, 13 (1978), at 243–79 at 271–2. Chater, 'Musical Patronage', 195, suggests that the other musician named in this letter is the French composer Bartolomeo Roy, active in Rome since 1570 and in the Kingdom of Naples in 1581 and 1583.

[11] Dinko Fabris, *Andrea Falconieri napoletano: Un liutista-compositore del Seicento* (Rome, 1987), 23–5. Actually, the suggestion that 'il cavalier del leuto' was Lorenzino was first made by Alberto Cametti, 'Orazio Michi "dell'Arpa", virtuoso e compositore di musica della prima metà del Seicento', *Rivista musicale italiana*, 21 (1914), 203–71 at 222.

(1553/54–99), and (Scipione?) Stella, (?1559–c.1610/30), who recently heard his works. The Cavalier del Leuto died in the cardinal's palace on 23 September 1608.[12]

Among the *staffieri* in the 1602 list is one Pier'Antonio *del leuto* and Marchio *cantore*, the latter of whom can be identified as the famous bass singer Melchior Palantrotti (Palontrotti, Palentrotti).[13] He was born on Peretti-family land in Venafro, trained at S. Luigi dei Francesi in Rome (1588–9), well paid at the court of Ferrara (1589–97), and appointed to the papal chapel in 1597.[14] In 1603 he spent an extended period performing for the Viceroy of Naples.[15] A letter of 29 July 1600 from Cardinal Del Monte to Grand Duke Ferdinando provides the first evidence that Palantrotti had joined Montalto's household:

As for the musicians of the papal chapel, between salary and gifts they get 25 scudi per month. Some of these singers are kept at the expense of some cardinal. I have one and Montalto has Melchiorre and others. During Lent they go to sing at [The Archconfraternity of] the Trinity [in the church of] S. Marcello, and they collect 20 scudi, some more and some less, according to their needs. And this is all [I have to report] about the musicians.[16]

According to the parish census of 1602, Palantrotti lived in Montalto's palace of the Chancellery, but in April of that year he received reimbursement for house rent retroactive to 19 January 1602.[17] These rent reimbursements continue until 8 July 1614.[18] He died on 18 September 1614.[19] While in Cardinal Montalto's service, Palantrotti sang in two of the earliest operas in Florence: Giulio Caccini's *Il rapimento di Cefalo* and Jacopo Peri's *Euridice* of 1600; in the Florentine intermedi of 1608; and in the first secular Roman opera, Montalto's *Amor pudico* of 1614 (see Ch. 9).[20]

A similar distribution among the ranks of Cardinal Montalto's household is found in the salary account books of 1612–20.[21] Among the *gentiluomini* is found

---

[12] I:Rav, S. Lorenzo in Damaso, 54, Morti II, fo. 60; see Chater, 'Musical Patronage', 195.

[13] I shall use the spelling of his name as he consistently signed it for the paymaster of the papal chapel, e.g. I:Rvat, Cappella Sistina, Cammerlingo 4 [payrolls for 1603], *passim*.

[14] A good summary of Palantrotti's career, with references to earlier scholarship and newly recovered documents, is provided by Anthony Newcomb, *The Madrigal at Ferrara, 1579–1597* (Princeton, 1980), i. 178–9.

[15] I:Rvat, Cappella Sistina, Cammerlingo 4, fos. 2ʳ, 31ᵛ.

[16] 'Quanto a' Musici la Cappella del Papa tra provisioni regaglie si fa conto che dia venticinque scudi il mese, alcuni di questi Cantori si accomodano per le spese con qualche Cardinale, io ne tengo uno, M.Alto tien Melchiorre, et altri; la Quarasima vanno à Cantare alla Trinita, S. marcello et buscano venti scudo chi piu chi meno secondo il bisogno; et questo è quanto alli Musici.' I:Fas, Mediceo del Principato, 3762, at the date 29 July 1600, Cardinal Del Monte to Bellisario Vinta. Quoted by Chater, 'Musical Patronage', 198.

[17] I:Rac, Archivio Cardelli, Appendice, vol. 33, 'Registro de' mandati e quiet.za, 1601–1602', under the date 30 Apr. 1602. The payment for six months is 12 scudi and 50 baiocchi.

[18] Ibid., vol. 37, 'Registro dei mandati, quietanze, e mandati di francitie dalli 1612 alli 22 di febraro 1616', *sub die*.   [19] I:Rav, S. Lorenzo in Damaso, Morti, II, fo. 77ʳ. Cited by Chater, 'Musical Patronage', 199.

[20] Chater, 'Musical Patronage', 198–9.

[21] I:Ras, Archivio Giustiniani, Busta 87. Chater, 'Musical Patronage', 218–21, transcribes names of musicians and painters from these lists, but he omits some through error.

the Cavaliere Cesare Marotta (*c.*1580–1630), the cardinal's most active composer of chamber music for solo voice and the central musician in this study. He was born with the name Vito at Sant'Agata in Puglia,[22] and, according to his wife's bitter testimony after his death, 'he was a pauper at the time [of his marriage], possessing nothing and earning his living by lending his personal services to various princes both in Naples and in Rome', before entering into Cardinal Montalto's service.[23] 'Cesarello' ('Little Caesar') Marotta, as he is called in the account book, was in Naples on 26 August 1604 when Montalto gave him and his wife 100 scudi for their transfer to Rome.[24] Probably because of this, Marotta is described as 'Napolitano' in the first parish document that records his presence in Montalto's neighbourhood on 4 August 1605.[25] The couple obviously settled in earlier, however, since their patron paid their apartment rent of 40 scudi for six months, retroactive to 6 November 1604.[26] According to the earliest census reports to mention them, Marotta and his wife were present in the parish of S. Lorenzo in Damaso (the neighbourhood of Cardinal Montalto's palace) in 1606, had 'gone to Naples' at Easter, at least, of 1607, and were back in Rome for the 1608 listing.[27] In all likelihood, Ippolita and Cesare had accompanied Cardinal Montalto on the trip to Naples that was extended to about six months because of the illness of Montalto's close friend, Cardinal Del Monte, as mentioned in the previous chapter.

Cesare Marotta and his wife, the famous singer Ippolita Recupito, immediately became the best-paid musicians in Cardinal Montalto's household, and it is probably for that reason that payments to them were made, for a time, in the form of *mandati*, which are something like present-day personal bank cheques, rather than through the usual mechanism, which was by monthly cash payment distributed by the *spendatore* of the household, who consulted a list normally called

---

[22] Cametti, 'Che era l'"Hippolita"', 116, describes Sant'Agata as a village in the province of Foggia, almost at the border of the province of Avellino, nestled in the Neapolitan Apennines at an altitude of about 800 metres.

[23] 'Erat adeo pauper, ut nihil possidebat et simplicem victum tantum ex personali servitude percepit, quam diversis Principibus tam Neapolis quam Romæ præstitæ'. Cametti, 'Chi era l'"Hippolita"', 118.

[24] I:Rac, Archivio Cardelli, Appendice, vol. 34, 'Registro de mandati, quietanze, e mandati di franchitie che comincia alli . . . di Gennaro 1603 e finisce alli XXI di Luglio 1607', at the date 12 Oct. 1604: 'S. Herrera e Cosa, ci darete debito delli *scudi* 100 di m.ta che havete fatti pagare in Napoli à Cesarello Marotta in 105 corr.te di Regno, al quale gli doniamo per fare un *nostro* Quieto, e V. S. di un con qui, di Bagnaia il di 12. di ottobre 1604, fatti buoni alli depos.i a 25 di ag.to pass.o *scudi* 100 m.ta.'

[25] I:Rav, S. Lorenzo in Damaso, 54, Morti II, fo. 51ᵛ, which records the death of Marotta's newborn son on 4 Aug. 1605; see Chater, 'Musical Patronage', 199. The same book of *Morti* records the death of another son of Cesare and Ippolita: Francesco, *putto*, died 15 Aug. 1609 (fo. 62ʳ). A female child was stillborn to the couple in March of 1611: see the letter of 18 Mar. 1611 in App. A, Letter 42. And yet another daughter, Anna Maria, age 4, died on 25 Sept. 1621 (Morti II, fo. 94ᵛ). The same book (fo. 140ᵛ) records Cesare Marotta's own death on 28 July 1630: 'Cesar Marotta annorum 50 circiter in communione S. Matris ecclesis animam Deo reddidit, cuius corpus die 29 sepultum est in hac ecclesia recepit sacramenta'. The year of his birth is calculated on the basis of this record.

[26] I:Rac, Archivio Cardelli, Appendice, vol. 34, at the date 26 Nov. 1604.

[27] I:Rav, S. Lorenzo in Damaso, 62, Stato d'Anime (1606–8), fo. 28ʳ.

the *ruolo de' salariati, lista della famiglia, libro de' provvisionati*, or something similar. I can think of two reasons for this special treatment. The salary payment was
explicitly for Cesare and Ippolita together. But women are rarely, if ever, found
on the household salary lists of cardinals, probably because it was prohibited
or discouraged by custom. Payment by *mandato*, therefore, kept Ippolita's name
off the cardinal's payroll. The other probable reason is that Cesare and Ippolita
received emoluments and reimbursements not given to any other members of
the household, and this fact, if widely known, might have caused jealousy, dissen-
tion, and bothersome, not to mention expensive, requests for similar treatment.

Cesare and Ippolita began receiving their salary via *mandati* on 8 June 1607,
with a large, overdue payment for services on an account that began in November 1604, when Cardinal Montalto also began to pay their rent:

Signori Herrero, etc., will pay to Cesarello Marotta 305 scudi in coins, which are the
balance and complement of the 725 scudi, which is the total of his salary and Lady
Hippolita's, his wife, for twenty-nine months, through the month of March past, of which
he has had 420 scudi on account from us, which were debited to his account. From the
Chancellery, 8 April 1607.[28]

Cesare and Ippolita continued to receive their salary of 25 scudi per month for
the rest of Cardinal Montalto's life. They were paid by means of *mandati* until 1617,[29]
when their monthly salary disappears from the registers.[30] No surviving *ruolo della
famiglia* has been found for the years 1617–19, but the roll for January 1620 provides an explanation for the disappearance. The 12 scudi per month that had been
allotted to Cesare Marotta, at first as *companatico* (food allowance) and later as a
nominal (and false) *provisione*, in the surviving lists of 1611–16,[31] is increased in
the first roll of 1620 by 25 scudi per month, exactly the *provisione* now missing
from the registers of *mandati*. It is clear, then, that the 'increase' in Cesare's salary,
as noted by Chater,[32] is merely the result of a transfer of the couple's joint salary
from the registers of *mandati* to the *ruoli della famiglia*.

In addition to the monthly 25 scudi salary, 12 scudi food allowance, and 6 and
two-thirds scudi rent reimbursement, Cesare Marotta received an allotment of
20 scudi, 20 baiocchi every six months for firewood from 1609 onwards,[33] and

---

[28] 'S. Herrero etc. pagarete à Cesarello Marotta scudi trecento cinque di m.ta quali sono per resto et
eccomp.to de scudi 725 ch'importa la sua provisione è di dama Hippolita sua moglie per mesi ventinove finiti
per tutto il mese di Marzo prossimo passato, che scudi 420 l'hà havuti a buon conto da noi, e datecene debito,
dalla Cancellaria il di 8 d'aprile 1607. scudi 305 m.ta', I:Rac, Archivio Cardelli, Appendice, vol. 34, *sub die* 8
Apr. 1607.   [29] Ibid., vols. 35 and 37, *passim*.

[30] Ibid., vol. 38, 'Registro de mandati, quietanze, e mandati di franchita, 1617–1622', contains no further
salary payments to the couple.

[31] I:Ras, Archivio Giustiniani, Busta 87; see Chater, 'Musical Patronage', 218–19.

[32] Chater, 'Musical Patronage', 200.

[33] I:Rac, Archivio Cardelli, Appendice, vols. 35, 37, 38, 54, and 55, *passim*.

even a hay allowance for his horse of 16 scudi, 25 baiocchi per semester in 1609–12.[34] In addition, Marotta had been awarded a 'pension' (a share in the ecclesiastical income of some individual or institution) by the end of 1615.[35] No one else in the cardinal's household enjoyed anything approaching this combination of benefits. And, as we shall see, Cesare and his wife received occasional gifts of money and goods, both from their patron and from their protector.

The title of courtesy *dama* given to Marotta's wife Ippolita in the *mandato* translated above suggests that she was from a family of some social pretension. There was, in fact, a Naples-born professor of theology at the Jesuit Collegio Neapolitano, author of erudite books in Latin, and 'very famous' preacher, by the name of Giulio Cesare Recupito, who, being born in 1595, could have been Ippolita's cousin.[36] In fact, it is not improbable that a professional singer like Ippolita Recupito could have a famous author for a relative: Adriana Basile, an equally renowned Neapolitan singer of Ippolita's generation, was the sister of the celebrated author Giovambattista Basile.

Cesare, however, is not given the corresponding dignity of *don* in Montalto's earlier registers, and it might be supposed that a difference between his and his wife's station became an irritant and one reason why the composer sought aristocratic status. The knighthood eventually conferred upon Marotta in 1612 might, on the other hand, be viewed as a reward for his artistic excellence, as we have been told was the case for two other of Montalto's household members: Il Cavalier del Leuto and the painter Giuseppe Cesari, Cavalier d'Arpino. But on 8 February 1612 Vincenzio Landinelli wrote from Rome to his patron, Marquis Enzo Bentivoglio,[37] in Ferrara:

Tomorrow morning in S. Agata à Monte Magnanapoli (since the pope has been at Montecavallo since yesterday), Sig. Cesare Marotti will receive the Cross of Savoy from the hands of the Ambassador. And present at this ceremony will be Cardinals Borghese, Sezza, and Capponi with a large representation of gentlemen and ladies. And Sig.ra

---

[34] Ibid., vol. 35, at the dates 6 Nov. 1609, 10 Nov. 1610, and 3 Dec. 1610; vol. 37, at the date 17 July 1612.

[35] He mentions this in his letter of 4 Dec. 1615, transcribed as Letter 102.

[36] Nicolò Toppi, *Biblioteca napoletana* (Naples: Bulifon, 1678), 167; and Philippe Alegambe, *Bibliotheca scriptorum Societatis Iesu* (Antwerp: Meursius, 1643), 288. Cametti, 'Chi era l'"Hippolita"', 120, points out that Giulio Cesare's father was named Giovan Paolo, whereas Ippolita's father was named Giovanni Tommaso, and he speculates that Giovan Paolo and Giovanni Tommaso could have been brothers, making Ippolita and Giulio Cesare cousins.

[37] Concerning Enzo Bentivoglio as patron of music, see Dinko Fabris, 'Frescobaldi e la musica in casa Bentivoglio', in *Girolamo Frescobaldi nel IV centenario della nascita: Atti del convegno internazionale di studi (Ferrara, 9–14 settembre 1983)*, ed. Sergio Durante and Dinko Fabris (Quaderni della Rivista italiana di musicologia, 10; Florence, 1986), 63–85. A book on this subject, with transcription of the extensive and valuable Bentivoglio correspondence, by Fabris is forthcoming under the title *Mecenati e musici: Documenti sul mecenatismo artistico dei Bentivoglio di Ferrara nell'epoca di Monteverdi (1585–1645)*. I am very grateful to Dr Fabris for reading the manuscript of my book, for his many useful suggestions, and for sharing much information and many transcriptions of letters prior to the publication of his book.

Hippolita will be there, too. So if, my Lord, you thought diplomacy were necessary, now that we invest these dignities in ordinary people, you are mistaken. It is quite true that he bought this dignity dearly, and this weighs upon Sig.ra Hippolita, since so far it has cost more than 300 scudi.[38]

Cesare Marotta considered Enzo Bentivoglio his protector,[39] as Giulio Caccini held Virginio Orsini to be his,[40] and he acquired his knighthood with a large measure of the marquis's help.[41] Cesare's relations with Bentivoglio can be traced back to 1607, when Enzo became involved in the three-way exchange of favours, involving Cardinal Montalto and Cardinal Scipione Borghese, which is detailed in Chapter 8.[42] Briefly, Bentivoglio helped Montalto collect his pension on the archbishopric of Ferrara and illicitly procured Ferrarese art treasures for Cardinal Borghese; Montalto lent Bentivoglio musicians and pleaded his case with Pope Paul V (uncle of Cardinal Borghese), whom he was instrumental in getting elected, through the cardinal-nephew; and Cardinal Scipione Borghese lent Montalto musicians and interceded with the pope on behalf of Bentivoglio's scheme to drain a vast marsh and claim the land as his own. Further complicating this web of *padroncinanza* and *clientela* is the fact that Cesare Marotta requested—almost demanded—that Enzo Bentivoglio intercede on behalf of two of Marotta's own clients, presumably as partial compensation for services rendered. In the first case, on 10 November 1612, he asks Bentivoglio for a recommendation in the appointment of a municipal judge for a five-year term by the Auditors of Ferrara. Marotta's client here is Pietro Santolino from Fano, Governor of Cervia in the duchy of Ferrara and brother of Francesco Santolino, *sottomaestro di casa* in Montalto's household (Letter 62). In the second case, on 1 October 1613, Marotta asks for 'a very warm letter, with a few words in your own hand' directed to the Commendatore of the Cavalieri dello Santo Spirito, a Church-based chivalric order similar to the Cavalieri della Croce di Savoia, to which Marotta bought an appointment (see above), except that apparently this order was for clerics. Bentivoglio's letter was to ask the Commendatore to make good on his promise of election, since the client, Don Giovanni Domenico de Rentijs, an archdeacon and a relative of Marotta, had fulfilled the Commendatore's conditions by founding an abbey (Letter 71). In both cases, one may presume that Marotta had received or expected from his client some reciprocation. Marotta's basis for appealing to Bentivoglio was obviously his perception of the current balance

---

[38] Entire letter transcribed in App. A, Letter 49.

[39] See the letter of 12 Nov. 1610, App. A, Letter 32.

[40] See his letter of 5 Mar. 1607, App. A, Letter 16.

[41] See Marotta's letters of 20.x.1610 (Letter 29), 12.xi.1610 (Letter 32), 8.xii.1611 (Letter 45), 14.xii.1611 (Letter 46), 14.xii.1611 (Letter 47).

[42] Cesare and Ippolita are first mentioned in correspondence to Bentivoglio in a letter of 28 July 1607, Letter 18.

in his exchange with the marquis. Bentivoglio, of course, must have had some credit with or power over the Auditors of Ferrara and the Commendatore dello Santo Spirito, and we know that he was beholden to Cardinal Montalto, whose tacit support of Marotta in things of this nature would have been part of his transaction with a valued household member, on the one hand, and a needy client, on the other.

Marotta's known correspondence with Bentivoglio is inaugurated in 1610, with a letter (Letter 27) that starts out with the playful deception that Cesare and Ippolita have already arrived in Ferrara after a long and arduous journey, which is described in imaginary detail, but continues with an abruptly concrete description of the cold realities of November in Rome. The cheeky tone of the first letter is continued in thirty-two others during the next five years, and after Marotta acquired his knighthood, it becomes even more familiar.

One of the most frequently recurring topics in letters to Bentivoglio from and about Marotta is the question of a visit to Ferrara, against which the ostensible impediment is Cardinal Montalto's apparent reluctance to order Cesare and Ippolita to go (Letters 50, 51, 74, and 75). One senses that Cesare and Ippolita feared not being taken back into the household if they accepted the cardinal's offer to go to Ferrara of their own volition. Even more letters mention gifts requested—four balls of soap from Bologna, a pair of black stockings from Ferrara, a hunting dog, a pistol, a pet monkey, a comb, a whisk broom, some ribbon, lace collars, salami, and money (Letters 39, 44, 45, 60, 72, 102–4, and 106)—and received: a box, eels, a watch, a necklace, stockings, gloves, salami, and money (Letters 28, 30, 35, 56, 67, and 89). Still more concern the training of singers for Bentivoglio's stage works in Ferrara—so many more that they will be the topic of Chapter 4. And almost as many are about Marotta's compositions for the marquis, which will be discussed in Chapters 6 and 8. The correspondence—and the relationship—comes to an impasse in 1616 with Marotta's repeated insistence that Bentivoglio pay him 20 scudi, which Marotta claims is owed him by Enzo's brother Ferrante, so that Marotta can replace the gold-wound strings cut away by thieves from one of Cardinal Montalto's harpsichords (Letters 102, 103, 104). Marotta's last known letter to Bentivoglio, in 1620, vainly requests the promised redemption of another debt, as will be explained shortly.

Almost everything we know of Cesare Marotta's activities as a composer is concentrated in the years 1611–16: music for Montalto's and Bentivoglio's stage works and monodies for Ippolita to sing at the Roman palaces of their patron and protector. What little we know about Marotta after Cardinal Montalto's death suggests a life in decline and disintegration. During his last two years, he obtained loans of 100 and 25 scudi through the mechanism of establishing an annuity (*census*) in favour of his creditor amounting to 5 per cent of the borrowed sum, a common method at that time of circumventing the Church rule against lending money at interest.[43] At Marotta's death, 28 July 1630, it was this creditor, and not any member of Cesare's family, who asked for his will to be opened.[44] Written on 19 May 1628, it provides for the support of his illegitimate daughter, Anna (born 11 April 1628), concedes only her clothes, a necklace, and two rings of her choice to his wife, Ippolita (plus 1,000 scudi in dowry if she should remarry), and the rest to his legitimate daughter Francesca.[45] Ippolita, however, successfully challenged the will, and was able to give her daughter a dowry of 3,000 scudi two years later.[46]

The principal argument that Ippolita Recupito (c. 1577–1650) used to challenge her husband's testament was that the wealth that he was disposing consisted mainly of her earnings. Implied in this claim is that the salary and other generous emoluments were given by Cardinal Montalto principally to retain her services. The claim would have rung true, since she was acknowledged to be one of the four great female singers of early Baroque monody, along with Vittoria Archilei (1550–c. 1620), Adriana Basile (c. 1580–c. 1640), and Francesca Caccini (1587–c. 1640). Although Vittoria Archilei was the first female virtuoso singer associated with the new styles of solo song that emerged towards the end of the sixteenth century, it was Pietro Della Valle's understanding that Ippolita surpassed her when they both sang in the festivities for the wedding of Cosimo II de' Medici in 1608,[47] a judgement in which the librettists Ottavio Rinuccini and Michelangelo Buonarroti the Younger and the composer Marco da Gagliano more or less concurred.[48] Ippolita's participation in the Medici festivities of 1608 prevented her from singing in Claudio Monteverdi's opera *Arianna*, for which her services had been sought from Cardinal Montalto by Duke Vincenzo Gonzaga of Mantua during the previous year.[49] Monteverdi considered Ippolita

---

[43] I:Rac, Archivio Generale Urbino, Sezione XXVI[a], Protocollo 3, *sub die* 19 July 1629, and Protocollo 4, *sub die* 1 June 1630.

[44] I:Ras, Archivio dei 30 Notari Capitolini, Ufficio 27, vol. 102, fos. 107 and 114. Cametti, 'Chi era l'"Hippolita"', mistakenly surmised that this creditor, Donna Margherita Ferraiola, was the mother of Marotta's illegitimate daughter.

[45] Ibid., fos. 110–11, dated 19 May 1628. A clausula of 20 May 1628 to the testament is noted in I:Ac, Archivio Generale Urbano, Sezione XXVI[a], Protocollo 2, fo. 85[r], but the clausula itself is missing.

[46] The details of Marotta's will, death, and burial, and of Ippolita's challenge and other later events in her life are provided with precise documentation by Cametti, 'Chi era l'"Hippolita"', 116–23.

[47] Pietro Della Valle, 'Della musica dell'età nostra che non è punto inferiore, anzi è migliore di quella dell'età passata [1640]', in Solerti, *Le origini del melodramma*, 164.

[48] Rinuccini said she 'passa tutte e di gran lungha', while Gagliano wrote, 'Se non fussi che la sig. Vittoria la supera di bontà di voce, direi assolutamente che ella [Ippolita] fusse più singolare'. Buonarroti's judgement was, 'Il vanto nella musica toccò alla S.ra Hippolita del S.re Car.le Montalto'. See Cametti, 'Chi era l'"Hippolita"', 113.

[49] Montalto's reply, communicated in a letter to the Mantuan court from their agent in Rome, Giovanni Magni, 30 Sept. 1607, is transcribed by Susan Parisi, 'Ducal Patronage of Music in Mantua, 1587–1627: An Archival Study' (Ph.D. diss., University of Illinois, 1989), 195.

comparable to Francesca Caccini and Adriana Basile, even when writing to the brother of the latter's patron.[50] And after Princess Giulia Felice d'Este wrote (24 June 1620), 'I heard Adriana sing to my greatest enjoyment . . . but it seems to me the Ippolita of Cardinal Montalto has a better voice', her brother, Cardinal Alessandro d'Este, replied (7 July 1620), 'Adriana pleased me quite a lot, and it is exactly as Your Illustrious Ladyship says, Montalto's Hippolita has a better voice'.[51] It seems that the cardinal's brother, Duke Cesare d'Este, had earlier complimented Cardinal Montalto on the singing of Ippolita, to which Montalto replied (9 July 1614):

The musician Ippolita has been favoured more than she herself could ever have desired, since Your Highness and those other nobles, my Lords, have been pleased to hear her singing, and I hold it most dear that it was a delight to them (Letter 79).

Enzo Bentivoglio, Ferrarese ambassador to Rome from 1608 to 1639 (Ch. 8), received regular reports from his household staff in Rome during his frequent retreats to his native Ferrara. These reports are full of exuberant praise of Ippolita's singing, and they frequently describe the extraordinary impression it made on guests at gatherings in Montalto's palaces and at those where the cardinal was an honoured guest. These are some samples:

The day before yesterday Cardinals Borghese, Caponi, and Leni came here to the music, in which Sig.ra Ippolita sang again, and they had the greatest pleasure. Also Sig. Enzo [Bentivoglio] has received a very great favour from Cardinal Montalto, who sent one of his household to my house to tell Sig.ra Ippolita that every time Sig. Enzo wishes it, she should immediately come to serve him, without asking permission any longer from his Illustrious Lordship, about which all Rome is astonished (1.v.1610, Alfonso Verati to Guido Bentivoglio, Letter 26).

Yesterday evening Cardinal Montalto came to visit the Duchess [Orsini, his sister] and some other Lords, and he did them the favour of having Sig.ra Ippolita come a little later to render them all speechless with her prodigious talent. The Lord Duke [Virginio Orsini], who seems to me to have the most delicate taste among all of them and is the most difficult to please, confessed that he had never heard a smoother and better controlled voice than hers, and he went so far as to say that he did not wish to hear another solo voice in order not to lose the taste that he had of this one (13.xi.1610, Francesco Belfiore to Enzo Bentivoglio, Letter 34).

[50] 'Avanti mi partissi da Roma udì la Sig.ra Hippolita molto ben cantare, a Firenze la Sig.ra filiola del Sig.r Giulio Romano, molto ben cantare et sonare di leutto chiaronato et clavicembano, ma a Mantova la Sig.ra Andriana benissimo cantare benissimo sonare et benissimo parlare ho udito . . .'. Claudio Monteverdi, *Lettere, dediche, e prefazioni*, ed. Domenico de' Paoli (Rome, 1973), 52.

[51] Alessandro Ademollo, *La bell'Adriana ed altre virtuose del suo tempo alla corte di Mantova* (Città di Castello, 1888), 263–4.

Thursday evening Sig.ra Ippolita came to sing in Your Most Illustrious Lordship's palace in the presence of Montalto, Mellini, Sig. Don Carlo, and the rest of the household. She stayed from the second to the fourth hour after sunset, and she did well. She sang five songs, but the last makes [a] stupendous [impression] because of the spinet that her husband played (17.xi.1610, Ercole Provinzale to Enzo Bentivoglio, Letter 37).

(The 'spinet' that made such an impression was the work of the Florentine Vincenzo Bolcione, and it was to be considered the best instrument in Rome because of its full sonority, which made it especially good for accompanying singing.[52] One secret of its tone was evidently the fact that its lower strings were wound with gold.[53])

The latest known description of Ippolita's singing, when she was about 44 years old, is found in a letter of 9 April 1621 from the famous singer and monody composer Francesco Rasi:

D. Ippolita [is] very beautiful and extremely courteous. And I am certain that if you heard her sing your lament of Andromeda and many of my madrigals you would be astonished.[54]

In addition to the salary, Ippolita earned considerable money from the *ad hoc* gifts of the cardinal and the nobility that heard her sing. For example, the Duchess of Massa gave her a diamond-encrusted wand after hearing her sing in 1610.[55] And among the items in the dowry that Ippolita gave to her daughter Francesca in 1632 was a necklace of pearls and rubies.[56] Sometime before 1620 Ippolita was able use such earnings to acquire a vineyard, but her husband sold it against her will, using the proceeds to buy shares in Bentivoglio's by then failed swamp-draining enterprise (to be explained in Ch. 8). In February of 1620 her husband had asked Enzo Bentivoglio to consummate an unspecified arrangement with the Marottas' landlord, as promised (Letter 111). Then in 1624 Ippolita, herself, wrote to Bentivoglio with the additional details, asking that he make good

[52] Thus, Montalto's musician Giovanni Giacomo Maggi wrote to Cardinal Ferdinando Gonzaga on 2 Mar. 1611: 'I remind you that you wanted to order a *cimbalo* to be made by master Vincenzo Bolcione, who really is a fine man in that occupation, and it is he who made the *cimbalo* belonging to S.ra Ippolita and S.r Cesare, which certainly turned out to be the best *cimbalo* in Rome because it has a great voice and one can sing to its accompaniment.' See App. A, Letter 41.

[53] This fact emerges in two letters of December 1615 from Cesare Marotta to Enzo Bentivoglio, in which Marotta claims that the gold strings of the *spinettina* were cut out and stolen. See App. A, Letters 102–3.

[54] 'D. Ippolita bella assai e garbatissima et io ho certo che se la sentissi cantare il vostro lamento di Andromeda . . . e molti miei madrigali che vi stupireste.' Rasi to Ercole Marliani, transcribed by Warren Kirkendale, *The Court Musicians in Florence during the Principate of the Medici with a Reconstruction of the Artistic Establishment* (Historiae musicae cultores biblioteca, 61; Florence, 1993), 595.

[55] As Cesare Marotta relates in his letter of 12 Nov. 1610, partially transcribed and translated in Anthony Newcomb, 'Girolamo Frescobaldi, 1608–1615: A Documentary Study in which Information also Appears Concerning Giulio and Settimia Caccini, the Brothers Piccinini, Stefano Landi, and Ippolita Recupito', *Annales musicologiques*, 7 (1964–77), 111–58 at 136–8. For the entire letter, see App. A, Letter 32.

[56] Cametti, 'Che era l'"Hippolita"', 119.

on his promise to take back the shares in exchange for a settlement with their landlord, meaning, presumably, the purchase from him of the apartment for them (Letter 112). Apparently Bentivoglio ignored that request,[57] for in her later years Ippolita lived in one of the apartments inherited by her grandson from his father, and supported herself and the boy, in part, through the occasional sale of his other property. She died on 10 June 1650 at the approximate age of 73.[58]

The rest of Cardinal Montalto's household musicians are listed below Cesare Marotta's rank of *gentiluomo*, precisely with the *staffieri*, in the salary rolls of 1612–20.[59] Among these, the first composer in dignity is Don Ippolito Macchiavelli (1568–1619). A notarized document of 1618 informs us that Macchiavelli was born in Bologna, the son of Agostino Macchiavelli,[60] and that information allows us to match him with the record of baptism on 28 May 1568.[61] Macchiavelli served in the household of Antonio Facchinetti della Noce (1574–1606), Cardinal of Santi Quattro (from 1591) and grand-nephew of Innocent IX,[62] as we learn in a letter to Enzo Bentivoglio of 28 August 1607 (Letter 24), a letter that implies that Macchiavelli was one of the earliest or one of the best (it is not clear which) composers of monody in Rome. He apparently entered Cardinal Montalto's household on 1 February 1607, the date on which he began receiving rent reimbursement from the cardinal.[63] The last semester of rents payments began on 1 July 1608,[64] after which Macchiavelli, a bachelor (and possibly a cleric, given his benefice, to be mentioned below), undoubtedly found lodging in Montalto's Chancellery palace, which is where he died on 14 May 1619.[65] In April and May

---

[57] It appears that Ippolita may have sued Bentivoglio over his refusal to honour his promise to redeem the shares. Dinko Fabris informs me that a series of letters written to Bentivoglio in 1627 refer to a suit brought by a 'Hippolita', the details of which are never speciffied. The letters will be transcribed in his forthcoming book on the patronage of the Bentivoglio family, mentioned earlier.

[58] Cametti, 'Che era l'"Hippolita"', 119–23.

[59] I:Ras, Archivio Giustiniani, Busta 87; Chater, 'Musical Patronage', 218–21.

[60] I:Ras, Archivio de 30 Notari Capitolini, Uffizio 25, Busta 61, fo. 541ʳ⁻ᵛ: 'Affictus reddituum, et alior. pro Ill. D. Hipolito Macchiavellio, Die 6 xbris 1618: Ill D. Hipolitus Macchiavellius q. Augustini Bononiensis mihi not. percognitus mi[?] alias provisum fuit de simplici beneficio sub invocat.ne S. Angeli de Ave tibaldesca . . .'.

[61] Macchiavelli's birth record is preserved in Bologna, Biblioteca Comunale dell'Archiginnasio, B.858, 'Cittadini maschi di famiglie bolognesi battezzati in S. Pietro come risultano dai libri dell'Archivio Battesimale, dal 1459 al 1809, compilazione del co. Baldassare Carrati, 1797–1809', 197, 28 May 1568: 'Ippolito di Agostino Malchiavelli [local equivalent for Macchiavelli] e di Elisabetta'. This is the only baptism of this name during the period 1540–69. This Ippolito Macchiavelli is not part of the large noble Macchiavelli family, according to Carrati's family tree.

[62] Concerning Cardinal Facchinetti, see Moroni, *Dizionario di erudizione storico-ecclesiastica*, xxi. 279–80.

[63] I:Rac, Archivio Cardelli, Appendice, vol. 34, *sub die* 16 Feb. 1607. The payment of 19 scudi was for six months' rent from 1 Feb.

[64] Further rent reimbursements to Macchiavelli of 19 scudi each are found in vol. 35, *sub diebus* 4 July 1607, 3 Apr. 1608, and 3 July 1608—the latter for the six months beginning on 1 July 1608.

[65] I:Rav, S. Lorenzo in Damaso, 54, fo. 90, *sub die* 14 May 1619: 'D. Hippolito Macciavello Cantore dell'Ill.mo Sig.r Card. Montalto in palazzo di S. S. Ill.ma'. The notice was first published by Paul Kast, 'Biographische Notizen zu römischen Musikern des 17. Jahrhunderts', *Analecta musicologica*, 1 (1963), 38–69 at 49.

Macchiavelli received grants of unspecified purpose from Montalto of 70 and 30 scudi, respectively,[66] but the earliest household list of November 1612 gives him a salary of 7 scudi plus a food allowance of 3 scudi.[67] His income was eventually augmented by a benefice that had an annual rental value of 50 scudi in 1618.[68] Macchiavelli's letter of 29 June 1613 to Ferdinando Gonzaga (Letter 66) alludes to a past service to the court of Mantua and asks, in unusually emotional terms, to serve or be of service to the duke in the future. This may indicate Macchiavelli's dissatisfaction with his service to Cardinal Montalto, or it may simply communicate the musician's willingness to take on additional duties for extra income. From the libretto of *Amor pudico* (1614), we learn that Macchiavelli was a theorbo player, and that instrument would seem to have conditioned his activity as composer, since all his known compositions are strophic variations for solo voice and basso continuo, a form closely tied to performance with chord-producing instruments.

The third composer in Cardinal Montalto's household during the period of the salary rolls was Giovanni Bernardino Nanino (*c.*1560–1618), who entered the cardinal's service in 1608 after seventeen years (1591–1608) as *maestro di cappella* at S. Luigi dei Francesi, one of the most important training institutions for boy singers in Rome at that time. Casimiri cites a contract of 21 January 1581 in which Nanino is obliged to teach Alessandro Costantini (d. 1657), who later became an important composer of monody in Rome.[69] Cametti shows that Nanino's students at S. Luigi dei Francesi included the future composers Gregorio Allegri, Domenico Allegri, Bartolommeo Allegri, and Antonio Cifra.[70] During his service with Cardinal Montalto, Nanino participated in training singers for performance in the new *stile recitativo* (see Ch. 4). The title *maestro di cappella* written after Nanino's name in the household account books refers to his position at Cardinal Montalto's titular church, San Lorenzo in Damaso, which was attached

---

[66] I:Rac, Archivio Cardelli, Appendice, vol. 34, *sub diebus* 4 Apr. and 4 May 1607.

[67] I:Ras, Archivio Giustiniani, Busta 87; Chater, 'Musical Patronage', 218. Later rolls for months with thirty-one days give Macchiavelli a total payment of 10 scudi and 10 baiocchi, because the traditional *companatico* payment was 10 baiocchi per day.

[68] In the document preserved in I:Ras, Archivio de 30 Notari Capitolini, Uffizio 25, Busta 61, fo. 541[r–v], and cited above, Macchiavelli rents his benefice to the abbot Pietro Giordano for three years at 50 scudi per year.

[69] Raffaele Casimiri, '"Disciplina musicae" e "mastri di cappella" dopo il Concilio di Trento nei maggiori istituti ecclesiastici di Roma: Seminario Romano, Collegio Germanico, Collegio Inglese (Sec. XVI–XVII)', *Note d'archivio per la storia musicale*, 15 (1938), 57.

[70] Alberto Cametti, 'La scuola dei *pueri cantus* di S. Luigi dei francesi in Roma e i suoi principali allievi (1591–1623): Gregorio, Comenico e Bartolomeo Allegri, Antonio Cifra, Orazio Benevoli', *Rivista musicale italiana*, 22 (1915), 593–641. For other details of Nanino's work at San Luigi, see Jean Lionnet, 'Quelques aspects de la vie musicale à Saint–Louis–des–Français de Giovanni Bernardino Nanino à Alessandro Melani (1591–1698)', in *Les Fondations nationales dans la Rome pontificale* (Collection de l'école française de Rome, 52; Rome, 1981), 333–75.

to the Palazzo della Cancelleria, Montalto's official residence.[71] Brought up in the Roman school of strict, a cappella counterpoint by Giovanni Maria Nanino, his elder brother, Bernardino published his first church music with basso continuo in 1610, shortly after entering Cardinal Montalto's service,[72] and his vocal monodies, written perhaps as early as 1612 (see Chs. 6 and 8), are preserved in manuscripts as well as in a printed collection of songs by Giuseppe Giamberti (*c.*1600–*c.*1662), who served and studied under Nanino as a boy soprano in the chapel of San Lorenzo in Damaso, 1615–16.[73]

In February of 1613 a fourth composer of solo songs was added to Montalto's household payroll, Orazio Michi *dell'arpa* (1594–1641) from Alife near Naples.[74] In time, Michi became Montalto's most favoured musician: by 1620 he received 15 and 3.10 scudi, respectively, for salary and *companatico*, which was more than Cesare Marotta's salary, if it is considered that Marotta's 37 scudi represented salary and food allowance for both himself and his wife. But this salary alone did not make Michi wealthy, as Chater supposed.[75] In 1622 Cardinal Montalto established an annual pension of 300 scudi for Michi made up of income from two of the cardinal's abbeys, Santo Stefano in Bologna and San Bartolomeo in Musciano.[76] And in his testament Montalto left Michi an additional pension of 2,000 gold scudi per year, an income worthy of a cardinal.[77] In 1639 the violist André Maugars estimated Michi's pension at 5,000–6,000 scudi, a figure partly to be explained by the rate of exchange between the gold standard stipulated in Montalto's testament and the silver standard used for accounting purposes.[78] But Maugars's appraisal probably also reflects the fact that Michi lived well. Indeed his testament eventually disposed of a carriage with horses, an organ, harpsichord, theorbo, and harp, a large library, a ruby that once belonged to Cardinal Montalto's mother, and 858 scudi in cash. His principal beneficiaries were the fathers of the Scuole Pie and the Congregazione dell'Oratorio di San Filippo Neri,

---

[71] An account book (I:Rav, S. Lorenzo in Damaso, 186, 2) names as *maestro di cappella* of San Lorenzo in Damaso both Nanino and Don Cesare Melotti, Cardinal Montalto's household secretary and canon in the church's chapter. Melotti seems to have served as a financial administrator, while Nanino was the actual musical director.   [72] See the entry in *New Grove* by Anthony Newcomb.

[73] I:Rav, S. Lorenzo in Damaso, 1816, *passim*. Giamberti's *Poesie diverse poste in musica . . . libro primo* (Rome: Soldi, 1623) includes Nanino's sonetto setting *Né lungo exilio mai, donna, mi mosse.* On the title-page of this collection, Giamberti identifies himself as a student of Nanino and of Paolo Agostini.

[74] A good summary of his career and bibliography by Gloria Rose is in *New Grove*.

[75] Chater, 'Musical Patronage', 204.

[76] I:Rac, Archivio Cardelli, Appendice, vol. 55, 'Copie di mandati, 1622–1627', *sub die* 6 May 1622: 'S.r Gio. Rotoli si compiacerà pag.re a Horatio Michi scudi 150 m.ta per la traslatione fatta in persona sua delli scudi 300 m.ta annoi riservatoci sopra li frutti delle nostre Badie, di S. Stefano di Bologna, e S. Bartolomeo di Musciano, e questi per il termine de S. Gio. Battista passato.'

[77] I:Ras, Archivio dei 30 Notari Capitolini, Officio no. 25, Busta 87, fos. 526–8, 545–7.

[78] Jean Lionnet, 'André Maugars: Risposta data a un curioso sul sentimento della musica d'Italia', *Nuova rivista musicale italiana*, 19 (1985), 681–705 at 691.

for which he composed a large number of sacred arias and cantatas during the last two decades of his life.[79]

Another monody composer, Pellegrino Mutij, is named in the parish census of 1611–12 and in the libretto of *Amor pudico* (1614) as a musician of Prince Michele Peretti but is not mentioned in any part of the payrolls for that period.[80] On the other hand, the payrolls do contain the name 'Don Pietro Torres' at the end of the section devoted to musicians: this could be Pietro Paolo Torre, whose canzonets, madrigals, and arias for one and two voices were printed in Venice in 1622.

The household of the 'adopted' Cardinal Andrea Baroni Peretti also contained a monody composer, or at least a musician who later became one. A letter of 5 June 1610 says that the harpist in Caterina Bentivoglio's household was soon to marry 'a lad who is with Cardinal Perreti',[81] and subsequent letters inform us that the woman's name is Lucrezia Urbani and the lad's is Domenico Visconti. Both of them moved to the Roman household of Enzo Bentivoglio later that summer, then transferred to the court of Don Antonio Medici in Florence by 17 April 1612. In 1616 Visconti sent Enzo Bentivoglio copies of his *Primo libro de madrigali a 5 voci* (Florence: Pignoni, 1615) and his *Primo libro de arie a 1 e 2 voci* (Venice: Amadino, 1616) with a letter that implies that Bentivoglio had not yet seen any of this music.[82] Thus, it is unlikely that any of it was composed in Rome. (Consequently, it will be considered beyond the scope of this study.)

The rest of Cardinal Montalto's musicians among the *staffieri* in the payrolls are five singers:

1. Melchior Palantrotti (a bass in the papal chapel, as mentioned earlier). He disappears from the rolls after the 1614 performance of *Amor pudico*.[83]

---

[79] Alberto Cametti, 'Orazio Michi "dell'Arpa"'; Lionnet, 'André Maugars'; Arnaldo Morelli, Il tempio armonico: *Musica nell'oratorio dei Filippini in Roma (1575–1705) = Analecta musicologica*, 27 (Laaber, 1991), 72–3.

[80] Monodies by Mutij were published in *Ghirlandetta amorosa*, comp. Fabio Costantini (Orvieto: Fei and Ruuli, 1621); *L'aurata cintia armonica*, comp. Fabio Costantini (Orvieto: Fei and Ruuli, 1622); and *Vezzosetti fiori di varii eccellenti autori* (Rome: Robletti, 1622). See John Walter Hill, 'Pellegrino Mutij e la nascente monodia in Polonia', *Quadrivium*, NS 1 (1990), 7–18, concerning the career of this interesting figure.

[81] 'Il marito e un giovanoto che sta col cardinal pereti.' Marchesa Bentivoglio to Giovanni Bentivoglio (I:FEas, Archivio Bentivoglio, Mazza 53, fo. 478'), quoted in Newcomb, 'Girolamo Frescobaldi', 135–6.

[82] These elements are brought together, with numerous transcriptions of unpublished letters, by Dinko Fabris, 'L'arpa napoletana, simbolismo estetico-sonoro di uno strumento musicale del primo Seicento', in Franco Fanizza (ed.), *Modernità e coscienza estetica* (Pubblicazioni della Cattedra di Estetica; Naples, 1986), 211–62.

[83] Palantrotti's name continues in the parish census of S. Lorenzo in Damaso through the year 1616, after which it appears no more: I:Rav, S. Lorenzo in Damaso, Stato d'Anime 63, fos. 17ᵛ and 51ᵛ. Palantrotti had been dismissed from the Sistine Chapel on 19 July 1603 for asking three months' leave to visit his home in Venafro, while it was known that he was actually going to serve the Viceroy of Naples. On 28 May 1608 he petitioned for readmittance but was denied on grounds that he was married: I:Rvat, Cappella Sistina, Cammerlengo 4, fo. 9ᵛ, and Diario 28, fo. 40ʳ⁻ᵛ.

2. Ercole Ferruzzi. He was another bass in the papal chapel, from 1594 until his death in 1626.[84] During the winter of 1611–12, Montalto made seven charitable contributions (*elemosina*) of 10 scudi each to a 'Hercole musico di casa' through the good offices of Duritio Isorelli, a friend of Emilio de' Cavalieri and member of the Congregazione dell'Oratorio in Rome.[85] The words 'di casa' make it appear that these payments were directed to Ferruzzi, perhaps because of a prolonged illness.

3. Lorenzo Mancini, from Perugia. A priest, he received an annual pension of 200 gold scudi in Cardinal Montalto's will.[86]

4. The 'Pier Antonio musico' who joins Montalto's payrolls when they resume in 1620 after a four-year gap is almost certainly the papal singer Pietrantonio Tamburini from Bologna,[87] since a letter to Enzo Bentivoglio, already in 1618, refers to one 'D. Pietro Antonio Bolognese musico del Card.le Montalto' (Letter 110). The same letter says that Don Pietro Antonio had already sung the part of Mercury in Enzo Bentivoglio's *torneo*, which may be the one presented in Ferrara in 1612,[88] or it may be the otherwise unidentified 'festa' that Bentivoglio presented there in 1614 and for which Cesare Marotta provided music (Letter 74); neither libretto is known to survive. In the one or the other case, the implication would be that Tamburini began his service to Cardinal Montalto in 1612 or in 1614.

5. 'Domenico Musico' in the salary rolls, 1612–20, is identified in the libretto of *Amor pudico* as 'Domenico Tombaldini dell'Illustriss. Montalto, Musico di Capella, perugino'. According to the manuscript collection of biographies left by his contemporary Paolo Aringhi, Domenico Tombaldini, as a boy, was a student of the Oratorian Duritio Isorelli, mentioned earlier.[89] On 2 September 1607 the singers of the papal chapel were asked to listen to a certain 'Domenico eunuco', presumably Tombaldini, but he did not come because he did not feel in good voice.[90] At his initiation in the papal chapel, 25 November 1609, Domenico Tombaldini is called 'fiorentino'.[91] Therefore, it is possible that the 'Domenico Fiorentino' listed with Cardinal Montalto's household in 1602 already refers to Tombaldini.[92] A list of extra singers at San Luigi for 25 August 1608 gives the name 'Domenico del Cardinal Montalto', which is the first unequivocal reference to

---

[84] For members of the papal chapel, see E. Celani, 'I cantori della cappella pontificia nei secoli XVI–XVIII', *Rivista musicale italiana*, 14 (1907), 764–75; and H.-W. Frey, 'Daș Diarium der Sixtinischen Sängerkapelle in Rom für das Jahr 1594', *Analecta musicologica*, 14 (1974), 455–505 at 499.

[85] I:Rac, Archivio Cardelli, Appendice, vol. 35, *sub diebus* 1 Oct., 25 Oct., 20 Nov., 1 Dec., 3 Dec. 1611; and vol. 37, *sub diebus* 14 Jan. and 16 Feb. 1612.

[86] I:Ras, Archivio dei 30 Notari Capitolini, Officio no. 25, Busta 87, fos. 526–8, 545–7, where he is given as 'R. D. Laur.o Mancino Perusino'.   [87] As suggested by Chater, 'Musical Patronage', 204.

[88] Mentioned in the 1613 preface *a' lettori* to the libretto of Antonio Ongaro, *L'Alceo* (Ferrara, 1614), to be discussed in Ch. 8.   [89] Kirkendale, *Court Musicians*, 283.

[90] I:Rvat, Cappella Sistina, Diario 27.   [91] Diario 29, fo. 32^r.

[92] I:Rav, S. Lorenzo in Damaso, 61, fos. 77^r–78^v.

his service in Montalto's household.[93] His name then appears on the salary rolls of Montalto's household from 1612 to 1620.

Another *musico* entered and left Montalto's service between the household lists of 1602 and 1612: Lorenzo Pozzo, whose rent was paid from 1 September 1608 through August 1609.[94] And the 1613 baptism record for the Marottas' daughter Francesca mentions Padre Gasparo Cassiani and Andrea Alberto da Belante, Milanese, as musicians of Cardinal Montalto,[95] although they cannot be traced in other documents.

'Giovan Giacomo Maggi dell'Illustrissimo Montalto' is named as a harpsichordist in the libretto of *Amor pudico*. Maggi had already played that instrument in a pastorale at Montalto's palace during carnival of 1611.[96] He is not included in any payrolls, probably because he was already a chaplain and possibly a canon of San Lorenzo in Damaso when he entered Montalto's circle of musicians on 17 September 1608, from which date the cardinal paid his rent for a full year.[97] In 1612 Duke Ferdinando Gonzaga of Mantua heard from his agent in Rome that Maggi was unwilling to leave Montalto's service because he held important benefices that depended upon the cardinal.[98] Since Maggi is known to have been a canon of San Lorenzo in Damaso at his death in 1634,[99] we may conclude that he was compensated with ecclesiastical income rather than salary during his association with Cardinal Montalto. It would seem likely that Maggi composed as well as played the harpsichord, but no surviving music is known to be attributed to him.

Among the lower servants of Cardinal Montalto, the payrolls include the trumpeter Gioachino Bacelli, who was in Montalto's service from at least 1610 to 1622.[100] In all probability his position was principally ceremonial rather than musical.

---

[93] Lionnet, 'Quelques aspects', 361.

[94] I:Rac, Archivio Cardelli, Appendice, vol. 35, *sub die* 9 Feb. 1609: 'S. Herrera etc. pagarete à Lorenzo Pozzo nuovo *nostro* musico *scudi* venti quali sono per pagare la pigione della casa ov'egli habita per un *semestre* cominciato al p.mo di sett.re passato 1608 e da finire a tutto febraio *presente*. E da.ne debito dalla Cancelleria il di 9 di febraio 1609.' A second six months' rent was paid on 9 May 1609 for the period beginning 1 Mar. 1609. There is no further trace of Pozzo in the documents used for this study.

[95] Cametti, 'Chi era l'"Hippolita"', 117 n. 2.

[96] See the letter of 2 Mar. 1611 from Maggi in Rome to Cardinal Ferdinando Gonzaga partially transcribed by Emil Vogel, 'Marco da Gagliano: Zur Geschichte des florentiner Musiklebens von 1570–1650', *Vierteljahrsschrift für Musikwissenschaft*, 5 (1889), 396–442, 509–68 at 562. A full transcription is given as Letter 41.

[97] I:Rac, Archivio Cardelli, Appendice, vol. 35, *sub die* 17 Sept. 1608, records the rent payment of 30 scudi to 'Gio. Giacomo Maggio Cappellano'.

[98] The letter from Paolo Faccone to Ferdinando Gonzaga, 29.xii.1612, in I:MAas, Archivio Gonzaga, Busta 1001, contains there lines: 'quanto poi a D. Gio. Giacomo del Card. Montalto, mi son informato che piutosto si darrebbe disgusto che altro; e lui si lascia intendere che mal volontieri si partirebbe dal Card. del quale n'ha ricevuto e tuttavia ne ha Beneficij d'importanza e poi per altri particolari quali mi resstelo dirgli a bocca a V.A. e perche importanto.' This transcription, based on one kindly shared with me by Susan Parisi, is somewhat hypothetical in a few details.   [99] Chater, 'Musical Patronage', 203.

[100] Ibid.

If the musicians in Cardinal Montalto's household were part of an inner circle around their patron, a larger concentric circle included the musicians of Montalto's titular church, San Lorenzo in Damaso. For while the performances of the household musicians served to entertain the friendly cardinals and nobility within Montalto's network of *clientela*, the music of his chapel was heard, potentially, by a cross-section of the local population, since San Lorenzo in Damaso was also a parish church. Cardinal Montalto supported the musical chapel of the church with the obligatory 20 scudi per month rent for the palace (that is, the palace belonged to the church and not the reverse) together with another 36 scudi monthly specifically for the musicians.[101] The size of this chapel diminished during the period for which we have records (1613–23) from eleven in 1613 (three sopranos, three altos, two tenors, two basses, and the *maestro di cappella*) to perhaps as few as four in 1623 (one tenor, two basses, and the *maestro di cappella*),[102] possibly reflecting a shift in emphasis from full-choir polyphonic works towards concerted motets for one, two, or three voices with organ continuo. Extra musicians were, however, engaged for special occasions.[103] When Cardinal Montalto took possession of San Lorenzo in Damaso as Vice-Chancellor in 1589, its *maestro di cappella* was the Flemish composer Ioanne Matelart (before 1538–1607),[104] who was succeeded by Giovanni Bernardino Nanino. The surviving records are not specific about Nanino's successor in 1619, but it is suggestive that one Paolo Agostino Nanino, perhaps a relative, joined the chapel payroll shortly before Nanino's death and continued thereafter for as long as records survive.

A third circle of clients around Cardinal Montalto included musicians who resided with him while on loan from service in other courts. In dedicating his first book of five-voice madrigals (1593) to Prince Michele Peretti, the Neapolitan composer Sebastiano Raval mentions that he had improvised some counterpoint at the Peretti palace in Rome in the presence of the Cavaliere del Leuto, Scipione Dentice (1560–*c*.1635), Luca Marenzio (1553/4–1599), and [Scipione] Stella

---

[101] I:Rav, S. Lorenzo in Damaso 167, opening 1, left, mentions these figures. The payments for the music are first recorded in I:Rac, Archivio Cardelli, Appendice, vol. 32, *sub die* 11 Jan. 1596, 'Al maestro di capella della musica di S. Lorenzo in Damaso scudi dieci di m.ta queli gli li doniamo dall Canc.ria a 11 gen.o 1596'. The higher level of support is recorded in the same volume *sub die* 1 Dec. 1598, 'per lemosina per la musica scudi 36' and is continued monthly thereafter.

[102] The singers listed in the surviving financial records of the church, I:Rav, S. Lorenzo in Damaso, 167 and 186, are Gregorio Bucchari, soprano (1613–14), Costantino Castiglione, contralto (1613–14), Antonio Fornai, contralto (1613–14), Francesco, soprano (1613–14), Bartolomeo Giovanardi, soprano (1613–16), Ferdinando Grappa, contralto (1613), Erminio Neroccio, tenor (1613), Michel'Arcangelo Nino, bass (1613–23), Curtio Pelliccia, bass (1613–23), Luca Sabbatelli, tenor (1613–14), Stefano Fabri, soprano (1614), Vergilio Puccitelli, soprano (1614), Claudio Perron de Rossi, tenor (1614), Bonifatio, soprano (1615), Giuseppe Giamberti, soprano (1615–16), Costantino di Cesare Fioricento, soprano (1616–18), Girolamo, soprano (1618–19), Giovanni Paolo, soprano (1619–21), Francesco Baranoli, soprano (1621), Jacomo Fabrica, contralto (1621–3), and the 'soprano di Don Erminio, putto' (1621–2).

[103] The second part of I:Rav, S. Lorenzo in Damaso 167 includes payments to Bernardino Nanino for 'musica straordinaria'.   [104] See the entry in *New Grove* by Godelieve Spiessens.

(?1559–c.1610/30), 'with whom and [with] other gentlemen of His Most Illustrious [Lordship] your brother [i.e. Cardinal Montalto] and of Your Excellency we
sang these little works various times'.[105] Although Raval's sentence makes it seem
as if the madrigal composers Dentice, Marenzio, and Stella were permanent
members of Montalto's household, we know that they were only occasional
guests of his during the 1580s and 1590s, compensated for their services, at least
in part, through Montalto's help and influence in obtaining permanent, paying
positions for them and their relatives.

Already in 1588 Montalto had recommended Marenzio to the care of the
Florentine Cardinal Del Monte on the eve of the composer's participation in the
intermedi that were to celebrate Grand Duke Ferdinando's marriage to Cristina
di Lorena in 1589.[106] After the wedding, Marenzio returned to Rome, where on
1 January 1591 he dedicated his fifth book of six-voice madrigals to Cardinal
Montalto's brother-in-law Virginio Orsini. In June of 1592, however, a place
was prepared for him in the household of Montalto himself.[107] It was at this time
that Sebastiano Raval encountered Marenzio at Montalto's palace in Rome.
Whether or not Marenzio actually transferred to Montalto's payroll, he seems to
have received patronage from several members of a tight circle of the cardinal's
relatives and friends: from late 1593 to October of 1595 Marenzio lived in the Vatican
apartments of Cinzio Aldobrandini, cardinal-nephew of Pope Clement VIII
and at the time a close ally of Montalto, but on 2 August 1595 it was to Flavia
Orsini, Montalto's sister, that Marenzio wrote, asking permission to go into the
service of Sigismund III of Poland.[108]

Scipione Dentice, also mentioned in Raval's 1593 account, is the musician with
the earliest documented connections with Cardinal Montalto. On 10 January 1587
Montalto acknowledges Dentice's letter of 3 January, in which the musician
reports his safe return to Naples (Letter 1). On 18 April 1587 our 17-year-old cardinal thanks the 27-year-old Dentice for some compositions sent and signs the
letter 'as a brother' (Letter 2). From these two letters we may conclude that
Dentice developed close relations with the young Cardinal Montalto during a
period in Rome beginning in 1586 or even earlier. It seems not unlikely that Dentice

---

[105] Sebastiano Raval, *Il primo libro de madrigali a cinque voci* (Venice: Vincenti, 1593), dedication: 'portai
a Roma, venendo da Urbino, & trovandomi al presente in servigio dell'Altezza Ser. del Duca mio Signore
si degnò V.E. nel Palazzo udirmi alcuni Contraponti, & altre habilità, che all'improviso fece innanzi del Sig.
Cavaliere del Liuto universal nel Mondo, del Sig. Scipion Dentici rarrissimo nel Cimbalo, il Sig. Luca Marentio
divino Compositore, & il mio Sig. Stella virtuosissimo in differenti Virtù, co i quali & altri Gentilhuomini
dell'Illustriss. suo fratello e di V.E. in differenti volte cantassimo di queste operine'.

[106] Montalto's letter of 28 June 1588 from Rome to Cardinal Del Monte in Florence is transcribed in James
Chater, 'Luca Marenzio: New Documents, New Observations', *Music & Letters*, 64 (1983), 2–11 at 4.

[107] Pietro Aldobrandini's letter to Virginio Orsini of 9 June 1592, transcribed by Steven Ledbetter, 'Luca
Marenzio: New Biographical Findings' (Ph.D. diss., New York University, 1971), 227, says: 'Parlai a monsignor Illustrissimo Montalto per il Marenzio e Sua Signoria Illustrissima si contenta di darli la medesima
provisione et lui receve per favore.'   [108] Ibid. 130–3.

gave Montalto music lessons. The cardinal's friend Vincenzo Giustiniani will later report that Cardinal Montalto played the harpsichord (see Ch. 3), which was Dentice's particular instrument, according to Raval's 1593 dedication; and the earliest evidence of Montalto's musical interests is a payment made on 14 May 1587 for two carved wooden legs of a table on which were to be placed the cardinal's harpsichord (*cimbalo*) and virginal (*spinetta*).[109] Other payments followed for 'adjusting the large harpsichord and other instruments' (1588),[110] for the purchase of 'a virginal . . . for our use and for other work in adjusting harpsichords' (1593),[111] for a harpsichord made by Giovanni Battista Bertarino (1594),[112] for several adjustments to the harpsichords (1595),[113] for a new harpsichord from Giovanni Battista Boni (1615),[114] and for two new harpsichords made by Girolamo Aciari in 1617[115] and 1620.[116]

Cardinal Montalto's letter of 18 April 1587 contains the earliest mention of compositions by Scipione Dentice. Another of the cardinal's letters, of 27 December 1591, acknowledges the receipt of other 'efforts' of the composer (Letter 11). Later, Dentice dedicated his first book of motets to Montalto (1594), and to Montalto's sister-in-law, Margherita della Somaglia, he dedicated his first book of madrigals (1596), which contained one setting of a text by Montalto's brother-in-law Virginio Orsini.[117] In the dedication of the motets, Dentice claims that they are Cardinal Montalto's because he, himself, belongs to the cardinal. And the dedication of the madrigals refers to the composer's service to Michele Peretti, Margherita's husband and Cardinal Montalto's brother. Indeed Vincenzo Giustiniani will claim that Scipione Dentice was in Montalto's *famiglia* (Ch. 3). However, in 1589 Montalto obtained for Dentice a place in the Roman household of Cardinal Antonio Maria Galli, Bishop of Perugia.[118]

Scipione Dentice is known to us exclusively as a composer of vocal music, and, in fact, no composer of keyboard music was ever in Cardinal Montalto's

---

[109] I:Rac, Archivio Cardelli, Appendice, vol. 30, 'Registro de mandati, 1587–1591', *sub die* 14 May 1587: 'ad Antonio Alegri falegname per doi piedi intagliati servono per tenervi sopra i *nostri* instrumenti cimbalo, et spinetta *scudi* 22'.

[110] Ibid., *sub die* 30 Dec. 1588: 'Gio. B*attista* da Pesaro . . . d'havere acconcio il cimbalo grande et altri instrumenti *scudi* 16'.

[111] Vol. 31, *sub die* 31 Jan. 1593: 'E più pagarette a m.ro Giorgio Bernieri m.ro di cimbali sc. 20 m.ta quali li facciamo pagare per una spinetta havuta da lui per servitio nostro et altre fatiche per accomodare cimbali.'

[112] Ibid., *sub die* 1 June 1594: 'a Gio B.a Bertarino per un cimbalo *scudi* 25'.

[113] Vol. 32, *sub die* 30 Aug. 1595: 'SS.r Giustiniani pagarete a Mastro Giorgio Cimbalaro da Trento scudi quindici di moneta per haver accomodato in più volte li cimbali'.

[114] Vol. 37, *sub die* 12 Nov. 1615: '*scudi* 30 m.ta a Gio. B*attista* Boni Cimbalaro per saldo d'un suo conto d'un Cimbalo nuovo et diverse sue modulare d'altri antichi'.

[115] Vol. 38, *sub die* 26 Apr. 1617: 'A di d.o *scudi* 16 m.ta a Girolamo Cimbalaro, a San Biaggio dell'anello, quali sono per il prezzo d'un cimbalo comp*ratto* da lui per ser.o della casa mia.'

[116] Vol. 54, fo. 34ᵛ, *sub die* 5 May 1620: 'Gir*onimo* Aciari cimbalaro a S. Carlo à Cattinari per il prezzo d'un cimbalo comperato da lui *scudi* 16'.

[117] Keith Austin Larson, 'The Unaccompanied Madrigal in Naples from 1536 to 1654' (Ph.D. diss., Harvard University, 1985), 561–2.   [118] Chater, 'Music Patronage', 189.

household, which instead always contained virtuoso singers and, with only one exception, composers exclusively occupied with accompanied vocal chamber music. Scipione Dentice seems to have been an early practitioner of this art, for on 22 December 1595 he was already at the keyboard accompanying the famous Neapolitan virtuoso bass singer Giulio Cesare Brancaccio.[119] It is reasonable, therefore, to hypothesize that Cardinal Montalto's harpsichords were used primarily for accompanied singing, which is where his musical patronage and personal interest remained focused from beginning to end.

The composers Costanzo Porta, Guglielmo Arnone, and Pompeo Stabile apparently had more distant relations with Cardinal Montalto during the early period.[120] As in the case of Scipione Dentice, Cardinal Montalto sought benefits on behalf of these musician-clients from individuals of nearly equal or lesser rank, in other words, from clients who depended or would depend in the future upon the cardinal for help in obtaining something for themselves or for their own clients. For Pompeo Stabile, for example, Montalto asked a lieutenancy in Civitanuova from Cardinal Farnese (3.x.1587), a household position from the Duchess of Torremaggiore (2.i.1588), and the order of St Maurice and St Lazarus from the Duke of Savoy (12.xii.1588).[121] However, when Montalto needed an intercession on Stabile's behalf (12.xii.1588) from the Viceroy of Naples, who was not a client, he sought the intermediation of the papal nunzio, who depended directly on Montalto in ecclesiastical matters.[122]

The same nunzio was enlisted to intercede with the Duke of Traetto (evidently a non-client) when Montalto sought (18.viii.1590) to obtain a 7-year-old girl singer for the service of his sister, the Duchess of Bracciano, but then abandoned the attempt (25.viii.1590), at least temporarily, citing his sister's indisposition.[123] The Duke of Traetto, at this time, was Luigi Carafa (1567–1630), who, since the death of his father, Antonio, in 1578, was also the Prince of Stigliano. The title Duke of Traetto (or Traetta) came to Luigi upon his marriage to Isabella Gonzaga, Duchess of Sabbionetta and of Traetto, in 1586.[124] Although we do not have any lists of Isabella's household, we do know that in 1610 it did include Adriana Basile, perhaps the most famous and sought-after singer of the period, because in 1610 Duke Vincenzo Gonzaga successfully concluded the protracted negotiation to bring Adriana to his court from the household of Isabella Gonzaga, Princess of

---

[119] Domenico Gnoli, *Vittoria Accoramboni: Storia del secolo XVI* (Florence, 1870), 324.

[120] Chater, 'Musical Patronage', 187–94.

[121] I:Rasv, Confalonieri 49, fos. 177ᵛ, 292ʳ⁻ᵛ (Letter 4), Confalonieri 50, fo. 426ᵛ (Letter 6); Chater, 'Musical Patronage', 189–90, gives incorrect dates for the second and third of these letters.

[122] I:Rasv, Confalonieri 50, fos. 426ᵛ–427ʳ; see Chater, 'Musical Patronage', 190.

[123] See Letters 8–10.

[124] Pompeo Litta, *Famiglie celebri italiane*, seconda serie, ii (Naples, 1913), tavola XLII—Carafa di Napoli; and Giuseppe Ceci, 'I feudatari napoletani alla fine del sec. XVI', *Archivio storico per le provincie napoletane*, 24 (1899), 122–38 at 127, 130.

Stigliano.[125] Since Adriana's birth date is usually estimated at *c.*1580,[126] it is possible that the 7-year-old girl in the Carafa household as of 1590 was none other than Basile. Twenty years later, Adriana Basile actually did visit the palace of Cardinal Montalto's sister, the Duchess of Bracciano, and from there on 7 June 1610 she wrote to the Duke of Bracciano, Virginio Orsini, who was in Rome, thanking him for favours and courtesies received in Rome and apologizing for not being in a position to do what he asked, which, presumably, was to remain in the service of the duchess.[127] An undated poem by Benedetto Maia implies that Montalto vied for Adriana in competition with the cardinals Borghese and Aldobrandini at this point.[128]

Cardinal Montalto was evidentally reluctant to ask a favour from a non-client because to do so might be taken as an obligation on his part or even an admission of his own client status, a status which he assumed almost exclusively in his relationship with popes. For instance, when the composer Costanzo Porta sent Montalto some music for seven voices, the cardinal expressed (7.i.1587) his willingness directly to remind his great-uncle, Sixtus V, of Porta's earlier service.[129]

Already in this early period, Montalto began to attract what might be called a fourth circle of musicians, consisting of composers whose only known association with the cardinal is their dedication of a collection of printed music to him. The first of these, Felice Anerio, dedicated his first book of six-voice madrigals to Montalto in 1590 and promptly received 25 scudi in consideration.[130] The same amount had been paid the previous year to Torquato Tasso for a collection of poems dedicated to Montalto's sister Flavia.[131] With these precedents, twelve other composers or compilers eventually followed suit:[132]

Felice Anerio, *Primo libro de madrigali a sei voci* (Venice: Amadino, 1590)
Mauro Chiauli, *Sacrarum cantionum . . . liber primus* (Venice: Amadino, 1590)

---

[125] Ademollo, *La bell'Adriana*, 7, 91–5.

[126] *New Grove*, s.v. 'Basile, Andreana'. Gioseppe Faccone's letter of 9 May 1609 to Vincenzo Gonzaga in Mantua says that Adriana Basile is about 19 years old, meaning she was born about 1590 and not 1580; Parisi, 'Ducal Patronage', 132, 181. But this may either be his estimate or a number put forward by the singer or someone connected with her in an effort to make her seem more desirable. She was already married at this time, and, after all, cinema actresses today have been known to misreport their ages.

[127] I:Rac, Corrispondenza epistolare di Virginio II Orsini, II C Prot. XXI.121, no. 3, letter 386.

[128] Ademollo, *La bell'Adriana*, 241.

[129] I:Rasv, Confalonieri 48, fo. 139ʳ; Chater, 'Musical Patronage', 188.

[130] I:Rac, Archivio Cardelli, Appendice, vol. 30, *sub die* 4 Mar. 1591: 'Mag. etc. pagarete à maestro Felice Anerio Musico scudi venticinque m.ta quali gli doniamo et ponete à nostro conto'.

[131] Vol. 30, *sub die* 25 Feb. 1590: 'Mag. etc. pagarete à maestro Torquato Tasso scudi venticinque m.ta quali li doniamo et ponete à nostro conto'. The collection was *Tempio fabricato da diversi coltissimi, e nobiliss. ingengni in lode dell'Illust.ma e Ecc.ma Donna Flavia Peretta-Orsina, Duchessa di Bracciano dedicatole da Uranio Fenice* [=Torquato Tasso] (Rome: Martinelli, 1591). Of the fifty-two contributing poets, only Tasso's name is familiar to modern readers. No musical setting of any of the poems contained in the book have come to light.

[132] The following list of musical prints dedicated to Cardinal Montalto is compiled from Chater, 'Musical Patronage', 225, and Larson, 'The Unaccompanied Madrigal', 561.

Scipione Dentice, *Motectorum quinque vocibus liber primus* (Rome: Coattino, 1594)

Ottavio Durante, *Arie devote* (Rome: Verovio, 1608)

Carlo Fiorillo, *Canzonette* (mentioned in his *Madrigali*)

Carlo Fiorillo, *Madrigali a cinque voci . . . libro primo* (Rome: Robletti, 1616)

Massimiano Gabbiani, comp., *Musica di diversi eccellentiss. auttori a cinque voci* (Venice: Gardano, 1604)

Ascanio Meo, *Il quinto libro de madrigali a cinque voci* (Naples: Carlino, 1608)

Giovanni Bernardino Nanino, *Madrigali a cinque voci . . . libro terzo* (Rome: Zannetti, 1612)

Pietro Pace, *Madrigali a quattro et a cinque voci . . . opera decima quinta* (Venice: Vincenti, 1617)

Sebastiano Raval, *Motectorum liber primus* (Rome: Coattino, 1593)

Sebastiano Raval, *Madrigali a tre voci* (Rome: Mutij, 1595) (one madrigal)

Scipione Stella, *Madrigali* (mentioned in the dedication of his *Hymnorum . . . liber*)

Scipione Stella, *Hymnorum ecclesiasticorum liber primus* (Naples: Carlini, 1610)

Vincenzo Ugolini, *Il secondo libro de madrigali a cinque voci* (Venice: Vincenti, 1615)

Ottavio Vernizzi, *Motectorum . . . liber primus* (Venice: Amadino, 1593)

With only one exception, these collections dedicated to Cardinal Montalto contained polyphonic vocal music rather than the accompanied vocal solos and duets produced by his inner circle of composers. This would seem to be no accident, as composers of polyphony for the most part remained distant from the cardinal, much as they would have preferred to join his inner circles. The one composer of polyphony in Montalto's household, Giovanni Bernardino Nanino, did compose monodies and church music accompanied by basso continuo once in the cardinal's service, and he played an important role in the training and preparation of solo singers, as he had at San Luigi earlier and as we shall see in the details provided by Chapter 4. The one collection of monody dedicated to Montalto, by a composer, Ottavio Durante, not in the cardinal's inner circles, contains failed imitations of Giulio Caccini's Florentine monodic style, a failure that Montalto and his musicians undoubtedly were able to detect.[133]

A fifth circle of musicians received Cardinal Montalto's patronage still more

---

[133] By contrast with Caccini's works, Durante's *Arie devote* (1608) use melismas, even on unaccented syllables, rather than speechlike declamation, as the primary means for text expression, and his bass lines reveal a polyphonic orientation through greater rhythmic and melodic activity. The division of some areas into sections defined occasionally by change of metre and often by relative degree of recitational versus metrical style, however, is typical of the monody composers in the circles around Cardinal Montalto, as we shall see in Chapters 3 and 6. The collection contains settings of twenty mostly anti-Calvinist texts, eighteen in Latin and two in Italian, perhaps reflecting Durante's view of Montalto's intention to lead the Counter-Reformation movement during his generation.

indirectly through his support of churches, monastic orders, and confraternities. The best example concerns the confraternity of Santissima Trinità dei Pellegrini, which maintained a very active and important programme of musical performance. Noel O'Regan has found that Montalto succeeded Ferdinando de' Medici as protector of the confraternity in 1588 and that he, his family, and relatives continued to be among its leading benefactors for decades afterward.[134]

We have said that the musicians with the earliest associations with Cardinal Montalto are already notable for their connection with accompanied solo singing, and this will become clearer in Chapter 3. Continuing this tendency, the musicians that he sought during a second period, roughly the decade from 1593 to 1602, were virtuosic vocal soloists associated with Florence. Montalto tried vigorously but unsuccessfully to recruit Giulio Caccini's prize student Francesco Rasi in 1593.[135] But at about the same time, two virtuoso solo singers from the Florentine court of Grand Duke Ferdinando de' Medici made important, extended sojourns at Montalto's court: the castrato Onofrio Gualfreducci and the brilliant and influential soprano Vittoria Archilei.[136] When he became Grand Duke of Tuscany in 1587, or shortly after, Ferdinando brought both of these singers from Rome, where they had long been active during the period of his cardinalate. In Florence, they became significant participants in the performance of court musical pageants and in the development of related innovations in the notation and performance of expressive and virtuosic solo singing that led to the productions of the earliest operas, in which both of them performed.

To some degree, the extended loan of Gualfreducci and Archilei symbolized Cardinal Montalto's *clientela* with Ferdinando de' Medici. This relation can be traced to the 1570s, when Ferdinando and Montalto's great-uncle, Felice, were both cardinals. Ferdinando became a protector of Felice, and eventually engineered his election to the papacy.[137] The connection was strengthened when Ferdinando arranged the marriage, in 1589, between his nephew Virginio Orsini and Cardinal Montalto's sister Flavia. At the time of Ferdinando's departure from Rome and the cardinalate to succeed his older brother as Grand Duke of Tuscany, he offered the loan of the entire Villa Medici for Montalto's private use.[138]

---

[134] Noel O'Regan, *Institutional Patronage in Post-Tridentine Rome: Music at Santissima Trinità dei Pellegrini 1550–1650* (Royal Musical Association Monographs, 7; London, 1996). My heartfelt thanks to Professor O'Regan for sending me a copy of the relevant chapter of his book before its publication.

[135] See Emilio de' Cavalieri's letter of 16 Dec. 1593 transcribed by Kirkendale, *Court Musicians*, 562.

[136] Chater, 'Musical Patronage', 195–9; Kirkendale, *Court Musicians*, 247–8, 265–70.

[137] For details, see Pastor, *History of the Popes*, xxi. 11–12.

[138] 'Il gran duca di Toscana ha dato ultimamente ordini alli suoi ministri qui [Roma], che faccino la fabricha del suo palazzo et giardino nel monte della Trinità, del quale had dato libero uso al signor cardinal Montalto, con tutti i mobili, che vi sono, poi ché S. A. non è altrimenti per venir più ad habitar in Roma': Orbaan, 'La Roma di Sisto V negli *avvisi*', 302, quoting from the *avvisi* of 28 Nov. 1587. As late as April of 1600, Cardinal

Cardinal Guido Bentivoglio described Montalto's relation with Ferdinando as 'friendship',[139] but that is a conventional euphemism of the time and does not necessarily mean what it does today. It was surely based on mutual need, as it was just as much in Ferdinando's interest to grant favours and honours to Montalto as it was in Montalto's to accept them. Ferdinando needed Montalto and his 'Sistine party' of cardinals (created by Sixtus V) to keep all Spanish-backed candidates from reaching the throne of St Peter; this was crucial for defence against the threat that Spanish hegemony in Italy posed to the independence of Tuscany.[140] And Montalto, of course, hoped that one day Ferdinando, through his surrogates in the curia like Cardinal Del Monte, would do for him what he had done for his great-uncle.

Montalto did not, however, always meet Ferdinando's expectations, as we have seen, and perhaps for a related reason, Cardinal Montalto seems to have avoided making a direct request to the Grand Duke for the services of singers, probably to maintain some measure of political independence, upon which his own power as *padrone* depended. Instead, Montalto relied on the mediation of Emilio de' Cavalieri, who was a client: on 31 April 1592 Cavalieri began to receive a lifetime pension of 5 gold scudi per month from Montalto in exchange for a large and valuable collection of paintings and statues,[141] and in a letter of 13 June 1592 Montalto promised to help Cavalieri's nephews.[142] The two other intermediaries in Montalto's requests for Medici singers were Cardinal Del Monte, a subordinate, and Virginio Orsini, who, as mentioned, was both brother-in-law to the cardinal and nephew to Grand Duke Ferdinando.[143] However, Montalto did agree to appeal directly to Pope Clement VIII, his patron in any case but one whom he was instrumental in electing (see above), and the pope's nephew

Montalto was still using the Villa Medici to entertain the Viceroy of Naples, upon whom Montalto depended for the enjoyment of his ecclesiastical income based upon churches and abbeys in the Kingdom of Naples (J. A. F. Orbaan, *Documenti sul barocco in Roma* (Rome, 1920), 151–4).

[139] Bentivoglio, *Memorie e lettere*, 58.

[140] The most thorough political history of the Medici grand duchy is still Riguccio Galluzzi, *Istoria del Granducato di Toscana sotto il governo della casa Medici*, 7 vols. (Cambiagi, 1781; 2nd edn., Livorno, 1820–1). Eric Cochrane, *Florence in the Forgotten Centuries, 1527–1800: A History of Florence and the Florentines in the Age of the Grand Dukes* (Chicago, 1973), includes an extensive and valuable bibliographic note, which admirably summarizes modern scholarship up to the date of publication, but the historical narrative, while rich in ideas and interpretation, tends towards the polemical. A more balanced overview, but without citation of sources, can be had from J. R. Hale, *Florence and the Medici: The Pattern of Control* (Plymouth, 1977). Samuel Berner has written the most interesting treatment of early grand-ducal politics, in the context of social, economic, and cultural history, in 'Florentine Political Thought in the Late Cinquecento', *Il pensiero politico*, 2 (1970), 177–99; and 'Florentine Society in the Late Sixteenth and Early Seventeenth Centuries', *Studies in the Renaissance*, 18 (1971), 203–46.

[141] I:Rac, Archivio Cardelli, Appendice, vol. 31, *sub die* 31 Apr. 1592. The collection of art that Cavalieri gave to Montalto in exchange for this pension included seven works by Giulio Romano and five 'quadreti' by Raphael. Further payments of this pension to Cavalieri are recorded in vols. 32 and 33 at uneven intervals.

[142] I:Rasv, Confalonieri 52, fo. 223ᵛ; Chater, 'Musical Patronage', 191.

[143] Chater, 'Musical Patronage', 199.

Cardinal Pietro Aldobrandini to help Gualfreducci obtain a canonry at Pistoia Cathedral in 1599.[144]

The exchange of favours between Montalto and Ferdinando de' Medici brought the cardinal to Florence on frequent visits. In 1595 Montalto served as godfather at the baptism of Ferdinando's fourth-born, Francesco, and in celebration of this event he heard the first pastorale *tutto in musica*, *Il giuoco della cieca*, by Emilio de' Cavalieri.[145] Early in the year 1600 Montalto was also present at the first performance of Cavalieri's *Rappresentatione di Anima, et di Corpo* in Rome.[146] During his visit to Florence in 1599, Montalto heard the first opera, *La Dafne* by Jacopo Peri.[147] Montalto's singer Melchior Palantrotti performed in the Florentine operas of 1600—Peri's *Euridice* and Caccini's *Il rapimento di Cefalo*.[148] (If the cardinal himself attended, he attracted no special notice.) In 1602 Montalto heard Caccini's setting of *Euridice* as well as the play *I morti e i vivi* with intermedi.[149] And finally, in 1608 his singers Ippolita Recupito and Melchior Palantrotti performed in *Il giudizio di Paride* to celebrate the marriage of Prince Cosimo, as already mentioned.[150]

As far as can be determined, Montalto's visits to Florence did not continue after 1602 or 1608, depending on whether or not he accompanied his singers there for Prince Cosimo's wedding. And the loan of Florentine singers comes to an end at about the same time. Montalto's role in the election of Pope Paul V, which so disgusted Cardinal Del Monte, may have something to do with this apparent cooling of relations. And Ferdinando's death in 1609 surely broke the major link between Montalto and the Medici. Coinciding with all this was Montalto's recruitment of Ippolita Recupito and Cesare Marotta in 1604, Ippolito Macchiavelli in 1607, Giovanni Giacomo Maggi, Giovanni Bernardino Nanino, and the Florentine Domenico Tombaldini in 1608. These additions to Montalto's household gave him considerably more ability to produce his own recitational solo singing in the new style that we associate with Florence.

Near what appears to be the end of his close relations with the Medici,[151] Cardinal

[144] Ibid. 197.

[145] Angelo Solerti, 'Laura Guidiccioni ed Emilio de' Cavalieri (i primi tentativi del melodramma)', *Rivista musicale italiana*, 9 (1902), 797–829 at 814.　　　　[146] Kirkendale, *Court Musicians*, 284.

[147] Frederick Sternfeld, 'The First Printed Opera Libretto', *Music & Letters*, 59 (1978), 121–38 at 133; Kirkendale, *Court Musicians*, 195–6.

[148] Claude V. Palisca, 'The First Performance of "Euridice"', in *Queens College Twenty–fifth Anniversary Festschrift (1937–1962)* (Flushing, NY, 1964), 1–23.

[149] Angelo Solerti, *Musica, ballo e drammatica alla corte medicea dal 1600 al 1637* (Florence, 1905), 23–6.

[150] Kirkendale, *Court Musicians*, 153, quotes from a letter of Giulio Caccini (15 Aug. 1608), which complains that Ippolita, her husband Cesare Marotta, a 'respectable matron', and a servant were quartered in his house during their stay.

[151] Montalto's opera *Amor pudico* of 1614 celebrates the triple alliance between the Peretti, Borghese, and Medici and defends it against unnamed enemies who wish to destroy it, as will be explained in the chapter devoted to the opera. This seems to be Montalto's last expression of *clientela* towards the Medici.

Montalto also tried to recruit Francesca Caccini, nominally to the service of his brother's wife. On 7 January 1607 (modern style) Giulio Caccini wrote from Florence to Virginio Orsini in Rome:

We are coming to Rome, my wife, Settimia, and I, to keep company with Cecchina [his nickname for Francesca], who is coming to serve the Princess Peretti [i.e. Margherita, first wife of Prince Michele Peretti], your sister-in-law [Orsini was married to Flavia, Michele's sister]; and we come in the good graces of Their Highnesses [the Medici], here, [they] having said to me that, since the service of Cardinal Montalto [i.e. the service is only nom-inally with Princess Margherita, for the sake of appearances] and theirs [i.e. the Medici's] is one and the same thing, they know that they will be able to send for Cecchina and for Signora Ippolita [Recupito] in every occasion with the same security with which His Most Illustrious Lordship [i.e. Cardinal Montalto] did when he wanted Signora Vittoria [Archilei].[152]

The Caccini family did not leave as soon as planned because negotiations hit a snag. Giulio Caccini writes, on 5 March 1607, 'For now our arrival there will be deferred to another occasion, because, having heard intimations from there that Cardinal Montalto had cooled off in the negotiations and, having sent him four lines [in a letter] in order to hear his pleasure, and, not having a reply, I find that it is true [i.e. he has cooled off], and, what worries me more, I am afraid that I have displeased him and lost his good grace'.[153] And Francesca's friend, the poet Michelangelo Buonarroti, il giovane, informed the Grand Duke the next day of the same thing.[154]

Apparently, Francesca's arrival in Rome was postponed some six years, and, once there, she did not stay long. On 3 March 1613 Piero Strozzi wrote to Virginio Orsini that Francesca and her husband were coming to Rome,[155] and on 4 May 1613 Francesca herself wrote to Orsini thanking him for gifts given during her recent visit there, because she had not been able to thank him personally at her

[152] 'Noi venghiamo à Roma, la mia Moglie, la Settimia, et io a tener compagnia alla Cecchina, la quale viene a servire la S.ra Principessa Peretti, sua Cognata, e venghiamo con buona grazia qui di lor Alt. avendomi detto, che, essendo il servizio del S.re Card.l Montalto, et il loro una cosa istessa, sanno di poter mandare per la Cecchina, e la S.ra Ipolita in ogni occasione con quell'istessa sicurtà, che ha fatto sua Sig.ria Ill.ma quando ha voluto la s.ra Vittoria.' I:Rac, Corrispondenza epistolare di Virginio II Orsini, II.C.Prot. XV.115, n. 1, lettera 133, par-tially transcribed by Ferdinand Boyer, 'Les Orsini et les musiciens d'Italie au début du xviie siècle', in Mélanges de philologie, d'histoire et de littérature offerts à Henri Hauvette (Paris, 1934), 301–10 at 305. Chater, 'Musical Patronage', 183, incorrectly assigns this letter to the year 1606 (it is dated 1606 Florentine style), and misin-terprets the passage to say that 'the service of Cardinal Montalto and theirs [Margherita's and Michele's] [is] one and the same'. In the context, this interpretation makes no sense. Kirkendale, Court Musicians, 151, tran-scribes the letter, but comments that 'Caccini was invited to visit Rome with his wife and daughters as house guests of Virginio Orsini', which is not at all stated in the letter.

[153] The full letter is transcribed in App. A, Letter 16.

[154] The draft of Buonarroti's letter is transcribed as Letter 17. Chater, 'Musical Patronage', who cites but does not quote this letter, assumes that 'the negotiations came to nothing', which this letter does not say (it says that the negotiation was 'at present quite cooled off') and which is contradicted by a later letter from Caccini to be quoted next.   [155] Kirkendale, Court Musicians, 313.

departure.[156] This makes me think that she did not depart from Orsini's palace but rather from Montalto's.

Later in the same month Francesca expresses her desire to return to Rome, and in March of 1614 she hopes to go there the following summer.[157] That summer visit did not materialize, as her father mentions in his letter to Orsini of 6 September 1614:

For the rest, I am infinitely pained that Your Most Illustrious Excellency did not again hear my daughter Francesca this summer because you cannot imagine the great strides that she has made since her departure from that city. It will be enough for several years to know that she has recently written 300 works in her own hand in three volumes, with all those spontaneous *passaggi* and other things that you can imagine and all the best expression and everything that can come from anyone who is a professional vocal soloist; and in the end she finally dissipated that timidity that held her back concerning poetry, and she has composed some madrigals and canzonette, both words and music, which have been much to the taste of everyone who has heard them.[158]

The correspondence that I have found says no more about visits to Rome,[159] and the three autograph volumes, which surely would have made Francesca Caccini the most prolific monodist of the era, have never been found. But a token, perhaps, of Francesca's stay in 1613 remained in Cardinal Montalto's library. It is a satirical *Egloga pastorale, Tirsi e Filli,* beginning 'Pascomi di sospir languendo e debile', which was later incorporated (along with other material clearly written earlier) into the 'favola' *Il Passatempo* by Michelangelo Buonarroti, *il giovane,* which was performed for the Medici court in Florence on 11 February 1614.[160]

---

[156] Letter 64. Also see Kirkendale, ibid.

[157] App., nos. 65 and 76. The second of these letters is cited by Kirkendale, ibid.

[158] 'Nel rimanente mi duole infinitam.te che V. E. Ill.ma non habbia udito di nuovo in questa estate la Fran.ca mia figl.a perché non voless.o ch'ella non giunge con l'immaginazione al grande acquisto, ch'ella ha fatto dopo la sua partenza che ella fece di costà, che basterà per qualche anno sapere che ella ha scritto di nuovo in tre libri di sua mano trecento opere, con tutti quei passaggi d'invenzione, che altri si possa immaginare, e con essi i migliori affetti, e tutti possino uscire da qualunq*ue* sia che professi di cantar solo, et in ultimo finalm.te ha disvolato quel timore, che la teneva, à freno intorno alla Poesia, et ha composto alcuni madrigali e canzonette le parole, e le musiche, che sono state di molto gusto, a chiunque l'ha udite.' I:Rac, Corrispondenza epistolare di Virginio II Orsini, II.C.Prot. XXV.126, n. 2, lettera 300, 6 Sept. 1614. Transcribed by Kirkendale, *Court Musicians,* 314.

[159] Francesca's later visit to Rome seems to have had nothing to do with Cardinal Montalto. In 1616 she was part of the entourage of Florentine musicians that Cardinal Carlo de' Medici brought with him to impress the Romans.

[160] A description of the performance from the court diary of Cesare Tinghi is transcribed in Solerti, *Musica, ballo e drammatica,* 81–5, in which volume (281–339) Solerti includes an edition of the text. Four versions of the text are found, in Buonarroti's hand, in Florence, Biblioteca Medicea Laurenziana, Buonarroti 62, the last of which contains much material not included in Solerti's edition. As Solerti explains (p. 282), only a portion of the text of *Il Passatempo*—*Il balletto della Cortesia*—was printed for the 1614 performance. The survival of this music for *Il Passatempo* by Francesca Caccini was mentioned in the handout for my paper 'Early Roman Monodies from the Circle of Cardinal Montalto', annual meeting of the American Musicological Society, Boston, 1981; the notice subsequently appeared in Kirkendale, *Court Musicians,* 313. Actually, there are two other pieces by Caccini that were used in *Il Passatempo.* See Ch. 5 for additional details.

Even in the years following the permanent addition of monody composers and
virtuoso solo singers to his household, Cardinal Montalto continued to patron-
ize musicians of these categories who were in the service of other courts. But,
in keeping with his shift in allegiance, these musicians tended to be associated
with the Borghese family rather than the Medici. In 1614, according to the published description,[161] he called upon Giovanni Domenico Puliaschi, Giacomo
Verovio, Pietro Ciamoricone, Cesare Zoilo, and a certain Ludovico to compose
music for *Amor pudico*, an opera in which he used the singers Francesco Severi,
Stefano (Landi?),[162] Cleria Agazzari, Giovanni Felice Sances,[163] and Pietro Paolo
Sabatini, and the theorbist Innocentio Menghi, in addition to the musicians of
his own household.[164] According to the description, Puliaschi,[165] Ciamoricone,
Severi,[166] and Menghi were in the service of the Borghese family, which included
Pope Paul V—who, as Cardinal Camillo Borghese, had been Cardinal Montalto's
client as Vice Legate to Bologna. Likewise in Borghese family service was the
composer Ottavio Catalani, who was in the household of Prince Marcantonio

[161] Romolo Paradiso, *Copia d'una lettera del Sig. Romolo Paradiso con quale dà avviso dell'apparato, e grandezza, con che si è rappresentato il festino dell'Eccellentiss. Sig. Principe Peretti* (Rome: Girolamo Discepolo, 1614), 64–7.

[162] Paradiso's description, 65, names only 'Stefano' as the singer of the role of Anterote. Stefano Landi was 27 or 28 in 1614. In 1611 Landi was paid to sing at the oratory of S. Marcello del Crocifisso (Domenico Alaleone, *Storia dell'oratorio musicale in Italia* (Milan, 1945), 337), for which Cardinal Montalto and his friend Vincenzo Giustiniani (see below) provided funds in 1595 and 1596 (Chater, 'Musical Patronage', 206). In 1616 Landi seems to be still in Rome, since his first printed work appeared then in Fabio Constantini, *Selectae cantiones* (Rome, 1616).

[163] Sances abruptly abandoned his position as boy soprano at the Jesuit German College on 1 Apr. 1614, shortly after his performances in *Amor pudico*. Thomas D. Culley, *Jesuits and Music, i: A Study of the Musicians connected with the German College in Rome during the 17th Century and of their Activities in Northern Europe* (Sources and Studies for the History of the Jesuits, 2; Rome, 1970), 141–2, suggests that Sances' departure resulted from his (or his father's) realization of the boy's potential outside the College. However, he is not correct in ascrib-ing to Cametti, 'Chi era l'"Hippolita"', the notion that Sances was already 'virtuoso of Cardinal Montalto' at the time of *Amor pudico*; neither Cametti's article nor the printed description of *Amor pudico* contains that suggestion. Likewise, I find no evidence to support the assertion of Rudolf Schnitzler and John Whenham (in the *New Grove* entry on Sances) that Sances 'became a musician in the service of Cardinal Montalto' after he sang in *Amor pudico*.

[164] Landi, Sances, and Sabatini were later to emerge as monody composers, as we shall see.

[165] On 9 Dec. 1606 Domenico Puliaschi resigned as *cantor sopranumerario* of the papal chapel because he had got married (I:Rvat, Cappella Sistina, Diario 26, fo. 33ᵛ). Parisi, 'Ducal Patronage', 105, transcribes a letter of 12 May 1612 from agent Paolo Faccone in Rome to Ferdinando Gonzaga in Mantua, which explains that Puliaschi had recently gained absolution from Pope Paul V to reenter the papal chapel and had, at the same time, passed from the service of Cardinal Aldobrandini into the household of Cardinal Scipione Borghese. For this period, the Borghese household account books are incomplete and disordered, but Jean Lionnet, 'The Borghese Family and Music during the First Half of the Seventeenth Century', *Music & Letters*, 74 (1993), 519–29 at 524, cites a payment on 5 May 1612 by Cardinal Scipione Borghese for candles for 'Sig. Gio. Dom.co . . . acetato in casa per musico'. Puliaschi's name can then be traced, from Jan. 1615 through 1622 (the year of his death), in the cardinal's household accounts, I:Rasv, Borghese 3946 and 3947. By coincidence, Puliaschi, as singer in the papal chapel, held his canonicate (from 2.xii.1614 to 9.vi.1622) in S. Maria in Cosmedin, the church to which Cardinal Montalto held the title in 1587, before becoming Vice-Chancellor and passing to the title of S. Lorenzo in Damaso. See *Serie cronologica degli eminentissimi e reverendissimi signori cardinali diaconi dell'insigne basilica di S. Maria in Cosmedin* (n.p., n.d.); a copy is in I:Rvat, S. Maria in Cosmedin, I-10, n. 18.

[166] Lionnet, 'The Borghese Family and Music', 523–4, shows that Severi, a native of Perugia, entered Cardinal Borghese's service in Jan. 1612.

Borghese from 1613 to at least 1621.[167] Catalani collaborated with Montalto *famigliari* Marotta and Macchiavelli in the rapid training of a boy singer, as we shall see in Chapter 4. If the singer called 'Stefano' was actually Stefano Landi, then another Borghese composer would be added to the list, because Landi studied at both the Collegio Germanico and the Seminario Romano and would go on to dedicate his opera *La morte d'Orfeo* (1619) to a familiar of Pope Paul V (Camillo Borghese) and to send a composition of his in that same year to Cardinal Scipione Borghese. The composer-singer identified in the description of *Amor pudico* only as Ludovico is designated as being in the service of Prince Bernardino Savelli, who later married the daughter of Cardinal Montalto's brother and was the brother of Cardinal Giulio Savelli, a creation of Pope Paul V and sponsor of a musical spectacle based on Tasso's *Gerusalemme liberata*, for which the Borghese lent Ottavio Catalani to provide some music, as will be explained below.

There is one other singer-composer in the third circle around Cardinal Montalto who contributed to *Amor pudico*, according to a manuscript source of the music,[168] but who is not mentioned in the printed description: 'Giuseppino', an often-mentioned virtuoso tenor and composer whom Nigel Fortune tentatively suggested should be identified as the papal singer Giuseppe Cenci,[169] citing Giovanni Battista Doni's 1635 reference to 'Giuseppe Cenci detto Giuseppino'.[170] A series of newly recovered documents confirms Fortune's and Doni's identification of Giuseppino. In the summer of 1615 Cardinal Montalto's client Enzo Bentivoglio, in Ferrara, received from Girolamo Fioretti, one of his agents in Rome, a letter, written on 8 July 1615 and mostly devoted to news of the activities of musicians in Montalto's household, that included this message: 'We shall have Giuseppino only a few days longer, since he has become completely mad, and he eats and sleeps very little. Of his madness one could write books, but it all belongs to his misery' (Letter 92). Actually, Giuseppino survived much longer than Fioretti anticipated, for a bit more than a year later, another of Bentivoglio's Roman agents, Ercole Provinzale, added a postscript to his letter of 11 July 1616, saying, 'Iosepino is dead, that is, the musician' (Letter 109). Now if we check the records of the papal chapel, we find that Giuseppe Cenci was absent due to illness

---

[167] Lionnet, ibid., 525, shows that Catalani entered Marcantonio Borghese's service in Apr. 1613. Catalani is still designated 'Musico de' Eccellentiss. Sig. Prencipe di Solmona [=Marcantonio Borghese]' in Giovanni Battista Robletti's anthology *Raccolta de varii concerti musicali* (Rome: Robletti, 1621).

[168] 'Anima bella, che in quel sen ti stai', from the Hora quarta of *Amor pudico*, is ascribed to 'Gioseppino' in I:Vc, Fondo Torrefranca, MS 250, 'Grilanda musicale di arie di diversi eccel.mi hautori', fos. 53ᵛ–56ᶠ, with concordances in I:Ru, MS 279; I:MOe, MS Mus. E 318; and I:Baf, MS 1424. See Ch. 5 and Vol. II, no. 17.

[169] Nigel Fortune, 'Italian 17th-Century Singing', *Music & Letters*, 35 (1954), 206–19 at 211.

[170] Giovanni Battista Doni, *Compendio del trattato de' generi e de' modi della musica* (Rome, 1635), 101. Although Cenci always signed his name 'Gioseppe Cenci' in the payrolls of the papal chapel (e.g. I:Rvat, Cappella Sistina, Cammerlingo 4 [payrolls for 1603], *passim*), I shall refer to him as either Giuseppino Cenci, thus incorporating the usual nickname given him, or Giuseppe Cenci, as he is called in all modern works of scholarship.

constantly during 1615 and the first half of 1616, that on 21 June 1616 'Sig. Giuseppe Cenci passed to the better life at forty minutes before sunset, as attested by Captain Severino', and that he was interred the next day in San Lorenzo in Damaso (Montalto's titular church).[171] The record of Cenci's death kept by the parish of Santa Maria in Via, where he died, and the inscription made at the parish of San Lorenzo in Damaso, where he was entombed, give the singer's name as 'Giosepino Cienso' and 'Gioseppino Cenci', respectively.[172] These parallels between the musician 'Giuseppino' mentioned in the letters to Enzo Bentivoglio and the papal singer Giuseppino Cenci cannot be mere coincidence.

The question of Giuseppino's identity arises in the first place because several musical manuscripts and writings of the period present us with the name 'Giuseppino' without surname (see Ch. 3). A possible explanation for this can be found in the hypothesis that Giuseppino and his friends preferred not to use his surname in order to avoid any association with the family of Francesco Cenci, which was made infamous by accusations of incest and patricide and was placed under arrest, en masse, in 1599.

Giuseppino Cenci entered the papal chapel in 1598.[173] The diaries of the Sistine Chapel make it clear that he was in the service of Cardinal Odoardo Farnese (1573–1626), the brother of Ranuccio I, Duke of Parma, from at least 1598 until 1608, when he apparently transferred to the service of Cardinal Scipione Borghese.[174] The chronic illness that led to Cenci's death seems to have begun in the spring of 1614.[175] This may explain why he did not sing in Amor pudico (1614) even though one of his arias was used and, hence, why he is not mentioned in the description printed after the event. The next chapter will begin to make clear Giuseppino Cenci's considerable significance in the history of early Baroque monody.

Cardinal Montalto's abiding interest in patronizing and surrounding himself with singers and composers involved with the new styles of dramatically expressive and virtuosic solo singing, while not unique among Italian cardinals and princes of his day, was sufficiently pronounced to inspire him to perform such

---

[171] I:Rvat, Cappella Sistina, Diario 34 (for 1615), passim; and Diario 35 (for 1616), passim and fo. 30ᵛ, sub die 21 June 1616: 'Il S.r Giuseppe Cenci passò a miglior vita a hore 23 1/3 come ne face fede il Capitan Severino' and sub die 22 June 1616: 'fu sepolto il S.r Giuseppe Cenci in S.to Lorenzo in Damaso a hore 22 dove fu il Collegio delli Sig.ri Cantori per accompagnare il Corpo secondo il solito et vennero delli SS.ri Giubilati.'

[172] I:Rav, S. Maria in Via, 11, Morti I, II (1571–1637), sub die 22 June 1616: 'morse il Signor Giosepino Cienso in cassa dal Capitan S.tro Severino fu sepulto a S.to Lorenzo in Damaso avendo avuti tuti li sacramenti'. I:Rav, S. Lorenzo in Damaso, 54, Morti II (1591–1644), fo. 82ᵛ, sub die 22 June 1616: 'Gioseppino Cenci Rom.o Musico del Papa da S. Maria in via sepolto quà'.   [173] Celani, 'I cantori della Cappella Pontificia', 765.

[174] Rome, I:Rvat, Cappella Sistina, Diario 22–35, passim.

[175] On 15 Apr. 1614 Giovanni Domenico Puliaschi and Francesco Severio are excused for service to Cardinal Borghese, but Cenci is not mentioned (I:Rvat, Cappella Sistina, Diario 33, fo. 16ᵛ), and in 1615 and 1616 he is continuously absent because of illness (Diario 34 and 35, passim), as mentioned earlier.

music himself and to attract Vincenzo Giustiniani's particular attention. It should be worthwhile to seek reasons for this preoccupation and to comment on its cultural significance. It is clear enough that Cardinal Montalto wished to emulate Ferdinando de' Medici, who was his benefactor, mentor, ally, and *padrone*—initially for historical and political reasons and then, perhaps, for personal motives as well. Both men, although already in prominent positions established for them by their families, strove for additional power and standing; neither was passive or conservative in behaviour. Both were well served by forms of patronage that produced a direct and strong effect on peers and clients. Palace and garden architecture and decoration produced such effects for them. Musical performance did likewise but with the additional advantages of greater personal association, as their palaces and gardens were largely inherited. By contrast, support of painters, contributions to church construction, founding of colleges, and payment for publication of books and music tended to produce results located separately and often at a distance from the patron. Musical performance by a soloist focuses attention on the heroic individual, who is, therefore, potentially a metaphorical representation of the prince himself. And the kind of solo singing that Cardinal Montalto and Ferdinando de' Medici promoted and presented was distinguished by its expressive spontaneity (sprezzatura, as explained in the next chapter) and virtuosity. These two features might easily be identified with more general values such as individuality, stupefaction, force, power, persuasion, influence, and domination: all usefully associated with men of great status and even greater ambition. And since this kind of music was new, not universally understood, and difficult to procure, its presentation by a patron might reflect acumen and efficacy.

Dramatically expressive and virtuosic solo singing was also valuable in musical pageantry, whose utility as an instrument of political persuasion Ferdinando had learnt well from his father, Cosimo, who had begun the celebrated series of aulic intermedi that was to climax in the first operas.[176] Cardinal Montalto and

---

[176] The idea that the Medici grand dukes had a distinct plan for the use of musical pageantry and spectacle as an instrument of politics originated with Galluzzi, *Istoria del Granducato di Toscana sotto il governo della casa Medici*. Modern and detailed analysis of grand-ducal pageantry from this point of view has been offered by Eve Borsook, 'Art and Politics at the Medici Court', *Mitteilungen des Kunsthistorischen Institutes in Florenz*, 12, 13, and 14 (1965, 1967, 1969); Giovanna Gaeta Bertelà and Annamaria Petrioli Tofani, *Feste e apparati medicei da Cosimo I a Cosimo II* (Florence, 1969); Ludovico Zorzi, 'Introduzione', in Mario Fabbri, Elvira Garbero Zorzi, and Annamaria Petrioli Tofani (eds.), *Il luogo teatrale a Firenze* (Spettacolo e musica nella Firenze medicea: Documenti e restituzioni, 1; Milan, 1975), 9–51; Zorzi, *Il teatro e la città* (Turin, 1977); id., *Il potere e lo spazio: La scena del principe* (Florence, 1980); Roy Strong, *Art and Power: Renaissance Festivals, 1450–1650* (Berkeley and Los Angeles, 1984); and Sara Mamone, *Il teatro nella Firenze medicea* (Problemi di storia dello spettacolo, 9; Milan, 1981). A more descriptive approach to the same material can be found in Nino Pirrotta and Elena Povoledo, *Music and Theatre from Poliziano to Monteverdi*, trans. Karen Eales (Cambridge Studies in Music; Cambridge, 1982); Alois Maria Nagler, *Theatre Festivals of the Medici, 1539–1637* (New Haven, 1964); Wolfgang Osthoff, *Theatergesang und darstellende Musik in der italienischen Renaissance (15. und 16. Jahrhundert)* (Tutzing, 1969); and Cesare Molinari, *Le nozze degli dèi: Un saggio sul grande spettacolo italiano nel Seicento* (Rome, 1968).

his brother understood this, too.[177] In 1596, in conjunction with Michele's first marriage, they announced plans for the first fully staged performance of Battista Guarini's pastorale tragicomedy *Il pastor fido*, with intermedi and other music. Although the Peretti apparently did not go through with the performance, it seems that the production may have been staged at a villa belonging to their friend and neighbour Cardinal Odoardo Farnese, and some of the music may survive (see Ch. 8). In 1603 Prince Michele organized a pageant, masque, joust, and horse race, all of which would have been accompanied by music. In 1605 Montalto followed a banquet with a musical stage performance that included dancing. Prince Michele presented a pastorale, which would have included singing, in 1609 at Montalto's chancellery palace.[178] Giovann Giacomo Maggi played harpsichord in a pastorale at Montalto's palace in 1611. That would seem to be distinct from the tragedy based on the myth of Psyche presented there during carnival of that year with intermedi that featured music performed on clouds (reminiscent of several earlier Florentine intermedi).[179] In 1612 Montalto presented a play with intermedi based on 'La priggionia, incantamento, et liberatione di Rinaldo', adapted by Guarini from Torquato Tasso's *Gerusalemme liberata*, for which some

---

[177] Documentation for the stage productions mentioned here is found in Chater, 'Musical Patronage', 208–10.

[178] I:Rvat, Urb. Lat. 1077, fo. 93ᵛ (28 Feb. 1609): 'La sera del med.mo giorno nell'appartam.to del Principe Peretti nel Palazzo della Cancell.a fù recitata da nobiliss.i giovanetti una pastorale, alla q.le intervenero li Car.li Montalto, Monti, Peretti, e Contestabile Colonna, che furno splendidam.te banchettati dal sud.o Prencipe Peretti'. Cited but not transcribed by Chater, 'Musical Patronage', 208.

[179] I:Rvat, Urb. Lat. 1079, fo. 119ᵛ (12 Feb. 1611): 'Mercoledi sera nella sala della Cancellaria fù recitata una tragedia composta dal Mastro di Don Francesco Peretti sopra la favola di Psiche, alla qual intervennero li Card.li Montalto, e Peretti, Il príncipe Peretti, et Duca di Bracciano [Virginio Orsini]. Et fù recitato dall'istesso Don Francesco Peretti et altri giovanetti nobili, tra questi si diportò[?] maravigliosam.te un nipote di Mons.r Ludovisio Aud.r di Rota. Et vi furono intermedij apparenti di musiche in nuvole, balletti e simili con belliss.i habiti e spesa notabile.' A second performance is described on fos. 127–8 (16 Feb. 1611): 'Lunedì sera nel Palazzo del Cardinal Montalto fu di novo ma più formatamente della prima volta recitata la scritta favola di Psiche con intervento delli Cardinali Cosenza, Monti, Borghese, Montalto, et Peretti et delli SS.ri Francesco Borghese, Ambasciatore di Savoia, Contestabile Colonna, Duca di Bracciano, Altaemps, et altri titolati; fu cominciato ad un'hora di notte et finita alle 5. et se per la qualità dell'opera, e nobilità de recitanti, come per gli habiti ricchi et pomposi et intermedi aparenti, buon ordine et silenzio, è riuscita la più nobile e degna materia che si sia fatta in Roma questo e molti anni dietro. E doppo esser spacciata la sala dove si recitava, fatta largo, essendovi ca. 30 Dame delle più principali e belle di Roma, vi fu danzato alquanto, et in fine l'istesso Principe Peretti, Don Ferdinando Orsini, con altri SS.ri e cavalieri tutti amorevoli con la testa scoperta, portarono una lautissima colatione di confetture, e altre esquisitezze per le Dame et cavalieri; oltre di ciò Sua Eccellenza mandato poi a casa a ciascuna Dama una canestrella di zuccaro con dentro paste confetture con statuette et altre galanterie degne non meno per l'artificio di quello si fossero dolci e delicate per la qualità della materia.' Both notices are cited by Chater, 'Musical Patronage', 208–9, but not completely transcribed. The second notice was transcribed in a handout for Margaret Murata's paper, 'Formal Entertainment and Opera for the Aristocracy in 17th-Century Rome', at the 1982 Congress of the International Musicological Society in Strasburg, but only an abstract was published in the report of the congress. The name of Don Francesco's tutor (*mastro*) has not been found, and no written materials relating to the tragedy or intermedi have been located, with the result that no surviving music can yet be linked to this very important musical stage work. The theatrical set designers at the Chancellery Palace must have been busy at this time, for on 5 Feb. 1611 the *avvisi* report, 'dal principe Peretti, ritornato col cardinal suo fratello dalle caccie di Cerveteri, una comedia, nella quale ogni atto si muterà la scena' (I:Rvat, Urb. Lat. 1078, fo. 122ᵛ).

music survives (see Ch. 8). And in 1614 Cardinal Montalto celebrated his brother's second marriage with the first secular Roman opera, *Amor pudico*, featuring 'musiche, di stile, che si dice recitativo' and other self-consciously Florentine elements. The political message of this opera was overt: the triangular alliance between the Peretti, Borghese, and Medici families must be defended against enemies who want to divide them (see Ch. 9).

In the known evidence there are indications of one more musical spectacle that may have had associations with Cardinal Montalto and his brother Michele. It is the play given in the Savelli palace during February of 1619, either itself derived from an episode from Tasso's *Gerusalemme liberata* or accompanied by one or more intermedi based upon such an episode.[180] The topic of the play or intermedio is identified in the rubrics given to one piece of music from it, which is preserved in three manuscripts connected with Cardinal Montalto's circles. One manuscript identifies the piece as 'Lamento cantato dalla Sig.a Olimpia Saponara nella comedia del Ill.mo Sig.r Cardinal Savelli'.[181] In a second manuscript, it is called 'Lamento di Ermenia cantato nella commedia di Savelli'.[182] And in a third manuscript it is simply ascribed to Ottavio Catalani, a musician connected with the Borghese family, as we have seen.[183] The 1619 performance is the only one mentioned in known documents that was presented in the Savelli palace during this period. A possible link to the Peretti (Cardinal Montalto and Prince Michele), beyond the presence of Catalani's lament in Montalto's music collection, is offered by a hypothetical occasion for the performance: the marriage of Bernardino Savelli, Duke of Riccia and brother of Cardinal Giulio Savelli, with Maria Felice, daughter of Prince Michele Peretti. The date of their marriage is unknown, but separate agreements between Michele Peretti and Prince Savelli pursuant to the marriage were consummated in 1618, 1619, 1620, and 1621.[184] Bernardino, who was born in 1606, would have been about 13 years old in 1619. This may have been too young to have one's marriage made public, but not at all too young to be married secretly: Michele himself, the father of the bride, was secretly married to Maria Felice's mother when he was 11 years old![185] So it is possible that a play or intermedi based on Tasso and performed at the Savelli palace in 1619 celebrated, semi-privately, the marriage of Bernardino Savelli and Maria Felice Peretti.

---

[180] I:Fas, Mediceo del Principato, Filza 3334 (Piero Guicciardini, agent in Rome, to the Secretary of State in Florence, 11 Feb. 1619): 'Hiersera nell'essere in Casa Savelli à una Commedia, dove era il Cardinale Borghese'. I:Rvat, Urb. Lat. 1087, fo. 68ᵛ: 'Si sono di questa settimana continuate le maschere, et corso de Pallij favorite dal tempo, et dal concorso di Popolo con grand.ma quiete, recitate diverse comedie in casa de part.ri una delle q.li molto bella, e principale nel Palazzo de SS.ri Card.le et Principe Savelli coll'Intervento delle più principali persone huomini, e donne di questa Citta con apparato magnifico.'

[181] I:Vc, Torrefranca 250, fos. 45ᵛ–48ʳ. See Ch. 5.   [182] I:Bc, CC.225, fos. 20ᵛ–24ʳ. See Ch. 5.

[183] I:Ru, MS 279, fos. 70ᵛ–74ʳ. See Ch. 5.

[184] I:Ras, Sforza-Cesarini, Iª parte (etichetta rettangolare), 72, AA56, no. 32, items 1, 8, and 9; and no. 33.

[185] See Ch. 7.

Cardinal Montalto certainly wished to emulate his *padrone* Ferdinando de' Medici in his patronage of expressive and virtuosic solo vocal music and in his use of musical spectacle as means of public presentation. Ottavio Durante's dedication of his monody collection, the first published in Rome (1608), makes Montalto's aesthetic orientation explicit, and his directions to performers, based as they are on Caccini's, make the same point implicitly:

Just as Castore Durante, my father, while he lived, was very much a servant of the Peretti house and demonstrated himself to be that, dedicating to the happy memory of Sixtus V his *Thesoro della sanità*, so I, wishing to follow in my father's footsteps, come to dedicate to Your Most Illustrious Lordship the present *arie*, knowing how much you delight in various arts and particularly in expressive music, as is clearly shown by the large number of *virtuosi* that you keep in your service, so that it can truly be said that this art shines today in your house as much as in any other place.[186]

But between Montalto's break with Ferdinando over the election of Pope Paul V in 1605 and Ferdinando's death in 1609, Montalto, whether by design or necessity, set out on a somewhat independent path, with the recruitment to his service of virtuosic singers and composers of monody from Naples and Rome. They brought traditions and developments to his court that were, to some extent, both cognate with and different from the Florentine fashions that the cardinal wished to emulate. What these traditions and developments were will be the subject of the next chapter.

---

[186] 'Si come Castore Durante mio Padre, mentre visse, era molto Servitore di casa Peretti, e si dimostrò tale, con dedicar alla felice memoria di Sisto V, il Thesoro della sanità; così volen'io imitar i vestigij paterni, vengo à dedicar à V. S.ria Ill.ma le presenti Arie, sapendo quanto diletto si prenda di diverse Virtù, e particolarmente della Musica affettuosa, come ne fa chiaro testimonio il copioso numero de' Virtuosi, che tiene al suo servitio; che si può dir con verità che questa Virtù risplenda hoggi in Casa sua, quanto in ogn'altro luogo. Gradisca dunq. V. S. Ill.ma questo mio affetto, e non risguardi alla debolezza dell'effetto ch'io trà tanto facendole humilissima riverenza, pregarò il s.r Iddio che conservi la Persona sua per molti e molti ann. Di Casa in Roma a di p.o di Gennaro 1608 di V. S. Ill.ma et R.ma Devotissimo Serv.e Ottavio Durante.' Ottavio Durante, *Arie devote* (Rome: Verovio, 1608), dedication.

3

Arie in stil recitativo, e cantativo

❧

IT seems to be frequently assumed or implied but rarely stated that Giulio Caccini's *Le nuove musiche* (Florence, 1602) is the fountainhead of Baroque chamber monody. Bukofzer makes this most explicit when he says, 'This famous publication opens a long procession of similar collections.'[1] Few today, however, would agree with Bukofzer that monody was 'a creation of learned intellectuals, the *Camerata* in Florence'.[2] Instead, Caccini's works are usually considered a fountainhead in the sense that all contributing factors and influences affecting Baroque monody flow into them, and all subsequent developments of that genre flow out of them. Tim Carter, for instance, who emphasizes most recently and perhaps more than anyone the roots of *Le nuove musiche* in earlier practices, makes his transition from Caccini to later monodists with this sentence: 'Moreover, serious "professional" composers (Monteverdi is a good example) seem to have been reluctant *to adopt the new Florentine style*: they may have looked askance at such trifles that gave little chance to display their hard-earned technical skills.'[3] The implication is that Italian composers of secular music *c.*1600–10 were faced with the choice either 'to adopt the new Florentine style' or to continue composing polyphonic madrigals, canzonette, or villanelle. Nowhere does Carter suggest that the widely diffused earlier practices that Caccini drew upon had any direct influence on non-Florentine monodists independently of Caccini's mediation. This, however, is precisely the conclusion that the music and documents from Cardinal Montalto's circles suggest. This thesis will be supported principally in this chapter and in Chapter 6, where the main body of music from Montalto's circles will be examined.

Caccini, of course, never claimed that monody was his invention or a creation of the Florentine *camerata*. Certainly everyone in Italian courtly life at that time knew that solo song accompanied by a lute, harpsichord, guitar, lira, or similar

---

[1] Manfred Bukofzer, *Music in the Baroque Era from Monteverdi to Bach* (New York, 1947), 29.
[2] Ibid. 26.
[3] Tim Carter, *Music in Late Renaissance and Early Baroque Italy* (London, 1992), 193 (emphasis mine).

instrument had a long history before 1602, even if today we cannot be sure how much music that comes to us in polyphonic notation was originally conceived for an accompanied solo voice. Caccini's extensive writing on the novelty of his music should be understood as a reply to Emilio de' Cavalieri's claim, voiced through his spokesman Alessandro Guidotti in the preface to the printed score of *La rappresentazione di anima et di corpo* (Rome, 1600), that Cavalieri's music was the first in modern times to resemble that with which the ancient Greeks and Romans moved audiences to various passions in their theatres, having varied dynamics, syllabic delivery, and accompaniment moulded to expression of the solo voice.[4] Caccini countered this in prefaces to the scores of his *Euridice* (Florence, 1600), *Le nuove musiche*, and *Nuove musiche e nuova maniera di scriverle* (Florence, 1614) and in an unpublished letter to Virginio Orsini in 1614.[5] Putting together these four writings, we can summarize Caccini's claims under six points:

1. That *Le nuove musiche* is the first publication to combine these three essential features:

(a) *basso continuato* (i.e. basso continuo), which is a notational convention, a set of performance techniques, and a compositional procedure in which the voice part is allowed considerable freedom in the creation of dissonances and in rhythmic delivery while the instrumental accompaniment, guided by the non-vocally conceived figured bass, remains relatively static;

(b) specifically notated ornaments and passaggi, which, by their restriction to accented syllables and their internal rhythmic variety, contribute to the expression of the passions implied by the text rather than to empty virtuosic display; and

(c) sprezzatura (nonchalance), which results from fluctuations in tempo and deviations from written rhythms in an attempt to capture in singing the spontaneously diverse syllable durations and accents of common speech. An annotation to one of the examples in the preface to the 1602 collection says: 'without measured rhythm, as if speaking in music with the abovesaid sprezzatura'.[6] Caccini's letter of 1614, quoted below, says much the same thing. To a great extent, Caccini's intent was to develop ever more precise means of capturing the sprezzatura of improvised and semi-improvised recitational singing in musical notation, as can be seen when earlier and later versions of his songs are compared.[7]

---

[4] Guidotti's introduction as well as all the other prefaces and claims of the Florentine pioneers of musical drama cited in this discussion, unless otherwise noted, are reprinted in Solerti, *Le origini del melodramma*.

[5] The political and personality conflicts that underlay Caccini's rivalry with Cavalieri are discussed by Nino Pirrotta, 'Temperaments and Tendencies in the Florentine Camerata', *Musical Quarterly*, 40 (1954), 169–89.

[6] 'Senza misura, quasi favellando in armonia con la suddetta sprezzatura.'

[7] Stephen Willier, 'Rhythmic Variants in Early Manuscript Versions of Caccini's Monodies', *Journal of the American Musicological Society*, 36 (1983), 481–97.

2. That an important novelty of this music is that, as a result of the points just mentioned, it is notated as it should be sung, rather than relying on the performers' musical invention and application of conventions.

3. That *Le nuove musiche* reveals the results of Caccini's study with Scipione del Palla,[8] who taught him the noble style of singing. (That study took place in Florence from 1565, at earliest, to Palla's death in 1569.)[9]

4. That Giovanni Bardi, at the time that his *camerata* was flourishing (*c.*1572–87),[10] declared this style to be the one used by the ancient Greeks when introducing song into their tragedies.

5. That Caccini first employed this style compositionally in three solo madrigals and a (lost) eclogue in about 1585.

6. That Caccini used this style in dramatic contexts first when he composed some music for *La Dafne*, then in *Euridice* (Florence, 1600).

Several of Caccini's most important claims, directed against those of Cavalieri, were forcefully summarized in a letter he sent to Virginio Orsini just as Caccini's second collection went to the printer in 1614:

I have sent to press if not for now all then at least some of my pieces of music, with a discourse about them in which I demonstrate that which is my taste concerning the true and noble manner of singing and how by means of this new style of mine—invented by me and called singing with nonchalance, like a new [kind of] speaking in music without observing measured rhythm—there was introduced in Florence the custom of acting stories while singing. And concerning all of this that I have done, without naming anyone and without giving offence to anyone, I demonstrate there that, notwithstanding that Sig.r Emilio de' Cavalieri, Roman gentleman of honoured memory, was the first here to let their Serene Highnesses hear such plays upon the stage, his was not the same style.[11]

---

[8] Kirkendale, *Court Musicians*, 100, reveals that Scipione's actual surname was Vecchi, according to Florentine court financial records. Kirkendale prefers 'Delle Palle' to 'del Palla' on grounds that 'it prevails in the contemporary sources'. I, however, am not convinced of that, and Kirkendale does not list the sources.

[9] Tim Carter, 'Giulio Caccini (1551–1618): New Facts, New Music', *Studi musicali*, 16 (1987), 13–32 at 13–20.

[10] Claude V. Palisca, 'The "Camerata Fiorentina": A Reappraisal', *Studi musicali*, 1 (1972), 203–36 at 205–7.

[11] 'Ho dato alla stampa si bene non per ancora il tutto, alcune mie Musiche con un Discorso in esse, nel quale io vengo à dimostrare qual sia stato il gusto mio intorno alla vera, e nobile maniera di cantare, e come mediante quel mio nuovo stile inventato da me, et appellato canto in sprezzatura quasi che una nuova favella in armonia senza osservanza di misura, fu introdotto in Firenze l'uso di rappresentar favole cantando, e intorno à questo tutto quello che è stato operato da me, senza nominar niuno, nè senza offesa per ciò di qualunche sia, mostrando appresso, che non ostante che 'l Sig.r Emilio del Cava:re Gentilhuomo romano d'onorata memoria fossi il primo qui, che facesse udire à quest'Alt. Ser.me su per le Scene dette favole, non fu per questo il med.o stile.' I:Rac, Corrispondenza epistolare di Virginio II Orsini, II.C.Prot. XXV.126, n. 2, lettera 300 —cited in Boyer, 'Les Orsini et les musiciens d'Italie', 306–7, but not transcribed completely. Many modern scholars have noted that, by contrast to the recitational styles of Caccini and Peri, Cavalieri's lacks rhythmic flexibility, interpretive word and syllable accentuation, and a rhythmically slower, non-vocal bass subordinated to the accents, pacing, and expression of the vocal line. Caccini seems to have been well aware of these crucial differences.

It will be noted that Caccini focuses his writing primarily against Cavalieri's claim to have been the first to use Greek-inspired recitative. Probably for this reason, he refers to the novelty and early date of his most declamatory solo madrigals, those with the most monotone recitation, limited ranges, syllabic text setting, ametrical rhythm, and static bass lines. All he says about his strophic canzonette is that their texts, mostly by Gabriello Chiabrera, are of a higher literary quality than those of earlier ones. He says nothing directly about his strophic variations, beyond his general remarks about his style of writing out embellishments and passaggi. He credits Bardi and his *camerata* with encouraging and steering him, but not with suggesting or inventing the compositional features of his music.

As far as those features are concerned, he leaves us with the strong impression that they can be traced back to his teacher Scipione del Palla. To a great extent, Caccini seems to be claiming simply to have found a way of reducing to notation the noble style of singing that he learned from Palla and later to have used it in dramas sung in their entirety. By implication, Jacopo Peri, on Caccini's view, may have been among the first to use this recitational style in an opera, but he neither invented it nor was the first to reduce it to notation.[12]

Because so many of Cardinal Montalto's leading musicians came from Naples it is worth emphasizing that before closing his career in Florence, Scipione del Palla was principally active in Naples. All the music by Palla known to survive is contained in the Neapolitan anthology *Aeri racolti insieme con altri bellissimi aggionti di diversi, dove si cantano sonetti, stanze e terze rime*, collected by Rocco Rodio, the second edition of which was published in 1577. The date of the first edition is unknown, but the contents of the collection seem to come from the 1550s. It contains settings of sonnets (16), capitoli in terza rima (4), stanzas of ottava rima (3), villanelle (3), and madrigals (3). Most of the items in the anthology resemble generic, all-purpose formulas for singing any poem of a particular form, although only two of them are designated as such by a rubric. In their notated form, these pieces are largely syllabic and narrow in range. In nearly all of them, recitation of several syllables on one pitch is a prominent feature. Most of the eleven-syllable poetic verses are provided with an eleven-note musical phrase, with minor embellishments added in some cases, ending with two relatively long notes, either on the same pitch or on a descending cadential formula, to accommodate the trochaic ending of the standard Italian *verso piano*.[13]

Vincenzo Galilei, the leading musician in the Florentine *camerata*, pointed out these same characteristics in certain mid-sixteenth-century villanelle and formulaic

---

[12] Peri's highly significant development of this style is analysed by Pirrotta, *Music and Theatre*, 237–80, and by Claude V. Palisca, 'Peri and the Theory of Recitative', *Studies in Music*, 15 (1981), 51–61.

[13] The most extensive and recent discussion of Rodio's anthology is Howard Mayer Brown, 'The Geography of Florentine Monody: Caccini at Home and Abroad', *Early Music*, 9 (1981), 147–68.

arie, which, in his opinion, would provide modern musicians with models of the essential features of ancient Greek music, along the lines of which modern solo singing might be reformed.[14] Galilei's interest in arias such as those in the Rodio anthology and in *madrigali ariosi* can be traced back to his first book of lute music (1563). That book, like the Rodio anthology, reveals the Neapolitan and Roman tendency to adapt the most serious Italian poetry—Petrarch, Bembo, Sannazzaro—to the recitational formulas of the unwritten tradition.[15] The content of Galilei's lute book, in fact, led Howard Mayer Brown to conclude that 'Galilei reveals himself to be musically a Roman' and that 'it was not just any native Italian song that served as one of the sources of Florentine monody but quite specifically Roman song'.[16]

Following the usual practice established for frottole early in the sixteenth century and continued for canzoni villanesche alla napolitana and related 'lighter' genres in the middle of the century and for villanelle and canzonetti in the later 1500s, Rodio's *arie* were provided to the public in settings for three and four voices, although their primary and, in many cases, original medium was solo voice accompanied by a chord-playing instrument such as lute, guitar, or harpsichord.[17] And in this repertoire, normal performance of the soprano melody is quite different from its customarily notated form.

Howard Brown has transcribed one of Rodio's *arie*, the anonymous sonnet setting *Vago augelletto che cantando vai*, together with an embellished version of it from a 1562 treatise on vocal ornamentation by a Neapolitan doctor named Camillo Maffei.[18] The piece had been published in the Rodio anthology as a conventional quasi-strophic setting (the same four phrases used for each of the two quatrains; phrases 1, 2, and 4 reused for each of the two tercets). But Maffei provides for each of the four segments of the text a different elaborate and complex collection of ornamental melismas, creating, in effect, a series of strophic variations quite similar to those in Caccini's printed collection of fifty years later: there is even a considerable degree of rhythmic variety within Maffei's ornamental passaggi. Since Maffei intended to teach common practice, we may conclude that Neapolitan professional singers were expected to create such strophic variations out of the very simple notation of strophic villanelle of a certain type. Since Brown has pub-

---

[14] Claude V. Palisca, 'Vincenzo Galilei and Some Links between "Pseudo-Monody" and Monody', *Musical Quarterly*, 46 (1960), 344–60.

[15] Howard Mayer Brown, 'Petrarch in Naples: Notes on the Formation of Giaches de Wert's Style', in Richard Charteris (ed.), *Essays on Italian Music in the Cinquecento* (Sydney, 1990), 16–50.

[16] Howard Mayer Brown, 'Vincenzo Galilei in Rome: His First Book of Lute Music (1563) and its Cultural Context', in Victor Coelho (ed.), *Music and Science in the Age of Galileo* (The University of Western Ontario Series in Philosophy of Science, 51; Dordrecht, 1992), 153–84 at 173.

[17] An excellent summary of this practice and of the mid-century repertoire is found in Donna G. Cardamone, *The canzone villanesca alla napolitana and Related Forms, 1537–1570* (Ann Arbor, 1981).

[18] Brown, 'The Geography of Florentine Monody', 155–7.

Ex. 3.1. Anon., *Vago augelletto* with embellishments by Camillo Maffei (1562)

lished the original sonnet and Maffei's variations in their entirety, only the first two phrases are given here as Ex. 3.1 (the tenor partbook for Rodio's anthology is lost). Maffei's embellished soprano is shown above the soprano and bass parts as given in Rodio's anthology.

In this context, we can appreciate the significance of the 1565 correspondence between Grand Duke Cosimo I de' Medici and his ambassador in Rome, Averardo Serristori.[19] Cosimo needed a boy soprano with 'a beautiful voice and

---

[19] Carter, 'Giulio Caccini', 13–17.

good grace in singing with embellishments in the Neapolitan manner' to sing in the projected intermedi for *La Cofanaria* later that year.[20] The boy fitting this description that Serristori eventually found for Cosimo in the Cappella Giulia of St Peter's was Giulio Caccini. Already capable, it would seem, of improvising strophic variations in Rome at the age of 14, Caccini could hardly claim to have invented the practice in Florence at the age of 51: he merely reduced it to notation.

Cosimo I was perfectly correct in assuming that singers in Rome at that time learnt Neapolitan embellishment practice. Another singer of the same description and generation came to the Florentine court in the Roman household of Cardinal Ferdinando de' Medici when he became Grand Duke in 1587: Vittoria Archilei. Her embellishment of *Dalle più alte sfere* in the Florentine intermedi for *La pellegrina* of 1589 was printed in 1591, and its passaggi are similar to both Maffei's and Caccini's in their rhythmic variety.[21] In the preface to his *Euridice* (1600), Caccini claimed that the style of ornamental passage work used by Vittoria Archilei was his invention, whereas Vincenzo Giustiniani says that her singing style was imitated by Caccini, as well as by Giuseppino Cenci and Giovanni Domenico Puliaschi in Rome, and by Francesco Rasi, an early student of Caccini.[22] It would be reasonable to say that Archilei, Caccini, Giuseppino, Puliaschi, and Rasi were all heirs to the same Neapolitan–Roman tradition of improvised *fioritura*. Caccini deserves some credit for restricting his passaggi to principal verse accents, although he is not always as good as his word in this respect.

An entirely different kind of extemporaneous treatment of another aria in the Rocco Rodio anthology is suggested by a description of a Neapolitan performance of intermedi in 1558:

Queen Cleopatra was [portrayed by] Fomia [i.e. Eufemia Jozola],[23] who, when she sings, cannot be compared to any earthly thing, but to the heavenly harmony. Musicians of great excellence and renown impersonated the characters of Mark Antony and others, within and outside of the boat: Cornelio was Mark Antony; Scipione delle Palle was Proteus outside the boat; Giovan Leonardo dell'Arpa, unique as a player of that instrument [the harp], was one of Mark Antony's servants. And as the boat came to face those ladies [the duchess and vice-reine, the Marquise del Vasto and others], Cleopatra stood and delivered some . . . stanzas *in a style midway between singing and reciting*, with the

[20] 'Vorremmo che havessi bella voce, et buona grazia di cantare con i suoi passaggi alla napoletana.'

[21] Transcribed by D. P. Walker (ed.), *Les Fêtes du marriage de Ferdinand de Médicis et de Christine de Lorraine*, i: *Musique des intermèdes de 'La Pellegrina'* (Paris, 1963), 120–1, and by Pirrotta, *Music and Theatre*, 217–18.

[22] Italian text of Giustiniani's 'Discorso sopra la musica de' suoi tempi [1628]' is printed in Solerti, *L'origine del melodramma*, 103–40. The translation published by Carol MacClintock in the American Institute of Musicology series Musicological Studies and Documents, 9, is unreliable, and the translations given later in this chapter will be my own.

[23] Identification of this singer and extensive information about her can be found in Larson, 'The Unaccompanied Madrigal in Naples', 91–2 (n. 204).

Ex. 3.2. Scipione del Palla, *Che non può far donna leggiadra*

instruments softly intoning rather than playing[?] after each verse, which resulted in great gracefulness and majesty.[24]

The musical setting of Cleopatra's stanzas ascribed to Scipione del Palla in Rocco Rodio's anthology (Ex. 3.2) consists of nothing more than two phrases that set the first distich syllabically and, to a great extent, monotonally in a soprano melody that covers a range of four steps and uses notes of just four different rhythmic values. The same formula would have been repeated for every two lines of the text, which consists of two stanzas of ottava rima. Not even Pirrotta's irregularly barred transcription can make this music seem 'midway between singing and reciting', however.[25] We are obviously in touch here with a second Neapolitan tradition and another way of creating variations upon a formulaic aria. For if we imagine that the singer, Eufemia, sang the notated rhythm with one sort of sprezzatura for the first distich, she surely must have made different alterations in the rhythms, perhaps also in the pitches, in order to conform to the

[24] Pirrotta, *Music and Theatre*, 198. The original language is transcribed in the earlier Italian version of Pirrotta's book, *Li due Orfei da Poliziano a Monteverdi* (2nd edn., Turin, 1975), 220: 'La regina Cleopatra era Fomia, la quale nel canto non si può comparare a cosa terrestre, ma all'armonia del cielo. Il Marc'Antonio e gli altri, dentro e fura della Nave, erano tutti musici eccellentissimi e famosissimi: Cornelio era il Marc'Antonio; Scipion delle Palle era Protea fuor della Nave; Giovan Leonardo dell'Arpa, unico in questo strumento, era de' servitori di Marc'Antonio. Giunta la Nave al cospetto di quelle signore [la duchessa viceregina, la marchesa del Vasto, ecc.], Cleopatra si levò inpiè e disse le . . . stanze, *con un modo, mezzo tra cantare e recitare*, ad ora ad ora, nel chiuder de' versi intonando, non già sonando gli istrumenti: il che dava grazia e maestà.' The italics are Pirrotta's. I have modified Karen Eales's translation of Pirrotta's transcription by rendering *disse* as 'delivered' rather than said, following the traditional use of that verb in the descriptive rubrics of 15th-c. *rappresentazioni sacre*, in which *disse* is used in a context that makes it clear that the lines were sung to a recitational formula. One could argue, along the same lines, that the word *modo* also alludes to the same practice of singing stanzaic poetry to a melodic formula alternatively called a *modo* or *modus dicendi*.

[25] Pirrotta, *Music and Theatre*, 199.

different accents and inflections of each subsequent pair of lines. Example 3.2 gives the surviving soprano and bass parts for Palla's *Che non può dar donna leggiadra e cara* as it was printed in Rodio's anthology. The kind of sprezzatura that a singer like Eufemia would have applied extemporaneously to formulas like this one in order to create a performance 'midway between singing and reciting' is reflected in notation, according to James Haar, in certain mid-sixteenth-century *madrigali ariosi* (predominantly by composers associated with Rome and Naples), in which extended syncopation and calculated anticipation of the beat create the musical impression of an individualized, rather than stereotyped, declamation of the poetry.[26]

Thus it seems that there were two very different kinds of extemporized modification made in the performance of mid-sixteenth-century villanelle and arie: one added ornamental melismas and thus created a cantillational style relatively liberated from the text being sung, while the other retained the syllabic setting of the notated song but modified its rhythm in order to create a recitational style even more closely controlled by the declamation of the text than the written music itself was. The result was a potential dichotomy in performance between *arie in stil recitativo, e cantativo*. This striking phrase, used as the title of this chapter, comes from a letter written by the composer Santi Orlandi in Mantua to Cardinal Ferdinando Gonzaga in Rome, 31 August 1612:

Regarding the person [to be Monteverdi's replacement] that your Illustrious Lordship will send [to Mantua], you know better than I the taste of the Most Serene [Duke Francesco Gonzaga]; but I wish, in any case, to remind you that he must be a capable man, that is, he must know how to compose motets and madrigals and, what is more important, arias in recitational style and cantillational style, ballets, etc., but everything rapidly.[27]

What is striking about the phrase is, of course, that it uses the older meaning of the word *aria* to signify a vocal melody as distinct from the text and, therefore, often a formula to which various texts could be sung. The later meaning of *aria* contrasts with *recitativo*, but for present purposes, it is important to remember that songlike and recitational styles could emerge from two different kinds of performance of the same or similar musical notation.

Arie in stil recitativo, e cantativo are already found as somewhat distinct types in the repertoire of mid-sixteenth-century villanelle and arie. For as Donna

---

[26] James Haar, 'The "Madrigale Arioso": A Mid-Century Devleopment in the Cinquecento Madrigal', *Studi musicali*, 12 (1983), 201–19.

[27] 'Circo il soggetto che mandarà Vostra Signoria Illustrissima sa meglio di me il gusto del Serenissimo; ma voglio in ogni modo ricordarli che bisogna sia valent'homo, id est, che sappi far mottetti; madrigali e quel che più importa arie in stil recitativo, e cantativo; balletti, etc. ma il tutto presto.' The letter, in I:MAas, Archivio Gonzaga 2725, is transcribed by Parisi, 'Ducal Patronge of Music in Mantua', 265.

Cardamone says, concerning the musical stage works that Scipione del Palla and his colleagues performed in Naples, 'These informal musical gatherings and theatrical entertainments fostered the development of aria styles that were uniquely southern and complementary: one in the tuneful dialectal [that is, using a text in local dialect] mode associated with the villanella alla napolitana and the other in the formulaic mode for singing high or low-style poetry'.[28] In fact, the anonymous *Vago augelletto che cantando vai* and Palla's *Che non può far donna leggiadra e cara*, both from the Rocco Rodio anthology, exemplify, respectively, the 'tuneful' and the 'formulaic' strains of Neapolitan song. We shall see that this double dichotomy between cantillational and recitational performance and compositional styles, brought to Rome from Naples by Montalto's musicians, will take on fundamental importance in shaping the style of the Roman monody repertoire in Montalto's circles and distinguishing it from Florentine monody, notwithstanding the fact that Galilei and Caccini were connected—albeit at some distance of time (Caccini) or space (Galilei)—with the Neapolitan–Roman traditions.

What of the instrumental accompaniment to Eufemia's 1558 aria, dimly represented in the printed arrangement by the usual two lower, texted vocal parts (of which the middle one is lost)? Are we to believe that the harp or lute shadowed Eufemia's subtly irregular minims and semiminims with flat-footed repetitions of chords? If we look to the many sixteenth-century printed and manuscript lute intabulations of madrigals, villanelle, and similar compositions, the answer would, surprisingly, be Yes. But I think that lute intabulations are frequently all-purpose arrangements just as much as the three-voice settings are. Often they merely reproduce the three voices of the polyphonic arrangement, even doubling the soprano vocal line, so that they could be used to play the music alone, without voices, as well as for accompaniment of singing.[29] And even when the soprano part is omitted, the lower voices tend to be intabulated very nearly as they are found in the polyphonic arrangement.[30] That method of accompaniment would seem suited to singing in relatively strict time but hardly adequate for 'a style midway between singing and reciting'. There is, however, another type of accompaniment that would seem more suitable and another kind of tablature that goes with it: chordal accompaniment on the five-course Spanish guitar and the alphabet tablature devised to transmit the practice.

---

[28] Donna G. Cardamone, 'The Prince of Salerno and the Dynamics of Oral Transmission in Songs of Political Exile', *Acta musicologica*, 67 (1995), 77–108 at 81. I am grateful to Donna Cardamone for allowing me to read her paper before publication.

[29] A list of printed vocal music that includes lute intabulation can be obtained from Howard Mayer Brown, *Instrumental Music Printed before 1600: A Bibliography* (Cambridge, Mass., 1965), by using Index III under the headings 'Lute and several voices' and 'Lute and solo voice' on p. 479.

[30] For example, in the Bottegari lute book (*c.*1574), edited by Carol MacClintock as number 8 in The Wellesley Edition series (Wellesley, 1965), or in Salomone Rossi's *Primo libro de madrigali a cinque voci* (1600).

Tablature for five-course Spanish guitar represents each chord, usually by means of a letter of the alphabet (one early system uses numbers). These letters were sometimes used in conjunction with a vocal part in staff notation, but more commonly they were placed above individual syllables of the text alone to show exactly where the indicated chords should be played; the singer was expected to remember the vocal melody without the aid of musical notation. The chords were meant to be strummed, and the pure strumming technique (*rasgueado*) admitted no possibility of reproducing the independent rhythms and pitch contours of individual vocal lines. Furthermore, chord repetition is normally not notated in the guitar-tablature accompaniments of songs. Guitar tablatures for dances often show up- and down-strokes of the player's right hand by means of short vertical lines extending up or down from a horizontal base line, and it has been suggested that the patterns of these lines indicate particular rhythmic patterns, depending upon metre.[31] Some songs with clearly metrical rhythms, *arie in stil cantativo*, might be well served by adding such rhythmically patterned chord repetitions, even when they are not notated. But there are plenty of other songs for which guitar-tablature accompaniments survive that are *arie in stil recitativo*, like Palla's recitational formula shown above. They contain no rhythmic patterns that the guitarist could follow, and they often do not even clearly suggest a single, constant metre. When we compare the guitar tablature for arias of this latter type with the staff-notation sources of the same pieces, we frequently see that the guitar chords are sparser than the harmonies created by the three-voice arrangement or, later, by the basso continuo accompaniment. This suggests the performance tradition that is reflected in staff notation by the slowly moving figured basses of Caccini's and Peri's *stile recitativo*, against which the vocal line might unfold with dissonance unrestricted by the traditional rules of counterpoint and with rhythms unfettered by accentual metre.

The major question is, however, how early were guitar accompaniments such as these performed? Juan Bermudo mentioned the strumming style, which he calls *música golpeada* ('strummed music') in 1555.[32] The expression arises in Bermudo's chapter on intabulation, and it contains some suggestive language that is worth quoting:

The music that you should intabulate at the beginning will be certain villancicos (first for two voices, then for three voices) with strummed music, in which [all notes in] the voices usually sound simultaneously. There is hardly any work in intabulating these because (since the notes stay together and are of the same value) the tablature numbers [for each voice] within each measure will be equal in number. Whoever wants to take

---

[31] James Tyler, *The Early Guitar: A History and Handbook* (Early Music Series, 4; Oxford, 1980), 68–70.
[32] Juan Bermudo, *Comiença el libro llamado declaracion de instrumentos musicales* (Ossuna: Juan de Leon, 1555), fo. 99ᵛ.

my advice: there is no use in playing those tablature numbers because it is not refined music, and one should not listen to it. Strummed villancicos do not have a good enough musical foundation to be sufficient for constructing and achieving good material for a fantasy. Thus take them for instruction or exercise in the art of intabulation for the instrumentalist; they are not worth more. After the player has practised on such villancicos, let him search out the villancicos by Juan Vazquez, which are [examples of] good music, and the works of a careful musician by the name of Baltasar Tellez.[33]

Recently Ivano Cavallini has argued that the noble singer-poet improvising to his lute was an ideal gradually fading from reality in Italy during the sixteenth century, his place increasingly filled by low-class popular entertainers in the piazzas, whose association with the guitar, rather than the lute, begins to be reflected in written sources near the turn of the seventeenth century, as well-born amateurs began to imitate this practice with the aid of tablature.[34] Thus, the Neapolitan Scipione Cerreto in 1608:

There are also the players of the Spanish guitar, who belong to the same status [as players of the double harp and lute]—not withstanding that [the guitar] has been used by people of low class and little worth, not to mention by clowns, who have used it at banquets—but that it was later used by cavaliers and by other important people came about because of the ease in playing this instrument, whose technique is learned rather for aria than for art.[35]

These points are well illustrated in the fascinating article by Donna Cardamone cited earlier, concerning a group of variously transmitted laments and responses attributed to Ferrante Sanseverino, Prince of Salerno. Sanseverino was an early patron of Scipione del Palla, of Palla's companions in the Rocco Rodio anthology Luigi and Fabrizio Dentice, and of the bass virtuoso Giulio Cesare Brancaccio, whom Giustiniani credits with a major role in the development

---

[33] 'La Musica que aveys de començar a cifrar: seran unos villancicos (primero duos, y despues a tres) de Musica golpeada, que communmente dan todas las bozes junctas. Para cifrar estos quasi non ay trabajo: porque (como los puntos quedan unos con otros sean de ygual valor) las cifras en los compases vernan yguales en numero. Quien quisiere tomar mi consejo: destas cifras no se aproveche para tañer: porque no es Musica de cudicia, y no se haga el oydo a ellas. Los villancicos golpeados no tienen tan buen fundamento en musica: que sean bastantes para edificar, y grangear buen ayre de fantasia. Pues tomense para ensayarse, o imponerse el tañedor en el arte de cifrar: que no son para mas. Despues que por estos villancicos estuviere el teñedor en alguna manera instruyo: busque los villancicos de Iuan Vazquez que son de Musica acertada, y las obras de un curioso musico que se llama Baltasar Tellez.'

[34] Ivano Cavallini, 'Sugli improvvisatori del Cinque-Seicento: Persistenze, nuovi repertori e qualche riconoscimento', *Recercare*, I (1989), 24–40.

[35] 'Vi sono ancora gli Sonatori di Chitarra alla Spagnola, alliquali si ben li tocca l'istesso grado, nondimeno per essere stata usata da gente basse, e di poco valore non dico da Boffoni, liquali se ne hanno servito ne i conviti, ma che fusse poi usato tal suono da Cavalieri, & da altri persone principali l'hà cagionato la facilità dello strometo, quale essercitio s'impara più tosto per aria, che per arte.' Scipione Cerreto, *Dell'arbore musicale* (Naples: Sottile, 1608), 37.

of extemporized passaggi; at the prince's palace in Naples, these composer-improvisers sang roles in musical plays during the 1540s. In 1552 the prince was exiled from Naples for conspiring with the French to depose the Spanish Viceroy, Pedro Toledo. It is Cardamone's thesis that the laments became attributed to the prince because he frequently sang them at the royal court of France, presumably to guitar accompaniment, as he had sung other Neapolitan songs during an earlier visit in 1544. By demonstrating that the musical settings of these laments consist largely of simple melodic formulas over standard chord progressions that were often used for improvisation (that is, they are examples of Bermudo's *música golpeada*) and that the many variants of the texts, both in Italian and in Spanish, that are preserved in manuscripts and prints reflect the typical results of oral transmission, Cardamone argues that the laments actually arose out of the extemporizations of Sanseverino's musicians and were transmitted, in large part, through their singing in Florence and, especially, in Rome. For present purposes, it is especially significant to note that although these laments were conceived as solo songs, they are preserved in notation exclusively as three- and four-part villanelle. Cardamone's article also illustrates the connection between Spanish and Italian musical practices and traditions that grew up in Naples during the long period of Spanish rule.[36] This connection helps to explain the importance of the Spanish guitar and its associated chordal style of accompaniment in Neapolitan music-making.

By the end of the sixteenth century, guitar accompaniment begins to find its way into written sources, evidently because literate people with money to spend on books began to want to learn how to imitate the earlier-established practices of illiterate street entertainers, as Cavallini has suggested. Thus, in 1596 the Spaniard Joan Carlos Amat described the use of the guitarist's strumming technique, now called *rasgado*, to accompany music that, in its polyphonic arrangement, was not strictly homorhythmic. For this end, he introduced a chordal tablature using numbers.[37] The intabulation technique that Amat explains is, to some extent, a variant of basso seguente practice, in which the guitarist takes each note of the lowest-sounding voice as the root or third of a triad, depending on the melodic intervals and contour of that voice part. One of Amat's practical examples, however, makes it clear that a guitar chord is provided only for each

---

[36] Another article that provides additional evidence of these connections is Keith A. Larson, 'Condizione sociale dei musicisti e dei loro committenti nella Napoli del Cinque e Seicento', in Lorenzo Bianconi and Renato Bossa (eds.), *Musica e cultura a Napoli dal XV al XIX secolo* (Quaderni della Rivista italiana di musicologia, 9; Florence, 1983), 61–77.

[37] Joan Carlos Amat, *Guitarra espanola de cinco órdenes la qual enseña de templar y tañer rasgado* (2nd edn., Lérida: Lorenço, 1627). No exemplars survive of the first edition of 1596, the date of which results from the imprimatur and the dedicatory letter still found in the second edition. See Monica J. L. Hall, 'The "Guitarra española" of Joan Carlos Amat', *Early Music*, 6 (1978), 362–73.

change of harmony and not for repeated pitches, leaps within a chord, passing notes, or suspensions. As a result, there will be times when only one chord per measure will be sounded. In effect, the style of guitar accompaniment that Amat describes does not duplicate the polyphonic vocal parts but simplifies them and abstracts their harmony. This is a type of accompaniment well suited to *arie in stil recitativo*. And, although it is not texted, Amat's illustration (Ex. 3.3) does seem to be the declamatory quatrain of a *romance*.[38]

The alphabet tablature for Spanish guitar that became standard all over Italy early in the seventeenth century seems to have originated in Naples during the 1590s. Although Daniel Devoto has claimed that the 'Palumbi' guitar manuscript dates from *c*.1595,[39] I concur with Richard Hudson's dating of *c*.1630.[40] The earliest securely dated source of the alphabet tablature is a manuscript with the year 1599 written on its title-page.[41] It is a collection of Spanish *romances* with guitar accompaniment inscribed to the 'Duchessa di Traetta'. In Chapter 2, we learned that in 1586 the fief of Traetta, or Traetto,[42] was in the dowry of Isabella Gonzaga when she married Luigi Carafa, Prince of Stigliano, who, by 1590, had become known as the *Duke* of Traetta. As of the date of her marriage in 1586, Isabella Gonzaga became both the duchess of Traetta and the princess of Stigliano.[43] It was by the latter title that Isabella was addressed in 1609, when Duke Vincenzo Gonzaga's agents were negotiating to bring Adriana Basile to serve in Mantua. Therefore the Traetta guitar manuscript belonged to Adriana Basile's first patroness. Accordingly, it seems almost certain that Basile knew this manuscript and sang its songs to her own accompaniment, inasmuch as she played the Spanish guitar and, at the time she was finally engaged to be Claudio Monteverdi's colleague at the Mantuan court (1610), was said to have a personal repertoire of 300 Italian and Spanish songs.[44] In this connection, it is relevant to note that

[38] Jack Sage, 'Romance, 1', *New Grove*, xvi. 123, describes this as 'a new, quasi-recitative style with repeated phrases and agitated rhythms' that came to characterize the quatrain of the Spanish *romance* at the end of the 16th c. A very good overview of the popular character of the *romance*, its improvisatory traditions, and its incorporation of traditional, migrating melodies is found in Louise K. Stein, *Songs of Mortals, Dialogues of the Gods: Music and Theatre in Seventeenth-Century Spain* (Oxford, 1993), 45–9, and in other literature cited there; an important overview of sources and editions of *romances* is found in Stein's first appendix, 354–60.

[39] F:Pn, MS Espagnol 390, 'Libro di Villanelle Spagnuol' et Italiane et sonate spagnuole Del Molt' Ill.e Sig. Mio Oss.mo il S.r Filippo Roncherollo Servo di V. S. Molt' Ill. Fran.co Palumbi'. Daniel Devoto, 'Encore sur "la" sarabande', *Revue de musicologie*, 50 (1964), 189–96.

[40] Richard Hudson, *The Folia, the Saraband, the Passacaglia, and the Chaconne*, ii: *The Saraband* (Musicological Studies and Documents, 35; Neuhausen-Stuttgart, 1982), p. xxxi.

[41] I:Rvat, Chigi Cod. L.VI.200, 'Libro de cartas y romançes españolas del Illustrissima Señora Duchessa di Traetta mi señora que Dios guarde mil años 1599'. The manuscript was first described by Giovanni Maria Bertini, C. Acutis, and L. Avila, *La romanza spagnola in Italia* (Turin, 1970), 176–84. Its place in music history and its concordances with staff-notation sources are discussed by John H. Baron, 'Secular Spanish Solo Song in Non-Spanish Sources, 1599–1640', *Journal of the American Musicological Society*, 30 (1977), 20–42.

[42] The place has been called Minturno since the 19th c. It is located about 14 km. east by north-east of Gaeta or about 70 km. north-west of Naples.   [43] See Litta, *Famiglie celebri*, s.v. 'Gonzaga' and 'Carafa'.

[44] Parisi, 'Ducal Patronage', 404 and 545.

Ex. 3.3. Intabulated guitar accompaniment by Joan Carles Amat (1596)

*source reads 5♭

Ippolita Recupito, the celebrated Neapolitan singer whom Cardinal Montalto recruited to his household in 1604, also played the guitar, but evidently not in the Italian style and therefore, presumably, in the Spanish manner, whatever that may have meant to a Roman gentleman in 1615 (Letter 92).

In the Traetta manuscript one finds some homorhythmic and metrically patterned accompaniments that follow the rhythms of the voices (as described by Bermudo) in part-song arrangements of *arie in stil cantativo*, but also accompaniments with sparse chords (as shown by Amat) for *arie in stil recitativo*. When these guitar intabulations accompany solo singing, as we assume they normally did, the melodic integrity of the lower voices is not maintained, as it is in lute and keyboard intabulations. The vocal bass line, in particular, is replaced by a slower moving abstraction that is strictly limited to the function of harmonic support and, because of its prevailing movement by leaps, is rather instrumental in character. I mention these factors because they are usually given as the characteristics that distinguish basso continuo from basso seguente.

An example of recitational style from the Traetta guitar manuscript is the first quatrain from the anonymous *romance Los rayos del sol impiden* (Ex. 3.4). The three-voice setting is preserved in a set of manuscript partbooks at the Biblioteca Nacional of Madrid usually referred to as 'Romances y letras'.[45] The guitar chords notated in alphabet tablature in the Traetta manuscript go best with the middle voice. This is especially evident in the *buelta* (refrain), which is not given in this example. The correspondence between the guitar chords and the middle voice has been noted in other concordances between guitar tablatures and three-voice Spanish *romances*,[46] leading to the hypothesis that the melody of an originally solo song is often harmonized with a soprano part above and a bass voice below in this repertoire. One notable feature of the guitar tablature for this *romance* is that the second and third quatrains are given their own set of chords, similar to those of the first quatrain but sufficiently different to suggest the possibility of strophic variations in recitational style. John Brande Trend, noting that the *Conde claros* tune was the subject of many written-out instrumental variations, hypothesized that 'variation form seems to have arisen in Spain, through the necessity of relieving the monotony of the lute-accompaniment during the recitation of a long *romance*'.[47] Evidence for variation is especially strong in the tablatures accompanying the second and third lines of the *Los rayos del sol impiden*, where the writing in the middle (presumably solo) voice is particularly recitational. The three-voice arrangement in the 'Romances y letras' partbooks, on the other hand, preserves only one setting for all three quatrains, as one would expect in a polyphonic arrangement. Another indication that the guitar tablature refers to a somewhat different, solo-voice version of this *romance* is the lack of correspondence between the tablature and the more contrapuntal parts of the *buelta* (refrain) as given in the partbooks.

---

[45] E:Mn, Sign. M. 1370, 1371, and 1372. A volume of works, including this one, from these partbooks was published as *Romances y letras a tres vozes*, ed. Miguel Querol Gavaldá (Monumentos de la música española, 18; Barcelona, 1956).   [46] Baron, 'Secular Spanish Solo Song', 34–8.

[47] John Brande Trend, *The Music of Spanish History to 1600* (London, 1926), 105.

Ex. 3.4. Anon., *Los rayos del sol impiden*, with guitar accompaniment

Giovanni Maria Bertini points out that the original part of the Traetta manuscript ends with folio 37^v, after which a different hand takes over.[48] Since *Los rayos
del sol impiden* is written on folio 41^{r-v}, there is no guarantee that it was entered
in the manuscript at or near the time indicated on the title-page (1599). However, in the original part of the manuscript there are a number of other *romances*
in which the guitar chords are just as sparse, with up to eight syllables of text accompanied by one chord. This is particularly evident in the quatrains, which, as has
been said, are noted for their quasi-recitational style. *Los rayos del sol impiden* was
selected for this example because it is the only one of this type in the Traetta
manuscript for which a staff-notation concordance has been found.

Thus we see that the tradition of *rasgueado* accompaniment on the Spanish guitar, which reaches back to the middle of the sixteenth century, contained all the
elements that distinguish the type of basso continuo accompaniment later associated with recitative vocal style: a slowly unfolding series of block chords set upon
a bass that is instrumental and not vocal in character and that is melodically and
rhythmically independent of the vocal part being accompanied. We have seen
that this style of guitar accompaniment was associated with the Spanish *romance*,
a genre that was historically connected with improvisational performance and
often featured contrast between sections of metrically defined music in the refrain
versus recitational passages in the quatrains. *Romances* with these features are
given guitar-chord accompaniments in the earliest source (1599) of the alphabet
guitar-chord tablature, the Traetta manuscript owned by the early patroness of
Adriana Basile, Isabella Gonzaga, duchess of Traetta and princess of Stigliano.
The Traetta manuscript, as we have said, contains only text and guitar chords.
Only one of its *romances* is found elsewhere in staff notation. But there are plenty
of other sixteenth-century *romances* with as much or more recitational music,
although we do not have specific guitar accompaniments for them.

Several such pieces are preserved in the so-called 'Cancionero musical de la
Casa de Medinaceli'.[49] Copied about 1560, it contains several more Spanish
songs prominently featuring a recitational style. *A beinte y siete de Março*, for
example, is an anonymous setting of the first strophe of the 'Romance de Juan
de Leyva a la muerte de Don Manrique de Lara', a poem first published in
1520.[50] The four-voice arrangement is mostly homophonic, and the melody is,
as usual, in the second *tiple* part. The setting is almost entirely syllabic. The range
of the second *tiple* is narrow within each phrase, and this voice has great deal

---

[48] Bertini, Acutis, and Avila, *La romanza spagnola in Italia*, 176.

[49] Madrid, Biblioteca de la Casa del Duque de Medinaceli, sig. 13230.

[50] This and the other songs cited here are published, with commentary, in *Cancionero musical de la Casa de
Medinaceli (Siglo XVI)*, i: *Polifonía Profana*, ed. Miguel Querol Gavaldá (Monumentos de la Música Española,
8; Barcelona, 1949).

of monotone recitation. Each line in the second *tiple* ends with a falling step-wise cadence figure or pitch repetition, usually in semibreves. The anonymous *romance Cavallero, sí a Francia ides*, the arias for Spanish octaves *Aquella boz de Cristo tan sonora* and *A su alvedrío*, and the aria for Spanish tercets *Aquella fuerça grande* are in this recitational style as well. It may be assumed that Spanish recitational arias of this sort were in circulation in Naples during the later sixteenth century. Others like them might be identified in the Traetta guitar manuscript if more concordances in staff-notation sources could be located. The possibility seems open, then, that the recitational style so prominent in the Neapolitan villanella and aria repertoire was influenced, encouraged, and enriched by contact with the Spanish *romance* during the long period of Spanish rule in Naples.

Caccini, as we have noted, derived his styles, forms, and formats from Neapolitan and Roman traditions, which he received as a boy in Rome, then as a student of Scipione del Palla in Florence, and finally as a colleague of Vincenzo Galilei in the Florentine *camerata*. Nearly all the composers and the most important singers in Cardinal Montalto's circles came from those same traditions. Developments in Naples and Rome after Caccini's departure must not have been exactly the same as those in Florence during the last quarter of the sixteenth century, since no repertoire of continuo-accompanied monody or opera emerged in those southern cities as early as it did in Florence. Rather, the course of solo singing and song-writing in Naples and Rome in the late Cinquecento was sufficiently parallel to that in Florence to permit singers and composers from the south to integrate their activities with Florentine musicians with relative ease, while it diverged sufficiently to produce some distinctive features once continuo-accompanied monody and opera appeared in Rome.

The basic compatibility of the Neapolitan–Roman traditions with the Florentine method of solo singing and notation is shown in the recruitment of singers from Naples and Rome for service in Florence and Mantua. It was extremely difficult to find musicians capable of singing in *stile recitativo*, even well into the seventeenth century, as will be shown in the next chapter. Evidently, the concept of *sprezzatura di canto* was quite foreign to most singers trained to perform polyphonic music exclusively. On the other side, many singers of recitational music did not read music.[51] And the requirement to improvise passaggi and to modulate the voice expressively were beyond the ability of the average vocalist. Nevertheless, we have seen that Cardinal Montalto's prized bass singer Melchior Palantrotti, who was born in Venafro, within the vice-realm of Naples, and trained in Rome, was able to sing leading roles in the two Florentine

[51] James Haar, '*Improvvisatori* and their Relationship to Sixteenth-Century Music', in his *Essays on Italian Poetry and Music in the Renaissance, 1350–1600* (Berkeley and Los Angeles, 1986), 76–99.

operas of 1600—Caccini's *Il rapimento di Cefalo* and Peri's *Euridice*—on relatively short notice.[52] He and Montalto's famous Neapolitan soprano Ippolita Recupito sang in the Florentine *intermedi* of 1608 alongside Jacopo Peri and the students, wife, and daughters of Giulio Caccini; and Ippolita was universally judged to have surpassed all the others.[53] And in 1610 the famous Neapolitan virtuosa Adriana Basile was recruited for the Gonzaga court in Mantua, where Florentine *stile recitativo* had recently taken root in the works of Claudio Monteverdi.[54]

The divergence during the last quarter of the sixteenth century between Neapolitan–Roman solo singing and Florentine monody is easy to see on the surface but difficult to penetrate deeply. On the surface we see different roles played by written and unwritten traditions. It seems clear enough that in sixteenth-century Italy the normal notational form of written music that was sung by an accompanied solo voice was the three- or four-voice predominantly homophonic arrangement of a villanella, canzonetta, aria, canzone, or madrigal. Some of Caccini's earliest works were written down in that form. One is *Amarilli, mia bella*, which survives as both a three-voice and a six-voice canzone and, of course, a continuo-accompanied solo madrigal.[55] Another is *Fillide mia, mia Fillide bella*, a canzonetta setting of what eventually became the second and fourth stanzas of *Fere selvaggie che per monti errate* when it was published in *Le nuove musiche*. *Fillide mia, mia Fillide bella* survives as a soprano vocal line with a lute-intabulation accompaniment in the Bottegari Lutebook, which was dated 1574 on the title-page and perhaps begun then.[56] But like nearly all Bottegari's intabulated accompaniments, the lute part for *Fillide mia* seems fairly clearly derived from the lower voices of a polyphonic model. In fact, when Bottegari's intabulation is unfolded into a hypothetical reconstruction of a four-voice arrangement of the song, the result (Ex. 3.5) closely resembles some of Luca Marenzio's villanelle published in the 1580s. The shape of Caccini's soprano voice closely resembles that of, for example, *Stride il lauro nel foco* in Marenzio's fourth book of *Villanelle* (1587).[57] Similar shapes can be found in Marenzio's *Dolce mia vita*, *Mia sorte empia e rubella*, *Se legete nel viso* (all three in his *Villanelle*, II, 1585), and *Se m'uccide crudele* (in his *Villanelle*, V, 1587). The relative amount of chordal versus rhythmically animated textures in *Fillide mia, mia Fillide bella* are also similar

---

[52] Palisca, 'The First Performance of "Euridice"', 1–23.

[53] Tim Carter, 'A Florentine Wedding of 1608', *Acta musicologica*, 55 (1983), 89–107.

[54] Parisi, 'Ducal Patronage', 405–10.

[55] Tim Carter, in 'Caccini's *Amarilli, mia bella*: Some Questions (and a Few Answers)', *Journal of the Royal Musical Association*, 113 (1988), 250–73, suggests that both of these may be derived from yet another, probably three-voice, polyphonic version, which may be the song's first notated form.

[56] I:MOe, Ms. Mus. C 311. A transcription is published in *The Bottegari Lutebook*, ed. MacClintock, 40.

[57] Similar views on resemblances between melodic shapes in Marenzio's villanelle and Caccini's monodies are presented by Tim Carter, ' "An Air New and Grateful to the Ear": The Concept of *Aria* in Late Renaissance and Early Baroque Italy', *Music Analysis*, 12 (1993), 127–45.

Ex. 3.5. Giulio Caccini, *Fillide mia*, arranged for four voices in accordance with Cosimo Bottegari's lute intabulation

Ex. 3.5. Cont'd

to those that typify Marenzio's villanelle. I am not suggesting any special relationship between Caccini's early music and Marenzio's villanelle. I refer to Marenzio's works as typical of the 1580s and because they happen to be at hand.

The double bars and repeat signs that I have used in Ex. 3.5 are not found in Bottegari's intabulation, although a repeat of the second part is found in the version that Caccini published in *Le nuove musiche* (1602). I have added them here in order to give my arrangement a more conventional appearance. The slightly concealed parallel fifths between the soprano and bass in the first measure are present in Bottegari's intabulation and are preserved even in the published version of 1602. The parallel fifths between the tenor and bass in bar 9 are also present in Bottegari's intabulation; Caccini's published version, of course, does not have a tenor part. Parallel fifths are a traditional feature of the villanella, although there is no general agreement as to why this is so.

Example 3.6 offers, for comparison, a villanella by the Cavalier del Leuto, who, as we learned in Chapter 2, was in the household of Cardinal Montalto, apparently from 1589 until his death in 1608. The piece, *Di pianti e di sospir notrisco il core*, is preserved in a manuscript together with villanelle of a similar type by Roman composers Paolo Quagliati (*c.* 1555–1628) and Giovanni Boschetto Boschetti (d. 1622), a composer in the Borghese household whose monodies were included in two prints that have many concordances with manuscript sources of Montalto's court music (see Ch. 5). The text of the Cavalier's villanella preserves the vestiges of ottava rima, as was typical of the early canzone villanesca. Its musical style is not dissimilar to that of my hypothetical four-voice reconstruction of Caccini's *Fillide mia* (see especially the closing formula). The manuscript that preserves it was ruled for lute intabulations on every page facing the three parts of the villanelle, as if to provide for solo performance; but *Di pianti e*

Ex. 3.6. Il Cavalier del Leuto, *Di pianti e di sospir*, I:MOe, Campori Ital. 1384.α.K.6.31

di sospir notrisco il core is one of the works for which the intabulation was never completed.

I would make no assumptions about how the early works of Caccini took form originally; they may well have been sung as accompanied solo songs before they were written down as part-songs. A letter from Caccini's Florentine colleague Alessandro Striggio specifies the alternative ways in which Caccini (or any other contemporaneous musician) would normally have accompanied polyphonically notated vocal music in 1584:

> Before I left Mantua I composed a dialogue with two embellished soprano parts in a different style from that of the first. And although I have not tried it out, in order not to let anyone see it, I am sending it to Your Most Serene Highness, waiting to hear which one will be suitable for [your] ensemble [of women]. Having, in addition, written the intabulation for the lute, I forgot it in Mantua at my departure. But it matters little, since Sig. Giulio [Caccini] will be able to play [an accompaniment] very well, either on the lute or on the harpsichord, using the bass part.[58]

While Caccini was developing the notation of basso continuo and *sprezzatura di canto*, and using both as platforms for new compositional elaboration, Roman and Neapolitan musicians continued to draw solo-singing repertoire from works that are known to us in the notational form of three- and four-part villanelle, canzonette, madrigali ariosi, madrigaletti, and the like. They continued to make three- and four-voice arrangements of works originally conceived as solo songs, to nourish the honoured tradition of improvising recitational and cantillational variations upon formulaic arias, and to add passaggi extemporaneously to written music. Although the Neapolitan Scipione Cerreto published (1601) instructions for improvising a chordal accompaniment for lira da gamba above a written bass line,[59] monodies with basso continuo accompaniment were not printed in Naples or Rome until 1607 and 1608 respectively. On the other hand, no significant body of villanelle or madrigaletti appears in Florence during the last three decades of the Cinquecento. And while Caccini was busy writing out

---

[58] 'Ma avanti io partissi di Mantova, io feci un Dialogo con dua soprani diminuiti d'un altro andare che non è il primo, e ancora che io non l'habbia provato per non lo lassar vedere a persona, io lo mando a V.A.S. Aspettando d'intendere qual più sarà al proposito per il conserto, havevo ancora scritto la intavolatura per il lautto et me lo scordai in Mantova nel mio partire. Ma impotarà poco, poi che il s' Giulio potrà benissimo sonare, o con il lautto, o con il cembalo sopra il basso.' Letter from Alessandro Striggio, 29 July 1584, first published in Riccardo Gandolfi, 'Lettere inedite scritte da musicisti e letterati appartenenti alla seconda metà del secolo XVI, estratte dal R. Archivio di Stato in Firenze', *Rivista musicale italiana*, 20 (1913), 527–54. My translation differs from that offered by Newcomb, *The Madrigal at Ferrara*, i. 55.

[59] Scipione Cerreto, *Della prattica musica vocale, et strumentale* (Naples: Carlino, 1601), 323–8, gives instruction for playing the 'lira in gamba' from staff notation. A bass part is shown, above which chords are added on three to five adjacent strings. If the bass runs in semiminims, only the first of each group of four is harmonized. When the bass ascends a fourth or falls a fifth, the first note is harmonized by a major third.

his embellishments in order to rein in his singers' exuberance, Roman singers as late as 1615 were still being trained to improvise florid melodies above a given harmonic bass, as will become clear in the next chapter.

It is relatively difficult to gain a precise idea of solo song in Naples during the late sixteenth and early seventeenth centuries because so many printed collections of Neapolitan villanelle and related genres from that period are missing one or more partbooks,[60] while other printed collections may be lost entirely. Perhaps Neapolitan composers during the last quarter of the sixteenth century actually turned their back for a time on the lighter genres of vocal music that were born in their city, turning their compositional attention to the intricate polyphony of the madrigal while maintaining the tradition of the native aria in performance. For surely when Scipione Dentice, Cardinal Montalto's client and, perhaps, his teacher, accompanied on the harpsichord the virtuosic singing of Giulio Cesare Brancaccio in Rome on 22 December 1585 at the rooms of Paolo Giordano Orsini's mistress, they did not perform any of Dentice's surviving vocal compositions, all of which are contrapuntal madrigals unsuited to solo performance.[61]

In this connection, it may be indicative that at the beginning of the seventeenth century the famous poet Giambattista Basile, brother of the singer Adriana Basile, expressed disdain for the newer contrapuntal villanella/canzonetta and enthusiastically endorsed the simpler formulaic villanelle and arie of the kind that were published in the Rocco Rodio anthology a quarter-century earlier.[62] Actually, Basile puts this judgement in the mouths of two friends, Micco and Ciullo, who ask a third friend, the musician Titta, to sing them a song. In the course of the dialogue, the three friends mention more than twenty villanelle by name, and

---

[60] In this category are the following:

Scipione Cerreto, *Primo libro di canzonette a tre voci* (Naples: Sottile, 1606)
Francesco Lambardi, *Villanelle a tre et a quattro voci, et arie . . . libro primo* (Naples: Sottile, 1607)
Grammatico Metallo, *Il secondo libro di canzoni a tre et quattro voci* (Naples: Cancer, 1577)
Giovanni Domenico Montella, *Prima libro di villanelle a tre et a quattro voci, con alcune arie* (2nd edn., Naples: Carlino, after 1602)
Giovanni Domencio Montella, *Secondo libro de villanelle et arie* (Naples: Sottile, 1604)
Giovanni Domencio Montella, *Terzo libro di villanelle a quattro et arie a due voci* (Napoli: Sottile, 1605)
Giovanni Domenico Montella, *Quarto libro di villanelle a quattro voci* (Naples: Sottile, 1606)
Donato Antonio Spano, *Il primo libro de madrigaletti ariosi et villanelle a quattro voci* (Naples: Bonino, 1607)
Giovanni Maria Trabaci, *Villanelle, et arie alla napolitana, a tre, & a quattro voci . . . libro primo* (Naples: Carlino, 1606).

[61] Gnoli, *Vittoria Accoramboni*, 324. The musicians' presence in this Roman palace on that date is recorded because they witnessed the assassination of Orsini's mistress by agents hired by Orsini's cousin Ludovico, protector of Virginio's son Paolo Giordano, who, in turn, became the father of the man who married Cardinal Montalto's sister.

[62] Elena Ferrari Barassi, 'La villanella napoletana nell testimonianza di un letterato', *Nuova rivista musicale italiana*, 2 (1968), 164–87.

they accept or reject each one according to the extent to which it represents or preserves the features of the classic villanelle of Gian Leonardo dell'Arpa published in 1565, 1566, and 1570, over and against examples of what Einstein called 'the new canzone' of the later sixteenth century.[63] Elena Ferrari Barassi has identified the evidently intended settings of several of these villanelle, both those approved and those rejected. And it is easy to see that the acceptable, classic examples are homophonic in texture, mostly syllabic in text-setting, narrow in melodic range, clearly articulated by cadences, and rhythmically compliant with the scansion of the text. The rejected songs are contrapuntal, sometimes melismatic, wide-ranging, less clearly articulated, and conditioned more by purely musical than by textual rhythms. The crucial factor, which Ferrari Barassi somehow overlooks, is that these villanelle are being proposed for performance by one singer, although all of them are preserved as part-songs. The features of the classic villanella are, in fact, the characteristics of the arie in the Rocco Rodio anthology and the traits of the popular traditional songs that Vincenzo Galilei recommended as models for the new monody. And it is easy to understand why the more recitational works of this type form a good basis for creating *arie in stil recitativo, e cantativo*, depending on whether and to what relative extent sprezzatura or passaggi were added to the notated music in performance. Basile's interlocutors needed what Nino Pirrotta calls *musiche ariose*, a category whose name he derives from the contemporaneous designation *madrigale arioso* and which is characterized by 'a straightforward (although by no means dance-like) rhythmic drive, and of simple well-designed melodic contours of the upper part, minimally affected by contrapuntal upsurges of the lower voices' as well as 'the quality [such music] appears to possess as being, as it were, precisely determined and inflected on an unavoidable course—no matter whether such unavoidability stems from tradition, repetition, and habit or from an inner sense of coherence and finality', in a word, a category of music characterized and conditioned by aria.[64]

The relatively few Neapolitan villanelle preserved from the period c.1575–1607 tend to have come out in print during the years 1602–7. (I have chosen the *terminus* 1607 because the first solo vocal music with basso continuo by a Neapolitan composer was published in that year.) And, as if responding to the same impulses that lead to Basile's criticism, the Neapolitan villanelle of 1602–7 tend to preserve important features of the classic villanelle, while reflecting some developments in the Neapolitan madrigal of the last quarter of the sixteenth century.

Il terzo libro di villanelle a quattro et arie a due voci (Naples: Sottile, 1605) by

---

[63] Einstein, *Italian Madrigal*, ii. 576–607.   [64] Pirrotta, *Music and Theatre*, 247–50.

Giovanni Domenico Montella (*c*.1570–1607) seems typical of the group.[65] Although only the tenor partbook survives, a number of the collection's features can be deduced from it. It contains twelve four-voice villanelle, all of which were evidently homophonic and syllabic in setting and arranged in the traditional AABB form. All these villanelle are written with the mensuration sign ¢, but one contains contrasting sections in 3/2 proportion, which is a feature found scattered through all these late Neapolitan villanella collections and one with a certain significance for Roman monody, as we shall see later. Two of Montella's arie are set for four voices, and they, too, are homophonic; one has a refrain. In the seven arie for two voices, the tenor is, fortunately for us, the upper voice, so these pieces can be reconstructed to a great extent. It should be pointed out that a certain number of works that are today considered monodies, by Jacopo Peri and later composers, come to us with texted bass parts and are, therefore, exactly like Montella's two-voice arie in notational format. Several works by Giulio Caccini that are elsewhere notated for solo voice and basso continuo are preserved in I:Bc, Q27.4, for soprano and texted, not figured, bass. Giuseppino Cenci's *Occhi un tempo mia vita*, for soprano and texted bass, is discussed towards the end of this chapter.

Montella's arie in the 1605 collection, like his villanelle, seem to be homophonic and syllabic and are cast in the traditional AABB repetition scheme; and likewise they frequently contain contrast between duple mensuration and triple proportion. Both the villanelle and the arie tend to be based on fairly intensive elaborations of short rhythmic motifs, a trait that they share with the Neapolitan madrigal of the same years.[66] This is a feature not particularly apparent in Caccini's monodies and one that, when found in the monodies of Cesare Marotta and his Roman colleagues, might be ascribed to the longer period of incubation that Neapolitan–Roman solo song spent in intimate association with polyphonic vocal music.

Another significant feature, found in Montella's aria *O novo mar d'amore* (Ex. 3.7), is contrast between recitational and cantillational styles. Depending on how those styles are defined, this may be the earliest known example of it in Italian

---

[65] Giovanni Domenico Montella became a lutenist in the *cappella* of the Viceroy of Naples in 1590 and a substitute organist there in 1601. He supplemented his income by giving private lessons to the nobility, and he was a reasonably prolific composer of both secular and sacred vocal music. Larson, 'The Unaccompanied Madrigal', 576, reports that there is no basis for the assertion that Montella was a student of Giovanni de Macque or that he participated in Don Fabrizio Gesualdo's academy; he also gives Montella's correct death date as January 1607. The most recent discussion of Montella's life and works is Iole Di Gregorio's introduction, 'Giovan Domenico Montella e il patrocinio musicale a Napoli tra Cinque e Seicento', in Giovanni Domenico Montella, *Il settimo libro de' madrigali a cinque voci*, ed. Iole Di Gregorio (Musiche del rinascimento italiano, 1; Florence, 1990), 5–19.

[66] See the discussion of Gesualdo's madrigals of the 1590s and the developments that led to them and followed from them in Larson, 'The Unaccompanied Madrigal in Naples'.

vocal music. The text of this aria could be called a canzone, and it is through-composed by Montella. In my reconstruction of it (Ex. 3.7) I have chosen to present the surviving tenor part as it would have been accompanied by a guitar in a solo-voice performance, which I think is even less conjectural than composing the inevitably homorhythmic bass voice, which itself would be easy enough to do.

The emergence of monody in Rome, parallel to its rise in Florence, within the context of recitational formulas and the accompanied solo performance of villanelle, arie, and madrigals that are preserved for us as part-songs, is succinctly narrated by Vincenzo Giustiniani, the close friend and frequent hunting companion to Cardinal Montalto, whom we met in the first chapter. Giustiniani's *Discorso sopra la musica* (1628) originated as a supplement to the same author's (now lost) treatise on the art of sustaining conversation and making it worthwhile. The conversation treatise, in turn, belonged to a series of essays addressed to newly created cardinals. As mentioned earlier, the other discourses treated hunting etiquette, palace architecture, art connoisseurship, and the social organization of a cardinal's household. In part, then, the purpose of Giustiniani's music treatise was to prepare newly created cardinals to appear informed and current in conversation. Indeed, Giustiniani confesses that he obtained much of the information contained in the discourse through conversations held in the palaces of musical dilettantes. One can easily imagine, therefore, that the changes of musical fashion that he describes were, in part, brought about and sustained by the social mechanism of conversations between cardinals and other nobility, the gentlemen of their households, and their guests at musical performances. Giustiniani's music discourse advises new cardinals about the recent history of musical fashion so that they can be well-informed patrons whose household musicians will reflect honour on them and produce effects in the souls of men, 'not only generally but particularly, corresponding to the individual inclinations of each one and to the tastes that in general prevail for distinct periods from time to time'.

The main thrust of Giustiniani's historical survey of musical taste is to account for and justify the new styles of accompanied solo singing that had emerged into a dominant position within his lifetime, while frequently referring to the influence of polyphonic music on the development of solo song. It is clear that he was well aware that the Florentines—Giulio Caccini, Ottavio Rinuccini, Jacopo Peri, and Marco da Gagliano—had claimed the leading role in the rise of these new styles for themselves. He presents his history, on the contrary, from a distinctly Roman perspective. I cannot agree with Carter, however, that Giustiniani reveals 'bias' or 'prejudice' in this respect.[67] Here, it is worth

---

[67] Carter, ' "An Air New and Grateful" ', 128–9.

Ex. 3.7. G. D. Montella, *O novo mar d'amore*, with hypothetical guitar accompaniment

Ex. 3.7. Cont'd

da si dol- ce boc-   ca a o- re fe- con- de   Ma più fe-

li- ce s'ha-   ve, ma più fe- li- ce s'ha-   ve, ma più fe-

li- ce s'ha-   ve In quel can- di- do sen por-   to so-

a-   ve,   ma più fel- li- ce s'ha-   ve in quel can-

di- do sen por-   to so- a- ve,   por-   to so- a- ve.

making the distinction between interest (which Giustiniani displays, as did the Florentines) and bias. The former may be said to consist of the writer's temperament, intentions, and hypotheses, whereas the latter, an extreme form of interest, can be detected by a crude selection of facts and notable lack of accuracy, order, logic, honesty, and self-awareness.[68] Carter does not give evidence of any of these, and, in what follows, the facts gathered in this research will tend to support rather than to discredit Giustiniani's account. This central part of his discourse is organized into eight numbered paragraphs, which will be translated or summarized and interspersed with commentary in what follows.

1. In my boyhood days, my late father sent me to music school, and I observed that the compositions of Arcadelt, Orlando di Lasso, Striggio, Cipriano de Rore, and Filippo di Monte were in use and were considered to be the best of that time, which, in effect, they were. For singing with a solo voice to the accompaniment of some instrument, preference for villanelle napoletane predominated, in imitation of which some of them were also composed in Rome, particularly by one Pitio, an excellent musician and noble comic actor.[69]

Given that Giustiniani was born in 1564 and that the year 1575 is mentioned later in his narration, we may assume that here he is referring roughly to the years 1570–5. Although 'Pitio' has never been completely identified, Newcomb quotes a dispatch of 6 June 1584 from the Este resident in Rome, which says that a Pitio was formerly in the service of Cardinal Louis Cornaro (1561–84), that he improvises both music and words for napolitane, and that he sings in a bass voice to the accompaniment of the lute.[70] Apart from Pitio, none of whose music is known to survive, only Alessandro Merlo (c.1530–after 1594) comes to mind as a Roman who published napolitane in the early 1570s. His works are not exactly imitations of Neapolitan villanelle but rather belong to a subsequent phase of Giustiniani's narrative.[71] The villanella by the Cavalier del Leuto, quoted earlier (Ex. 3.6), may represent a Roman imitation of the simple Neapolitan style, and it could date from the early 1570s if the Cavalier is truly to be identified

---

[68] I am paraphrasing the widely used textbook by Jacques Barzun and Henry F. Graff, *The Modern Researcher* (5th edn., Forth Worth, 1992), 185–92, 44–7.

[69] 'Che nella mia fanciullezza mio padre b. m. mi mandò alla scola di musica, et osservai ch'erano in uso le composizioni dell'Archadelt, di Orlando Lassus, dello Strigio, Cipriano de Rores e di Filippo di Monte, stimate per le migliori di quei tempi, come in effetto erano; e per cantare con una voce sola sopra alcuno stromento prevalesse il gusto delle Villanelle Napoletane, ad imitazione delle quali se ne componevano anche in Roma, e particolarmente da un tal Pitio musico bravo e buffone nobile.'

[70] Newcomb, *The Madrigal at Ferrara*, i. 47.

[71] His first two books of canzoni alla napolitana were published in 1570 and 1571 respectively. Ruth I. DeFord, 'Musical Relationships between the Italian Madrigal and Light Genres in the Sixteenth Century', *Musica disciplina*, 39 (1985), 107–68 at 114, is correct in saying 'Merlo's villanelle were considerably more independent of the Neapolitan style and more like madrigals, both textually and musically, than the early villanelle of Ferretti.'

as the lutenist Lorenzini, who was in the service of Cardinal Ippolito d'Este at Tivoli in 1570–1.

2. Within a short span of time, musical taste changed, and there appeared compositions by Luca Marenzio and by Ruggiero Giovannelli with the invention of new delights, those [compositions] to be sung by several voices as well as [others] for one [voice] alone accompanied by some instrument, the excellence of which consisted in a new aria pleasing to the ears with some easy points of imitation without extraordinary artifice. And at the same time Palestrina, Soriano, and Giovanni Maria Nanino composed things to be sung in church.[72]

It is striking that Giustiniani mentions compositions by Marenzio and Giovannelli for one voice alone accompanied by some instrument. All the surviving music known by these two composers, of course, comes to us only as partsong. Music by Marenzio or Giovannelli that was published in polyphonic form but which would have been typically sung by an accompanied solo voice would include Marenzio's villanelle issued in five books, 1584–7, Giovannelli's first book of villanelle and arie alla napolitana, 1588, some canzonette by each of them published, with lute and keyboard intabulations, in several of Simone Verovio's anthologies, 1586–95, and, hypothetically, some of their madrigals in which the full text appears, with few or no interruptions, in the canto part. If Giustiniani is referring here to music that became known after 1575, then the events that he narrates under Point 2 overlap with those described under Point 3, below. If not, it is hard to know whether he had in mind earlier music, now lost, by these two composers, or whether some of the pieces by them published between 1584 and 1595 were actually written much earlier—and if so, which. Be that as it may, some of Marenzio's villanelle are comparable in style to Giulio Caccini's *Fillide mia*, which, as mentioned earlier, was copied into a volume dated 1574 on its first page. Since Marenzio began his Roman residence in 1574, or shortly before, when he entered the service of Cardinal Cristoforo Madruzzo, it is possible that villanelle similar to his were known in Rome by 1575. If Giovannelli were born about 1560, as now thought, it would seem unlikely that villanelle by him were known in Rome by 1575. Indeed the surviving villanelle and canzonette by Giovannelli are generally more contrapuntal and madrigal-like than is typical of Marenzio's, so they seem to belong to a later phase of the genre's history.

The first known publication of a madrigal by Marenzio occurred in 1577, while his first complete book of five-voice works appeared in 1580. Giovannelli's

---

[72] 'In poco progresso di tempo s'alterò il gusto della musica e comparver le composizioni di Luca Marenzio e di Ruggero Giovannelli, con invenzione di nuovo diletto, tanto quelle da cantarsi a più voci, quanto ad una sola sopra alcuno stromento, l'eccellenza delle quali consisteva in una nuova aria et grata all'orecchie, con alcune fughe facili e senza straordinario artificio. E nell'istesso tempo il Pellestrina, il Soriano e Gio. Maria Nanino composero cose da cantarsi in chiesa.'

madrigals were anthologized by 1582 and collected in his first book by 1585. The early madrigals by these two composers are notable for sharing features drawn from the canzonetta, particularly in the choice of light-hearted texts, clear and directional harmony, moderate use of dissonance, and textures and melodic lines dominated by short, rhythmically distinctive motifs, frequently including groups of three or more texted fusae (eighth notes).[73]

Although such groups of three or more texted fusae had been known in the Neapolitan villanella since the mid-1560s,[74] they seem to have been introduced into the madrigal in Rome by Giovanni de Macque in the mid- to later 1570s.[75] According to Ruth DeFord, these strings of texted fusae produced a change in the nature of rhythmic contrast, helped to create rhythmic patterns that were more distinctive and memorable, increased the speed of declamation so that the poetic line now could occupy a motif instead of a phrase, opened the way to intensive imitation and frequent repetition of distinctive rhythmic patterns, and fostered the transition from fluid, text-based tactus rhythm to more rigid structures approaching accentual metres.[76] To this, I would add that strings of texted fusae promote a more dramatic declamation of the text because they increase the range in rates of syllabication, and, owing to the tendency to repeat and elaborate on short text-based motifs made up of fusae, they tend to correlate with rhetorical figures derived from various kinds of intensified repetition; furthermore, since fusae belong to the rhythmic level of diminution, more of them can be introduced with greater freedom within the duration of each essential consonance, as might be represented by a note in a basso continuo part or by a chord strummed on a guitar. For these reasons, it is not surprising that texted fusae are ubiquitous in the recitative style employed in the earliest operas.

On the other hand, groups of three or more texted fusae are not especially common in Giulio Caccini's 1602 *Nuove musiche*; fewer than half the solo madrigals in the collection contain any at all. This may be a reflection of the fact that this device was introduced into the Roman madrigal after Caccini left for Florence and of the fact that no Florentine madrigalist was yet following this Roman trend at the time when the earliest pieces in *Le nuove musiche* were written.

---

[73] Ruth Irene DeFord, 'Ruggiero Giovannelli and the Madrigal in Rome, 1572–1599' (Ph.D. diss., Harvard University, 1975), 34–42; 192–5.

[74] Giovan Leonardo Primavera, *La villanella quand'all'acqua vai*, *Mira la villanella*, and *Dirudiridido padrona mia*, all three in his second book of *canzone napolitane* of 1566; Francesco Celano, *Così scolpita a gl'occhi miei ti porto*, in *Canzon napolitane a tre voci* (Venice: Scotto, 1566). I am very grateful to Donna Cardamone for pointing out these examples and for much additional help with the earlier *villanella* repertoire.

[75] *Poi che 'l camin m'è chiuso di mercede* and *Ahi disperata vita* in Macque's first book of six-voice madrigals (1576); *Non al suo amante più Diana piacque* and *Di coralli e di perle ha fatt'Amore* in his book of madrigals for four, five, and six voices (1597). Also see *Talhor mi s'avicina* in his second book of *madrigaletti* of 1582.

[76] Ruth I. DeFord, 'The Evolution of Rhythmic Style in Italian Secular Music of the Late Sixteenth Century', *Studi musicali*, 10 (1981), 43–74.

Caccini's presumably later monodies tell a different story: all but two of the madrigals and all but one of the strophic variations in his 1614 *Nuove musiche e nuova maniera di scriverle* have abundant strings of texted fusae. The major manuscript anthologies of early Florentine monody show something of the same thing. In the Brussels manuscript, for instance, with its 140 compositions, only ten of the anonymous works (that is, excluding those known to be by Caccini and his younger followers) have strings of three or more texted fusae, and three of these are late additions to the manuscript.[77] The more dramatic style of declamation found in Caccini's 1614 collection and later Florentine monody can be traced, I believe, to a growing awareness of the Roman canzonetta-madrigal.

By contrast, the two earliest datable continuo-accompanied monodies ('true monodies') from the Roman–Neapolitan orbit are rich in texted fusae, and, since they pre-date the publication of Caccini's *Nuove musiche*, they appear to reflect slightly different traditions, or at least they seem to have absorbed the rhythmic style of the Roman canzonetta-madrigal earlier than Caccini's did. These Roman–Neapolitan monodies can be dated only approximately by the death or retirement of their composers, and so their placement at this point in Giustiniani's narrative is a hypothesis based partly upon the presence of texted fusae and other points of similarity with the polyphonic madrigals of Marenzio and Giovannelli. Before we examine these monodies, the way in which they are preserved requires careful explanation.

The earliest datable monodies from the Roman–Neapolitan orbit are continuo-accompanied solo madrigals by Bartolomeo Roy (*c.*1530–99) and Sebastiano Raval (*c.*1550–1604). They are preserved in a dual-purpose format in Pietro Maria Marsolo's *Secondo libro dei madrigali a quattro voci* (1614). Lorenzo Bianconi published an edition of this collection with extensive, highly informative commentary in 1973.[78] Marsolo offers a four-voice polyphonic paraphrase of the monodic original as well as a continuo part that can be used to accompany either the arrangement or the original solo voice part, which he aligns with the continuo part under the rubric *partitura*. In his preface, Marsolo explains precisely how the original solo aria upon which each of his four-voice madrigals is based can be reconstituted:

When singing [an aria] for solo voice, the singer should not observe any of the rests written into his part, but should pass immediately to the following notes, just as the accompanist should omit from his part just so many notes as are represented by the rests indicated in

---

[77] Concerning the dating, ascriptions, and scribes of this manuscript, see William V. Porter, 'A Central Source of Early Monody: Brussels, Conservatory 704', *Studi musicali*, 12 (1983), 239–79; 13 (1984), 139–67.

[78] Pietro Maria Marsolo, *Madrigali a quattro voci sulle monodie di Giulio Caccini e d'altri autori, ed altre opere*, ed. Lorenzo Bianconi (Musiche rinascimentali siciliane, 4; Rome, 1973). Neither Bianconi nor any subsequent writer has called attention to the historical significance of these two solo madrigals, as mentioned above.

Ex. 3.8. Giulio Caccini, *Vedrò 'l mio sol*: (*a*) B:Bc, MS 704; (*b*) arrangement for four voices by Pietro Marsolo

the singer's part, which he can see immediately, without any mental distraction, following the partitura from which he is playing. And he should pause on the same notes upon which the singer pauses.[79]

Example 3.8 gives a representative sample of this process.

In his preface and in the body of the work, Marsolo makes it clear that the madrigals arranged polyphonically in his collection were originally composed for solo voice, and he carefully distinguishes between madrigals that have been arranged 'sopra l'aria' of such-and-such a composer and madrigals designated simply 'aria' by a certain composer:

I say, therefore, that these madrigals are composed for four voices upon the arias for one voice alone by various excellent musicians. In some of them our composer has held to the entire [original musical] text until the end, and in some he has only taken the motifs

[79] 'quando si canta a una voce, non si ha da tener pausa nissuna notata nella parte, ma passare immediatamente alle note sussequenti si come anche il suonatore deve tralasciar nella sua parte tante note quanto sarà il valor delle pause notate nella parte di quello che canta, il che in un batter d'occhio, senza deviamento alcuno di mente potrà vedere mediante la partitura sopra la quale suona. Fermandosi sopra l'istessa nota dove il cantore si ferma.'

Ex. 3.8. Cont'd

Ex. 3.8. Cont'd

to be imitated and some ancillary figures, [and thus] guiding the conduct of his leading melodic line, he has arranged the parts according to his taste. Those in which the entire [original musical] text is used will be recognized by this inscription in the margin above the continuo: 'aria by so-and-so'. The other by this: 'upon the aria by so-and-so'.[80]

Madrigals 'sopra l'aria' are free adaptations, and comparison with known originals shows that the partitura cannot be used reliably to reconstitute the original monody. But the partiture of madrigals designated as simply 'aria' preserve the source monody exactly, as Marsolo claims. This has been verified by comparing them with surviving originals by Giulio Caccini, Francesco Rasi, and Giuseppe Cenci. Bianconi has done this comparison for *Parlo, misero, o taccio?*, *Vedrò 'l mio sol*, *Occhi, soli d'Amore*, *Sfogava con le stelle*, *A me che tanto v'amo*, and *Deh come invan chiedete* by Caccini and *Schiera d'aspri martiri* by Francesco Rasi. More recently, Susan Parisi shows 'how close the solo version extracted by Lorenzo Bianconi from the polyphonic madrigal was to Gioseppino's original monody', *Occhi un tempo mia vita*, which Bianconi did not know at the time.[81] None of the arias arranged by Marsolo has been traced to a polyphonic or 'pseudo-monodic' part-song.

It would be difficult to guess Marsolo's motivation for bringing out polyphonic arrangements of monodies in 1614, but there is a pattern in his choice of works: they all have some possibility of having been composed before 1600. Bianconi, in the introduction to his edition of Marsolo's collection (p. xxiv), argues that, on stylistic grounds, all the works included seem to have been composed during the 1590s. But Caccini himself claims to have composed *Vedrò 'l mio sol* (no. 13 in Marsolo's book) in about the year 1585. And I would say that some of the works could have been composed even as early as 1580. None of Marsolo's arrangements of Caccini's monodies is based upon the 1602 published version; rather they are all derived from pre-publication versions preserved in manuscript. Each of the other composers represented in Marsolo's anthology of arrangements either must have written his arie before 1600 or could have done so; no one who began to compose only after 1600 is included. Specifically, Achille Falcone died on 9 November 1600. Giuseppino Cenci's main activities as composer can be assigned to the decade of the 1590s, as we shall see later. Francesco Rasi began his studies with Caccini, supported by a stipend from the Florentine court in 1588, was heard as a solo singer in Rome in 1593, and was composing at the court of Mantua by 1595.[82] Bartolomeo Roy died in 1599. Sebastiano Raval retired from

[80] 'Dico dunque, che questi Madrigali sono composti a quattro sopra l'Arie d'una voce sola di diversi Eccellentissimi Musici, in alcune de quali il nostro Autore si è obbligato a tutto il testo sino al fine, e in alcune ha solamente prese le fughe, e commesse guidando il procedere della sua Cantilena ha disposte le parti a suo gusto. Quelli de quali si serve di tutto il testo saranno conosciuti con questa inscrizione nel margine superiore del Continuo: Aria del tale. E gli altri con questa: Sopra l'Aria del tale.'   [81] Parisi, 'Ducal Patronage', 74.

[82] Warren Kirkendale, 'Zur Biographie des ersten Orfeo, Francesco Rasi', in *Claudio Monteverdi: Festschrift Reinhold Hammerstein zum 70. Geburtstag* (Laaber, 1986), 297–335 at 300–1.

Rome in 1595, finishing his career in Palermo, where he died in 1604. Lelio Bertani had composed madrigals by 1571; all three collections bearing his name were published in 1584–5, and he retired as *maestro di cappella* of Padua Cathedral in 1604. Madrigals by Gioseffo Guami began to appear in 1562. The two other composers named by Marsolo—Capovia and Angelo da Napoli—remain unidentified.

Bartolomeo Roy held church positions in Rome from 1570 to 1581. In 1583 he was appointed *maestro di cappella* to the Viceroy of Naples, but by 1589 he was in the service of Cardinal Montalto in Rome.[83] He died at Naples in 1599, securing for us a *terminus ad quem* for his solo madrigal. Sebastiano Raval served in the household of Marc'Antonio Colonna, Gran Contestabile of the Kingdom of Naples, while Colonna was serving as Viceroy of Sicily from 1577 to 1584. Raval passed briefly into the service of Marc'Antonio's son Cardinal Ascanio in Rome, and by 24 March 1593 was in the Roman service of the grandson, also named Marc'Antonio Colonna.[84] The dedication of his five-voice madrigals (10 May 1593) says that the works had been composed in Urbino. This has led Steven Ledbetter (*New Grove*, s.v.) to surmise that Raval had been for some time at the court of Duke Francesco Maria II della Rovere. This conclusion, however, does not square with Raval's account of his own career given in the dedication of his *Canzonette a quattro voci*. Shortly before Colonna's death in 1595, Raval moved to Palermo, where he finished out his remaining nine years as *maestro* of the Cappella Palatina. Since the younger Marc'Antonio Colonna was Cardinal Montalto's brother-in-law, it is not surprising that Raval dedicated music to Montalto and his brother, Michele Peretti, that he described a performance of his five-part madrigals by household musicians in Montalto's palace, and that he was inspired to compose his three-voice madrigals by the singing of Vittoria Archilei while she was on loan from Grand Duke Ferdinando de' Medici to Cardinal Montalto—technically to Montalto's sister Flavia and her husband, Virginio Orsini.[85] The period of Vittoria Archilei's visit to Rome, 1593–4, would seem the most likely time for the composition of Raval's sole surviving solo madrigal.

My reconstructions of Roy's and Raval's solo madrigals from Marsolo's arrangements—following Marsolo's own instructions—are given as Ex. 3.9 and Ex. 3.10. They are predominantly syllabic in setting. Melismas with a variety of rhythms occur exclusively on primary verse accents. The vocal line is confined to narrow ranges within phrases, and monotone recitation is used frequently at the beginnings of verses; syllables are set to a wide range of note values (24:1). They

---

[83] Chater, 'Musical Patronage', 195.

[84] This information is taken from Raval's dedication, 24 Mar. 1593, of his *Primo libro di canzonette a quattro voci* (Venice: Vincenti, 1593).

[85] Chater, 'Musical Patronage', 199 n. 108. Raval's dedication of the *Madrigali a tre voci* (Rome: Mutij, 1595), 21 Feb. 1595, contains the reference to Vittoria Archilei; it also mentions Raval's close connection with Cardinal Montalto and Michele Peretti.

Ex. 3.9. Bartolomeo Roy, *O dolce anima mia*, reconstructed from Marsolo's arrangement

O dol- ce a- ni- ma mia   dun- que è pur ve- ro Che can- gian- do pen-

sie- ro Per al- trui   m'ab- ban- do-   ni?   Se cer- chi un

cor   che più t'a- do- ri ed a-   mi, In- giu- sta- men- te bra- mi   Se

cer- chi le- al- ta, mi- ra che fe-   de   mi- ra che fe- de.   A-

mor, quan- do al- trui do- ni La mia ca- ra mer- ce- de   E la spe- ra- ta

Ex. 3.9. Cont'd

Ex. 3.10. Sebastiano Raval, *Ecco si ferma a gran stupore*, reconstructed from Marsolo's arrangement

have non-vocal, largely non-imitative bass lines that are usually slow-moving and sometimes static. *Seconda prattica* dissonance treatment can be found in Ex. 3.9, bars 3, 8, and 11; and in Ex. 3.10, bars 7, 13, and 18.

These two madrigals respect poetic enjambment: the music avoids closure because the meaning in the text carries over between lines in Ex. 3.9, bars 3,

Ex. 3.10. Cont'd

4, 11, and 16; and in Ex. 3.10, bars 3 and 10. Both madrigals use syncopation effectively to set off secondary accents in cases of hypotaxis. This can be seen in Ex. 3.9, bars 11 ('*quando* altrui doni . . .'), 13 ('*dolce* pietade'), 16, and 21 ('*in* questo core'); and in Ex. 3.10, bar 12 ('*grida* mio core in tanto'). These and other syncopations together with the wide range of syllabication rates contribute substantially to the effect of written-out *sprezzatura di canto* that I believe these two works possess.

Roy and Raval adhere to the Roman–Neapolitan practice of elaborating on short motifs with sharp rhythmic profiles, in part a corollary to their use of texted fusae. As a result, their music often parallels or creates rhetorical figures in their texts. In Ex. 3.9, bars 9–10, for instance, the repetition of the motif that sets the plea 'mira che fede' creates a classic *iteratio*. But the rhetorical figures are not confined to intensified repetition. In Ex. 3.9, bars 10–12, the poet's *apostrophe* to the god of love is set off by the only melodic interjection in the bass found in the madrigal. In bars 14–16, the two elements of the *antithesis* 'Non mirar me cor mio, mira te stessa' ('Do not look upon me, my dear, look upon yourself') are set apart musically by the opposition of one melodic and harmonic gesture converging on E flat against a second phrase cadencing on a C major chord. In Ex. 3.10, bars 1–5, the tension that accumulates in the static preparation for what will be told (*procatascene*), 'Ecco si ferma a gran stupore il sole | E così fisso tiene | Lo sguardo in voi luci d'amor serene' ('Behold, the sun stops in amazement and, thus, holds its gaze fixed upon you, gentle lights of love'), is underscored by first a half-cadence then a full cadence to A major chords in the context of an opening, continuation, and conclusion on G major chords. The rising vocal line in bars 3–4 certainly contributes to this tightening of tension as well. In Ex. 3.10, bars 15–16, there are three questions, 'O che sento? o che veggio? e dove sono?' ('Oh, what do I hear? Oh, what do I see? And where am I?'), that are answered by three replies 'Odo d'angelo il canto | Miro d'angelo il viso | O me beato i' sono in paradiso!' ('I hear the angel's song. I see the angel's face. Oh, blessed me, I am in paradise'). The three questions, placed in climactic order (*auxesis*), are set to three phrases whose final notes rise by degrees, B, C♯, and D. The first two questions also form an *anaphora* because they begin with the same words, and the two musical phrases that set them are the two members of a melodic sequence, naturally with parallel initial gestures. And the three replies likewise are set to two members of a sequence (descending so as to respond musically to the rising line of the questions) plus a concluding third phrase. The entire passage of text, therefore, forms an *anthypophora*, which the music faithfully mirrors, rising to D through the questions and descending to G in the answers. By contrast, very few instances of rhetorical figures created or supported by the music are found in Giulio Caccini's *Nuove musiche*, beyond the immediate repetition of a word or phrase of text to music that forms the second member of a sequence. Nothing as elaborate as the examples just discussed can be found in Caccini's early works.

The solo madrigals by Roy and Raval, possessing as they do true basso continuo and *sprezzatura di canto* in the service of interpretive declamation, seem comparable to Caccini's early works in the genre in that respect. But the fact that they contain considerably more abundant strings of three or more texted fusae and a related concentration of motivic elaboration and rhetorical figuration are reasons for believing that they are not mere imitations of Caccini's monodies. They seem to relate to developments in the Roman and Neapolitan madrigals from which Caccini, in Florence, remained sheltered until after the turn of the century. The solo madrigals of Roy, Raval, and Caccini may have been to some extent products of parallel developments with common roots in Roman–Neapolitan traditions but with different relations to developments in the madrigal that took place in Rome and Naples after Caccini's move to Florence.

Curiously, neither monody by Roy or Raval resembles in any important way these composers' polyphonic madrigals and canzonette. In fact, it seems ironic that while Roy's monody is remarkable for its numerous series of texted fusae, his polyphonic madrigals are notable for 'unimaginative combinations of half notes and quarter notes'.[86] However, the works in Roy's only known book of madrigals were collected by the Roman Pietro Paulo Quartieri and published in 1591, well after Roy's 1583 departure for Naples. It therefore seems likely that Quartieri collected pieces that Roy had left in Rome before 1583, and, judging from the style of the madrigals, they may well have been composed during the 1570s. Roy's monody, on the other hand, reflects changes that occurred in the Neapolitan and Roman madrigals during the 1580s and even the 1590s, as we have said. There is actually some hint at those developments in two of Roy's madrigals that were anthologized in the 1580s: *Una bianca cervetta* in *Dolci affetti: Madrigali a cinque voci* (Venice: Scotto, 1582) and *Verdi piaggie, fiorite* in *Il lauro verde* (Ferrara: Baldini, 1583). Both of these use texted fusae, but no more than two of them at a time. Both of them also display more supple, naturally declamatory rhythms than are found in the Roman collection of Roy's madrigals. So perhaps his monody represents further change in the same direction.

The only feature of Raval's monody that can be detected in his polyphonic madrigals and canzonette (published in 1593 and 1595) is the interest in melismas. But the melismas in his polyphonic works are treated motivically and involve notes no faster than fusae, whereas there is only one melisma in Raval's monody, and, replete with semifusae and fusellae, it clearly represents a spontaneous gesture not likely to be repeated, imitated, or elaborated. One is practically left to conclude that, in composing *Ecco si ferma a gran stupore*, Raval referred himself to models and procedures in no significant way connected with those that he used in writing his polyphonic works. This would not be remarkable, however. Many composers of simple villanelle and arie also wrote intricate madrigals and elaborately contrapuntal church music.

---

[86] DeFord, 'Ruggiero Giovannelli', 182. Only *Quand'io ripenso, Amore* in Roy's first book of five-voice madrigals (1591) contains pairs of texted *fusae*, but no groups of three or more.

As a hypothetical example of the type of model and procedures that either Roy or Raval could have used, I offer solo madrigal with basso continuo accompaniment (Ex. 3.11) that I have derived exclusively from the soprano part and the harmony of Ruggiero Giovannelli's *Tu nascesti di furto* (Book 2, five voices, 1593).[87] Virtually the only modifications made to Giovannelli's original soprano part involved removing some repetitions of text segments with their accompanying repetitions and elaborations of musical motifs. The harmonies are exactly Giovannelli's. The melisma in bar 5 is taken from G. B. Bovicelli's 1594 ornamentation treatise.[88] The point here is not that Roy or Raval actually arranged previously written polyphonic madrigals in composing their monodies. My hypothetical example is only meant to show the basic stylistic compatibility between the earliest known Roman–Neapolitan monodies and polyphonic madrigals of the kind that Marenzio and Giovannelli composed.

This point is further demonstrated by the fact that a major portion of an actual monody from Montalto's circle shares nearly all its basic motivic material with a five-voice madrigal by Marenzio, that is, the anonymous monody *Ecco Silvio colei che 'n odio tanto* (bb. 63–96, from the line 'Anima cruda si, ma però bella') and Marenzio's *Anima cruda sì, ma però bella* (Book 6, a 5, 1594). The text is from *Il pastor fido*, and the question of which setting was written first will be taken up in Chapter 7.

3. In the Holy Year of 1575, or shortly after, there began a style of singing very different from the earlier one, and [it continued] thus for some years afterward, especially as regards the style of singing with one voice alone to the accompaniment of an instrument, following the example of one Giovanni Andrea of Naples and of Giulio Cesare Brancaccio and of Alessandro Merlo of Rome, all of whom sang in a bass voice with a range of 22 degrees of the scale, with a variety of passaggi that were new and gratifying to everybody's ears. These [singers] stimulated the composers to write works both to be sung by several voices as well as for one [voice] alone accompanied by an instrument, in imitation of the aforesaid [singers] and of a woman named Femia, but obtaining [in their compositions] superior invention and artifice. And there emerged, as a result, some mixed villanelle [combining aspects of] polyphonic madrigals and villanelle, many books of which are seen today by the aforesaid composers and by Orazio Vecchi and others. But, since villanelle acquired greater perfection by means of more artful composition, each composer, in order that his compositions would be pleasing to taste in general, also took care to advance himself in the style of composing for several voices, and particularly Giaches de Wert in Mantua and Luzzasco [Luzzaschi] in Ferrara.[89]

---

[87] Transcribed by DeFord, 'Ruggiero Giovannelli', App., 68–75.

[88] Giovanni Battista Bovicelli, *Regole, passaggi di musica* (Venice: Vincenti, 1594), 23.

[89] 'L'anno santo del 1575 o poco dopo si cominciò un modo di cantare molto diverso da quello di prima, e così per alcuni anni seguenti, massime nel modo di cantare con una voce sola sopra un istrumento, con l'esempio d'un Gio. Andrea napoletano, e del sig. Giulio Cesare Brancaccio e d'Alessandro Merlo

Ex. 3.11. Ruggiero Giovannelli, *Tu nascesti di furto*, arranged as a solo madrigal

Ex. 3.11. Cont'd

Giulio Cesare Brancaccio (*c*.1515–*c*.1585) was born and trained in Naples, spent extended periods in Rome, and participated with important results in the *musica segreta* of Ferrara.[90] Although Giustiniani vouches for his influence on composers, we have nothing composed by him or transcribed directly from his singing. The five-voice madrigals (1554, 1565), four-voice villanelle (repr.? 1579) and five-voice canzoni alla napolitana (1570, 1571) of Alessandro Merlo are certainly interesting examples of music largely intended for solo performance but published in the form of part-songs. In most respects they belong to the stages in the history of Roman monody, discussed earlier, that precede the compositions of Raval's and Roy's monodies. But, in their published form, they give no overt hint of the innovative style of singing that Giustiniani mentions here.

romano, che cantavano un basso nella larghezza dello spazio di 22 voci, con varietà di passaggi nuovi e grati all'orecchie di tutti. I quali svegliarono i compositori a far opere tanto da cantare a più voci come ad una sola sopra un istrumento, ad imitazione delli soddetti e d'una tal femina chiamata Femia, ma con procurare maggiore invenzione et artificio, e ne vennero a risultare alcune Villanelle miste tra Madrigali di canto figurato e di Villanelle, delle quali se ne vedono oggi dì molti libri de gl'autori suddetti e di Orazio Vecchi et altri. Ma sì come le Villanelle acquistarono maggior perfezione per lo più artificioso componimento, così anche ciascun autore, a fin che le sue composizioni riuscissero di gusto in general, procurò d'avanzarsi nel modo di componere a più voci, e particolarmente Giachet Wert in Mantova, il Luzzasco in Ferrara.'

[90] Newcomb, *The Madrigal at Ferrara*, 185–6; *Dizionario biografico degli italiani*, s.v. 'Brancacio, Giulio Cesare'.

The 'villanelle [combining aspects of] polyphonic madrigals and villanelle' are associated with Alessandro Merlo, Girolamo Conversi, Giovanni Piccioni, Giuseppe Caimo, and Giovanni Ferretti, in addition to Orazio Vecchi, whom Giustiniani names. The general features of these works, whether called villanelle, canzoni, or canzonette, are the retention of the characteristic binary form, clear phrasing, and lively rhythm of the villanella and the absorption from the polyphonic madrigal of a more contrapuntal texture, greater length, and musical illustration of the text.[91] These are Einstein's 'new canzoni', to which Giambattista Basile objected, as we have seen. I see this genre as tangential to early monody and without very much influence on it.

The florid style of madrigal, inspired, according to Giustiniani, by the virtuosic singing of Giovanni Andrea of Naples, Giulio Cesare Brancaccio, Alessandro Merlo, and 'Femia' (Eufemia Jozola, mentioned earlier for her recitative-style performance of Scipione del Palla's aria at Naples in 1558), is associated above all with Ferrara. Although many of these works were written for the conventional five voices, the madrigals for one, two, and three sopranos with written-out keyboard accompaniment composed by Luzzasco Luzzaschi and published in Rome in 1601 seem more relevant to the emergence of monody. Anthony Newcomb argues that these madrigals by Luzzaschi were actually composed in Ferrara during the 1580s by reason of their old-fashioned embellishments and the four-voice texture of their accompaniments, which reflect the madrigale arioso of the period 1550–80, and because that was the decade during which Luzzaschi was involved with the court's famous *concerto delle dame*.[92] Giustiniani, in a long passage that I shall not transcribe or translate here, credits the singing ladies of Ferrara with a style of diminution, expression of passions, use of echoes, dramatic gestures, and clear declamation of the words that produced influences felt in Mantua, Naples, and Rome. This may be so, but the accompanied madrigals by Luzzaschi had little to offer Roy, Raval, or later monodists in Rome; in them there are never more than two consecutive texted fusae, almost no monotone recitation, neither opportunities for nor notation of *sprezzatura di canto*, no basso continuo, and in general a melodic line that is anything but self-determined. These, of course, are observations that betray the extreme acuity of hindsight. Only Giulio Caccini and a few others in 1601 might have noticed that Luzzaschi's accompanied madrigals were not in 'the same style' (referring to Caccini's 1614 letter against Cavalieri) as his and some Romans'. Pirrotta makes the plausible suggestion that Cavalieri might have encouraged Luzzaschi's 1601 publication in Rome, as Cavalieri could have imagined that they supported his contention that Caccini's monodies were not entirely innovative, and he further suggests that

---

[91] DeFord, 'Musical Relationships'.   [92] Newcomb, *The Madrigal at Ferrara*, 57–67.

the publication may also have been an expression of rivalry directed at Grand Duke Ferdinando de' Medici by Cardinal Pietro Aldobrandini, to whom Luzzaschi's collection was dedicated.[93] And, I would add, perhaps an expression of Aldobrandini's rivalry, as patron of music, with Cardinal Montalto, with whom the earliest Roman monodies could have been associated.[94]

Luzzaschi's unpublished solo madrigals had actually been the object of Cardinal Montalto's intensive searches since 1605, shortly after Ippolita Recupito and her husband Cesare Marotta joined his household. On 11 December 1605 Duke Vincenzo Gonzaga of Mantua replied to Montalto, through his agent in Rome, that his sister Margherita had the words but not the music for the madrigals requested, because Luzzaschi had made sketches and then taught the singing ladies of Ferrara by rote.[95] A few of Luzzaschi's madrigals were sent on 7 January 1606, and Montalto acknowledged receipt of them on 21 January.[96] But these must not have sufficed, for on 2 March 1606 Duke Vincenzo wrote to the Marquis of Scandiano, asking his help in obtaining more madrigals directly from Luzzaschi; on 31 March Duke Vincenzo acknowledges their receipt.[97] Whether these were not of the type that Montalto sought, or whether Duke Vincenzo never forwarded them to him cannot be determined. But during the summer of 1607 Cardinal Montalto still had Bernardo Bizzoni write to Enzo Bentivoglio in Ferrara asking Bentivoglio for his help in persuading Luzzaschi, himself, to send Montalto's singer Ippolita Recupito specifically some of his unpublished *opere passagiate* so she could sing them in Florence at the Medici festivities of 1608. Luzzaschi declined, citing old age.[98]

This may have been a crucial episode in Montalto's musical patronage, for although monodies more advanced than Luzzaschi's (from our viewpoint) had already been composed in Rome, Montalto spent a year and a half in a vain attempt to provide his newly acquired prize singer with unpublished embellished madrigals that Luzzaschi had sketched and taught to the ladies of Ferrara twenty years earlier. With these Montalto presumably sought to rival Grand Duke Ferdinando de' Medici, his Florentine singing ladies, and their embellished monodies by Giulio Caccini. In the event, however, Montalto did not manage to get the embellished solo madrigals by Luzzaschi that he sought, and perhaps this became one motivation for turning to his own and other Roman monodists for more of the solo songs that would be comparable to those of Florence (as Montalto hoped) while retaining some particularly Roman and Neapolitan features (as his composers could not entirely avoid).

---

[93] Pirrotta, *Music and Theatre*, 240.
[94] Concerning this rivalry, see Annibaldi, 'Il mecenate "politico"'.
[95] The letter is transcribed in Parisi, 'Ducal Patronage', 184–5.   [96] Ibid.   [97] Ibid. 185.
[98] See the letters of 28 July 1607 and 22 Aug. 1607 in App. A, Letters 18 and 20.

4. With the examples of these courts [Mantua and Ferrara] and of the two Neapolitans who sang in a bass voice in the aforesaid style, they began in Rome to vary the style of composing for several voices extemporizing and in notated polyphony and also for one and two voices accompanied by some instrument.[99]

I cannot suggest which Roman composers of accompanied solos and duets pursued the virtuosic style of Luzzaschi during the 1580s, if not Giuseppino Cenci and some others of Cardinal Montalto's circles whose music is either lost or not securely datable to those early years. And so, skipping again over Giustiniani's following remarks about Gesualdo and other Neapolitan madrigalists, we come back to Roman singers.

5. At the same time [1571–87], Cardinal Ferdinando de' Medici, who was later Grand Duke of Tuscany, stimulated both by his own taste and by the example of the abovesaid princes, strove to have excellent musicians, and especially the famous Vittoria [Archilei], from whom the true style of singing for women practically had its origins, since she was the wife of Antonio di Santa Fiore, thus named because he was from boyhood a prized musician of Cardinal Santa Fiore. And with this example, many pursued this style of singing in Rome, so that they prevailed over all the other musicians of the abovesaid places and princes. Thus came to prominence Giulio [Caccini] the Roman, Giuseppino [Cenci], Giovanni Domenico [Puliaschi], and [Francesco] Rasi, who emerged in Florence from [the school of] Giulio [Caccini] the Roman; and they all sang bass and tenor with a range of many notes and with exquisite styles and embellishments and with extraordinary expression and a particular talent to make the words well heard.[100]

This segment goes over mostly familiar ground, but what is interesting is that Giustiniani lumps Caccini together with Cenci, Puliaschi, and Rasi as essentially Roman followers of Vittoria Archilei. On the basis of what biographical information we have about these composers, it is quite possible that they were writing florid and wide-ranging monodies already in the mid- to late 1580s, as Giustiniani suggests. Caccini's collection of 1614 and Puliaschi's of 1618 do, indeed, contain monodies that combine the bass and tenor voice ranges.[101]

---

[99] 'Coll'esempio di queste Corti e delli due napolitani che cantavano di basso nel modo suddetto, si cominciò in Roma a variar modo di componere a più voci sopra il libro e canto figurato, et anche ad una o due al più voci sopra alcuno stromento.'

[100] Nell'istesso tempo il Cardinale Ferdinando de' Medici, che fu poi Gran Duca di Toscana, stimolato e dal proprio gusto e dall'esempio degli altri suddetti Prencipi, ha premuto in aver musici eccellenti, e specialmente la famosa Vittoria, dalla quale ha quasi avuto origine il vero modo di cantare nelle donne, perciocchè ella fu moglie d'Antonio di Santa Fiore, così cognominato perchè era stato fino da fanciullo musico per eccellenza del Cardinal di Santa Fiore. E con questo esempio molt'altri s'esercitarono in questo modo di cantare in Roma, in guisa tale che prevalsero a tutti gli altri musici dei luoghi e Prencipi suddetti, e vennero in luce Giulio Romano, Giuseppino, Gio. Domenico et il Rasi, che apparò in Firenze da Giulio Romano; et tutti cantavano di basso e tenore con larghezza di molto numero di voci, e con modi e passaggi esquisiti e con affetto straordinario e talento particolare di far sentir bene le parole.

[101] H. Wiley Hitchcock, 'Caccini's "Other" *Nuove musiche*', *Journal of the American Musicological Society*, 27 (1974), 438–60.

Giustiniani continues with general praise for the falsettists Giovanni Luca Conforto, Ottavio Durante, Simoncino, and Ludovico, and the castrati Onofrio Gualfreducci, the Spanish Mathias, and Giovanni Girolamo Rosini of Perugia, all active in Rome at the end of the sixteenth century.

6. Then Cardinal Montalto succeeded Cardinal Ferdinando de' Medici, and he delighted in music no less than the latter, because he moreover played the harpsichord very well and sang in a sweet and affecting manner and kept in his household many of the [musical] profession who rose above the average, among them the Cavaliere del Leuto and Scipione Dentici, harpsichordist, excellent instrumentalists and composers, then Orazio [Michi], rare player of the double harp, and for singers Onofrio Gualfreducci, castrato, Ippolita [Recupito] of Naples, Melchior [Palantrotti], bass, and many others, to whom he gave large salaries. And with the example of these and all the aforesaid others, the cultivation of music was revived, so that many nephews of popes and other cardinals and princes delighted in it. Indeed, all the *maestri di cappella* had to undertake to train various castrati and other boys to sing with embellishments and in expressive and new styles. Among these [*maestri*], Giovanni Bernardino Nanino, *maestro di cappella* at San Luigi, and Ruggiero Giovannelli turned out students with great success, which [students] being still living and very numerous I will leave off naming them for now.[102]

This is Giustiniani's main statement about Cardinal Montalto and his pivotal role in the history of solo singing and solo song in Rome and in Italy. The singers and composers whom he names have been identified and discussed in Chapter 2.

In the meantime, Giustiniani goes on to say, the polyphonic madrigal style of Gesualdo was developed further by Claudio Monteverdi, G. B. Nanino, Felice Anerio, and others. Then he finishes his brief chronological survey by concluding:

7. From all these things one can recognize what I said above, that is, that the style and manner of singing changes from time to time according to the different tastes of the great lords and princes who delight in it, just as with the style of dress, which constantly changes appearances according to what is introduced in the courts of great nobles: as for example, in Europe, dressing in the style of France or Spain.[103]

[102] 'Successe poi al Cardinal Ferdinando de' Medici il Cardinal Montalto, che niente meno di lui si dilettò della musica, perché di più sonava il Cimbalo egli per eccellenza, e cantava con maniera soave et affettuosa, e teneva in sua casa molti della professione che eccedevano la mediocrità, e tra gli altri il Cavaliere del Leuto e Scipione Dentici del Cimbalo, sonatori e compositori eccellenti, e poi Orazio sonatore raro d'Arpa doppia, e per cantare aveva Onofrio Gualfreducci eunuco, Ippolita napoletana, Melchior Basso, e molt'altri a' quali dava grosse provigioni. E con l'esempio di questi e di tutti gl'altri suddetti si ravvivò l'esercizio della musica, a segno che se ne sono dilettati poi molti Nipoti di Papi, et altri Cardinali e Prencipi; anzi tutti i Maestri di Cappella hanno intrapreso di ammaestrare diversi eunuchi, et altri putti a cantare con passaggi e con modi affettuosi e nuovi; tra quali Gio. Bernardino Nanino Maestro di Cappella in San Luigi, e Ruggero Giovannelli hanno fatto allievi di gran riuscita, che per esser vivi et in gran numero tralascio di nominare per ora.'

[103] 'E da tutte queste cose si viene chiaramente a conoscere quel che dissi di sopra: cioè che il modo e maniera di cantare si va di tanto in tanto variando alli varij gusti de' Signori e Prencipi grandi che se ne dilettano,

After this, he considers styles systematically and aesthetically, rather than historically.

In this systematic account, Giustiniani begins by explaining that there are national and regional vocal styles, which are reflected in various formulas (arie) for improvised singing of standard verse forms. For example, 'the *aria Romanesca* is unique and considered very beautiful, and it is sung everywhere with great delight, since it is exquisite and capable of receiving all sorts of ornaments and of being accompanied by [the harmony of] every mode with perfect ease'.[104] He goes on to mention local arie for Palermo, Messina, Catania, Siracusa, Genoa, Milan, Florence, Bergamo, Urbino, Ancona, Foligno, and Morcia.

Next, Giustiniani pays respect to the strict contrapuntal style that produces compositions in which every note is derived from a tightly unified motivic and thematic structure. Polyphonic compositions, however, are best if their material is easy, flowing, and melodious (*ariosa*). This melodious quality is especially necessary in 'arie da cantarsi ad una o poco più voci sopra stromenti', meaning continuo-accompanied strophic and largely syllabic settings of texts with regular patterns of rhyme and metre.

Aria and *grazia* are, for Giustiniani, the essential aesthetic qualities of vocal music of his time. With a long series of metaphors and analogies, he makes *grazia* seem the equivalent of Baldassare Castiglione's sprezzatura, 'apparently inborn spontaneity and relaxed self-confidence',[105] a term that enjoyed a great vogue during the sixteenth century and which, as mentioned earlier, Giulio Caccini used in the prefaces to his two printed monody collections (1602 and 1614) to describe the rhythmically free and spontaneous manner of singing that imitated the effect of the spoken language. Giustiniani's last examples are Cardinal Montalto, 'who played and sang with much *grazia* and *affetto*, although he had an appearance more martial than Apollonian, and who had a scratchy voice',[106] and Giulio Caccini, 'who . . . was practically the inventor of a new manner of singing'.[107]

After rehearsing some of the ancient myths of the miraculous powers of music (useful, at least, for entertaining conversation), Giustiniani describes the new styles of solo singing that had recently emerged in Italy:

---

appunto come segue nel modo di vestire, che si vanno sempre rinnovando le foggie, secondo che vengono introdotte nelle Corti de' grandi; come per esempio in Europa il vestire a modo di Francia e di Spagna.

[104] 'L'aria *Romanesca* è singolare e riputata bellissima e per tutto si canta con molto diletto, come esquisita e atta a ricevere ogni sorte di ornamento e accompagnata con ogni tuono e con gran facilità.'

[105] Pirrotta, *Music and Theatre*, 245–6.

[106] 'Sonava e cantava con molta gratia ed affetto, se bene aveva un aspetto più tosto martiale che apollineo, et una voce da scrivere, come si suole dire.' Cardinal Montalto evidently also played the lute, with which he might have accompanied his own singing, for on 17 Jan. 1604 he wrote to Cardinal Alessandro d'Este in Modena, thanking him for his advice concerning lute strings (Modena, Archivio di Stato, Marchionale poi Ducale Estense, Estero, Carteggio di Principi e Signore, Italia, Roma, Busta 150, under the date cited).

[107] 'e così anche Giulio Romano, che come ho detto fu quasi inventore d'una nuova maniera di cantare'.

8. In the present part of our age, music [i.e. musical training] is not much in use [by the upper classes], not being pursued in Rome by gentlemen, nor is it usual to sing polyphonically from books, as in bygone years, notwithstanding that it is a very good opportunity to unify and extend conversation. Indeed, music-making has been reduced to an unusual and almost novel perfection, being undertaken by a great number of good [professional] musicians, who, being trained by the abovesaid good masters, give much delight to those who hear, with their artful and smooth singing. For, having abandoned the past style, which was quite rough, and also the excessive passage work with which it was ornamented, they now cultivate, for the most part, a recitative style embellished by *grazia* and by ornaments appropriate to the conceit, along with an occasional melismatic passage drawn out with judgement and articulation, and with appropriate and varied consonances [above the bass part], marking the end of each period, within which the composers of today are [otherwise] apt to produce boredom with excessive and frequent cadences. Above all, they make the words well understood, applying to each syllable a note now soft, now loud, now slow, and now fast, demonstrating with their face and in their gestures the conceit that is sung, but with moderation and not excessively. And one voice or, at most, three voices sing to the accompaniment of one's own instrument: a theorbo, guitar, harpsichord, or organ, according to the circumstances. Furthermore, within this [recitative] style there has been introduced singing *alla spagnola* or *all' italiana*, similar to the foregoing but with more artifice and ornament, as much in Rome as in Naples and Genoa, with the invention of new arie and of new ornaments, for which composers strive, for instance in Rome the German theorbo player named Johann Hieronymus [Kapsberger].[108] In Naples [Antonio] Gutiérrez began [to sing in this style],[109] and his son Pietro, [Vincenzo?] Gallo,[110] and others followed. And in Genoa, a certain Cicco composes and sings excellently, giving great delight to those ladies in conversations and in evening parties, which are the custom there more than elsewhere.

This recitative style was already customary in [*sacre*] *rappresentazioni* sung by ladies in Rome, as even now is the case.[111] But it is performed so simply and without variety of consonances [above the bass] and of ornament that if the boredom felt were not

[108] Giustiniani undoubtedly refers to Kapsberger's books of *Arie passeggiate a una voce* (Rome, 1612) and *Mottetti passeggiati a una voce* (Rome, 1612).

[109] Giustiniani seems to be referring to Antonio Gutiérrez and his son Pedro. According to documents cited by Parisi, 'Ducal Patronage', 451–2, Antonio Gutiérrez was employed at the Mantuan court between 1594 and 1599, as well as on an unspecified earlier occasion. He also performed in his native Naples, Brussels, Modena, Florence, and the courts of the Prince of San Severo, Cardinal Montalto, and the Duke of Serra. He died at Naples in 1608. His son Pedro performed in all the same places. In August 1610 he sent Ferdinando Gonzaga in Mantua, from Naples, a dialogue in *stile recitativo*, which would seem to be the earliest use of that term (and precisely that style) in Naples. Putting this information together, it is possible to understand Giustiniani to mean that Antonio Gutiérrez introduced recitative singing in Naples during the 1590s, but there is, at this time, no evidence to corroborate this interpretation.

[110] Vincenzo Gallo was a Sicilian composer, *c.*1560–1624, whose two known madrigal collections are now considered lost. Another possibility is the Neapolitan harpist Domenico Gallo mentioned by Cerreto, *Della prattica musica vocale et strumentale*.

[111] Giustiniani is referring to the practice of using an aria formula to sing the stanzas of ottava rima, in which the traditional *sacra rappresentazione* was written. See Bianca Becherini, 'Un canta in panca fiorentino: Antonio di Guido', *Rivista musicale italiana*, 50 (1948), 241–7; and ead., 'La musica nelle "sacre rappresentazioni" fiorentine', *Rivista musicale italiana*, 53 (1951), 193–241.

moderated by the presence of those actresses, the audience would leave their benches and the hall would be completely empty.

Giulio [Caccini] Romano and Giuseppino [Cenci] were those, as I have mentioned above, who were almost the inventors [of recitative style], or at least they gave it good form. And then by degrees it has been perfected to the point where little more can be added to it in the future, having been introduced into the singing of the Latin verses of hymns and odes, even those full of holiness and devotion, with smoothness and great decorum, causing the conceits and the words to be heard well and with distinctness.[112]

One is struck, once again, by how Giustiniani's account of the emergence of recitative and related early Baroque monody styles differs from those offered in modern texts, which derive from the writings of Florentines, such as Giulio Caccini, Jacopo Peri, Ottavio Rinuccini, Marco da Gagliano, Severo Bonini, and Pietro de' Bardi.[113] However, the Florentine Giovanni Battista Doni absorbed something of the Roman point of view expressed by Giustiniani, when writing in that city (1635):

Much different, then, and somewhat contrary to [counterpoint] is solo singing, which is accompanied by some instrument, having returned, so to say, from death to life in this century, largely through the efforts of Giulio Caccini, called 'il Romano', but with the help and direction of those virtuous Florentine academy members, as I have more

---

[112] 'Nel presente corso dell'età nostra, la musica non è molto in uso, in Roma non essendo esercitata da gentil uomini, nè si suole cantare a più voci al libro, come per gl'anni a dietro, non ostante che sia grandissime occasioni d'unire e di trasmettere le conversazioni. È ben la musica ridotta in un'insolita e quasi nuova perfezione, venendo esercitata da gran numero de' buoni musici, che disciplinati dalli suddetti buoni maestri porgono col canto loro artificioso e soave molto diletto a chi li sente. Perché avendo lasciato lo stile passato, che era assai rozzo, et anche li soverchi passggi con li quali si ornava, attendono ora per lo più ad uno stile recitativo ornato di grazia et ornamenti appropriati al concetto, con qualche passaggio di tanto in tanto tirato con giudizio e spiccato, e con appropriate e variate consonanze, dando segno del fine di ciascun periodo, nel che li compositori d'oggi dì con le soverchie et frequentate cadenze sogliono arrecar noia; e sopra tutto con far bene intendere le parole, applicando ad ogni sillaba una nota or piano, or forte, or adagio, or presto, mostrando nel viso e nei gesti segno del concetto che si canta, ma con moderazione e non soverchi. E si canta a una o al più 3 voci concertate con istrumenti proprii di Tiorba o Chitarra o Cimbalo o con Organo, secondo le congiunture; e di più in questo stile si è introdotto a cantare o alla spagnola o all'italiana, a quella simile ma con maggior artificio e ornamento, tanto in Roma, come in Napoli e Genova, con invenzioni nuove dell'arie e de gli ornamenti; nel che premono i compositori, come in Roma il Todesco della Tiorba nominato Gio. Geronimo. In Napoli cominciò il Gutierrez, e poi hanno seguitato Pietro suo figlio e Gallo et altri; et in Genova un tal Cicco per eccellenza compone e canta, porgendo gran diletto a quelle signore nelle conversazioni e nelle veglie, ch'ivi più che altrove si costumano.

Questo stile recitativo già era solito nelle rappresentazioni cantate dalle donne in Roma, come or anche è in uso; ma riesce tanto rozzo e senza varietà di consonanze nè d'ornamenti, che se non venisse moderata la noia che si sente dalla presenza di quelle recitanti, l'auditorio lascierebbe li banchi e la stanza vuoti affatto.

Giulio Romano e Giuseppino furono quelli, come ho di sopra accennato, che quasi furono gl'inventori, o almeno che le diedero la buona forma, e poi di mano in mano s'è andato perfezionato a segno, che poco più oltre pare che per l'avvenire possa aggiungere, essendosi anche introdotto a cantare versi latini in inni et ode anche piene di santità e devozione, con soavità e gran decoro, e con far sentir bene e spiccati li concetti e le parole.'

Giustiniani next mentions that church music is no longer strictly contrapuntal, as in previous times, but ornamented and concerted with several choirs of voices and instruments. He concludes with an account of instruments in use, with names of outstanding performers.

[113] For the original texts, see Solerti, *Le origini del melodramma*.

amply explained in my *Trattato della musica* and as he himself confesses. The improvement in this sort of melody that music has produced is quite notable, since, in addition to the artifice of the compositions (which, in the case of Caccini, was expected somewhat more, at first, than was produced), there have been set theatrical dramas and non-theatrical dialogues, which delight extremely in their style called *recitativo*. And the quality of expression (a very important part of practical music) has been refined greatly, and its decorum has been increased through reduction of those repeated notes and through the perfection of the ornaments of this [recitative] singing, that is, through accents, melismas, trills, turns, and so on, first through the efforts of the said Caccini and then through the experiments and just aims of other singers, mostly of this city [Rome], and particularly Giuseppe Cenci, called 'Giuseppino'.[114]

A letter written during Giuseppino's lifetime (28.viii.1607), briefly mentioned in the previous chapter, seems to support the claims of Giustiniani and Doni regarding Giuseppino's historical position:

Don Ippolito [Macchiavelli], excellent musician from Bologna, who previously was in the service of the late Cardinal [Facchinetti] of S. Quattro and who is now in the service of Cardinal Montalto, is considered to be the first after Sig. Giuseppino. He has given me the enclosed new madrigal, which here is judged to be very beautiful. For that reason I send it to Your Illustrious Lordship. The truth is that the arias of Rome, here, succeed better when heard sung than when written down.

The antiquity of the aria and of the words of the Romanescas that I sent you cannot be expunged. Sig. Giuseppino, who is the author of them, removed their other imperfections in [the act of] writing them down for me in his own hand, as is the case with the other aria that I sent, which begins 'Vezzosetta pastorella'.[115]

Giuseppino's monodies were being collected vigorously in 1604 by the Roman agent of Duke Vincenzo Gonzaga of Mantua, in spite of Monteverdi's availability at his court,[116] and these efforts continued in 1607.[117]

In conformity with Giustiniani's narration, Pietro Della Valle, another Roman

---

[114] 'Molto diverso poi, & quasi contrario à questo [contrappunto], è il Canto d'una Voce sola, che s'accompagna col suono di qualche instrumento: ritornato si può dire, da morte à vita in questo secolo; per opra massimamente di Giulio Caccini, detto il Romano; ma con la scorta & indirizzo di quei virtuosi Accademici Fiorentini; come nel Trattato della Musica Scenica, più ampiamente ho discorso, & egli medesimo confessa. Il miglioramento che ha fatto la Musica per questa sorte di Melodie, è molto notabile: poiche oltre la finezza de' Componimenti (alla quale, ad esempio del Caccini s'è atteso alquanto più che prima non si faceva) vi si sono modulate attioni Sceniche, e Dialoghi fuor di Scena; che dilettano grandemente nello stile detto Recitativo: & la qualità dell'espressione (parte molto importante nella Musica operativa) s'è raffinata assai: e cresciuto il decoro, col risecamento di molte di quelle Repliche; e perfettionati gl'ornamenti di esso Canto; che sono gl'accenti, passaggi, trilli, gorgheggiamenti, e simili; prima per l'industria del medesimo Caccini; e poi per l'esperienza, e buona dispositione d'altri Cantori, per lo più di questa città, & particolarmente di Giuseppe Cenci detto Giuseppino.' Giovanni Battista Doni, 'Discorso sopra la perfettione delle melodie', in his *Compendio del trattato de' generi e de' modi della musica* (Rome, 1635), 100–1.

[115] Bernardo Bizzoni (Rome) to Enzo Bentivoglio (Ferrara); App. A, Letter 24.

[116] Ademollo, *La bell'Adriana*, 40–1.

[117] Parisi, 'Ducal Patronage', 561, transcribes a letter to that effect written 4 Aug. 1607 by the singer Francesco Campagnolo, who had been sent to Rome to learn the local styles, develop his reputation, and gather monodies.

contemporary, places Giuseppino's main activities, at least as a singer, in the 1590s. Della Valle's treatise[118] is dated 16 January 1640 at its conclusion, and the point of departure of his narrative is 'la musica da cinquanta anni in qua', which means about 1590. He begins his discussion of singing (Solerti, 161) with a reference to a falsettist, Lodovico, whom he had heard as a boy (Della Valle was born in 1586). He places Giuseppino's activity 'nell'istesso tempo, o poco dopo' and claims that the singing of Giuseppino and his contemporaries (e.g. Melchior Palantrotti, Giovanni Luca Conforti, and 'Orazietto') lacked expressivity (Solerti, 162), which was introduced in Rome when Emilio de' Cavalieri transferred the Florentine style there, presumably with his *Rappresentatione* of 1600, at the first performance of which Della Valle claims to have been present (Solerti, 163). Giovanni Battista Doni, as we have seen, identified Giuseppino as the papal singer Giuseppe Cenci, who died in 1616, and unpublished documents tend to confirm that identification, as discussed in Chapter 2.

Only seven works by this composer have been previously known: a strophic canzonetta in the Barbera manuscript ascribed to 'Giuseppino',[119] three solo madrigals by 'Giuseppino' preserved as polyphonic arrangements by Pietro Marsolo, of which only one could be reconstructed as a monody—although it never has been[120]—and three compositions posthumously ascribed to Giuseppe Cenci in printed anthologies of the 1620s.[121] However, among the monody manuscripts uncovered in the course of this research, there are eight additional works ascribed to Giuseppino. Altogether, among the fifteen works of Giuseppino now known, there are seven strophic variations, four solo madrigals, two dialogues, one strophic canzonetta, and one strophic duet (see Table 3.1). The prominence

---

[118] *Della musica dell'età nostro* . . . ; modern edition in Solerti, *L'origine del melodramma*, 148–79.

[119] *Fuggi, fuggi da questo cielo.* See Federico Ghisi, 'An Early Seventeenth Century Manuscript with Unpublished Monodic Music by Peri, Giulio Romano and Marco da Gagliano', *Acta musicologica*, 20 (1948), 46–60. An unreported lute intabulation of this canzonetta is in Brescia, Private Collection Franchi, MS without call number, 15. A description of this manuscript, without concordances, is found in Victor Anand Coelho, 'The Manuscript Sources of Seventeenth-Century Italian Lute Music: A "Catalogue Raisonné" ' (Ph.D. diss., University of California at Los Angeles, 1989), 32–3, 143–50. Further, see Luigi Ferdinando Tagliavini, 'Il Ballo di Mantova, ovvero "Fuggi, fuggi da questo cielo," ovvero "Cecilia," ovvero . . .', in Bernhard Hangartner and Urs Fischer (eds.), *Max Lütolf zum 60. Geburtstag: Festschrift* (Basle, 1994), 135–75.

[120] *Ahi com'a un vago sol cortese giro*, 'sopra l'aria di Gioseppino'; *Occhi un tempo mia vita*, 'sopra l'aria di Gioseppino'; and *Occhi ch'alla mia vita*, 'aria di Gioseppino'. Only the last of these could be reconstructed from Marsolo's arrangement. The other two survive as anonymous monodies in manuscripts never before described in the scholarly literature: *Ahi com'a un vago sol cortese giro* in US:PHu, MS Ital. 57, fos. 9ᵛ–10ᵛ; and *Occhi un tempo mia vita* in I:Bc, Q27.4, fo. 124ʳ. A comparison between Marsolo's arrangement and the original monodic version of these two madrigals shows sufficient communality of material to establish the connection between the versions but enough difference to demonstrate that the monody could never have been reconstructed from the polyphonic arrangement.

[121] *Più non amo più non ardo* and *Se perche à voi mi tolga* in *Raccolta de varii concerti musicali a una et due voci*, comp. Giovanni Battista Robletti (Rome: Robletti, 1621); and *Vita della mia vita egl'è pur vero* in *Le risonanti sfere da velocissimi ingegni armonicamente raggirate*, comp. Giovanni Battista Robletti (Rome: Robletti, 1629). The first and last of these are also found, unascribed, in USA:PHu, MS Ital. 57, as was the madrigal by 'Giuseppino' mentioned in the previous note. This is a circumstance that tends to lend support to Doni's identification of Giuseppino with Giuseppe Cenci.

TABLE 3.1. Compositions by Giuseppino Cenci

Incipit	Sources	Genre	Edition (Vol. II)
Ahi com'a un vago sol cortese	US:PHu, MS Ital. 57, fos. 9ᵛ–10ᵛ; Marsolo, *Secondo libro dei madrigali* (1614) ('sopra l'aria di Gioseppino')	solo madrigal	no. 101
Amorosa Licori	I:Vc, Torrefranca 250, fos. 29ᵛ–34ʳ ('Giuseppino'); I:Baf, MS 1424, fos. 35ᵛ–42ʳ; I:Ru, MS 279, fos. 37ᵛ–44ᵛ; *Il maggio fiorito* (1623)	dialogue	no. 10
Anima bella che nel sen ten stai	I:Vc, Torrefranca 250, fos. 53ᵛ–56 ('Giuseppino'); I:Baf, MS 1424, fos. 5ᵛ–9ʳ ('Giuseppino'); I:Ru, MS 279, fos. 17ʳ–20ᵛ; I:MOe, Mus. E 318, fos. 7ᵛ–9ʳ	strophic variations	no. 17
Deh dolc'anima mia	I:Vc, Torrefranca 250, fos. 87ᵛ–88ʳ ('Giuseppino')	solo madrigal	no. 33
Dunque Clorida mia per questi prati	I:Vc, Torrefranca 250, fos. 62ᵛ–66ʳ ('Giuseppino'); I:Baf, MS 1424, fos. 1ᵛ–5ʳ ('Giuseppino')	strophic variations	no. 19
Fuggi, fuggi da questo cielo	I:Fc, MS Barbera, fo. 158ʳ ('Giuseppino'); Brescia, Private Collection Franchi, MS s.s., fo. 15 (lute intabulation)	strophic canzonetta	no. 157
Io che l'età solea viver nel fango	I:Vc, Torrefranca 250, fos. 48ᵛ–51ʳ ('Giuseppino'); I:Baf, MS 1424, fos. 29ᵛ–32ʳ ('Giuseppino')	strophic variations	no. 15
Leggiadri occhi sereni	I:Baf, MS 1424, fos. 9ᵛ–13ʳ ('Giuseppino'); I:Bc, CC.225, fos. 24ᵛ–27ʳ ('Giuseppino'); US:PHu, MS Ital. 57, fos. 22ᵛ–24ʳ; I:MOe, Mus. E 318, fos. 11ᵛ–13ʳ	strophic variations	no. 49
Occhi ch'alla mia vita	Marsolo, *Secondo libro* (1614) ('aria di Gioseppino')	solo madrigal	no. 155
Occhi un tempo mia vita	I:Bc, Q27.4, fos. 124ᵛ–125ʳ Marsolo, *Secondo libro* (1614) ('sopra l'aria di Gioseppino'); GB:Lbm, Add. 36877, fo. 36ʳ	solo madrigal (Guarini)	no. 154
Perché non togli o Clori i pesci al fiume	I:Vc, Torrefranca 250, fos. 41ᵛ–45ʳ ('Giuseppino'); I:Baf, MS 1424, fos. 42ᵛ–46ʳ ('Giuseppino'); Costantini, comp., *Ghirlandetta amorosa* (1621) ('Paolo Quagliati')	dialogue	no. 13
Più non amo più non ardo	Robletti, comp., *Raccolta de varii concerti musicali a una e due voci* (1621) ('Giuseppe Cenci'); US:PHu, MS Ital. 57, fos. 25ᵛ–26ʳ	strophic duet	no. 148
Se 'l dolce sguardo di costei m'ancide	I:Baf, MS 1424, fos. 50ᵛ–53ʳ ('Giuseppino')	strophic variations	no. 84
Se perché voi mi tolga	Robletti, comp., *Raccolta de varii concerti* ('Giuseppe Cenci')	strophic variations	no. 153
Vita della mia vita egl'è pur vero	Robletti, comp., *Le risonanti sfere* (1629) ('Giuseppe Cenci'); US:PHu, MS Ital. 57, fos. 16ᵛ–17ᵛ	octave set as strophic variations	no. 156

of strophic variations in this distribution is typical of Roman monody repertoires of the early seventeenth century: we have already seen that strophic variations reflect the sixteenth-century Neapolitan–Roman tradition of performing aria formulas with either extended embellishment, recitational sprezzatura, or both in alternation or opposition. With this repertoire in hand, it is possible to comment to some degree on the monodies of this nearly legendary figure.

Unfortunately, none of Giuseppino's works preserved in manuscript can be securely dated to the 1590s, the period of his major activity, according to comtemporaneous commentary. (The chapter on *Il pastor fido* will present circumstantial evidence that one of his solo madrigals, *Deh dolc'anima mia*, may have been composed for the performance of Guarini's pastorale given at the villa of Giuseppino's patron, Cardinal Odoardo Farnese, in 1596.) Inasmuch as Giuseppino died in 1616, assessing the style of his pre-1600 monodies on the basis of the surviving repertoire is much like judging Caccini's early works on the basis of the 1614 *Nuove musiche*: we know that some of the works must be early ones, but we cannot be entirely sure which ones they are. In any case, the surviving works as a whole do offer a general stylistic profile that can be compared with Caccini's.

The surviving work by Giuseppino that appears, by its format and notation, to be the least modern (and, therefore, perhaps the oldest) is the two-voice (tenor and bass) madrigal *Occhi un tempo mia vita*, on a text by Battista Guarini. It is preserved in two partbooks (labelled 'canto' and 'basso') that contain, among other things, several works by Giulio Caccini that are notated in other sources for solo voice and basso continuo, although they, like all the other pieces designated in this manuscript as 'a due', have bass voices that are texted and not figured. These works by Caccini and Giuseppino are, therefore, preserved here in a notational format that is no different from the one used in late sixteenth-century collections of two-voice madrigals and villanelle.

In its two-voice version (Vol. II, no. 153), Giuseppino's *Occhi un tempo mia vita* could be taken for a reduction of a four-voice, homophonic madrigal of a type that can be found scattered around the repertoire during most of the madrigal's history. The amount of monotone recitation and the texted fusae, of course, tend to place the work in the last two decades of the sixteenth century.

This madrigal is also preserved as a text with alphabetic guitar tablature but without staff notation for the voice part.[122] In Ex. 3.12 these guitar chords have been joined with the upper (tenor) vocal line from the two-voice version. The chords indicated by the tablature concord with the vocal line in all but two places, which have been adjusted to fit and are indicated by brackets in

---

[122] In GB:Lbm, Add. 36877, fo. 36ʳ. This manuscript will be discussed in Chapter 5.

Ex. 3.12. Giuseppino Cenci, *Occhi un tempo mia vita*, with guitar accompaniment

Ex. 3.12. Cont'd

the example. There are, however, many places where the guitar chords do not accord with the bass vocal line, certainly indicating that the chords were not intended to accompany the two-voice form of the madrigal that we know but rather, probably, a solo-voice performance of it. The reconstructed solo madrigal with guitar accompaniment is strikingly different from the two-voice version because of its much slower harmonic rhythm, which seems almost magically to transform the work from a homophonic madrigal into an early form of recitative. We do not know the history of this guitar accompaniment, but the two versions of this madrigal certainly are suggestive of a role for the Spanish guitar in the emergence of monody, as suggested earlier in this chapter.

Giustiniani claimed that Giuseppino was co-inventor, with Caccini, of the recitative style. *Occhi un tempo mia vita*, when sung by a solo voice with the guitar accompaniment, certainly illustrates that claim, although it cannot prove it. We can test the claim further by searching for other examples of recitative style in Giuseppino's known works.

The most purely recitational of Giuseppino's works is the dialogue *Perché non togli o Clori i pesci al fiume* (Vol. II, no. 13).[123] Here, the amount of monotone recitation and static bass exceeds that which is found in Caccini's *Perfidissimo volto*, the most recitational of his madrigals and one of the three that he claims were composed as early as 1585. But if it is unfair to compare a dialogue with a madrigal,[124] consider Giuseppino's madrigal *Occhi ch'alla mia vita* (Vol. II, no. 154). In this mostly syllabic and frequently monotone madrigal, each verse is limited to the range of a fourth. A similar style is found in the strophic variations *Se 'l dolce sguardo di costei m'ancide* (Vol. II, no. 84). In contrast to Caccini's recitational madrigals, however, all three of these examples, and Giuseppino's monodies generally, reflect less *sprezzatura di canto* in their narrower rhythmic range of syllabication—no syllables set to semifusae and less exaggerated difference between accented and unaccented syllables within a phrase—and they have less specifically *seconda prattica* dissonance treatment. Of course, Jacopo Peri revolutionized Florentine recitative style during the 1590s, but apart from Monteverdi, who followed Peri's lead rather closely, the majority of early operatic recitative elsewhere,

---

[123] I:Vc, Torrefranca 250, fos. 41ᵛ–45ʳ; and I:Baf, MS 1424, fos. 42ᵛ–46ʳ. These two manuscripts derive from materials once in the private collection Cardinal Montalto, as I will argue in Ch. 5. The same dialogue is ascribed to Paolo Quagliati in the anthology *Ghirlandetta amorosa*, comp. Fabio Costantini (Orvieto: Fei & Ruuli, 1621). From 1605 to 1608 Quagliati was in the service of Cardinal Odoardo Farnese, a period overlapping with Giuseppe Cenci's service in the same household, 1598–1608. At the time the *Ghirlandetta* was published, Quagliati, who died in 1628, was still living, while Giuseppe Cenci, who died in 1616, was not in a position to defend his authorship of this dialogue. Although there are other works by Giuseppino that use a similar recitative style, there are none comparable among Quagliati's other known works. These are the reasons why I favour the ascription of *Perché non togli o Clori i pesci al fiume* to Giuseppino.

[124] Although dialogues are not inevitably recitational in style. Giuseppino's other dialogue, *Amorosa Licori*, in *Il maggio fiorito* is set entirely in a metrical canzonetta style.

certainly in Rome, adheres father more to the rhythmically simpler and contrapuntally more moderate style exemplified in Giuseppino's monodies.

Of particular interest in Giuseppino's works, at least from the perspective of his Roman successors, is the contrast between recitational and cantillational styles incorporated into such works as *Io che l'età solea viver nel fango* (Vol. II, no. 15) and *Anima bella che nel sen ten stai* (Vol. II, no. 17). In *Io che l'età*, the recitational style of the first three verses of the sonnet is relieved in bar 16 by the measured, scalewise descent in the vocal line and the sequentially patterned bass, which supports ornamental divisions upon its repetition. Here, the contrast of style does not seem to be motivated by the text. Instead, the antithesis that occurs between lines 2 and 3 of the first quatrain is underscored in bar 6 by a shift in harmony—a mutation that illustrates the words 'hoggi mutato il cor'. And in Parts 2 and 3 of the sonnet, the shift to melismatic ornamentation occurs progressively earlier, only to return to the shape of Part 1 in the final Part 4. In fact, it could be argued that, notwithstanding the fact that all four *parti* are built upon the same bass, only Parts 1 and 4 contain substantial sections of recitative style, while Parts 2 and 3 are mostly given over to ornamental arioso and metrical aria styles. Thus, the three principal styles found in early strophic variations—recitational, ornamental arioso, and metrical aria—are contrasted here; and the contrast is deployed even more between strophes than within them. Giulio Caccini's 1614 setting of the same text contains no comparable contrast of recitational and cantillational styles, as ornamental passaggi abound in all parts of each variation. The only similar case in early strophic variations that I know of is the anonymous sonnet *Passer mai solitario in alcun tetto* in the Florentine manuscript anthology Brussels 704, as mentioned in William Porter's dissertation.[125] This contrast of recitational and two kinds of cantillational style between variations—juxtaposing *stil recitativo, e cantativo* through various renditions of an aria—is fraught with implications that will be explored in Chapter 6, where the argument begun in this chapter will be completed. For now, I can offer four intermediate conclusions:

1. Florentine and Roman monody and recitative styles are based, at least remotely, on common traditions of composition and performance that are revealed in activities centred in Naples and Rome. The three principal features of these traditions are (i) the spontaneous alteration of rational, measured rhythm to create a recitational style mid-way between speech and song, (ii) the improvisational addition of ornamental passaggi, and (iii) a form of chordal accompaniment that abstracts underlying harmony. This form of accompaniment was derived from basso seguente practices, was established fundamentally in the

---

[125] William Vernon Porter, 'The Origins of the Baroque Solo Song: A Study of Italian Manuscripts and Prints from 1590–1610' (Ph.D. diss., Yale University, 1962), 209.

Spanish–Neapolitan style of strummed guitar accompaniment, and was crystallized in basso continuo notation.

2. Unlike Caccini's earliest monody, the earliest written vocal solos with basso continuo from the Rome–Naples orbit reveal traces of a rhythmic style closely associated with developments in the madrigal that unfolded, from Macque to Marenzio and Giovannelli, in those two cities after Caccini moved from Rome to Florence; thus, the earliest Roman monody transmitted some aspects of its musical ancestry independently of influence from Caccini.

3. Using the rhythmic style of the Roman and Neapolitan madrigal, vocal lines that create or parallel rhetorical figures in the text are more characteristic of the earliest Roman monodies than of Caccini's early works.

4. Large-scale contrast between recitational and two kinds of cantillational style appears to be native to Roman and not to Florentine monody.

4

Quanto sia difficile questo cantare solo

༒

THE previous chapter established that to a great extent Italian monody emerged in the decades surrounding the year 1600 out of a process of reducing to musical notation features of accompanied solo singing that had grown out of unwritten performance traditions. These features were principally embellishment, especially by the overlay of melismatic divisions or passaggi; *sprezzatura di canto*, which resulted in rhythms thought to reflect those of common or heightened speech; and accompaniment by an instrumentally conceived, harmonically oriented basso continuo, which represented by means of abbreviated staff notation the relatively slow and simplified progression of chords that had for some time been produced by *rasgueado* technique on the Spanish guitar. We may hypothesize several reasons why this transference from unwritten to written means occurred.

1. Composers like Giulio Caccini wished to take control of these features, thereby improving and refining them for new aesthetic purposes then being embraced by musicians and their patrons. Caccini's preface to *Le nuove musiche* offers this explanation.

2. Solo singers trained in the older unwritten traditions had become rare by the end of the sixteenth century, and in any case they were probably not accustomed, in general, to the restrictions and requirements of written passaggi and recitative style, if indeed they could read music at all. They would be, therefore, of little use in achieving the goal stated under Point 1. On the other hand, musicians trained only for polyphonic music probably lacked the ability to take suitable liberties with the written rhythms of older music, to add acceptable improvised ornamental passage work, and to shade the voice in dramatically expressive ways. One solution to these problems obviously was to reduce these characteristics and subtleties of the unwritten tradition to notation from which polyphonic singers could perform. But even with the aid of the newer notational practices, singers capable of performing the various forms of cantillational and

recitational solo vocal music remained difficult to find for a full generation after the emergence of written monody. This difficulty has already been illustrated in Chapter 2 by the narration of Cardinal Montalto's recruiting efforts, and further evidence will be presented in this chapter.

3. Patrons became interested in advertising the abilities of their virtuoso singers beyond the circle of those able and permitted to hear and see them. The printing of music for intermedi and early operas, which seem not intended principally to promote further performances of these works, suggests this motive. The printed music, thus, served a purpose similar to the published description and libretto.

However, in spite of the emergence of written monody, unwritten traditions of solo singing did not suddenly disappear at the beginning of the seventeenth century. In this chapter we shall see that, in Rome, training in techniques of improvisation were conjoined with notation-based instruction in the preparation of young singers well into the seventeenth century. The evidence to be presented here suggests that these unwritten traditions were continued and preserved because even the newer kind of more specific notation pioneered by Giulio Caccini was considered inadequate to convey fully the impression of spontaneity, which was a major aesthetic goal in early monody. And to some extent, too, the more specific notation was not readily embraced in Rome, where the improvisational aspects of singing were perhaps more deeply rooted than in Florence and therefore maintained their prestige longer. Hence, Bernardo Bizzoni wrote from Rome to Enzo Bentivoglio (28.viii.1607): 'The truth is that arias of Rome, here, succeed better when heard sung than when written down' (Letter 24). This implies that Roman arias did not specify details in notation as completely as, say, Florentine arias did. On the other hand, we shall see that the ornamental passages written into some early Roman monodies from Cardinal Montalto's circles often seem to be transcriptions of improvisations or reminders for novice singers of embellishments customarily left to the performer by Roman *maestri*—instances of the latter are documented in letters.

The information to be presented here about singers in Rome and their various uses of notated and unnotated details comes from letters written between 1612 and 1616 to Enzo Bentivoglio, who produced a series of musical spectacles in Ferrara during those years, culminating with the intermedi that are the subject of Chapter 8. Bentivoglio used his connections with Cardinals Montalto and Borghese both to recruit singers who were already trained and to enlist Roman *maestri* in crash programmes of instructing beginners.

Bentivoglio managed to borrow at least two singers from Cardinal Montalto's household: Don Pietro Antonio Tamburini for the *torneo* of 1612 or 1614 (Letter

110) and Ippolita Recupito some time in 1615 (as we may infer from the reference to Cesare Marotta's visit in Letter 94). But usually it proved impossible to obtain completely formed, virtuoso singers for his stage works. The comical story of Bentivoglio's attempts to recruit a castrato by the name of Cesare illustrates both the range of honest and dishonest strategies that were employed and the powerful reasons that prevented an established singer from leaving Rome.

We first hear of Cesare in a letter to Bentivoglio of 20 June 1615 from his Roman agent Girolamo Fioretti:

As for Cesare, the castrato at [the church of] San Giovanni [Laterano],[1] he replied in the negative to Signor Ottavio Catalano, although the same Signor Catalano then told Signor Landinelli that the young man had said that he wanted to think about it. However, Cavalier Marotta decided that he should speak with him about it with me, which we have done, but without any profit at all, even though we told him that no one more than Your Most Illustrious Lordship could help him attain the place in the [Sistine] Chapel, to which he aspires, and that he should think carefully before displeasing Signor Catalano, who asked him almost as a favour to come to serve Your Most Illustrious Lordship, showing him how he is very beholden to the said Signor Catalano and that he could hope for new benefices, in addition to the advantages that he would have as a result of Your Most Illustrious Lordship's favours and gifts, and a thousand other things. I also told him that I am staying in Rome by orders of Your Most Illustrious Lordship only to carry on this negotiation with him, because you know that there is a very close friendship between us, and that, because of that, you have judged that he could be more easily induced to come to Ferrara where we would be happily in company. And at the time I described for him a thousand delights that he would have in that fellowship, always adding that he would have higher earnings there than in Rome. Finally, neither Cavalier [Marotta] nor I were able to draw out from his mouth any response other than that he was very intent in not wishing to leave Rome, and he was astonished that we were trying to persuade him to do the contrary. I left him, saying that I did not wish to accept this veto and that Cavalier [Marotta] would write to Your Most Illustrious Lordship that he wanted to think about it, just as Signor Catalano had said, although he denied that at once and maintained that he had also given the latter a negative reply. Cavalier [Marotta] ordered me to write to Your Most Illustrious Lordship [describing] everything that is taking place, adding that he is certain that the young man will not want to leave Rome. And I believe it because I have information that he lives, we might say, a disordered life, keeping company with certain people who are entirely given up to greed and lust. Actually he himself confessed to Cavalier [Marotta] and me that he is in love with a young lady in such a way that he does not think he could live for one hour far away from her. Your Most Illustrious Lordship may consider to what state Cupid is reduced if he gets mixed up with castrati. In

---

[1] If the church truly is San Giovanni Laterano, then the singer in question must be Cesare Puntirolo, who joined that chapel as a boy singer on 1 May 1593. See Raffaele Casimiri, *Cantori, maestri, organisti della Cappella Lateranense negli atti capitolari (sec. XV–XVII)*, ed. Laura Callegari [Hill] (Biblioteca di 'Quadrivium', Note d'Archivio: Bibliografia, biografia e storia, 6; Bologna, 1984), 113.

conclusion, it has been decided to have him speak again with Signor Catalano, considering that Signor Landinelli does not provide such a good means in this business, since, as Your Most Illustrious Lordship knows very well, he sought many times to turn your intentions away from such expenses as he judged amounted to throwing money into the sea. In the meantime, we shall be attentive to Your Most Illustrious Lordship's commands, begging you to believe that every effort is being made so that you will be served in this matter, since you have reminded us of the obligation that we have to obey you with all faith and diligence (Letter 90).

In fact, Cesare Marotta wrote to Bentivoglio that same day, but not with the falsely encouraging report that Fioretti requested of him:

I have told Signor Girolamo [Fioretti] that he should give Your Most Illustrious Lordship an account of what we have negotiated with the castrato, who does not wish to come in any way. And both Signor Girolamo and I have said that we might as well have converted a stone. Notwithstanding that, we shall not fail to speak with him again together with Signor Ottavio Catalano, and we shall do everything possible so that Your Most Illustrious Lordship is served. I have not discussed this with Signor Landinelli both because he has a thousand other matters on his mind and because I recognize that he is not in favour of Your Most Illustrious Lordship doing these things (Letter 91).

It was eighteen days before Fioretti reported again to Bentivoglio on this matter on 8 July 1615, by now trying to portray Cesare in a negative light so as to discourage the marquis from further efforts:

As for the castrato, I have made every effort to make him submit to Your Most Illustrious Lordship's wishes, but the matter is desperate because this beast is so arrogant that even if he were the first [ranking] man in the world he would not say such impertinent things, not recognizing the opportunity and his risk. In the end, he has no other merit than that little bit of voice accompanied by a thousand vices, so that certainly in a short time Your Most Illustrious Lordship would be disgusted with him. And then as far as that goes, it you want him to be of use, he has need both of a teacher and of everything else that he might sing there, because he is accustomed to singing the *Kyrie eleison* like a madman without taking into account any restraint (Letter 92).

The last sentence in this quotation requires some explanation. Fioretti is claiming that Cesare has no repertoire of pieces that could be worked into a stage production, as seems to have been Bentivoglio's practice (see Ch. 8). He would need to be provided with pieces, and they would have to be taught to him. 'Singing the *Kyrie eleison* like a madman without taking into account any restraint' seems to refer to the kind of improvised *contrappunto in compagnia*, sometimes called *sortisatio*, in which several singers in an ensemble extemporized simultaneously on the basis of a chant cantus firmus that was seen in notation, hence *cantare super librum*, as Tinctoris called it.[2] This sort of florid improvised counterpoint was widely criticized in late sixteenth-century treatises because it often violated the 'restraints' of written counterpoint, but it nevertheless had its enthusiastic adherents, even among music theorists.[3] Mastery of the technique had been required of singers auditioning for the papal chapel since 1545,[4] and Adriano Banchieri reported in 1614 that it was still used there and in innumerable other Italian chapels.[5]

By 22 July 1615 matters had become so urgent that Fioretti was willing to try outright deception in order to induce Cesare to come to Ferrara, ostensibly for a short visit:

I resolved to give a new assault to Cesare, which I did today, assailing him suddenly with the ploy of having new instructions from Your Most Illustrious Lordship to ask him that since he does not wish to go to serve you, at least he should want to oblige you by doing the service of singing in this occasion of the play, which you wish to do in the space of a few days, for which effect Your Most Illustrious Lordship promised to regale him in a manner that would make him content and that he would be paid travelling expenses. To this he again gave me the usual negative reply, saying that he does not wish to leave Rome, neither for a little while nor for a long period. Once I heard that, I added, almost with resentment, that I had express orders if he did not want to reach an agreement that I should have recourse to the Abbot Pignattelli, who, in addition to the authority that he has over [Cesare] as Canon of San Giovanni [Laterano], would have had also Cardinal Borghese command him, and thus Your Most Illustrious Lordship would have had your wish without having any obligation towards him. These words made him put his brain into action, so that he decided to promise that for this occasion he would come if I would obtain leave for him from the Chapter, which I immediately promised to do, or rather even more, that I would obtain from the Chapter itself the assurance that upon his return he would have the same place in that chapel that he has at present. Signor Ottavio Catalano, who had earlier been informed as to what I wanted to accomplish, additionally promised Cesare that upon his return, if he were not immediately given a salary, he would keep him in his house at his expense and wanted that I promise him to have him given that which he would have earned in that chapel, until he was accommodated. I was content to agree, knowing that once Your Most Illustrious Lordship has him there you will not let him leave, and in any case Signor Pignattelli would provide for him immediately at the request of Your Most Illustrious Lordship. It remained, then, to speak with a Canon called Signor Rodolfini, who protects Cesare to a very great

[2] Johannes Tinctoris, *Liber de arte contrapuncti* (1477), II. xx.

[3] The controversy is summarized by Ernest T. Ferand, '"Sodaine and Unexpected" Music in the Renaissance', *Musical Quarterly*, 37 (1951), 10–27; and Ferand, 'Improvised Vocal Counterpoint in the Late Renaissance and Early Baroque', *Annales musicologiques*, 4 (1956), 129–74.

[4] Ernest T. Ferand, *Die Improvisation in der Musik* (Zürich, 1938), 195–6.

[5] Adriano Banchieri, *Cartella musicale nel canto figurato fermo et contrapunto* (3rd edn., Venice: Vincenti, 1614), 230.

extent. They are closer than brothers, and that is enough. We went to find him in the congregation, and we begged him to concur in order to give this satisfaction to Your Most Illustrious Lordship, adding, as much as it seemed to me necessary to tell him, that you are also beloved by Cardinal Borghese, telling him of your greatness, and many other details. He made several objections, which I refuted expertly, but I could not yet overcome the difficulty that he raised, saying that as far as it was up to him, he would not suggest nor would want in any way that [Cesare] leave Rome before the end of Leo [22 August]. I replied to him as best I could, citing the example of Cavalier Marotta, who had returned from there to Rome, but finally no argument availed, since the negotiation could not conclude in any other manner than it being promised that Cesare would come to serve Your Most Illustrious Lordship in the occasion of the play and would take up his journey at the first rain of August. Thus we made a commitment. And I used this trick to send him there, since it seemed to me that I could not find a better way of serving you. Now it remains for you to write a letter to the Abbot Pignattelli crediting me for this agreement so that [Cesare] can have his leave, and in this matter I ask you to recommend me to him warmly but as your servant, not being able to do things in any other way, it being necessary for me, if I want to serve Your Most Illustrious Lordship here in Rome, as I wish to always, and to attend to your business, that I depend upon the Abbot for everything that could happen. Likewise you will be able to write (and this is essential) a letter to Signor Mario Rodolfini, who is that Canon mentioned above, saying that you have heard from me of his willingness, etc., and that you beg him to bring the negotiation to its end. And you should enlarge upon that, because in this consists the point. You can address him as Most Illustrious, because he is from a good family. You can also write to Signor Catalano on the same subject; and in this Your Most Illustrious Lordship will be served by your goodness in recommending me as your servant, because in music [Catalano] can do me many relevant services, from which, God willing, Your Most Illustrious Lordship will receive some satisfaction (Letter 94).

Here the essential point to understand is that under the laws and customs of feudalism, a noble patron had the power to retain a courtier, by force if necessary, once he had entered into service. It will be remembered that Alfonso d'Este kept Torquato Tasso under a sort of house arrest for seven years following an altercation. This is one reason why it was important to have a protector, someone equal in rank to one's patron who could petition for justice or mercy should need arise. In fact, in the last letter in this series concerning Cesare we learn that the Abbot Pignattelli offers to be the singer's protector with respect to Marquis Bentivoglio (Letter 99).

The reason that Cesare could not leave before the end of the *sol leone* becomes clear in Fioretti's letter of 12 August 1615:

Cesare the castrato is going with Rodolfini to Tivoli for the celebration that is being made there for [the feast of] Saint Lawrence. As soon as I hear that he has returned, I shall present the letter to the Abbot Pignatelli, so that he will speak to [Cesare] and obtain what

Your Most Illustrious Lordship desires. I have given Signor Catalani the letter addressed to him, and he wishes to be remembered as a servant of Your Most Illustrious Lordship, saying that he will serve you with all readiness (Letter 96).

Fioretti's optimism reaches its apex with Cesare's return from Tivoli:

I heard that Cesare the castrato has returned to Rome, so yesterday morning I presented Your Most Illustrious Lordship's letter to the Abbot Pignatelli, informing him fully of your desire. He showed himself to be ready to do the favour, and Sunday, which will be tomorrow, he should have spoken to [Cesare]. But since this young man is very given to good times, [the Abbot] doubted that [Cesare] would be induced to leave Rome to stay there for a long time, because he has been so much led astray and is so unwilling that the space of only six months would seem a long time to him. I shall return for the reply, and tomorrow I shall present the letter to Signor Rodolfini so that the Abbot will be more disposed to comply, although I am very sure that owing to his close friendship with Cesare he would not gladly consent that he be absent for a long time from Rome. I have given your letter to Signor Catalani, and he has promised to favour the negotiation and me, as well as [to do] everything that he can do (Letter 97).

But in the end, Cesare could thumb his nose at Bentivoglio—from a distance:

As for Cesare the castrato, the business has been dispatched, since neither the authority of the Abbot Pignattelli, nor the exhortations of Signor Catalani, nor my entreaties have been sufficient to dispose him to promise to serve Your Most Illustrious Lordship for six months, but rather to everyone he has responded with equal impertinence, having always the absolute negative in his mouth, which displeased the Abbot extremely, who treated [Cesare] in this negotiation with every term of courtesy, offering his perpetual protection with respect to you. But nothing availed since, as the Abbot said at the beginning, he is too much given to good times, not to say to the vices in which he abounds to such an extent that, after being dismissed from this conversation, he returned to the choir, since we spoke to him at San Giovanni [Laterano]; he joked, and said that if Your Most Illustrious Lordship wished to enjoy him you yourself would have to come to Rome (Letter 99).

The imbalance between supply and demand that permitted a mere chorister to treat a well-connected marquis with such contempt must have been caused by a rather rapid shift in musical taste and the fashion for musical stage works at the beginning of the seventeenth century. Singers capable of performing chamber monody and recitative could not be trained fast enough. This is illustrated by the case of a young woman named Francesca.

Cesare Marotta begins to write to Enzo Bentivoglio about Francesca during the summer of 1613. She must have begun her studies somewhat earlier, for on 13 July 1613 Marotta reports that she has begun to learn a new sonnet setting of his—a work undoubtedly in the form of strophic variations, as were most Italian sonnet settings at this time. And, Marotta adds, 'I am going to adjust those two pieces of mine that she sang poorly' (Letter 67). This is the first of several indications found in this correspondence that monodies were tailored to the abilities of specific performers. Two weeks later, Marotta claims to be devoting all available time to Francesca (Letter 68), and on 7 September 1613 he reports that Francesca has nearly learnt a new arietta (Letter 69). By 25 September Marotta is already preparing to send Francesca to Ferrara, but he is worried that the time has not been sufficient.

I am sorry not to be able to be there, too, to serve you, especially on the occasion of Francesca's arrival, because, since she is such a beginner, it would be necessary to have her teacher with her, as playing [the pieces] is half the battle in singing, and, on the contrary, playing them badly [loses half the battle]. The two works that she has learnt I have given to her in writing so they can jog her memory over there. If she happens to forget something Your Illustrious Lordship will have pity, since she is a beginner, also knowing how difficult solo singing is (Letter 70).

From this letter we gain the impression that Francesca was being taught her repertoire by rote, without the aid of musical notation, and that impression is reinforced by a further letter from Marotta dated 1 October 1613, which, like the previous, speaks of providing her with the written music as if it were a departure from his ordinary practice.

Signora Francesca is coming there, as Your Lordship knows, and I am sorry that she is not very secure in those things that she sings as well as I would wish, so that Signor Enzo would be better satisfied. All things considered, I believe that he will keep in mind the short time she has been learning and that, since this solo singing is such a difficult occupation, one has to allow a lot of time. I am not talking about months but years. I believe, however, that Signora Francesca will give some satisfaction, if only by putting her together with someone who plays those works well, all of which I have given her written exactly in the way that she has learnt them. And if she forgets anything in the meantime, she can remember it by looking at the written version (Letter 71).

Once in Ferrara, Francesca needed more written music from Marotta, which he sent with his letter of 3 March 1614.

I am sending Your Most Illustrious Lordship the Romanesca that you command from me, even though I was reserving it for myself to demonstrate it to Signora Francesca, so that you might hear it from her in the manner in which I would like it to be sung. For I argue that demonstrating it is not easy for someone who is not well practised in it, because although it is a Romanesca, I nevertheless called it a *Romanesca bastarda* since in many places it must be sung with passion (*cantato con affetto*) and in others with sustained notes, short embellishments, and other niceties (*con tenute di voci, accenti, et altre diligenze*) that cannot be written but require the spoken word (Letter 74).

Here, again, Marotta explains that he normally teaches Francesca by rote, and not because she cannot read music but because notation is insufficient to communicate the essential elements of his monodic style. He had already warned Bentivoglio about the unwritten conventions of recitative in his letter of 16 May 1612: he sends pieces already learnt by a singer sent to Ferrara from Rome and adds, 'whoever is in charge of rehearsing them needs to be trained in that manner of recitational music' (Letter 55).

Francesca seems to have continued to learn by rote, for on 18 April 1615 it is Enzo Bentivoglio, himself, who writes to Antonio Goretti, his music supervisor: 'The aria that Francesca recently learnt I have never had from Cavalier [Marotta] nor did the secretary, who could not leave it for that reason, in addition to which, one can say that Francesca did not know it to any extent' (Letter 81). But the last letter about Francesca, 25 April 1615, reveals that she actually could read music and could play the harpsichord. 'Do not forget', writes Bentivoglio to Goretti, 'to have Francesca practise the works written in her book, which I should like her to learn to play on the keyboard' (Letter 82).

Early in the correspondence about Francesca we learnt that Marotta adjusted some arias to her capabilities. In another letter, of 25 September 1613, he reveals that he first taught a singer named Francesco a relatively unembellished version of an arietta, which he calls a sketch (*abozzo*)—presumably lacking its melismatic passages—with the intention of teaching him the completely ornamented work at a later time.

Two days ago I gave [Francesco] an arietta, but very, very difficult, and I am sorry that, for the brevity of time, I cannot show it to him as I would like. You will, in the meantime, hear a sketch of it. Then upon his return I will offer to have him sing it in a better way (Letter 70).

There are, in fact, multiple versions of monodies from Montalto's circle that illustrate the practice of tailoring embellishment to an individual singer and that show the difference between a sketch and a fully realized work. If we compare two versions of Cesare Marotta's *O dell'ombrosa notte amati orrori* (Vol. II, nos. 47 and 47a), it is reasonably clear that the melismas in no. 47a have been adjusted so as to avoid the lower register, particularly the c', which is notably exploited in no. 47. In some cases the low-lying passaggio has been eliminated (bb. 26, 52), while in others it has been completely recomposed so as to remain in a distinctly higher register (bb. 12–15, 16–18, 64–7). The version transcribed as no. 47 requires a contralto voice, or at least a mezzo-soprano, whereas no. 47a could be sung comfortably by a soprano. On the other hand, the version of Pellegrino Mutij's *Questi spirti gentil* from *Amor pudico* (1614), in Vol. II, no. 4a, when compared with the reading in Vol. II, no. 4, shows more caution with the upper tenor range (e'-a'), particularly at the beginnings of phrases, where notes a fourth, fifth, or octave lower are substituted. In modern terms, the version of *Questi spiriti gentil* in no. 4 requires a countertenor voice, whereas the other reading, in no. 4*a*, could be sung by an ordinary tenor. In both works, *O dell'ombrosa notte amati orrori* and *Questi spiriti gentil*, the overall range is not different in the alternative versions, nor even the general tessitura, but rather it is the placement of the passaggi in the first pair of versions and the placement of the exposed attacks in the second pair that differ.

Of course there are pairs of versions of the same piece that differ only in the degree of technical difficulty produced by the amount and kind of embellishment written out. For example, a passaggio in one version of Cesare Marotta's *Suavissimi lumi al cui splendore* (Vol. II, no. 23, b. 86) consists entirely of sixteenth notes, while another version (Vol. II, no. 23*a*, b. 86) begins with sixteen running thirty-second notes. But both passaggi cover exactly the same pitches. In at least one case, a completely unembellished version of a canzonetta can be compared with another in which different embellishments are added to each strophe: the anonymous *A sì duri lamenti* (Vol. II, nos. 78 and 78*a*). When compared with the unembellished, purely strophic version (no. 78*a*), even the first *parte* of the multipartite version (no. 78) is already an embellished variation, with the conjunctly moving quarter notes in the bass, typical of early Roman strophic variations, and the short, simple melismas in the vocal line, which are replaced by more rapid and difficult passaggi in later variations. Indeed, the unadorned, strophic *A sì duri lamenti* resembles precisely a Roman or Neapolitan villanella of the period *c.*1560–75. Compared with the varied version, it is nothing more or less than a sketch—the potential basis of a series of improvised variations, as explained in Chapter 3, or a starting place in the teaching process, as indicated in Cesare Marotta's letter of 25 September 1613 (Letter 70), quoted above.

The full curriculum used in Cardinal Montalto's circles to prepare a singer for monody and recitational stage music is described in the correspondence relating to a boy by the name of Baldassarre. We first hear of him in Girolamo Fioretti's letter to Enzo Bentivoglio of 8 June 1615:

As for Baldassarre, I retrieved the letters for Cavalier [Cesare] Marotta and for Signor [Giovanni Bernardino] Nanino, and I gave them to both of them, because neither of these men ever goes to the post office for letters. They continue to teach him and they continue to complain about the defect in intonation, which they judge not to be able to remedy, concluding from this that the boy is older than was said to Your Most Illustrious Lordship and that, as a result, his voice will last but little. They have, however, asked that I write to Your Most Illustrious Lordship that they will clarify the matter soon and that I should assure you that they will not fail to do everything so that you will know them to be true and most devoted servants. Cavalier [Marotta] has finished teaching him the sonnet, although nevertheless he will take care to have him practise it in order to bring it totally to perfection. And meanwhile he is composing a new aria to teach him. Signor Nanino also continues to teach him with every diligence, and he gives thanks to Your Most Illustrious Lordship for honouring him with your letter. In addition to the usual lessons that he gives Baldassarre in singing and composing, he is also teaching him to play upon the part [that is, to realize a basso continuo], since I have advised him that Your Most Illustrious Lordship would like this particularly. I will also meet with Signor Frescobaldi as I have with Signora Ippolita, who tells me that Your Most Illustrious Lordship will recognize from the results that she has served you. For the rest, Your Most Illustrious Lordship should not doubt that the boy is being launched because I am giving particular thought to it, recalling, thus, the duty that I have to obey your every command (Letter 87).

We recognize in this letter that Baldassarre is being taught individual pieces, as were Francesca and Francesco. But there are several additional details is this report. The 'defect in intonation' ('diffetto dell'Intonatione') of which Marotta and Nanino complain is mentioned in every subsequent letter about Baldassarre. In the next to be quoted, Fioretti reports that Nanino and Marotta complain 'that he is very faulty in intoning' ('che pecca assaissimo nell'Intonare'). And in the subsequent one, he writes that Nanino spends two hours daily with Baldassarre, the first 'in having him sing and intone well' ('in farlo cantare ed intonare bene'). These derivatives and uses of the verb *intonare* practically rule out that intonation in the modern sense is at issue. Rather, it would seem that Baldassarre's teachers are talking about intonation in the sense described in Giulio Caccini's preface to *Le nuove musiche* (1602):

The first and most important foundations [to the profession of the singer] are the intonation of the voice in all the pitches, not only so that nothing is lacking beneath or so that [the voice] grow to advantage but so that it have the good manner of intoning, as it should have, which [manner] is usually of two [types]. . . . There are, then, some [singers] who, when intoning the first pitch [of a phrase], begin a third below, and others, singing the first note at its proper pitch, always make it swell, saying that this is the good manner of placing the voice with grace. As for the first, it cannot be [the] general rule, since in many harmonies [the lower third] is not consonant, and where it can be used it has become, by now, a manner so ordinary that, instead of having grace, I would say that it is rather unpleasant to hear, also because some [singers] hold the third below too long, whereas it should be barely suggested, and that for beginners in particular it should seldom be used, as [something] rather rare. I would choose, instead of that, the second [manner, which is] swelling the voice.[6]

[6] 'I primi et più importanti fondamenti sono l'intonazione della voce in tutte le corde, non solo, che nulla non manchi sotto, o cresca di vantaggio, ma abbia la buona maniera, come ella si deve intonare, la quale per essere usata per lo più in due. . . . Sono adunque alcuni, che nell' intonazione della prima voce intonano una terza sotto, et alcuni altri detta prima nota nella propria corda, sempre crescendola, dicendosi questa essere la

Furthermore, we learn, Nanino is teaching Baldassarre composition and playing 'upon the part', which is the expression that Nanino himself uses in his counterpoint treatise, to be discussed later, when he offers guidance for the realization of a figured bass. Whether Baldassarre was singled out for special treatment or whether Francesca and Francesco, too, were given lessons in composition and basso continuo realization is not clear, although it did seem that Francesca was being taught repertoire more by rote than by notation. Nevertheless, some women were taught composition as a component of their preparation as singers, as we know from the examples of Francesca and Settimia Caccini.

Fioretti's second letter about Baldassarre, dated 13 June 1615, provides several additional details. Evidently, Enzo Bentivoglio had personally arranged for the boy's training during a recent visit to Rome, so recent that Fioretti had received word of Bentivoglio's safe return to Ferrara within the previous five days, that is, since writing his previous letter. After giving thanks for the marquis's safe arrival there, Fioretti reports on his young charge:

I shall not fail to advise you with every dispatch of Baldassarre's progress. He continues to take lessons from Signor Nanino, Ghenizzi always accompanying him, as he does when he goes to the keyboard school of Signor Girolamo [Frescobaldi]. Cavalier Marotta has decided to give him three or four lessons per day, but only a little each time, having judged that it is good not to confuse him in his learning. But both Signor Nanino and the same Cavalier [Marotta] say that he is very faulty in intoning, which, however, they will try to correct with all their ability (Letter 89).

The news in this letter is that Baldassarre is studying keyboard performance with Frescobaldi. This is, incidentally, the first notice to have been found that Frescobaldi maintained a regular school. One imagines that if the boy were being prepared to do no more than play his vocal repertoire at the keyboard it would be unnecessary to have lessons from a person of Frescobaldi's stature. Fioretti's letter of 20 June 1615, however, provides even more interesting information.

[Baldassarre] continues to go to Nanino every day, where I am, too, every morning, and [Nanino] gives him two good hours of lessons, dividing them into one [hour] in having him sing and intone well and the other [hour] in having him attend to the study of improvised counterpoint and composition, for which, however, I have provided him with two

buona maniera per mettere la voce con grazia: la quale, in quanto alla prima, per non essere regola generale, poi che in molte consonanze ella non accorda, benché ov'ella si possa anco usare, è divenuta ormai maniera cotanto ordinaria, che invece d'aver grazia (perché anco alcuni si trattengono nella terza sotto troppo spazio di tempo, ov'ella vorrebbe a pena essere accennata) direi ch'ella fosse più tosto rincrescevole all'udito, e che per li principianti particolarmente ella si dovesse usare di rado, e come più pellegrina, mi elleggerei in vece di essa la seconda del crescere la voce.' Giulio Caccini, 'Ai lettori', Le nuove musiche (Florence, 1602), transcribed in Solerti, Le origini del melodramma, 62–3; my translation.

other books, which he needed. Cavalier [Marotta] continues to have him sing several times a day, as I told Your Most Illustrious Lordship. Likewise he goes to take a lesson from Signor Girolamo Frescobaldi every day at 10:00 a.m. (*16 hore*). In this connection, it is my duty to warn Your Most Illustrious Lordship that the boy formed bad habits in the beginning, and I am aware that when he can Cavalier [Marotta] stays with him. For that reason, I would think that Your Most Illustrious Lordship would be well advised to order Ghenizzi by letter to accompany [Baldassarre] when he goes to take a lesson. But I ask that you not make me the author [of that request] because Cavalier [Marotta] might not like it. But my duty to Your Most Illustrious Lordship does not require anything else (Letter 90).

Here we learn that Baldassarre also studies improvised counterpoint. Fioretti's term for this is *contrappunto alla mente*, but it is clearly the equivalent of *sortisatio* or *cantare super librum*, terms mentioned earlier. After reviewing the few subsequent letters about Baldassarre, we shall examine Giovanni Bernardino Nanino's treatise on *contrappunto alla mente* in order to find out exactly what this boy was being taught.

On 20 June 1615 Cesare Marotta himself wrote to Enzo Bentivoglio, promising that Marotta's wife, Ippolita, will also begin teaching Baldassarre as soon as the rash on his hands is cured (Letter 91). This explains the beginning of the following passage from Girolamo Fioretti's letter of 8 July 1615:

Concerning Baldassarre, I can tell you that he does not have the rash on his hands any more, since he was made to wash with a soap, which after two or three times cured him. Now he will be at the disposition of Signora Ippolita, who will teach him how to play the guitar. And I shall not fail to remind her of Your Most Illustrious Lordship's wishes in this regard. In the meantime, you will be able to give those orders that seem appropriate to you so that Baldassarre will have a guitar with which to study, since Signora Ippolita does not have a guitar to lend him. I, too, will teach him what little I know, so that on some occasion he will be able to sing also the pieces of music that he will know in the Italian manner. For the rest, he is continuing the usual studies, and I have again exhorted Cavalier [Marotta] and Signor Nanino as well as Signor Frescobaldi, who says that he will teach him to play upon the part [that is, to realize basso continuo] as Your Most Illustrious Lordship commands. Likewise, Signor Nanino will have him practise this same skill, since I asked him to do it on behalf of Your Most Illustrious Lordship. Signor Landinelli has written you, really with too much exaggeration, saying that the boy's voice had changed and that he was learning nothing at all. But since he is not of this profession, and, as a consequence, does not understand its language, he deserves to be excused, especially since he has no other object than that Your Most Illustrious Lordship should not incur this expense without being able to derive some satisfaction. . . . But actually these gentlemen are firm in the first opinion that [Baldassarre's] shortcoming in intonation cannot be a natural defect. Care will be taken, as I have said, to get him to study. Cavalier [Marotta] has begun to teach him the octave *Non havete a temer ch'in forma nova*, a really beautiful work, as well as to have him practise the sonnet that he had given him to learn, so that [Baldassarre] learns to sing it and to play it by memory without the book when he will have to do it (Letter 92).

The new piece of information here is that Baldassarre is learning to accompany himself on the guitar, as do Ippolita Recupito, a virtuosa singer, and Girolamo Fioretti, an aristocratic dilettante. At the time this letter was written, song collections with guitar tablature were just beginning to appear in print. Additionally, Fioretti seems to be saying that his personal instruction will allow Baldassarre to accompany himself in singing pieces in the Italian manner, with the implication that Ippolita's instruction alone would not allow the boy to do so. If that interpretation is correct, it raises the question as to whether Ippolita, being a Neapolitan, sang to the guitar in the Spanish manner, whatever that may have been.

Girolamo Fioretti's letter of 22 July 1615 (Letter 94) makes only brief mention of Baldassarre, but the next, of 29 July 1615, confesses that the boy's change of voice may be at the root of his problems:

Cavalier Marotta has set to music the madrigal O *solenne vittoria*, having adorned it with passaggi tailored to the ability of Baldassarre, to whom he has begun to teach it, so that, if Your Most Illustrious Lordship wishes to have him give service in the play, as you have written, [Marotta] can send him to Ferrara at your command. Signor Nanino, too, does not fail to teach him with every diligence, although with little hope of profit, since the boy does not cease to have the inborn defect of bad intonation, rather it is increasing, for which reason it is feared that his voice is changing. These two *virtuosi* despair that a candidate has come into their hands who is so little able to do them honour in the service of Your Most Illustrious Lordship, to whom, as they have asked, I give expression of their displeasure, assuring you that they have not failed to employ every thought so that Your Most Illustrious Lordship may be served as is their duty, which they wish to retain (Letter 95).

Fioretti's last two letters about Baldassarre (App. A, Letters 94 and 95) repeat and elaborate upon the despairing tone of the previous. Only Pompeo Lasco, apparently a member of Bentivoglio's household, could muster any optimism, in his letter of 29 August 1615:

As for [Baldassarre's] voice, which, I am told, has changed several days ago, I take this to be a good sign, since it will not make another change, and it is necessary that his teacher make him sing as high as possible (Letter 98).

Having completed the narration of Baldassarre's training, in so far as we know it, we may now return to the matter of *contrappunto alla mente* and Giovanni Bernardino Nanino's treatise on the subject. Nanino's treatment of *contrappunto alla mente* actually takes the form of a series of annotated musical examples imbedded within an anonymous counterpoint treatise that survives in two eighteenth-century copies (I:Bc, MS B 124 and 125) that once belonged to Giovanni Battista Martini. In his *Storia della musica*, Martini refers to this as a 'manuscript counterpoint treatise with the rule for making *contrappunto a mente* by Giovanni Maria and Bernardino Nanino, his nephew'.[7] Apart from the fact that Giovanni Maria and Giovanni Bernardino Nanino were brothers, Martini's description leaves it unclear as to whether the entire treatise was by the Nanino brothers or only the 'rule' for *contrappunto alla mente*. This ambiguity extends to the manuscript copies, as on fo. 22[r] of the fair copy (B 124), Martini's annotation reads:

In an old Roman manuscript lent to me by Sig. Don Girolamo Chiti, *maestro di cappella* at the Lateran, the following words are written: 'This rule, which follows, [is] for learning how to make *contrappunto alla mente*, both above and below the cantus firmus. The method is very beautiful, it is by Sig. Giovanni Maria Nanino, and it can be very easily committed to memory. But even more easily would you be able to read the [rules] by Sig. Giovanni Bernardino Nanino that follow immediately after, in which [Giovanni Bernardino] has specified ascent and descent by step and ascent and descent by third and fourth, fifth and sixth, and octave, and in which he has shown very well the method of making counterpoint, both above as well as below [the cantus firmus] in one [note] or in several notes within the same [rule?].'[8]

The title-page of the fair copy merely says:

This treatise is a copy of an old manuscript formerly possessed by D. Girolamo Chiti or existing in one of the libraries of Rome during his time. See an annotation about this by Padre Martini on folio 22 in the present manuscript.[9]

Towards the end of the nineteenth century, Gaetano Gaspari claimed to have seen the source of Martini's copies in the Biblioteca Corsini in Rome, and he says that it then lacked a title-page. Nevertheless, he found a note, presumably at the end of the manuscript, attesting that the copy was made by Orazio Griffi, a

---

[7] 'Trattato MS. di Contrap. con la regola per far Contrappunto a mente di Gio. Maria, e Bernardino Nanini suo nipote'; Giovanni Battista Martini, *Storia della musica*, i (Bologna: Volpe, 1757), 461.

[8] 'In un M.S. vecchio di Roma prestatomi dal Sig. D. Girol.o Chiti M.o di Cap. del Laterano stanno notate le seguenti parole[:] Questa Regola, che segue per imparare a fare Contrappunto a mente, tanto sopra quanto sotto il Canto Fermo[.] Il modo è bellissimo et è del Sig.r Gio: Maria Nanino et facilissimamente si pole mandare a memoria. Ma più facilissimamente potrete leggere quelle del Sig. Gio: Bell.o Nanino quali seguitano immediatamente dopo questa dove ha destinto ascenso et discenso di grado et ascenso, o discenso di 3.a e 4.a 5.a e 6.a e 8.a dove anco ha disteso benissimo il modo di far contrappunto, tanto sopra, quanto sotto in una ovvero più note nella istessa.' I:Bc, MS B 124, fo. 22[r].

[9] 'Questo Trattato è copia d'un antico MS posseduto già da D. Girolamo Chiti ò alistente in alcuna della Biblioteche di Roma al suo tempo—Veggasi su ciò un' annotazione del Padre Martini nella carta vigesimaseconda del presente manoscritto.' I:Bc, MS B 124, fo. 1[r]. Concerning this and other sources of theoretical works by the Nanino brothers, see Ferand, *Die Improvisation in der Musik*, 218–19 n. 5; and id., 'Improvised Vocal Counterpoint', 160 n. 1. The foul copy, I:Bc, MS B 125, contains neither this inscription nor the annotation translated above, but in all other essentials it is identical to the fair copy in content.

papal singer, and was finished on 5 October 1619, and Gaspari claims that Martini's transcriptions matched Griffi's *ad litteram*.[10] About a century after Gaspari described Griffi's copy, the Biblioteca dell'Accademia Nazionale dei Lincei e Corsiniana no longer possessed any manuscript treatise by the Nanino brothers. It does preserve a 1757 inventory of Girolamo Chiti's music collection, which lists two treatises by the brothers, one entitled 'Regole per il contrappunto' and the other 'Regole per imparare à fare il contrappunto sotto il canto fermo'.[11] Another inventory, of musical works bought in Rome by Girolamo Chiti for Marquis Flavio Chigi Zondadari in 1756, describes one item as follows:

Rules for learning to sing and make counterpoint; a book that seems [to have been written in] manuscript in 1606, deducing this from page 68. From the same page 68, from page 65, and from page 80, which is the last page, one deduces that these rules are by *Signori* Giovanni Maria and Giovanni Bernardino Nanino (these were brothers . . .).[12]

In Martini's copy, the page following the annotation mentioning the Nanino brothers begins with the rubric, 'This rule serves for learning how to make *contrappunto alla mente*, both above and below the cantus firmus.'[13] Then follow four pages of examples that systematically exemplify contrapuntal figures, first above bass lines in whole notes ascending and descending by step and by leaps of various intervals, then below soprano lines in whole notes likewise ascending and descending by step and by various combinations of leaps. After these examples, a second series begins (fo. 24ᵛ), showing canonic imitation above bass lines ascending and descending by step and leap. It is unclear from Martini's description whether these examples of canonic imitation begin Giovanni Bernardino's 'rule', or whether they form the conclusion of the first set of examples by Giovanni Maria Nanino. On the whole, I believe that they conclude the first set. What follows (fos. 25ᵛ–43ᵛ), however, is unambiguously covered by Martini's description of Giovanni Bernardino's 'rule'. This final series of examples displays some recommended florid contrapuntal figures over, then under, cantus-firmus lines ascending by step, descending by step, ascending by third and fourth, ascending by third

---

[10] Gaetano Gaspari, *Catalogo della biblioteca del Liceo Musicale di Bologna*, i (Bologna, 1890), 302.

[11] I: Rli, Musica II, 'Inventario di G. Chiti, 1757', fo. 21ᵛ.

[12] 'Regole per imparare a cantare et fare contrappunto. Libro, che sembra manoscritto nel 1606, deducendosi questo dalla pag: 68, dalla 65, e dalla 80, che e l'ultima pagina si deduce, che queste Regole sono delli SS.ri Gio: Maria, et Gio: Bellardino Nanini (Questi furono fratelli . . .)'; I:Rli, Musica C8, 'Catalogo di libri musicali teorici manoscritti, e stampati esposti con ordine cronologico . . . 1756 Raccolta di Libri Pratici, e Teorici, e manoscritti Fatta dall'Ill.ma Sig. Marchese Flavio Chigi Zondadari per il suo Archivio Musicale di Siena Per la pale molto hà cooperato d'indagare e comprare D. Girolamo Chiti in Roma senza pregiudizio del suo Archivio, e Inventario Musicale . . .', 13–14. The manuscript in question is identified as '1606 H', and on fo. 3ʳ of the inventory, we learn that the letter *H* designates books acquired by Marquis Chigi for his collection in Siena. Inquiries to the current Count Chigi in Siena have gone unanswered.

[13] 'Questa regola serve per imparare à fare Contrappunto a mente tanto sopra quanto sotto il Canto fermo.' I:Bc, MS B 124, fo. 22ᵛ.

and descending by fourth, descending by third and ascending by fourth, ascending by fourth and descending by fifth, and so on. Since we are concerned here with the training of a boy soprano for singing to a basso continuo, only Giovanni Bernardino Nanino's illustrations of counterpoint above the cantus firmus are transcribed in Vol. II, nos. 165–91.

It should be clear from what has already been said that Giovanni Bernardino Nanino's *regole* are not 'rules' in the commonly accepted modern sense of a set of written instructions. Although I shall continue to refer to them as 'rules' for the sake of an easy reference to the original language, a better translation of the word *regole* would, perhaps, be 'models'. It is in this sense that Giovanni Battista Bovicelli uses the word in the title of his 1594 treatise on vocal ornamentation, *Regole, passaggi di musica, madrigali, e motetti passeggiati*, since he presents, in that order, brief samples of ornamentation intended as models in the construction of complete embellishments (i.e. *regole*), then longer examples that consist of complete elaborations of specific melodic shapes (he calls these 'Diversi modi di diminuire', and they correspond to the 'passaggi di musica' in his title), and finally complete elaborations of soprano parts to madrigals and motets (the 'madrigali, e motetti passeggiati' promised in his title). In a similar sense, Giulio Caccini, in the preface to his 1602 *Nuove musiche*, wrote:

The *trillo*, which I illustrated on one single pitch, was demonstrated in this way for no other reason than that in teaching it to my first wife and, now, to my other, living one, [who is] with my daughters, I have used no other *regola* than the very one that is written for both the one and the other [ornament], that is, beginning with the first quarter note and re-striking each note with the throat upon the vowel *à* until the last breve, and likewise the *gruppo*.[14]

Caccini's *regola* is actually a very brief musical example illustrating how the *trillo* is to be sung and practised.

Ferand, who devotes several pages of his 1956 article to the Naninos' examples, assumes that their sole purpose was to prepare singers to improvise above a plainchant cantus firmus.[15] However, repeated melodic patterns such as up a sixth, down a fifth; down a sixth, up a fifth, or up and down an octave (Vol. II, nos. 165–96) are hardly normal in plainchant. Now, Ferand could not deny that G. B. Nanino's 'rule' exemplifies improvisation by a solo voice rather than an ensemble, since they are replete with intervals of a sixth, which are universally forbidden in *contrappunto alla mente in concerto*.[16] And in an earlier article, in fact,

---

[14] 'Il trillo, descritto da me sopra una corda sola, non è stato per altra cagione dimostrato in questa guisa, se non perchè nello insegnarlo alla mia prima moglie et ora all'altra vivente, con le mie figliuole, non ho osservato altra regola che la stessa nella quale è scritto, e l'uno e l'altro, cioè il cominciarsi della prima semiminima, e ribattere ciascuna nota con la gola sopra la vocale *à* finto all'ultima breve, e somigliantemente il groppo.'

[15] Ferand, 'Improvised Vocal Counterpoint', 160–4.   [16] See e.g. ibid. 166.

Ferand quoted two seventeenth-century treatises that link *contrappunto alla mente* to the style of sixteenth-century villanelle.[17] These considerations, taken together with the fact that young Baldassarre was being taught *contrappunto alla mente* as preparation for singing in a stage work, lead towards the conclusion that an important purpose of Giovanni Bernardino Nanino's examples was to show how one might improvise above a basso continuo, as, for example, in the creation of strophic variations on the basis of a chordal bass pattern, such as the Romanesca, Ruggiero, or Passamezzo, or by taking a simple villanella or canzonetta as the point of departure. It will be recalled that as early as 1553, Diego Ortiz, master of the viceregal chapel in Naples, demonstrated how to improvise counterpoint above segments of plainchant as well as above the bass patterns (with chords added) now generally called La Spagna, Romanesca, and Passamezzo, using the same techniques regardless of the source of the cantus firmus.[18]

Ferand is correct, however, in comparing the figures proposed by Giovanni Bernardino Nanino to the patterns shown in late sixteenth-century treatises on melodic ornamentation.[19] And to some extent, both improvised florid counterpoint and extemporized embellishment can serve similar ends and produce similar results. But ornamentation depends upon a given melody and tends to produce only various sets of rapid melismas more or less directly linked to a constant, underlying melodic structure, whereas *contrappunto alla mente* requires only a cantus firmus, that is, a chordal bass pattern, and can produce new syllabically set melodies and a series of variations in which each is quite different from the others in outline.

Again, Ferand is not entirely incorrect to call Nanino's florid counterpoints 'of a conspicuously instrumental character',[20] although I cannot say which instrument's character he had in mind. The specific idioms of neither the organ, the harpsichord, the violin, the lute, nor the trumpet are particularly in evidence. I suspect that he is referring to the wide range of some—up to an octave and a fifth—the precipitous rise and, especially, fall encountered at times, and the strongly angular profile of many, which flirt with the melodic tritone now and then. Some of these features, however, result from the hypothetical and inclusive nature of the examples, showing as they do a variety of possibilities even within a three- or six-bar example, and from the organization of the cantus firmus by sequentially repeating patterns that often force the counterpoint to cover a wide range. In keeping with the abstract character of the examples, most of the upper lines are written in the alto clef, while the rest are notated in the mezzo-soprano clef, which never occurs, as far as I can remember, in monody sources, where treble,

---

[17] Ferand, '"Sodaine and Unexpected" Music', 22–4.
[18] Diego Ortiz, *Trattado de glosas sobre clausulas y otros géneros de puntos en la música de violones* (Rome: Dorico, 1553). [19] Ferand, 'Improvised Vocal Counterpoint', 164.
[20] Ibid.

soprano, tenor, and bass clefs are the rule. Likewise, Nanino's cantus firmi are set out with the baritone instead of the bass clef customary in the basso continuo accompaniments of monodies.

Although Nanino's cantus firmi are sequentially patterned, except for those consisting of one pitch repeated, his counterpoints usually are not. For although his florid melodies often repeat one melodic figure at various pitch levels, the pattern traced by those transpositions is often at odds with the configuration of the cantus firmus, forming a different set of intervals with it at each rendition of the melodic pattern. In some cases Nanino has contrived to repeat a phrase at one and the same pitch level while the cantus firmus rises or falls against it, or vice versa. And in a few instances he repeats a rhythmic pattern in the counterpoint that is one or two beats longer or shorter than the semibreve measure established by the notation and the steady march of the cantus firmus. Likewise, the counterpoints conform to the broadly construed norms of dissonance and perfect-consonance treatment of late-Renaissance polyphony while avoiding a slavish conformity to the dictates of the cantus firmus. Thus, a tie is often found where a suspension is not present but rather a consonance at the end of the tie and a dissonance following. In these ways, Nanino suggests improvised counterpoint that produces somewhat eccentric melodic profiles, flaunts a rather specific degree of independence from the authority of the cantus firmus, and eschews predictability while still demonstrating casual melodic self-determination and effortless mastery over obstacles, five important facets of the early-monody aesthetic that reflect some central cultural values of courtly life in Montalto's Rome and elsewhere in Italy at that time.

It could be assumed that singers and composers who trained with Giovanni Bernardino Nanino would tend to incorporate his contrapuntal strategies and style of figuration into their improvisations and compositions. And although the composers in Cardinal Montalto's circles were colleagues rather than students of Nanino's, we shall examine their works in Chapter 6 for those characteristics, on grounds that Nanino's examples probably reflect the general practice of a group of musicians in Rome at the beginning of the seventeenth century more than any of his personal ideas or idiosyncrasies. To some extent, and as suggested in Chapter 3, early monodies can be considered to be vocal improvisations, idealized or actual, more or less specifically notated. And to this extent, the conceptual framework and specific details that we have encountered in this chapter will serve as a guide as we explore the Montalto monody repertoire. But before we can embark on that exploration, it will be necessary to examine the sources that preserve the repertoire, in order to assess the authenticity and dating of ascribed works, the probable provenance of the anonymous items, the relative authority of variant readings, and the information transmitted by the distribution and groupings of genres and subtypes within sources.

5

The *Grilanda musicale* and its Companions: Sources of Music from Cardinal Montalto's Circles

୯ଓଡ଼ିହ

CARDINAL Montalto's library in the Villa Peretti is reported to have held 1,682 volumes, all of which had disappeared from the palace by 1696.[1] Of the wealth of music that the cardinal's library must have contained, only one volume can be identified today. It consists of nine printed collections of Roman monodies by Ottavio Durante, Antonio Cifra, Paolo Quagliati, and Andrea Falconieri from the years 1608–18 bound together under a leather cover on which Cardinal Montalto's coat of arms has been tooled.[2] Of these nine collections, only the first, by Durante, was dedicated to Montalto, and none of the composers of these works is known to have been directly in the cardinal's service. The manuscript music books that Cardinal Montalto so jealously guarded during his life seem to have vanished after his death. Fortunately, at least some of them came into the hands of a commerical copyist and one or two printers shortly after the cardinal died, and those men created a group of secondary sources that preserve a considerable amount of vocal music for chamber and stage by composers in Montalto's circles.

All together ten manuscripts and eight printed anthologies with music from Cardinal Montalto's circles are known to survive. Only one of these has ever been discussed in relation to Montalto, however, and several of the manuscripts have never been mentioned as sources of monody in scholarly literature. While it seems

[1] Massimo, *Notizie istoriche*, 153, 165. An inventory of the library in the Peretti palace was made in 1655 at the death of Francesco Peretti, the third Cardinal Montalto. Several sets of printed music books are listed, without reference to composer or genre, but no music manuscripts are mentioned. The inventory is in I:Ras, Notai Archivio Capitolino n. 6645 (J. Simoncellus), 13.v.1655, fos. 1190–217.

[2] The volume is in the library of the Conservatorio di Musica Santa Cecilia with the shelf mark G.CS.2.D.16. It contains Ottavio Durante, *Arie devote* (Rome, 1608); Antonio Cifra, *Scherzi sacri . . . libro primo* (Rome, 1616); Antonio Cifra, *Scherzi sacri . . . libro secondo* (Rome, 1618); Antonio Cifra, *Li diversi scherzi . . . libro primo* (Rome, 1613); Antonio Cifra, *Li diversi scherzi . . . libro secondo* (Rome, 1613); Antonio Cifra, *Li diversi scherzi . . . libro quarto* (Rome, 1615); Antonio Cifra, *Li diversi scherzi . . . libro quinto* (Rome, 1617); Paolo Quagliati, *Affetti amorosi* (Rome, 1617); and Andrea Falconieri, *Libro primo di villanelle* (Rome, 1617).

clear enough that neither these ten manuscripts nor the related prints were ever in the cardinal's private collection, the evidence to be presented here suggests that these sources represent five distinct types of relation to music books that actually were in Montalto's library: (1) four manuscript anthologies (1*a–d*) prepared by copying directly from manuscripts in Montalto's library shortly after the cardinal's death in 1623; (2) four manuscripts (2*a–d*) collateral with sources in Montalto's library; (3) one print closely related to manuscripts in Montalto's library; (4) seven other prints (4*a–g*) with music by composers in Montalto's circles; and (5) two guitar-tablature manuscripts (5*a–b*) perhaps derived from prints in categories 3 and 4, or perhaps indirectly from Montalto's original manuscripts, including material otherwise lost.

A final section (6) will describe the sources of music by Orazio Michi, who served Cardinal Montalto from 1613 to 1623. Michi lived until 1641, and it would seem that most, if not all, of his surviving works were composed after Montalto's death, since none of the sources that relate directly or indirectly to manuscripts in Montalto's library contains any music ascribed to Michi, and no source preserving Michi's music contains any concordances with sources so related.

1. Manuscript Anthologies Copied from Montalto's Manuscripts

1*a*. I:Vc, Torrefranca 250

The manuscript Venice, Conservatorio di Musica 'Benedetto Marcello', Fondo Torrefranca 250 (hereafter I:Vc, Torrefranca 250), was linked to Cardinal Montalto in a little-known article published by Fausto Torrefranca in Italy during the war years.[3] Nigel Fortune, who was allowed only a very brief examination of this manuscript, reported its contents to be Roman in style.[4] A more precise physical description of the book was given by Irving Godt,[5] and an inventory has been published by Franco Rossi.[6] No concordance with other sources has previously been attempted, and no ascription or other identification of anonymous items is found in earlier discussions.

The most obvious link with Cardinal Montalto, and the one noticed by Torrefranca, is the presence of eight compositions by Don Ippolito Macchiavelli,

[3] Fausto Torrefranca, 'Il lamento di Erminia di Claudio Monteverdi', *Inedito: Quaderno musicale*, 2 (1944), 31–42; supplement, 1–8.

[4] Nigel Fortune, 'Italian Secular Song from 1600 to 1635: The Origins and Development of Accompanied Monody' (Ph.D. diss., Gonville and Caius College, Cambridge, 1953), App., 53–4.

[5] Irving Godt, 'A Monteverdi Source Reappears: The "Grilanda" of F. M. Fucci', *Music & Letters*, 60 (1979), 428–39.

[6] Franco Rossi, *I manoscritti del Fondo Torrefranca del Conservatorio Benedetto Marcello: Catalogo per autori* (Historiae musicae cultores, 45; Florence, 1986), 155–64.

five by Cavaliere Cesare Marotta, and one by Pellegrino Mutij, all three composers in the household of Cardinal Montalto. Music by these composers is preserved almost exclusively in the group of interrelated manuscripts being considered in this chapter.

Six works in I:Vc, Torrefranca 250 can be ascribed to Giuseppino Cenci, a Roman musician, discussed in Chapter 3, whose connection with Montalto is otherwise established by his contribution of at least one aria to the cardinal's opera *Amor pudico* (1614). At the time when that opera was produced, Cenci was in the service of Cardinal Scipione Borghese, one of Montalto's closest friends and allies. Likewise, Ottavio Catalani, who is represented by one piece in this manuscript, was a Borghese composer. In a printed Roman anthology of 1621, he is titled 'Musico dell'Eccellentiss. Sig. Prencipe di Solmona' (Marc'Antonio Borghese);[7] he dedicated a pastorale to Camillo Borghese, from whom, as Pope Paul V, he later received benefices; and he served as composer at the Collegio Germanico, which was protected by Cardinal Scipione Borghese.[8] Very little is known about Abundio Antonelli, who is likewise represented by one composition in I:Vc, Torrefranca 250. Carlo Schmidl, who often reports biographical details of obscure Italian composers based on documents seen by no one else, says that Antonelli served in Cardinal Montalto's church of S. Lorenzo in Damaso before becoming *maestro di cappella* of S. Giovanni in Laterano in 1608.[9] Ties of friendship and politics may explain the presence in I:Vc, Torrefranca 250 of one composition by Marco da Gagliano, who served at the Medici court of Florence. Two pieces by the Florentine Raffaello Rontani may likewise represent Montalto's link with Florence, although Rontani was also active in Rome, serving there as *maestro di cappella* of San Giovanni dei Fiorentini from 1616 until his death in 1622. I:Vc, Torrefranca 250 preserves versions of the pieces by Gagliano and Rontani that do not depend on their printed sources. On the contrary, the manuscript versions of all three works, but especially the two by Rontani, have the characteristics of prepublication drafts: more moderate ornamentation and simpler rhythm.

A biographical event apparently explains the presence of the famous *Lamento d'Arianna* from Monteverdi's *Arianna* (1608) in I:Vc, Torrefranca 250. Torrefranca refers to Monteverdi's well-known visit to Rome in 1610, where he tried to obtain a place in the Collegio Montalto in Bologna for his son. On this occasion, a copy of the famous lament would have made a very suitable gift to the melomane founder

[7] *Raccolta de varii concerti musicali a una et due voci de diversi eccellentissimi autori* (Rome: Robletti, 1621), 6–7.
[8] Jerome Roche, 'Catalani, Ottavio', *New Grove*.
[9] Carlo Schmidl, *Dizionario universale dei musicisti*, i (Milan, 1937), 59. Antonelli's appointment to S. Giovanni in Laterano is substantiated by an early 18th-c. document from that church (I:Rvat, Codice Vat. lat. 8039A) transcribed in Casimiri, *Cantori, maestri, organisti della cappella lateranense*, 188.

of that college. The version of the lament in I:Vc, Torrefranca 250 differs in as many details from the authorized monodic print (Venice: Gardano, 1623) as it conforms to the reading in Giovanni Battista Rocchigiani's anthology *Il maggio fiorito* (Orvieto: Fei and Ruuli, 1623), where it appears without ascription. The coincidence of the publication date of these two prints suggests a hypothesis: the closely related versions of the lament in I:Vc, Torrefranca 250 and in *Il maggio fiorito* both derive from the copy that Cardinal Montalto retained from Monteverdi's visit in 1610, a copy that was sequestered with the rest of the cardinal's music until his death in 1623. It may be imagined that, upon seeing an outmoded version of his lament printed without ascription in the Rocchigiani anthology, Monteverdi would have rushed into print with an uncharacteristically small collection of his own works, consisting of the lament and two *lettere amorose* with a title-page that announces the name of the composer and his position in large type.

I:Vc, Torrefranca 250 is a very unusual manuscript in several respects (see Fig. 5.1). Its large vertical format (33 × 21 cm.), illuminated initials, and the fully written-out poetic text preceding every musical setting are unique among surviving monody sources. It begins with a title-page after the style of early seventeenth-century printed anthologies: 'Grilanda musicale di arie di diversi eccel.mi hautori scritta da Francesco Maria Fucci, Romano'. The words 'Di Cesare Antonino Cavagnolo' have been added by hand to a small cartouche at the bottom of the printed border provided for the title-page of the index. Nothing further is known of either Fucci or Cavagnolo. But the copyist's self-advertisement on the title-page certainly suggests that the manuscript was produced on speculation rather than on commission.

A further unusual feature of I:Vc, Torrefranca 250 is the motto 'Il non s'impresta' ('Not to be lent') written in a special cartouche on the top of the main title-page. Since this warning was part of the original plan of the title-page and is written in Fucci's hand, it must relate to the contents of the collection rather than to the lending policies of its eventual owner, who was presumably unknown to Fucci when he prepared the title-page. Since the manuscript contains two arias from the opera *Amor pudico* (1614), music that Cardinal Montalto personally gathered up after the performances in order to prevent its circulation (Letter 74), we may imagine that either the motto 'Il non s'impresta' was copied directly from a manuscript in Montalto's library or that it was intended to boast of a repertoire whose exclusivity was guaranteed by Montalto's reputation for jealously guarding his artistic property.

In truth, the music in I:Vc, Torrefranca 250 was not as exclusive as its motto suggests by the time the manuscript was copied. As we shall see, the same Francesco Maria Fucci produced at least three other manuscripts containing many of the same compositions. The motto 'Il non s'impresta', therefore, would not have

Fig. 5.1. I:Vc, Torrefranca 250, fo. 1ʳ

remained valid for very long after Fucci sold I:Vc, Torrefranca 250 to its first buyer. In fact, the pattern of concordances between this manuscript and other sources is instructive in this regard (see App. B, Table 1). These concordances are concentrated in the three other anthologies known to survive in Fucci's hand: eight in I:Bc, CC.225; seven in I:Baf, MS 1424; and five in I:Ru, MS 279. The three manuscripts presumed to be collateral with Montalto's original material each contain two concordances with I:Vc, Torrefranca 250: I:Bc, Q140; I:MOe, Mus. E 318; and US:PHu, MS Ital. 57. Two concordances are found in GB:Lbm, Add. 36877, a guitar-tablature manuscript derived in part from a print of 1623 but in part, perhaps indirectly, from original materials in Montalto's library now lost. One piece is found in Fabio Costantini's Roman anthology *Ghirlanda amorosa* (Orvieto: Fei and Ruuli, 1621), where it is ascribed to Paolo Quagliati, although in I:Baf, MS 1424, it is given to Giuseppino Cenci. Two pieces by Raffaello Rontani were printed in his collection *Le varie musiche . . . libro terzo* (Rome: Soldi, 1619), and one by Marco da Gagliano was published in Pietro Benedetti's *Musiche . . . libro secondo* (Venice: Amandino, 1613), as stated earlier. All the other concordances relate to Monteverdi's *Lamento d'Arianna*, whose presence says little about the derivation of a particular manuscript. With these latter concordances aside, then, we see that I:Vc, Torrefranca 250 is in no way connected with the manuscript tradition of Florence or of any centre of early monody other than Rome, and that it contains nothing printed after 1621 and nothing that cannot be reasonably associated with Cardinal Montalto.

I think that we may conclude from the coincidence of all these facts that this manuscript was probably copied from materials in Montalto's library shortly after the cardinal's death in 1623.

Some of the peculiarities in the physical make-up of I:Vc, Torrefranca 250 permit a reconstruction of its assembly and invite some hypotheses about the number and type of manuscripts from which it may have been copied. It consists of thirty-five gatherings of different sizes, ranging from bifolios to octerns (some with one or two folios cut away), on paper with two watermarks or possibly a watermark and its countermark. The crown watermark appears roughly centred and vertically oriented on only one half of each bifolio in Gatherings 3–18 (fos. 9–72), 22–7 (fos. 88–107), and 34 (fos. 132–5). The fleur-de-lis mark appears similarly oriented and distributed in Gatherings 1–2 (fos. 0–8), 19–20 (fos. 73–80), 28–33 (unnumbered fos. 108–31), and 35 (fos. 135–6). A mixture of the two watermarks is found in Gathering 21.

All the folios containing the crown watermark were used before the folios with the fleur-de-lis were employed. We can deduce this from the table of contents at the end of the manuscript. It does not follow the order of compositions in the finished manuscript. Instead, the table was begun by entering the title of the pieces copied to date in assembled order. Then new pieces were entered in the order in which they were copied. Afterward blocks of gatherings were substantially reordered. Following this, the folios were numbered by the scribe, and the numbers were added to the table of contents. Table 5.1 is a map of the manuscript in its present state, showing the order and structure of the gatherings, the distribution of watermarks, the arangement of compositions within and across the gatherings, the order in which the pieces were copied, and the order in which the blocks of gatherings were assembled.

From the information summarized in Table 5.1, we may deduce in detail

TABLE 5.1. Watermarks, gatherings, folios, contents, and assembly order of I:Vc, Torrefranca 250

		Folios	Contents	
Fleur de lis	1	0	Title Page	
		1		
		2	*Ama pur ninfa gradita*, Don Ipolito [Macchiavelli]	46
		3		
		4		
	2	5		
		6	*Dolce auretta*, D[on] Ipolito [Macchiavelli]	47
		7		
		8		
Crown	3	9	*Occhi meco piangete*, [Anon.]	23
		10		
		11	*Questi spirti gentil di te ragionano*, [Pellegrino Mutij, *Amor pudico*]	24
		12		
	4	13	*Porto celato il mio nobil pensiero*, [Anon.]	25
		14		
	5	15	*Ahi dispietato Amor come consenti*, [Anon./B. Tasso]	26
		16		
		17		
		18		
		19		
		20	*Venuto pur quel lagrimabil giorno*, Don Ipolito [Macchiavelli]	27
	6	21		
		22		
		23	*Somiglia foglia a cui fa guerra il vento*, [Anon.]	28
		24		
	7	25		
		26		
		27	*Solingo augello che piangendo vai*, D[on] Ipolito [Macchiavelli/Bembo]	29
		28		
	8	29		
		30		
		31	*Amorosa Licori*, Giuseppino [Cenci]	30
		32		
	9	33		
		34		
		35	*Quando il ciel vago s'infiora*, Don Ipolito [Macchiavelli, Intermedi, 1616]	31
		36		
	10	37		
		38		
		39	*Dhe Filli vita mia se mai ti punsero*, Don Ipolito [Macchiavelli]	32
		40		
	11	41		
		42	*Perche non togli o Clori i pesci al fiume*, Giuseppino [Cenci]	33
		43		

Assembly order: 6 (gatherings 1–2), 3 (gatherings 3–10)

TABLE 5.1. Cont'd

	⌐44 / 45 / 46		
12	⌐47 / 48 / 49 / 50	*In che misero punto hor qui me mena*, [Ottavio Cattalani/T. Tassso], Comedia dell Ill.mo Sig.r Cardinal Savelli	34
		Io che l'età solea viver nel fango, Giuseppino [Cenci/Della Casa]	35
13	⌐51 / 52 / 53 / 54	*Dolcissime pupille ond'io mi vivo*, [Anon./Guarini]	36
14	⌐55 / 56 / 57 / 58	*Anima bella che nel sen ten stai*, Giuseppino [Cenci, *Amor pudico*]	37
15	⌐59 / 60	*Occhi belli occhi rei*, [Anon.]	38
16	⌐61 / 62 / 63 / 64		
17	⌐65 / 66 / 67 / 68	*Dunque Clorida mia per questi prati*, Guiseppino [Cenci]	39
18	⌐69 / 70 / 71 / 72	*Lasciatemi morire*, [Claudio] Monteverdi/[Rinuccini, *L'Arianna*]	40
		Dove, dove ten fuggi anima bella, [Cesare] Marotti	41
19	⌐73 / 74 / 75 / 76	*O durezze amarissime d'amore*, [Cesare] Marotti [Intermedi, 1616]	42
		Suavissimi lumi al cui splendore, [Cesare] Marotti	
20	⌐77 / 78 / 79 / 80	*Vita della mia vita egl'e pur vero*, D[on] Ipolito [Macchiavelli/B. Tasso]	43
		Io pur deggio partire, Ipolito [Macchiavelli]	44
21	⌐100 / 81 / 82 / 83	*Io piango tu non torni il duol non sciema*, [Anon.]	45
		Io vorrei pur morir cosi mi preme, [Anon.]	16
		Dunque da me ten fuggi ho mio tesoro, [Anon.]	17
		Alma afflitta che fai, [Anon./Marino]	18
22	⌐84 / 85 / 86 / 87	*Temer donna non dei*, [Anon./Marino]	19
		O quanto sei gentile car'augellino, [Anon./Guarini]	20
		Donna per acquetar vostro desire, [Anon./Gottifredi]	21
		Deh dolc'anima mia, Giuseppino [Cenci/Guarini, *Il pastor fido*]	22
	⌐88 / 89	*Amiam fillide amiam ah non rispondi*, [Anon./Guarini]	1

Fleur de lis

5

TABLE 5.1. Cont'd

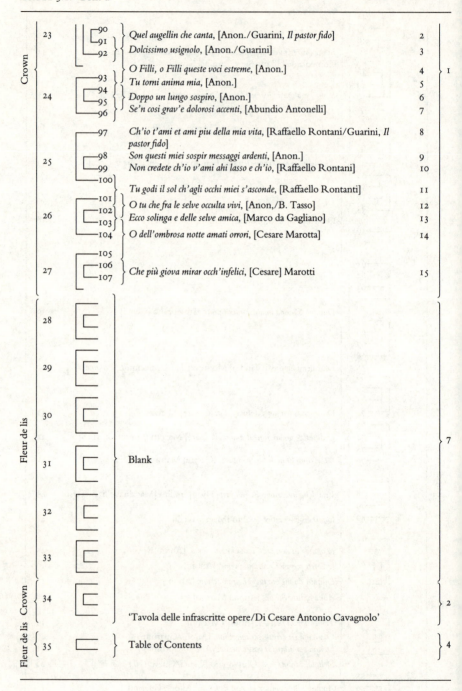

Crown	23	90 91	*Quel augellin che canta,* [Anon./Guarini, *Il pastor fido*]	2
		92	*Dolcissimo usignolo,* [Anon./Guarini]	3
			O Filli, o Filli queste voci estreme, [Anon.]	4
	24	93 94	*Tu torni anima mia,* [Anon.]	5
		95	*Doppo un lungo sospiro,* [Anon.]	6
		96	*Se'n cosi grav'e dolorosi accenti,* [Abundio Antonelli]	7
		97	*Ch'io t'ami et ami piu della mia vita,* [Raffaello Rontani/Guarini, *Il pastor fido*]	8
	25	98	*Son questi miei sospir messaggi ardenti,* [Anon.]	9
		99	*Non credete ch'io v'ami ahi lasso e ch'io,* [Raffaello Rontani]	10
		100	*Tu godi il sol ch'agli occhi miei s'asconde,* [Raffaello Rontanti]	11
	26	101 102	*O tu che fra le selve occulta vivi,* [Anon,/B. Tasso]	12
		103	*Ecco solinga e delle selve amica,* [Marco da Gagliano]	13
		104	*O dell'ombrosa notte amati orrori,* [Cesare Marotta]	14
	27	105 106 107	*Che più giova mirar occh'infelici,* [Cesare] Marotti	15

'Tavola delle infrascritte opere/Di Cesare Antonio Cavagnolo'

Table of Contents

and with considerable certainty the method used to construct I:Vc, Torrefranca 250. The first two blocks of compositions to be copied must have been those in the original quaternions of Gatherings 23–7, 34, and 21–2 (fos. 89–107, 132–4, and 81–7). The last folio of Gathering 27 and the first folio of Gathering 21, which probably contained a linking composition, were cut away before the table of contents was drawn up. Gatherings 3 and 5–18 were completed next, then enlarged through the insertion of two works: *Porto celato il mio nobil pensiero* on its own bifolio, Gathering 4 (fos. 13–14), and *Ahi dispietato Amor come consenti*, on two single folios attached to the beginning of Gathering 5. Copying then came to a temporary halt, leaving the last two folios of Gathering 18 blank. The block made up of Gatherings 3–18 were then placed in front of the block made up of Gatherings 23–7, 21–2, and 34. All the paper used up to this point bears the crown watermark. Now the table of contents was begun, recording, in order, the works contained in the gatherings assembled so far.

The table of contents was the first portion of the manuscript written on paper with the fleur-de-lis watermark. That paper was used next to copy the contents of Gatherings 19–20, which were inserted after Gathering 18. The pieces in Gatherings 19–20 were entered into the table of contents at this point, beginning with Cesare Marotta's *Dove, dove ten fuggi anima bella,* begun on the last two folios (71–2) of Gathering 18, which had been left blank. (This proves that Gatherings 3–18 form the last block of paper with the crown watermark to have been incorporated into the manuscript.) Then the copyist used some fleur-de-lis paper to produce Gatherings 1–2. He inserted these in front of Gathering 3 and entered their contents into the table at this point. Now Gatherings 21–2 were removed from their position at the end of the manuscript and placed between Gatherings 20 and 23. A link between Gatherings 20 and 21 was forged by Ippolito Macchiavelli's *Io pur deggio partire*, which was begun at the end of Gathering 20 (fo. 79^v) and completed on a separate folio, with fleur-de-lis watermark, bound to the beginning of Gathering 21, where it replaces the cut-away folio mentioned above. This was the last item entered in the table of contents. The composition that had been at the end of Gathering 22 since the time its contents were entered into the table, Giuseppino Cenci's *Deh dolc'anima mia* (fos. 87^v–88^r), concludes on a separate folio that was evidently cut away from the beginning of Gathering 34; that folio was now attached to the beginning of Gathering 23. At this point the folios were numbered and the numbers entered into the table of contents. The title-page of the entire manuscript, which is not taken into account in the folio numbering, was then attached, as a single folio, to the beginning of Gathering 1. The rest of the fleur-de-lis paper was then collected in regular quaternions (Gatherings 28–33), prepared for new music, inserted between Gatherings 27 and 34, but left blank. Whether Fucci's work was interrupted at this point or whether he decided to make the manuscript's contents expandable by deliberately leaving blank folios at the end is difficult to say.

The blocks of folios thus considered from the standpoint of their original makeup and chronology display interesting patterns of consistency in content. The copyist began with compositions for which he apparently had no ascriptions. None of them was part of the stage works produced by Cardinal Montalto during the years 1612–14 for which we have librettos. Six pieces, including the first four to be copied, are settings of texts by Guarini, three from *Il pastor fido*.

The works towards the middle of the first block to be copied are of a different description. First come two pieces ascribable to Raffaello Rontani through the presumably later printed versions followed by two echo madrigals, the second ascribable to Marco da Gagliano through a later print and the first (*O tu che fra le selve occulta vivi*) sufficiently related in text and musical style that one might postulate Gagliano's authorship on the basis of circumstances. These four works might well have been taken from a second manuscript.

The first block continues with the first works by a composer in Montalto's household, the first taken from the cardinal's later stage works, and the first to carry ascriptions. These are two compositions by Cesare Marotta: *O dell'ombrosa notte amati orrori* (fos. 103ᵛ–105ᵛ), which is musically linked to another piece, *Suavissimi lumi*, mentioned by Marotta in a letter of 1611; and *Che più giova mirar occh'infelici*, which Marotta added in 1616 to intermedi composed for Cardinal Montalto in 1612. This latter work was the first actually ascribed by the copyist of this manuscript. The last piece to be copied in this block is the work that begins on the last page of Gathering 22 and concludes on a folio attached to the beginning of Gathering 23 after it was finished: *Deh dolc'anima mia*, ascribed to Giuseppino [Cenci].

The two pieces by Marotta and one by Cenci at the end of the first block of folios to be copied may have been taken from a third manuscript, one that contained principally pieces by composers active in Montalto's household and immediate circle during the second decade of the seventeenth century. The reason for suggesting this is that the next compositions to be copied are dominated by further pieces of this description. In particular, the block marked '3' in Table 5.1, which eventually became folios 9–72, contains five works by Giuseppino Cenci, four by Ippolito Macchiavelli, and one each by Pellegrino Mutij, Ottavio Catalani, and Claudio Monteverdi. Only six are anonymous. Four of the arias come from stage works, two of these from Montalto's production of *Amor pudico* (1614). The copyist must have had a motive for eventually placing this block of compositions ahead of those already copied, and I suppose that he considered them more important, given the fact that they were ascribed to composers closely associated with Cardinal Montalto.

Blocks 5 and 6 continue the same pattern of contents as Block 3: four compositions by Ippolito Macchiavelli and three by Cesare Marotta, both composers in Cardinal Montalto's household. None of the pieces in these blocks is anonymous. The copyist eventually chose to frame Block 3 with Blocks 6 and 5, creating in the first half of the manuscript and at the very end two concentrations of pieces ascribed to composers in Montalto's circle and leaving anonymous settings of Guarini for the second half of the book.

The significance of the source material from which the Blocks 3, 5, and 6 were eventually copied must have become clear to the copyist only after he began to put some of its contents into Block 1. Certainly he did not survey all that was available to him before beginning to his work. Even the table of contents, as explained earlier, follows the order of work rather than the eventual order of pieces in the 'Grilanda'. In fact, the disorder of the table of contents suggests that Fucci began I:Vc, Torrefranca 250 with a much smaller project in view, one initially limited to a copy of a collection of anonymous monodies focused upon settings of Guarini's texts.

Among other things, these considerations suggest caution in linking to Cardinal Montalto's household the contents of Gatherings 21–7. By the same token, the six anonymous works in Gatherings 3–18 are more likely to have been the work of composers with close associations to the cardinal.

1*b*. I:Bc, CC.225

The manuscript Bologna, Civico Museo Bibliografico Musicale, CC.225 (hereafter B:Bc, CC.225), has never been mentioned in the scholarly literature as a source of monody. There is no entry for it in Gaspari's 1893 catalogue of the Martini collection,[10] while the current card catalogue of the Bologna library describes it as a manuscript of anonymous eighteenth-century cantatas. It is, however, a close companion of I:Vc, Torrefranca 250, copied at nearly the same time and at the same place. The title-page begins with the same warning, 'Il non s'impresta', and it carries the same copyist's name in conjunction with another title that would be typical of a printed anthology of Roman monodies in the early seventeenth century: *Selva musicale di arie e villanelle di diversi eccellentissimi autori con il suo basso per sonare sopra a hogni sorte d'istrumento scritto da Francesco Maria Fucci Romano*.

I:Bc, CC.225 has concordances in very nearly the same group of manuscripts as I:Vc, Torrefranca 250, as will be seen in Appendix B, Table 2. The major difference is that I:Bc, CC.225 has six items in common with I:Fn, MS Cl. VII, 1222

---

[10] Gaspari, *Catalogo della Biblioteca Musicale G. B. Martini*, iii.

bis, and five in common with GB:Lbm, Add. 36877. As will be shown below, these are two very similar guitar-tablature and text manuscripts with close relations to an anthology with connections to nearly all the 'Montalto' manuscripts, an anthology printed in 1623, the year of Cardinal Montalto's death. Both these guitar-tablature manuscripts contain one aria from Montalto's *Amor pudico* that is preserved nowhere else.

Although similar in title-page, nearly parallel in range of concordances, and partially overlapping in content, I:Bc, CC.225 differs substantially from I:Vc, Torrefranca 250 in form and overall content (see Fig. 5.2). It is much smaller: quarto format, 22 × 16.1 cm., sixty-one numbered folios plus title-page. It is homogeneous: one kind of paper is used throughout, and all the gatherings are simple quaternions, with three exceptions—a title-page was added to the first gathering, the last folio of Gathering 10 has been cut away, and the last gathering, which holds the table of contents, is a bifolio. The original copyist of I:Bc, CC.225, Fucci, left the last six folios (54–9) blank, before writing the table of contents. A later scribe added music to those folios, which, therefore, cannot be assumed to have come from the repertoire upon which Fucci drew. And although I:Bc, CC.225 begins with a group of solo madrigals and strophic variations—the categories of works that make up the entire Torrefranca manuscript—the remainder, and by far the largest part contains strophic canzonette (called 'Villanelle' in the table of contents and title-page), a type not found at all in I:Vc, Torrefranca 250.

All the paper used in I:Bc, CC.225 bears the same crown watermark as the paper with which Fucci began I:Vc, Torrefranca 250; none of it bears the fleur-de-lis mark of the paper used to complete the Torrefranca manuscript. Therefore, we may posit that Fucci compiled I:Bc, CC.225 before he began I:Vc, Torrefranca 250. The content of I:Bc, CC.225 bears out that supposition: it begins with eight compositions that are found in the portions of I:Vc, Torrefranca 250 written on paper with the crown watermark. Five of these concordant works occur in nearly the same order in which they are written in the oldest block of I:Vc, Torrefranca 250—only two of them are reversed. And there are no other concordances between I:Bc, CC.225, and I:Vc, Torrefranca 250. The ninth composition in I:Bc, CC.225, *Leggiadri occhi sereni*, concludes the first group of works, all of which are strophic variations or madrigals, like the pieces in I:Vc, Torrefranca 250. It seems reasonable to assume that these nine works were copied from the same one or two sources that Fucci used to begin I:Vc, Torrefranca 250. But after this point he used a source or sources to which he did not return in creating his other manuscripts.

The segment that contains the balance of the pieces in I:Bc, CC.225 starts at the beginning of Gathering 8. Actually, the last page of Gathering 7 (fo. 28^v) was ruled with six staves, like all the previous pages, but no music was entered. Folio

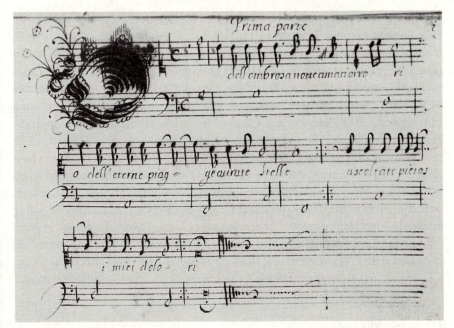

Fig. 5.2. I:Bc, CC.225, fo. 1ʳ

29ʳ, however, was ruled with only two staves, like all the following recto sides, in order to accommodate the residual text, from the second strophe onward, of a canzonetta. But Fucci used the blank space, instead, to write what appears to be the name 'Luigi' with interwined flowering branches. (The only doubt about the name arises from the fact that the letter 'G' looks like a letter 'C'.) It seems that the copyist had first intended to use this opening for a strophic canzonetta but decided, probably before going on, to use it as a sort of title-page for the second segment of the manuscript. If that is so, then he must have been referring, in some way, to the authorship of what follows or to a name written on the new source manuscript from which he began to copy at this point. If 'Luigi' refers to a musician so well known by 1623 as to be recognized by his first name only, the only choice would be Luigi Rossi, who since 1620 had been a musician in the household of Marc'Antonio Borghese, Prince of Sulmona, the brother of Cardinal Montalto's close friend and ally Cardinal Scipione Borghese.[11]

---

[11] The dates of Rossi's service to Marc'Antonio Borghese were first given by Henri Prunières, 'Notes sur la vie de Luigi Rossi', *Sammelbände der Internationalen Musikgesellschaft*, 12 (1910–11), 12–16, and this been repeated ever since without documentation. Actually 'Alousice Rossi' first appears in the prince's account book, Rome, Archivio Vaticano, Borghese 8237, fo. 20ᵛ, where his monthly salary as 'sonatore' of L.3.2.0 was the second to highest in the household. Salaries and miscellaneous payments in subsequent years are found in Borghese 8310 (for 1625), Borghese 3949 (for 1626–32), and Borghese 3951 (for 1635–6). Rossi's salary in this

The segment of the manuscript introduced by the name 'Luigi' does not, however, contain exclusively music by Luigi Rossi. *Voi partite sdegniose* (fos. 31^v–32^r) is found in Raffaello Rontani's *Le varie musiche* (1618); *Dhe mirate luci ingrate* (fos. 32^v–33^r) was ascribed to Giovanni Domenico Puliaschi in the anthology *Ghirlandetta amorosa* (1621); and *Voi mi dite ch'io non v'ami* is given to Ottavio Catalani in Robletti's *Raccolta de varie concerti musicali* (1620). It may be relevant to point out, however, that Puliaschi and Catalani were, like Rossi, associated with the Borghese family when this manuscript was assembled.[12]

It is not at all improbable that Cardinal Montalto could have come into possession of a performing repertoire manuscript marked with the name of Luigi Rossi before 1623, given his very close association with the Borghese family. As with the first manuscript discussed in this chapter, I:Bc, CC.225 contains no music known to have been composed or printed after Cardinal Montalto's death in 1623. The pattern of concordances and the use of the motto 'Il non s'impresta', in common with I:Vc, Torrefranca 250, again suggest that Fucci also copied I:Bc, CC.225 in 1623 from materials from the library of the late Cardinal Montalto.

1c. I:Baf, MS 1424

The manuscript Bologna, Accademia Filarmonica, MS 1424 (hereafter I:Baf, MS 1424), is written in the hand of Francesco Maria Fucci on paper with the fleur-de-lis watermark, the same paper with which Fucci finished I:Vc, Torrefranca 250. Therefore, we may suppose that he copied this manuscript after completing I:Vc, Torrefranca 250—indeed it contains concordances with blocks of the Torrefranca manuscript copied on fleur-de-lis paper, as well as pieces from earlier portions of that manuscript. With fifty-three folios, it is nearly the length of I:Bc, CC.225 but somewhat larger and more ornate (see Fig. 5.3). It is in quarto format, 28.4 × 20.5 cm., and consists of thirteen gatherings, all of them quaternions with three exceptions: the first gathering, which begins with a title-page, is a sextern; Gathering 8 is a bifolio, and the last folio has been pasted on to the end of Gathering 13. None of these irregularities is the result of a rearrangement. However, the last composition to begin within the original four folios of

last book is L.3.—.7; and his last payment was received in Sept. 1636. At this point it is thought that he moved over to the service of Cardinal Antonio Barberini, although he appears in that cardinal's household accounts in Jan. 1642 (I:Rvat, Barberini [no signature], 'Salarii e companetici della famiglia del Ecc.mo S.r Card.le Ant.o Barberini', under the heading 'Cappelani e musici' and the date cited).

[12] Puliaschi is listed from the beginning to the end of two Borghese family account books that probably belonged to Cardinal Scipione: Rome, Archivio Vaticano, Borghese 3946 (for the years 1615–18) and Borghese 3947 (for the years 1618–22). Catalani's associations with the Borghese family are mentioned earlier in this chapter.

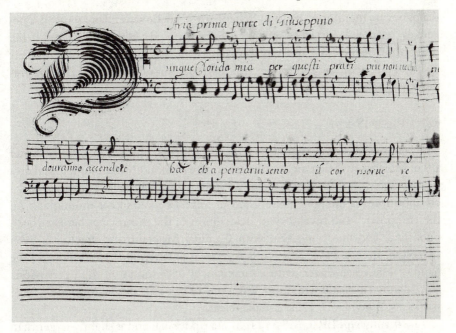

FIG. 5.3. I:Baf, MS 1424, fo. 1ʳ

Gathering 13, *Se 'l dolce sguardo di costei m'ancide* (fos. 50ᵛ–53ʳ), is a sonetto miss-ing its last tercet, which should have been set to a fourth strophic variation.

Although the motto 'Il non s'impresta' does not appear on this manuscript, the majority of the works in it can be traced to the circle around Cardinal Montalto (see App. B, Table 3). Seven of the sixteen pieces in I:Baf, MS 1424 are concord-ant with items in I:Vc, Torrefranca 250; and one other concords with I:Bc, CC.225. Of the eight remaining compositions, two can be ascribed to Montalto's prin-cipal composer, Cesare Marotta, because they are mentioned in the composer's letter of 14 October 1611; and another is ascribed here to Giuseppino [Cenci]. This leaves five pieces with no demonstrable link to Cardinal Montalto. None of these five has concordances in any known staff-notation manuscript, and only one of them carries the name of a composer: *Questa ch'el cor misura*, by Stefano Landi. It is ironic, then, that some later scribe supplied this manuscript with the title 'Dialoghi del Sig:r Stefano Landi'. In fact, the only two dialogues in I:Baf, MS 1424 are ascribed in it to Giuseppino [Cenci].

Although the manuscript was briefly described in a catalogue published in 1914, it has been ignored in subsequent surveys of monody sources.[13] Two of its

---

[13] Alfredo Bonora and Emilio Giani, *Catalogo delle opere musicali . . . città di Bologna: R. Accademia Filarmonica—Collezione privata Ambrosini—Archivio e Museo di S. Petronio* (Parma, 1914–39), 19.

dialogues are mentioned by John Whenham, who, however, apparently did not actually see the manuscript.[14] Likewise, Silke Leopold lists this manuscript in her dissertation on Stefano Landi with the remark 'nicht eingesehen'.[15] No complete inventory, concordance, or other thorough account of this manuscript has previously appeared.

1*d*. I:Ru, MS 279

The manuscript Rome, Biblioteca Universitaria Alessandrina, MS 279 (hereafter I:Ru, MS 279), was first mentioned as a source of monody in a biographical dictionary entry on Francesca Caccini written by Lina Pannella.[16] Stefano Landi's compositions in this source are listed in Silke Leopold's later monograph on the composer.[17] No inventory or description of the manuscript has ever been published, and no connection with Cardinal Montalto has previously been suggested. In fact, I:Ru, MS 279 is another Roman monody anthology in the hand of Francesco Fucci, with concordances with several of the other Montalto manuscripts, and with music from one or two of Cardinal Montalto's stage works, as Appendix B, Table 4 makes clear.

The manuscript I:Ru, MS 279 is in quarto format and is slightly larger than I:Bc, CC.225, measuring 27.7 × 20.6 cm., probably because it has not been trimmed as much (see Fig. 5.4). It contains 102 folios arranged in forty gatherings, all quaternions, except for one bifolio (fos. 77–8). With the exception of one sheet,[18] all the paper used in this manuscript, bearing the watermark of the fleur-de-lis, is of the type with which Fucci completed I:Vc, Torrefranca 250. Thus, I:Ru, MS 279 most probably was copied just after I:Vc, Torrefranca 250.

In its present state, I:Ru, MS 279 contains neither title-page nor table of contents, but it may once have had both. The very large initials on folios 1 and 9, done in red and black ink, suggest that this manuscript, like the two previously discussed, was made to be sold to a collector. That at least one segment of the manuscript was removed at some point is indicated by the fact that Gathering 32 (fo. 69) begins with the fourth part of a set of strophic variations by Ippolito Macchiavelli that is found complete in I:Vc, Torrefranca 250. The last two folios of Gathering 33 are blank and are followed by seven entirely self-contained

---

[14] John Whenham, *Duet and Dialogue in the Age of Monteverdi* (Ann Arbor, 1982), ii. 156–7. Whenham places a question mark before each of his concordances with this source, from which I conclude that he was unable to verify them through an examination of the manuscript's contents.

[15] Silke Leopold, *Stefano Landi: Beiträge zur Biographie—Untersuchungen zur weltlichen und geistlichen Vokalmusik* (Hamburger Beiträge zur Musikwissenschaft, 17; Hamburg, 1976), i. 116.

[16] Lina Pannella, 'Caccini, Francesca', *Dizionario biografico degli italiani*, xvi (Rome, 1973), 19–23.

[17] Leopold, *Stefano Landi*, i. 116–17.

[18] The sheet used to form fos. 38–9 has the watermark of a kneeling figure, but this sheet, which forms the middle of the twentieth quaternion, is continuous in content with the surrounding folios.

FIG. 5.4. I:Ru, MS 279, fo. 1ʳ

gatherings filled exclusively with duets ascribed to Stefano Landi, who has no known direct link to Cardinal Montalto. The rest of the manuscript contains only works for accompanied solo voice by composers connected with Cardinal Mont-alto or the Borghese family—with the exception of one set of strophic vari-ations ascribed to Landi. It therefore seems possible that the last segment of the manuscript, which begins with the only bifolio gathering, was not at first intended to be joined to the first thirty-three gatherings and that its contents came from a different source. The current binding is marked simply 'Libro di Musica' on its spine, and the words 'ex legato Josephi Carpani I.V.B.' are written in modern pencil at the bottom of fo. 1.

In I:Ru, MS 279 Cardinal Montalto's household composers Ippolito Mac-chiavelli, Cesare Marotta, and Bernardino Nanino are joined by their usual com-panion Giuseppino Cenci, the Borghese composers Giovanni Ottavio Catalani and Domenico Puliaschi,[19] the aforementioned Stefano Landi, and Francesca Caccini of the Medici household in Florence.

---

[19] Puliaschi's salary payments as 'Musico' in the household of Prince Marc'Antonio Borghese from 1615 to 1622 are recorded in Archivio Segreto Vaticano, Borghese 3946 and 3947. Although Puliaschi was formally

The work by Francesca Caccini, *Pascomi di sospir languendo e debile*, is given the rubric 'Egloga pastorale, Tirsi e Filli', and it takes the form of a satirical dialogue, largely in recitative style, concluding with a two-strophe aria for Tirsi, which is provided with ornamentation for the second strophe. The first tercet of the text is taken from a capitolo by Petrarch, and indeed the object of the satire is the pastoral convention of unrequited love, since in this dialogue Filli immediately accedes to Tirsi's opening supplication, leaving the shepherd with nothing to sing afterwards but expressions of comically empty and awkward rejoicing.

As mentioned in Chapter 2, the text, and presumably Francesca Caccini's setting of it, was incorporated into the 'favola' *Il Passatempo* by Michelangelo Buonarroti, the younger, which was performed for the Medici court in Florence on 11 February 1614. I say 'incorporated' into it because *Il Passatempo* seems to have been a pastiche of songs, dances, skits, and dramatic scenes—some of them written much earlier than 1614—paraded successively across the stage for the amusement of Pastime, Laughter, Recreation, Tranquillity, Playfulness, Peace, and Quiet while they await the climactic performance of *Il balletto della Cortesia*.[20] Each presentation becomes the subject of the onlookers' satirical remarks. Beside the eclogue, two other texts sung in *Il Passatempo* were set by Francesca Caccini and later printed in her *Primo libro delle musiche* (1618).[21] Assuming that Francesca Caccini composed the eclogue of Tirsi and Filli at least a year before it was incorporated into *Il Passatempo*, Cardinal Montalto had the opportunity of obtaining a copy of it when she was in Rome during the spring of 1613, as was established in Chapter 2.

Udite Amanti udite (fos. 9ʳ–16ᵛ) is another work with links to Florence, at least as far as the poetry is concerned. The poem was entitled *Favola dell'ape, e d'Amore*, under the rubric *Recitativi*, when it was published in the posthumous *Poesie* of the Florentine poet Andrea Salvadori (1591–1635),[22] whose earliest datable stage work was performed at carnival 1616. This printed version begins with twenty-two lines not set here and ends with a madrigal, *Contro di me s'adira*, which is,

admitted to membership in the papal chapel in 1612, as noted in all reference works, he was admitted to that choir as a supernumerary on 2 Feb. and remained until 9 Dec. 1606 at the request of Cardinal del Monte, one of Montalto's closest friends and allies (I:Rvat, Cappella Sistina, Diario 26, fo. 7ᵛ). However, on 9 Dec. 1606 Puliaschi was removed from the papal chapel for having taken a wife (fo. 33ᵛ). This marriage must have been annulled later, since he rejoined the papal chapel on 3 May 1612, and on 2 Nov. 1614 he was made a canon of the basilica of S. Maria in Cosmedin, in which capacity he became a colleague of Cardinal Montalto (I:Rvat, S. Maria in Cosmedin, I-10, and Giovanni Maria Crescimbeni, *L'istoria della basilica diaconale collegiata, e parrocchiale di S. Maria in Cosmedin di Roma* (Rome, 1715), 277, where Puliaschi's death date—unreported in modern scholarship—is given as 9 June 1622). In the libretto of Cardinal Montalto's *Amor pudico* (1614), Puliaschi, who composed and sang for the spectacle, is listed as 'dell'Illustriss. Borghese'.

[20] I:Fl, Buonarroti 84, fos. 400ᵛ–407ʳ, contains a description and text for an allegorical cart with a note that it was first written in 1605, revised in 1611 for a narrative rather than dramatic presentation, and then inserted into the 'festa' *Il Passatempo* in 1613 (1614 modern style). Throughout the four versions of *Il Passatempo* one sees entire entertainments added and deleted many times.

[21] These are 'Chi desia di saper che cosa è Amore' and 'Io veggio i campi verdiggiar fecondi'.

[22] Andrea Salvadori, *Le poesie*, i (Rome: Ercole, 1668), 480–5.

likewise, not found in the monody sources from Cardinal Montalto's circles. The fact that Salvadori was Florentine has little bearing on the provenance of the music, however, since poetry by Salvadori's Florentine contemporary Jacopo Cicognini, set by several of Cardinal Montalto's musicians, is found in several of the sources discussed in this chapter, because the music and poetry formed part of Montalto's opera *Amor pudico* (1614). There were many ways and many opportunities for Salvadori's poem to be transmitted to Cardinal Montalto or to one of his musicians.

2. Collateral Manuscripts

2a. US:PHu, MS Ital. 57

The catalogue of the Rare Book Collection of the University of Pennsylvania Library (Philadelphia) describes US:PHu, MS Ital. 57, as a collection of sixteenth-century madrigals and canzonette.[23] The manuscript actually contains fourteen compositions for solo voice with unfigured bass and seven duets, likewise with continuo accompaniment (see App. B, Table 5). The catalogue description is correct only in so far as five of the solo-voice works set madrigal texts, and the manuscript may have been begun during the last decade of the sixteenth century. Based upon the handwriting (diamond-shaped note heads and semi-calligraphic text) and musical style of the repertoire ('pseudo-monody' in reduced-polyphonic style, strophic variations, strophic canzonette for one and two voices, but nothing in true recitative style), this may well be the earliest Roman monody source and one of the earliest manuscripts to preserve continuo-accompanied solo song from any Italian centre (see Fig. 5.5). It has never previously been described as a source of monody.

   Diplomatically, US:PHu, MS Ital. 57 has nothing in common with the four Fucci manuscripts described above. The paper, bearing the simple cross-on-shield watermark, is gathered into five fascicles: octern, quaternion, quaternion, octern, and quaternion. The first gathering seems to have been assembled separately from the other four. The principle scribe of the manuscript, who wrote out the contents of Gatherings 2–5, entered three items in the first gathering, beginning on fo. 1^v, ending with fo. 5^v, and leaving fos. 6–8 blank. Gatherings 2–5, however, are filled continuously by pieces in the principle hand that link all four gatherings together. The manuscript consisting of Gatherings 2–5 was begun on the verso of its first folio, just as Gathering 1 was. After Gathering 1 was bound

---

[23] Norman P. Zacour and Rudolf Hirsch, *Catalog of the Manuscripts in the Libraries of the University of Pennsylvania to 1800* (Philadelphia, 1965), 103.

FIG. 5.5. US:PHu, MS Ital. 57, fo. 1ʳ

to the beginning of the original manuscript (Gatherings 2–5), two additional compositions were added by a second hand on fos. 6ᵛ–9ʳ, thus linking the two fascicles. On the first page, a third scribe wrote a phrase of a solo song (*Ah fuggite fuggite*) together with three sketches of various ornamental diminutions of it. On the same page a fourth hand has added the beginning of what appears to be a contrapuntal exercise. Unlike the Fucci manuscripts, US:PHu, MS Ital. 57 has no title-page, table of contents, decorative initials, or attributions to composers. It is bound in what appears to be a period cover of lightweight vellum. The handwriting is neat but informal. Thus, diplomatic evidence suggests that, unlike the Fucci manuscripts, US:PHu, MS Ital. 57 seems not to have been copied for sale to a collector.

The unimposing appearance of US:PHu, MS Ital. 57 suggests that it may have been a repertoire manuscript of a singer. This suggestion finds some support in the further observation that all the solo songs in this manuscript are written in tenor clef rather than the soprano clef, which is much more common in the monody repertoire. Indeed, all the compositions in US:PHu, MS Ital. 57 that have concordances elsewhere are preserved in the other sources in soprano rather than tenor clef. If the identity of the singer-compiler of the manuscript is sought, the candidate who emerges immediately is Giuseppino Cenci, considering that all the compositions in this manuscript that can be ascribed through concordances can, at least with some degree of probability, be attributed to him, and considering that he was a well-known virtuoso tenor. On the chance that the Philadelphia manuscript should turn out to be an autograph of Giuseppino Cenci, a comparison was made with his signatures attesting receipts of his monthly salary in the Sistine Chapel, 1603 and 1605, but the comparison proved inconclusive.

Different though it may be in form and function from the Fucci manuscripts, US:PHu, MS Ital. 57 is linked with them and with the Montalto circle through content. Of the fifteen items in it that are also found in other sources, four have concordances in one or more of the Fucci anthologies, and another eight have concordances in one or more of the 'collateral' sources.

Although US:PHu, MS Ital. 57 is thus linked to sources connected with the Montalto circles, it does not derive from any of them. The readings preserved in the Philadelphia manuscript are independent in every case, as a scrutiny of the concordances in Volume II will confirm. In a couple of cases they are preferable (*Donna, per acquetar vostro desire* and *Vita de la mia vita egl'è pur vero*). And all four duets in US:PHu, MS Ital. 57 that are printed in the anthology *Concerti amorosi* (1623) are transcribed in the latter source as solo songs, sometimes borrowing from now one, now the other voice of the original. Evidently the versions in the other sources derive from a different avenue of transmission.

2b. I:MOe, Mus. E 318

Nigel Fortune describes Modena, Biblioteca Estense, Mus. E 318 (hereafter I:MOe, Mus. E 318) as 'a small, ugly manuscript' containing songs in a Roman style.[24] Indeed, it consists of a single sextern of coarse paper (no watermark is discernible) with an additional folio pasted on at the beginning. The handwriting is hurried and crude throughout. No composers' names are given in the manuscript, but through concordances with all the Fucci manuscripts and one

---

[24] Fortune, 'Italian Secular Song from 1600 to 1635', Appendix I(b), 47.

Floentine source, ascriptions to Giuseppino Cenci (2), Ippolito Macchiavelli,[25] and Cesare Marotta—the central composers in Montalto's circle—can be established with some degree of certainty (see App. B, Table 6).

In the three cases of concordances with the Fucci manuscripts, the readings preserved in I:MOe, Mus. E 318 are different enough to suggest independent transmission. Even in the cases of *Suavissimi lumi al cui splendore* and *Anima bella che nel sen ten stai*, in which the versions in I:MOe, Mus. E 318 are close enough to the Fucci manuscripts that a common source is possible, the more careful use of accidentals in the Modena source tends to preclude the possibility that it was merely copied from one of the Fucci anthologies. In the case of *Leggiadri occhi sereni*, I:MOe, Mus. E 318 combines features found in two of the Fucci sources with others that are contained in US:PHu, MS Ital. 57.

2c. I:Bc, Q140

The manuscript Bologna, Civico Museo Bibliografo Musicale, Q140 (hereafter I:Bc, Q140), has never been examined in print. As Appendix B, Table 7 shows, this manuscript contains two items from Cardinal Montalto's production of *Amor pudico*, one of them preserved nowhere else, three concordances with items in two of the Fucci manuscripts, two concordances with US:PHu, MS Ital. 57, and one concordance with I:MOe, Mus. E 318. On the other hand, it is the first manuscript discussed so far with items, like Caccini's *Dovrò dunque morire* and Piccinini's *Filli gentile perché fug'ogn'hora*, that cannot be linked with Cardinal Montalto in any plausible way.

In fact, I:Bc, Q140 is a heterogeneous manuscript diplomatically as well as repertorially. It consists of six gatherings, as shown in Table 5.2. Each of the six gatherings is independent in content: none of them is linked by a connecting composition. They could have been copied at different times and places then bound together later. In fact, the principal copyist of I:Bc, Q140 finished entering compositions in what eventually became Gathering 1 with *Lasso perché mi fuggi* on fo. 4ʳ. Later a second copyist added *Ben è ver, ch'ei pargoleggia* on fo. 6ʳ, but the surrounding pages were left blank. Furthermore, Gatherings 1 and 2 have one watermark, Gathering 3 has a second one, and Gatherings 4–6 have a third. Finally, Gathering 3 itself is a composite of at least two independent fascicles:

---

[25] Fortune, ibid. 47, suggests that the initials 'H. M.' attached to *Questa tenera angioletta* in I:Fn, Magl. XIX.23, stand for '[H]orazio Michi'. He omits mentioning, however, that the initials in that manuscript are actually 'D. H. M.' Fortune did not know of the existence of Don Hippolito Macchiavelli when he wrote his dissertation. If he had, one suspects that Macchiavelli would have seemed to him a more likely candidate, since Michi—another Montalto composer—is not known to have composed any strophic variations like *Questa tenera angioletta*. Indeed, compositions of this type were out of fashion by the time Michi's surviving works were composed—evidently sometime after the assembly of the manuscripts from which Fucci copied his, as they contain nothing ascribable to Michi.

TABLE 5.2. Watermarks, gatherings, folios, and contents of I:Bc, Q140

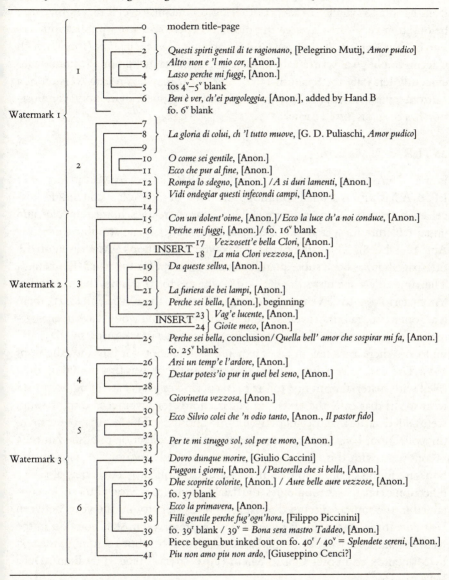

	0	modern title-page
	1	
	2	*Questi spirti gentil di te ragionano*, [Pelegrino Mutij, *Amor pudico*]
	3	*Altro non e 'l mio cor*, [Anon.]
1	4	*Lasso perche mi fuggi*, [Anon.]
	5	fos 4ᵛ–5ᵛ blank
	6	*Ben è ver, ch'ei pargoleggia*, [Anon.], added by Hand B
Watermark 1		fo. 6ᵛ blank
	7	
	8	*La gloria di colui, ch 'l tutto muove*, [G. D. Puliaschi, *Amor pudico*]
	9	
2	10	*O come sei gentile*, [Anon.]
	11	*Ecco che pur al fine*, [Anon.]
	12	*Rompa lo sdegno*, [Anon.] /*A si duri lamenti*, [Anon.]
	13	*Vidi ondegiar questi infecondi campi*, [Anon.]
	14	
	15	*Con un dolent'oime*, [Anon.]/*Ecco la luce ch'a noi conduce*, [Anon.]
	16	*Perche mi fuggi*, [Anon.]/ fo. 16ᵛ blank
	INSERT 17	*Vezzosett'e bella Clori*, [Anon.]
	18	*La mia Clori vezzosa*, [Anon.]
Watermark 2	3	19	*Da queste sellva*, [Anon.]
	20	
	21	*La furiera de bei lampi*, [Anon.]
	22	*Perche sei bella*, [Anon.], beginning
	INSERT 23	*Vag'e lucente*, [Anon.]
	24	*Gioite meco*, [Anon.]
	25	*Perche sei bella*, conclusion/*Quella bell' amor che sospirar mi fa*, [Anon.]
		fo. 25ᵛ blank
	26	*Arsi un temp'e l'ardore*, [Anon.]
	4	27	*Destar potess'io pur in quel bel seno*, [Anon.]
	28	
	29	*Giovinetta vezzosa*, [Anon.]
	30	*Ecco Silvio colei che 'n odio tanto*, [Anon., *Il pastor fido*]
	5	31	
	32	*Per te mi struggo sol, sol per te moro*, [Anon.]
	33	
Watermark 3	34	*Dovro dunque morire*, [Giulio Caccini]
	35	*Fuggon i giorni*, [Anon.] /*Pastorella che si bella*, [Anon.]
	36	*Dhe scoprite colorite*, [Anon.] / *Aure belle aure vezzose*, [Anon.]
	37	fo. 37 blank
	6		*Ecco la primavera*, [Anon.]
	38	*Filli gentile perche fug'ogn'hora*, [Filippo Piccinini]
	39	fo. 39ʳ blank / 39ᵛ = *Bona sera mastro Taddeo*, [Anon.]
	40	Piece begun but inked out on fo. 40ʳ / 40ᵛ = *Splendete sereni*, [Anon.]
	41	*Piu non amo piu non ardo*, [Giuseppino Cenci?]

the quaternion consisting of the present folios 17, 18, 23, and 24 was inserted between the outer and inner quaternions, as shown by the fact that *Perché sei bella* begins on fo. 22 but concludes on fo. 25.

The table reveals that all the music linked to Cardinal Montalto, either through *Amor pudico* or through concordances with the Fucci manuscripts, is located in

Gatherings 1 and 2 of I:Bc, Q140. The content of other gatherings may not derive from Montalto's circle. In fact, Gathering 6 contains several pieces that may belong to a very early layer of the monody repertoire: a pre-publication version of *Dovrò dunque morire* from Giulio Caccini's *Le nuove musiche* (1602), which Caccini implies was written about 1585; a canzonetta by Filippo Piccinini, who evidently left Italy for Spain in 1597;[26] and what may be an early version of a canzonetta by Giuseppino, whose reputation as a pioneer in monody composition has been discussed earlier.

2d. I:Rsc, A.Ms.247

Rome, Conservatorio di Musica 'Santa Cecilia', Biblioteca, A.Ms.247 (hereafter I:Rsc, A.Ms.247) is a small commonplace book of sixty folios containing miscellaneous poems, instructions for children's games, recipes, home remedies, and guitar tablature for a large number of dances, modes,[27] and strophic songs (see App. B, Table 8). The name of the male owner of the book was written on the title-page but has been subsequently cut away, except for the word 'Romanus'. The same title-page bears the date 1618, whereas fo. 51^r carries the inscription 'Aromatario venuto da Venetia l'anno 1656'. Between these pages, on fo. 21^r, there is a 'Sonetto sopra la morte del Card.le Montalto', which would have been written in 1623. On fos. 58^v–59 there is an account of a clock made in 1625, and on fo. 60^v there are a few notes of expenses and receipts for July and August of 1625. These dates certainly suggest that this notebook was first bound up then filled with material from first to last over a period of years extending from 1618 to 1656. In that case, the texts and guitar chords for seventeen strophic songs were added to the manuscript between 1618 and 1623. The fact that one item in this collection, *Voi partite sdegnose*, was printed in a collection published in 1623 is consistent with this hypothesis. The fact that only two of the songs in this book are found in other sources from Cardinal Montalto's circle may also be a reflection of relative chronologies: the datable items from Montalto's circles contained in the sources discussed so far tend to cluster around the years between 1611 and 1616. One item, *Per torbido mare*, is preserved in staff notation in the hand of composer Marc'Antonio Pasqualini (1614–91), but a setting of the text by Montalto's composer Orazio Michi (1594–1641) is praised by Pietro Della Valle in 1640.[28]

---

[26] According to Pier Paolo Scattolin in his entry on Alessandro Piccinini in *New Grove*.

[27] See Richard Hudson, 'The Concept of Mode in Italian Guitar Music during the First Half of the 17th Century', *Acta musicologica*, 42 (1970), 163–83.

[28] Robert R. Holzer, ' "Sono d'altro garbo . . . le canzonette che si cantano oggi": Pietro della Valle on Music and Modernity in the Seventeenth Century', *Studi musicali*, 20 (1991), 253–306, favours the ascription to Michi.

3. One Print Closely Related to Manuscripts in Montalto's Library

3a. Concerti amorosi: terza parte delle canzonette in musica raccolte da Giovanni Stefani (Venice: A. Vincenti, 1623)

Between 1618 and 1625, Giovanni Stefani compiled at least four anthologies of strophic canzonette for accompanied solo voice: *Affetti amorosi* (1618), *Scherzi amorosi* (2/1622), *Concerti amorosi* (1623), and *Ariette amorose* (1626), all published by Giacomo Vincenti in Venice. At least the first three were reissued in subsequent editions; the fourth, once known to Fétis, seems now to be lost.[29] Stefani's principal place of activity is unknown, but his repertoire, in so far as it can be traced, is Roman and Florentine.

The collection *Concerti amorosi* contains twelve canzonette that are found among six of the Montalto repertoire manuscripts described above, principally I:Bc, CC.225 (see App. B, Table 9). At the same time, seven of its items are found among three Florentine monody manuscripts: I:Fn, Magl. XIX.24; I:Fn, Magl. XIX.25; and I:Fc, Barbera. Two Romans, Ottavio Catalani and Giuseppe Cenci, and one Florentine who moved to Rome, Raffaello Rontani, can be identified as composers. Two closely related guitar-tablature manuscripts—I:Fn, MS Cl. VII, 1222 bis and GB:Lbm, Add. 36877—contain entire segments copied from each of the three Stefani prints.

It cannot be a mere coincidence that *Concerti amorosi* (1623), published in the year of Cardinal Montalto's death, contained so many pieces that presumably were preserved in the manuscripts that he jealously guarded during his life, and that the two Stefani anthologies published before Montalto's death contain virtually nothing that can now be traced to that repertoire. The collection *Affetti amorosi* (1618) (see App. B, Table 10) contains just three canzonette also found in I:Bc, Q140, a manuscript with mixed Roman and Florentine contents, while the anthology *Scherzi amorosi* (2/1622) contains nothing traceable to Montalto (see App. B, Table 11). Both these earlier prints, however, do include pieces from I:Fc, Barbera, a Florentine manuscript with repertoire covering the first quarter of the seventeenth century,[30] and the only composer identifiable in either of them is Jacopo Peri.

[29] Nigel Fortune, 'Stefani, Giovanni', *New Grove*.
[30] See Ghisi, 'An Early Seventeenth Century Manuscript', 46–60; and Nigel Fortune, 'Postscript' in his article 'A Florentine Manuscript and its Place in Italian Song', *Acta musicologica*, 23 (1951), 124–36 at 134–6.

4. Other Prints with Music by Composers in Montalto's Circles

Whether or not by coincidence, all but one of the Italian chamber monody anthologies known to have been published between 1621 and 1623 are Roman in origin, and of these all but the three compiled by Remigio Romano contain music by composers in Cardinal Montalto's circle or have concordances with sources of music by the cardinal's musicians. Three of these anthologies, compiled by Giovanni Stefani, were discussed in the preceding section. The seven further collections to be explored here were compiled by either Fabio Costantini (2), Giovanni Battista Robletti (3), Giovanni Battista Rocchigiani (1), or Giuseppe Giamberti (1), only the latter of whom had a direct connection to Cardinal Montalto, as far as we know.

4a. Ghirlandetta amorosa, arie, madrigali, e sonetti di diversi eccellentissimi autori . . . poste in luce da Fabio Costantini Romano . . . opera settima, libro primo (Orvieto: Fei and Ruuli, 1621)

This collection includes one work each by Pellegrino Mutij and Giovanni Bernardino Nanino, two musicians in Cardinal Montalto's household at this time, and one by Abundio Antonelli, who was once *maestro di cappella* of Montalto's church of San Lorenzo in Damaso (see App. B, Table 12). In addition, there is one piece by Giovanni Domenico Puliaschi, a Borghese composer who contributed music to Cardinal Montalto's production of *Amor pudico* in 1614; his contribution to this print, *Deh mirate luci ingrate*, is also found in I:Bc, CC.225, a manuscript with direct connections to Montalto's circle. Further, this anthology contains one item, *Perché non togli, o Clori*, that is here ascribed to Paolo Quagliati but is given to Giuseppino [Cenci] in two other 'Montalto' manuscripts. Two other composers represented in this print have less direct connections to Cardinal Montalto: Francesca Caccini, whom the cardinal tried to recruit for his sister's household in 1607 and who visited him in 1613, and Girolamo Frescobaldi, who collaborated with several of Montalto's musicians in the training of a boy singer in 1615, as recounted in Chapter 4. Nothing is known about Teofilo Gargarij. The compiler of this volume, Fabio Costantini, may have been in possession of some of Cardinal Montalto's manuscripts.

4b. Giardino musicale di varii eccellenti autori (Rome: Robletti, 1621)

This anthology, compiled and printed by Giovanni Battista Robletti and dedicated to the composer Paolo Quagliati, contains music by only one composer who had a position in one of Cardinal Montalto's musical establishments,

Abundio Antonelli. However, several of the other composers represented in this print also have music in one or more of the 'Montalto' manuscripts: Catalani, Landi, and Rontani (see App. B, Table 13). Like Catalani and Landi, Alessandro Costantini and Giovanni Boschetto Boschetti had links to the Borghese family through their associations with the leading Jesuit institutions of Rome, Costantini as *maestro di cappella* of the Collegio Germanico (1620–1) and Boschetti as *maestro* at the Seminario Romano in 1619. Costantini, however, had a more direct connection with Cardinal Montalto, since he had been a student of Montalto's *maestro di cappella*, Giovanni Bernardino Nanino. Frescobaldi's link to Montalto's musicians has already been mentioned. We have no biographical information about Francesco Cerasolo.

4c. Raccolta de varii concerti musicali a una et due voci da diversi eccellentissimi autori (Rome: Robletti, 1621)

This collection contains music by four composers who were in one of Cardinal Montalto's musical establishments at one time or another: Abundio Antonelli, Ippolito Macchiavelli, Pellegrino Mutij, and Giovanni Bernardino Nanino (see App. B, Table 14). In addition, it has pieces by three other composers with indirect links to the cardinal: Ottavio Catalani, Giuseppino Cenci, and Stefano Landi. Only the young Domenico Mazzocchi, among these composers, has no known connection to Montalto. The piece by Antonelli is found in I:Vc, Torrefranca 250, the largest and most central of the 'Montalto' manuscripts.

4d. L'aurata cintia armonica, arie, madrigali, dialogi, e villanelle di diversi eccellentissimi autori (Orvieto: Fei and Ruuli, 1622)

This is another anthology compiled by Fabio Costantini and printed by Fei and Ruuli in Orvieto (see App. B, Table 15). Most of the composers represented in it have been mentioned earlier. Two of them—Mutij and Antonelli—had posts in one of Montalto's musical establishments. Ferdinando Grappuccioli later became a singer in the papal chapel (1630–7).

4e. Vezzosetti fiori di varii eccellenti autori (Rome: Robletti, 1622)

This collection adds several composers not represented in the Robletti anthologies already discussed (see App. B, Table 16). Pietro Paolo Sabbatini sang in Cardinal Montalto's *Amor pudico* as a boy in 1614. Giovanni Giacomo Porro had been in the service of the Duke of Savoy since 1618, but in 1623, if not at the time this anthology was printed, he was *maestro di cappella* of Cardinal Montalto's church of San Lorenzo in Damaso. Pellegrino Mutij, of course, had been one of

Montalto's musicians since at least 1614. Francesco Severi and Nicolò Borboni were students of Ottavio Catalani. The piece by Severi in this collection is also found in I:Bc, CC.225, the second most important of the 'Montalto' manuscripts. We have no information about the patronage that supported Giovanni Antonio Todini, Gregorio Veneri, Enrico Torsianello, Antonio Granata, or Francesco Pesce.

4f. Il maggio fiorito arie, sonetti, e madrigali à 1. 2. 3. de diversi autori (Orvieto: Fei and Ruuli, 1623)

The most significant item in this anthology, from both the artistic and philological points of view, is the Lamento d'Arianna, Lasciatemi morire, from Claudio Monteverdi's otherwise lost opera L'Arianna (Mantua, 1608). The hypothesis presented towards the beginning of this chapter, apropos of I:Vc, Torrefranca 250, was that Cardinal Montalto obtained a copy of the Lamento from Monteverdi during the composer's visit in 1610 and that the unique similarities between the version printed in this anthology and the one preserved in I:Vc, Torrefranca 250 can be explained by their mutual dependence upon that copy. If that is so, then it would be reasonable to suspect that other items in this anthology were likewise copied from manuscripts in Cardinal Montalto's collection shortly after his death in 1623. We see from the inventory given in Appendix B, Table 17, however, that only one other piece in Il maggio fiorito has concordances in other 'Montalto' manuscripts: Amorosa Licori by Giuseppino Cenci. And only one further item in the collection is known to be by a Montalto composer: Pellegrino Mutij's Mille scherzi, e canti belli. Otherwise, with the exceptions of Giulio Caccini's Amarilli io mi parto and Giovanni Francesco Anerio's Pastorelle vagh'e belle, the contents of this collection remain, for the present at least, anonymous. However, the presence of a piece by Caccini might offer a clue to the origins of this print. I believe that it is the only composition by Giulio Caccini to appear in a Roman anthology, and Cardinal Montalto was Caccini's principal contact in Rome in his later life (he died in 1618), if we consider that Virginio Orsini, Caccini's protector and Montalto's brother-in-law, resided principally in Bracciano. By 1623 no one, I should think, was still collecting pieces by Giulio Caccini, so the hypothesis that a Caccini composition found its way anonymously into a Roman anthology by way of a manuscript of Cardinal Montalto seems plausible.

4g. Poesie diverse poste in musica da Gioseppe Giamberti Romano . . . con due aggiunte una di Gio. Bernardino Nanini, l'altra di Paolo Agostini ambidoi miei maestri (Rome: Soldi, 1623)

During the years 1615–16, at least, Giuseppe Giamberti was a singer in the chapel of S. Lorenzo in Damaso, the church attached to Cardinal Montalto's official residence, the Palazzo della Cancelleria. Although Giamberti's birth date is not yet known, it seems likely that he was still a boy during those years. The print described here is his first opus, and the title-page declares that two of the pieces that it contains are, respectively, by Giovanni Bernardino Nanino and Paolo Agostini, both teachers of his (see App. B, Table 18). Nanino, as we have seen, entered Cardinal Montalto's service in 1608 as *maestro di cappella* of S. Lorenzo in Damaso as well as member of the cardinal's private household; he died in 1618. Agostini, student and son-in-law of Nanino, was vice *maestro di cappella* at S. Lorenzo in Damaso from 1619 to 1626. These facts would fit well with the hypothesis that Giamberti studied with both teachers while he sang in the S. Lorenzo chapel, from at least 1615 to 1618 with Nanino and from 1619 to 1623 with Agostini. Perhaps as early as 1624 he became *maestro di cappella* at the cathedral of Orvieto, a position mentioned on the title-page of his Op. 3 in 1628. The monodic settings in his *Poesie diverse* (canzonette, sonetti, madrigals, a dialogue, and an ottava rima) must certainly be reckoned to emanate from one of the circles around Cardinal Montalto, if not the innermost circle. That this print contains no concordances with the Montalto manuscript sources would seem most likely a reflection of the relatively late date of their composition: probably around the year 1620. Orazio Michi, Montalto's favourite musician towards the end of his life, is not found in these manuscript sources either.

5. Guitar-Tablature Manuscripts Closely Related to the Foregoing Manuscripts and Prints

5a. GB:Lbm, Add. 36877

Additional Manuscript 36877 in the British Library, London, is a very large (146 folios) anthology identified on its title-page as 'Villanelle di più sorte con l'intavolatura per sonare, et cantare su la chitarra alla spagnola di Giovanni Casalotti' ('Villanelle of Various Kinds with Intabulation to Play and Sing with the Spanish Guitar by Giovanni Casalotti'). Although the manuscript is listed in Tyler's history of the early guitar,[31] no information is available about Giovanni Casalotti, the compiler of the anthology. The manuscript contains 149 texts in Italian (134 canzonette, 4 madrigals, 4 sonnets, 3 dialogues, 2 capitoli in terza rima, 1 stanza of ottava rima, and 1 cantata) and sixteen in Spanish (all *romances*) (see App. B, Table 19). Most of the texts in both languages have the typical early seventeenth-century alphabet chord tablature for five-string Spanish guitar above the words,

---

[31] Tyler, *The Early Guitar*, 145.

but no staff notation. The presence of Spanish texts tends to suggest Naples as the city of origin, although Spanish songs are found in early seventeenth-century manuscripts from all parts of Italy.[32]

The most immediate connection that this manuscript has with Cardinal Montalto is the presence here (fo. 118ʳ) of one aria, *Questi spirti gentil di te ragionano*, from the cardinal's *opera Amor pudico* (1614) and one aria, *Lagrimosa pietà, che più consolami*, from the 1616 production of the intermedi on texts by Guarini, which were first performed at Montalto's palace in 1612. The guitar chords for the aria from *Amor pudico* concord with the two staff-notation sources for the same number; no staff-notation source for the other aria is known. The manuscript contains concordances with five monody manuscripts with repertoire from the Montalto circle: I:Baf, MS 1424 (2), I:Bc, CC.225 (6), I:Bc, Q140 (5), I:Vc, Torrefranca 250 (3), and US:PHu, MS Ital. 57 (2). In addition, items found in this manuscript are also contained in the two Stefani anthologies with connections to the Montalto repertoire: *Affetti amorosi* (7) and *Concerti amorosi* (4). Unlike the manuscripts discussed above under other categories, this guitar-tablature anthology contains a significant number of concordances with Florentine monody manuscripts, particularly B:Bc, MS 704 and others in I:Fn. Since at least one staff-notation source served as a model for each entry in any guitar-tablature manuscript, a significant quantity of lost monody sources, many of them doubtless Roman, is reflected in the rather large number of items in GB:Lbm, Add. 36877 for which there are no concordances listed in the table.

Monody prints with concordances with GB:Lbm, Add. 36877 were published from 1602 to 1623, but no concordances with prints that appeared after 1623 have been found. Montalto, of course, died in 1623, and we have surmised that his jealously guarded musical repertoire became available to copyists and anthology compilers at that date. The pattern of concordances in the present manuscript tends to conform to that hypothesis.

There is, in addition, one concordance with a 1597 print of part-songs: *Più che mai vagh'e bella* by Gemignano Capilupi, which was published in *Canzonette à tre voci* (Venice: Gardano, 1597). Actually, the guitar chords in Add. 36877 seem to refer to a slightly different version of this canzonetta, one that included some extra repetition in its first section and two additional strophes of text not found in the print. Some of the guitar chords are at odds with Capilupi's three-part harmony, but in every case they accord with the printed soprano part, if sung alone. A set of guitar chords that does follow Capilupi's harmony exactly accompanies another version of the song in I:Fn, Magl. XIX.25, which consists of the soprano and bass (texted) of the three-voice printed version by Capilupi. Both sets of

---

[32] Cesare Acutis, *Cancioneros musicali spagnoli in Italia (1585–1635)* (Pisa, 1971); and Baron, 'Secular Spanish Solo Song'. Neither Acutis nor Baron mentions this manuscript as a source for Spanish songs, however.

guitar chords correspond to the staff notation only if the song is transposed down a fifth, as could happen if the 'chiavette' interpretation of the high clefs of the two staff-notation versions were employed. Since this is one of the few concordances known between guitar-chord tablature and a pre-1600 Italian part-song published without continuo, it would be interesting to know whether Add. 36877 preserves a later expansion for solo voice of Capilupi's three-voice canzonetta, or whether Capilupi's version is an arrangement of a song normally and earlier sung as a guitar-accompanied solo. The evidence at hand is not decisive on this point.

No items in guitar-chord tablature manuscripts have previously been concorded with staff-notation sources of Italian monody. The number of such concordances in Appendix B, Tables 19 and 20 demonstrates that guitar-chord tablatures are normally performing materials for solo songs whose melodies have been memorized by the singer. Earlier hypotheses that these tablatures represent 'instrumental accompaniment to a spoken dialogue' or mere frameworks for improvisation can be discarded.[33]

The practical value of GB:Lbm, Add. 36877 is that its guitar chords help to clarify chord selection and placement in accompaniments realized on the basis of the much less specific basso continuo notation in other sources. The manuscript also testifies to the broad diffusion and reception of the Montalto repertoire after the cardinal's death.

5b. I:Fn, Cl. VII, 1222 bis

Manuscript Cl. VII, 1222 bis in the Biblioteca Nazionale Centrale of Florence is quite similar in size and scope to the British Library anthology just described, with the notable difference that it does not contain any texts in Spanish. It contains exactly 200 Italian texts, most with guitar-tablature letters, including 196 canzonette, two stanzas of ottava rima, one madrigal, one sonnet, and one dialogue (see App. B, Table 20). It begins with a key to the 'intavolatura per la guitarra spagnola', followed by tablatures for forty-eight dances.[34] This manuscript has never been listed or described as a musical source.

The pattern of concordances between I:Fn, Cl. VII, 1222 bis and staff-notation sources is very similar to that shown in the table for GB:Lbm, Add 36877, with one major difference: there are entire blocks of texts that were copied into this manuscript in the same, or nearly the same, order in which they occur in the three printed anthologies compiled by Giovanni Stefani: *Affetti amorosi* (26), *Scherzi amorosi* (17), and *Concerti amorosi* (33). Either these parts of I:Fn, Cl. VII, 1222 bis were copied from the Stefani prints, or both were copied from a common (Roman)

---

[33] See Baron, 'Secular Spanish Solo Song', 25–8.

[34] Including a 'Ballo di Palazzo' not listed by Warren Kirkendale, *L'Aria di Fiorenza, id est il Ballo del Gran Duca* (Florence, 1972).

source or sources. Otherwise the usual manuscripts containing repertoire from the Montalto circles are found among the other concordances: I:Baf, MS 1424 (2), I:Bc, CC.225 (9), I:Bc, Q140 (6), and US:PHu, MS Ital. 57 (8). And the printed sources that concord with this manuscript were published between 1610 and 1623, the majority of them Roman in origin. Therefore it seems likely that I:Fn, Cl. VII, 1222 bis, like the British Library anthology discussed previously, was copied about 1623 or shortly after and includes repertoire that became available to the public only after the death of Cardinal Montalto in that year.

6. Sources of Music by Orazio Michi

Because there are no concordances between sources of music by Orazio Michi and the prints and manuscripts described under the previous five headings, I shall dispense with the tables of contents in this final portion of the chapter.

Compositions ascribed to Orazio Michi are preserved in five manuscripts and one print that are known at present. Two of the manuscripts, I:Rcas, MS 2472 and I:Rcas, MS 2490, are anthologies in oblong, four-stave format at the Biblioteca Casanatense, and they seem to be of Roman provenance, like the others of the same type in that library. These two Casanatense manuscripts are in one and the same hand, and both bear the imprint of a seal whose design incorporates a cross braced at its base by the initials 'A' and 'R'. Specialists working on this group of Casanatense manuscripts have not yet suggested an interpretation of these initials, so I will advance the hypothesis that they stand for 'Alouisce Rossi' or 'Alouigi Rossi', which are the forms of Luigi Rossi's name that appear in the Borghese account books of the 1620s and may, therefore, reflect the form that Rossi used during his early years in Rome. The manuscripts are not, however, in Rossi's hand, as even a cursory comparison with GB:Lbm, Add. 30491 demonstrates.[35] The contents of these two anthologies are complementary, consisting largely of works by composers active in Rome during the 1630s.[36] Only

---

[35] A sample of Rossi's hand from GB:Lbm, Add. 30491 is reproduced in the entry on Rossi in *New Grove*, xvi. 218.

[36] In I:Rcas, MS 2472:

Odoardo Ceccarelli (*c.*1605–68), papal chapel singer, 1628–58
Stefano Landi (1586/7–1639), papal chapel singer, 1629–39
Cieco Lombardi, i.e. Francesco Lambardi (*c.*1587–1642), in Naples
Giovanni Marciani (*c.*1605–*c.*1663), singer at the Collegio Romano
Domenico Mazzocchi (1592–1665), Aldobrandini musician with ties to the Barberini
Orazio Michi (1594–1641); after Montalto served Cardinal Maurizio of Savoy in Rome
Giovanni Minilli (Manelli?)
Gioacchino Moriani (=?)
Raffaelle Rontani (d. 1622), *maestro di cappella* of San Giovanni dei Fiorentini in Rome, 1616–22
Luigi Rossi (*c.*1597–1653), Borghese musician, 1620–41; Barberini household, 1641–53

two composers are represented in both manuscripts, Orazio Michi and Luigi Rossi, and Michi dominates both, accounting for twenty-two of the fifty-two items in I:Rcas, MS 2472 and thirty-two of the fifty-five pieces in I:Rcas, MS 2490. Pieces ascribed to Stefano Landi and Raffaello Rontani in I:Rcas, MS 2472 form the only concrete links between these two sources and the manuscripts from the Montalto circles described above.

Two other manuscripts with ascriptions to Orazio Michi are the nearly twin Florentine anthologies apparently copied during or shortly after Luigi Rossi's stay there in 1635: CS:Pnm, II.La.2, the so-called 'Roudnici manuscript',[37] and I:Bc, Q49.[38] Here, again, Michi and Rossi keep company, as they do in Vincenzo Bianchi's printed anthology *Raccolta d'arie spirituali a una, due, e tre voci* (Rome: Bianchi, 1640), whose collection of composers is very similar to those of the two Casanatense manuscripts.[39] In I:Rvat, Chigi Q.IV.8 Michi and Rossi are the only composers named, with two works each out of a total of thirty-six pieces.

A sixth manuscript, I:Rn, Ms. Mus. 56, identical in format with the Casanatense and Chigi anthologies, carries no ascriptions, although four of its pieces are assigned to Michi in three of the manuscripts just mentioned. A modern pencil annotation on the flyleaf of this manuscript says: 'Sono di Orazio Michi dell'Arpa cantore del Card. Montalto—M. Pacifico 1948', but I do not know who M. Pacifico is or was or how he or she came to that conclusion. The author

Mario Savioni (1608–85), papal chapel singer, 1642–85

In I:Rcas, MS 2490:

Giacomo Carissimi (1605–74), *maestro di cappella* of the Collegio Germanico, 1629–74
Giovanni Paolo Costa (fl. 1610–14), *maestro di cappella* of Treviso Cathedral
Vigilio Mazzocchi (1597–1646), *maestro* of the Cappella Giulia, Rome, 1629–46
Orazio Michi, as above
Luigi Rossi, as above
Paolo Tarditi, led music for the Arciconfraternità di Ss. Crocifisso, Rome, 1602–23; still living in 1649
Giuseppe Zamponi (*c.*1610/20–62), Roman; moved to Brussels in 1648

Michi's *Veggio nel tuo costato aspra ferita*, I:Rcas, MS 2490, fos. 56ᵛ–58ʳ, carries the inscription 'Sonetto di Papa Urbano VIII sopra Christo crocifisso', which means it was copied after Maffeo Barberini became Pope Urban VIII in 1623.

[37] An inventory and description is found in Paul Nettl, 'Über ein handschriftliches Sammelwerk von Gesängen italienischer Frühmonodie', *Zeitschrift für Musikwissenschaft*, 2 (1919–20), 83–93.
[38] Inventory and description in Fortune, 'A Florentine Manuscript'.
[39] Bianchi's anothology contains works by:

Giuseppe Giamberti (*c.*1600–62/4); served and studied under G. B. Nanino as a boy soprano in Montalto's chapel of San Lorenzo in Damaso, 1615–16; *maestro di cappella* of S. Maria Maggiore in Rome, *c.*1630–45
Domenico Massenzio (d. 1650), Seminario Romano, 1612; Collegio Inglese, 1624–6; Cappella Giulia, 1626–7
Virgilio Mazzocchi, as above
Domenico Mazzocchi, as above
Orazio Michi, as above
Luigi Rossi, as above
Loreto Vittori, as above
Giuseppe Zamponi, as above

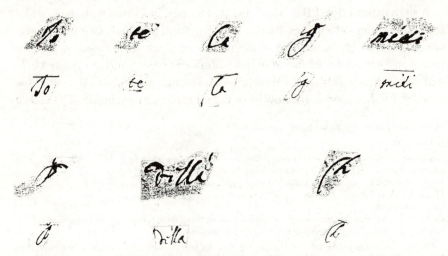

FIG. 5.6(a). Michi's autograph endorsement of his testament in 1641

FIG. 5.6(b). Individual letters, combinations, and words from the testament (above) compared with parallel samples of handwriting from I:Rn, Ms. Mus. 56

of the catalogue of the music collection of the Biblioteca Nazionale in Rome asserts that this manuscript is a probable Michi autograph.[40] Indeed, a detailed comparison between the text writing in I:Rn, Ms. Mus. 56, and the autograph authentication of Michi's testament of 1641 (Fig. 5.6) reveals a large number of significant similarities in letter forms, angles, and curvatures and no consistent dissimilarities that cannot be explained by the blunter or softer quill and coarser

[40] Arnaldo Morelli, *Catalogo del fondo musicale della Biblioteca Nazionale Centrale Vittorio Emanuele II di Roma* (Rome, 1989), 26.

paper used for the testament authentication.[41] Nearly all the pieces in I:Rn, Ms. Mus. 56 contain some compositional revisions, and all its concordances result in ascriptions to Michi and to no other composer. For all these reasons it makes sense to accept, provisionally, all the compositions in this manuscript as works by Michi.

On the basis of the foregoing, it is possible to list ninety-six or ninety-seven compositions as works by Michi, keeping in mind that those contained only in I:Rn, Ms. Mus 56 are incorporated in the list only by virtue of their inclusion in an autograph manuscript, and *Per torbido mare* only because Pietro Della Valle praised a setting of that text by Michi (see Table 5.3).[42]

---

[41] Michi's autograph authentication of his testament is reproduced in Cametti, 'Orazio Michi', 266.
[42] See above, n. 28.

TABLE 5.3. Provisional list of works by Orazio Michi

Incipit	Sources	Genre[a]
A pena il giorno	I:Rcas, MS 2472, fos. 47ᵛ–48ʳ	canzonetta text set strophically
Afflitto mio core	I:Rcas, MS 2490, fos. 13ʳ–14ʳ	canzonetta text set as a strophic trio
Al mio penoso ardore	I:Rvat, Chigi Q.IV.8, fos. 5ʳ–7ʳ	canzonetta text set as a strophic trio
All'hor che ridente	I:Rcas, MS 2490, fos. 82ᵛ–83ʳ	canzonetta text set strophically
Alma che ti sollievi a un dolce lume	I:Rn, Ms. Mus. 56, fos. 23ᵛ–24ᵛ	canzonetta text set strophically
Ben ratta fuggesi	I:Rcas, MS 2490, fo. 86ʳ	canzonetta text set strophically
Cari lumi che pietosi	I:Rn, Ms. Mus. 56, fos. 34ᵛ–35ʳ	canzonetta text by Francesco Balducci set strophically
Cari lumi che pietosi	I:Rn, Ms. Mus. 56, fos. 15ᵛ–16ʳ	canzonetta text by Francesco Balducci, of which only one strophe is given
Che legge è questa o Dio	I:Rcas, MS 2472, fos. 31ᵛ–32ᵛ	canzonetta text set strophically; mixed styles
Chi fe le stelle e 'l sole	I:Rcas, MS 2472, fos. 58ʳ–59ʳ	canzonetta text set strophically; mixed styles
Chi non dimanda aita	I:Rvat, Chigi Q.IV.8, fos. 1ʳ–4ᵛ	canzonetta text set as a strophic trio
Chi può mirar le stelle	I:Rcas, MS 2472, fos. 13ᵛ–14ʳ	canzonetta text set strophically
Chi puo mirarti	I:Rn, Ms. Mus. 56, fos. 25ᵛ–26ʳ	canzonetta text, of which only one strophe is given
Cieco mondo io t'abbandono	I:Rcas, MS 2490, fo. 78ʳ⁻ᵛ	canzonetta text, of which only one strophe is given
Cint'al crin di ricchi bende	I:Rn, Ms. Mus. 56, fos. 5ᵛ–6ʳ	canzonetta text, of which only one strophe is given
Collinetta chi di fiori	I:Rn, Ms. Mus. 56, fos. 26ᵛ–27ʳ	canzonetta text by Francesco Balducci set strophically
Colmo il sen d'ardente zelo	I:Rcas, MS 2490, fos. 48ᵛ–49ʳ; I:Rn, Ms. Mus. 56, fos. 9ᵛ–10ʳ	canzonetta text, of which only one strophe is given
Cor mio se questa fera	I:Rn, Ms. Mus. 56. fos. 36ᵛ–37ʳ	canzonetta text set strophically
Correte correte	I:Rn, Ms. Mus. 56, fos. 13ᵛ–14ᵛ	canzonetta text, of which only one strophe is given; mixed styles
Dal più profondo	I:Rcas, MS 2490, fo. 88ʳ⁻ᵛ	canzonetta text set strophically; mixed styles
Dalle squalide tombe al cielo uscita	I:Rcas, MS 2490, fos. 58ᵛ–60ʳ	sonetto text set as strophic variations, modified
Desio mortale	I:Rcas, MS 2472, fos. 46ᵛ–47ʳ	canzonetta text set strophically
Di fiamme e d'oro adorno	I:Rn, Ms. Mus. 56, fos. 8ᵛ–9ʳ	canzonetta text set strophically; mixed styles
Dicano i monti	I:Rcas, MS 2490, fos. 49ᵛ–51ʳ	canzonetta text set strophically
Disdegnoso il Ciel fremea	I:Rcas, MS 2472, fos. 55ʳ–56ʳ	canzonetta text set strophically
Disperato partirò	I:Rn, Ms. Mus. 56, fos. 30ᵛ–31ʳ	canzonetta text set strophically
Disse il folle entro sé	I:Rcas, MS 2490, fos. 18ᵛ–19ʳ	canzonetta text set as a strophic duet
Dolce frutto amor compose	I:Rn, Ms. Mus. 56, fos. 71ᵛ–72ʳ	canzonetta text, of which only one strophe is given

TABLE 5.3. Cont'd

Incipit	Sources	Genre[a]
Dolci sospiri	I:Rn, Ms. Mus. 56, fos. 21ᵛ–22ʳ	canzonetta text by Ottavio Rinuccini set strophically
Ecco di rose infiora	I:Rn, Ms. Mus. 56, fos. 6ᵛ–7ʳ	canzonetta text, of which only one strophe is given
Empio cor, core ingrato	I:Rcas, MS 2472, fos. 64ʳ–65ʳ	madrigal or monostrophic canzonetta set as a cantata
Fermate homai fermate	I:Rn, Ms. Mus. 56, fos. 47ᵛ–49ʳ	canzonetta text by Francesco Balducci set as strophic variations
Fierissimo dolore	CS: Pnm, II.La.2, fos. 62ʳ–64ʳ	lamento text set as recitative
Folle, folle chi crede	I:Rcas, MS 2490, fos. 84ᵛ–85ʳ	canzonetta text set strophically
Fugga la notte homai	I:Rn, Ms. Mus. 56, fos. 7ᵛ–8ʳ	canzonetta text, of which only one strophe is given
Fuggite amanti	I:Rcas, MS 2490, fos. 42ʳ–43ᵛ	canzonetta text set as a strophic duet
Giovanetti dhe non alletti	I:Rcas, MS 2490, fo. 79ʳ⁻ᵛ	canzonetta text set strophically
Gite gite sospiri	I:Rcas, MS 2490, fos. 22ʳ–23ʳ; I:Bc, Q49, fo. 4ʳ	madrigal text set as a trio
Guarda guarda mio core	CS:Pnm, II.La.2, fo. 4ʳ	canzonetta text set strophically
Hor che dal Tebro smaltano	I:Rn, Ms. Mus. 56, fos. 18ᵛ–19ʳ	canzonetta text by Francesco Balducci, of which only one strophe is given
Hor che la notte del silentio amica (i),[b]	I:Rn, Ms. Mus. 56, fos. 19ᵛ–20ᵛ	canzonetta text by Francesco Balducci, of which only one strophe is given; mixed styles
Hor che la notte del silentio amica (ii)	I:Rn, Ms. Mus. 56, fos. 59ᵛ–63ᵛ	canzonetta text by Francesco Balducci set as a cantata incorporating the preceding setting of the first strophe
Hor che scherza l'auretta	I:Rcas, MS 2490, fos. 16ᵛ–18ʳ	madrigal text set as a trio
Hor che si asconde	I:Rn, Ms. Mus. 56, fos. 31ᵛ–32ʳ	canzonetta text set strophically
I di sen volano tacit'ali	I:Rcas, MS 2472, fos. 51ᵛ–52ʳ	canzonetta text set strophically
I diletti del mondo	Bianchi, comp., *Raccolta d'arie spirituali a una, due, e tre voci di diversi eccellentissimi autori* (Rome: Bianchi, 1640), fos. 27ʳ–28ʳ	canzonetta text set strophically
Il tempo fugge i giorni Volano	I:Rn, Ms. Mus. 56, fos. 16ᵛ–17ʳ	canzonetta text by Francesco Balducci set strophically
Io che del mondo amante	I:Rcas, MS 2472, fos. 52ᵛ–53ᵛ	madrigal text or monostrophic canzonetta; mixed styles
Io son'amante sì	I:Rn, Ms. Mus. 56, fos. 27ᵛ–28ᵛ	canzonetta text, of which only one strophe is given
Ite voi del mio cor desiri ardenti	I:Rcas, MS 2472, fos. 59ᵛ–60ᵛ	canzonetta text set strophically; mixed styles
La mia pallida faccia	I:Rn, Ms. Mus. 56, fos. 65ᵛ–68ʳ	canzonetta text by Francesco Balducci set as strophic variations
La vita mortale	I:Rcas, MS 2490, fos. 81ʳ–82ʳ	canzonetta text set strophically
L'ardor che poco fà	I:Rn, Ms. Mus. 56, fos. 29ᵛ–30ʳ	canzonetta text, of which only one strophe is given

TABLE 5.3. Cont'd

Incipit	Sources	Genre[a]
Mio cor se cor tu sei	I:Rcas, MS 2472, fos. 50ᵛ–51ʳ; Bianchi, comp., *Raccolta d'arie* (1640), fos. 22ʳ–23ʳ	canzonetta text set strophically; mixed styles
Mira o stolto core	I:Rn, Ms. Mus. 56, fos. 4ᵛ–5ʳ	canzonetta text, of which only one strophe is given
Ne la bella stagion ch'ai raggi tepidi	I:Rn, Ms. Mus. 56, fos. 55ᵛ–59ʳ	canzonetta text by Francesco Balducci set as strophic variations
No, no ch'io non vo seguir	I:Rcas, MS 2490, fos. 9ʳ–10ᵛ	canzonetta text set as a strophic duet
Non chinate egri mortali	I:Rcas, MS 2490, fos. 53ᵛ–54ᵛ	canzonetta text set strophically
Non diffidar cor mio	I:Rcas, MS 2472, fos. 62ᵛ–63ᵛ	canzonetta text set strophically; mixed styles
Non festeggi al mio dolore	I:Rn, Ms. Mus. 56, fos. 21ᵛ–22ʳ	canzonetta text set strophically
Notturno velo	I:Rcas, MS 2472, fos. 56ᵛ–57ᵛ	canzonetta text set strophically
O che rigidi strali	I:Rcas, MS 2490, fos. 14ᵛ–16ʳ	madrigal text set as a duet
O luci che fate	I:Rcas, MS 2472, fos. 61ʳ–62ʳ	canzonetta text set strophically; mixed styles
O mas que Venus hermosa	I:Rn, Ms. Mus. 56, fos. 35ᵛ–36ʳ	villancico text set strophically
O mio cor che paventi	I:Rcas, MS 2490, fos. 20ʳ–21ᵛ	madrigal text set as a trio
Occhi leggiadri e belli	I:Rn, Ms. Mus. 56, fos. 73ᵛ–74ʳ	canzonetta text, of which only one strophe is given
Peccai signor peccai	I:Rcas, MS 2472, fos. 28ᵛ–29ᵛ	canzonetta text set strophically
Pensier ch'al ciel sen' va	I:Rcas, MS 2490, fo. 85ᵛ	canzonetta text set strophically
?*Per torbido mare*	I:Rvat, Barb. lat. 4151, fos. 246ᵛ–48ʳ (in Pasqualini's hand); I:Rsc, A.Ms.247, 14ᵛ	canzonetta text set strophically
Per tue gioie o mondo misero	I:Rcas, MS 2490, fos. 90ᵛ–91ᵛ	canzonetta text set strophically
Perché ahi lasssa torno a me	I:Rcas, MS 2472, fos. 48ᵛ–49ʳ	canzonetta text set strophically
Perché fiero al mio fallire	I:Rcas, MS 2490, fos. 89ᵛ–90ʳ	canzonetta text set strophically
Perché perché cor mio	I:Rcas, MS 2490, fos. 86ᵛ–87ᵛ	canzonetta text, of which only one strophe is given; cantillational and recitational styles
Perdan quest'occhi il sole	CS: Pnm, II.La.2, fos. 65ʳ–68ʳ; I:Rn, MS. Mus. 56, fos. 50ᵛ–54ᵛ	composite text by Francesco Balducci set as a cantata
Piangete afflitti lumi	I:Rcas, MS 2490, fos. 6ᵛ–8ᵛ	canzonetta text set as a strophic duet
Più non armi la mia lingua	I:Rn, Ms. Mus. 56, fos. 32ᵛ–33ᵛ	canzonetta text by Francesco Balducci set strophically
Quando Filli parti l'ondi piangevano	I:Rn, Ms. Mus. 56, fos. 70ᵛ–71ʳ	canzonetta text, of which only one strophe is given
Quando l'alba in Oriente	I:Rn, Ms. Mus. 56, fos. 12ᵛ–13ʳ	canzonetta text by Gabriello Chiabrera, of which only one strophe is given
Quanti quanti sospiri	I:Rcas, MS 2490, fos. 51ᵛ–52ʳ	canzonetta text, of which only one strophe is given; cantillational and recitational styles

Table 5.3. Cont'd

Incipit	Sources	Genre[a]
Quel Signor che fè l'aurora	I:Rcas, MS 2472, fos. 24ᵛ–25ʳ; Bianchi, comp., Raccolta d'arie (1640), fo. 24ʳ	canzonetta text set strophically
Se giocondo il cor si sta	I:Rcas, MS 2490, fo. 80ʳ⁻ᵛ	canzonetta text set strophically
Si dileguà è di distrugge	I:Rcas, MS 2490, fo. 47ʳ⁻ᵛ; I:Rn, Ms. Mus. 56, fos. 10ᵛ–11ᵛ	canzonetta text set strophically
Sino a quel segno o Dori	CS:Pnm, II.La.2, fos. 57ʳ–61ʳ; I:Bc, Q49, fos. 7ʳ–9ʳ; I:Rn, Ms. Mus. 56, fos. 42ᵛ–47ʳ	canzonetta text set as strophic variations
Sola fra suoi più cari	I:Rcas, MS 2490, fos. 60ᵛ–63ʳ; I:Rn, Ms. Mus. 56, fos. 37ᵛ–42ᵛ; I:Bc, Q43, fos. 92ʳ–96ʳ	canzonetta by Giovanni Battista Marino's text set in a mixture of expressive recitative and arioso style
Son mie Signor son mie	I:Rcas, MS 2472, fos. 54ʳ⁻ᵛ	canzonetta text, of which only one strophe is given; cantillation and recitational styles
Sospiri ch'uscite dall'arco mio sen	I:Rn, Ms. Mus. 56, fos. 64ᵛ–65ʳ	canzonetta text, of which only one strophe is given
Splendete ardete	I:Rcas, MS 2490, fos. 11ʳ–12ᵛ	canzonetta text set as a strophic duet
Stral'amor tal m'avventò	I:Rn, Ms. Mus. 56, fos. 68ᵛ–70ʳ	canzonetta text by Francesco Balducci, of which only one strophe is given
Su duro tronco esangue	I:Rcas, MS 2472, fos. 30ʳ–31ʳ; Bianchi, comp., Raccolta d'arie (1640), fos. 25ʳ–26ʳ	canzonetta text set strophically; mixed styles
Su fuggite mortali	I:Rcas, MS 2490, fos. 52ᵛ–53ʳ	canzonetta text set strophically
Su l'oriente	I:Rcas, MS 2490, fos. 55ʳ–56ʳ	canzonetta text, of which only one strophe is given; mixed styles
Tempo fu che sovente	I:Rcas, MS 2472, fos. 45ᵛ–46ʳ	canzonetta text set strophically; mixed styles
T'offesi e me ne pento	I:Rcas, MS 2472, fos. 49ᵛ–50ʳ; Bianchi, comp., Raccolta d'arie (1640), fo. 21ʳ	canzonetta text set strophically; mixed styles
Veggio nel tuo costato aspra ferita	I:Rcas, MS 2490, fos. 56ᵛ–58ʳ	sonetto text set as strophic variations
Vermiglia l'Aurora	I:Rcas, MS 2472, fos. 16ᵛ–17ʳ	canzonetta text set strophically
Vita de la mia vita/Se fai partita	I:Rn, Ms. Mus. 56, fos. 72ᵛ–73ʳ	canzonetta text, of which only one strophe is given
Zefiretti che spirante	I:Rn, Ms. Mus. 56, fos. 17ᵛ–18ʳ	canzonetta text by Francesco Balducci, of which only one strophe is given

[a] The ascriptions of poetry are taken from Holzer, 'Music and Poetry in Seventeenth-Century Rome', 110–13.

[b] Caluori, *The Cantatas of Luigi Rossi*, ii. 57, ascribes this piece to Luigi Rossi ('It is highly probable that the music is Luigi's') solely on grounds that Pietro Della Valle in 1640 praised a setting of this text by Rossi. Holzer, 'Pietro della Valle on Music and Modernity', follows Caluori in that ascription. Both authors would surely admit that both Michi and Rossi might well have set the same text. Neither Caluori nor Holzer knew that I:Rn, Ms. Mus. 56 is in Michi's hand. On balance, it seems more likely that the setting in the Michi holograph I:Rn, Ms. Mus. 56 is by Michi rather than Rossi.

6

The *Romanesca bastarda* and Other Arias

❧❧

RESUMING, now, the discourse begun in Chapter 3, we may ask how the monodies preserved in the *Grilanda musicale* and its companions drew and elaborated upon the earlier *arie di stile recitativo, et cantativo* and how subsequent monodists received the styles and procedures thereby created in the circles around Cardinal Montalto. The ordering of topics in the first part of this chapter derives from the organization of *Grilanda musicale* (I:Vc, Torrefranca 250), which appears to be the central surviving source preserving monodies from the circles around Cardinal Montalto. It is by far the longest, largest in format, and most elaborately decorated of Francesco Fucci's manuscripts. It also seems to have been his first, for the history of its construction—deduced from the constellation of its gathering structure, watermarks, index, pagination, and contents—reveals that Fucci changed his mind about its components and their ordering more than once during the process of assembling them. His other manuscripts seem to have been created after he was more familiar with his materials and was relatively certain about their ordering, as they show no comparable signs of indecision.

When information about the content and structure of the Torrefranca manuscript, shown in Appendix B, Table 1, and Table 5.1 of Chapter 5, is combined with some rudimentary observation of styles and' types, some pregnant facts emerge. Fucci began to assemble the manuscript with a particularly homogeneous group of pieces setting overwhelmingly non-strophic poetry (fos. 81–107). There are only three strophic variations in this segment, and two of those are in a recitational style rarely encountered in conjunction with that form. Actually, the first portion of this section to be copied (Gatherings 23–7, consisting of fos. 88–107) contains most of the recitative to be found in the manuscript. The second portion to be written (Gatherings 21–2, consisting of fos. 80 bis–88) includes a series of madrigals with reduced polyphonic texture (fos. 80ᵛ bis–85) that incorporates the majority of such works found in the manuscript. The most modern aspect of these otherwise archaic pieces are the two texts by Giovanni Battista Marino, *Alma afflitta, che fai?* and *Temer donna non dei*, but these were published

(1602) in the second volume of his *Rime* and were, therefore, in the poet's port-
folio during his service to Cardinal Pietro Aldobrandini (1604–8),[1] who was
then Cardinal Montalto's friend and ally. The most concrete suggestion of the
age of these madrigals is the presence of *Deh dolc'anima mia* by Giuseppino
Cenci, who may have composed it for a performance of *Il pastor fido* that his patron,
Cardinal Odoardo Farnese, produced in 1596, according to arguments to be
advanced in Chapter 7. Gatherings 23–7 include an anonymous *Quel augellin che
canta*, likewise from *Il pastor fido*, as well as apparently early versions of Raffaello
Rontani's works that were published, presumably later, in 1614 and 1619. Most
of the works in both portions of this original segment are unascribed in the
Grilanda; only the last work in each portion carries the name of a composer,
'Giuseppino' and 'Marotti', respectively.

Madrigals in Reduced Polyphony

Madrigals in reduced polyphony designates settings of madrigals (poems with irregular alternations of seven- and eleven-syllable lines and unpredictable rhyme
schemes) in which the accompanying bass line has a vocal character (even if
somewhat attenuated), being rather similar to an actual vocal line in degree and
kind of rhythmic activity. In meaning, the term has certain parallels with Einstein's
'pseudo-monody',[2] but has no pejorative connotation. The best-known example of it is Giulio Caccini's *Amarilli mia bella*, which he published as a solo madrigal with basso continuo accompaniment in his 1602 *Nuove musiche*, although
it was printed earlier in a version for six voices.[3] Although this texture is not
typical of the early Florentine monodists, other examples can be located, for
instance, in Caccini's *Queste lagrim'amare*, *Se in questo scolorito languido volto*, and
S'io ivo, anima mia, and in Jacopo Peri's *Ho visto al mio dolore*. Although reduced
polyphony would logically appear to represent an early stage in the development
of Baroque monody and seems to have been abandoned by the Florentines rather
early on, it is represented in the first group of solo madrigals printed in Rome,
that is, in *Era dunque ne fati occhi miei cari* and *Lagrimosa pietà che più consolami*
in the appendix to Paolo Quagliati's *Carro di fedeltà d'amore* (Rome: Robletti, 1611).
And the type continues in the madrigal settings of the Roman Giovanni Francesco
Anerio published in 1611–21, well after it was out of favour elsewhere. Indeed,

---

[1] James Mirollo, *The Poet of the Marvelous: Giambattista Marino* (New York, 1965), 21–7.
[2] Einstein, *Italian Madrigal*, 836–49.
[3] Tim Carter, 'Caccini's *Amarilli, mia bella*: Some Questions (and a Few Answers)', *Journal of the Royal Musical Association*, 113 (1988), 250–73.

Anerio may be the composer of some of the unascribed madrigals of this kind found in the sources described in Chapter 5.

Temer donna non dei is a particularly clear instance. It appears in the *Grilanda musicale* as a continuo-accompanied solo madrigal, while it is preserved in I:Bc, CC.225 as an accompanied duet for soprano and bass voices. A comparison between the two versions shows that the continuo part, which is essentially the same in both, is really derived from the bass voice of the duet version, in which imitation between the voice lines is more clearly brought out (see Vol. II, nos. 30 and 30*a*).

All but one of the madrigals in reduced polyphony in Gatherings 21–2 of the *Grilanda* actually employ extensive imitation between the vocal and bass parts (the exception is *Io vorrei pur morir così mi preme*, Vol. II, no. 27, which tends towards a homophonic texture). These pieces (Vol. II, nos. 26–30) generally reveal the habits of Roman/Neapolitan polyphonic madrigalists in their concentration on short, rhythmically incisive motifs that are elaborated through sequential repetition and the concomitant reiteration of both short and long segments of the text. Their rhythms tend towards the square and metrical, and at best their vocal lines tend to conform to the accents of the text but never imaginatively interpret it through declamation. Considering that these pieces are notated here for accompanied solo voice, they are remarkably devoid of ornamental passaggi, which factor contributes further to their archaic appearance. Like many late sixteenth-century polyphonic madrigals, these musical settings tend to project the texts by means of illustration and harmonic structure. For example, in *Alma afflitta che fai* (Vol. II, no. 29), the words *Chi ti darà più vita* are accompanied by a sudden shift from lugubrious to lively rhythm, and the phrase *Hai son ben foll'e cieco* is introduced by an abrupt *mutatio toni* signalled by the juxtaposition of G minor and F major chords.[4]

We know of only one other manuscript produced by Francesco Fucci, I:Bc, CC.225, that includes a similar group of madrigals in reduced polyphony, and it contains all five of those found in the original segment of the *Grilanda musicale*, copied in the same order, reproducing the same idiosyncrasies of beaming, and perpetuating the same errors. These pieces were therefore derived either from a common source or from the *Grilanda* itself. After finishing I:Bc, CC.225, which is second to the *Grilanda musicale* in length and elaboration, Fucci apparently abandoned this group of madrigals when assembling his other anthologies.

Among the collateral manuscripts, only US:PHu, MS Ital. 57 incorporates similar compositions. But while these are madrigals in reduced polyphony, they are

---

[4] Concerning Athanasius Kircher's (1650) terms *mutatio modi* (shift of system) and *mutatio toni* (shift of mode), see Eric Chafe, *Monteverdi's Tonal Language* (New York, 1992), esp. p. 23.

otherwise quite different from Fucci's, as they include very little imitation but a considerable number of decorative melismas. Also by way of difference, musical and textual repetition in them tends to be restricted to the reprise of the final section, setting the acumen or concluding 'point' of the text, as was customary in both the polyphonic and the solo madrigal.

In Giuseppino Cenci's setting of *Ahi com'a un vago sol cortese giro* (Vol. II, no. 101), the two roughly synonymous verbs of the acumen, *sanai* and *salda*, are emphasized (bb. 34–42) by brief ornamental gestures. In the repetition of the point (bb. 43–53), the first of these is expanded into a longer passaggio, and in the additional elaboration of the last line, the second of the verbs receives an even more extended treatment. Thereby, the idiom of embellished solo song is mustered in the service of text expression, creating a series of climaxes of increasing weight and urgency, as the last lines of the poem seem by degrees to be filled with the singer's spontaneous and nearly uncontrollable emotion.

Guarini's poem is disposed in three sentences, the second of which, in some respects, is a clarification and amplification of the first:

Ahi com'a un vago sol cortese giro	Ah, as to a charming single kind turn
De' duoi begl'occhi ond'io	of two beautiful eyes, whence I
Soffersi il primo e dolce strale d'Amore,	suffered the first sweet dart of Love,
Pien d'un novo desio,	full of new desire,
Sì pronto a sospirar torn'il mio core.	so ready to sigh, my heart turns.
Lasso, non val nascondersi ch'omai	Alas, there is no use hiding it, since by now
Conosci i segni che il mio cor m'adita	you know the signs that my heart reveals to me
Dell'antica ferita.	of the ancient wound.
Et è gran tempo pur ch'io la sanai;	And although I long ago healed it,
Ahi, che piaga d'amor non salda mai.	ah, Love's scar never closes!

The first sentence builds considerable syntactic tension through the anticipation by an adverbial extension (itself expanded with a relative clause) and two appositional phrases of the principal clause *torn'il mio core*. Giuseppino effectively underscores the moment of arrival with an extended cadential gesture on the highest closing note of the piece (bb. 16–18). On the other hand, he found no means to parallel the adverbial clause with musical hypotaxis. Neither did Monteverdi (in Book V). The articulation of the madrigal at the word *Lasso* is accomplished by recourse to the cliché of the descending third to broadened rhythm, here with a slight vestige of imitation in the bass (bb. 19–22). The extended approach to climax through expansions of melismas in the repetitions of the acumen and its last line, mentioned earlier, is enhanced by the rising lines and growing level of rhythmic activity in the bass during the later portion of the madrigal (bb. 34–68).

Recitational Madrigals and Recitatives

The madrigals that fill the original core of the *Grilanda musicale* (fos. 89–107) form another remarkably consistent set, unified in this case by their extraordinary concentration on recitational style. In this type, early accompanied monody made its most decisive break with the polyphonic madrigal. It was with understandable pride that Giulio Caccini pointed to his settings of *Perfidissimo volto*, *Vedrò 'l mio sol*, and *Dovrò dunque morire* as among his earliest works, because they are the madrigals in his 1602 *Nuove musiche* with the greatest concentration of the features that define this style, which he called *favellare in armonia* ('speaking in music'): predominantly syllabic text-setting, narrow vocal range within phrases, wide range of note values assigned to syllables, frequent use of monotone, and a bass mostly in mimims, semibreves, and breves and without many vestiges of a vocal melodic or rhythmic character. Although *Ite amari sospiri* and *Per pianto la mia carne si distilla* in Quagliati's *Carro di fedeltà d'amore* (1611) give a prominent place to this style, it has not been associated with Roman monody to any great extent in modern scholarship prior to the discovery and identification of the sources described in Chapter 5.

In the Fucci manuscripts, the pastoral element is unusually strong in the madrigals of this type. The anonymous settings of Guarini's *Amiam Fillide amiam ah non rispondi* (Vol. II, no. 34) and Bernardo Tasso's *O tu che fra le selve occulta vivi* (Vol. II, no. 45) incorporate the echo device native to the dramatic pastorale. *Quel augellin che canta* (Vol. II, no. 35) and *Ch'io t'ami et ami più della mia vita* (Vol. II, no. 41) are actually from *Il pastor fido*, while *Dolcissimo usignolo* (Vol. II, no. 36) could easily be inserted into that play immediately after *Quel augellin*, as happens in the *Grilanda*. In each of these madrigals, the recitational style is relieved by one or more bursts of florid melismas, and in several of them, cantillational passages, both syllabic and melismatic, with both active and static bass lines, alternate with recitative.

In *O Filli, o Filli queste voci estreme* and *Tu torni anima mia*, cantillational style is introduced with a change to 3/2 metre precisely at the beginning of the acumen. In the former (Vol. II, no. 37) this corresponds to the last two lines of the madrigal:

O Filli, o Filli, queste voci estreme	O Phyllis, o Phyllis, these last words,
Per estremo dolor tratto dal core.	out of extreme pain, I speak from the heart.
Ascolta di chi more.	Hear him who is dying!
O Filli, o Filli questo pianto amaro	O Phyllis, o Phyllis, this bitter tear
Ch'amaramente versand'agl'occhi fuori:	bitterly pouring forth from my eyes:
Rimira a chi more	gaze upon him who is dying
Ch'il tuo morir t'è grato.	for your death gives you pleasure.

Vedilo almeno o cruda;	Look upon it, at least, o cruel lady;
Aprime gl'occhi insin che gl'occhi chiuda.	Open your eyes to me until my eyes close.

The recitative style used in this madrigal is melodically more expressive and musically organized than would be expected in the narrative recitative used for most dialogue in early opera. Both expression and organization are served by the reharmonized sequential repetition of the opening line (bb. 1–6), the inversion of the initial motif for the second apostrophe to Filli (m. 16), and the parallel treatments of *ascolta, ascolta* (bb. 10–12) and *rimira, rimira* (bb. 24–6). Expressive details such as the diminished fifth leap to a discord on the word *pianto* and the chromatic inflection at the end of *amaramente* (b. 20) are used sparingly. The unnamed composer uses more rhythmic variety and somewhat slower delivery than is typical in narrative recitative, but the extent of monotone delivery and the largely static bass of bars 1–31, often remaining on a single pitch for two and three semibreves, leave no room for confusion with typical early Florentine solo-madrigal style. The acumen in the last two lines is introduced by a passage in 3/2 metre that lasts only three bars, but cantillational style remains after the return to common time. It is marked by an avoidance of monotone recitation, a more active bass line that even participates in imitation (bb. 47–50), and a melismatic preparation for the final cadence. The poem, incidentally, is conspicuously Marinist in tone and cannot be understood, I think, in any other than sexual terms.

Tu torni anima mia (Vol. II, no. 38), which follows immediately in the *Grilanda musicale*, is sufficiently similar in style to the foregoing that it could be by the same composer. Even the motif and treatment employed here at the words *tu torni, tu torni* resemble those used for *ascolta, ascolta* and *rimira, rimira* in the previous work. But now the cantillational style is mixed with the recitational throughout the body of the poem. And, after the prefatory eighth line is repeated to the by now familiar device of the reharmonized sequence (bb. 53–6), the acumen begins with a much more extended songlike period in 3/2 (interrupted at the end in order to prolong the cadence), in which the initial phrase (57–63), ending inconclusively on the D major chord, is answered by its own closed variant concluding on the modal final, G. The last line is delivered in a style situated somewhere between recitational and cantillational.

Comparable to the two foregoing in many ways but with an even longer cantillational treatment of the acumen is the anonymous setting of Battista Guarini's *O quanto sei gentile* (Vol. II, no. 31). The recitative style is drier and more distinct from madrigalian arioso than that heard in either *O Filli, o Filli queste voci estreme* or *Tu torni anima mia*, while the frequent alternation between recitational and cantillational styles is more like the latter of those two. The acumen, consisting of the last two lines of text, is much longer, occupying the last thirty-six bars and incorporating a varied repeat, like the one found in *Tu torni anima mia*. This section achieves its extreme length, in part, because the first half of the last line, *Vivi cantando*, is sung six times in all. The recurring threefold repetition of the these words creates a metrical verse rhythm, reflected in the triple proportion of the musical setting, which brings about a departure from the prose-like unpredictability of accentuation pattern that is normal for madrigal verse. A similar process, although resulting in duple-metre canzonetta style, is achieved earlier (bb. 12–15) with the metrical repetitions *Tu prigion, io prigion, tu prigion, io prigion*. In effect, the composer, through these repetitions, creates a temporary shift to metrical, canzonetta-like verse, a feature that decades later will be built into the poems themselves in order to accommodate exactly this kind of contrast between recitative and songlike aria.

The jewel of the recitational pieces in this original section of the *Grilanda musicale* is the anonymous *Doppo un lungo sospiro* (Vol. II, no. 39). The poem by itself is no masterpiece but offers the composer a useful contrast between its narrative frame and the direct discourse of its central part as well as some fluctuations of tempo and a few expressive exclamations. Beyond this, its brutal concision favourably accommodates this composer's dramatic style and evokes a brief musical utterance, which gathers a power not entirely dissipated at the conclusion. The text is unusual for pastoral verse, as the protagonist and quite possibly the narrator are women.

Doppo un lungo sospiro	After a long sigh,
Apena puote dir queste parole	scarcely could she say these words,
La bellissima Nisa al suo bel sole:	the very beautiful Nisa, to her fair sun:
'Crudel, per te sospiro,	'Cruel man! For you I sigh,
Per te l'anima spira,	for you my soul expires,
E non m'aiuti e non mi porgi aita!	and you help me not nor render me aid.
Voi ch'io lasci la vita.	You want me to leave this life.
Morrò, morrò s'a te ben mio t'involi.	I shall die! I shall die if you, my beloved, desert me.'
Ma il pastor più crudel gli disse, 'mori'.	But the cruel shepherd said, 'Die.'
Cadd'ella tramortuta in gremb'ai fiori.	She fell, stunned, onto the bosom of flowers.

The composer develops the first line of the poem into an ominous procatascene by isolating the words *doppo* and *un lungo sospiro* with aposiopeses, solemnly intoning the first one on the fifth degree while maintaining the D minor harmony through four measures. The slight optimism in the balance of the opening narration, generated by accelerated pace, the melodic ascent at *la bellissima Nisa*, and the rapid movement to C major harmony, serve to set off the shift to E major, the delayed vocalization, and the chromatic cross-relations of Nisa's despairing *Crudel per te sospiro, per te l'anima spira*. The intensified repetition of the central accusation, *Voi ch'io lasci la vita*, is rendered more powerful by a reharmonization that produces an expansive mutation from D major to C major at bar 22.[5] Another shift, from E major to D minor, introduces Nisa's cataplexal epizeuxis *Morrò, morrò, morrò*, which intensifies the same faltering rhythm of her first imprecations through two unprepared discords. The narrator, intensely sympathetic from beginning to end, braces for the shepherd's reply with rising line and accelerated repetition of *gli disse, gli disse*, but the cold response, *mori*, shatters the melodic line—and possibly the harmony, if the omission of the sharp from the last note of bar 34 is intentional. The narrator's climactic peroration resumes where she left off. From that point an extraordinary cascade of thirds descends to the $c\sharp'$ at the end of *tramortuta*, which presses and yearns for the final d'. Once again, the reharmonized sequential repetition of the vocal phrase creates an appalling dissonance (b. 38), as the music rapidly expires.

While the style of *Doppo un lungo sospiro* could be described as expressive recitative merging with arioso, there are examples elsewhere in the Fucci manuscripts of nearly unrelieved narrative recitative. The most extended example of this is *Udite Amanti udite* in I:Ru, MS 279 (Vol. II, no. 85). Andrea Salvadori's poem is a curious concatenation of rhymed septenarial couplets retelling the ancient tale of 'Cupid and the Bee' in the tradition of Anacreon but with no known model in the abundant derivative literature.[6] It disposes the story in eight segments: (1) Cupid wanders through the meadows, shooting birds but also wounding the narrator (bb. 1–12). (2) He spies a rose half-opened, which he attempts to pick (bb. 12–35). (3) A bee, hidden in the flower, stings him on the lip; he runs to his mother, Venus (bb. 35–60). (4) Cupid complains that he has been bitten by a winged serpent (bb. 60–75). (5) Venus smiles and reminds him that his arrows cause much more painful wounds (bb. 76–108). (6) In exchange for Cupid's promise to give only pleasure and no pain with his arrows, Venus soothes his stung lips with a kiss, after which he flies away (bb. 109–38). (7) The narrator blames Venus for not letting Cupid die of his bee sting, for the young god immediately resumes his dolorous archery (bb. 139–59). (8) The narrator hopes that the next time faithless Cupid is stung in the meadow it will be by a viper rather than a bee (bb. 160–74).

The unidentified composer of *Udite Amanti udite* marks the end of each of these eight segments with a major cadence and signals the beginning of most of the

---

[5] At bars 21, 23, 40, and 42 I have added editorial major thirds not shown by bass figures, following the invariable practice of contemporary lute intabulations of continuo accompaniments to monodies and the uniform advice of the earliest Italian treatises on the subject, as I have reported in 'Realized Continuo Accompaniments from Florence, *c.* 1600', *Early Music*, 11 (1983), 194–208.

[6] The ancient sources and modern versions of this tale are discussed by James Hutton, 'Cupid and the Bee', *Publications of the Modern Language Association*, 56 (1941), 1036–58; and Joseph G. Fucilla, ' "Cupid and the Bee": Addenda', *Publications of the Modern Language Association*, 58 (1943), 575–9. *Udite Amanti udite* was not known to these authors, and it does not specifically resemble any of the versions that they cite.

ensuing episodes with a harmonic mutation. But the setting articulates the poem on both a larger and smaller scale, by full stops and double bars after Episodes 3, 5, 6, and 7, and by several lesser cadences, some followed by mutations.

The setting of *Udite Amanti udite* is almost entirely syllabic with only occasional cadential melismas, such as might be found in many early operatic recitatives. The vocal range within phrases is narrow, and the composer has frequent recourse to monotone recitation. Since it has little chromaticism, dissonance, and rhythmic variety, it would belong to the category of narrative style, in Giovanni Battista Doni's scheme.[7] As in the operas of Caccini, Peri, Monteverdi, and Gagliano, syllables are set to note values ranging from the semibreve to the semifusa, and the bass moves predominantly in semibreves and minims, rarely semiminims and never fusae. The setting seems to be made more for rapid delivery than for expressive detail, although there are a few interpretive touches, as in the not entirely expected projection of dejection, though slow delivery, pause, and downward inflection, at the beginning. The numerous unprepared and repeated dissonances (bb. 42, 55, 57, 58–9, 63, 72–3, 78, 84, 89, 103–4, 110, 121, 148, and 173) are motivated by the text and reveal that the composer was more oriented towards the *seconda prattica* than were Cavalieri, Agazzari, Landi, and most later Roman opera composers.

Occhi belli occhi rei (Vol. II, no. 18) is another poetic curiosity set, in the *Grilanda musicale*, likewise entirely in recitative style. The anonymous poem, which might be described as an experimental mutation of a canzone, consists of six long strophes of eighteen settenari each, organized by a very complex rhyme scheme, plus a *residuo* whose four lines combine a reprise of the poem's first verse with the rhyme scheme of the last quatrain of the first strophe. The *residuo*, however, makes no reference to the canzone itself. The form is further obscured by five anomalies in the rhyme scheme (modifications of the original text or errors in transmission?) and a musical setting that frequently runs lines together in order to preserve poetic enjambment. The musical style is narrative recitative with narrow range, much pitch repetition, and very slow-moving bass, as in *Udite Amanti udite*. Syllables to successive semifusae are not found, although the unnamed composer has the peculiar habit of using patterns of dotted fusae and semifusae, which I cannot recall encountering in any other Italian recitative. There are no obvious interpretive details in the declamation and no use of *seconda prattica* dissonance. Unlike *Udite Amanti udite*, this work includes several ornamental passaggi as preparations for cadences.

Recitative style is also found in nine of the thirteen dialogues preserved in the

---

[7] Giovanni Battista Doni, *Annotazioni sopra il compendio de' generi e de' modi della musica* (Rome: Fei, 1640), 60–3.

sources described in Chapter 5.[8] *Perché non togli o Clori* (Vol. II, no. 13) is ascribed to Giuseppino in the *Grilanda musicale* but (less plausibly) to Paolo Quagliati in *Ghirlandetta amorosa* (1621)—less plausibly because nothing else ascribed to Quagliati is in a similar recitative style. Monotone recitation and static bass are abundant, but harmonic movement is not restricted to the support of primary verse accents, as often in Peri and Monteverdi. Also unlike those two, Giuseppino here does not set syllables to semifusae. Most segments of recitative have some short melismas for relief, not unlike the recitatives of Gagliano or Landi. There is no *seconda prattica* dissonance. The rhythm is rather stiff, not as reflective of *sprezzatura di canto* as Peri's or Monteverdi's, but the overall style is more purely recitational and operatic than is found in any of Giuseppino's works discussed in Chapter 3.

We may conclude from the foregoing that several types of recitative style were known in Cardinal Montalto's circles, none of them precisely like Peri's or Monteverdi's, some of them similar to those of later Roman opera, but all of them fully differentiated from the older recitational styles rooted in aria formulas, villanelle, or declamatory madrigals. Altogether, nine through-composed madrigal settings in Fucci's *Grilanda musicale* contain some sort of juxtaposition between recitational and cantillational styles, as we saw emerging in the earlier Roman and Neapolitan villanelle and madrigals discussed in Chapter 3.[9] To a limited extent, these juxtapositions conform to the tendency, observed by Nigel Fortune in the solo-madrigal repertoire of the second and third decades of the seventeenth century, to introduce 'aria-like' passages at or near the conclusions, not infrequently involving a shift to triple metre.[10] But among the examples that Fortune cites,

---

[8] *Ecco ch'all'apparire*, Fabio Costantini, *Ghirlandetta amorosa* (1621), 21–2
Ecco Maggio pastori, anon., *Il maggio fiorito* (1623), 16–19
Ecco l'alma staggione, Giuseppe Giamberti, *Poesie diverse poste in musica* (1623), 27–33
Fiammeggiante del ciel fulgida, Fabio Costantini, *L'aurata cintia armonica* (1622), 5–6
O bella Clori, Fabio Costantini, *L'aurata cintia armonica* (1622), 33
Pargoletta son'io, Alessandro Constantini, *Vezzosetti fiori di varii eccellenti autori* (1622), 15–17
Pascomi di sospir languendo e debile, Francesca Caccini, I:Ru, MS 279, fos. 61ʳ–68ᵛ
Perché non togli o Clori i pesci al fiume, Giuseppino [Cenci], I:Vc, Torrefranca 250, fos. 41ᵛ–45ʳ; also ascribed to
       Paolo Quagliati in *Ghirlandetta amorosa* (1621), 23
S'ardo il mondo com'io, Fabio Costantini, *Ghirlandetta amorosa* (1621), 24–5
       The two dialogues set in canzonetta style, without recitative, are:
Amorosa Licori, Giuseppino [Cenci], I:Vc, Torrefranca 250, fos. 29ᵛ–34ʳ
Ove ne vai pastor così doglioso, anon., I:Bc, CC.225, fos. 53ᵛ–54ʳ
       Two further dialogues are preserved with guitar chords but no staff notation for the voice:
Quando miro il vago volto, anon., GB:Lbm, Add. 36877, fo. 15ʳ
Son prontissimo sempre a voler far, anon., I:Fn, Cl. VII, 1222 bis, fos. 102ʳ–103ᵛ

[9] *O quanto sei gentile car'augellino*, *Donna per acquetar vostro desire*, *Deh dolc'anima mia*, *Amiam Fillide amiam ah non rispondi*, *Quel augellin che canta*, *Dolcissimo usignolo*, *O Filli, o Filli queste voci estreme*, *Tu torni anima mia*, and *Doppo un lungo sospiro* (Vol. II, no. 39), which fill adjacent folios, 85ᵛ–95ʳ, in the manuscript.

[10] Fortune, 'Italian Secular Song from 1600 to 1635', 284–98.

none employs recitative as clearly marked as *O quanto sei gentile*, and only one, Andrea Falconieri's madrigal *Deh dolc'anima mia* (Book 6, 1619), even approaches the recitational style of *O Filli, o Filli queste voci estreme* and *Tu torni anima mia*. Fortune also found that in the chamber monodies available for his study there was very little recitative in general, and nearly all that he did find was in *lettere amorose* and laments,[11] examples of which mostly postdate the Montalto repertoire. Clearly there is something extraordinary in the extensive use of recitative in the pieces that Francesco Fucci copied into his manuscripts and in the large-scale contrast between recitative and songlike aria in several of these through-composed madrigals. We already saw some of this contrast in the music of Giuseppino examined in Chapter 3. Several of the examples considered so far in this chapter are anonymous. It would seem quite probable that some of them are by Giuseppino himself. Others may well be by Cesare Marotta, who, we know from letters and librettos, wrote recitatives (now lost) for the intermedi (1612–16) discussed in Chapter 8 and for the opera *Amor pudico* (1614), to be examined in Chapter 9.

Florid Arioso Madrigals

Between the extremes of reduced polyphony and recitative falls the florid arioso that is the most common in early Florentine solo madrigals. It is remarkable, therefore, that the Fucci manuscripts contain no madrigals that exactly conform to that style. *Crud'Amarilli, che col nom'ancora* (Vol. II, no. 102) and *Vorrei baciarti, o Filli* (Vol. II, no. 103) in US:PHu, MS Ital. 57 would be examples of this type, in which the distinctly non-vocal bass moves constantly at a slower pace than the voice, mostly in minims with occasional semibreves, while the vocal line moves freely over its full range and neither remains on one pitch for long nor interprets the text through musically controlled or particularly rapid declamation. The brief and modest melismas that are notated in these two works resemble those that one finds in early manuscript sources of Caccini's solo madrigals,[12] including the unpublished version of his *Dovrò dunque morire* (Vol. II, no. 139) in I:Bc, Q140, which can be conveniently compared with the two previously mentioned. *Care lagrime mie* (Vol. II, no. 97) in US:PHu, MS Ital. 57 is also similar to those two, but its bass is both less angular and more active and motivic, although not as much so as *Ahi com'a un vago sol cortese giro* and other madrigals more obviously written in a reduced polyphonic style.

---

[11] Fortune, 'Italian Secular Song from 1600 to 1635', 270–3.

[12] See Nancy Maze, 'Tenbury Ms 1018: A Key to Caccini's Art of Embellishment', *Journal of the American Musicological Society*, 9 (1956), 61–3; H. Wiley Hitchcock, 'Vocal Ornamentation in Caccini's *Nuove Musiche*', *Musical Quarterly*, 56 (1970), 389–404; and Tim Carter, 'On the Composition and Performance of Caccini's *Le nuove musiche* (1602)', *Early Music*, 12 (1984), 208–17.

TABLE 6.1. Works ascribed to Cesare Marotta

Incipit	Main source[a]	Genre	Edition (Vol. II)
Che più giova mirar occh'infelici	I:Vc, Torrefranca 250, fos. 106ʳ–107ᵛ	ottava rima, strophic variations on the Romanesca, from the 1616 intermedi	no. 48
Dove, dove ten fuggi anima bella	I:Vc, Torrefranca 250, fos. 71ʳ–73ᵛ	canzonetta, strophic variations	no. 21
O dell'ombrosa notte amati orrori	I:Vc, Torrefranca 250, fos. 103ᵛ–105ᵛ	terza rima, composite strophic variations	no. 47
O durezze amarissime d'amore	I:Vc, Torrefranca 250, fos. 73ᵛ–75ʳ	ottava rima, strophic variations on the Romanesca from the 1616 intermedi	no. 22
Può ben fortuna far ch'io m'allontani	I:Baf, MS 1424, fos. 46ᵛ–48ʳ	canzonetta, strophic variations	no. 83
Suavissimi lumi al cui splendore	I:Vc, Torrefranca 250, fos. 75ᵛ–77ʳ	canzonetta, strophic variations	no. 23
Tu dormi e 'l dolce sonno[b]	I:Ru, MS 279, fos. 48ᵛ–52ᵛ	canzonetta, strophic variations	no. 89

[a] For other sources see the appropriate table in Appendix B.
[b] Also ascribed to Jacopo Peri.

Strophic Variations and Verse Forms

The last three segments of music that were added to Francesco Fucci's *Grilanda musicale* (designated 6, 3, and 5 at the extreme right side of Table 5.1 in the previous chapter) contrast markedly in content with the original part of the manuscript (number 1 at the right side of Table 5.1). Whereas anonymous settings of madrigal texts predominate in the oldest section of the *Grilanda*, the portions added to it last overwhelmingly contain strophic variations, many of which are specifically ascribed to Cardinal Montalto's musicians Cesare Marotta and Ippolito Macchiavelli and their sometime collaborator Giuseppino Cenci. This apparent coincidence between a category of musical style and the presence of attributions is probably the factor that most plausibly explains why all the known works of Marotta (see Table 6.1), and all but one of Macchiavelli (see Table 6.2), take the form of strophic variations: works of other kinds by these composers probably survive, but, if so, they most likely remain among the anonymous pieces in the earliest layer of the *Grilanda musicale*.

The term 'strophic variations' will refer, here, to monodies or duets that are divided into *parti*—usually four or more, customarily labelled 'Prima parte', 'Seconda parte', and so on. The bass line of each ensuing *parte* either repeats that

TABLE 6.2. Works ascribed to Ippolito Macchiavelli

Incipit	Main source[a]	Genre	Edition (Vol. II)
Ama pur ninfa gradita	I:Vc, Torrefranca 250, fos. 1ʳ–4ʳ	canzonetta, strophic variations	no. 1
Dhe Filli vita mia se mai ti punsero	I:Vc, Torrefranca 250, fos. 37ᵛ–41ʳ	canzonetta, strophic variations	no. 12
Dolce auretta	I:Vc, Torrefranca 250, fos. 4ᵛ–8ᵛ	canzonetta, strophic variations	no. 2
Fuggi fuggi dolente mio core	*Raccolta de varii concerti*, 17	canzonetta, strophic	no. 148
Io pur deggio partire	I:Vc, Torrefranca 250, fos. 79ᵛ–80 bisʳ	canzonetta, strophic variations	no. 25
Quando il ciel vago s'infiora	I:Vc, Torrefranca 250, fos. 34ᵛ–37ʳ	canzonetta, strophic variations, from the 1616 intermedi	no. 11
Solingo augello che piangendo vai	I:Vc, Torrefranca 250, fos. 25ᵛ–29ʳ	sonetto, strophic variations	no. 9
Venuto è pur quel lagrimabil giorno	I:Vc, Torrefranca 250, fos. 17ʳ–21ʳ	ottava rima, strophic variations on the Ruggiero	no. 7
Vita della mia vita egl'è pur vero	I:Vc, Torrefranca 250, fos. 77ᵛ–79ʳ	ottava rima, strophic variations on the Romanesca	no. 24

    [a] For other sources see the appropriate table in Appendix B.

of the first or forms a variation (and possibly also an abbreviation) of it. On the basis of this series of repeated or varied bass lines, the vocal lines of the *parti* form a series of variations. As we learned in Chapter 3, strophic variations arose out of the notating of the sort of extemporaneous melismatic embellishment, sprezzatura, and melodic contour manipulation that, in earlier decades, provided a different rendition of an aria formula or strophic villanella for each stanza. The poetry is either truly strophic or is treated as if it were. For purposes of creating strophic variations, stanzas of ottava rima are normally divided into four couplets, sonetti into two quatrains plus two tercets, and capitoli in terza rima into tercets with one quatrain at the end. Fortune reserves the term 'strophic variations' for settings of strictly strophic poetry, placing this category on a parallel footing with the classic forms of the sonetto, ottava rima, and capitolo and using the term 'sectional songs' to encompass them all.[13] The difficulty of this system, in my view, is that it obscures the fact that many of the 'sectional songs' in classical forms, which

---

[13] Fortune, 'Italian Secular Song from 1600 to 1635', 329–84. He continues this usage, although less obviously, in 'Italian Secular Monody from 1600 to 1635: An Introductory Survey', *Musical Quarterly*, 39 (1953), 171–95; and in his chapter 'Solo Song and Cantata', in *The Age of Humanism, 1540–1630*, ed. Gerald Abraham (New Oxford History of Music, 5; Oxford , 1968), 125–217.

are not strictly strophic, use the same compositional procedure as 'strophic variations', while other 'sectional songs' in those poetic forms do not. Furthermore,
in Fortune's usage the terms 'sonetto', 'ottava rima', and 'capitolo', on the one
hand, and 'strophic variations', on the other, are not parallel, the first group
referring to poetic forms, the last term to a compositional procedure. In what I
believe is the more common usage, the strophic character or treatment of the text
is united with the technique of writing a series of *variations* in the vocal line, giving rise to the expression 'strophic variations'.

Fortune associated strophic variations above all with Rome, and he was always
impatient with their long and difficult melismas, which he considered to be
mechanical and inexpressive, and their slowly moving basses, which he condemned
as contrary to the progressive trends of style in this genre. It is clear that he and
others have based their assessment, both of strophic variations and of Roman
monody in general, to a great extent upon the various collections of *Scherzi*
(*diversi* or *sacri*) by Antonio Cifra, which were published between 1613 and 1618.
Although the 'Montalto' repertoire of monody contains some examples of the
type of strophic variation described by Fortune, it includes a notable variety of
other styles within this category, a variety that has not been adequately described
in the earlier literature on Baroque monody.

Fucci, himself, seems to have made a distinction among several types of
strophic variation when assembling his *Grilanda musicale*. For he chose to place
the music in what turned out to be Gatherings 19 and 20, written on paper with
the fleur-de-lis watermark, after the section of the manuscript written on paper
with the crown watermark (number 3 in the right-hand column of Table 5.1),
whereas he elected to put the music in what are now Gatherings 1 and 2, likewise written on fleur-de-lis paper, in front of the 'crown' segment. Why this separation of the fleur-de-lis paper into two separate portions of the manuscript?
Evidently Fucci noticed that the two sets of strophic variations on the fleur-de-
lis paper of Gatherings 1 and 2 were of the same type as three of the four sets that
were, at that point, already in place at the beginning of the 'crown' segment,
whereas two of the three sets of variations that are found on the rest of the fleur-
de-lis paper, in what we now number as Gatherings 19 and 20, are of an entirely
different kind. In order to understand this better, it will be useful to make some
distinctions among types of variations and to correlate those types with poetic
metres. The real purpose of this, of course, is to illuminate further the musical
repertoire under discussion.

In the monody repertoire, strophic variations are used to set only four types
of poem: (1) sonetti, (2) ottave rime, (3) canzonette, which category will include
poems that could be designated by the older name villanella, and (4) terze rime.

A sonetto invariably has fourteen lines of eleven syllables each, divided into two
quatrains and two tercets, as has been said. The quatrains always have a rhyme

scheme of ABBA, whereas the two tercets, taken together as a sextet, may use any one of a number of symmetrical schemes, the most common being CDC DCD. When composed as strophic variations, a sonetto is customarily divided into four parts, consisting of the two quatrains plus two tercets, and these are set, respectively, to four variations.

Ottava rima, in this period, refers to the rhyme scheme ABABABCC applied to eleven-syllable lines. It should be understood here and with respect to the terza rima, to be discussed next, that the term 'eleven-syllable line' refers to a theoretical construction based on the normal expectation that a line of Italian poetry ends on the next syllable after the final, primary accented one, in which case it is called a *verso piano*. If, on the other hand, the line ends with an accented syllable, an extra, imaginary syllable is added for purposes of counting, and the line is called a *verso tronco*. Similarly, if the line ends with not one but two unaccented syllables, the last one is ignored for purposes of classification, and the line is called a *verso sdrucciolo*. Ottava rima can be found in single stanzas of eight lines or as a repeating pattern in book-length epic poems, such as Ariosto's *Orlando furioso* or Tasso's *Gerusalemme liberata*. It is normal to divide a stanza of ottava rima into four parts of two lines each when setting it as four strophic variations.

The term 'canzonetta', at this time, refers to a strophic poem whose stanzas are made up of lines whose lengths and rhyme schemes, while not conforming to any of the 'classic' metres defined above, nevertheless form a pattern repeated in each strophe. Some canzonette have refrains or other vestiges of the older villanella, itself a derivative of the ottava rima. A few are written with eleven-syllable verses, but most deploy shorter lines, often with regularly recurring accents, as opposed to the variable and unpredictable accentuation schemes that are found in endecasillabi and in settenari when they are mixed with endecasillabi in madrigals and operatic dialogue set to recitative. Each strophe of a canzonetta is normally set to a single, complete *parte* in strophic variation sets.

'Terza rima' refers to the rhyme scheme ABA BCB CDC, etc., applied to lines of eleven syllables. Terza rima deployed in relatively brief poems and closed by a final stanza of four lines, YZYZ, results in a capitolo. Otherwise, terza rima is used in long poems, such as the books of Dante's *Commedia divina*. In strophic variations, each three-line stanza of terza rima is set to its own variation.

Although it is convenient to refer to sonetti, ottave rime, terze rime, and canzonette of these kinds by the collective term strophic variations, there are important differences between the settings that poems of each type typically receive in the monody repertoire. Or at least such differences are reasonably clear in the Montalto repertoire contained in the sources described in Chapter 5. These differences are found in the rhythmic and melodic character and the overall construction of the bass, and in the style of the vocal line.

Sonetti

Of the eighteen sonetti in the Montalto repertoire, fifteen have a relatively slow-moving bass part dominated by semibreves and minims, a bass part that is altered, moderately or radically, from variation to variation, even more than is needed for accommodating to a tercet the bass originally deployed to accompany a quatrain. The distinguishing characteristic in the vocal line of these fifteen sonetti is a heterogeneous mixture of recitational style with very rapid, long, and complex ornamental passaggi. Considering that recitational style, passaggi, and static bass lines all imply sprezzatura, it can be hypothesized that sonetti of this type were meant to be performed with even less than the usual degree of adherence to a regular beat or tempo. Indeed, it may be this seemingly spontaneous, emotive, and personalized manner of performance—a reflection of the lyric quality of most sonetti—that determines the notated character of both the arie and the strophic variations that set poems of this category in the sixteenth and seventeenth century. If so, it would be significant that the three sonetto settings in this repertoire that do not mix recitational with melismatic vocal writing are entirely recitational. Two of them are through-composed entirely in recitative: *Non credete ch'io v'ami ahi lasso e ch'io* (Vol. II, no. 43) and *Tu godi il sol ch'agli occhi miei s'asconde* (Vol. II, no. 44), both by Raffaello Rontani.[14] The other one (*Amor il mio tormento e la mia pena*, in *Affetti amorosi*), which also has a slow-moving bass and much monotone recitation, is strophic and, thus, resembles the formulaic arie for reciting sonetti found in the sixteenth-century villanella sources mentioned in Chapter 3. Indeed, the recitational character of earlier *arie da cantare sonetti* is probably the determining historical factor that most influenced the style of our monodic sonetti set as strophic variations, which reflect in notation the proper method, according to Camillo Maffei (Ch. 3), of performing sonetti that are notated as if they were strophic. Table 6.3 lists the sonetto settings found in the staff-notation sources described in Chapter 5.

Giuseppino's setting of Giovanni della Casa's religious sonnet *Io che l'età solea viver nel fango* (Vol. II, no. 15) was singled out towards the end of Chapter 3 for its deployment of recitational and cantillational styles as a principle of formal design. The same composer's sonnet *Anima bella che nel sen ten stai* (Vol. II, no. 17) from the opera *Amor pudico* was mentioned as a similar case, and it will be considered further in Chapter 9. The same pattern of recitational beginning and melismatic

---

[14] Concerning these sonetti by Rontani and G. B. Doni's critique of using recitative for this poetic form, see John Walter Hill, 'Frescobaldi's *Arie* and the Musical Circle around Cardinal Montalto', in Alexander Silbiger (ed.), *Frescobaldi Studies* (Durham, 1987), 157–94; also in Italian as 'Le *Arie* di Frescobaldi e la cerchia musicale del cardinal Montalto', in *Girolamo Frescobaldi nel IV centenario della nascita*, ed. Sergio Durante and Dinko Fabris (Quaderni della Rivista italiana di musicologia, 10; Florence, 1986), 215–32.

TABLE 6.3. Sonetto settings in staff-notation sources

Incipit	Composer	Source	Genre	Edition (Vol. II)
Amor il mio tormento e la mia pena	Anon.	*Affetti amorosi*, 8	strophic	no. 17
Anima bella che nel sen ten stai	Cenci	I:Vc, Torrefranca 250, fos. 53ᵛ–56ʳ	variations	no. 150
Disse costei e gl'occhi fu le gote	Nanino	*Raccolta de varii concerti*, 3–4	variations	
Gioisce l'aria il ciel	Anon.	*Ghirlandetta amorosa*, 11–12	duet without variations	
Io che l'età solea viver nel fango	Cenci	I:Vc, Torrefranca 250, fos. 48ᵛ–51ʳ	variations	no. 15
Liete, verdi, fiorite, e fresche valli	Catalani	*Giardino musicale*, 3–6	cantata	
Né lungo exilio mai donna mi mosse	Giamberti	Giamberti, *Poesi diverse poste in musica*, 5–8	variations	
Non credete ch'io v'ami ahi lasso e ch'io	Rontani	I:Vc, Torrefranca 250, fo. 99ʳ⁻ᵛ	recitative	no. 43
Non dormo no, non sognio	G. F. Anerio	*Ghirlandetta amorosa*, 7–8	through-composed, almost variations	
Pace non trovo, e non ho da far guerra	Anon.	US:PHu, MS Ital. 57, fos. 3ᵛ–5ᵛ	variations	no. 98
Per cercar terra ignota e pelegrina	Nanino	Giamberti, *Poesi diverse poste in musica*, 9–12	variations	no. 151
Quel rosignol ch'in sì soavi accenti	Rontani	*Giardino musicale*, 14–15	variations	no. 84
Se 'l dolce sguardo di costei m'ancide	Cenci	I:Baf, MS 1424, fos. 50ᵛ–53ʳ	variations	no. 40
Se 'n così grav' e dolorosi accenti	Antonelli	I:Vc, Torrefranca 250, fos. 95ᵛ–96ᵛ	variations	no. 9
Solingo augello che piangendo vai	Macchiavelli	I:Vc, Torrefranca 250, fos. 25ᵛ–29ʳ	variations	no. 8
Somiglia foglia a cui fa guerra il vento	Anon.	I:Vc, Torrefranca 250, fos. 21ᵛ–25ʳ	variations	no. 44
Tu godi il sol ch'agli occhi miei s'asconde	Rontani	I:Vc, Torrefranca 250, fos. 100ʳ–101ʳ	recitative	no. 123
Vidi ondegiar questi infecondi campi	Anon.	I:Bc, Q140, fos. 12ᵛ–14ᵛ	variations	

closing can be seen in the portions of Giuseppino's *Se 'l dolce sguardo di costei m'an-cide* that remain in the copy in I:Baf, MS 1424, made incomplete by the removal of a folio (Vol. II, no. 84).

Somiglia foglia a cui fa guerra il vento (Vol. II, no. 8) and *Solingo augello che piangendo vai* (Vol. II, no. 9), the second ascribed to Ippolito Macchiavelli in the *Grilanda musicale*, where they are found on adjacent pages, make a unique pair of sonnets since they are founded upon one and the same bass. If the bass conformed to a standard pattern, such as the Romanesca, this would be of no consequence. But this one corresponds to no known archetype. In both pieces, there is less monotone recitation than typically found in Giuseppino's works, while virtuosic melismas are more evident in all portions of these variations. Both works exhibit extreme contrast as a prevailing aesthetic principle. Macchiavelli's *Solingo augello che piangendo vai* will serve to illustrate this point.

Solingo augello che piangendo vai	Solitary bird, who go weeping for
La tua perduta e cara compagnia,	your lost and dear companion,
Meco ne vien ch'io piango anco io la mia;	come with me, since I, too, weep for mine;
Insieme potrem far' i nostri lai.	together we can sing our lamentations.
Ma tu la tua fors'hoggi troverai;	But you will perhaps find yours today,
Io la mia quando? E tu pur tuttavia	I mine when? And you, however,
Ti stai nel verde; io fuggo indi ove sia	are in the foliage; I flee from where I am.
Chi mi conforta ad'altro ch'a trar guai.	Who comforts me for other than to cause pain?
Privo in tutto son'io d'ogni mio bene,	I am deprived entirely of my happiness,
E nudo e grave e solo e pellegrino	and naked and doleful and alone and wandering
Vo misurando i campi e le mie pene.	I go measuring the fields and my sorrows.
Gli occhi bagniati, porto il viso chinno,	With tearful eyes, I carry my face bowed down.
Il cor in doglia e l'alma fuor di spene,	My heart in pain and my soul beyond hope,
Né d'haver cerco men fero destino.	Nor do I seek to have a less harsh destiny.

All four variations begin with very slow declamation over a static G in the bass. I think that we may assume that the vocal line is intended to sustain the written pitches without embellishment at these points because melismatic elaborations, both short and long, are specified with a high degree of precision elsewhere in the sonnet. This slow and static music corresponds to the first poetic phrase of each text segment, bounded by the caesura of the verse in three of the four cases. And in these three instances, this opening phrase is well served by its sombre musical treatment, as it establishes the doleful tone for the remainder of the quatrain or tercet: 'Solitary bird', 'I am deprived entirely', 'With tearful eyes'. In all but the first instance, Macchiavelli includes the unusual leap of a diminished fourth to an unprepared F♯ against the sustained G of the bass, a clear example of *seconda prattica* dissonance treatment in a work ascribed to one of Montalto's household musicians. A similarly static and sustained musical treatment is given to the likewise expressive parallel conclusion of each part of the poem in its first presentation: 'our lamentations' (bb. 21–3), 'to cause pain' (bb. 55–7), 'my sorrows' (bb. 87–9), and 'harsh destiny' (bb. 110–12). These solemn and slow passages are contrasted with very rapid melismas that are concentrated at, but not limited to, the varied repeat of the last verse that closes each variation. For the most part, these outbursts of *fioritura* are not motivated by a particular word or phrase, as is demonstrated by the fact that the conclusion of each quatrain or tercet, which is first sung in a melodically, harmonically, and rhythmically static and subdued fashion, is eventually repeated in groups of very rapid melismas.

This use of virtuosic passage work to set sorrowful words is neither confined to *Solingo augello che piangendo vai* nor to the pieces ascribed to Macchiavelli: it is found all over the early monody repertoire, in Florence as much as in Rome. Compare, for instance, Giuseppino's setting of Giovanni della Casa's penitential sonnet *Io che l'età solea viver nel fango* (Vol. II, no. 15) with Caccini's in *Le nuove musiche e nuova maniera di scriverle* (1614). In the Italian text, below, the words set to melismas are singled out: Giuseppino's in italics, Caccini's underlined:

Io che l'età solea viver nel fango,
Hoggi mutato il cor da quel che soglio,
D'ogn'immondo pensier mi purgo e spoglio,

E 'l mio grave fallir correggio e piango.
Di servir falso duce io mi rimango;
A te mi dono, ad ogn'altro mi toglio;

Né rotta nave mai partì da scoglio
Sì pentita dal mar com'io rimango.
E poi ch'a mortal rischio e gita in vano
E senza frutto i cari giorni ha spesi,

Questa mia vita in porto homai t'accolgo.
Reggami per pietà tua santa mano,

Padre del ciel, che poi che a te mi volgo;
Tanto t'adorerò quanto t'offesi.

I, who for for so long used to live in mud,
today, my heart changed from what I wont,
of every impure thought I purge and divest myself,
and my grave error I correct and repent.
Serving a false leader I renounce.
To you I give myself; cut myself off from every other.
Nor did any broken ship escape from the rocks
as wary of the sea as I am.
And since at mortal risk and wandering in vain
and without profit, it has spent its precious days,
this life of mine I now welcome to port.
Extend to me, for pity's sake, your sacred hand,
heavenly Father, for now that I turn to you,
I will adore you as much as I have offended you.

This comparison shows that Caccini tends to confine his melismas to the last word of a verse, although he does not do so exclusively. Giuseppino decorates more words, without concern for their position within the line, except that he tends to *avoid* the last word. In both settings the passaggi neither illustrate the text nor express the emotion implied by any particular category of word. With respect to meaning and, in Giuseppino's case, with respect to placement within the verse, the melismas seem to occur haphazardly or, much more to the point, unpredictably.

When Pietro Della Valle criticized Giuseppino for indiscriminate use of passaggi, he at once unfairly singled out one person who really represented a widespread norm and applied an aesthetic judgement based upon the practice of polyphonic madrigalists but not of monodists:

However, at the same time or a little after [the heyday of the falsettist Lodovico] the tenor Giuseppino also flourished, and he, for the same reason of knowing his talent and taking advantage of it, did just the opposite. Giuseppino's voice was not good, but he had very great agility, and of art he did not know the most in the world. But passaggi were natural for him. Therefore, he sang with judgement with respect to himself, because he took advantage of his own talent. One hardly ever heard from him a long note that did not tremble with a *trillo*. All his singing consisted in passaggi. But with respect to the others he did not sing with judgement, because often he placed passaggi where they should not go. One never knew whether his singing was cheerful or melancholy, because it was always of one kind, or, to say it better, in every case, however appropriately or inappropriately, it was always cheerful because of the rapidity of the notes that he continued to produce, without himself knowing, I believe, what notes they were.[15]

Della Valle probably did not hear Giuseppino in his prime; having been born in 1586, he would barely have entered adolescence when Giuseppino completed his best decade. Furthermore, Della Valle wrote this account from distant memory, twenty-four years after Giuseppino's death. Whether or not Giuseppino could sing sustained notes towards the end of his life, he put them into his compositions often enough. And he certainly must have known what notes were in his passaggi when he wrote them out. We have already established that in the early monody repertoire at large there is no exclusion or particular limitation of passaggi in settings of sorrowful texts. Indeed, Della Valle, who travelled widely in the Islamic world and even married an Egyptian woman, must have frequently heard lamentations sung with very rapid ornamental melismas, if present-day oral traditions in that part of the world are any indication. An Arabic *mawwal* recorded in Cairo, for instance, projects with many short and long vocal quivers a text that says, 'I try to smile, although my heart is weeping. How could I but

---

[15] 'Però nell'istesso tempo, o poco dopo, fiorì anche Giuseppino tenore, il quale per la medesima ragione di conoscere il suo talento e valersene, faceva tutto il contrario. La voce di Giuseppino non era buona, ma aveva egli grandissima disposizione e dell'arte non sapeva tanto che finisce il mondo: ma i passaggi gli erano naturali. Cantava egli perciò con giudizio quanto a sè stesso, perchè si valeva del proprio talento: non si sentiva da lui quasi mai una nota lunga, se non era con trillo tremolante; tutto il suo cantare erano passaggi; ma quanto agli altri non cantava con giudizio; perchè più delle volte metteva i passaggi, dove non andavano: non si sapeva mai se il suo cantare era allegro o malinconico, perchè era sempre di una sorte, o, per dir meglio, in ogni cosa, o a proposito o a sproposito che fosse, era sempre allegro per la velocità delle note, che egli di continovo profferiva; senza sapere, credo io, egli stesso quali note fossero.' Pietro Della Valle, 'Della musica dell'età nostra', in Solerti, *L'origine del melodramma*, 161–2.

weep under such cruel tribulations, yet I must smile to conceal my tears'.[16] And some of the most ornate and melismatic of the Sicilian folk songs that Alberto Favara transcribed early in this century are religious laments.[17] Clearly, rapid passaggi are accepted as appropriate in songs of lamentation in several Mediterranean cultures, as they were generally in the monody repertoire of early seventeenth-century Italy.

The conflict between the complaint against passaggi in sorrowful songs and their widespread use in composition and singing in writings about music at the turn of the seventeenth century may be symptomatic of a struggle between Mediterranean and northern aesthetics, in which the former, issuing northward through Naples and then Rome, dominated, for a time, that form of solo singing based on southern traditions, without displacing the latter in the literary conventions surrounding music-making. This conflict is clearly seen, for example, in Giovanni Battista Bovicelli's 1593 treatise on passaggi:

Likewise it would be very prejudicial to the poet when the words are sad to accompany them with cheerful notes or [to put] sorrowful notes under cheerful words. Thus, in singing, one should, as much as possible, imitate the words, that is, [one should] not embellish sorrowful words with passaggi but accompany them, so to say, with small ornaments (*accenti*) and a weak voice. If the words are cheerful, [one should] use passaggi and even give them liveliness, producing varied notes, as one sees below.

In any case, as the proverb says, there is an exception to every rule. Thus, it will be allowed sometimes to create some passaggi under sorrowful words (if, in doing so, one seeks out the consonance and harmony of the parts), even if, perhaps, [the passaggi] do not express entirely the sorrow that the words imply, which, however, should not be done without judgement and with occasional use of appropriate passagi.[18]

---

[16] On the recording *Taqasim and Layali Cairo Tradition*, in the Unesco Collection: Modal Music and Improvisation, VI-5, Philips 6586 010.

[17] Alberto Favara, *Corpus di musiche popolari siciliane*, ed. Ottavio Tiby (Accademia di Scienze Lettere e Arti di Palermo, Supplemento agli Atti, 4; Palermo, 1957), ii, nos. 664–73. Nino Pirrotta, 'New Glimpses of an Unwritten Tradition', in Laurence Berman (ed.), *Words and Music: The Scholar's View* (Cambridge, Mass., 1972), 271–91, finds some features of Favara's folk songs in some ballate of the Italian *Ars nova*, which attests to a high degree of long-term continuity in southern Italian oral tradition.

[18] 'Come sarebbe disdicevole molto a chi scrive, se le parole sono molte [meste], accompagnarle con note allegre, ò note meste sotto parole allegre: Cosi nel cantare si devono più che si può, imitare le parole; cioè parole meste, non adornarle con Passaggi, ma accompagnarle, per cosi dire, con accenti, & voce flebile; se le parole sono allegre, usar Passaggi, e darli anco vivacità, facendo note variate, come si vede qui sotto. [Example] Ad'ogni modo, come per proverbio si dice, ogni regola patisce qualche eccettione: onde sarà lecito alcuna volta anco

And indeed, Bovicelli's first three examples of complete soprano parts of madrigals and motets with passaggi added (38–49) all have quite sorrowful texts: Palestrina's *Io son ferito hai lasso*, the same composer's *Ave verum corpus*, and Rore's *Ancor che co 'l partire*, compositions in which Bovicelli adds passaggi to words such as *lasso, moro, partito, ferito, passum, immolatum*, and *morire*.

If in the context of a lament, a very rapid vocal ornament might be taken as a musical representation of a quavering voice, which is quite the impression that they often make in modern recordings of Arabic improvisations and Sicilian folk songs, at other times something more pleasant and emotionally neutral seems to be intended, as, for example, when a decorative melisma imitates birdsong. An obvious example of this is Raffaello Rontani's *Quel rosignol ch'in sì soavi accenti*, a sonnet setting printed in Robletti's anthology *Giardino musicale di varii eccellenti autori* (1621) along with pieces by several other composers with links to Cardinal Montalto. In this case, the song of the nightingale is depicted by brief passaggi that incorporate series of thirty-second notes repeating a single pitch, the ornament that Caccini calls the *trillo*.

Recordings of Sicilian *cantastorie*, Arabic *sha'er*, and nightingales encourage me to accept the conclusions supported by historical evidence and consideration for the pacing of the words and syllables in the recitational portions of sonetti: these pieces with their long strings of sixteenth notes and groups of up to twenty-eight thirty-second notes were sung at tempos in the neighbourhood of 60–80 half notes per minute. This conclusion rests on the observation that the tactus tempo traditionally equated with a leisurely walking pace (*c.*80 per minute),[19] the human pulse (*c.*70 per minute),[20] or the pendulum of a clock (60 per minute),[21] relates, by the beginning of the seventeenth century, to the minim.[22] Notwithstanding such a rapid tempo, passaggi, even in thirty-second notes, were sung cleanly

sotto parole meste (se cosi recerca la consonanza, & armonia delle parti) far alcuni Passaggi, se ben forsi non isprimessero tutta quella mestitia, che ricercano le parole, che però non si deve far senza giuditio, e con occasione di Passaggi, che lo ricerchino.' Bovicelli, *Regole, passaggi di musica*, 15.

[19] e.g. by Hans Buchner, *Fundamentbuch von Hans von Constanz* (1550).

[20] e.g. by Giovanni Maria Lanfranco, *Scintille di musica* (1533).

[21] e.g. by Lodovico Zacconi, *Prattica di musica* (1592). Thus, in summary, John Playford, *Introduction to the Skill of Musick* (rev. edn., London, 1694), 25: 'First, I shall speak of Common-Time, which may be reckond three several sorts; the first and slowest of all is marked thus C: 'Tis measured by a Semibreve, which you must divide into four equal Parts, telling *one, two, three, four*, distinctly, putting your Hand or Foot down when you tell *one*, and taking it up when you tell *three*, so that you are as long down as up. Stand by a large Chamber-Clock, and beat your Hand or Foot (as I have before observed) to the slow Motions of the Pendulum. . . . The second sort of Common Time is a little faster, which is known by the Mood, having a stroak drawn through it thus ₡. . . . The third sort of Common Time is quickest of all, and then the Mood is retorted thus; you may tell *one, two, three, four* in a Bar, almost as fast as the regular Motions of a Watch.'

[22] The basic evidence for this is laid out by J. A. Bank, *Tactus, Tempo and Notation in Mensural Music from the 13th to the 17th Century* (Amsterdam, 1972), 223–59, a book that admittedly presents some difficulties, but not in this particular respect. Specific application of Bank's primary sources to monody is promoted by Putnam Aldrich, *Rhythm in Seventeenth-Century Italian Monody* (London, 1966), with valuable corrections provided by Paul Brainard, 'Proportional Notation in the Music of Schütz and His Contemporaries', *Current Musicology*, 50 (1992), 21–47.

and clearly because each note was articulated by a light glottal stop, as Caccini implied in the preface to his first *Nuove musiche* (1602):

The *trillo*,[23] which I illustrated on one single pitch, was demonstrated in this way for no other reason than that in teaching it to my first wife and now to my other, living one, together with my daughters, I have used no other model than the very one that is written for both the one and the other [ornament], that is, beginning with the first quarter note and re-striking each note with the throat upon the vowel *à* until the last breve, and likewise the *gruppo*.[24] This *trillo* and *gruppo*, to the extent that the abovesaid model was learnt superbly by my late wife, I will leave to be judged by whomever heard her sing in her day, as likewise I leave it to the judgement of others who can hear in what an exquisite manner it is produced by my other, living [wife]. For if it is true that experience is the mistress of all things, I can, with some certainty, affirm and declare that one cannot use a better means to teach it nor a better model to describe it, since both the one and the other are expressed [in this way]. This *trillo* and this *gruppo*, being the necessary stairway to many things that are described [below], are consequences of that grace which is sought most of all for good singing.[25]

Likewise, Bovicelli: 'Thirty-second notes, beyond agility of the voice, need to be well separated.'[26] And in his *Harmonie universelle* (1636–7), Marin Mersenne says that the most rapid notes that can be sung in an articulated fashion, either on several pitches or on one pitch, are sixteen per second, which means thirty-second notes at half note = 60; and he adds that this is the same maximum velocity that is attainable on the harpsichord or on the viol.[27]

The import of Caccini's instructions, as I understand them, is that in performing both the repeated-note *trillo* and the oscillating *gruppo* each note is begun with a glottal stop, and the rapid notes in all *passaggi* are likewise articulated. In effect, this form of articulation is the vocal counterpart to the separate bow

[23] Caccini's musical examples make it clear that the *trillo* consists of an accelerating repetition of a single pitch.

[24] Caccini's musical examples make it clear that the *groppo* is formed by an oscillation between two adjacent degrees of a diatonic scale.

[25] 'Il trillo, descritto da me sopra una corda sola, non è stato per altra cagione dimostrato in questa guisa, se non perchè nello insegnarlo alla mia prima moglie e ora all'altra vivente, con le mie figliuole, non ho osservato altra regola che la stessa nella quale è scritto, e l'uno e l'altro, cioè il cominciarsi della prima semiminima, e ribattere ciascuna nota con la gola sopra la vocale *à* fino all'ultima breve, e somigliantemente il gruppo, il qual trillo e gruppo quanto con la suddetta regola fosse appreso in grande eccellenza dalla mia moglie passata lo lascierò giudicare a chiunque ne' suoi tempi l'udì cantare, come altresì lascio nel giudizio altrui, potendosi udire, in quanta squisitezza sia fatta dall'altra mia vivente: che se ver è che l'esperienza sia maestra di tutte le cose, posso con qualche sicurezzo affermare e dire non si potere usare miglior mezzo per insegnarlo, nè miglior forma per descriverlo, come si è espresso e l'uno e l'altro. Il quale trillo e gruppo, per essere scala necessaria a molte cose che si descrivono e sono effetti di quella grazia che più si ricerca per ben cantare.'

[26] 'Le biscrome poi, oltre la disposition della voce devono esser spicatte bene.' Bovicelli, *Regole*, 14.

[27] *Harmonie universelle* (Paris, 1636–7), Book 3, fo. 137ᵛ. A recent summary of the history of tempo that supports what I have written here is found in Klaus Miehling, *Das Tempo in der Musik von Barock und Vorklassik: Die Antwort der Quellen auf ein umstrittenes Thema* (Wilhelmshaven, 1993). My remarks about glottal articulation of very rapid melismas are supported by Robert Greenlee, '*Dispositione di voce*: Passage to Florid Singing', *Early Music*, 15 (1987), 47–55.

strokes and wind articulation syllables, such as *te-re-te-re*, that are prescribed for the performance of ornamental *passaggi* and diminutions by early seventeenth-century manuals on instrumental performance.[28]

Whereas there are a number of recordings in which these instrumental articulations are expertly demonstrated, I have heard vocal ornaments and *passaggi* sung in the way Caccini describes only in isolated instances, nearly always confined either to a *trillo* or a rapidly rising scale. Until we can hear complex *passaggi* sung as Giuseppino, Ippolito Macchiavelli, and Giulio Caccini customarily heard them, we must continue to rely on our imagination to supply some major reasons why Ippolita Recupito, Francesca Caccini, Adriana Basile, and Vittoria Archilei were so highly paid and widely praised.

Ottava rima

Of the twenty settings of ottava rima stanzas in the sources described in Chapter 5, eighteen take the form of strophic variations. Two settings, both in printed anthologies assembled by Giovanni Stefani, are strophic formulas that would provide raw material for improvisation, like the arie included in sixteenth-century lute books and collections of villanelle.

Eleven of the ottava rima settings use the Romanesca chordal bass pattern, which is rarely found in the monody repertoire at large in conjunction with any other poetic metre.[29] The bass and chord pattern associated with the Romanesca in early seventeenth-century vocal and instrumental music can be generalized to the series of notes B♭ F G D ‖ : B♭ F G D G : ‖ . These bass notes are the roots of major triads, the 'framework chords',[30] which, in seventeenth-century variations, are customarily prolonged by passing, auxiliary, or parenthetical harmonies or varied, particularly by the substitution of an E♭ triad or other pre-dominant chord, for G harmony when it precedes a D chord.

More than eighty years ago, Hugo Riemann noticed that in Giulio Caccini's *Ahi, dispietato amor come consenti* (among the musical examples in the preface to *Le nuove musiche* of 1602) and in 'many other compositions up to the middle of the seventeenth century' the framework chords of the Romanesca are evenly spaced at intervals of three minims.[31] In Riemann's judgement, this produces the effect

[28] A summary of this argument and reference to treatises that support it are found in Richard Erig's Introduction to *Italienische Diminutionen: Die zwischen 1553 und 1638 mehrmals bearbeiteten Sätze*, ed. Richard Erig and Veronika Gutmann (Prattica musicale, 1; Zürich, 1979), 9–57.

[29] Alfred Einstein, 'Die Aria di Ruggiero', *Sammelbände der Internationalen Musikgesellschaft*, 13 (1911–12), 446–7, cites a duet setting of Petrarch's sonnet *Ite, caldi sospiri* over a Romanesca bass in Francesco Dognazzi's *Primo libro de varii concenti a una et a due voci* (Venice: Gardano, 1614). I cannot supply an additional example.

[30] Richard Hudson, 'Romanesca', *New Grove*.

[31] Hugo Riemann, 'Der "Basso ostinato" und die Anfänge der Kantate', *Sammelbände der Internationalen Musikgesellschaft*, 13 (1911–12), 531–43 at 533–4.

of 3/2 metre in spite of the modern connotation of the half-circle mensuration sign, which Caccini and nearly all other monodists used in notating their
Romanescas. Caccini, for one, uses the half circle with the vertical line that originally denoted diminution. By the beginning of the seventeenth century, however, the vertical line merely suggests a slightly faster tempo in most cases.[32] The
half circle still signified imperfect tempus and prolation, although perfect tempus
was completely out of use by Caccini's day, and perfect prolation was met but
rarely. The tactus lines customarily employed in conjunction with the half-circle
mensuration sign in monody sources set off either the value of a semibreve or
a breve, or either indiscriminately and not necessarily correlating with the
presence or absence of the diminution line. Riemann correctly recognized that
twentieth-century musicians frequently assume that those tactus lines have the
meaning of modern barlines as indicators of metrical accentuation. The difficulty,
which Riemann, perhaps, did not sufficiently appreciate, is that the accentual connotation of tactus lines was, about 1600, in the middle of a historical process of
spreading from *proportio tripla* (3) and *sesquialtera* (3/2), where it had possessed that
meaning for about a century, to compositions and their parts where *integer valor*
or *proportio dupla* holds sway.

About forty years later, Helga Spohr extended Riemann's triple-metre interpretation of Caccini's example to virtually all monodies using the Romanesca
pattern.[33] And she explained what she saw as the Romanesca's metrical consistency by arguing that it was originally a dance as well as an *aria da cantare*. In order
to sustain that thesis, it was necessary for her to reject Kastner's arguments that
the Romanesca originated in Spain, where it first showed itself in written music,
taking its name, according to Kastner, from the *romance*, the category of epic poem
that was, so he maintained, sometimes sung to its chords (see the discussion of
the *romance* in Ch. 3).[34] Spohr needed to reject the theory of Spanish origin principally because all the dance versions of the Romanesca are Italian. It is, nevertheless, significant that the earliest written (Spanish) examples of this chordal bass
pattern, including the first to be associated with the name *Romanesca*—the two
pieces entitled *Romanesca O guárdame las vacas* in Alonso Mudarra's *Tres libros de
música en cifras para vihuela* (Seville, 1546)—render the music in triple proportion,
making its pattern of metrical accentuation unequivocal.

Twenty years later, Ernst Apfel pointed out that, although the three-minim

[32] Brainard, 'Proportional Notation', 21–47.

[33] Helga Spohr, 'Studien zur italienischen Tanzkomposition um 1600' (Ph.D. diss., Albert-Ludwigs-
Universität zu Freiburg im Breisgau, 1956), 31–45.

[34] Spohr refers to the manuscript of Kastner's book on Antonio de Cabezón, lent to her by the author. The
book eventually published, however, Macario Santiago Kastner, *Antonio und Hernando de Cabezón: Eine
Chronik dargestellt am Leben zweier Generationen von Organisten* (Tutzing, 1977), contains no discussion of the
origin of the Romanesca.

Ex. 6.1. Cesare Marotta, *O durezze amarissime d'amore* (1616), the bass of the first two *parti* with the framework chords marked

rhythm of the framework chords prevails in most seventeenth-century variations on the Romanesca, many of them contain anomalies that do not permit a uniform transcription in 3/2 metre. He concluded that the Romanesca was originally constructed out of eight triple bars divided into two phrases of equal length. In the monody repertoire it typically begins that way, with or without an anacrusis, but becomes 'metrically variable or unsettled' towards the middle of the pattern.[35]

Indeed, among the variations on the Romanesca in the Montalto repertoire, it is common to find the framework chords disposed at three-minim intervals in the first *parte* but then to discover that disposition substantially distorted in subsequent variations. As an illustration of this, I offer the bass of the first two *parti* from Cesare Marotta's Romanesca *O durezze amarissime d'amore* (1616), in which I have marked the framework chords, or their replacements, with an 'X' (see Ex. 6.1). In other cases the distortions begin already in the first *parte* (for

---

[35] Ernst Apfel, 'Rhythmisch-metrische und andere Beobachtungen an Ostinatobässen', *Archiv für Musikwissenschaft*, 33 (1976), 48–53.

example, the anonymous *Se terrena beltà passa e non dura* in Giovanni Stefani's anthology *Affetti amorosi*). In order not to compromise the metrically unsettled character of these Romanescas, I have chosen not to impose modern metres, even changing metres, upon them in my transcriptions, barring them instead according to tactus, with the understanding that the framework chords, or their substitutes, and the associated syllables of text should, in many cases, receive some slight emphasis.

The operative metre of the Romanescas may be variable or unsettled from time to time, probably because monody composers, as usual, attempted to render in notation the departures from notated regularity customarily taken by accomplished singers when they improvised passaggi or introduced sprezzatura for the sake of more natural or impassioned declamation of the text. But the Romanesca variations still have an underlying reference to accentual metre that is generally lacking in the sonetti, which are normally even more recitational and rhapsodic, by turns. This reference to accentual metre correlates with the somewhat more active bass of the Romanesca settings of ottava rima when compared with the sonetti. This difference is subtle rather than overwhelming, and one or two examples cannot really convey it. But it is illuminating to count the semiminims in each bass part and divide by overall length as measured in semibreves, yielding some indication of rhythmic activity. (Similar results could be obtained by counting all the notes in the bass and dividing by the length; my reason for counting semiminims will become clear during the discussion of canzonetta texts set as strophic variations.) The result of this arithmetic is an average of .52 for the sonetti contained in the sources described in Chapter 5 versus an average of .87 for the Romanescas (.83 for all settings of ottava rima). In other words, the basses of the Romanescas, and indeed of all the settings of ottave rime in this repertoire, are, on average, 1.67 times more active. One reason why the figure for Romanescas is so similar to the number relating to all settings of ottave rime is that fully half of our ottava settings are Romanescas, to which are added one setting based on the Ruggiero pattern and another on the Passamezzo moderno, both of which have rhythmic qualities similar to those of the Romanescas. And there are other ottava settings with basses likewise similar to the Romanescas with regard to rhythm but not harmony. On the other hand, there are also a few in recitational style. These will be discussed a bit later.

This typical difference between the bass parts of sonetti and ottava rima settings correlates with parallel distinctions in the prevailing vocal styles. Whereas the sonetti, as said before, usually contrast phrases in recitational style with extended and highly virtuosic passaggi, both implying a high degree of spontaneous-sounding freedom from regular beat and metre, the ottava rima settings tend to avoid both extremes, inclining more, in general, towards a more fluid lyricism, more moderate embellishment, and, probably, a somewhat more regular beat and at least occasional metrical accentuation in performance.

It is instructive to see how these features are deployed in Ippolito Macchiavelli's Romanesca setting of the ottava rima stanza *Vita della mia vita egl'è pur vero* by Bernardo Tasso (Vol. II, no. 24). As with all ottave set to the Romanesca, each *parte* sets two lines of text to one statement of the chordal bass pattern. Indeed, each verse corresponds to one phrase of the Romanesca design, in which the second phrase, beginning like the first but ending with a cadence on G, responds to the first phrase, which ends with pre-dominant harmony resolving to the dominant chord, D. The melodic line that frequently goes with the Romanesca bass—so frequently that it, rather than the chordal bass pattern, is sometimes called the *Aria della Romanesca*—can be detected behind the embellishment, at least in the first *parte* of this setting. It parallels the shape of the chordal bass pattern in that the second phrase completes the descent from d'' to g', which had been left incomplete on a' in the first phrase. This simple open-and-closed musical relation of the two phrases corresponds here, as in many ottava settings, to the linguistic pattern of the poetry, in which the second line of each couplet completes or responds to the meaning of the first. Then, as is typical of Romanesca settings of ottave, the second line of each couplet is repeated to a variation upon the second musical phrase, immediately preceding.

Vita della mia vita, egl'è pur vero	Life of my life, it is really true
Ch'io vivo senza te misero e solo,	that I live without you miserable and alone
Se non quanto col'ali del pensiero,	unless, with wings of thought,
Pien d'ardente desio m'innalzo a volo	full of ardent desire, I lift myself in flight
E vengo per drittissimo sentiero	and come, by the most direct path,
A sfogar vosco il mio angoscioso duolo.	to pour forth to you my grievous sorrow.
Ma sì brev'è la gioia e sì fugace,	But so brief is my joy and so fleeting
Ch'io non ho col mio ben tregua né pace.	that I have with my beloved neither rest nor peace.

The overall descending outline that underlies the embellished surface contours of the melodic line of each phrase guarantees, to some extent, that Macchiavelli's vocal line will have at least something of a flowing character, even if local activity commands much of our attention. Monotone recitation makes only one brief appearance (bb. 31–2), where the vocal line, momentarily held fast against the descending bass, afterward releases its static energy in accelerated declamation of syllables to a rising line climaxing on the word *volo*, simultaneously illustrating the literal meaning and expressing the underlying passion of the clause 'full of ardent desire, I lift myself in flight'. Here, once again, a simple musical dynamic, this one of stasis and release, parallels and underscores the linguistic relation of the two component phrases of text, the first expressing desire and the second describing its fulfilment.

No other line in this poem divides into reciprocally balanced expressions of desire and fulfilment, but every line is split by a caesura, as is all but inevitable in an endecasyllabic verse. Because the placement of the poetic caesura is variable, it does not always fall in the same place relative to the Romanesca pattern. Nevertheless, Macchiavelli marks each caesura with some gesture of articulation in the vocal line: the two minims in bar 3 followed by the semimimim rest, the minim at the beginning of bar 9 followed by the new melodic process of a rising melisma of fusae, the end of the passaggio on semifusae followed by the cadential preparation in bar 16, the same gesture in bar 22, and so on.

Macchiavelli varies the pace of declamation to extremes, and I take this as a source of musical *chiaroscuro*, developed here in compensation for the Romanesca pattern, which excludes all marked harmonic or hexachordal contrasts. He also controls musical declamation for an impassioned interpretation of the text through delivery: 'Vita de*lla* mia vita, egl'è pur vero ch'io *vi*vo senza te *mi*sero e solo, ch'o vivo *senza TE* misero e solo.' These emphases derive from local melodic apexes (bb. 2, 8, and 14), a leap from anacrusis to thesis (bb. 7–8), and by exceptional prolongation effected by arresting the motion of a passaggio at its end (bb. 9–10 and 15–16). It is symptomatic of a dramatic monodist that Macchiavelli emphasizes syllables as an actor would and ignores the recurring vowel *o*, which gives the stanza its dark colour and which a polyphonic madrigalist may well have underscored musically. Furthermore, whoever transmitted the text replaced Bernardo Tasso's word *voi* with the word *te* in the second line, thereby reducing the level of alliteration.[36] The poet's own intentions concerning the text reflect, I think, an older aesthetic, in which alliteration and vowel coloration meant more than dramatic declamation: 'I have used considerable artifice, so that they satisfy the world, for although I have no judgement of music, at least I can judge how works made for singing ought to go. They are full of purity, of amorous passions, of colours, and of figures accommodated to harmony.'[37]

Even more severe in its contrasts is Macchiavelli's *Venuto è pur quel lagrimabil giorno* (Vol. II, no. 7), an ottava setting in the form of strophic variations over the Ruggiero chordal bass pattern. The *prima parte* begins with a solemn intonation of the first ten syllables on *g'*, beginning with four semibreves ('At last has come that mournful day'), which is answered by the first ten syllables of the second line on *a'*, most as syncopated minims, one of them attacked, after a rest, above a *B* in

---

[36] The text set to the music differs from the one published in Bernardo Tasso's *Rime* (Venice: Giolito, 1560), 19, also in the last line, where Tasso has 'Ch'io non ho col disio tregua, ne pace'.

[37] 'Io ho usato grandissimo artificio, affine che sodisfacciano al mondo, perchè etiandio, ch'io non habbia giudicio di musica, ho almeno giudicio di conoscer quali debbiano essere le compositioni, che si fanno per cantare. Elle son piene di purità, d'affetti amorosi, di colori, & di figure accommodate a l'armonia.' Quoted from Tasso's letter written from Antwerp in 1544 by Edward Williamson, *Bernardo Tasso* (Rome, 1951), 48–9.

the bass ('that day of sighing, that fatal day'). In the *terza parte*, however, syllables are set to fusae for entire phrases, while in the *quarta parte* there are composite *trilli* in thirty-second notes and runs that include sixty-fourth notes. Performance of a composition like this one obviously requires control, expressive shading, and incredible agility; the effect can only be imagined.

The Montalto repertoire contains two ottava settings in recitational style: the anonymous *O fiamma del mio cor luce amorosa* in Stefani's anthology *Concerti amorosi*, which is strophic; and Ottavio Catalani's *In che misero punto hor qui mi mena* (Vol. II, no. 14), which was originally a set of strophic variations—hence both are truly *arie in stil recitativo*.

The text set by Catalani is from Torquato Tasso's *Gerusalemme liberata*, xix. 105–8, from which the first two lines of narrative introduction have been removed, yielding a text that is entirely direct discourse, in order to conform to the dramatic requirements of a 'Lamento di Ermenia cantato nella commedia di Savelli'.[38] The ground plan of the work consists of an unusual, rondo-like alternation of three bass patterns spread over the four stanzas thus:[39]

Stanza:	I	II	III	IV
Bass segments:	A B (inc.)	C B	A B	C A
Measures:	1–23	24–53	54–86	87–105

This ground plan would have more naturally accommodated four complete stanzas without the omission of the first two lines, and perhaps that is the way it was conceived. The adaptation of the plan to accommodate the alteration of Tasso's text, however, was made by a composer, presumably Catalani, and not merely by a copyist, because the musical abbreviation in the setting of Stanza I does not occur in the first bass segment, A, where the missing lines would have been set, but rather in Bass Segment B, marked incomplete in the plan given above. Indeed, although the other two variations on Bass Segment B set four verses, the first Bass Segment B (bb. 12–23) is incomplete because it accommodates only lines 7 and 8 of Stanza I, Tasso's original lines 3–6 having been sung to Bass Segment A (bb. 1–11). These observations suggest that Catalani had composed this work earlier with four complete stanzas of text and later modified it to accommodate the excision of the first two lines of narration required by its use in a stage work.

The style of Catalani's 'Lamento di Ermenia' seems to reflect some non-Roman influence, perhaps from Monteverdi's 'Lamento d'Arianna', *Lasciatemi morire*, a copy of which was evidently in Cardinal Montalto's library, perhaps as a memento of the composer's visit in 1610. It is Catalani's syllabic setting of many semifusae that is so uncharacteristic of Roman recitative yet typical of the Florentine and Mantuan varieties. But Catalani's composition has less of the chromaticism and *seconda prattica* dissonance treatment that characterize Monteverdi's

---

[38] I:Bc, CC.225, fo. 20ᵛ.   [39] Based on Fortune, 'Italian Secular Song from 1600 to 1635', 347.

more famous work. And the alternation between the recitational style of the vocal parts that go against Bass Segments A and C with the cantillational style that goes with the much more active Bass Segment B is typical of monody from Montalto's circles and not of music from elsewhere at this time (1619).

Canzonette

The segment that Francesco Fucci finally awarded place of honour, at the beginning of the *Grilanda musicale*, deliberately separating it from the other gatherings copied on fleur-de-lis paper, consists of two strophic variations. Both are in the same style as three of the four works that begin the segment that, up to that point, had been the first one in the manuscript. This style is marked by a rhythmically active bass with a significant concentration of semiminims, a bass that is unvaried or varied only slightly from strophe to strophe, and a flowing, often syllabic vocal line that eschews both the monotone recitational and the florid cantillational techniques that are the normal components in sonetti. Fortune, as said earlier, restricts his use of the term *strophic variations* for songs of this type—when he does not call them 'strophic-bass cantatas'. I choose to call this the canzonetta style in strophic variations, both because the texts of these pieces are almost invariably strophic canzonette and because the melodic and rhythmic conduct of both the vocal and bass parts are derived from the purely strophic canzonetta, with modest divisions, usually in fusae, added as embellishment in the voice, and conjunct semiminims added as passing notes in the bass.

The derivation of the canzonetta style of strophic variations from the strophic canzonetta would have remained a mere hypothesis were it not for the survival of the two anonymous settings of *A sì duri lamenti* mentioned in Chapter 4. The development of the one setting from the other is demonstrated by a comparison between the first *parte* from the variations (Ex. 6.2*b*) with the entire strophic version (Ex. 6.2*a*). The Xs beneath the bass notes of the two versions show that both basses share a common framework of twelve notes that occur in each under the same twelve syllables of text. But the bass of Ex. 6.2*b*, when compared with that of Ex. 6.2*a*, has been reworked in two ways. Several minims and semibreves in the simpler version have been replaced by groups of semiminims, almost in the manner of a division upon the unembellished bass. And the rhythm of Ex. 6.2*b* has been rearranged so as to suggest an alternative metre of 3/2, as frequently happens in ottava rima variations, particularly those founded upon the Romanesca chordal bass pattern, as we have seen. In order to show this clearly, Ex. 6.2*b* has been rebarred on the staves in 3/2, while the tactus of the original imperfect tempus and prolation are shown with lines between the

Ex. 6.2. Anon., *A sì duri lamenti*: (*a*) strophic setting with framework notes marked; (*b*) strophic variations with framework notes marked

staves. We see that all the syllables of text and the framework bass notes in the two versions are oriented in the same way with respect to barlines *only* when Ex. 6.2*b* is rebarred in this manner. This is evidence that supports Riemann's triple-metre interpretation of pieces like Ex. 6.2*b*. We also note that in the varied repetition of the last line of text in Ex. 6.2*b*, the words *solo e pur* are rhythmically expanded, whereas the words *piangend'il* are reciprocally contracted, producing a simple example of that sprezzatura—here actually *tempo rubato*—mentioned above in connection with ottava rima variations.

The sources described in Chapter 5 in fact contain a substantial number of strophic canzonette that already have the rhythmic characteristics of Ex. 6.2*b*, even though they have not been subjected to the process of variation. The Fucci manuscript I:Bc, CC.225 (the *Selva musicale*), for example, contains the following eight anonymous strophic canzonette with rhythmic and harmonic structures that imply 3/2 metre; five of them have a concentration of semiminims in the bass (shown in parentheses) equal to or greater than the average among canzonetta variations:

Occhi stelle fatali, Vol. II, no. 50 (1.87)
Dhe mirate luce ingrate, Vol. II, no. 53 (.87)
Ho pur d'or il crin anc'io, Vol. II, no. 55 (1.56)
Questa bell'Amor, Vol. II, no. 56 (2.39)
Aure placide volanti, Vol. II, no. 61 (1.52)
Bella Clori non fuggire, Vol. II, no. 65 (.67)
Ferma, ferma non percotere, Vol. II, no. 67 (1.00)
Dhe girate, Vol. II, no. 70 (2.00)

The strophic variations in the sources discussed in Chapter 5 that are based on canzonetta texts have an average concentration of 1.56 semiminims per semibreve measure, three times greater than the sonetti and almost twice as great as the ottave rime. This, of course, is neither a good thing nor a bad thing; it means simply that the styles of strophic variations in this repertoire are heavily dependent upon traditions tied to poetic forms, that they conform to different norms, and that they evidently have somewhat different aesthetic goals. For comparison with these canzonetta variations, the concentration of semiminims in the bass of Giulio Caccini's *Ard'il mio petto*, which Fortune cites as initiating this style, is 1.06. The coefficient in Ippolito Macchiavelli's *Ama pur ninfa gradita*, which Fucci placed at the beginning of the *Grilanda musicale*, is 2.31. The much later works by Giovanni Pietro Berti, Alessandro Grandi, and Carlo Milanuzzi that Fortune calls 'strophic-bass cantatas' have basses with long stretches of continuous semiminims and coefficients over 3. But the figure for Girolamo Frescobaldi's *O bell'occhi che guerrieri*, one of two works that Fortune describes approvingly as 'strophic variations on the point of turning into strophic-bass cantatas', is only 1.61.[40] I do not subscribe to Fortune's view that it was the historical and aesthetic mission for strophic variations to evolve into 'strophic-bass cantatas', but it is worth pointing out that his recurring stereotype of Roman strophic variations as having 'sluggish basses' and 'otiose festoons of semiquavers',[41] however inadequate those phrases may have been as a critical response to Roman sonetti and ottave rime, is simply not applicable to the canzonetta variations in the Montalto repertoire. It does seem, on the other hand, that Francesco Fucci's choice of concentrating canzonetta variations at the beginning of the *Grilanda musicale* implies a somewhat retrospective view of the music that he was assembling, not unlike Fortune's, we might say. This view is revealed in Fucci's choice to give special prominence to pieces that must have seemed the most up to date in 1623.

Of all the types of monody in the repertoire under discussion, strophic variations on canzonetta texts seem the least closely bound to text and the most likely to exploit principles and techniques of purely musical design and structure. And so it is with Macchiavelli's *Ama pur ninfa gradita* (Vol. II, no. 1). Like most strophic canzonette, this work employs binary form, which is reproduced in each of its variations. Many of its melodic and harmonic features are governed by its Mixolydian mode, which is the preferred major mode generally in early seventeenth-century monody. The five cadence points, the goals of melodic and harmonic movement, are, as usual, the final, G (bb. 15 and 32 in the *prima parte*), and the boundary pitches of the repercussion and species of mode 8: C (bb. 6 and 29) and D (m. 22).[42] The contour of the vocal line leading to each of these cadences forms a broad, lightly decorated, asymmetric arch, which helps unify rather long phrases, even across articulating rests (bb. 8 and 29 in the *prima parte*). In four of the five cases, the top of the arch is the fifth above the next cadence pitch, the exception being the third phrase, which descends from the octave of the mode, g'', to d''. Overall melodic unity is also aided by elaboration on the opening three-note rising motif, setting the text *Ama pur*. It is immediately taken up by the bass, which expands it into a four-note motif, and worked into two overlapping sequences. In the second phrase, the bass initiates an inversion of that motif, at once adapted by the voice to the words *Hor che sei*, which are then repeated to the original form of the motif. Whether or not the descending sequence within the text phrase *hor che sei nel età verde* (bb. 8–10) is heard as the descending form of this motif enlarged, the same words are repeated (bb. 10–12) to a semi-sequential

[40] Fortune, 'Italian Secular Song from 1600 to 1635', 373–4.

[41] Ibid. 24. These phrases are repeated in Fortune, 'Italian Secular Monody from 1600 to 1635', 188.

[42] Delbert Meacham Beswick, 'The Problem of Tonality in Seventeenth-Century Music' (Ph.D. diss., University of North Carolina, 1950), shows that the fourth above the final is the preferred secondary cadential point in 17th-c. Mixolydian compositions regardless of whether the modal ambitus is authentic or plagal, as is also the case with Phrygian-mode works in this period.

expansion of this figure, accelerated by a rolling anapaestic rhythm, which returns in each of the other variations. Against this rising semi-sequence in the voice, the bass traces a broad, scalewise descent from *a* to *G*, in preparation for the medial cadence in bar 15. The first phrase of the second half of the *prima parte* outlines the broadest melodic arch of all, while the harmony progresses by fourths, *G*, *C*, *F*, and *B♭*, to its most remote point. A recapitulation (bb. 23–32) combines motifs and features from both component periods of the first half. Then analogous patterns unfold in each of the ensuing variations.

I have belaboured these details in order to demonstrate that the flowing melodic style and directed harmonies that Fortune associates with non-Roman monody of later years were being created in Cardinal Montalto's circles, obviously before Macchiavelli's death in 1619. In fact, three works of comparable style by the cardinal's household composers can be dated even earlier. Cesare Marotta mentions his *Suavissimi lumi al cui splendore* (Vol. II, no. 22) in a letter of 14 December 1611 (Letter 47). Macchiavelli's *Quando il ciel vago s'infiora* (Vol. II, no. 11) was included in the 1616 production of intermedi on texts by Battista Guarini discussed in Chapter 8. And Pellegrino Mutij's *Questi spirti gentil di te ragionano* (Vol. II, no. 4), similar in style although based on terza rima, is from the opera *Amor pudico* of 1614. The Fucci manuscripts and the other Roman sources described in Chapter 5 contain seventeen other canzonetta variations with similarly active basses, many either unascribed or undated, although a number of them include more rapid and extended passaggi than *Ama pur ninfa gradita* and the three pieces named in this paragraph.[43]

Although sharing a similar level of movement in the bass and formed on the Mixolydian matrix in much the same way as Macchiavelli's *Ama pur ninfa gradita*, Cesare Marotta's *Dove, dove ten fuggi anima bella* (Vol. II, no. 21) is both more bound to its text and more acquiescent to the voice than Macchiavelli's piece. Marotta exploited his wife's singing by including passaggi that, while not reaching the

---

[43] *Dolce auretta*, I:Vc, Torrefranca 250, fos. 4ᵛ–8ᵛ, D. Ipolito [Macchiavelli] (Vol. II, no. 2)
Porto celato il mio nobil pensiero, I:Vc, Torrefranca 250, fos. 13ʳ–14ᵛ, anon. (Vol. II, no. 5)
Dhe Filli vita mia se mai ti punsero, I:Vc, Torrefranca 250, fos. 37ᵛ–41ʳ, Don Ipolito (Vol. II, no. 12)
Dolcissime pupille ond'io mi vivo, I:Vc, Torrefranca 250, fos. 51ᵛ–53ʳ, anon. (Vol. II, no. 16)
Dunque Clorida mia per questi prati, I:Vc, Torrefranca 250, fos. 62ᵛ–66ʳ, Giuseppino [Cenci] (Vol. II, no. 19)
Io pur deggio partire, I:Vc, Torrefranca 250, fos. 79ᵛ–80 bisʳ, Ipolito [Macchiavelli] (Vol. II, no. 25)
Leggiadri occhi sereni, I:Vc, I:Bc, CC.225, fos. 24ᵛ–27ʳ, [Giuseppe Cenci] (Vol. II, no. 49)
A sì duri lamenti, I:Baf, MS 1424, fos. 14ᵛ–16ʳ, anon. (Vol. II, no. 78)
Voi pur mi promettesti occhi sereni, I:Baf, MS 1424, fos. 19ᵛ–22ʳ, anon. (Vol. II, no. 79)
Felice che discior tra fiamme ardenti, I:Baf, MS 1424, fos. 32ᵛ–35ʳ, [Stefano Landi] (Vol. II, no. 82)
Può ben fortuna far ch'io m'allontani, I:Baf, MS 1424, fos. 46ᵛ–48ʳ, [Cesare Marotta] (Vol. II, no. 83)
Infelice colui che s'innamora, I:Ru, MS 279, fos. 33ʳ–36ᵛ, anon. (Vol. II, no. 87)
Chi vuol veder il sole, I:Ru, MS 279, fos. 45ʳ–48ʳ, Gio[vanni] Domenico [Puliaschi] (Vol. II, no. 88)
Amor io ben sapea, I:Ru, MS 279, fos. 53ᵛ–56ʳ, Stefano Landi (Vol. II, no. 90)
Questa tener angioletta, I:MOe, Mus. E 318, fo. 9ᵛ, D. H. M. [Don Ippolito Macchiavelli?] (Vol. II, no. 118)
Alla gloria alli honori, Ghirlandetta amorosa, 3–4, Girolamo Frescobaldi
O bell'occhi che guerrieri, Giardino musicale, 8–10, Girolamo Frescobaldi

extremes of virtuosity and passion that characterize the composer's sonetti or ottave rime, exceed what is typical of canzonetta variations. Marotta's variations, however, do not merely decorate a given framework but accommodate and interpret the shepherd's lament as it unfolds.

Dove, dove ten fuggi anima bella?	Whereto, whereto are you fleeing, beautiful soul?
Dunque queste campagnie e questi poggi	Thus, will these fields and these hills
Non ti vedran più d'oggi?	no longer see you after this day?
Dunque per altri prati a coglier fiori	Thus, in other meadows to gather flowers,
Move il bel piè, e per più lieti campi	will you set your delicate foot, and upon other happy
Scintilleran de tuoi begl'occhi i lampi?	fields will your beautiful eyes shine their lights?
Dhe, che farem o pastorelle o ninfe	Ah, what shall we do, o shepherds and nymphs,
Senza quel sol ch'innamorar il cielo?	without that sun to enamour heaven?
Ahi, tutto parmi già tenebre e gielo.	Ah, everything already seems dark and cold!
Sospirate augelletti, aure piangete,	Sigh, little birds; breezes weep;
Piangete antri frondosi e colli adorni,	weep leafy grottos and beautiful hills;
Fin che moss'a pietà con noi soggiorni.	dwell with us until you are moved to pity.
Odi bel angioletta i nostri pianti;	Hear, beautiful little angel, our weeping.
Raccogli le bel ali e ferma il volo;	Draw in your wings and stay your flight.
Non ten fuggir, non mi lasciar qui solo.	Do not go; to do leave me here alone.

Although the chamber monody repertoire is full of shepherds' laments, this one gives the impression of originating in a stage work because of the erotesis to shepherds and nymphs in the third strophe. In the *Grilanda musicale*, it follows two other laments: Giuseppino Cenci's *Dunque Clorida mia per questi prati* and *Lasciatemi morire* from Claudio Monteverdi's opera *Arianna* (1608). Marotta's *Dove, dove ten fuggi anima bella*, a lament upon the death of the beloved like Cenci's, could be from Montalto's 1611 'pastorale', mentioned in Chapter 2. No matter if it is. We shall see in Chapters 7, 8, and 9 that Montalto's stage works made use of the same forms and genres, and sometimes the same pieces of music, that were otherwise or originally employed in chamber performances.

Marotta sets the first strophe almost syllabically, but not in recitative. Nor can his style here even be called arioso, since the bass is just as rhythmically active as the voice. Even so, dramatic declamation and not melodic design rules. The repetition of *dove* urgently anticipates the second tactus, *fuggi* is given an interrogative inflection, and *anima* is prolonged without strong accentuation through syncopation. The third verse is begun twice, each time with realistically different accentuation provided by melodic contours and patterns of durations: 'Non ti ve*dran*, non *ti* vedran più d'oggi.' Then the shepherd restates the entire sentence a fourth lower, as if in somber reflection.

The shepherd becomes somewhat more animated in the second and third strophes, when he recalls, in grief, how his beloved tripped through the meadows gathering flowers, lit up the fields with her eyes, and inflamed the sky with her warmth. His agitation is projected by accelerated delivery of the text and rapid, rising melismas on *prati*, *move*, *scintilleran*, and *innammorar*. But he reverts to lethargy in the fourth strophe, where *sospirate* is uttered with waning syncopation, *aure* follows *augelletti* without a breath, and *piangete* requires a sobbing *trillo*. And he sinks further into despair with the shift to *cantus mollis*, reminiscent of *Tu sei morta* in Monteverdi's *Orfeo* (1607), in the *quinta parte*, which begins with the cruel cross-relation that results from the continuo realization at *odi*.

It is true that the most extensive *passaggi* are found in the last part of Marotta's lament, but here and elsewhere in the piece they often promote text accentuation, not by stressing the syllable treated melismatically but by serving as anacruses to the emphasized word immediately following. Thus, 'Ahi *tutto* parmi già *tenebre*' (bb. 49–52), 'con noi *soggiorni*' (bb. 69–72), 'con *noi* soggiorni' (bb. 74–5), 'Odi bel angioletta i *nostri* pianti' (bb. 77–81), and 'ferma il *volo*' (bb. 84–7).

There are three sectional, non-strophic canzonetta settings preserved in the sources described in Chapter 5 that, venturing even further in the service of text declamation, arrive at recitative of one kind or another: *Occhi meco piangete*, *Tu parti Anima mia*, and *Tu dormi e 'l dolce sonno*. None of them takes the form of strophic variations strictly speaking, but each uses variation technique to some extent. Two of these works are laments, which, like those mentioned earlier, could easily have come from musical stage works. However that may be, by inclusion in the Fucci manuscripts these two recitative laments, along with Catalani's *In che misero punto hor qui mi mena*, Marotta's *Dove, dove ten fuggi anima bella*, and Cenci's *Dunque Clorida mia per questi prati*, take their place near the head of the long line of monodic laments, written or adapted for chamber use in emulation of, and often, as here, in the company of Monteverdi's *Lasciatemi morire*.[44]

Only two vestiges of strophic-variation procedure can be traced in the anonymous *Occhi meco piangete* (Vol. II, no. 3): its division by rubrics into *parti* and the musical refrain at the end of each *parte*, which is varied textually by a different last word each time and musically by a small amount of additional embellishment in two of its four appearances. In singing these verses, the distraught shepherd constantly shifts styles and harmonic regions, creating some of the most prolonged and jolting musical contrasts that can be found in the monodic literature. In the first fifteen bars alone the harmony moves through the regions of E major

---

[44] This tradition is discussed in summary by Lorenzo Bianconi, *Music in the Seventeenth Century*, trans. David Bryant (Cambridge, 1987), 209–19. Of the monodic laments mentioned here, Bianconi refers only to *In che misero punto hor qui mi mena*, without, however, identifying its composer.

(bb. 1–3), C major (b. 4), A major (b. 5), B♮ major (b. 9), and A major, again (b. 15). The expressive recitative heard at the beginning and throughout the work gives way to an outburst of diminution over a static bass (bb. 12–13) or melts into a cantillational style (e.g. bb. 16–24, 34–6, 48–56, 62–9, 75–95, 101–21), which also admits passaggi, over basses moving in semiminims, however. At the other extreme, uninflected narrative recitative makes a brief appearance in the *terza parte* (bb. 70–3). The musical refrain, basically a descending scale in syncopated minims over an active bass, represents a fourth style. At one point, before the final addition of the two segments copied on fleur-de-lis paper, Francesco Fucci intended *Occhi meco piangete* to be the first piece in the *Grilanda musicale*, and it is easy to understand why it would have made a strong impression on him and his clients.

The anonymous *Tu parti Anima mia* (Vol. II, no. 86) is an oddity. Its text, although organized by stanzas, is not precisely strophic. The first three stanzas, each of which begins with the same first line, have seven, six, and five verses respectively. The only poetic regularity is that each stanza ends with a different rhymed couplet. In spite of their disparate lengths, however, the first three stanzas are set as variations, but in recitative style. Stanzas 6 and 8 also form a pair of variations, but not on the bass used for stanzas 1–3. The entire poem of nine stanzas is set in an expressive recitative style unrelieved by melismas or lyrical interludes. Indeed, a partial copy of this work carries the rubric 'Aria stile ricitativa' in a Florentine manuscript, I:Fn, Magl. XIX.23, which also preserves *Questa tener angioletta*, ascribed to 'D. H. M.', probably Don Hippolito Macchiavelli, less likely Don Horatio Michi,[45] who was born a bit too late to emulate Monteverdi. In fact, several of Macchiavelli's works begin with just the sort of slow, solemn intonation that opens each of the first three *parti* here. The rubric 'Aria stile ricitativa' recalls the phrase 'arie in stil recitativo' used in the letter of 1612 written from Rome to Mantua by the Florentine Santi Orlandi, cited in Chapter 3, and it raises the question as to whether I:Fn, Magl. XIX.23 is a collection of monodies sent or carried back to Florence by Orlandi during period 1609–12, when, in the service of Cardinal Ferdinando Gonzaga, he lived in Rome but visited Florence. Of all the laments in the Montalto repertoire, this one comes closest to Monteverdi's *Lasciatemi morire* in style and technique. One is tempted to say, however, that only a Roman would have thought to include five strophic variations when setting nine asymmetrical stanzas of *versi sciolti* as recitative.

The third set of stanzas in recitative style is *Tu dormi e 'l dolce sonno* (Vol. II, no. 89). Both the poetry and the music have some points in common with *Tu*

---

[45] Fortune, 'A Florentine Manuscript', 135, observed that the songs in I:Fn, Magl. XIX.23 are Roman in style. He read the initials 'D. H. M.' as 'DI H:M:' and suggested that they referred to 'Horatio Michi'.

parti Anima mia. Although each of the three stanzas has eleven lines, the pattern of line length is different in each. Each stanza begins with the rhyme scheme ABB and ends with FFGG, but lines 4–7 have a different pattern in each stanza. The music, too, is irregular in form, as the bass of each *parte* merely hints at the structures of the other two. The piece is ascribed to Cesare Marotta in one of the Fucci manuscipts, I:Ru, MS 279. Two other sources, however, assign it to Jacopo Peri, and in a third it is anonymous. Francesco Fucci must have derived his attribution to Marotta from a manuscript in Cardinal Montalto's music collection, and it is hard to imagine how it could have been misattributed to Marotta there, of all places. Luigi Rossi, however, assigns it to Peri in a manuscript that he apparently copied in Naples, before moving to Rome in 1620.[46] It is unascribed in the Florentine manuscript I:Fc, Barbera, which contains monodies, both Florentine and Roman, in several hands, from the first quarter of the seventeenth century but focuses on works from the earlier part of that period. But then it is given to Peri in a later Florentine source, CS:Pnm, II.I.a.2, a manuscript including works by Roman composers Luigi Rossi, Domenico Mazzocchi, and Orazio Michi that seems to have been copied about the time of Rossi's stay at the Medici court in 1635, two years after Peri's death. It is, therefore, possible that the ascription to Peri in CS:Pnm, II.I.a.2 stems from Rossi and not from a Florentine tradition. Fortune considered the style of *Tu dormi e 'l dolce sonno* 'rather dated by 1630' and suggested that Peri may have composed it 'many years earlier'.[47] Tim Carter, who, like Fortune, did not know of the conflicting attribution to Marotta, lists eleven features of harmonic style found in this work that he considers to be among 'Peri's characteristic expressive devices . . . exploited to an unprecedented extreme', and yet he judges the piece to be 'essentially conservative' and 'somewhat forced and self-conscious'.[48] The eleven traits that Carter lists are also found in the works of composers from Montalto's circles, although, as in the general run of Peri's works, they are not present in the same concentration as in *Tu dormi e 'l dolce sonno*.[49] No definitive resolution of this conflicting attribution seems possible at present.

---

[46] GB:Lbm, Add. 30491, fos. 42ᵛ–43ᵛ. See Roland Jackson (ed.), *Neapolitan Keyboard Composers, circa 1600* (Corpus of Early Keyboard Music, 24; Rome, 1967), pp. x–xi.

[47] Fortune, 'Italian Secular Song from 1600 to 1635', 372.

[48] Tim Carter, *Jacopo Peri, 1561–1633: His Life and Works* (New York, 1989), i. 268–9.

[49] The traits, with reference to works in the Montalto repertoire, are:

(1) mixture of recitative and arioso: Cesare Marotta, *O dell'ombrosa notte amati orrori* (Vol, II, no. 47), *passim*

(2) non-harmonic tones: Ippolito Macchiavelli, *Venuto pur quel lagrimabil giorno* (Vol II, no. 7), bb. 13–14

(3) awkward harmonic progressions: Cesare Marotta, *O dell'ombrosa notte amati orrori* (Vol. II, no. 47), b. 11

(4) superimposition of natural and altered versions of the same note: Ippolito Macchiavelli, *Dhe Filli vita mia se mai ti punsero* (Vol. II, no. 12), b. 76

(5) juxtaposition of major triads on D and E: Ottavio Catalani, *In che misero punto hor qui me mena* (Vol. II, no. 14), bb. 88–9

(6) irregular cadences: Giuseppino Cenci, *Io che l'età solea viver nel fango* (Vol. II, no. 15), bb. 4–5

(7) chromaticism: Ottavio Catalani, *In che misero punto hor qui mi mena* (Vol. II, no. 14), b. 56

Terza rima

The variety of formats found among the six terza rima settings in the Fucci manuscripts probably stems from the dual nature of this poetic form. It is one of the classic metres, like ottava rima and the sonetto, but, consisting of symmetrical tercets, it can be treated as if strophic, like the canzonetta. Consequently, among these terze rime there are a strophic setting, a set of strophic variations in sonetto style, two strophic variations of the canzonetta type with active bass, one of them *passaggiata* and the other not, and two composite strophic variations with a mixture of techniques.

The strophic *Arsi et ardo per voi ma nel ardore* (Vol. II, no. 58) combines an active bass with an almost completely syllabic text setting, which uses enough repeated pitches that it could pass for the simple, mechanical type of recitative were it combined with a static accompaniment. This type of strophic song may be a holdover from the sort of recitational villanella mentioned in Chapter 3, perhaps in deference to the classic terza rima text. However, the two other strophic songs in this style set modern canzonetta texts. One of these is *Voi partite sdegniose* (Vol. II, no. 52) by Raffaello Rontani, who seems to have specialized in using recitational style in unusual contexts.[50] The anonymous *D'una guancia alma e ridente* (Vol. II, no. 54) is similar and may be Rontani's work as well.

The text of *Son questi miei sospir messaggi ardenti* (Vol. II, no. 42) consists of three stanzas of irregular or corrupted terza rima. Instead of the classic ABA BCB CDC rhyme scheme, these endecasyllabic verses end *-enti, -ore, -enti / -ene, -ate, ene / -ade, -eno, -ade*, which is close enough to reveal a kinship to terza rima but sufficiently different to suggest some corruption in transmission. The anonymous setting of this text alternates between a largely syllabic and often monotone recitation over a slow-moving or static bass (bb. 1–12, 16–24, 29–32, 35–9) with brief passaggi in semifusae. This alternation in the context of strophic variations brings to mind the typical sonetto setting. But the passaggi, much shorter and simpler here than is customary in sonetti, amount to somewhat extended cadential decorations.

Towards the opposite extreme from these two recitational settings are the terze rime set as strophic variations in canzonetta style. Pellegrino Mutij's *Questi spirti gentil di te ragionano* (Vol. II, no. 4) has an unvaried bass that is somewhat more active than the average canzonetta variation in the Montalto repertoire. Each *parte*

---

(8) juxtaposition of major triads a minor third apart: Ippolito Macchiavelli, *Solingo augello che piangendo vai* (Vol. II, no. 9), bb. 8–9

(9) interrupted cadence: Ippolito Macchiavelli, *Quando il ciel vago s'infiora* (Vol. II, no. 11), bb. 2–3

(10) irregular resolution of suspensions: Cesare Marotta, *Che più giova mirar occh'infelici* (Vol. II, no. 48), b. 1

(11) affective melodic leaps: Ippolito Macchiavelli, *Solingo augello che piangendo vai* (Vol. II, no. 9), b. 9

[50] Hill, 'Frescobaldi's *Arie*', 163–6.

is divided by a strong medial cadence and double bar, which are typical of strophic canzonette of this period. Mutij's syllabic text setting in a clearly metrical, cantillational vocal line is relieved by brief, modest melismas, almost entirely in fusae. The easy, graceful, simple, and gentle style of this aria is appropriate to its dramatic context within the opera *Amor pudico*, which will be explained in Chapter 9. Giuseppino Cenci's *Se perché a voi tolga e più non v'ami* (Vol. II, no. 152) combines an even more active bass with a vocal line decorated by the rapid passaggi for which the composer was noted, even if they are somewhat more moderate than found in his sonetti.

The most remarkable of the terza rima settings are the two that juxtapose recitational and cantillational styles from one *parte* to the next. One of these works is Giovanni Domenico Puliaschi's *La gloria di colui, che 'l tutto muove* (Vol. II, no. 122), which has an unequivocal ascription and date (1614). But since it was part of the opera *Amor pudico*, a detailed examination of it will be postponed until Chapter 9.

The other composite setting of terza rima can be ascribed and dated only through indirect evidence. It is *O dell'ombrosa notte amati orrori* (Vol. II, no. 47), which appears anonymously towards the end of the original fascicles of Fucci's *Grilanda musicale*. However, the curiously chromatic, non-standard bass of its first and fourth *parti* is identical with the one used in the canzonetta variations *Suavissimi lumi al cui splendore* (Vol. II, no. 23), ascribed to Cesare Marotta in the same manuscript and mentioned in Marotta's letter of 14 December 1611 (Letter 47). Because of this, I think we should also ascribe *O dell'ombrosa notte amati orrori* to Marotta and conclude that it was written near to the time when *Suavissimi lumi al cui splendore* was composed, that is, about 1611.

Marotta's text is a capitolo formed of five stanzas of terza rima, the last extended in the traditional manner by one verse in order to achieve closure in the rhyme scheme.

O dell'ombrosa notte amati orrori,	O beloved horrors of dark night,
O dell'eterne piagge aurate stelle,	o shining stars of eternal shores,
Ascoltate pietos'i miei dolori.	listen with pity to my sorrow.
Voi che i venti movete e le procelle,	You who move winds and storms,
E tu ch'a venti folgori tonanti	and you who hurl thundering lightning in the wind,
Dal ciel volando le sembianze belle.	chasing away the serene countenance from the sky,
Deh frena l'ira a questi dolci canti,	restrain your wrath at the sound of these sweet songs,
Se può cantar un che languisc'e more,	if one who languishes and dies can sing;
E dagl'occhi distil'amari pianti.	and from his eyes sheds bitter tears.

Amante io son che non ho spirto e core,	I am a lover who has no spirit or heart left,
E s'io spiego miei doglie al ciel sereno,	and if I expound my grief to the still heavens,
Sol me da spirto e cor il mio dolore.	only my sorrow gives me heart and spirit.
Vive l'anima mia dentro un bel seno,	My soul dwells within a beautiful breast,
Né si cura tornar dov'è fuggita,	nor does it care to return whence it fled,
Tal che la morte ha di mia vita il freno,	so that death has control of my life
E non mi sdegna e non mi trahe di vita.	and neither rejects me nor takes my life.

The invocation to nocturnal phantoms is an impassioned incantation, intensifying at the prolongation of O in line 2, waxing in the vehemently sputtered *dell'eterne piagge*—the syllables set, without precedent in early recitative, to thirty-second notes—declining by a full octave from initial exclamation to final entreaty, and waning to a minim on the accented syllable of *dolori*.

The single sentence uniting stanzas 2 and 3 of this work combines a more extended invocation with a more specific entreaty, as narratio after exordium. Here, the tone becomes more lyrical, and Marotta changes to that canzonetta style which suggests an alternative barring in 3/2 metre. It is at this point that he borrows the bass from his own *Suavissimi lumi al cui splendore*, as I have said. The text of that earlier work spoke of a soul full of 'most agreeable martyrdom' and horror 'mercifully calmed'. In the present stanzas we have winds, storms, and lightning to be calmed by the sweet songs of one who languishes and dies. It would appear that the similar themes and expressions of the new text recalled the earlier work to Marotta's mind, and this would seem to be another argument in favour of ascribing O *dell'ombrosa notte amati orrori* to him.

After the climactic allusion to 'thundering lightning' sweeps from the lowest to the highest note of the piece, the *terza parte*, which speaks of 'sweet songs' and languishing, flattens the melodic curves and reins in the pace somewhat. The return to the bass of the second variation imparts the gesture of a new beginning to the *quarta parte* while reverting to the feeling of *amabilissimo martire*, perhaps embodied in the sinuously tortured chromaticism with which this bass line begins. In this variation the climactic phrase from the *seconda parte* is expanded by the longest passaggio of the work at *spiego miei doglie al ciel*, after which the vocal line lapses into phlegmatic monotones. The recitative that begins the last stanza of Marotta's setting proves to be a variation on the first *parte*. Thus the peroratio grows out of the exordium. But the last line rounds out the whole by recalling the attenuated cantillational style of the middle stanza.

In this way, Marotta embeds localized contrast within a large-scale plan that opposes recitative and aria (in the modern sense) from stanza to stanza. It is the earliest vocal composition to do so: in many other sectional settings of strophic texts, for example, Jacopo Peri's *Se tu parti da me* (1609), contrast between recitative and aria occurs *within* each strophe, whereas in Marotta's O *dell'ombrosa notte amati orrori* the styles are maintained throughout each strophe and the contrast occurs *between* strophes. This work is not isolated, of course, and really belongs, as we have seen, to a group of monodies from Cardinal Montalto's circle that juxtapose recitational and cantillational styles, harking back to presumably earlier works of Giuseppino and certain Neapolitan villanelle described in Chapter 3. Marotta was conscious of this type of contrast as a relatively novel compositional technique and aesthetic principle, for in a letter of 3 March 1614 (already quoted in Ch. 4), he refers to an unnamed Romanesca in this way:

I am sending Your Most Illustrious Lordship the Romanesca that you command from me, even though I was reserving it for myself to demonstrate it to Signora Francesca, so that you might hear it from her in the manner in which I would like it to be sung. For I argue that demonstrating it is not easy for someone who is not well practised in it, because although it is a Romanesca, I nevertheless called it a *Romanesca bastarda* since in many places it must be sung with passion (*cantato con affetto*) and in others with sustained notes, short embellishments, and other niceties (*con tenute di voci, accenti, et altre diligenze*) that cannot be written but require the spoken word. I do a great deal when I obey my patrons. I also beg you not to hand it about because I have not presented it, and I never wanted to release it, although I have had a thousand requests for it (Letter 74).

This passage is difficult to interpret precisely, which is why I have included two samples of the original wording in parentheses. Marotta must be referring here to departures from the normal manner of singing a Romanesca. His words 'cantato con affetto' recall to mind the expression 'cantare con affetto, solo' ('to sing with passion, alone'), which is one of the formulations that Giulio Caccini used to designate the new monodic style in the preface to his 1614 *Nuove musiche*. There, Caccini asserted that to sing well with passion, alone, requires three things: passion, variety of the same, and sprezzatura (that is, rhythmic freedom, as explained in Ch. 3), which, therefore, links *cantare con affetto* with recitational styles of singing, as Monteverdi must have thought when he instructed performers that the lament of the nymph, proper, in his *Non havea Febo ancora* (Book 8, 1638), was to be sung with the rhythmic freedom dictated by the expression of passions ('va cantato a tempo dell'affetto del animo, e non a quello de la mano'). *Tenute di voci*, literally 'sustaining of pitches', and *accenti*, meaning 'short embellishments', appear to characterize something different from *cantare con affetto* and, therefore, cantillational styles, in all likelihood. So, although this letter refers primarily to unnotated details in performance, it also tells us that these details are of different kinds, that they are appropriate in different places, and that, on the whole, the *Romanesca bastarda* combines different styles, much as the viola bastarda and trombone bastardo combine bass, tenor, and alto voice ranges. Since we do not know which piece Marotta was describing, we can only use his letter as a confirmation of our view that this type and extent of internal contrast between recitational

TABLE 6.4. Lost music mentioned in letters transcribed in Appendix A

Donna bella, et crudele (no. 74)

Non havete a temer ch'in forma nova (no. 92, 96)

O quante volte in van cor mio te chiamo (nos. 96, 99)

O solenne Vittoria (nos. 94, 95, 96)

O tu che ne vai altiero (no. 27)

Se quel dolore (no. 32)

---

and cantillational styles were, for him, a significant novelty that other composers sought to imitate.

Reception

Much of Cesare Marotta's music is now lost or inaccessible to us: many pieces named in his letters and his *musiche* for stage works of which we have titles and even word books have disappeared without a trace (see Table 6.4 for a list). The same must be true of much work by his colleagues in Cardinal Montalto's circles. It seems unlikely that Marotta actually composed only one *Romanesca bastarda* like *O dell'ombrosa notte amati orrori*, and more likely that he produced others that remain unknown to us. But the most original and ambitious works by the principal composer in the household of the most prestigious and generous music patron in Rome must have received attention, admiration, and emulation at that time. Indeed, further along in the 1614 letter just cited, Marotta claims that some of the arias that he composed for *Amor pudico*, 'which had the fortune to please universally' were 'requested by many, many people' and that 'some beginnings of these (arias) were stolen while they were being sung, for some curious musicians deftly wrote them down while hearing them'. (For a list of the arias, see below, Table 9.2.)

If *O dell'ombrosa notte amati orrori* was composed about 1611, as seems likely, then the first known emulation of it was Puliaschi's *La gloria di colui, che 'l tutto muove*, composed, as has been said, for *Amor pudico* in 1614. This work sets a capitolo in terza rima, exactly the poetic form of Marotta's piece. In it, the first and third stanzas are in recitative style and are related by variation, while the second and fourth stanzas are in cantillational style, the fourth beginning as if it would be a variation on the second but then digressing. In other words, Puliaschi's *La gloria di colui, che 'l tutto muove* is quite like Marotta's *O dell'ombrosa notte amati orrori* in poetic and musical form.

After this, there is a steady, if narrow, stream of similar works that survive in the monody and early cantata repertoires. By Marotta's sometime instructional collaborator Girolamo Frescobaldi we have *Alla gloria alli honori* (1621) and *Così mi disprezzate?* (1630), both of which set strophic poetry to a mix of variation and non-variation *parti*, alternating between recitative and aria styles.[51] Giovanni Felice Sances, who sang Marotta's music in *Amor pudico* as a boy, later published *Misera hor sì ch'il pianto* in the second book of his *Cantade* (1633), a work likewise containing recitative and aria contrast in which three of the strophes are related as variations while two are not. Later, in the fourth book of his *Cantate, et arie* (1636), Sances included *Non sia chi mi riprenda*, a strophic poem set as variations in metrical aria style with two strophes of poetry composed as non-variation arioso.

In the meantime, compositions that are comparable in several respects began to appear in the Venetian orbit. *Occhi miei tristi*, in Giovanni Pietro Berti's *Cantade et arie* (1624), sets eight stanzas of terza rima as recitatives and arias, although not in variation relationship. Pellegrino Possenti's *Accenti pietosi d'Armillo* (1625) included *Ecco Filli, o pastori*, in which a series of strophic variations in arioso style are interrupted by an unrelated *parte* in 3/2 metre; and *Udite s'a raggion* in the same collection consists of two sets of interlocking variations, much like Puliaschi's *La gloria di colui, che 'l tutto muove*. *Quanto t'inganni Amor* in the third book of Martino Pesenti's *Arie* (1636) has a strophic text set to alternating recitatives and arias, among which two of the *parti* are variations while the others are not.

Back in Rome, this thread was taken up by Luigi Rossi (*c.*1597–1653). We have learnt that in 1620 he entered the service of the Borghese family, with whom Cardinal Montalto exchanged musicians and maintained the closest alliance (celebrated in *Amor pudico*, as we shall see). Most of Rossi's works are preserved in manuscripts and cannot be securely dated, but some of what seem to be his earliest ones elaborate on one or more of the principles that made Marotta's *O dell'ombrosa notte amati orrori* innovative. In Rossi's *Giusto così va detto*, in GB:Lbm, Harley 1265, the strophes of text that are set as recitatives form a discontinuous series of variations, while the other strophes, which are set in metrical aria style, are not related by variation. This work is based upon Rossi's *Questi caldi sospiri et humil gridi* in I:Bc, Q49, a Florentine manuscript assembled *c.*1635.[52] Rossi's *Presso un ruscel*, in I:Rvat, Barb. lat. 4208, sets strophic poetry to an interlocking structure of varied recitatives alternating with varied arias, unrelated to the recitatives. Among his other works, *Precorrea del sol l'uscita*, *Già nell'oblio profondo*, and *Ingordo uman desio* are strophic variations in which each *parte* is divided between recitative and aria.

What distinguishes all these works, save the last three mentioned, is that recitative–aria contrast occurs *between* the major sections rather than within them.

⁵¹ Hill, 'Frescobaldi's *Arie*', 157–94.   ⁵² Fortune, 'A Florentine Manuscript'.

Canzonette and strophic variations with this dichotomy *within* each *parte* are more common,[53] and madrigals that incorporate some differentiation between recitational and cantillational styles are spread relatively thickly upon the ground.[54] But Marotta's *Romanesca bastarda* and its successors are the first compositions in which the recitatives have ample time to establish their character and the arias are closed movements.

In apparent response to this musical procedure, poems were eventually written with asymmetrical stanzas to accommodate the opposing musical styles —canzonetta verse for the arias and *versi sciolti* for the recitatives. Francesco Bracciolini (1566–1645), secretary to Maffeo Barberini both before (1601–5) and after the latter became Pope Urban VIII (1623), took that step in at least four texts: 'In verde bosco ombroso',[55] 'Quando miro l'innamorata Dido',[56] 'Taci taci o mio core',[57] and 'Addolorata amante'.[58]

Other paths to a similar destination led, over time, from canzonette and madrigals in mixed styles to musical and poetic elaborations and expansions that achieve higher levels of sectional definition and closure. There is one canzonetta in the Fucci manuscripts where recitative and aria styles are juxtaposed within each strophe: *Bella e vaga Filli vezzosa* (Vol. II, no. 77). But madrigals with this sort of opposition were produced abundantly in the Montalto circles, beginning with the works of Giuseppino Cenci, and they are among the most characteristic productions of this group of composers. As stated earlier, nine such works are found in the original fascicles of the *Grilanda musicale*.

Orazio Michi (1594–1641) followed the path initiated by this part of the Montalto repertoire, and, in doing so, he selected and elaborated upon some features of its styles. Michi, it will be recalled, served in Cardinal Montalto's household from 1613 to 1623, but he lived and composed for eighteen years after Montalto's death. As established in Chapter 5, none of the sources that preserve Michi's music has any connection with the manuscripts derived from material in Montalto's library. Indeed, the sources of Michi's music overwhelmingly contain music by composers active in Rome during the 1630s. For these reasons, Michi's

---

[53] Fortune, 'Italian Secular Song from 1600 to 1635', 424–36; Porter, 'The Origins of the Baroque Solo Song', Ex. 35; Gloria Rose Donington, 'The Cantatas of Carissimi' (Ph.D. diss., Yale University, 1959), 35–43; James Forbes, 'The Nonliturgical Vocal Music of Johannes Hieronymus Kapsberger (1580–1651)' (Ph.D. diss., University of North Carolina, 1977), 95, 142.

[54] Eugen Schmitz, *Geschichte der Kantate und des geistliche Konzerts*, i: *Geschichte der weltlichen Solokantate* (2nd edn., Leipzig, 1955), 44–53; Jan Racek, *Stilprobleme der italienischen Monodie: Ein Beitrag zur Geschichte des einstimmigen Barockliedes* (Opera Universitatis Purkynianae Brunensis Facultas Philosophica, 103; Prague, 1965), 166–80; Donington, 'The Cantatas of Carissimi', 34; Fortune, 'Italian Secular Song from 1600 to 1635', 30, 295–7, 430, 434.

[55] I:Rn, Vitt. Em. 43, fos. 13ᵛ–14ᵛ, 'Versi per musica in stil recitativo', consisting of *versi sciolti* at the beginning and a strophic canzonetta at the end.   [56] Ibid., fos. 11ʳ–12ᵛ, 'Lamento di Didone per musica'.

[57] Ibid., fos. 9ᵛ–10ʳ, 'Versi per musica in stil recititivo', *versi sciolti* followed by a strophic canzonetta.

[58] I:Rn, Vitt. Em. 43, fos. 219ʳ–220ᵛ, *versi sciolti* interspersed with metrical sections marked for arias and duets.

TABLE 6.5. Francesco Balducci, 'Su l'Oriente' (*Rime*, 1630)

1.	Su l'Oriente	D'un bel candore	Ostro ove ondeggia	Servirò à l'empio
2.	L'Alba ridea	Misto il cinabro	Sangue innocente	L'altrui ruine.
3.	Forse perché vedea	D'una guancia, ò d'un labro	De' pianti altrui ridente	E fabricarò al fine
4.	fulminata la notte, e l'ombre spento;	Fea del giorno d'amor rider l'albore;	Fea d'un Tiranno insuperbir la reggia.	Consecrati al suo fasto, o Casa, o Tempio;
5.	Quando repente	Quando un pallore	Ma in Ciel fiammeggia	Ma fù di scempio,
6.	Altra nebbia levossi, e 'l Sol rapì.	Subito il ricoperse, e scolorì	Stella, cui di saette il Fato armò.	Non di riparo, e non rimase in piè.
7.	Poi co i fati del dì	Come tosto sparì	Stella ch'insanguinò	Quanto ordì, quanto fè
8.	Vid'io guardando in giro	De la bocca odorata	Con la morte de gli empi	Gli cadde in testa, e fù sua sepoltura
9.	Che rapide fuggiro,	La porpora animata	La chioma, e con gli scempi	La superba struttura.
10.	Come s'avesser l'ali,	Comme fuggir le rose	De' popoli, e de' Regni	Al suol valsero d'armi
11.	Le Vite de' mortali.	De le guance amorose	Che provocar gli sdegni	Di vendetta quei marmi.
12.	E la speme, e 'l desio schernito fu.	E la speme, e 'l desio schernito fu.	Ne' Numi, e 'l vil desio schernito fu.	Ch'ei ne divulse, e 'l reo schernito fu.
13.	Folli noi di quà giù;	Folli noi di quà giù;	Folli noi di qua giù;	Folli noi di quà giù;
14.	Rio fugace è 'l piacer, ch'al mar sen va;	Rio fugace è 'l piacer, ch'al mar sen va;	Rio fugace è 'l piacer, ch'al mar sen va;	Rio fugace è 'l piacer, ch'al mar sen va;
15.	E per Tantalea sete acqua non ha.	E per Tantalea sete acqua non ha.	E per Tantalea sete acqua non ha.	E per Tantalea sete acqua non ha.

undated works can be more safely considered as reception of the Montalto monody repertoire than part of it.

Contrast between recitational and cantillational style is a major component of Orazio Michi's music, as it was in the earlier Montalto repertoire. But it does not occur between stanzas in the context of modified strophic variations, as it does in some of Rossi's works. The closest he comes to this procedure is *Dalle squalide tombe al cielo uscita* (I:Rcas, MS 2490, fos. 58^v–60^r), a 'Sonetto della morte di Christo Signor Nostro', which is divided into four *parti* (mixing recitative and arioso in accordance with the tendency observed in our earlier discussion of sonetti), the fourth of which is almost a variation on the first. But contrast between cantillational and recitational styles is most frequently encountered in Michi's works within the strophes of canzonette.

Of the ninety-six or ninety-seven pieces by Orazio Michi listed in Table 5.3 in Chapter 5, six are trios and six are duets. The remaining eighty-four compositions are accompanied vocal solos. Of these, forty-eight are strophic settings of canzonetta texts, and at least an additional twenty-one are settings of single canzonetta strophes. In all, twenty-one pieces by Michi combine some form of cantillational and recitational styles. Thirteen of these are monostrophic or are traditional polystrophic settings of canzonetta texts. Some of these are rather brief and basically cantillational in style, having only a few measures of recitative. But others have substantial, well-developed, and closed sections of recitative and aria.

It is, in fact, a vexing question whether Michi's settings of single canzonetta strophes should be considered a distinct type. It is quite possible that some or all of these pieces were intended as strophic songs and that the additional stanzas of text were simply not copied into the manuscripts that preserve them. Balducci's *Cari lumi che pietosi* is set to music in Michi's autograph manuscript, I:Rn, Ms. Mus. 56, fos. 15^v–16^r, as a single strophe, while the same text, in a different setting, is given additional stanzas of text on fos. 34^v–35^r in the same manuscript. And the first strophe of Balducci's *Hor che la notte del silentio amica* is set as a monostrophic canzonetta in I:Rn, Ms. Mus. 56, fos. 19^v–20^v, whereas the same text in the same setting is preserved on fos. 59^v–63^v of the same manuscript as the first of four strophes set to distinct sections of recitative, arioso, and metrical aria.

However, in no case is the same musical setting that is preserved as a monostrophic canzonetta in one source found as a normal multistrophic canzonetta with full text in a second source. Indeed, in some cases subsequent strophes of the poem could not be sung to Michi's setting of the first strophe. A clear instance is *Su l'oriente* (Vol. II, no. 162). The text of all four strophes as they were printed in Francesco Balducci's *Rime* (1630) is given in Table 6.5. The third line of the first strophe, although a settenario *piano*, is set in its first appearance as if it had only six syllables by interpreting the word *vedea* ('saw') as if it had two rather than three syllables, an interpretation made possible by the attachment of *fulminata*, which is isolated from its position as the first word of line 4. Thus, *Forse perché vedea fulminata* is set syllabically to ten notes (bb. 5–8). That setting is absolutely impossible for any of the following strophes. The second phrase of Michi's music amplifies the third line of text with typical repetitions: *forse, forse perché, perché vedea*. The three segments of this phrase, thus, contain two, four, and five syllables each, respectively, beginning twice on the first word and once on the second word of the line. While this treatment might be possible for line 3 of strophe 2, it is out of the question for the parallel places in strophes 3 and 4. Again, line 8 of the first strophe, another settenario *piano*, is set to music as if it had eight syllables by eliminating the elision between the fifth and the sixth (b. 35). None of the ensuing strophes has a word break after the fifth syllable of line 8, hence none could be sung to Michi's music for the first strophe.

Michi's setting of the first strophe of Balducci's *Hor che del Tebro smaltano* is split between triple-metre aria and duple-metre arioso, to which other stanzas of the poem cannot be accommodated on account of text repetition. The recitative and aria sections that set the first strophe of *Hor che la notte del silentio amica* are likewise moulded to the text, so that when Michi wanted to add the rest of Balducci's poem, he had to compose new music for each strophe. Michi's strophic setting of *Cari lumi che pietosi* accommodates all five stanzas of Balducci's text to uniformly metrical music, but his monostrophic setting of the first stanza, divided between triple-metre aria and duple-metre arioso, could not because of partial verse repetitions. Even the two monostrophic settings of Balducci canzonette entirely in triple metre—*Stral'amor tal m'avventò* and *Zefiretti che spirante*—could not be adapted to all the stanzas of those poems. The complete poems from which Michi drew the single stanzas of texts of his other monostrophic canzonette have not come to hand, and so we cannot conclude that they could not have been intended to be sung strophically. But all Michi's monostrophic settings of Balducci's canzonette seem to have been composed for only one stanza of text. They appear to be symptomatic of the composer's struggle against the restrictions of existing text forms. And they provide further support for my hypothesis—adumbrated apropos of the modified strophic variations that followed Cesare Marotta's *Romanesca bastarda*—that the musical procedures typical of the mid-century chamber cantata emerged earlier than the eventually associated text structures, which therefore must have resulted from poets' accommodation to composers.

It is difficult, at times, to distinguish Michi's monostrophic canzonette from his solo madrigals, for many of his monostrophic texts consist of seven- and eleven-syllable *versi sciolti*, as do many of the strophic canzonette, except, of course, that in the case of strophic canzonette a rhyme scheme that was unpredictable in the first stanza becomes predictable thereafter. In general, I consider a work to be a monostrophic canzonetta when the text contains lines of other than seven or eleven syllables or when the verses, although exclusively settenari and ende-casillabi, are entirely or largely *tronchi* or *sdruccioli*. Texts of this latter sort tend to establish regular patterns of accentuation, which is one of the characteristics that distinguishes canzonette from madrigals.

A good example of the problems involved in this judgement is *Empio cor, core ingrato* (Vol. II, no. 163):

Empio cor, core ingrato,	Wicked heart, ungrateful heart,
M'han le tue colpe a questo legno affisso,	your strokes have nailed me to this cross,
E 'l mio petto svenato	and my eviscerated breast
Apre per te, d'ogni tesor l'abbisso.	opens, for you, the greatest of all treasures.
Strale d'amor più forte	A stronger dart of Love
M'ha già ferito a morte;	has already mortally wounded me.
Già languisco, già moro e non rispondi.	I already languish, already die, and you do not respond.
Cor ingrato, empio cor, dove t'ascondi?	Ungrateful heart, wicked heart, where are you hiding?

As it consists entirely of settenari and endecasillabi, I would tentatively clas-sify the poem as a madrigal, although it could be the isolated first strophe of a canzonetta. Unlike a typical madrigal, it has a fairly regular rhyme scheme ABABCCDD, and the fifth and sixth lines establish the metrical rhythm $- \smallsmile \smallsmile - \smallsmile - \smallsmile$. Michi responds to this poetic property exactly as the anonymous com-poser of *O quanto sei gentile* (Vol. II, no. 31) did, following the scansion of the more metrical lines by a shift to triple metre and the regularly accented rhythms of aria style.

Michi begins *Empio cor, core ingrato* with twenty-eight measures of recitative, relieved by many small ornaments, a few short melismas, and one major passag-gio, almost a sort of cadenza, which leads to the full cadential closure of this sec-tion. This corresponds to the first sentence of the text, which is considerably expanded through repetitions that provide strong rhetorical reinforcement to a poem already exaggerated in this imagery and fervour. Here, as usual, Michi writes expressive recitative in which strong dissonance and a very wide vocal range con-tribute to extravagantly impassioned expression. His wide leaps, sudden shifts of register, and broadly sweeping contours bring to mind the monodies of Sigis-mondo d'India, Michi's sometime colleague in the service of Cardinal Maurizio of Savoy. But these features can also be found in several of the anonymous mad-rigals with recitative in the Montalto repertoire, for instance, the anonymous *Doppo un lungo sospiro* (Vol. II, no. 39), discussed earlier in this chapter.

The second sentence of Michi's *Empio cor, core ingrato* is set in 3/4 metre as a closed aria (bb. 29–53), which is subdivided by a Phrygian half-cadence (b. 35), a full cadence on B♮ (b. 46), and several non-cadential phrase endings. Harmonic

shape, melodic contour, and the elaboration of a few motifs and metrical patterns seem to be the point of this section more than any specific reinforcement
of poetic meaning, either local or general. In this respect, Michi's setting is
symptomatic of a new generation of Italian composers whose works eventually
predominated in the 1650s.

The last two lines of *Empio cor, core ingrato*, perhaps a madrigalian acumen, form
a third sentence, which, having returned to the prosaic accents of endecasillabi,
is set in a style that hovers between expressive recitative and florid arioso (bb. 54–
76). Like the first section, this one opens with a rising anapaest, an emphatic
declamatory gesture that begins so many of Michi's phrases of recitative as to be
considered something of a personal signature. Likewise typical for Michi is the
separation, often by a rest, of syllables that normally ought to be elided. This contributes further to his characteristically assertive style of delivery and clarity of
enunciation.

Not that Michi always sets *versi sciolti* as recitative. In *Quanti quanti sospiri*
(I:Rcas, MS 2490, fos. 51ᵛ–52ʳ), a single stanza entirely made up of settenari and
endecasillabi is put to music mostly in triple-metre aria style, relieved briefly by
arioso and recitative.

Michi's *Perché, perché, cor mio* (I:Rcas, MS 2490, fos. 89ʳ–90ʳ) is one among many
of his pieces comparable to *Empio cor, core ingrato* in that one stanza of text contains verses of divergent character that point to their setting as recitative and aria,
but in the case of *Perché, perché, cor mio* the presence of ottonari clearly indicates
the canzonetta as frame of reference:

Perché, perché, cor mio,	7
Ad'ogn'aura di diletto	8
Apre folle il tuo desio	8
Alle gioie, a l'alma e 'l petto?	8
Ah, non t'alletti così,	8t
Sereno splendore che liet'appari;	11
Per fuggire, inpenna l'ale	8
E l'estremo del riso il pianto assale.	11

Su l'oriente (I:Rcas, MS 2490, fos. 55ʳ–56ʳ, discussed above) has a similar but much
longer text, set predominantly as triple-metre aria occasionally interrupted by a
bit of recitative and some duple-metre florid arioso.

If *Empio cor, core ingrato* can be considered an expansion of *versi sciolti* through
the interpolation of canzonetta-like verses, *Perdan quest'occhi il sole* (Vol. II, no. 164)
sets a composite of two strophic structures.[59]

---

[59] This work is ascribed to Michi in CS:Pnm, II.La.2, fos. 65ʳ–68ʳ, and is also contained in Michi's autograph collection, I:Rn, Ms. Mus. 56, fos. 50ᵛ–54ᵛ.

Perdan quest'occhi il sole	May these eyes lose their sun
Pria che tramonti di mia vita il giorno,	before my life's day sets,
Né mai faccia ritorno	nor may ever return
Alba che mi console,	the dawn that consoles me,
Né rischiari per me l'ombra importuna	nor may the ray of a star or moon
Raggio di stella o luna.	light up for me the dreary shadow.
Piova la notte horrenda	May horrendous night rain
Fiamme di torti fulmini e di lampi,	flames of twisted thunderbolts and lightning,
Né sia chi me ne scampi,	nor may there be anyone to rescue me,
Né sia chi mi difenda.	nor may there be anyone to defend me;
Manchi la terra ove mai pos'il piede	may the earth give way wherever I set my foot
Pria ch'i manchi di fede.	before I lack faith.
Empia, così giurasti,	Wicked woman, thus, you swore,
E 'n segno che la fè perir dovea,	and as a sign that my faith should perish,
La man di morte rea	your hand, mortally guilty,
Di congiungervi osasti.	you dared to offer.
Vendetta, o cieli! hor chi la suso a cura	Revenge, o heaven! Now that he above takes care
Di punir la spergiura.	to punish the perjurer.
Piovete, o fulmini,	Rain, o thunderbolts, upon the wicked head,
Su l'empio capo il sol di nubi involgasi,	engulf the sun with clouds
O 'ndietro volgasi,	or turn yourself around
S'atterri e fulmini	if you strike down and fulminate
La fallace ch'altrui 'ngannando va,	the false woman who deceives others,
L'empia che fè non ha.	the wicked woman who has no faith.
Manchili sotto ai piè	May the offended earth give way under her feet
La terra offesa, e fin dal centro squotasi	and the heaven that revolves
Lo ciel che rotasi.	be shaken to its centre.
Vendichi la mia fè.	Avenge my faith!
Ma che priego? saette il ciel non ha	But what do I want? heaven does not have thunderbolts
Per punir la beltà.	to punish the beauty.
Più chiari splendono	Those wicked eyes shine more brightly
Quegl'occhi rei che la mia morte bramano.	that long for my death.
Gli dii che l'amano	The gods that love her
Lei non offendono.	do not hold her back.
E mentre i cieli amici a lei si voltano,	And while her heavenly friends turn towards her,
Me non ascoltono.	they give no heed to me.

Although Balducci maintains the same rhyme scheme throughout the poem, he changes to a different, if related, verse structure at mid-point. The first three strophes maintain the pattern 7 11 7 7 11 7, whereas stanzas 4–6 introduce variants of it based on *versi sdruccioli* and *versi tronchi* as follows:

Strophe 4:	5s	11s	5s	5s	11t	7t
Strophe 5:	7t	11s	5s	7t	11t	7t
Strophe 6:	5s	11s	5s	5s	11s	5s

The verse lengths are actually less irregular than they appear, since the real syllable count for quinternari *sdruccioli* and settenari *tronchi* are the same, and both types of verse, in this poem, could be sung to the same music with only minor barbarisms. A more serious anomaly is the substitution of an endecasillabo *sdrucciolo* in strophe 6 where there should have been an endecasillabo *tronco*.

The first three strophes of Balducci's poem, consisting, as they do, of seven- and eleven-syllable lines that bear some resemblance to *versi sciolti*, are set as through-composed recitative. But the bass speeds up abruptly at the word *piovete* (b. 44), which begins the fourth strophe, signalling a change to a cantillational style related to the canzonetta type of strophic variations. The stanzas are separated in this part of the piece by cues for a ritornello in both sources of the work, although neither manuscript provides the required instrumental interlude. (A suitable one could easily be found in one or another contemporaneous guitar- or lute-tablature manuscript.) Michi responds to the metric anomaly of the penultimate verse by reverting to a more recitational style at bars 97–108.

Michi's *Hor che la notte del silentio amica* (I: Rn, Ms. Mus. 56, fos. 59ᵛ–63ᵛ) is comparable to *Perdan quest'occhi il sole* in that successive stanzas of a canzonetta are set to music that passes through various shades of recitational and cantillational style. But only one canzonetta structure is used, and the contrasting sections of music do not correspond to the divisions of the text. Of this piece Holzer says: 'With the exception of the arioso writing in measures 56–72, his setting consists entirely of recitative, not the tuneful measured style of *Per torbido mare*.'[60] But the passage that he calls 'arioso' (which actually begins in b. 58) has a bass line that moves mostly in quarter and eighth notes and a predominantly melismatic vocal line. It may not be 'tuneful and measured' in the sense that it does not elaborate upon metrical formulas, but it is hardly arioso, either. Arioso (and not recitative) might more adequately describe bars 20–33 or 95–114, where the bass often moves in half and quarter notes and the vocal line alternates between syllabic, sometimes broken, recitation and several types of melismatic writing. But the whole point of a piece like *Hor che la notte* is that it moves, sometimes fluidly, sometimes abruptly, across various shadings of style as defined by parameters that do not always change in concert.

Clearly, then, Orazio Michi composed works that conform to the most narrow and restrictive definition of the term *cantata* that can be found in recent scholarship: 'The cantata is a piece of vocal chamber music whose text combines *versi*

---

[60] 'Pietro della Valle on Music and Modernity', 274. The work is transcribed in the same article on pp. 302–4.

sciolti and canzonetta verses and whose music generally sets these elements with recitative and aria; it can also be a series of unrelated canzonettas set in recitative and/or aria style.'[61] By that token, the same author's pronouncement that 'Orazio Michi . . . wrote canzonettas but no cantatas'[62] is not correct and cannot be used to support his contention that the cantata, as he understands it, emerged only during the 1640s. For not only does Michi's death in 1641 provide a terminus ad quem for dating his works but the inclusion of *Perdan quest'occhi il sole* in CS:Pnm, II.La.2 indicates that it was probably composed before 1635, the year in which that manuscript appears to have been copied.

Other works by Michi that come into the field of the emerging cantata, more broadly defined, are his recitative laments *Fierissimo dolore* (CS:Pnm, II.La.2, fos. 62^r–64^r) and *Sola fra suoi più cari* (I:Rcas, MS 2490, fos. 60^v–63^r; I:Rn, Ms. Mus. 56, fos. 37^v–42^r), the first on a poem in *versi sciolti* but the second to the text of a strophic canzonetta rendered all but unrecognizable by its treatment as recitative—much like *Occhi belli occhi rei*, *Occhi meco piangete*, *Tu parti anima mia*, and *Tu dormi e 'l dolce sonno* (Vol. II, nos. 18, 3, 86, and 89) in the *Grilanda musicale*.

No one can claim that Orazio Michi originated the fully fledged chamber cantata. In addition to the many earlier works, mentioned above, that follow Cesare Marotta's *O dell'ombrosa notte amati orrori* in opposing entire stanzas of recitative and aria, there were other compositions before 1635 that based extended recitational and cantillational sections on non-strophic poetry. In the second book of *Cantade* (1633) by Giovanni Felice Sances there are two such. His 'cantada in stil recitativo' *Risiede più che mai* begins with *versi sciolti* to a long recitative, which is followed by an ample and well-developed aria in triple metre based on endecasillabi and settenari, many of them *tronchi*, that establish a more regular pattern of rhyme. And his *Filli mirando il ciel* begins with three lines of *versi sciolti* in recitative and continues with a triple-metre aria, twice interrupted by arioso, setting more rhythmic settenari and endecasillabi, one of them *tronco*. Madrigal texts set in contrasting recitative and aria sections are abundant in the Fucci manuscripts, as we have seen. There are several in Johann Kapsberger's *Primo libro di arie passeggiate* (Rome, 1612), too. A non-strophic poem consisting of five-syllable rhymed couplets, *O miei pensieri*, was set as recitative followed by a brief aria in 3/2 as early as 1606 in Domenico Brunetti's *L'Euterpe*.[63]

It is not claimed that the monody repertoire of Montalto's circles necessarily provided models for Rossi and Michi, only that it contains sufficient prototypes for important features of these composers' works. Rossi and Michi could

---

[61] Holzer, 'Music and Poetry', 256.   [62] Ibid. 257.

[63] Fortune, 'Italian Secular Song from 1600 to 1635', 430, incorrectly calls this a madrigal text and claims that it is the earliest example of recitative and aria.

conceivably have found models for those features elsewhere, especially in somewhat later compositions, but none with which they had as much documented
contact. Rossi and Michi selected and elaborated upon some of the same significant attributes that the older composers in Cardinal Montalto's circles, in their
turn, had been among the first to receive and among the most active to develop
along similar lines from earlier villanella and aria composers of the Rome–Naples
orbit. To a great extent, then, Michi and Rossi transmuted the features of the
Romanesca bastarda into those of the Roman chamber cantata, next to opera and
oratorio 'the most important and ubiquitous form of vocal music of the Baroque
period'.[64]

---

[64]   Nigel Fortune, 'Cantata', I. 1, *New Grove*, iii. 694.

7

L'aria pastorale—Il pastor fido

❦

T HE overwhelming majority of the poems set to music in the Montalto monody repertoire are in the pastoral tradition, and indeed they are largely confined to various expressions of sorrow and pain caused by loss or failure to gain
the intensely desired union between shepherd and shepherdess or nymph. Given
that these works were performed in a cardinal's palace and often in the presence
of other churchmen, how is their subject matter to be reconciled with the religious life and vows of chastity to which these men, at least publicly, bound themselves? Why did Montalto's monodists not set equally passionate religious texts,
as Orazio Michi did later in his life?

If these questions had been posed at a social gathering in Cardinal Montalto's
palace—as they quite likely were—we could image several possible answers.
Vincenzo Giustiniani would probably have observed that cardinals are princes.
As such, they must display the same level of taste, sensibility, and knowledge of
fashion expected of their secular counterparts. Battista Guarini would have argued
that the acute sorrow and amorous longing expressed by the poems, intensified
by their musical settings, and conveyed to the listener by an expressive voice, may
cause that kind of purgation which purifies and cleanses such emotions, freeing
them from their vileness and making them perfect in their nature, thereby removing 'that part which by overflowing its natural bounds corrupts the symmetry
of life', 'making it conform to reason'. Thus, worldly and physical love, sorrow,
and pity would be purged, leaving behind their spiritual counterparts, which
contribute to virtue.[1] Cardinal Montalto, himself, may have quoted Petrarch's
sonnet 229:

> Cantai, or piango; et non men di dolcezza
> Del pianger prendo che del canto presi,

---

[1] Baxter Hathaway, *The Age of Criticism: The Late Renaissance in Italy* (Westport, Conn., 1962), 268–73, who
bases his summary and interpretation upon Guarini's *Compendio della poesia tragicomica* (1601).

Ch'a la cagion, non a l'effetto intesi
Son i miei sensi vaghi pur d'altezza.

(I sang, now I weep, and I derive no less sweetness
from weeping than I took from singing,
for my senses, yearning for elevation, are intent
upon the cause and not on its perceived effects.)

Of course, none of these poems embodies voices from the real world of
Cardinal Montalto and his courtiers, as religious poems might. The shepherds
and nymphs who populate these texts and in whose mouths they are placed are
figures of mythology, far removed from contemporaneous life. They are more
like metaphorical symbols of human beings than likenesses of them. And they
refer to the Golden Age of antiquity, the return to which had been for nearly a
century a central political theme in all the arts cultivated by Europe's ruling élite.[2]

Another stage of removal results from the fact that the words of the shepherd
were frequently sung by a female musicians, just as, on the contemporaneous dramatic stage, the parts of women were played by boys. The singer, then, may be
thought of as an actress giving voice to a mythical being in figural speech set out
in rhymed and measured verses and sung to music that adhered to various traditions of form, style, and technique.

The singer of these monodies was like an actress, too, in that the text sung was
often taken from a stage work. Arias from Montalto's opera *Amor pudico* and
Monteverdi's 'Lamento d'Arianna' are included in Montalto's monody anthologies and were evidently sung *in camera*. Other texts came from epic poems
and pastoral plays sufficiently well known to listeners that both the personage and
the dramatic situation could readily be called to mind. Thus they could become
metonyms of narrative. Even the texts that were not from stage works and epics
were so similar to those that were that they could be imaginatively located in
conventional dramatic contexts. And some monodies that were originally composed for chamber performance were eventually incorporated into actual theatrical productions. Catalani's 'Lamento d'Ermenia' has already been mentioned,
and several more examples will be discussed in Chapter 8. In chamber dialogues
a small segment of dramatic continuity is actually incorporated, while the texts
of many solo songs contain references to interlocutors (usually unheard): almost
always the beloved but quite frequently other nymphs, shepherds, gods, spirits,
echoes, and the like.

In these respects, an evening of monody at Cardinal Montalto's palace was
a bit like attending the performance of a pastoral play, just as some plays incorporated musical performances. For example, in *L'amoroso sdegno*, a *favola pastorale*

---

[2] Harry Levin, *The Myth of the Golden Age in the Renaissance* (Bloomington, Ind., 1969).

that Francesco Bracciolini wrote in Rome about 1590,[3] Aminta invites Bargeo to sing with him (Act II, Scene v). Aminta then intones the first strophe of a canzonetta, and Bargeo replies with the second strophe, after which Aminta proposes another song, which Bargeo continues. In all, they sing the first two stanzas of eleven canzonette. A similar musical eclogue concludes Act III of Giovanni Maria Avanzi's *Il Satiro* (Venice: Sessa, 1587), a *favola pastorale* that was dedicated to Cardinal Montalto's brother, Michele. Here Calandro tunes his lyre to Mirtillo's, after which the two shepherds alternate stanzas of terza rima, until Florindo interrupts, 'I want to sing, too; give me my lyre'. Whereupon he sings two strophes of a canzonetta. Each of the other four acts of this play concludes with a sonetto, each of which is sung by an individual named in the text. In the first intermedio incorporated into Vincenzo Jacobilli's *Miracoli d'Amore* (Rome: Facciotto, 1601), Orfeo sings two stanzas of terza rima to the accompaniment of his lyre. The title-page of this *favola pastorale* tells us that it was performed for Ranuccio Farnese, Duke of Parma and brother of Giuseppino Cenci's patron, Cardinal Odoardo Farnese, presumably at the latter's palace in Rome with music by Cenci, in which case the composer probably appeared as the musical demigod.[4] In *Partenia* by Barbara Torelli Benedetti,[5] the scene is set in the garden of Duke Farnese's villa, and several of the speeches of individual personages, which take the form of madrigals, were sung, as shown by remarks such as 'I have no other delight than to gaze upon your beauty and to hear the harmony of your voice' (fos. 62^v–63^r) and 'That harmony, those accents so sweet, which incline me to conform to your wishes, I shall never hear again' (fo. 88^v). Thus, the poetic-musical forms sung in these theatrical concerts are precisely those of chamber monody. And as scenes in plays became concerts, musical evenings at Montalto's palaces could seem ever more like dramatic spectacles.

Il pastor fido, by Battista Guarini, was, of course, the most celebrated pastoral play in Italy and all over Europe during Cardinal Montalto's lifetime. It was the most important prototype of early-modern pastoral tragicomedy, the model for countless imitations, among which are a large proportion of seventeenth-century opera libretti. The five monodic settings of speeches from Guarini's play that are preserved in Montalto's repertoire testify that it was a dramatic presence in the cardinal's palace. Four of these five texts, like most of the passages from *Il pastor fido* favoured by composers, belong to the tragic portions of the drama,[6]

---

[3] The 1602 edition brought out by Ciotti in Venice (I:Ra, RR.1.67) includes the printer's dedication to Battista Guarini dated 6 Feb. 1597, which says that Bracciolini wrote the play six or seven years earlier, at the time, therefore, when he was in Rome. [4] I:Ra, RR1.38.3.

[5] I:Ra, MS 1690/1.

[6] A preliminary survey of musical settings of texts from *Il pastor fido* was undertaken by Arnold Hartmann, Jr., 'Battista Guarini and *Il Pastor Fido*', *Musical Quarterly*, 39 (1953), 415–25. A more extensive listing should be forthcoming from James Chater in a congress report be entitled *Guarini e la musica*.

as identified and explained by Guarini himself in the *Compendio della poesia tragi-comica* (1601).[7] The exception is *Quel augellin che canta* (Act I, Scene i), which encapsulates Linco's attempt to persuade Silvio to surrender himself to love. Although the scene that it summarizes belongs to the comic order, according to Guarini, the madrigal itself is amorous, not humorous. On the other hand, *Crud'Amarilli, che col nom'ancora*, which begins the second scene of Act I, is Mirtillo's most bitter love lament. In *Ch'io t'ami et ami più della mia vita*, Mirtillo pleads his case after Amarilli is tricked into kissing him instead of Corisca at the climax of the blind man's buff (Act III, Scene iii). Amarilli's long reply to Mirtillo includes *Deh dolc'anima mia*, which expresses the tragic conflict between love and duty that torments her. And in *Ecco Silvio colei che 'n odio tanto* (Act IV, Scene ix), Dorinda berates Silvio for wounding her instead of returning her love. Guarini classifies Dorinda as a comic rather than tragic character because of her low station, and her appeal plants seeds that produce a seasonable harvest in Act V. The madrigal itself, however, is caustic and accusing in tone.

Surely for everyone in Cardinal Montalto's circles, these poems powerfully invoked dramatic contexts in Guarini's familiar play. For many at his court, they would also have restored memories of a rare staging of the enormously long pastorale that they had witnessed in 1596. One or more of these pieces may even have been sung in that performance. *Deh dolc'anima mia* is preserved in the *Grilanda musicale*, where it is ascribed to Giuseppino Cenci, who belonged to the cardinal's circle of musicians and was already composing monodies during the 1590s, as we have seen. *Quel augellin che canta* is found in the same fascicle of the *Grilanda* and, being similar in style to *Deh dolc'anima mia*, might also be by Giuseppino. The same could be said for *Crud'Amarilli, che col nom'ancora* in US:PHu, MS Ital. 57, and *Ecco Silvio colei che 'n odio tanto* in I:Bc, Q140. On the other hand, *Ch'io t'ami et ami più della mia vita* was eventually printed—albeit in a rhythmically and ornamentally more elaborated form—in Raffaello Rontani's *Le varie musiche . . . libro primo* (Florence, 1614). Rontani's date and place of birth are at present unknown. The first known publication of his music was issued in 1610, by which time he was in the service of Don Antonio de' Medici in Florence. In 1616 he moved to Rome, where he died in 1622. These dates are actually not very dissimilar to Jacopo Peri's, who published his first monodies in 1609 and died in 1633. But it would be too perilous to suppose that Rontani's music was available for a Roman performance of *Il pastor fido* in 1596. Exploring the possibility that the other pieces might have been available will at least shed some light on the context for the 1596 production, which became, from a certain point of view, background to these monodies even when they were performed off-stage.

[7] For a discussion, see Marvin T. Herrick, *Tragicomedy: Its Origin and Development in Italy, France, and England* (Urbana, Ill., 1962), 130–42.

The point of departure for this exploration is an *avviso* sent to Urbino from Rome on 28 February 1596:

Don Michele Peretti, who had determined to do some beautiful things for his wedding, has not wanted to do anything because of the death of Contestabile Colonna [his brother-in-law], although it is said that after Easter he wants to produce, in the hall of the Chancellery, a performance of Guarini's tragicomedy *Il pastor fido*, resolving to spend, for the intermedi and other things, two or three thousand scudi.[8]

Michele, who was only 19 years old at this time, maintained no more than a token staff, and he lived more or less as his elder brother's dependant. In this as in other cases, Don Michele's name was attached to a spectacle that was evidently conceived and produced by Cardinal Montalto. This may have been done to avoid a close connection between the prominent cardinal and theatrical entertainment.

Considering the long preparations for performances of *Il pastor fido* in Ferrara, Turin, Florence, and Mantua and the extended periods of gestation that preceded the production of Florentine intermedi and early operas,[9] it seems inconceivable that Cardinal Montalto and his brother had the idea of presenting Guarini's pastorale no earlier than 28 February, since the performance was to have taken place shortly after Easter, which fell on 14 April in 1596. Based on everything we know about elaborate musical theatre at this time, it seems far more likely that preparations had begun a year or more in advance and that music for it had already been in rehearsal for several months. If so, the early preparations for the performance began when the wedding plans were much different. For although Don Michele Peretti planned to celebrate his marriage to Margherita della Somaglia publicly during the first three months of 1596, a year earlier his intended bride had been Donna Caterina Gonzaga, daughter and only heiress of the recently deceased Alfonso Gonzaga, marquis of Castelgoffredo (d. 1592). Arranging for a marriage between Donna Caterina and Don Michele had been a major concern at the Gonzaga court of Mantua during the years 1593–5.

In fact there had been three official candidates for matrimony with Don Michele Peretti: Caterina Gonzaga, Margherita della Somaglia, and a certain Marquise Potenza. The choice of Margherita was favoured by the Spanish, and

---

[8] 'il signore Don Michele Peretti il quale haveva disegnato per le sue Nozze di far cose belle, non hà poi voluto per causa della morte del Contestabile Colonna far cosa alcuna, benche si dica che dopo Pasqua voglia nella sala della Cancelleria fare recitare la Tragicomedia del Cavaliere Guarini detta il Pastor Fido, resolvendosi di spendere nelli intermedj et altri 2 o m/3 scudi.' I:Rvat, Urb. Lat. 1064, fo. 122ᵛ. Transcribed in Chater, 'Musical Patronage', 207.

[9] For preparations of *Il pastor fido* see the accounts in Alessandro D'Ancona, *Origini del teatro italiano* (Turin, 1891), ii. 535–75; and Vittorio Rossi, *Battista Guarini ed Il pastor fido: Studio biografico-critico* (Turin, 1886). Long preparations for Florentine intermedi are described in Iain Fenlon, 'Preparations for a Princess: Florence 1588–89', in Della Seta and Piperno (eds.), *In cantu et in sermone*, 259–81; and Carter, 'A Florentine Wedding of 1608', 89–107. Extensive preparations for early operas are described in Palisca, 'The First Performance of "Euridice"'; and Stuart Reiner, 'Preparations in Parma—1618, 1627–28', *Music Review*, 25 (1964), 273–301.

Cardinal Montalto was advised to choose her for his brother because so many of Michele's feudal holdings and the cardinal's ecclesiastical benefices were in the Spanish Vice Realm of Naples. On the other hand, Montalto himself continued to urge the pope to favour a marriage with Donna Caterina precisely in order to free himself and his brother from dependency upon the Spanish. It was probably for this reason that Grand Duke Ferdinando de' Medici also favoured the Gonzaga union. And it was pointed out that a statute in the state of Milan, where many of Donna Margherita's feuds were located, forbade giving property in dowry to other than subjects of Spanish Milan.[10]

In seems clear that Cardinal Montalto was favouring a marriage with Donna Caterina throughout 1594 and up to June 1595, by which time the details of the wedding (in Mantua) were being arranged.[11] All the negotiation on the bride's side was done by Duke Vincenzo Gonzaga himself, who even travelled to Rome to complete the marriage contract and sign it. And he required very elaborate mollification when the contract was eventually broken.[12] The Mantuan court learnt of their defeat in a letter of 8 July 1595, in which their Roman agent finally revealed that the pope had ruled that Don Michele Peretti had validly married Margherita della Somaglia in secret when he was 11 years and eight months old, that is, in 1588 or 1589.

This explains why the *avvisi* from Rome in 1595–6 make no mention of Don Michele's marriage to Margherita and why there was no public word about a celebratory spectacle until the *avviso* of 28 February 1596, quoted towards the beginning of this chapter. Indeed, from all that we have learned of the negotiations of 1594–5, we may safely conclude that the idea to perform *Il pastor fido* originated in the context of a projected Peretti–Gonzaga wedding.

The years of negotiation aimed at accomplishing this marriage followed immediately upon the period 1591–3, during which the Mantuan court was intensely occupied with very difficult preparations for their own performance of *Il pastor fido*. In effect, Don Michele and Cardinal Montalto intended to continue where the Mantuan preparations left off, perhaps to profit from that experience, and, at the same time, to pay homage to the Gonzaga court by achieving the much-desired

---

[10] All this is related in letters dated 13 Sept. through 3 Dec. 1594 from Annibale Chieppio, agent in Rome, to Duke Vincenzo Gonzaga of Mantua, I:MAas, Archivio Gonzaga, Busta 963, fos. 458–63, 563–8, and 670–4.

[11] I:MAas, Archivio Gonzaga, Busta 963, fos. 505–8, 563–8, 607–10, 619–26, 670–4, 678–80; Busta 964, fos. 11–12, 52–4, 76–9, 97–100, 112–13, 134, 157–9, 198–200, etc.

[12] Correspondence about the marriage negotiations between Rome (Mantuan agents, Camilla Peretti, and her grandsons, Cardinal Montalto and Michele Peretti) and Mantua (Duke Vincenzo Gonzaga and his secretary, Annibale Chieppo) is preserved in I:MAas, Archivio Gonzaga, Buste 961–7. A copy of the marriage contract between Michele Peretti and Caterina Gonzaga is found in the same series, Busta 223, fos. 150–9. When Cardinal Montalto sent his secretary, Tommaso Cospi, on a three-month mission to mollify Duke Vincenzo, Feb.–Apr. 1596, Pope Clement VIII wrote a letter to the duke asking him to accept Cardinal Montalto's expressions of loyalty and affection (Busta 967, fos. 86–9).

performance of Guarini's pastorale. It may even be that the Mantuan performance was postponed precisely on account of the projected wedding celebration, at first planned for Rome but changed to Mantua by the summer of 1595. In that case, Guarini himself may have helped the Peretti prepare their production when he was in Rome during the winter of 1594–5.[13] The Mantuan connection would also help to explain the eventual cancellation of the Peretti production of *Il pastor fido*, the symbolism of which could have been found unsuitable for a marriage with Margherita della Somaglia.

The problem with performing *Il pastor fido* in honour of the Peretti–Somaglia wedding may have even gone beyond the pastorale's Mantuan associations. For someone could easily have noticed that its plot is resolved when a reason is found to dissolve an earlier, expedient engagement in order to permit a different union compelled by new circumstances. In the play, Amarilli and Silvio have been betrothed by their fathers in their attempt to satisfy the oracle of Diana, who, like the pope, requires obedience to ethical standards—chastity and fidelity— and a marriage of demigods (i.e. nobility). Satisfying the oracle would release the Arcadians from the obligation of annual maiden sacrifice (the burdens of Spanish domination?). The obstacle in the way of this is that Amarilli secretly loves her suitor Mirtillo, while Silvio is the object of Dorinda's desires. The denouement follows the discovery that Mirtillo fulfils the oracle's conditions just as well as Silvio and that Mirtillo was once actually called by the name Silvio, so that Amarilli can marry him with at least casuistical justification. One can imagine that grounds even more far-fetched were being suggested to the pope (Clement VIII, an Aldobrandini, who normally tried to reduce Spanish influence over the papacy whenever he could) in an attempt to dissolve the secret childhood marriage between Michele Peretti and Margherita della Somaglia. When these arguments failed, there would have been, perhaps, little for the Peretti to celebrate. Furthermore, problems between the newly-weds had become the subject of malicious gossip.[14]

[13] Rossi, *Battista Guarini*, 112.

[14] Thus the Ferrarese agent Giuseppe Bastiano Malatesta wrote to Duke Alfonso II on 6 Apr. 1596: 'Il Cospi che fù a Mantova, et a Ferrara è tornato qui con la buona reconciliatione tra 'l S. r Duca di Mantova, et questi Sig.ri Peretti, i quali haveranno ogni dì più à invidiare la fortuna di quella Dama, che ricusarono, et da pentirsi di quest'altra, che hanno presa, la quale altra una sua strana disparatezza, che ogni dì apparisce maggiore, è opinione quasi certa che sia sterile, et infeconda, prima per una sua macrezza, et deboltà di complessione grandissima, et poi perche dà un catarro, hebbe alcuni anni sono tale offesa nell'osso spihale della schiena, che ne rimasse col collo alquanto attratto, et piegato sopra la spalla onde i medici dicono che quando ben'ella concipisse, il che reputano difficile, non potria poi reggere il concetto per la causa predetta di quell'osso in cui nello zone si appoggia il parto, ò reggendolo pure andarebbe per la gran violentia che in ciò sentirebbe à indubitato rischio di morte atteso massime il suo pochissimo vigore, onde non hà adosso senon pochissima carne, et quella enervata. Con le quali sue parti se ella non può dare molta soddisfatt.ne al marito giovane, et ben complesso non può ne anche ricevere da lui sicome intendo già fin a quest'hora che tra loro passi più tosto quiete per honor del mondo che molta affett.ne.' I:MOas, Cancelliere Ducale, Estero, Ambasciatori, Italia, Roma, under the date cited.

During the preparations up to July 1595, perhaps until the Peretti performance was abandoned after Easter of 1596, any music to be used in *Il pastor fido* would have been assembled in Rome. I think, therefore, we should explore the possibility that one or more of the monodies in the Montalto repertoire with texts from *Il pastor fido* were in existence in time for the 1596 Roman performance. And we should review the often-debated question as to whether solo singing was ever a part of *Pastor fido* performances during Guarini's lifetime.

There are really three pieces of evidence about music in *Il pastor fido*, none of them new but two of them sometimes misinterpreted:

1. Angelo Ingegneri, in three sentences in his treatise *Della poesia rappresentativa e del modo di rappresentare le favole sceniche*, a work very closely associated with Guarini's drama, mentions three categories of music in pastorales: 'cori', 'intermedi', and 'altre musiche':[15]

I come, now, to music, the third and last aspect of the performance. In comedies and in pastorales that do not have choruses, [the music] will be arranged by someone else [other than the poet] to serve for intermedi or to accompany [these plays] in some other way, so that they turn out more enjoyable.[16]

In the plays that have choruses, if in addition to them there will be intermedi or other music, the abovementioned style will be used, and it will be sufficient that they are sung very simply, so that they only seem different from ordinary speech.[17]

But where choruses are used for intermedi or where there is no other music, [the choruses] must be sung with greater elaboration.[18]

2. Giovanni Battista Doni's *Compendio* was published much later, in 1635, and overall it advocates, for the performance of pastorales, a mix of singing with spoken dialogue on a model in use at the court of Duke Ferdinando Gonzaga in Mantua. But, when writing historically about the period before 'they began to sing entire plays',[19] he reports, 'In every epoch, it has been the custom to mix into dramatic works some sort of singing, either in the form of intermedi or else within the act itself, for some reason relating to the subject portrayed'.[20]

[15] Antonio Ingegneri, *Della poesia rappresentativa, e del modo di rappresentare le favole sceniche* (Ferrara, 1598), 78–9, as transcribed by Carol MacClintock, *Giaches de Wert (1535–1596): Life and Works* (Musicological Studies and Documents, 17; [Rome], 1966), 181.

[16] 'Vengo alla musica terza et ultima parte dela rappresentazione, la quale nelle Commedie et nelle Pastorali, che non avranno cori, sarà ad arbitrio altrui, per servire per intermedi overo per accompagnarli in altro modo, ch'essi riescono più dilettevoli.'

[17] 'Nelle favole ch'aranno i cori, se oltre di lor vi saranno intermedii, ovvero altre musiche, in queste serbandosi il sopradetto stile, basterà che i detti sono cantati semplicissimamente, e tanto che paiono solo differenti dal parlare ordinario.'

[18] 'Ma dove i cori verranno per intermedii, o dove non sarà altra musica, si dovranno cantare con arte maggiore.'   [19] 'Si cominciassero a cantare tutte le azioni intere.'

[20] 'In ogni tempo si è costumato di frammettere alle azioni dramatiche qualche sorta di cantilene, o in forma d'intermedi tra un atto e l'altro, o pure dentro l'istesso atto, per qualche occorrenza del soggetto rappresentato.' Giovanni Battista Doni, *Compendio del trattato de' generi e de' modi della musica* (Rome, 1635), 22, as

3. Guarini himself provides justification for mixing singing into the acts of pastoral plays in his *Compendio della poesia tragicomica* when he says, 'Now it is not to be marvelled that the shepherds of Arcadia, especially the noble born, embellished their speech with poetic expressions, since they, more than all other nations, were most beloved by the muses', and he continues, citing Polybius, to the effect 'that all the Arcadians were poets, so that their principal study and their principal practice was that of music, which they began as children, which their laws obligated them to do'.[21]

Although three of the texts set in the Montalto monody manuscripts match the corresponding passages in *Il pastor fido* with near exactness, the other two texts differ in some details. Paradoxically, one of these two differing texts may constitute evidence in favour of the hypothesis that it could have been used in the projected performance of 1596, and indeed may have been composed expressly for it. It is *Deh dolc'anima mia*, shown below together with the corresponding passage in *Il pastor fido* and a similar text set by Antonio Bicci as a madrigal and published in Marenzio's seventh book of five-voice madrigals.

Set by Giuseppino Cenci, I:Vc, Torrefranca 250, fos. 87ᵛ–88ʳ	Set by Antonio Bicci, in Marenzio, Book 7 *a* 5 (1595)	*Il pastor fido*, Act III, Scene ii
		Orsù, Mirtillo, è tempo che tu ten vada; e troppo lungamente
Deh dolc'anima mia,	Deh dolc'anima mia,	hai dimorato ancora.
Partiti e ti consola	Non pianger più se m'ami e ti consola	Pàrtiti; e ti consola,
Ch'infinita è la schiera	Ch'infinita è la schiera	ch'infinita è la schiera
Degl'infelici amanti.	Degl'infelici amanti.	degli infelici amanti.
Vive ben altrui in pianti	Vive ben altri in pianti	Vive ben altri in pianti
Sì come tu, Mirtillo.	Sì come tu, mio core.	sì come tu, Mirtillo. Ogni ferita
Ogni ferita a seco il suo dolore,	Ogni ferita ha seco il suo dolore,	ha seco il suo dolore,
Né sei tu solo a lagrimar d'Amore.	Né se' tu solo a lagrimar d'Amore.	né sei tu solo a lagrimar d'amore.

transcribed by Solerti, *L'origine*, 207. It is clear from the context that Doni is referring to dramatic performances before 1600.

[21] 'Or non è meraviglia se i pastori d'Arcadia, massimamente nobili, abbellivano di vaghezze poetiche i loro ragionamenti, essendo essi, più di tutte l'altre nazioni, amicissimi delle muse', e continua poi citando Polibio a testimonianza del fatto 'che tutti gli arcadi eran poeti, che 'l principale studio, il principale esercizio loro era quel della musica, che l'apparavano da fanciulli, che le leggi a ciò fare li costringevano'. As cited by Nino Pirrota, *Li due Orfei da Poliziano a Monteverdi* (2nd edn., Turin, 1975), 304–5.

As has been said, this passage comes towards the end of the antagonistic dialogue between Mirtillo and Amarilli, just after the game of blind man's buff (*il gioco della cieca*). Although Amarilli sends Mirtillo away, her words hint at sympathy for him and her own suffering. I do not necessarily assume that the version in Guarini's printed playbook was written earlier and that the text set by Bicci was the revision. It could be the other way around. But it is clear that the text set by Giuseppino Cenci is a conflation of the two earlier ones (unless Cenci's text predates one or both of them). It takes the much gentler and more singable first verse from Bicci's text in preference to the rather harsh exhortation from the printed version of *Il pastor fido* while drawing from the playbook the name Mirtillo and the command *partiti*, crucial to the action of the drama. In a performance, of course, Giuseppino's *Deh dolc'anima mia* could well be sung after Amarilli speaks the first three lines of the passage from the playbook.

In *Quel augellin che canta*, the name of Silvio does not appear, as it does in the printed versions of *Il pastor fido*. But it is not replaced by the generic *o Tirsi*, as in the text set by Marenzio:

I:Vc, Torrefranca 250, fos. 90ᵛ–91ʳ	*Il pastor fido*, Act I, Scene i
Quel augellin che canta	Quell'augellin, che canta
Sì dolcemente e lascivetto vola	sì dolcemente e lascivetto vola
Hor dall'albero al faggio	or da l'abete al faggio
Et hor dal faggio al mirto,	e or dal faggio al mirto,
S'havesse umano spirto,	s'avesse umano spirto,
Direbbe, 'ardo d'Amore, ardo d'Amore'.	direbbe: 'Ardo d'amore, ardo d'amore'.
Ma ben arde nel core	Ma ben arde nel core
E parla in sua favella,	e parla in sua favella,
Sì che l'intende il suo dolce desio.	sì che l'intende il suo dolce desio.
Et odi a punto il suo dolce desio,	E odi a punto, Silvio,
Che gli risponde, 'ardo d'Amore anch'io'.	il suo dolce desio,
	che gli risponde: 'Ardo d'amore anch'io.'

The line that begins *Et odi apunto* is extended, in the musical text, to eleven syllables with the words *il suo dolce desio*, which appear as a separate line of seven syllables in the printed version of *Il pastor fido*. Without wishing to argue strongly one way or the other about priority, I would merely point out that the kind of parallelism that results between the antepenultimate and penultimate lines of the monody text *Quel augellin che canta* is rather commonly encountered elsewhere in Guarini's pastorale. Certainly the interjection of the name Silvio in the *Pastor fido* text interrupts the flow of the syllables and produces a less satisfactory vocal text. In any case, there is no need to assume that the name was removed in order to make the text less specific. Proper names of personages occur in three of the other four *Pastor fido* texts set to music in the Montalto manuscripts.

Would solo singing in Cardinal Montalto's production of *Il pastor fido* make an already overly long pastorale impossible to perform? One hears that extensive cuts were made in the play when it was performed in Guarini's lifetime, and indeed it would be quite feasible to perform only specific episodes of the play without losing the thread of its plot. Montalto, in fact, witnessed an entirely sung performance of the *gioco della cieca* episode of *Il pastor fido* at exactly the time during which he must have been arranging his own production of the play: Emilio de' Cavalieri's setting of this scene, modified by Laura Guidiccioni, was performed in Florence on 29 October 1595, the day after Montalto held Prince Francesco de' Medici at the baptismal font.[22]

The music itself contains additional evidence of interest. *Ecco Silvio colei che 'n odio tanto* (Vol. II, no. 137) is composed in what seems to me an early recitative style, perhaps too early to fit into one of Giovanni Battista Doni's categories, but, if not, then somewhere between *stile narrativo* and *stile espressivo* or *rappresentativo*. The basic features of the style evident in this piece are a rather static bass, a syllabic vocal line using speech-like rhythms that avoid metrical patterning, a rather narrow vocal range within most phrases, some monotone recitation, *seconda prattica* dissonance treatment, and vestiges of the verse-ending formulas typical of the aria formulas of the sixteenth century. Syllabication no faster than the fusa, semibreves at other places in addition to the cadences, and the use of the *proportio dupla* sign place *Ecco Silvio colei che 'n odio tanto* very early in the history of *stile recitativo*. These features are found in Jacopo Peri's *Qual nova meraviglia*, the only example of *recitativo narrativo* that survives from *La Dafne* (1598), but they occur nowhere in the recitatives of Cavalieri's *Rappresentatione di anima, et di corpo* (1600), Peri's or Caccini's *Euridice* (1602), Monteverdi's *Orfeo* (1607), or Gagliano's *Dafne* (1608).

On the other hand, several factors place this example well beyond the formulaic aria in compositional sophistication. Prolonged but syncopated notes are used tellingly to produce interpretive accentuation without restricting the musical and syntactical motion towards hierarchically ordered points of repose and articulation: for example, 'Bramastila ferir: ferita l'ai | Bramastila tua preda: eccola preda | Bramastila al fin morta: eccola morta.' The regular phrase rhythm of the formulaic aria is broken up, not only by the unequal lengths of Guarini's *versi sciolti* but by the musical fusion of verses (e.g. bb. 35 and 83) or interruption of lines (e.g. bb. 29 and 74), following the meaning rather than the poetic structure of the text.

Both *Ecco Silvio* and *Quel augellin che canta* gain considerable expressive force by artfully interpreting the rhetorical features of Guarini's poetry. In *Ecco Silvio*,

---

[22] Chater, 'Musical Patronage', 214.

Dorinda, accidentally wounded by Silvio's arrow and carried to her beloved's house, begs for his love with what seems might be her last breath. The setting begins slowly and with little inflection, as if portraying Dorinda's weakened condition: 'Ecco Silvio colei che 'n odio [hai] tanto.' It begins to gain animation, as if through anger ('Eccol'in quella guisa'), but sinks back from the effort ('Che la volev'a punto'). Beginning in bar 10, Guarini's anaphora is dramatized through an ascending series of climaxes in parallel phrases, each a musical reflection of the poet's anthypophora: 'Bramastila ferir: ferita l'ai | Bramastila tua preda: eccola preda | Bramastila al fin morta: eccola morta.' The first major closure (b. 28), in mid-verse, sets off the second apostrophe, which takes the form of another anaphora and which introduces a series of antitheses that form a kind of refutatio. This anaphora is, again, underscored through musical parallelism that unfolds into a peristasis, extended through intensifying chromaticism (bb. 34–5) and musico-poetic enjambment: 'Ahi garzon crudo | Ahi cor senza pieta tu non credevi | La piaga che per te mi fei amore.' The use of *credevi* here, in preference to the word *credesti* of Guarini's printed text, clarifies the antithesis that the composer underscores in the following passage through a shift in style—more active bass, wider vocal range within the phrase, and less monotone recitation: 'Poi tu questa negar della tua mano.' The second antithesis, beginning in bar 44, is rhythmically and melodically similar to the first (compare bb. 40–2 with 48–50). The refutatio concludes with Guarini's litotes, intensified by the composer's rising repetition and by rapid movement from soft to hard hexachords and back, and by a third anaphora underscored by parallel music: 'Non mi negar, *non mi negar,* ti prego | Anima cruda sì, ma però bella | Non mi negar al ultimo sospiro | Un tuo solo sospir.' Momentum is decreased but tension increased through two aposiopeses in the peroratio. The first breaks off in mid-verse after the composer's iteratio ('Beata morte, *beata morte* | Se l'adolcissi tu . . .'), while the second interrupts the flow of two conjoined verses ('con questa sola | Voce cortes'e pia: . . .'). Cadences on the two competing harmonic centres of the setting, F and G, set Dorinda's final words: 'Va in pace anima mia, *va in pace anima mia.*'

A possible indication of the age of *Ecco Silvio colei che 'n odio tanto* may be found in the form of its bass. Clearly someone has transcribed it into staff notation from arch-lute tablature. In bars 90–1, for example, the bass notes c–e–F result in a completely unmotivated leap of a major seventh downward. A better transcription of the tablature would have omitted the e as belonging to the tenor voice of the accompaniment and prolonged the c in its place, in spite of the fact that the e was to be played on the c course (in G tuning). Or else the F, sounded on the first diapason string and enriching the F major chord that resolves the cadence in bar 91, should have been recognized as a contrabass note and replaced in the transcription by the true bass note, f, which undoubtedly was found in the intabulated chord at this point and which would have properly resolved the *e*. But it is evident that the transcriber mechanically derived his bass from the lowest notes sounding in the tablature. This leads to a similar anomaly in bars 92–4. Here, voice and bass repeat the music of bars 87–9 transposed upward by approximately one scale-degree. The intabulation obviously exploited the third diapason string, *D*, in forming a contrabass line, *G–D*, in bars 91–2. The instrument in question, however, must not have possessed a fourth diapason, *C*, because there was no parallel contrabass in bars 87–8. For a similar reason, the bass line is forced to leap upward from *D* to *b♮* between bars 93 and 94, transposing the pattern first given in bar 89 upward by a ninth instead of a step, because an *F♯* was not available on the instrument, *G* being the lowest string on the fretboard, below which the unfretted diapason strings would have been arranged by descending diatonic step, *F, E, D*. The fact that the accompaniment for *Ecco Silvio colei che 'n odio tanto* had earlier been written in arch-lute tablature may be an indication that its composer or its intended performer was not yet familiar with basso continuo notation. For, while it is true that other intabulated accompaniments for Italian monody are found well into the seventeenth century, they are derived from basso continuo notation and not the reverse.

James Chater has pointed out to me that the portion of *Ecco Silvio colei* from the line *Anima cruda sì, ma però bella* to the end shares several motifs with the setting of the same text segment published in Luca Marenzio's sixth book of five-voice madrigals in 1594. Indeed, I find that there are no fewer than seven shared motifs setting the same phrases of text—easily more than coincidence or idiom could explain. They are shown in Examples 7.1 and 7.2. Marenzio, it will be recalled, was living in the Vatican apartments of Cardinal Aldobrandini at the time his sixth book of madrigals was published, and he was very much a part of Montalto's circles, having been considered for a place in the cardinal's household in 1592 and mentioned as one of the musicians who sang at the Chancellery Palace in 1593.

But which setting of this text came first, Marenzio's or the one for solo voice? Chater judges Marenzio's *Anima cruda sì, ma però bella* to be compositionally superior in a number of respects. Does this mean that Marenzio improved upon the original or that the monodist bowdlerized Marenzio's madrigal? The history of music is, of course, full of examples in which composers, emulating earlier works, have sought to improve upon their models as a form of competition.[23] On the basis of secondary literature, however, no case comes to mind in which the emulator obviously fell short of the prototype. Along the same lines, most results of emulation belong to more important genres, while the models

---

[23] See Howard Mayer Brown, 'Emulation, Competition, and Homage: Imitation and Theories of Imitation in the Renaissance', *Journal of the American Musicological Society*, 35 (1982), 1–48.

Ex. 7.1. Anon., *Ecco Silvio colei che 'n odio tanto*, I:Bc, Q140, fos. 30ʳ–31ʳ, seven motifs marked

Ex. 7.1. Cont'd

Ex. 7.1. Cont'd

Ex. 7.1. Cont'd

tend to come from lesser ones: the mass, motet, polyphonic chanson, and madrigal draw on the popular tune, frottola, and villanella and not the reverse, normally. When a villanella quotes a madrigal, we usually think of it as a humorous send-up, and the quotation normally consists of just one phrase, not a series of motifs that encompass most of the model's melodic material, as is the case here. To the extent, then, that the polyphonic madrigal was the more prestigious, important genre and monody the lesser one, we may weigh this factor in favour of a conclusion that Marenzio meant to improve upon the monody.

There are other examples of monodies and polyphonic madrigals that share musical motifs in setting the same text. Giulio Caccini's *Ahi dolente partita*, in GB:Ob, Tenbury MS 1018, fo. 40ʳ, is part of such a web of connections that includes Marenzio's setting in his sixth book of five-voice madrigals (1594), Giaches de Wert's in his eleventh (1595), and Claudio Monteverdi's in his fifth (1605). The Tenbury manuscript that contains Caccini's *Ahi dolente partita* preserves what are thought to be the earliest known versions of several other of his works—meaning that they could date from the 1580s—even if the manuscript itself is probably not as old as some of its contents.[24] Likewise Caccini's *Sfogava con le stelle*, in *Le nuove musiche* (1602) and several manuscripts including GB:Ob, Tenbury MS 1018, shares significant features with Monteverdi's madrigal on the same text (fourth book *a 5*, 1603). In this instance, Imogene Horsley gave precedence to Caccini, but Tomlinson is not sure.[25] In both these cases, diplomatic evidence eliminates neither possibility, and I cannot bring to mind any case of emulation between a monody and a polyphonic madrigal (as opposed to an arrangement) in which such evidence is conclusive. These discussions, therefore, tend to involve analytical criteria.

Let us start with the hypothesis that our anonymous monodist ineptly wove seven motifs from Marenzio's *Anima cruda sì, ma però bella* into his inferior *Ecco*

[24] Maze, 'Tenbury Ms 1018', 61–3; and Hitchcock, 'Vocal Ornamentation in Caccini's *Nuove Musiche*', 389–4. Gary Tomlinson, *Monteverdi and the End of the Renaissance* (Oxford, 1987), 100–1, mentions the connections between the settings by Wert, Marenzio, and Monteverdi, but does not include Caccini in the discussion.

[25] Imogene Horsley, 'Monteverdi's Use of Borrowed Material in "Sfogava con le stelle"'. *Music & Letters*, 59 (1978), 316–28; Tomlinson, *Monteverdi*, 92.

Ex. 7.2. Luca Marenzio, *Anima cruda sì, ma però bella* (1594), only canto texted, seven motifs marked

Ex. 7.2. Cont'd

Measures 37-54 essentially repeat measures 19-36.

Ex. 7.2. Cont'd

Silvio colei: where would that premiss lead us? We should have to concede that this incompetent composer found textually appropriate ways of preparing for the striking chromatic ascent with which Marenzio begins his madrigal, corresponding to bars 63–5 in the monody, by prefiguring it in bars 34–6 ('cor senza pietà tu non credevi') and in bars 51–3 ('Ma se con la pietà non è in te spenta'), and we should have to believe that the same incapable composer also thought to expand the motif taken from Marenzio's phrase 'Non mi negar' (bb. 10–11 in the madrigal, bb. 68–9 in the monody) and use it to set 'Ahi garzon crudo'

earlier in his piece (bb. 29–31)—both places in the monody have no counterpart in the madrigal, which begins with text found a few lines further along in *Il pastor fido*. But then this same composer, now seemingly not entirely without ability or imagination, passes up Marenzio's dramatically effective leap of a minor sixth and outline of a diminished seventh at 'a l'ultimo sospiro un tuo solo sospir' (Ex. 7.2, bb. 12–18)—perhaps the most memorable passage in Marenzio's madrigal—in favour of the bland and somewhat misaccented setting of the same words that he put in his monody (Ex. 7.1, bb. 70–4).

These reflections incline me to believe that the anonymous monody *Ecco Silvio colei* was the model for Marenzio's *Anima cruda sì, ma però bella*. If this were so, then *Ecco Silvio colei* was composed before 1594, making it the earliest datable example of *stile recitativo*. That date would help explain why it had been written with an accompaniment in arch-lute tablature rather than in basso continuo notation. It would tend to place *Ecco Silvio colei* and its composer in Rome, because Marenzio was there at the time when he presumably would have encountered this monody. And it would mean that *Ecco Silvio colei* could have been incorporated into the 1596 production of *Il pastor fido*.

Three other *Pastor fido* settings in the Montalto manuscripts tend more towards the declamatory monodic madrigal style of Caccini's *Perfidissimo volto*, *Vedrò il mio sol*, and *Dovrò dunque morire*, compositions from the mid-1580s, which, according to Caccini's claim, prefigured the recitative style that he employed in setting *L'Euridice*. They are predominantly syllabic. *Quel augellin che canta* (Vol. II, no. 35) contains the most melismas, which illustrate or underscore the words *canta*, *vola*, and *ardo*, but the other two, *Deh dolc'anima mia* (Vol. II, no. 33) and *Crud'Amarilli, che col nom'ancora* (Vol. II, no. 102), contain mostly brief ornamentations of notes whose durations, unornamented, would not have stood out from the context.

These three madrigalian settings differ from *Ecco Silvio* in their slightly more active bass lines and less frequent monotone recitation. Their bass lines, however, are distinctly less active than their melody lines and in no way resemble vocal parts. Narrow vocal range with occasional monotone recitation also distinguishes these settings from all but the very most declamatory polyphonic madrigals of the 1590s.

Both *Deh dolc'anima mia* and *Crud'Amarilli, che col nom'ancora* use the distinctive rising chromatic line for expressive intensification that we noticed in *Ecco Silvio*. Also similar to *Ecco Silvio* in *Deh dolc'anima mia* are the delayed exclamations (bb. 1, 6) and the contrast between the slowly paced opening exhortation (bb. 1–14) and more rapid delivery of syllables in the following narratio. And like *Ecco Silvio*, the three madrigalian pieces strongly project the rhetorical structures of the text, or else impose such structures through simple modifications:

in *Deh dolc'anima mia* and *Quel augellin che canta* several added text repetitions are set to quasi-sequential melodic constructions, while in *Crud'Amarilli, che col nom'ancora* the loose anaphora of the last five verses is mirrored in extended parallelism between bars 64–75 and 76–89: 'Parlerà nel mio volto | La pietade e 'l dolore | E, se fia muta ogn'altra cosa, al fine parlerà il mio morire | E ti dirà la morte il mio martire.'

Even if four of the five *Pastor fido* settings in the Montalto repertoire could have been available for inclusion the 1596 production of the pastorale, it still remains to see what further evidence arises from the circumstance of the play's performance in that year. I have already said that the Peretti production at Cardinal Montalto's Palazzo della Cancelleria evidently did not take place: the *avvisi* would have mentioned it if it had. But Cardinal Odoardo Farnese, Giuseppino Cenci's principal patron, did produce a performance of the play at his secondary country villa, in Ronciglione, on 2 September 1596. The circumstances are described in a letter to Battista Guarini written by a member of the cardinal's court. Having taken his household and many important guests to his villa at Caprarola, Cardinal Farnese transferred them all to Ronciglione, likewise located in the province of Viterbo, in order to escape the heat. The transference to Ronciglione was completely unforeseen. There, *Il pastor fido* was performed with very little preparation or forethought, for it is clear from this letter that Farnese's production was not actually planned for Ronciglione. The performers had come from Rome to Caprarola along with the cardinal and his household only a few days earlier. And a little later, the performance had to be repeated for other noblemen and prelates who came out from Rome to marvel at the apparently unplanned production. The letter says that there was no scenery and that costumes were very simple. But the actors were very well prepared and were not merely household members but rather 'very capable members of academies, most of them scholars and well read'.[26] Guarini's informant makes much of the fact that *Il pastor fido* was, thus, successfully produced in a small provincial city, while the major centres of northern Italy had failed in several attempts to mount a performance of it.[27]

Under the circumstances I can suggest only one explanation for the apparent ease with which Cardinal Farnese was able to produce a well-rehearsed performance of *Il pastor fido* without advance planning: the production was the fruit of the long and elaborate preparations made by Cardinal Montalto and his brother, preparations that would have gone to waste once their festive performance was

---

[26] 'Academici molto virtuosi, e la maggior parte scolari, e di belle lettere.'

[27] The letter, written by a certain 'Bambasi di Reggio d'Emilia, famigliare del cardinal Farnese' on 4 Sept. 1596, is reprinted in D'Ancona, *Origini*, 563–5, from a transcription published in Bartolomeo Zucchi, *Idea del segretario* (Venice, 1614), 37.

cancelled. It would have been quite like Montalto to garner favour with a potential friend or ally by allowing him to share artistic property.[28] This is exactly what Montalto did for Enzo Bentivoglio with Guarini's last stage work in 1612, as we shall see in the next chapter. And if Giuseppino Cenci were already in Cardinal Farnese's household by the fall of 1596, this would constitute an additional reason for transferring the production from the Palazzo della Cancelleria to a Farnese villa. Or if Cenci joined Cardinal Farnese's household shortly after the production—the only alternative—his music for *Il pastor fido* may have been what attracted the cardinal's attention.

It is still quite possible that the settings of texts from *Il pastor fido* in the Montalto manuscripts are no different in their origins from the scores, perhaps hundreds, of other similar works in the madrigal and monody repertoire: concrete invocations of the *aria pastorale* that pervaded Italian secular vocal music about the turn of the seventeenth century. But those who sang these songs and those who listened participated in the same extended metaphor about politics, culture, and society, whether they sang and listened in the undecorated hall of the Farnese villa in Ronciglione or in the chambers of Montalto's Palazzo della Cancelleria in Rome.

---

[28] The Farnese palace and Montalto's Palace of the Chanellery were located in adjacent piazzas, and the two cardinals belonged to the same small social circle. So, for example, the banquet offered by Cardinal Odoardo Farnese on Sunday, 1 July 1601, included as guests only Cardinals Montalto and (Pietro) Aldobrandini, Montalto's brother, Michele, and Michele's future father-in-law, Paolo Emilio Cesi. See the document transcribed by Waźbiński, *Il Cardinale Francesco Maria Del Monte*, 352.

8

La priggionia, incantamento, et liberatione di Rinaldo: Guarini's Last Stage Work

✧❦✧

ON 24 April 1610 Cardinal Montalto in Rome wrote to Cardinal Alessandro d'Este in Modena: 'Since Guarini, who gave me Your Lordship's letter, is a person of such good and honourable qualities, as you write, he deserves every assistance on his own account. I would gladly apply myself in his behalf for that reason and to obey Your Lordship, wherever I am aware that I can benefit him' (Letter 25). He was, of course, referring to Battista Guarini, the most prestigious living poet in Italy and, perhaps, in all of Europe. It is likely that Montalto had already met Guarini, if not during the preparations for the planned performance of *Il pastor fido* in 1596, then perhaps in Florence during the period surrounding Grand Duke Ferdinando's wedding in 1589.

By March of 1612 Guarini had obtained the purpose of his visit: a favourable ruling on his claim to the feudal possessions formerly held by Bradamante d'Este in the Duchy of Ferrara.[1] Guarini had judged well where to place his appeal: Montalto was the closest and most powerful ally of Pope Paul V, Montalto's former Vice Legate, and of the Cardinal-Nephew, Scipione Borghese. But now Guarini had a debt to pay in the form of service.

The first mention of the work that Guarini wrote for Cardinal Montalto early in 1612 comes from a letter of 3 March 1612 to Enzo Bentivoglio, Ferrarese ambassador to Rome: 'Tomorrow evening in the house of Cardinal Montalto a comedy will be performed, and Sig.ra Hippolita is prepared to sing in an outstanding fashion.'[2] The description of the event found in the *avvisi* from Rome four days later, 7 March 1612, specifies that the singing would be heard in intermedi at the ends of the acts of the play:

---

[1] I:MOs, Cancelleria ducale, Ambasciatori, Roma, busta 201, no. 267, letter from Febo Denatio to Cesare d'Este, 28.iii.1612. Bradamante was the illegitimate daughter of Francesco, son of Duke Alfonso I d'Este.

[2] 3.iii.1612: Giacinto Landinelli (Roma) to Enzo Bentivoglio (Ferrara): 'Domani a sera si recita in casa di Mont'Alto una comedia, e la S.ra Hip.ta s'è preparata di cantare egregiamente.' I:FEas, Archivio Bentivoglio, mazzo 64, fo. 16ʳ.

Among the other comedies, one was performed almost without planning last Sunday evening in the house of Cardinal Montalto. At the end of every act, as an intermedio, there was sung, by the most select voices and excellent musicians that are in Rome, the imprisonment, enchantment, and liberation of Rinaldo, invented by Torquato Tasso in his epic poem *Gerusalemme liberata*, with the most beautiful and rich costumes that can be imagined, at which Cardinals Monte, Borghese, Niccarola, Peretti, and Capponi, and Father Francesco Borghese were in attendance, and they were presented with a very sumptuous dinner.[3]

Torquato Tasso is the only author mentioned so far, but Guarini's role in this production gradually becomes clear in further letters. The first of them was written by Montalto's principal composer, Cesare Marotta, to Enzo Bentivoglio in Ferrara on 16 May 1612:

Your Most Illustrious Lordship . . . will have already received four intermedi that Cavalier Guarini, in your name, had me compose. . . . I know that they have turned out short. This is not my fault. I will be waiting for Cavalier Guarini to make additions to them, and then I will serve you immediately in this respect. . . . And he who has charge of rehearsing them must be practised in that style of recitative music (Letter 55).

Marotta seems to be writing about a commission that Guarini fulfilled for Enzo Bentivoglio, but it can be deduced that at least three of these intermedi are the same ones performed for Cardinal Montalto in March. A process of building up by accretion from earlier stages was already under way, as will be gradually revealed in what follows.

It is quite likely that the additional texts that Marotta needed in order to lengthen his intermedi were not, in fact, written by Guarini, who died in Venice five months later, on 7 October 1612. It is, indeed, not until nineteen months later that Marotta next informs Bentivoglio of his progress (the reason for this delay will become clear later):

I am sending the pieces of music that you commanded me to compose. . . . Friday evening, the thirteenth of this month, the words were given to me . . . and today, Tuesday morning, I have finished everything (Letter 72).

These additions were not enough, and on the first day of the year 1614, Marotta explains that he had to extend some of the music he had already sent:

I see that Your Most Illustrious Lordship is too partial to my things, which he favours too much. In those things sent to you, I aimed at brevity in order not to cause boredom.

---

[3] 7.iii.1612: *Avvisi* from Rome to Urbino: 'Frà l'altre [commedie] quasi ch'al'improviso ne fù recitata Domenica sera in casa del Card.l Montalto nella quale in fine degl'atti fù per intermedio cantata dalle più scelte voci, et ecc.ti musici, che siano in Roma la priggionia, incantamento, et liberatione di Rinaldo, inventata da Torquato Tasso nel suo poema heroico di Gerusalem liberata con habiti belli e richi quanto si possa imaginare, alla quale intervennero li Card.li Monti, Borghese, Niccarola, Peretti, Capponi, et il P. Francesco Borghese, che furno regalati d'una cena molto sontuosa.' I:Rvat, Urb. lat. 1080, fo. 211ᵛ.

Now that you command me to make an addition, I have done so immediately. . . . And I have made this addition blind, not having a copy of those pieces of music sent, which were needed in order that I could use the motifs. Considering all that, I have done as well as possible (Letter 73).

And more than a year later, Enzo Bentivoglio was in Rome, still looking for more music for his play, as he explains to Antonio Goretti, the supervisor of his music:

I ask Your Lordship to attend to the pieces of music in the comedy, for which I, here, shall not forget to procure some vocal works to be sung in various ways, and I shall send them directly to Your Lordship to give you the enjoyment of them. In this endeavour I am finding out that no one ever bestirs himself to give you any music for nothing (Letter 81).

A letter of 8 July 1615 from Bentivoglio's agent in Rome finally mentions a specific new text, which is an octave from Ariosto's *Orlando furioso* (XLIV. lxv):

Of Baldassarre, then, I can say that . . . Cavalier Marotta has begun to teach him the ottava *Non havete a temer ch'in forma nova*, a truly beautiful work . . . (Letter 92).

In a letter of 22 July the same Roman agent mentions another piece of music that Marotta is composing for the same singer:

Baldassarre . . . continues to learn, and for him will be composed the ornamented music on the words *O solenne Vittoria*, since I have recovered the letter and presented it to Signor Marotta (Letter 94).

The last music was composed and sent to Ferrara in August of 1615:

As soon as I received Your Illustrious Lordship's letter, I took the enclosed words of the Furies to Cavalier Marotta, explaining your intentions to him and informing him about the music that comes before and after the said words, so that he will not compose them in some mode that will make it difficult to insert them in the middle of the other pieces of music (Letter 97).

Finally, on 6 January of 1616, the composer wrote to Enzo Bentivoglio with satisfaction:

I have felt particular pleasure in hearing that over there the comedy and other festivities are in active preparation (Letter 104).

The comedy to which Cesare Marotta referred was Alessandro Guarini's *Bradamante gelosa*, and the subject of all these letters was the set of intermedi performed with it in Ferrara in 1616. Some history of these intermedi, which begins to explain the years-long delay in performing them, is offered in the description published with the playbook:

When Signor Enzo Bentivoglio (a little less than two years ago), to celebrate better the arrival in this city of the Illustrious Lord Cardinal Rivarola, Legate to Romagna, staged *Idalba*, a tragedy by Mafeo Venieri, the intermedi that accompanied it pleased very much. . . . Having, therefore, selected a new tragedy and since the author is Signor Alessandro Guarini, worthy son of our Apollo, I thought to unite the intermedi of the father to the noble play of the son. . . . With the changes made in them and with the addition of the most stupendous and surpassingly beautiful machines, [the intermedi] have thus changed appearance to the extent that in many places they will scarcely be recognized.[4]

The earlier performance of the intermedi to which this preface alludes, in February 1614, is also represented by a printed description, one that had, however, been prepared for a still earlier production of the same play that was to have taken place a year before. This is from the preface to the 1613 edition:

Here, kind readers, Arsiccio, who last year presented you with the description of that magnificent and royal tournament, now makes bold to return before you with the same mask, describing the stupendous intermedi with which Signor Enzo Bentivoglio has staged *Alceo*, a fisherman's tale by Antonio Ongaro. . . . Enzo Bentivoglio began the project at the beginning of December, and at the end of January he had completed everything and had it transcribed, too.[5]

To this the pasted-in 1614 preface adds:

When the Most Illustrious Signor Enzo Bentivoglio decided fifteen months ago [1 December 1612] to stage *Alceo*, the fisherman's tale, with the intermedi by the late Cavalier Guarini, illustrious ornament of this city and glory of the present century, I, on the basis of a single rehearsal, which was seen publicly by a large crowd, thought how fine and marvellous it would appear at the time when it would be seen on stage with formal

---

[4] 'Quando il Signor Enzo Bentivogli (già sono poco men, che due anni) per solennizzar maggiormente la venuta in questa Città dell'Illustriss. Sign. Cardinale Rivarola Legato di Romagna, fece ponere in iscena l'Idalba Tragedia di Mafeo Venieri, piacquero tanto gl'Intramezzi da' quali fu accompagnata. . . . Fece dunque elezione d'una Tragedia nuova, e . . . l'Autore, . . . è il Sig. Alessandro Guarino degno figliuolo del nostro Appolo. . . . Alla nobile favola del figlio penso d'unire gl'Intramezzi del padre . . . che con le mutazioni fatte pur anche in essi, e con la giunta di stupendissime machine, e belle oltra modo, hanno in guisa mutato sembiante, che in molti luoghi saranno appena riconosciuti per dessi.' *Descrizione degl'intramezzi co' quali l'Ill.mo Sig. Enzo Bentivogli ha fatto rappresentare la tragedia del Sig. Alessandro Guarini intitolata* Bradamante gelosa (Ferrara: Baldini, 1616), Preface. This description has been unknown to modern scholarship. Rossi, *Battista Guarini*, 156 n. 2, cites the title of this libretto but confesses not to have been able to consult it. His citation is based on Giusto Fontanini, *Biblioteca dell'eloquenze italiana* (Parma, 1803), i. 447. The exemplar of the 1616 *Descrizione* consulted for this study is in I:Rn, 34.3.A.27.4.

[5] 4.iii.1613: *L'Arsiccio a' lettori*: 'Ecco, cortesi Lettori, che quell'Arsiccio, che l'anno addietro v'appresentò la discrizione del pomposo, e real Torneo, ora col raccontamento degli stupendissimi Intramezzi, co' quali il Signor Enzo Bentivogli ha fatto porre in iscena l'Alceo Favola Pescatoria d'Antonio Ongaro, di tornarvi, con la stessa maschera, pur anche davanti, ha preso ardire. . . . [Enzo Bentivoglio] cominciò l'opera nell'entrata di Dicembre, e all'uscita di Gennaio d'avea compiuta del tutto, e fatta trascrivere ancora.' 'Lo stampatore a' lettori', Antonio Ongaro, *L'Alceo, favola pescatoria . . . con gl'intramezzi del Sig. Cavalier Batista Guarini* (Ferrara: Baldini, 1613/14). Exemplar in I:Rvat, Dramm. Allacc. 288, int. 4.

and most lavish splendour. For that reason, I hastened to procure the description of those intermedi in order to present everything to you at the same time in which they were to be performed. It [the description] was obtained, by order of Signor Enzo, from Arsiccio, not only with the step-by-step explanations, but with the addition of many essays about each intermedio. But because the arrival of those personages, to whom such a noble spectacle was dedicated, was delayed, and since Signor Enzo had to go to Rome on business, we were deprived of that noble and generous spectacle. I did not think twice about [not] printing [the description] on this account, considering it certain that, upon the return of Signor [Enzo], the general expectation would be satisfied. This thought was not entirely mistaken, since the work has been done, but very differently, not only because the intermedi have, in more than one place, received some alteration, as can be seen, but also because Signor Enzo wanted them to appear on stage and in print not with *Alceo* but with the tragedy *Idalba*. Nevertheless, since I had already undergone the expense of [printing] *Alceo* and the first intermedi, and since I judge that the work, both on account of the essays as well as for the descriptions and for other considerations, is not entirely unworthy of your attention, I have decided to present it to you, begging you courteously to forgive Arsiccio's errors and my own on account of the rapidity with which each of us worked to complete the present volume. Farewell.[6]

The final knot that ties these Ferrarese intermedi by Guarini together with those that he had done for Montalto in Rome can be found in their content, which can be summarized as follows:

Synopsis of the intermedi performed in Ferrara in 1613 and 1614

Madrialetti in place of a prologue: Faith and Hope.
Primo intramezzo: Medea is angry at Jason's abandonment. Moon provides Medea with a chariot drawn by two dragons, with which to pursue her revenge. Jason defies Medea, who kills their children in rage. Jason laments.
Secondo intramezzo: Armida descends from the sky in a chariot, carrying Rinaldo, asleep.

---

[6] '[28.ii.1614]: Quando l'Illustriss. Sig. Enzo Bentivogli si dispose, gia sono da quindici mesi [= 1.xii.1613], di far rappresentar l'Alceo Favola Pescatoria, con gl'Intramezzi del già Signor Cavalier Guarini, illustre fregio di questa Città, e gloria del presente secolo, Io, dalla riuscita della sola prova, che pubblicamente, e con tanto concorso se ne vide, feci ragione quanto riguardevole, e maravigliosa sarebbe ella comparsa allor, che con pompa solenne, e generosissima veder si dovea in iscena. La onde m'affrettai d'aver la descrizione di essi Intramezzi, per presentarvi ogni cosa nello stesso punto, che si sarebbe recitata. L'ebbi, per ordine del Signor Enzo, dall'Arsiccio, non pur con le dichiarazioni di passo in passo, ma con la giunta di molti Discorsi sopra ciascheduno Intramezzo. Ma perché la venuta di quei personaggi, a' quali principalmente sì nobile rappresentazione era dedicata, si dileguò, e al Signor Enzo convenne per suoi affari condursi a Roma, di così nobile, e magnanimo spettacolo, fummo privati. Io non rifletti per questo di stampare; tenendo per fermo, che al ritorno di quel Signore si sarebbe alla comune aspettazione soddisfatto. Il pensiero non m'è del tutto fallito, poiché l'opra s'è fatta, ma molto diversa, sì perché gl'Intramezzi hanno in più d'un luogo ricevuta qualche mutazione, come si vede; e sì ancora perché non più con l'Alceo, ma con l'Idalba Tragedia, ha voluto il Sig. Enzo, che compariscano in iscena, ed in istampa. Contuttocciò avendo io già fatta la spesa dell'Alceo, e de' primi Intramezzi, e stimando, che l'opra, e per li Discorsi, e per le dichiarazioni, e per altri riguardi, non sia del tutto indegna del vostro cospetto, ho diliberato d'apprentarlavi. Pregandovi, a condonnar cortesemente gli σ[e]rrori dell'Arsiccio, ed i miei alla fretta velocissima con laquale, e l'uno, e l'altro ci studiammo in dar compimento al presente volume, e vivete felici.' Ibid.

A palace arises. Armida reassures Rinaldo, and they invoke Venus. [*Gerusalemme liberata*, XIV]

Terzo intramezzo: Armida and Rinaldo, singing of their love, are surprised by Ubaldo and Carlo, who persuade Rinaldo to rejoin them in battle. Armida, unable to keep Rinaldo, vows revenge on him. [*Gerusalemme liberata*, XVI]

Quarto intramezzo: Cynthia counsels Proserpina to remain a virgin in heaven, but Venus, enticing her with love, prevails. Proserpina descends with Pluto in his chariot.

Quinto intramezzo: The gods argue whether or not Proserpina should return to heaven. Jove decides that she will spend six months of each year with her mother and six with Pluto, her husband.

As we would have suspected, considerable material has been added, but we can see the outlines of the Rinaldo episodes in the second and third intermedi. The problem is that the *avvisi* from Rome in 1612 mention three episodes: 'imprisonment, enchantment, and liberation of Rinaldo'. The Ferrarese wordbook of 1613/14, however, includes just two. And Cesare Marotta's letter of 16 May 1612, quoted above, says that he is sending to Ferrara four intermedi on texts by Guarini. The solution to this problem, I believe, is to be found in the wordbook printed for the 1616 Ferrarese revival of these intermedi. Here is a summary of their content, with elements not found in the 1613/14 printing set in italics:

Synopsis of the intermedi performed in Ferrara, 1616

Primo intramezzo: Faith and Hope (as before). *Then Alcina descends on a flying dragon. 'Recitò cantando alcuni versi'* [*Non avete a temer ch'in forma nuova*].

Secondo intramezzo: Medea is angry at Jason's abandonment. Moon provides Medea with a chariot drawn by two dragons, with which to pursue her revenge. Jason defies Medea, who kills their children in rage. Jason laments.

Terzo intramezzo: Armida descends from the sky in a chariot, carrying Rinaldo, asleep. A palace arises. Armida reassures Rinaldo, and they invoke Venus. [*Gerusalemme liberata*, XIV] *A boat appears, guided by Fortune and carrying Carlo and Ubaldo. Following Fortune's descriptions and advice, the two knights climb to the mountain top, defeat the serpent, lion, and monsters, reject the temptation of a Siren, and enter Armida's palace.* [*Gerusalemme liberata*, XV]

Quarto intramezzo: *In his grotto, Pluto incites his Furies to help Armida and kill her enemy. The Furies lament their fate. Smoke covers the scene.* [*Gerusalemme liberata*, IV] *When it clears, we see* Armida and Rinaldo, singing of their love. They are surprised by Ubaldo and Carlo, who persuade Rinaldo to rejoin them in battle. *Ubaldo refutes Armida's accusations. Armida calls Rinaldo cruel and laments her loss.* Armida, unable to keep Rinaldo, vows revenge on him. *She flies off on the seven-headed Hydra.* [*Gerusalemme liberata*, XVI]

Quinto intramezzo: Cynthia counsels Proserpina to remain a virgin in heaven, but Venus, enticing her with love, prevails. Proserpina descends with Pluto in his chariot. *Amphitrite celebrates love's victory (O solenne vittoria), and sings a duet with Neptune.*

Sesto intramezzo: The gods argue whether or not Proserpina should return to heaven.

Jove decides that she will spend six months each year with her mother and six with Pluto, her husband. *Time, Beauty, and Youth dispute over which one will have the most influence over the future happiness of Proserpina.*

In this version, the third and fourth intermedi each have an additional episode not found in the earlier source. The addition to the third intermedio is based on Canto xv of *Gerusalemme liberata*, and it forms the link between the Canto xiv and Canto xvi episodes, which were in the earlier wordbook. The addition to the fourth intermedio in the 1616 print is out of sequence and is more difficult to explain. It is based on Canto iv of *Gerusalemme liberata*, but with fundamental changes. In Tasso, Pluto incites the Furies to wage war on the Franks. In the course of this war, the magician Idraote sends his niece Armida against the Christians, eventually to take Rinaldo prisoner. Perhaps in the original 1612 Roman version, this underworld episode from Canto iv introduced the 'imprisonment of Rinaldo', as narrated by the 'vecchio onesto' in Canto xiv. Here, in the 1616 version in the intermedio, Pluto commands his Furies to pursue Rinaldo, since Carlo and Ubaldo are about to free him.

I think that the underworld episode in the fourth intermedio was altered for the 1616 production. Pluto's opening speech in it begins with the first four lines of Tasso's Canto iv, stanza 9, but it concludes with four new lines that introduce the altered circumstances. The description says: 'Pluto proudly sang the following very beautiful verses, part taken from the great Tasso and part added by a most delicate pen just for the present invention.'[7] The 'finissima penna' may well be that of Enzo Bentivoglio, since he was a poet and made the arrangement of these intermedi in his own hand.[8] Furthermore, the words sung by the Furies in the second portion of this addition were written and set to music only in 1615, as we learned from Geronimo Fioretti's letter of 22 August 1615, quoted above. In addition, Fioretti's letter of 22 July 1615 mentioned *O solenne Vittoria*, which was added to the fifth intermedio in the 1616 wordbook.

But the letters make no mention of texts belonging to the two Rinaldo episodes that were added to the 1616 wordbook. The reason for this, I submit, is that they were two of Guarini's four intermedi originally sent to Enzo Bentivoglio

---

[7] 'Plutone orgogliosamente cantò li seguenti bellissimi versi parte tolti dal gran Tasso, e parte da finissima penna a proposito della presente invenzione aggiunti.'

[8] Poetry by Enzo Bentivoglio is contained in *Applausi poetici alla gloria della Signora Leonora Baroni* (Bracciano, 1639), 110–12; and *Rime scelte dei poeti ferraresi* (Ferrara, 1713), 263–8. Bentivoglio's manuscript copy of these intermedi is in I:FEc, MS Cl. I, 309, on the spine of which is inscribed '[Intramez]zi del S.r Enzo Be[ntivoglio]'. Giuseppe Antonelli, *Indice dei manoscritti della Civica Biblioteca di Ferrara, Parte prima* (Ferrara, 1884), 161, describes this as 'Intramezzi di Enzo Bentivoglio ferrarese alla tragedia del S.r Alessandro Guarini intitolata: Bradamante gelosa. . . . Questi Intramezzi, che sono autografi, furono impressi'. A comparison of this manuscript with Bentivoglio's autograph letters of 1615, in the same library, tends to confirm Antonelli's claim. Another possibility is that the text was completed by Ottavio Magnanini, who, under the academic name 'Arsiccio', wrote the descriptions of the Ferrarese *torneo* of 1612 and intermedi of 1613/14, as will be shown below.

in 1612. They were not included in the performances of 1613 and 1614, I suppose, because at that time Bentivoglio did not yet have the necessary singer or singers at his disposal. In fact, the process of assembling the cast of the 1616 intermedi in Ferrara entailed efforts to discover, train, recruit, borrow, and practically kidnap singers over a period of four years (see Ch. 4). Some further additions to Battista Guarini's text are not mentioned in the correspondence but can be deduced from surviving musical sources.

Altogether certainly three, but possibly four or five, arias survive from Guarini's last stage work, or at least from the version of it printed in 1616. *Quando il ciel vago s'infiora* (Vol. II, no. 11) is sung by Fortune, commenting upon the enchantment of Rinaldo by Armida, in the episode based on Tasso's Canto xv in the Terzo intramezzo of 1616. The music is ascribed to Ippolito Macchiavelli, one of Cesare Marotta's colleagues in the household of Cardinal Montalto. The two strophes of text are set as four variations in the canzonetta style, with rhythmic, unvaried bass and lyrical vocal line that is mostly syllabic in the first stanza but varied by short melismatic ornaments in subsequent strophes. The 1616 wordbook describes the music in this way:

Fortune arrived singing as we said. The aria was so graceful and so filled and embellished by such beautiful passages and ornaments that the spectators were more astonished by its extraordinary and excessive sweetness than if they had been hearkening to the mortal songs of the Sirens. Rather, if the music of those very beautiful sea creatures had been as rare and soft as this, Ulysses would not have fled but would have met a most adventurous death and would have fainted away quite delightfully.[9]

The description is certainly public-relations hyperbole, and much of the spectators' real delight might well have been their reaction to the almost legendary singing of Ippolita Recupito. The notated music, however, does give a glimpse of grace and astonishing ornamentation. One remarkable feature of the aria is the rhythmic disposition of the eight-syllable verses. In this aria Macchiavelli plays against the predictable hemiola pattern, which, in scores (perhaps hundreds) of strophic canzonetta settings, mechanically follows the invariable accentuation scheme of ottonari *piani*. He places the primary accent of the seventh syllable and the secondary accent of the third syllable at the customary distance of three minims, in most cases, but delightfully stretches or compresses that distance just often enough to break the monotony while preserving the basic, implied 3/2 metre. The ornamental sixteenth notes, particularly in the second and third variations,

[9] 'Venne [Fortuna] cantando come dicemmo; ed era l'aria sì graziosa, e di passaggi, e di spiriti bellissimi, si ripiena, ed ornata, che gli spettatori per l'inusitata, ed eccessiva dolcezza, piu attoniti restarono, che se al canto micidial delle Sirene fossero stati intenti. Anzi, che se sì cara, e soave al pare di questa stata fosse l'armonia di qelle bellissime fiere del mare, non avrebbe Ulisse fuggita, ma incontrata cosi avventurosa morte, ed un cosi dilettevole venir meno.' *Descrizione degl'Intramezzi*, 26–7.

actually enhance the rhythmic lilt of the aria by running up to the principal anacrusis in several verses. The vocal line is constantly flirting and teasing with the
rock-solid motion of the bass. This playful style seems well suited to the tone
and imagery of Fortune's words, which prepare Carlo and Ubaldo for the scene
about to unfold, as they enter Armida's enchanted garden (the text here follows
the wordbook; variants occur in the musical source):

Quando il Ciel vago s'infiora	When charming heaven enflowers itself
Su l'aurora, e di viole	above the dawn, and with violets
Carca il Sole, il carro aurato,	the sun loads up the gilded chariot,
E su 'l prato sparge quelle	and scatters these upon the meadows
Al suo par vezzose, e belle.	as charming and beautiful as himself,
Cristallina, e pura Linfa	Crystalline and pure water
Bella Armida ha per suo speglio,	serves Armida for her mirror.
Vedi il meglio, e 'l più gentile	Behold the best and noblest part
Del suo Aprile, e fassi altera	of her April, and spring becomes proud
A sua riva Primavera.	on her banks.
Mira lei Rinaldo amante,	The loving Rinaldo gazes on her
E le tante sue bellezze	and her great beauties
Le vaghezze singolari	and singular charms,
I suoi rari pregi mira,	and views her rare excellences
E ne piange, e ne sospira;	and weeps and sighs for them;
I sospiri, e 'l pianto viene	The sighs and weeping arise
Ch'ella tiene in seno ascoso	from her holding hidden in her breast
Orgoglioso, e rigid'angue,	a haughty and stiff serpent,
Che del sangue degl'Amanti	that feeds only on the blood
Sol si nutre, e sol di pianti.	of lovers, and only on tears.

The change of poetic expression in the last stanza is mirrored in the music by a
disintegration of the lilting rhythms and sobbing reverse-dotted figures on the
words *e sol di pianti* ('and only tears', b. 81).

From the same episode and also sung by Fortune is *O dolcezze amarissime
d'Amore*, in which Fortuna tells Carlo and Ubaldo, just after they leap ashore, that
he who is imprisoned by earthly love cannot attain fame and honour. Again, the
wordbook describes the music:

While the knights strove to reach [the mountain top] and to defeat the magic obstacles,
the lady [Fortune] began to sing the following octave with so much grace and such a
delicate melody that she overcame herself. And while in the preceding song she surpassed
the Sirens of the sea, in this one she nearly equalled those of heaven.[10]

---

[10] 'Mentre i Cavalieri s'affaticavano di giunger colà, e di vincere i magici intoppi, la donna si diede a cantare
la seguente Ottava, con tanta grazia, con si leggiadra melodia, che vinse se stessa. E se con la passata Canzone
si lasciò addietro le Sirene del mare, in questa pareggiò in un certo modeo quelle del Cielo.' *Descrizione
degl'Intramezzi*, 29.

This is Fortune's warning to all, based upon the misfortune of Rinaldo:

O dolcezze amarissime d'Amore,	Oh bitter sweetness of love
In cui si giace un cor vivo e sepolto.	in which a heart lies living yet entombed!
Splender non può giammai spirto, o valore,	Neither spirit nor valor can shine any longer
S'egli è fra l'ombra di lascivia involto.	if he is ensnared in the shadow of lasciviousness.
Non speri d'aquistar fama, ed onore,	He may not hope to acquire fame and honour
Chi da terreno amor non è disciolto.	who is not liberated from earthly love.
Sì, sì fuggite amor, fuggite amanti,	Yes, yes, flee from Love, flee, lovers
Ch'egli ha del suo piacer seguaci i pianti.	for the consequences of his pleasure are tears.

Cesare Marotta's setting of this text (with *durezze* rather than *dolcezze* in the first line—Vol. II, no. 22) takes the form of a fairly typical set of variations on the Romanesca chordal bass pattern. The bass marks out a 3/2 metre with the space of three minims between each of the framework harmonies in the first *parte*, while that pattern is distorted by extensions and contractions in the subsequent variations, as frequently happens, to produce the effect of *sprezzatura di canto* in the context of an essentially lyrical, cantillational style. The extensive use of syncopation in the vocal line also contributes to the same effect, while the many long and unpatterned passaggi evoke the spontaneity and eccentricity that form important components of the aesthetic embraced by Cardinal Montalto's composers. The passaggi in this work are among the most difficult to be found in the monody repertoire, particularly those in the *Quarta parte*, where the singer is required to perform scales, leaps, many reversals of direction, and pitch repetition all in one series of twenty-eight thirty-second notes.

The third surviving aria is *Che più giova mirare occhi infelici*. It was sung by Megera, one of the Furies, in the second portion of the inferno scene in the Quarto intramezzo of 1616, while she rises slowly through the flames towards the upper world, in compliance with Pluto's directive.

Che più giova mirare, occhi infelici,	What pleases you more to see, unhappy eyes,
Del questo Sol la luce amata, e cara.	than the beloved and dear light of this sun?
E sospirando i dì lieti e felici,	And, sighing for the happy, blessed days,
Pianger la notte gelid'et amara.	to weep for the frigid and bitter night?
Troppo al ben nostro, ohimè, furo inimici	Too much against our well-being, alas, were enemies
Il destino e la sorte iniqua e avara.	destiny and wicked, cruel fate.
Vano è il desir, e vana è la speranza,	Vain is desire, and vain is hope,
Che pianger solo, e di sospirar n'avvanza.	which promote only weeping and sighing.

Although called a 'madrigale' in the playbook, it is, in reality, a stanza of ottava rima, which Cesare Marotta set as strophic variations over a Romanesca bass (Vol. II, no. 48). In keeping with the subdued expression of the text, the bass here is far less active than it is in any of the other Romanesca settings in the Montalto repertoire. It also gives no hint of the 3/2 metre that underlies most of the other Romanescas. The text juxtaposes syllabic, almost recitational phrases with brief bursts of extremely rapid embellishment, almost like a typical sonetto. The syllabic phrases, however, are rarely monotonal. Instead, a halting, tenuated arioso effectively projects the extreme dejection and pessimism of the text. The melodic contours are fragmented, and any sort of patterning is avoided and defeated in order to suggest a spontaneous outpouring of bitter hopelessness.

The first of the two questionable cases is the text *Coglier la rosa in sul mattino adorno*, which appears as the *Quarta parte* of Giovanni Bernardino Nanino's *Dhe mira egli cantò spuntar la rosa* (Vol. II, no. 91). The text set is a modified version of the last four lines of Tasso's Canto XVI, stanza 15. In *Gerusalemme liberata* these descriptive verses are spoken by the magical bird just before Carlo and Ubaldo find Rinaldo and Armida. In the wordbooks of 1613/14 and 1616 these lines are quoted just at the point when, about to leave Armida's enchanted garden, Rinaldo thinks he hears the comforting words of the magical birds. Whether these words were sung, off-stage for instance, is not clear to me. Here is the description, which is the same in both editions of the wordbook:

And when [these words] were finished, [Rinaldo] turned his back in anger on the luxuriant and very soft lodging. And since it seemed to the ears of his own consciousness that the little birds, earlier, encouraged him so sweetly to

> gather the rose that adorns the morning
> of this day, which soon loses its tranquillity;
> gather the rose of love, and love while
> you can be loved in return,

the murmuring of the breeze, the rustling of the leaves, the whispering of the crystalline waves, and the charming laughter of the flowered gardens were no longer seductive notes tempered by the heated sighs of love.[11]

Singing the four lines taken from *Gerusalemme liberata* to the last of Nanino's four strophic variations as Rinaldo pauses before leaving would, I think, have been theatrically effective. If, on the other hand, they were not sung, it is difficult to imagine why these verses were printed in the wordbook.

---

[11] 'E finite, che l'hebbe, voltò con dispetto le spalle al lussuriante, e morbidissmo albergo. E perchè all'orecchie della sua propria conscienze pareva, che quegli uccelletti, che prima sì dolcemente il confortavano a

> Coglier la rosa in sul mattino adorno
> Di questo dì, che tosto il seren perde:
> Coglier d'Amor la rosa, amare, or quando
> Esser si puote riamato amando,

che 'l mormorar dell'aura, il garrire delle foglie, il susurrar dell'onde cristalline, e 'l riso vezzoso di quei fioriti giardini non piu fossero lascivette note temprate a i cocenti sospiri d'Amore.' Ongaro, *L'Alceo*, 103–4.

The second questionable case is *Lagrimosa pietà, che più consolami*, a lament sung by Armida in the Quarto intramezzo at Rinaldo's departure with Carlo and Ubaldo. The aria was added for the 1616 performance, and the text was obviously not composed for the occasion. It consists of three stanzas of *versi sdruccioli* in terza rima, one of them imperfect, as it lacks a line and breaks the rhyme scheme. The complete and proper text, with a minor variant, survives in two different musical settings. The text as given in the 1616 libretto is compared with the version closest to it from a guitar-tablature manuscript of early seventeenth-century Roman origin, described in Chapter 5:

Wordbook of 1616	GB:Lbm, Add. 36877, fo. 118ᵛ
Lagrimosa pietà, che più consolami.	Lacrimosa pietà, che più consolami
Or, che sì gran dolor il cor mi macera,	Hor che l'altrui dolor il cor mi macera
Ed di me stessa la più parte involami.	E nell'interno nott'il sonn'involami.
Sento l'alma dolente afflitta, e lacera,	Veggio più del Pastor la gregge macera
E come nel dolo tutta disperdesi.	E come in pochi dì tutta disperdesi
	Ne' boschi errando sconsolata, e lacera.
Crudel'Amor così la vita perdesi.	Crudel Amor' così la vita perdesi,
Né per lagrime, o prieghi miserabili	Né per lacrime, ò prieghi miserabili
La speme degli amanti unqua rinverdesi.	La speme delli amanti unqua riverdesi.
O doglie sempeterne, o gioie labili,	Oh dogli sempiterno, oh gioie labili,
Itene consumando afflitta l'anima,	Itene consumando afflitti gl'animi
Ch'io canterò d'amor l'ire durabili.	Ch'io canterò d'Amor' l'ire durabili.

The reference to slumber in line 3 of the full text and the imagery of the shepherd's flock in the second tercet have been removed in the wordbook of 1616 as they would make no sense in the dramatic context of the Quarto intramezzo. And in the last tercet, the generalized reference to all afflicted souls in the original version is appropriately replaced by a single soul in the wordbook.

It is obvious that this text was added to the intermedio in order to use an existing setting of its music. There would be no other reason to modify—indeed to lacerate—an existing text instead of composing entirely new words.

As mentioned, two different settings of the original form of the text are known to survive. One is through-composed in madrigalian style and published in Paolo Quagliati's *Carro di Fedeltà d'Amore* (Rome, 1611), and the other is found in the Roman guitar-tablature songbook cited above. Quagliati had no known connection with the circles around Cardinal Montalto, and, indeed, his music is conspicuously absent from the sources that emanate from Montalto's ambience. The London guitar manuscript, on the other hand, contains many concordances with manuscripts and prints related to Montalto's circle. The guitar tablature shows the chords to be strummed in the accompaniment of the song, but one cannot reconstruct the voice and bass lines from it. However, since the guitar chords are given for the first tercet only, we can deduce that they were repeated for each of the following tercets as well. This means that the setting was either strophic or strophic variations. Given that the text is in terza rima, strophic variations is the more likely form of the music. Strophic-variation procedure is also suggested by the description of the singing in the libretto, which says that Armida sang these verses with 'maniere, e passaggi dilicatissimi', referring, therefore, to ornamental divisions. The number and frequency of the chords show that the harmonic rhythm was moderately rapid, certainly more rapid than would be typical for recitative. Therefore in both probable form and style, the setting represented by the guitar tablature conforms better than Quagliati's madrigalian setting to the prevailing character of the other surviving arias from these intermedi and with the repertoire of songs from Montalto's circle in general. Furthermore, it would have been difficult to adapt a through-composed, madrigalian monody by cutting out one line of text and replacing two others. But this is relatively easy to do with strophic variations; and indeed exactly this was done in the case of Ottavio Catalani's lament *In che misero punto hor qui mi mena* when it was sung in Cardinal Savelli's comedy based on *Gerusalemme liberata*, as was explained in Chapter 6.

Each of the other arias also sets a text that, in the musical source, is slightly different from the one given in the 1616 wordbook. As with *Lagrimosa pietà*, each version printed in the wordbook makes specific reference to the drama, while the version in the musical manuscript is non-specific. Again, analysis shows that the non-specific texts were the originals and were subsequently altered to fit the intermedi. The best example among these others is *Quando il ciel vago s'infiora*. The *Seconda parte* in the musical source begins *Cristallin' e pura linfa | Bella ninfa ha per suo speglio*. This internal rhyme (*linfa* and *ninfa*) is found at the corresponding place in each of the other strophes, except in the second strophe of the wordbook version, where the rhyme scheme is destroyed precisely by the substitution of Armida's name for the generic *ninfa*: *Cristallina, e pura linfa | Bella Armida ha per suo speglio*. The variations between the text of the wordbook and that of the musical source in each of the other cases can be discovered by consulting the relevant musical transcriptions in Volume II.

All the surviving arias from the 1616 intermedi, therefore, had already been composed with other texts and for other purposes before they were pressed into service for this stage work. Even so, they could have been part of the original intermedi prepared by Guarini in Rome. The *avvisi* from Rome of 7 March 1612 mention a hasty preparation that might, therefore, have necessitated inclusion of existing music from singers' repertoires. And later these arias are not mentioned in the correspondence between Rome and Ferrara along with the additions to the intermedi that were settings of new texts provided to Cesare Marotta. If they were already composed, there would have been no need to mention them.

I have not been able to identify the author of these altered texts, but I think Apostolo Zeno in effect endorsed an identification early in the eighteenth century.[12] When he reported someone's suggestion that additions to the 1616 version of these intermedi were made by Girolamo Preti, I suspect that the evidence upon which the suggestion rested was a copy of one of these added aria texts with an ascription to Preti. It probably did not occur to Zeno or his informant that in all likelihood Preti had nothing to do with the insertion of his poetry, but rather that Marotta or one of his colleagues had already set Preti's poem and that the setting was subsequently added to the intermedio with textural modifications. Indeed, Preti was among the poets frequently set by composers in the Montalto circle.

It cannot be fairly said that the addition of these texts destroyed the poetic integrity of Guarini's last stage work. It contained verses not by Guarini from the beginning—verses by Tasso. Table 8.1 offers a sample of the process by which Guarini incorporated and modified Tasso's stanzas to create dramatic dialogue. Guarini frequently alters the first line of Tasso's stanza to transform direct quotation into dialogue, as at lines 3, 43, and 47 in this sample. At other times, he simply excises narrative verses, as at lines 1–2, 25, 35–6, and 71. Guarini's complete recasting of Tasso's verses, on the other hand, seems to be aimed at producing language more direct, forceful, concrete, and impassioned—language that derives its effect more from accents, inflections, pacing, articulations, and small-scale patterning rather than from elaborate rhetorical figures, impersonal constructions, and polysyllables. In the process, he replaces the predictable metre of ottava rima with more spontaneous and varied *versi sciolti*. Where Guarini left Tasso's stanzas intact, he evidently intended them to be set as arias, whether rhythmic and melodious, ornate and madrigalian, or formulaic and recitational. Where he transformed them into *versi sciolti* he intended the new theatrical recitative styles, as is clearly indicated by the descriptions in both versions of the wordbook. These are not, however, the first verses that Guarini composed to be set to recitative, as we shall see later.

We have seen that the complex history of Guarini's last stage work extended well beyond the death of the poet. It was propelled beyond that point through the efforts and interests of Enzo Bentivoglio, whose political motives help place this musical spectacle in a broader context.

At the death of Alfonso d'Este in 1597, Pope Clement VIII refused to recognize the claim to the papal fief of Ferrara laid by Cesare d'Este, son of the late Duke Alfonso's illegitimate half-brother, and he consequently reincorporated the

[12] Rossi, *Guarini*, 156 n. 2, cites Venice, Biblioteca Nazionale Marciana, It. Cl. X, 79, letter G, p. 88. The same information is found among Zeno's annotations in Fontanini, *Biblioteca*, i. 484, note b: 'Chiama nuovi gl'intermezzi dell'*Idalba*, come se fossero diversi da quelli già fatti dal *Guarini* per l'*Alcéo*: ma quegli sono gli stessissimi trattone alcune mutazioni necessariamente fattevi, e forse a parere del sig. *Barotti da Girolamo Preti*.'

TABLE 8.1. Tasso's *Gerusalemme liberata* compared with Guarini's *Terzo intramezzo* from the *Alceo* playbook of 1613/14

Gerusalemme liberata, XVI. 21–2, 25, 32, 34, 40, 53–4, 59, 73		Guarini, *Terzo intramezzo* (1613/14)
L'uno di servitù, l'altra d'impero	1	
Si gloria, ella in sé stessa ed egli in lei.	2	
Rinaldo:		
—Volgi, —dicea—deh volgi—il cavaliero	3	Volgi Armida, deh volgi
—A me quegli occhi onde beata bèi,	4	A me quegli occhi, onde beata bei,
Chè son, se tu no 'l sai, ritratto vero	5	Che son ritratto vero,
De le bellezze tue gli incendi miei;	6	Delle bellezze tue gl'incendi miei,
La forma lor, la maraviglia a pieno	7	La forma lor, le meraviglie a pieno,
Più che il cristallo tuo mostra il mio seno.	8	Più, che 'l cristallo tuo, mostra il mio seno.
Deh! poi che sdegni me, com'egli è vago	9	Deh poi chè sdegni me, com'egli è vago
Mirar tu almen potessi il proprio volto;	10	Mirar tu almen potessi il proprio volto,
Chè il guardo tuo, ch'altrove non è pago,	11	Che 'l guardo tuo, ch'altrove non è pago
Gioirebbe felice in sè rivolto.	12	Gioirebbe felice in sé rivolto.
Non può specchio ritrar sì dolce imago,	13	Ne puo specchio ritrar sì dolce imago,
Nè in picciol vetro è un paradiso accolto:	14	Ne in picciol vetro è un Paradiso accolto,
Specchio t'è degno il cielo, e ne le stelle	15	Specchio t'è degno il Cielo, e nelle stelle
Puoi riguardar le tue sembianze belle.—	16	Puoi risguardar le tue sembianze belle.
Armida:		
Teneri sdegni, e placide e tranquille	17	Ben'è ragion cor mio,
Repulse, e cari vezzi, e liete paci,	18	Che tu faccia nel seno
Sorrise parolette, e dolci stille	19	Delle bellezze mie dolce conserva,
Di pianto, e sospir tronchi, e molli baci:	20	Perchè tanto son bella
Fuse tai cose tutte, e poscia unille	21	Quant'a te piaccio. Or posa
Ed al foco temprò di lente faci,	22	Mentr'io parte, e ritorno.
E ne formò quel sì mirabil cinto	23	Pegno in tanto de' miei desir veraci
Di ch'ella aveva il bel fianco succinto.	24	Ti sian questi dolcissimi miei baci.
Ubaldo incominciò parlando allora:	25	
Ubaldo:		
—Va l'Asia tutta e va l'Europa in guerra:	26	Và l'Asia, e tutta
Chiunque e pregio brama e Cristo adora	27	Seco l'Europa in guerra;
Travaglia in arme or ne la siria terra.	28	
Te solo, o figlio di Bertoldo, fuora	29	
Del mondo, in ozio, un breve angolo serra;	30	
Te sol de l'universo il moto nulla	31	Te sol dell'universo il moto nulla
Move, egregio campion d'una fanciulla.	32	Muove, egregio campion d'una fanciulla?
	33	Mira quì dentro, e guata,
	34	Se tu Rinaldo, o femmina sfacciata?
Tacque, e 'l nobil garzon restò per poco	35	
Spazio confuso e senza moto e voce.	36	
Rinaldo:		
Ma poi che diè vergogna a sdegno loco,	37	Perchè terra non t'apri, e non m'inghiotti?
Sdegno guerrier de la ragion feroce	38	Squarcio i panni di fuore,
E ch'al rossor del volto un novo foco	39	Come mi squarcia la vergogna il core.
Successe, che più avampa e che più coce,	40	
Squarciossi i vani fregi e quelle indegne	41	
Pompe, di servitù misera insegne.	42	
Armida:		
Forsennata gridava:—O tu che porte	43	Ove ne vai crudele? ah che tu porti
Teco parte di me, parte ne lassi,	44	Teco parte di me, parte ne lassi

Table 8.1. Cont'd

Gerusalemme liberata, xvi. 21–2, 25, 32, 34, 40, 53–4, 59, 73		Guarini, Terzo intramezzo (1613/14)
O prendi l'una o rendi l'altra, o morte	45	O prendi l'una, o rendi l'altra, o morte
Dà insieme ad ambe: arresta, arresta i passi,	46	Dà insieme ad ambe, arresta, arresta i passi.
. . . .		
		[Gerusalemme liberata, xvi. 47–50, follow.]
Rinaldo:		
Poi le risponde:—Armida, assai mi pesa	47	Armida assai mi pesa,
Di te; sì potess'io come il farei,	48	Ch'habbi per me, che senza pro t'ascolto,
Del mal concetto ardor l'anima accesa	49	Del mal concetto ardor l'anima accesa.
Sgombrarti: odii non son, nè rammento offesa;	50	
Nè serva tu, nè tu nemica sei.	51	
Errasti, è vero, e trapassasti i modi,	52	Errasti, è vero, e trapassasti i modi,
Ora gli amori essercitando, or gli odi;	53	Ora gli amori esercitando, or gli odi.
Ma che? son colpe umane e colpe usate:	54	Ma che? son colpe umane, e colpe usate:
Scuso la natia legge, il sesso e gli anni.	55	Scuso la natia legge, il sesso, e gli anni.
Anch'io parte fallii; s'a me pietate	56	
Negar non vuo', non sia ch'io te condanni.	57	
Fra le care memorie ed onorate	58	Tra le care memorie, ed onorate,
Mi sarai ne le gioie e ne gli affanni,	59	Mi sarai nelle gioie, e ne gli affanni,
Sarò tuo cavalier quanto concede	60	Sarò tuo Cavalier, quanto concede
La guerra d'Asia e con l'onor la fede.	61	La guerra d'Asia, e con l'honor la fede.
Armida:		
Vattene pur, crudel, con quella pace	62	Vattene pur crudele.
Che lasci a me; vattene, iniquo, omai.	63	
Me tosto ignudo spirto, ombra seguace	64	
Indivisibilmente a tergo avrai.	65	Ch'avrai me tosto a tergo
Nova Furia, co' serpi e con la face	66	Nuova furia; va pur, ch'ovunque andrai
Tanto t'agiterò quanto t'amai.	67	Tanto t'agiterò quanto t'amai.
. . . .	68	O spiriti infernali
	69	Mandatemi un de' vostri
	70	Più furiosi, e più veloci mostri.
—Io n'andrò pur,—dicea ella—anzi che l'armi	71	
De l'Oriente il re d'Egitto mova.	72	Caro Drago opportuno
Ritentar ciascun'arte e trasmutarmi	73	Levati a volo, e portmi in Soria
In ogni forma insolita mi giova,	74	Campo fatal della vendetta mia.
Trattar l'arco e la spada, e serva farmi	75	Andrò colà fra l'armi,
De' più potenti e concitargli a prova:	76	Tentarò, soffrirò, cangierò forma,
Pur che le mie vendette io veggia in parte,	77	Perchè le mie vendette io veggia in parte,
Il rispetto e l'onor stiasi in disparte.	78	Il rispetto, e l'onor stiasi in disparte.

duchy into the Papal States proper. When Cesare took compensatory possession of the imperial fiefs of Modena and Reggio, Ippolito Bentivoglio, his military commander, followed. This left Ippolito's brother Enzo at the head of the Bentivoglio family in Ferrara.[13]

---

[13] A general account of Enzo Bentivoglio's rise to prominence and of his patronage of the arts in this connection is found in Janet Southorn, *Power and Display in the Seventeenth Century: The Arts and Their Patrons in Modena and Ferrara* (Cambridge, 1988), 78–87. As mentioned in Ch. 2, a book by Dinko Fabris devoted to the musical patronage of Bentivoglio is soon to be published.

Although Enzo Bentivoglio was immediately made one of the twenty-seven counsellors of the first order under the new regime, his further rise to power began at the election of the Borghese pope, Paul V, in 1607. In that year, Enzo began procuring a very large number of Ferrarese art treasures for the gallery of Scipione Borghese, the new cardinal-nephew. Most of these formerly belonged to the Este family and were obtained, to a great extent, by fraud and deceit. This work continued for many years but was concentrated in the period 1607–9. Correspondence recently published shows that Enzo received, in direct exchange for these art works, papal permission to undertake the massive drainage of Ferrarese wetlands with funds raised from the sale of bonds.[14] As a reward for this undertaking, Enzo was given personal title to half the 11,581 hectares (28,605 acres) that were drained.[15] Almost as important, he held power over the eventual distribution and regulation of the remaining land. The diary of Marc'Antonio Guarini contains the believable accusation that Enzo Bentivoglio had begun to assert absolute power in these matters:

By order of Enzo Bentivoglio, it was announced to the interested parties in the Polesine of Ficarolo that on the twentieth of January he would be in the said Polesine in order to mark boundaries and to circumscribe that land that he claimed should be included in the drainage project. . . . But . . . he went there secretly . . . and put up boundary markers according to his own whim, enclosing in the said circumscription that land which had, for centuries, already been drained, . . . which occasioned loud complaints by the interested parties. But they will not be heard because of the interests of the Borghesi, to whom he has paid many thousands of scudi. . . . And he succeeded in doing as he pleases and wins out not as private citizen but as if he were absolute lord and *padrone*.[16]

This was certainly a good start towards establishing Bentivoglio hegemony in Ferrara, as the family had done earlier in Bologna. Furthermore, in 1607 Enzo's brother Guido was named papal nuncio to Flanders, and in 1608 Enzo was made Ferrarese ambassador to Rome.

---

[14] Giulio Marcon, Silvia Maddalo, and Giuliana Marcolini, 'Per una storia dell'esodo del patrimonio artistico ferrarese a Roma', in *Frescobaldi e il suo tempo nel quarto centenario della nascita* (Venice, 1983), 93–112.

[15] Aldo Berselli (ed.), *Storia della Emilia Romagna* (Bologna, 1977), 224–6.

[16] 10.iii.1611: Ferrarese diary of Marc'Antonio Guarini: 'D'ordine di Enzo Bentivoglio venne publicato à gli Interessati del Polezine di Ficaruolo che il vigesimo giorno di Genaio si ritrovarebbe nel detto Polezine per ponere i termini, et far il circondar di que tereni ch'egli pretendeva che dovessero esser compresi nella bonificatione. . . . Ma . . . vi andò furtivamente, . . . et pose i termini à voglia sua chiudendo nel d.o circondario que terreni che per centenaia d'anni erano bonificati . . . della qual cosa ne venne fatta gran doglianza da gli Interessati. Ma non vennero uditi, et questo per lo interesse che vi havevano gli Borghesi ai quali . . . gli e sominstrate molte migliaia dis scudi. . . . E gli riusci facendo à voglia sua quanto gli tornava bene non come privato cittadino ma come s'egli ne fusse stato assoluto signore, et padrone.' 'Diario descritto da Marc'Antonio Guarini di tutte le cose all suo tempo accadute nella nobilissima Città di Ferrara', I:MOe, α.H.2.17, 316–17.

Shortly after this sudden rise to prominence, Enzo Bentivoglio began producing a series of lavish carnival entertainments in Ferrara, outdoors for the general
public and indoors for visiting dignitaries.[17] The first of these of which some
trace has been found is the *Campo aperto*, a musical-dramatic mock-tournament
(*barriera*) performed 6 February 1610.[18] The wordbook for the spectacle includes
four extensive dialogues by Alessandro Guarini in *versi sciolti* specifically indicated to be sung—presumably, therefore, in recitative. For carnival of 1612, two
musical spectacles were to have been united under the conceit that the marriage
between Apollo and Bellona was to be celebrated with a pastorale in honour
of the poet-god and a tournament in tribute to the goddess of war. The printed
description includes details and text for the tournament only and mentions that
the pastorale, by Alessandro Guarini, was cancelled owing to the death of Duke
Vincenzo Gonzaga of Mantua, who had been the current prince of the Accademia
degl'Intrepidi, which was to have staged the drama.[19] Dinko Fabris has found a
diary entry specifying that the pastorale was to have been 'La Bonarella, pastoral
eclogue adorned by intermedi and a variety of machines'.[20] Tim Carter cites a
letter of 1627 that attributes the music of the cancelled intermedi to Sigismondo
d'India.[21] The published description of the events begins with the initial *invenzione*, essentially an extended intermedio or a short opera, in which the celebrations
for the marriage of Apollo and Bellona are planned, with extensive dialogue, once
again, in recitative. The libretto does not make clear who wrote the text of this
invenzione, but the diary of Marc'Antonio Guarini does:

In the expectation that the Duke of Mantua, who was Prince of the Accademia
dell'Intrepidi, and other cardinals would be in Ferrara for carnival, Enzo Bentivoglio prepared for them a very beautiful tournament on foot and horseback and other inventions
with artful machines, which represented some very delightful stories, earlier invented
by Cavalier Battista Guarini and by Alessandro, his son. But with all that happened after
the death of the said duke, and because the cardinals did not come, everything was performed in the presence of Cardinal Spinola, the papal legate, and Cardinal Pio, with the

---

[17] See Elena Povoledo, 'Ferrara', *Enciclopedia dello spettacolo*, v (Rome 1958), 182.

[18] *Del campo aperto mantenuto in Ferrara l'anno M.DC.X la notte di carnovale; dell'Illustriss. Signor Enzo
Bentivogli, mantenitore della querela, pubblicata nel sequente disfida da un'Araldo, à suon di trombe, il dì 6. febrario, su
'l corso, pieno di tutta la città mascherata, sontuosissima, e magnifica invenzione, inventore, ed autore il S. Alessandro
Guarini* (Ferrara: Baldini, 1610).

[19] *Relazione del torneo a cavallo, e a piedi, fatto questo carnevale in Ferrara per ordine dell'Accademia dove s'intende
il grande apparato, e la marvigliosa invenzione del Sig. Enzo Bentivogli nel comparire a mantenerlo con la descrizione delle
pompose livree de' cavalieri combattenti compilata dall'Arsiccio Accademico Ricreduto* [=Ottavio Magnanini] (Ferrara:
Baldini, 1612), 21.

[20] This reference to Alessandro Guarini's *La Bonarella* is found in the entry for 5 Mar. 1612 in the diary of
one C. Randoni. The full citation and transcription of the entry will be given in Dr Fabris's forthcoming book
on the artistic patronage of the Bentivoglio family.

[21] Tim Carter, 'Intriguing Laments: Sigismondo d'India, Claudio Monteverdi, and Dido *alla parmigiana* (1628)',
Journal of the American Musicological Society, 49 (1996), 32–69 at 35–7.

attendance of many visiting and local cavaliers, everything succeeding very happily, this day 5 [March 1612].[22]

Enzo Bentivoglio tried repeatedly to get Ippolita Recupito to come to Ferrara to sing in this *invenzione*, but she held back, Bentivoglio's correspondents citing the need for Cardinal Montalto's express command, Ippolita's pregnancy, and the fact that Adriana Basile from Mantua was going to be singing there (Letters 48–53). The letters fail to mention, however, that Ippolita was singing in the first version of Guarini's Rinaldo intermedi in Rome at the same time.

Under the circumstances, it is easy to interpret Enzo Bentivoglio's entertainments as *pubblicità* whose purpose was to help win legitimacy for his emerging power. And we can even understand the eventual form of Guarini's last stage work as propaganda with a specific message.

Tasso's *Gerusalemme liberata*, at one level, was intended to embroider a myth about the glorious origins of the house of Este, of which Rinaldo represents the founder. At a more general level, therefore, the poem embodied a patriotic view on Ferrara's past greatness. This is why, I suppose, Enzo Bentivoglio had the frieze of the Sala dei Giganti in his palace at Gualtieri decorated with scenes from *Gerusalemme liberata*.[23] For the central intermedi in his productions of 1613/14 and 1616, Bentivoglio chose the episodes encompassed in Guarini's last stage work, which culminate in Rinaldo's liberation from amorous bondage. The same theme is echoed in the other intermedi: the story of Jason and Medea, the struggle between Cynthia and Venus over the fate of Proserpina, and the lament of Alcina, which was added to the first intermedio for the 1616 production. All together, I take this as a thinly veiled endorsement of relative political independence for Ferrara supported through a moral and philosophical allegory, and my warrant for this interpretation is found in the 1613/14 wordbook itself.

In that wordbook, 'Arsiccio', who can be identified as Ottavio Magnanini (1574–1652), secretary of the Accademia degl'Intrepidi of Ferrara,[24] provided twenty-five long and erudite discourses commenting upon Guarini's intermedi. Here are their titles:

---

[22] 'La speranza che si haveva che il Duca di Mantova, ch'era Prencipe dell'Accademia dell'Intrepidi, et altri Card.li dovevero ritrovarsi à far il Carnevale in Ferrara cagionò ch'Enzo Bentivoglii preparasse loro un bellissimo torneo à piedi, et a cavalo, ed altre invenzioni di machine artificiose che rapresentavano alcune favole molto diletevole pria inventate dal Cavalier Battista Guarini, et d'Alessandro suo figliuolo. Ma con tutto che ne sucedesse poi la morte di detto Duca, et che gli Card.li non vi si ritrovassero, venne però il tutto rapresentato alla presenza del Card. Spinola legato, et del Card. Pio con l'intervenuto di molti Cavalieri forestieri, e paesani riuscendo il tutto con molta felicità questo di 5 d.o [marzo 1612].' I:MOe, α.H.2.17 (Ital. 387), 345.

[23] Anna Maria Fioravanti Baraldi, 'Pier Francesco Battistelli e l'impresa bentivolesca di Gualtieri in un carteggio', in *Frescobaldi e il suo tempo*, 161–72 at 166.

[24] Luigi Ughi, *Dizionario storico degli uomini illustri ferraresi* (Ferrara, 1804), ii. 46–7.

1. Introduction, in which he speaks to the spectators

About the Prologue

2. Why faith and hope are placed on guard at the Temple of Love

About the first intermedio

3. Concerning the origin of the intermedio
4. Concerning killing oneself

About the second intermedio

5. The conflict between the sensual and the rational parts

About the third intermedio

6. That either liberty or the reign of reason is lost
7. That reason regains the lost reign

About the fourth intermedio

8. Discourse in praise of virginity
9. Concerning the natural necessity of marriage
10. Concerning the moral necessity of marriage
11. Concerning the political necessity of marriage
12. That it makes sense to make allegories of fables with moral and philosophical materials
13. What is free will, and why it is so called
14. The opinions of some, who believed that [free will] should either be abolished or limited
15. These opinions refuted
16. Plato maintains that vices are voluntary
17. Neither heaven nor the stars extinguish or impair free will

About the fifth intermedio

18. Concerning the origin and necessity of counsel
19. Concerning the difficulty of giving counsel
20. Concerning the condition of the counsellor
21. Divine Providence is proven in the doctrine of Mercurio Trismegisto
22. Understood and taught by Plato
23. Recognized and professed by Aristotle
24. The same is confirmed in the testimony of the most illustrious poets
25. That the misfortunes that occur to good people do not disprove Providence[25]

---

[25] 'Tavola de' discorsi dell'Arsiccio sopra gl'Intramezzi del Cavalier Guarini.

1. Introduzione, dove si parla degli spettacoli.
Sopra il Prologo.
2. Perchè la Fede, e la Speranza sieno poste in guardia del Tempio d'Amore
Sopra il Primo Intramezzo.
3. Dell'origine dello'ntramezzo.

Discourse 12 argues for interpreting fables as moral and philosophical allegories, which is exactly what the other twenty-four discourses do. Their overall thrust is that, in those things that come under human control rather than under Divine Providence, man and his institutions should be guided by reason freely exercised in deliberative counsel rather than by fatalism. Applied to politics, this view would argue for secular rule by parliaments of the wisest, rather than by absolute monarchs, and for the absolute authority of the Church in religious matters. With reference to Ferrara at that time, it would mean that the city should be governed by the Consiglio, of which Enzo Bentivoglio was the dominant member. By this means the city might regain its past glory, symbolized by the Rinaldo episodes from *Gerusalemme liberata*.

4. Dell'amazzar se stesso.
   Sopra al Secondo Intramezzo.
5. Del contrasto tra la parte sensitiva, e la ragionevole.
   Sopra il Terzo Intramezzo.
6. Che la libertà, ò lo'mperio della ragione si perde.
7. Che la ragione racquista il perduto impero.
   Sopra il Quarto Intramezzo.
8. Discorso in lode della Virginità.
9. Della necessità naturale delle nozze.
10. Della necessità morale delle nozze.
11. Della necessità politica delle nozze.
12. Che si convegna allegorizzar le favole con materie Morali, e Filosofiche.
13. Che cosa sia libero arbitrio, e perchè così chiamato.
14. Opinioni d'alcuni, che d'ammortarlo, o raccorciarlo si credettero.
15. Le proposte opinioni si ribattono.
16. Platone vuole, che i vizi sieno volontari.
17. Ne il Cielo, ne le stelle spegnono, ne storpiano il libero arbitrio.
    Sopra il Quinto Intramezzo.
18. Dell'origine, e della necessità del Consiglio.
19. Della malagevolezza del consigliare.
20. Delle condizioni de' Consiglieri.
21. La Providenza di Dio si prova in dottrina di Mercurio Trismegisto.
22. Intesa, e insegnata da Platone.
23. Conosciuta, e confessata da Aristotile.
24. La medesima si conferma col testimonio de' Poeti piu illustri.
25. Che le sciagure, che avvengono a i buoni non tolgono la Providenza.'

9

Amor pudico

❧

THE climax of Cardinal Montalto's programme of musical patronage, as far as surviving sources permit us to know it, was certainly the production of *Amor pudico*, during the Carnival season of 1614, to celebrate the wedding of Prince Michele Peretti and Princess Anna Maria Cesi. Although the prince himself officially presented the entertainment, the project bears the marks of Montalto's patronage and politics. The cardinal's own musicians were the leading composers and performers in the production; Montalto's close friends and allies in the Borghese family provided most of the other musicians; the choice of poet, theatrical genre, scene designer, scenic emblems, and musical style reflect the cardinal's client relationship with Grand Duke Ferdinando de' Medici; the theme of the whole plot and the climatic scenic display paid homage to Montalto's current principal patron, Pope Paul V; and the spectacle was performed in the Palazzo della Cancelleria, Cardinal Montalto's official residence.

As far as we know, no musical spectacle so grandiose or stylistically current had previously been undertaken in Rome. Emilio de' Cavalieri's *Rappresentatione di anima et di corpo* of 1600, although sung throughout, had been performed by boys using a musical style devoid of both the virtuosic flair and dynamically charged recitative that was emerging in musical drama at that time, especially in Jacopo Peri's *Euridice* (Florence, 1600) and Claudio Monteverdi's *Orfeo* (Mantua, 1607) and *Arianna* (Mantua, 1608). The same can be said about Agostino Agazzari's moral pastorale *Eumelio* (Rome, 1606), which, even more than Cavalieri's *sacra rappresentazione*, relies on metrically regular recitation matched to a rhythmically active bass according to the dissonance-treatment norms of *prima prattica* counterpoint. Agazzari's 'recitatives' actually resemble the skeletal recitation-formula arie preserved in the Rocco Rodio anthology, the Bottegari lute book, and the lute intabulations of Vincenzo Galilei, the type of recitational style that Vincenzo Giustiniani said could still be heard in the 1620s in the *sacre rappresentazioni* performed by convent girls: with its syllabication predominantly in semiminims, its pervasively stepwise melodic motion, and repeated pitches reserved to mark the ends of poetic lines, it lacks interpretive inflection, speech-like rhythms, the sustained bass that would make *sprezzatura di canto* feasible, rapid monotone recitation to set off subordinate clauses, and *seconda prattica* dissonance treatment for expressive piquancy and syntactical tension.[1] If *Eumelio* was performed by students at the Jesuit Seminario Romano, as seems likely, the rendition heard in 1606 might not have differed markedly from the written version, since the ability to sing with *grazia* or sprezzatura and to improvise the kind of ornaments mentioned by Giustiniani and Doni was the relatively rare accomplishment of a few highly trained professionals at this time (Ch. 4)—the kind of professionals that Cardinal Montalto attracted to his circles through patronage.

The theme of Montalto's musical spectacle, 'chaste Love', may have seemed ironic to a cynical observer of Peretti family life. Michele's bride, actually his second wife, had been engaged to marry his son, Francesco, since 1609, when the boy was only 12 or 13 years old (Anna Maria's age is not known).[2] When, however, Michele's own child bride, Margherita, died in February 1613, the prince did not hesitate to marry his son's fiancée within the year: 13 November 1613. Francesco, by this time aged 16 or 17 years, whether out of heartbreak, humiliation, or obedience, left for Naples, where he entered the priesthood, never to return to Rome until after his father's death.[3] And it seems that Anna Maria entered a convent within a few years after the marriage. The evidence for this is the dedication of Paolo Quagliati's *Affetti amorosi spirituali* (Rome: Robletti, 1617) 'all'Ill.ma et Molto Rev.ma Suor Anna Maria Cesi, monaca di S.ta Lucia in Seleci'. The title-page of Quagliati's collection is adorned with a design that incorporates the three-tiered mountain topped by a tree, which are two elements in the Peretti coat of arms, and four crowns, possibly symbolizing the titles of Princess of Venafro, Marquise of Incisa, Countess of Celano, and Baroness of Piscina, which Anna Maria obtained by marriage. Quagliati's dedication says that 'these same compositions, first caressed and favoured by you, when, at times, it pleased you to sing them and to embellish them with your artistic ornaments and

---

[1] The term 'recitative' is used in descriptions of this musical pastorale by Margaret F. Johnson, 'Agazzari's *Eumelio*, a "Dramma Pastorale"', *Musical Quarterly*, 57 (1971), 491–505, and Carolyn Gianturco, 'Nuove considerazioni su *il tedio del recitativo* delle prime opere romane', *Rivista italiana di musicologia*, 18 (1982), 212–39. Johnson points out (p. 497) that Agazzari limits himself to only six different recitational formulas, which observation points to the historic roots of the style used, as suggested above. Gianturco argues (pp. 226–9) that, although much of the music in *Eumelio* is not in *stile recitativo*, only one solo segment, 'Sento al cor un dolce foco', can be considered an 'aria' in the later sense of being characterized by rhythmic, harmonic, and melodic regularity. The rest is 'mezz'aria' or 'arioso', according to her. I prefer to consider all the solo singing in *Eumelio* in the light of the recitational aria formulas as they are preserved for us in 16th-c. sources, only accidentally resembling later operatic recitatives, arias, and 'ariosi' from time to time and from a retrospective point of view.   [2] Chater, 'Musical Patronage', 185.

[3] Cametti, 'Chi era l'"Hippolita"', 115 n. 1. Francesco became a cardinal in 1641, as mentioned in Ch. 1.

sweetest voice, want no other protection than yours'.[4] Much later, in 1640, Pietro Paulo Sabbatini likewise praised Anna Maria Cesi as a singer in dedicating to her his *Canzoni spirituali ad una, a due, et a tre voci . . . libro secondo, opera decimaterza* (Rome: Grignani, 1640), which has led two recent researchers to hypothesize that Pietro Della Valle had Anna Maria in mind when, in the same year (1640), he praised the singing of the nuns of Rome and added, in particular, 'Everyone knows how much renown the nun at Santa Lucia in Selice has'.[5] Not surprisingly, Prince Michele's marriage with Anna Maria did not produce offspring. As a result the Peretti were eventually forced to repay the dowry of 200,000 scudi to the Cesi family.[6] Cardinal Montalto's wedding gift of a villa in Frascati, which he bought on 21 April 1614 from the Cardinal of Sant'Eusebio for 20,000 scudi,[7] remained with Michele.

The story portrayed in *Amor pudico* is, of course, quite different from reality. It is a political allegory in large part. In the beginning, Venus returns to earth and finds ancient Rome in ruins. Love reveals to her his intention to redeem his bad reputation (for causing mischief with the gods) by inspiring chaste love in two worthy mortal hearts. Venus opposes this plan as futile where death holds sway. Anteros, the second son of Venus, however, offers Love his help. Cupid then discards his arrows, which had in the past inspired only mischievous and impure infatuation. Venus, angered by her sons' defiance, threatens Jove's discipline. Love and Anteros nevertheless call down Hymen, the god of marriage. Rome, personified, reciprocates for the honour of the gods' visit and for Love's purification by changing her outward aspect from ancient ruins to modern splendour in a spectacular scenic transformation. Here in modern Rome, Love, Hymen, and their followers—Delight, Laughter, Play, Beauty, Dance, and Youth—celebrate the joys of chaste love in dance and chorus.

For the second act, the scene is set in heaven. Venus enlists the aid of Mars, Sun, Moon, and Mercury in her opposition to Love's plan. While she attempts to pursuade Jove to join her effort, Fame arises from earth to describe the principal glory of modern Rome: the Vatican (recently brought to completion by the Borghese pope, Paul V). Fame reports that Love has been embraced by Cesi and Peretti in pure ardour, amidst rejoicing. Jove then decides to send Mercury to persuade Love to return to heaven. At the end of the act, a chorus of Medicean

---

[4] 'che gli stessi componimenti accarezzati prima, & favoriti da lei, quando tal volta s'è compiaciuta cantarli, & abbellirli con le sue artificiose maniere, & soavissima voce; altra protettione non bramano, che la sua'.

[5] 'La monaca di Santa Lucia in Silice ognun sa di quanta fama sia.' Pietro Della Valle, *Della musica dell'età nostra*, in Solerti, *L'origine del melodramma*, 166. The connection with Anna Maria Cesi is made by Susan C. Cook and Thomasin K. LaMay, *Virtuose in Italy, 1600–1640: A Reference Guide* (New York, 1984), 143.

[6] Nicola Ratti, *Della famiglia Sforza* (Rome: Il Salamoni, 1794), ii. 353.

[7] I:Ras, Archivio Sforza-Cesarini, I* parte (etichetta rettangolare), vol. 61, 'Libro 2.do dell'istrumenti del S.r Card.l Montalto dal 1610 al 1620', fos. 46–50.

Stars (the four moons of Jupiter recently discovered by Galileo Galilei) implore
Love to return to heaven and to obey the commands of the supreme god.

The next act is set again in modern Rome, where Mercury finds a chorus celebrating chaste love. He argues unsuccessfully with Love, who refuses to return to
heaven. In the course of this argument, the beauties, charms, and virtues of the bride
are extolled, and Love points out that *Amor* spelt backwards is *Roma*. Mercury
then turns to the underworld for help, assisted by another visible mutation of the
scene. Here Mercury finds Anger, the worst enemy of Love. But in the end Love
overcomes Anger and inspires even the monsters of the inferno to dance and sing.

The fourth act returns to the setting of modern Rome. In appreciation for
having seen such virtue, beauty, glory, and honour on earth, Love takes Rome
to hear the great spirits of the past happily singing in the Elysian Fields, to which
location the scene abruptly changes. Here Love and Rome encounter Dante's
Beatrice and Ariosto's Orlando. Dante, Petrarch, Ariosto, Tasso, Sannazzaro, and
Anguillara sing new versions of their most famous verses, which are transformed through paraphrase into praises of the bride (see Table 9.1). They are seconded by a chorus of modern poets along with Eternity, while the Peretti arms
appear in the sky. Hymen invites the wedding couple to lead a dance.

The scene in the last act is the ocean. To celebrate the rebirth of Rome
through Love, Sun (Apollo), Golden Age, and the nine muses are called down
from heaven. Venus, too, descends to offer her blessings; Neptune rises from the
sea, and Amphitrite appears. Finally Jove, from on high, approves and is seconded
by a chorus of gods. Having accomplished his purpose, Love agrees to return to
heaven. All join in celebrating the return to Rome of the Golden Age.

In the context of court spectacle of the period, it is rather to be assumed that
the scenario of *Amor pudico* was intended allegorically, at least to some extent.[8]
Certainly the scenic theme of the first act—the ruins of ancient Rome transformed
into modern splendour—is, in part, a deliberate reference to the programme of
urban renewal of Rome that was the outstanding feature of the pontificates of
both Sixtus V, great-uncle of Cardinal Montalto and Prince Michele Peretti, and
the current Borghese pope, Paul V, former protégé and current patron of Cardinal
Montalto,[9] as is made explicit in Romolo Paradiso's description of the costumes
and stage effects:

---

[8] A recent exponent of this assumption, Strong, *Art and Power*, gives some detailed interpretation of
late 16th-c. Medici court pageantry. The symbolism of early Florentine opera scenarios and musical style is
treated further in my chapter 'Florence: Musical Spectacle and Drama, 1570–1650', in Curtis Price (ed.), *The
Early Baroque Era from the Late 16th Century to the 1660s* (Music and Society, ed. Stanley Sadie; New York,
1993), 121–45.

[9] Cardinal Montalto's close alliance with the then-current Cardinal-nephew of the pope, Scipione Borghese, has been mentioned frequently in earlier chapters. Beside the scenic theme of Rome's modern renewal
and the prominent use of Borghese family musicians in the performance, the libretto of *Amor pudico* includes
a third homage: it was dedicated to Cardinal Borghese by the author, Jacopo Cicognini.

TABLE 9.1. The words of the poets in Act IV of *Amor pudico* and their models

---

Dante

La gloria di colui, che 'l tutto muove,
Con lo suo raggio penetra, e risplende
In una parte più, e meno altrove.
Ne lo tuo volto real Donna scende
Più ch'in fattura, ch'uscisse giamai
Da quel Fattor, che sol se stesso intende.
Talche i begli occhi, onde superba vai,
Potriano in terra, se mancasse il giorno,
Dar luce al mondo con suoi raggi gai.
L'anime stanno à tua beltade intorno,
Come l'api davanti à lor Regina:
Però che porti ne lo viso adorno
La maestà, cui tutto 'l mondo inchina.

Paradiso, I, ll. 1–12

La gloria di colui che tutto move
Per l'universo penetra, e risplende
In una parte più e meno altrove.
Nel ciel che più della sua luce prende
Fu'io, e vidi cose che ridire
Né sa né può chi di là su discende;
Perché appressando sé al suo disire,
Nostro intelletto si profonda tanto,
Che dietro la memoria non può ire.
Veramente quant'io del regno santo
Nella mia mente potei far tesoro,
Sarà ora materia del mio canto.

Petrarch

Anima bella, che in quel sen ti stai,
E di te stessa altera mente godi,
E con atti soavi, e dolci modi
Giri di quei begli occhi i chiari rai:
In sì begli anni, io pur lieto mirai
Roma gioir de' tuoi beati nodi,
E rinovarsi in te l'altere lodi,
Che un tempo amando del mio Sol cantai.
Ma pianse Citerea, che nuova stella
Scorse qua giù, che 'l nobel vanto fura
A l'amorosa sua chiara facella.
Al nascer tuo conobbe alta ventura
Il mondo, e parve ogni beltà men bella:
E si stupì de l'opra su Natura.

Sonnet 305

Anima bella da quel nodo sciolta,
Che più bel mai non seppe ordir natura,
Pon dal ciel mente a la mia vita oscura
Da sì lieti pensieri a pianger volta.
La falsa opinion del cor s'è tolta,
Che mi fece alcun tempo acerba, e dura
Tua dolce vista: omai tutta secura
Volgi a me gli occhi, e i miei sospiri ascolta.
Mira 'l gran sasso, donde Sorga nasce,
E vedra'vi un, che sol tra l'erbe, e l'acque
Di tua memoria, e di dolor si pasce.
Ove giace 'l tuo albergo, e dove nacque
Il nostro amor, vo' ch'abbandoni, e lasce,
Per non veder ne' tuoi quel, ch'a te spiacque.

Ariosto

Le Donne, i Cavalier, l'armi, e gli amori
Io già cantai con sì felice canto,
Che, cinto il crin di sempre verdi allori,
Lieto me'n vivo à i più famosi accanto.
Hor dirò come Amor stringa due cori'
Nel laccio d'Himeneo pudicò, e santo;
Se i versi spira a questa tromba mia
La beltà, la virtù d'ANNA MARIA.

Orlando furioso, I. i

Le Donne, i Cavallier, l'arme, gli amori,
Le cortesie, l'audaci imprese io canto;
Che furo al tempo, che passaro i Mori
D'Africa il mare, e in Francia nocquer tanto
Seguendo l'ire, e i giovenil furori
D'Agramante lor Re; che si diè vanto
Di vendicar la morte di Troiano
Sopra Re Carlo Imperator Romano.

Tasso

O Diva tu, che di caduchi allori
Non circondi la fronte in Helicona,
Ma cinto il biondo crin di gemme, e d'ori
Hai di stelle terrene alta corona?
Tu spira al petto mio soavi ardori,
Ond'il Tebro felice hoggi risuona;
E questa degli Heroi famosa tromba
Faccia quella tacer, ch'hoggi rimbomba.

Gerusalemme liberata, I. ii

O Musa, tu che di caduchi allori
Non circondi la fronte in Elicona,
Ma su nel cielo infra i beati cori
Hai di stelle immortali aurea corona,
Tu spira al petto mio celesti ardori,
Tu rischiara il mio canto, e tu perdona
S'intesso fregi al ver, s'adorno in parte
D'altri diletti, che de' tuoi, le carte.

Sannazzaro

Questi spirti gentil di te ragionano,
I tuoi spiegando ogn'hor pregi ammirabili;
Onde'i superbi colli hoggi risuonano.
Non son le glorie tue fugaci, e labili,
Né per volar de gli anni al Tempo cedono;

Arcadia, end of scene 1

Quest'alberi di lei sempre ragionano;
Et ne le scorse scritta la dimostrano:
Ch'a pianger spesso, e a cantar mi spronano,
Per lei li tori, & le arìeti giostrano.
. . . .

TABLE 9.1. Cont'd

Poiché splendono in te virtù durabili.
Strali d'invida sorte unqua non fiedono
La bellezza de l'alma, e in te rimirasi
Gratia, che i sommi Dei la sù possiedono.
Per te, Donna reale, al Cielo aspirasi,
E gli affetti terreni al tutto mancano,
E del tuo Sol, ch'à noi benigno girasi,
I Cigni di cantar mai non si stancano.

Anguillara	Le metamorfosi di Ovidio ridotte da Gio. Andrea Dall'Anguillara in ottava rima, Libro primo, stanza 3
Pria che 'l ciel fosse, il mar, la terra, e 'l foco,	Pria che 'l ciel fosse, il mar, la terra, e 'l foco
E distinti dal ciel la terra, e 'l mare,	Era il foco, la terra, il cielo, e 'l mare:
Era ne l'alta Idea quel casto foco,	Ma 'l mar vendeva il ciel, la terra, e 'l foco,
Che difonde di gratie un'ampio mare:	Deforme il foco, il ciel, la terra, e 'l mare
Poi nacque in terra l'impudico foco,	Che ivi era e terra, e cielo, e mare, e foco;
Ch'Amore ha spento in sì felice Mare,	Dove era e ciel, e terra, e foco, e mare:
E svegliando ne i cor beato foco,	La terra, il foco, e 'l mare era nel cielo;
Nel ciel muove d'invidia un dolce foco	nel mar, nel foco, e ne la terra il cielo.

It was recognized by everyone that [the scene] was the new Rome, which seemed all the more beautiful because, shortly before, it was seen miserable and deformed. It [Rome] was born under the guidance of [Emperor] Octavian, and it was seen to be gloriously reborn, and raised from the ruins under which it was buried, by the liberating hand of Sixtus V and then regenerated through the magnanimity of the present Most Holy Pontiff [Paul V]. . . . and in the background the front of the Temple of the Vatican [S. Pietro] with the inscription and arms of His Holiness [Paul V] was shown in all its beauty.[10]

The scenery and description, then, tell us that the revival of modern Rome is the result of the initiatives of Sixtus V and Paul V and is, therefore, a symbol of the alliance between the Peretti and Borghese families, whose arrivals in Rome, like those of Love and Hymen, were the cause of this renewal.

The other family symbols in *Amor pudico* are the four Medicean Stars in the second act:

Surrounding [Jove] were four boys, like bodyguards, with silver armour and golden helmets upon each of which, amidst many azure feathers, was mounted a star. I was told that these four stars represented those that have the name of the Most Serene House of the Highnesses of [Florence]. It seems to me that Sig. Cicognini has not only demonstrated

---

[10] 'Fù conosciuta da tutti esser la nuova Roma; la quale parve altrettanto più bella, quanto poco innanzi si era veduta miserabile, e difformata: e quale a punto già nacque sotto la cura di Ottaviano; e qual si vede gloriosamente rinata, e sollevata dalle ruine, ove era sepolta, e da mano liberatrice di SISTO V, e rigenerata poi dalla magnanimità del presente Santissimo PONTEFICE . . . e nel luogo più ultimo facea mostra delle sue bellezze la parte anteriore del Tempio del Vaticana con l'iscrittione, & arma di Sua Beatitudine'; Paradiso, *Copia d'una lettera*, 18–20.

devotion towards his Prince but also the affection that he feels for Sig. Galileo, who was the first observer of the said stars.[11]

The four MEDICEAN STARS, with the sweetness that others said or believed of the Sirens of Heaven, sang of the power of Jove, which extends even over the power of Love.[12]

It seems likely that the Medicean Stars are attributes intended to identify Jove as the allegorical symbol of Grand Duke Ferdinando de' Medici, who was, after all, the most powerful secular sovereign ruler in Italy. And if Jove represents Ferdinando de' Medici, then the allegory emerges rather clearly. The alliance between Cardinal Montalto and the Borghese family was opposed at first by the Grand Duke (this is true, as we have seen in Ch. 3) because of the intervention of some fourth party (Venus). In the end Jove (the Grand Duke) is persuaded to favour the alliance by a series of deistic endorsements, beginning with that of Apollo, who promises to 'spread sweet song among the muses'.[13] Apollo, son of Jove, who invokes the muses, symbols of the fine arts and humanistic learning, and who strikes from afar with his bow, may well represent Cardinal Montalto himself, renowned patron of musicians, artists, and scholars, formidable hunter, and successor to Ferdinando de' Medici as prime mover in the Sacred College.[14] Be that as it may, it is notable that the crucial turning-point in the plot is the descent of this musician-god, symbol of arts patronage.[15] The sun god's descent to earth means the arrival of a new Golden Age, which, personified, sings another capitolo and a duet with Apollo with choral response. The new Golden Age, of course, implies some similarity with the earlier one, which was evoked in the previous act by the famous poets of the past, who endorsed the union wrought by chaste Love.

[11] 'Attorno a lui erano quattro Giovanetti, a guisa di custodi, con armature d'argento, & elementi dorati; da quali tra molti pennacchi di color turchino sorgeva in ciascuno per cimiere una stella. Fummi detto, che questi quattro, quelle stelle rappresentavano, le quali hanno il nome dalla Serenissima Casa di coteste Altezze. Parmi, che in ciò il Sig. Cicognino habbia non solo mostrato devotione verso il suo Principe; ma anco l'affettion, che porta al Sig. Galileo, che di dette Stelle è stato il primo osservatore'; Paradiso, *Copia d'una lettera*, 27–8.

[12] 'Le quattro STELLE MEDICEE, con quella soavità, ch'altri disse, o credè delle Sirene del Cielo, cantarono del poter di Giove; il qual si stende ancor sopra la podestà di Amore'; Paradiso, *Copia d'una lettera*, 30.

[13] 'Spiegarò tra le Muse il dolce canto' is the last line of Apollo's capitolo, p. 35 in the libretto. The stage direction above this text says 'Sole [i.e. Apollo] scendendo dal Cielo'.

[14] According to Vincenzo Giustiniani; see Ch. 3.

[15] This conceit is similar to the one ruling the intermedi performed with *La pellegrina* for Ferdinando de' Medici's wedding of 1589: the first five intermedi retell the ancient myths of music's power in the first Golden Age of Greek antiquity; the last depicts the return of the gods, at the onset of a new Golden Age, with their gifts of song and dance, in answer to Ferdinando's entreaties. In other words, Ferdinando's encouragement of a new musical style (the one sought by the Camerata of Giovanni Bardi, original ideator of the intermedi), inspired by descriptions of ancient Greek music, is presented as a symbol of cultural and political renewal. A somewhat similar reference to the symbolic importance of arts (especially musical) patronage is found in the scenarios of the first two Florentine operas, *Dafne* (1597) and *Euridice* (1600), whose musician-god protagonists, Apollo and Orpheus, respectively, complete the cycle of life, death, and rebirth with an eternally enduring monument of artistic glory. For further on this argument, see Hill, 'Florence: Musical Spectacle and Drama, 1570–1650'.

When the chorus of the muses finally arrives, having been invoked earlier by Apollo, only the two singers among them are given their own stanzas of ottava rima. Clio, symbol of history who sings of glory, declares:

> Formerly, the celebrated stories of invincible warriors
> I made to resound among mortal men;
> Now pious soldiers and religious kings
> Have obscured and extinguished those ancient glories.
> Today Rome praises another CAMILLO
> Who has made her happy and reborn
> While likewise praising the valiant fame
> Of the new SCIPIO with pride.[16]

Her references are, of course, to Camillo Borghese, who was Pope Paul V, and Cardinal Scipione Borghese, the pope's nephew. And Calliope, muse of poetry, who sings her verses with a beautiful voice, praises the beauty of the bride.

Whether or not we can reliably identify Venus or Anger and his monsters of the inferno, who are eventually charmed by music (are they the Aldobrandini and other erstwhile enemies?), the allegory of *Amor pudico* is quite clearly a celebration of the restored triangular alliance between the Peretti, Borghese, and Medici families. It has precious little to do with the unlucky bride or her family.

The libretto calls *Amor pudico* a 'festino, e balli', but the *avvisi* sent from Rome to Urbino mention dancing between the acts of the spectacle only at its second performance, when a large number of ladies were included among the guests.[17] The description of the first performance in the *avviso* of 8 February also implies a different order of scenes than is preserved in the known libretti, and it raises some interesting questions of generic terminology:

[16]
> 'Già di Guerrieri invitti i chiari fregi
> Fei risonar tra la caduca gente,
> Hor pietosi Guerrieri, e sacri Regi
> L'antiche glorie hanno oscurate, e spente,
> Roma d'altro CAMILLO hoggi si pregi,
> Fatta per lui felice, e rinascente,
> Né prezzando d'altrui fama guerriera,
> Di nuovo SCIPIO homai se 'n vada altera.'

[17] I:Rvat, Urb. Lat. 1082, fos. 74^{r-v} and 80^r–81^r, which refer to the first performance of 5 Feb., do not mention dancing, which, however, is described with reference to the second performance on 9 Feb. on fos. 101^{r-v} and 106^v–107^r. A thrid performance on 11 Feb. is mentioned only briefly on fo. 101^v. See Chater, 'Musical Patronage', 209–10. I have seen two editions of the libretto for *Amor pudico*: the one in a smaller format, bound together with Romolo Paradiso, *Copia un'una lettera . . . con la quale dà avviso dell'apparato, e grandezza, con che si è rappresentato il festino dell'Eccellentiss. Sig. Principe Peretti* (Rome: Girolamo Discepolo, 1614), is presumably the later of the two (I:Fn, Magl. 3.E.8.239, and I:Fn, Palat. 12.7.5.40); the other, in a larger format and lacking the dedication to Cardinal Borghese and the accompanying letter by Paradiso, is presumably the earlier (I:Fn, Magl. Misc. 70.20). Both editions, however, mention dancing by 'Dame e Cavalieri' at the close of each act. Although Chater, in n. 177 (p. 210), says there were three editions of the libretto for *Amor pudico*, he describes only the 'third', which contains the dedication and is bound with Paradiso's *Copia d'una lettera*.

Wednesday evening in the hall of the Chancellery the Prince Peretti's *commedia* in five acts (written by the Florentine poet Cicognini), which is like a *trionfo* of chaste Love, was sung for the first time with costumes and intermedi. And the intermedi are born of the theme of the *commedia* itself. The first [intermedio] was a ball ordered by Love, who sent, for the purpose, Laughter and Play to celebrate the wedding of the said prince. The second was Rome destroyed, who, throwing off her ancient apparel, takes on new raiments, and likewise the scene changes from the antiquities and ruins of ancient buildings to the most beautiful construction of modern ones. In the third, Venus angered, meaning lascivious love, having been scorned by chaste Love, gathers the friendly gods to avenge herself. In the fourth the Elysian Fields are portrayed, from which emerge the Italian poets with laurels, and each one of them sings in the style of his poetry, applauding the said marriage. And in the fifth there appear a sea and a boat that passes along the sea with the muses, and these, too, sing in praise of the marriage. And in the end there arrive on a cloud two lady singers representing Thetis and placated Venus, made friendly with chaste Love. The costumes, intermedi, proportion, and quality of the musicians and the actors turned out to be something singular and worthy of being seen, since in attendance were Cardinals Bandini and Bevilacqua and many prelates and members of cardinals' households, Princess Peretti with Duchesses Cesarini and Cere, and other ladies of her court.[18]

The five intermedi described in this *avviso* correspond to portions of the second part of the first act, the first part of the first act, the second act, the fourth act, and the fifth act, respectively, of the libretti. And within these acts, the 'intermedi', which 'are born of the theme of the *commedia* itself', seem to consist more precisely of the last episode or scenic effect of each act, rather than something outside the scenario of *Amor pudico* as it appears in the printed libretto. The 'intermedi' are, therefore, built into the opera, and there does not seem to have been a spoken play for which these acts were, at first, used as intermedi. Indeed, according to this *avviso*, the entire *commedia* was sung. Thus, when the principal composer of *Amor pudico*, Cesare Marotta, writes about his current project on 17

---

[18] 'Mercorì sera nella sala della Cancelleria fù per la p.a volta con habiti et intermedij cantata la comedia del Prencipe Peretti opera del Cicognino poeta fiorentino di 5. atti che è quasi un trionfo d'amor pudico et dal tenore della comedia istessa nascono gl'intermedij che fecero primo un ballo ordinato d'amore che manda perciò il riso et il giuoco per allegrezza delle nozze di detto prencipe, 2° Roma destrutta che gettando gl'habiti vecchi prende i nuovi et si cambia anco la sciena d'anticaglie et ruina d'edifitij antichi et appariscono le bellissime fabricche de moderni, 3° Venere sdegnata significando amor lascivo per esser sprezzata da Amor pudico, congrega le deità amiche per vendicarsi, 4° si rappresentano i Campi elisi di dove escono li poeti italiani con la laurea et cantarono ciascuno nella qualità del suo poema, applaudendo a detto matrimonio, et nel 5° apparisce un mare et una nave che passa il mare con le Muse che ancor esse cantorono in lode del matrimonio et in fine in una nuvola comparvero due dame cantatrici representanti Teti et Venere placata et fatto amico d'Amor pudico, essendo gli habiti, gl'intermedij et la proportione et bontà de musici et rectanti reuscita cosa singolare et degna di esser veduta, essendovi intervenuti li card.li Bandini et Bevilacqua et molti prelati et fam.ri di card.li, Pri*n*cipessa Peretti con la Duchessa Cesarina et Cere et altre dame familiari di casa.' *Avviso* of 8 Feb. 1614 (I:Rvat, Urb. lat. 1082, fo. 74^{r-v}), transcribed by Orbaan, *Documenti sul barocco in Roma*, 214–15, adjusted in some details to conform better to the manuscript.

December 1613, he says: 'I am so busy, having to compose so many *intermezzi* for the wedding of the prince' (Letter 72). And on 3 March 1614 he refers to his composition as *tramezzi*, a variant of the same word (Letter 74). It seems natural enough that a new genre would be called by the name of an older but closely related form, and thus these references raise the question whether the *commedie* with intermedi *Psiche* (1611) and *Gerusalemme liberata* (1612) were not also entirely sung dramatizations with built-in intermedi like *Amor pudico*.

The *avvisi* from Rome actually contain another complete description of the first performance of *Amor pudico*, which makes some of these points clearer:

In the hall of the Chancellery, Wednesday [5 February], the story that was planned in honour of Prince Peretti's wedding was acted for the first time, as was reported, with very extensive preparation and royal expenditure for all these days. The subject was the descent of the god of love from heaven to earth; having fallen vehemently in love with it, and not caring therefore ever to return above whence he departed, all the other gods appeared in heaven, even down to Pluto, the god of the underworld, begging him and threatening him so he would leave this lower and earthly dwelling place. All the action of it was contained in five scenes, and all the actors, dressed in royal garb, were made to speak in music (*parlare in aria musicale*). Between the scenes, various devices were displayed as intermedi, which stupified the spectators. Among others there were ancient Rome, Rome destroyed, and another [Rome] restored, which is the modern [Rome], the Elysian Fields, and a lake with Charon's boat, full of various and excellent musical performances and instruments. And since the same story is to be acted another time with dancing accompanying the intermedi, they say that this will follow tomorrow and that most of the cardinals, ambassadors of princes, and leading ladies of the city will be invited.[19]

Likewise, the second performance of 9 February is reported twice in the *avvisi*.[20] In the first of them, *Amor pudico* is described as a 'veglia alla fiorentina', a term

---

[19] 'Nella sala della Cancellaria mercordi fù rappresentata per la p.a volta la favola che come si avvisò con grand.mo studio, et spesa reale, tutti questi giorni si è meditata in honore delle Nozze del Sig.r Principe Peretti il cui soggetto è stato il discenso del Dio d'amore dal cielo in terra della quale inamoratosi fieramente ne curandosi per cio di ritornare più la su donde si era partito comparivano in cielo tutti li altri dei, et fino à Plutone dio dell'inferno pregandolo et minacciandolo accio lasciasse questa inferiore et terrestre habitatione, tutte le quali attioni si compirno in cinque scene facendosi parlare in aria musicale tutti l'interlocutori vestiti di vesti reali, tra li quali scene si fecero anco apparire varij artificij per intermedij che facevano stupire le spettatori, essendo tra li altre cose apparsi Roma antica Roma distrutta, et per un altra restaurata che è la moderna, li campi elisij et un pelago con la barca di Caronte piena di vari et eccellenti musiche et instrumenti et dovendosi l'istessa favola un altra volta rappresentare con il ballo accompagnato alli intermedij si dice che q.sto seguira dimani, et che vi saranno invitati la maggior parte di card.li, amb.ri di principi et dame principali di questa città.' I:Rvat, Urb. Lat. 1082, fos. 80ᵛ–81ʳ.

[20] I:Rvat, Urb. lat. 1082, fo. 101ʳ⁻ᵛ: 'La Dom.ca sera [9 febbraio] poco avanti l'Avemaria si cominciò di nuova di recitare la Comedia, ò sia una veglia alla fiorentina del Principe Peretti con l'intervento dell'Ambasciatore et Ambasciatrice di Spagna, oltre alcuni di questi Ill.mi trà quali li Card.li Zappata et Borgia, Borghese, et alcune sue Creature, et di Montalto et li Baroni et li soliti romani parenti, et amici trà quali particolarm.te il Duca di Bracciano et il Principe di Sulmona et oltre a 70 Dame, li Ambasciatori di Venetia, et Malta, Duch.a d'Urbino, et altri.

used to describe a long entertainment lasting well into the night, that is, a vigil. Hence, each of the five acts of *Amor pudico* is called an 'hora'.

The *veglia* belongs to a family of musical spectacles that includes the *mascherata*, *trionfo*, *festa da ballo*, *barriera*, mock naval battle, *intermedi*, and several others, all of which use extensive allegorical scenery, props, costumes, and pantomime in order to establish a narrative or dramatic context for pieces of vocal music, which are separated from one another by action or scenic transformation accompanied by instrumental interludes or (relative) silence. Like the *veglia*, these other related types of musical spectacle progress through a series of scenes or tableaux that can either narrate a single story, relate to a single allegorical or mythological theme, comment on successive events in a play, or have no evident unifying principle at all. In all of them, some complementary activity intervenes between the scenes, either dancing (in the *mascherata*, *festa da ballo*, and *veglia*), mock combat (in the *barriera* and naval battle), spoken drama (in the case of *intermedi*), or other elements of pageantry (in the case of the *trionfo*). These kinds of musical spectacle gradually lost their central position in court culture with the spread of recitative-style singing (in opera, serenade, cantata, and oratorio), which provided a purely musical–poetic means of establishing the narrative or dramatic context for the textual and affective content of metrical musical numbers. In this respect, the early seventeenth century was a period of transition, in which operas retained some narrative features of staging, while the older forms of musical spectacle absorbed recitative for the same purpose.

The Florentine poet Jacopo Cicognini (1577–1633), who wrote the libretto of *Amor pudico*, had collaborated on another one of those older types of musical spectacle, a *barriera*, for the previous carnival, of 1613, at the Tuscan Grand Ducal court in Florence.[21] The general scheme of a *barriera* is always the same: one knight, the *mantenitore* (sometimes more than one), proclaims his view or opinion on some

La Comedia fù in tutto simile à quanto se ne scrisse con li passati; vi furno di più nell'occorrenza dell' Intermedij li balletti de S.ri et Dame che vi erano presenti, et nel fine del 4.o Atto fù data una collatione di confetture condite et paste di Genova con altre cose esquisite (portata dall'istesso *Principe* Peretti et Francesco suo fig.lo, et figli minori del Duca di Bracciano, et altri Card.i à parata superba) havendone le Dame, et sue Damigelle, et Matrone magnato, et immanicato per la bondanza, et moltitudine delle confetture, et prontezza, et liberalità con la q*ua*le gl'erano presentati avanti, et oltre di ciò li fù poi à ciascuna Dama mandato sino à Casa un regalo nobilissimo arrivando in tutto la spesa circa à 3 [mila?] sc.

Et perche la Comedia durò fino alle 7 hore di notte D. Fran.co Peretti ritenne seco à Cena il *Principe* di Sulmona, et li 4 figli del Duca di Bracciano avendovi rimasto anco à dormire, et la mattina à pranzo il S. *Principe* Sulmona, et havendosi il med.o D. Francesco Peretti levato lo scorruccio che portava per esser finito l'anno della morte della S.ra *Principe*essa sua madre.'

These elements are repeated in a second report of the 9 Feb. performance in I:Rvat, Urb. lat. 1082, fos. 106^v–107^r.

[21] The details are preserved in the *Descrizzione della barriera e della mascherata fatte in Firenze a' XVII et a' XIX di febbraio 1612* [1613 modern style] *al serenissimo signor prencipe d'Urbino* (Florence: Sermartelli, 1613), and in the court diary of Cesare Tinghi, partially transcribed by Solerti, *Musica, ballo e drammatica*, 69–72.

courtly subject (the *disfida*) and challenges all who disagree to (mock) combat. Thus, in the middle of a ball at the Pitti Palace honouring the Prince of Urbino on 3 February 1613, a herald proclaimed that Love, disturbed by lovers' complaints and lamentations, has banished from his realm Venus, his mother, and all the Passions born of her, so that he might live in tranquillity. To this end, he is leaving Cyprus and coming to establish his empire in Tuscany, where the Cavalier Fidamante (The Knight Faithful Lover) and the Cavalier dell'immortale Ardore (The Knight of Undying Ardour) will sustain his edict by erecting a temple and two fortresses, which they will defend against all comers. On the announced evening of 17 February, in the great hall of the *commedie* above the Uffizi, Fame began this *barriera* by descending on a cloud while singing an elaboration of the *disfida* in forty-eight *versi sciolti*, presumably set in a recitative style. A list was displayed containing the names of those banished from the realm of Love: Venus, Hatred, Sorrow, Anger, Jealousy, Wrath, Discord, Fury, Deception, Ingratitude, and Desperation. Love entered, accompanied by the two *mantentiori*, and sang a canzonetta, declaring his intentions in establishing his new realm in Tuscany. Following this, there were eight entries (*comparse*) of challengers, each group arriving on a different fantastic conveyance inspired by mythology. The leader of each group sang verses promoting the claims of certain banished Passions (personified by a lady), after which the attacks by her champions—courtiers named in the description—were warded off by the *mantenitori*. In the entry written by Cicognini, Jove appeared in support of Amorous Deception, and he was accompanied by the four Medicean stars recently discovered by Galileo Galilei. In the last entry, Venus rose from the sea on a shell to plead her own case in a canzonetta. The ensuing battle was interrupted by Divine Love, who appeared in the heavens singing five octaves that commanded an end to the hostilities and counselled, instead, pity, kindness, and reconciliation on earth, while true joy would be sought only in heaven. The *mantenitori* concluded by declaring the peaceful reign of Love in Tuscany.

It is easy to see how much the Florentine *barriera* of 1613 had in common with the Roman opera/*veglia* of 1614, *Amor pudico*. Each involved a dispute between Love and Venus concerning the nature of love and its role in defining the ethos of a polity. Each used action and scenic effect to establish the narrative and dramatic context for musical numbers. Each employed recitative style only to a limited extent. In each, the musical-dramatic scenes were separated by a complementary activity (dancing or mock fighting). And in both, Jove was accompanied by the four Medicean stars in homage to the Grand Duke of Tuscany and his family.

As in other early operas, the dialogue in *Amor pudico* is contained in *versi sciolti* of seven and eleven syllables set in recitative style. Paradiso's *Lettera* says:

The musical segments in the so-called recitative style of the first and second *hore* were composed by Sig. Cavalier Cesare Marotta, member of the Most Illustrious Cardinal Montalto's household. . . . His Excellency Prince Michele's [household member] Sig. Pellegrino Mutij composed the musical segments in the third [*hora*]. The other [musical segments] in the fourth and fifth [*hore*] were by Sig. D. Ippolito Macchiavelli, [household member] of the said Most Illustrious [Cardinal].[22]

The word *musiche*, which I translate in this context as 'musical segments' in the second and third sentences of this quotation, must be understood to imply *musiche di stile recitativo*, in parallel with the first sentence, since the letter goes on to ascribe some non-recitative portions of the fourth and fifth acts to other composers: Marotta provided the music sung by Amphitrite and Venus in the last *hora*, while in the fourth act each singer who portrayed a poet composed his own aria. The possibility of spoken dialogue is to be ruled out because the *avviso* quoted above says that the *commedia* was entirely sung and because Romolo's letter tells us that the actors' singing was continuously accompanied by two harpsichords, two theorbos, and an organ, to which was added a harp when the muses sang in their boat.[23] It is true, however, that the first two acts contain much more dialogue in *versi sciolti* than the others; the fourth contains rather little, and the last almost none, especially if several of the more lyrical and extended speeches with closed rhyme forms were actually set as solo madrigals.

Of the approximately twenty-nine closed, lyrical segments, connected by dialogue recitative, the distribution of poetic forms is, again, similar to that found in the earliest Florentine and Mantuan opera libretti (see Table 9.2). Eight consist of one or more stanzas of ottava rima, five are quaterne chiuse, four are capitoli in terza rima, six are strophic canzonette, two are sonetti, one is a sestina narrativa, and perhaps three take the form of madrigals.[24] Ottava rima, quaterne chiuse, and terza rima are the most common metres at the *luoghi oziosi* in the

---

[22] 'Le Musiche, di stile, che si dice recitativo dell'hora Prima, e Seconda, furono opera del Sig. Cavalier Cesare Marotta famigliare dell'Illustris. Sig. Card. MONTALTO. . . . Compose il Sig. Pellegrino Mutij dell'Eccellentiss. Sig. Principe PERETTI, le Musiche della Terza. Furono l'altre della Quarta, e della Quinta del Sig. D. Hippolito Macchiavelli del detto Illustrissimo'; Paradiso, *Copia d'una lettera*, 64–5.

[23] 'Formavano l'armonia dietro le Scene con due Cimbali il Cavaliero Marotta, & il Sig. Giovan Giacomo Maggi dell'Illustrissimo Montalto. V'erano due Tiorbe, l'una suonò il Sig. Innocentia Menghi dell'Illustriss. Sig. Card. BORGHESE. L'altra il detto Sig. Macchiavelli. Tutti questi istrumenti, e dovea dirlo à V. S. dà principio, con l'organo del Sig. Nanino, sempre accompagnarono il canto de' Rappresentanti. . . . Suonò l'Arpa maravigliosamente dentro la Nave il Sig. Horatio Michi dell'Illustrissimo Montalto, Napolitano'; Paradiso, *Copia d'una lettera*, 65, 67.

[24] Since there is no pattern of verse lengths or predictable rhyme scheme that distinguishes madrigals from the surrounding *versi sciolti* of recitative dialogue, they cannot be identified with certainty in the libretto alone, without recourse to the score. However, the passages named above are set apart by a closed rhyme scheme or pattern of line lengths as well as a lyrical expression of feeling that seems not intended to be heard by interlocutors present on stage. Other text segments that could well have been set as madrigals include *Nobil desir mi spinse* and *O di Permesso Vergini canore*, both sung by Amore in the last act. One of the two duets in *Amor pudico*, *Stringhiamo in breve giro un mar di gloria*, is also a madrigal.

TABLE 9.2. The arias in *Amor pudico* (1614)

Incipit	Verse form	Sung by	Act	Composer	Music in Vol. II
Amor io vidi a real Donna in grembo	quaterna chiusa	Fama	II	Marotta	
Anima bella, che in quel sen ti stai	sonetto	Petrarca	IV	Cenci	no. 17
Bella Madre d'Amore	madrigal	Giove	V	Macchiavelli	
Cinte le chiome del mio casto alloro	capitolo in terza rima	Sole	V	Macchiavelli	
Da i negri alberghi, e tenebroso centro	strophic canzonetta	Mercurio and Sdegno (one strophe each)	III	Mutij	
Deh lasciate	strophic canzonetta	Anfitrite	V	Marotta	
E voi non men, che saggie, honeste, e belle	ottava rima	Sole	V	Macchiavelli	
Ecco di Maia il generoso figlio	quaterna chiusa	Amore	III	Macchiavelli	
Et io fregiando il crin di quelle fronde	capitolo in terza rima	Età de l'oro	V	Macchiavelli	
Felici spirti, per virtù famosi	sonetto	Amore	IV	Macchiavelli	
Già di Guerrieri invitti i chiari fregi	ottava rima	Clio	V	Macchiavelli	
Io che sprezzo di morte il crudo strale	quaterna chiusae	Eternità	IV	Macchiavelli	
Io di tanta dolcezza ho colmo il seno	madrigal	Amore	V	Macchiavelli	
Io nel teatro dei real diletti	quaterna chiusa	Amore	IV	Macchiavelli	
La gloria di colui, che 'l tutto muove	capitolo in terza rima	Dante	IV	Puliaschi	no. 122
Le Donne, i Cavalier, l'armi, e gli amori	ottava rima	Ariosto	IV	Ludovico	
Ninfe per rimirar l'alto stupore	ottava rima	Nettuno	V	Macchiavelli	
Non mai rapida fiamma, o neve algente	ottava rima	Amore	IV	Macchiavelli	
Non più madre di sdegno	strophic canzonetta	Venere	V	Macchiavelli	
Non si muove aura serena	strophic canzonetta	Venere	V	Marotta	
O bellissime Donzelle	strophic canonetta	Himeneo	I	Marotta	
O de l'Olimpo regnator possente	madrigal	Fama	II	Marotta	
O Diva tu, che di caduchi allori	ottava rima	Tasso	IV	Verovio	
O valor de l'arco d'oro	canzonetta	Venere and Anfitrite	V	Marotta	
Per ricercar del pargoletto Arciero	strophic canzonetta	Mercurio	III	Mutij	
Pria che 'l ciel fosse, il mar, la terra, e 'l foco	ottava rima	Anguillara	IV	Zoilo	nos. 4 and 4a
Questi spirti gentil di te ragionano	capitolo in terza rima	Sannazzaro	IV	Mutij	
Se da l'eterno, e luminoso Impero	quaterna chiusa	Venere	I	Marotta	
Sovra carro d'Honor Sposa oradita	ottava rima	Calliope	V	Macchiavelli	

TABLE 9.3. The choruses in *Amor pudico* (1614), set by Giovanni Bernardino Nanino

Incipit	Verse form	Sung by	Act
Al gran Dio, che 'l Mondo regge	strophic canzonetta	Coro di Stelle Medicee	II
Bella pianta avventurosa	madrigal	Coro di Poeti innominati	IV
Deh qual splendor, deh quai bellezze regnano	strophic canzonetta	Coro de gli Dei	V
D'Himeneo cantiam gli honori	madrigal	Coro de' seguaci d'Amore	I
D'Iffion la cruda rota	strophic canzonetta	Coro di Mostri d'Inferno	III
Dolcemente il mondo infiamma	strophic canzonetta	Ninfe e Serene del Mare	V
E voi non men, che saggie, honeste, e belle	madrigal	Sole with the muses	IV
Mentr'Amor trionfa in Terra	madrigal	Coro di Mostri d'Inferno	III
Non più se 'n vada altero	madrigal	Coro di Poeti innominati	IV
Nudo Arcier, che i petti avvampi	strophic canzonetta	Coro delle Muse	IV
O del Cielo aure serene	madrigal	chorus, 'col canto de gli ucelli'	IV
O memorabil giorno	strophic canzonetta	Ninfe e Serene del Mare	V
Qual superbo havrà possanza	strophic canzonetta	Coro de' seguaci d'Amore	III
Qui d'Amor la gloria ammirasi	madrigal	chorus	II
Tal bellezza	strophic canzonetta	Coro di Poeti innominati	IV

earliest libretti of Rinuccini, Chiabrera, and Striggio, while Rinuccini favoured canzonette and madrigals in his later works.[25] Only the presence of *sonetti* distinguishes the libretto of *Amor pudico* from the texts of other early operas.

The poetic forms of *Amor pudico*'s arias also correspond precisely with those of the chamber repertoire preserved in the sources derived from Cardinal Montalto's musical circles, as we learned in Chapter 6. This correspondence probably explains the distribution of poetic forms as much as does any theory of poetic verisimilitude, according to which gods, muses, and great poets of the past ought to sing in the classic poetic metres. Or more precisely, both that theory of verisimilitude and the poetic forms of the chamber repertoire were influenced by the continuous Italian tradition of poetic and vocal improvisation in the forms of ottava rima, terza rima, and sonetto that reached well back into the fifteenth century.

The sixteen choruses in *Amor pudico*, composed by Giovanni Bernardino Nanino, are either madrigals or strophic canzonette (see Table 9.3). In addition to providing reflection and commentary on the action, seconding the expressions of the protagonists, or setting the words of collective interlocutors in dialogue, several choruses give musical structure to the acts of the drama through

---

[25] See Barbara Russano Hanning, *Of Poetry and Music's Power: Humanism and the Creation of Opera* (Studies in Musicology, 13; Ann Arbor, 1980), 131–80.

their patterns of recurrence: in the Elysian Fields (fourth act), three renditions of the chorus with bird songs, *O del Cielo aure serene*, are interspersed among the dialogues and quatrains that introduce the great Italian poets of the past. In the first and fourth acts, choruses frame solo songs,[26] while the last act ends with four repetitions of the chorus *O memorabil giorno* (heard once earlier) that form a refrain to the three strophes of Venere's canzonetta *Non si muove aura serena*.

To judge on the basis of the three surviving arie, the strophic or stanzaic poetry that predominates among the lyrical solos in *Amor pudico* was composed in styles that represent several branches of the tradition of strophic variations. All three surviving arie come from the fourth *hora*, in which the great poets of the past praise the bride with new variants of their most famous verses.

Dante, who was on the right side, recognizing again the power over him of Him who called forth from him such genius while he lived, turning his eyes upward, as if praying to none but his Beatrice, to gain help from her, began, with a style full of sweet gravity, to praise the most beautiful bride with a short capitolo. His voice was sonorous and great, and well represented that which still resounds in all academies and literary gatherings.[27]

Thus the supplement to the libretto describes Giovanni Domenico Puliaschi's bass voice singing his own setting of *La gloria di colui che 'l tutto muove*, one of the most extraordinary and historically significant early seventeenth-century monodies (see Ch. 6 and the music in Vol. II, no. 122). Each of the four stanzas of the capitolo (three tercets and a quatrain) is set to its own self-contained *parte*, as usual in monodic settings of poems in this form. But only stanzas 1 and 3 are related as the customary strophic variations. Both of them begin with relatively rapid syllabic text setting, many repeated pitches, and static bass, a style probably very similar to the *stile recitativo* of the preceding dialogue. In this way the transition into the aria must have been nearly imperceptible, and the dramatic illusion of spontaneity would have been preserved while the poet began with an invocation to God, gradually warming his passions into song.[28] Only at the end of the first stanza does he break into a melisma, preparing for the more lyrical style of the second *parte*, in which the poet begins to describe the beauties of the bride: here the bass moves mostly by step in half notes and quarter notes,

---

[26] *D'Himeneo cantiam gli honori* in the first act and *Bella pianta avventurosa* in the fourth.

[27] 'DANTE, che si era locato à destra, riconoscendo ancora sovra di se la forza di colui, che gl'inalzò tanto l'ingegno mentre visse, sollevando gli occhi, quasi che non pregasse altri, che la sua Bice, à prestargli aiuto; incominciò con stile pieno di soave gravità, à lodar la bellissima Sposa, con un breve Capitolo. La sua voce era sonora, e grande, e ben rappresentante quella di lui, che ancor risuona per tutte l'Academie, e radunanze de letterati'; Paradiso, *Copia d'una lettera*, 43.

[28] Girolamo Mei's theory about the spontaneity of *parti recitative* in blank verse versus the premeditated character of the *luoghi oziosi* in fixed metres and closed forms, within 16th-c. plays, is explained and developed in Hanning, *Of Poetry and Music's Power*, 44–5.

forming metrical patterns suggestive of 3/2 in spite of the imperfect mensuration, while the vocal line gradually expands its range and extends its syllables with short melismas. In other words, the contrast between the first two stanzas is between an *aria di stile recitativo* and an *aria di stile cantativo*. The third stanza returns to the recitational style and the bass pattern of the first, but with a much longer melisma at the end. The final stanza begins as if to form a variation on the second, and is explicitly notated in 3/2 proportion. But it develops differently, even if in the same measured and somewhat melismatic, songlike style.

'Petrarch had a more tender and sweet voice, such as have those who accompany the softness and delicacy of poetry with the gentleness of love.'[29] His sonetto, *Anima bella che nel sen ten stai*, was performed by the Borghese singer Pietro Ciamoricone according to the supplement to the libretto, but composed by 'Gioseppino' (Giuseppino Cenci) according to the musical source.[30] Its form is the usual four strophic variations (one each for the two quatrains and the two tercets), and its style is that of madrigalian monody according to the tradition that G. B. Doni later observed:

Sonnets, which correspond quite closely to the hymns, paeans, nomoi, and similar Greek poems, normally should be set for one voice alone, but in the madrigalian style (as regards the variety of pitches and intervals) rather than the recitative style, which, being the simpler and easier style, is apt above all for ottava rima and epic poems, whether long, such as *La Gerusalemme [liberata]* by [Torquato] Tasso, or short, such as *L'Oronta* by [Girolamo] Preti.[31]

Cenci's broad melodic contours, wide leaps, and flowing melismas respond to the softness and delicacy of Petrarch's lyrical sonetto (Vol. II, no. 17). Although expressive text inflection still influences the melodic shape of the vocal line, as in the more recitational style of Dante's (Puliaschi's) first and third stanzas, affectively significant words and brief expressions are given enough individual

---

[29] 'Havea il PETRARCA, più tenera, e più soave la voce; come quegli, che tenea ben accompagnata la mollitia, e delicatezza del verso con la mansuetudine d'Amore'; Paradiso, *Copia d'una lettera*, 43.

[30] This apparently constitutes an exception to the remark made in the *Copia d'una lettera del Sig. Romolo Paradiso*, 65, that 'each of the poets composed the aria that he sang according to his own taste' ('ciascuno de' Poeti compose secondo il proprio gusto l'aria, laquale cantò'). It must have been that remark which led Claudio Monteverdi to refer ironically to 'Cardinal Montalto, who presented a play in which every personage who appeared in it composed his own part' ('Sig. Cardinal Mont'Alto che fece una comedia che ogni sogetto che in essa intervienevi si compose la sua parte'); Monteverdi, *Lettere, dediche e prefazioni*, ed. de' Paoli, 87, letter of 9 Dec. 1616.

[31] G. B. Doni, 'Discorso sopra la perfettione de' concenti', 118: 'I Sonetti, che corrispondono assai à gl'Inni, Peani, Nomi, e simil Poesie Greche, comunemente se dovrebbono modulare à una voce sola; ma più tosto in Stile Madrigalesco (quanto al ricercare molte corde, & intervalli) che Recitativo: il quale, come quello ch'è più semplice e facile, sopratutto s'accomoda all'Ottava rima, & à' Poemi Heroici; ò siano qui lunghi, come la Gierusalemme del Tasso; ò brevi, come l'Oronta del Preti.'

attention (see *godi, chiari, dolci, nodi, cantai, altere lodi, stella, sua chiara facella, stupì,* and *opra tua natura*) that the continuity of declamation frequently dissolves into lyrical introspection or rhetorical illustration. The bass, however, is mostly static or slowly moving, and it never maintains the metrical patterning or active rhythm that helped to define the *aria di stile cantativo* in Dante's second and fourth stanzas.

A fourth style is found in Sannazzaro's *Questi spirti gentil di te ragionano* (Vol. II, no. 4), composed and performed by Pellegrino Mutij, according to the libretto supplement, which describes the aria in this way: 'Sannazzaro, showing that noble simplicity with which he formerly sang his *Arcadia*, made himself heard with a capitolo whose verses were *sdruccioli*, to the sound of his instrument, and he finished with applause.'[32] 'Noble simplicity', perhaps, corresponds to the clear triple metre projected (again, in spite of imperfect mensuration) by the rhythmically active bass, which produces a full cadence at the end of each line of poetry and which remains unchanged in each of the four variations. The vocal line, too, is simple in its very modest technical demands, small vocabulary of rhythmic figures, and rounded melodic contours, which pay little heed to the demands of declamation or other sources of expression. Although this simple, rhythmic sort of strophic variations is closest in style to the villanelle and canzonette of the sixteenth century, it is rare in early monody sources: after Caccini's *Ard'il mio petto* of 1602, nothing of this sort appears in the printed monody repertoire until 1616, except for Orfeo's aria *Qual honor di te sia degno* in Claudio Monteverdi's *Orfeo* (Mantua, 1607). As said in Chapter 6, Nigel Fortune attributes great importance to this more rhythmic type of strophic variation because the first pieces to be called 'cantata', published by Grandi and Berti in Venice, 1620–7, are of this kind.[33] We have seen, however, that the monody repertoire from the circle of Cardinal Montalto is rich in this type of aria.

In sum, then, the arias in *Amor pudico* use forms and styles that are typical of the chamber repertoire in the Montalto manuscripts. We are again reminded, therefore, how much in common stage works and chamber repertoire share in this period of Italian opera history.

Perhaps too little music survives from *Amor pudico* for us to judge its reception by subsequent composers of Roman opera. In particular, we are hampered by not having any sample of its dialogue recitative. But we can say that the relative proportion of *luoghi oziosi*, both solo arias and choruses, to *parti recitative* is greater than in earlier operas, that broad 3/2 metre already makes its appearance

---

[32] 'Ma il SANAZZARO, mostrando quella nobil simplicità, con la quale già cantò l'altro la sua Arcadia, con un capitolo, i cui versi erano sdruccioli, al suono del suo stromento fece sentirsi: e terminò con applauso'; Paradiso, *Copia d'una lettera,* 43–4.   [33] Fortune, 'Italian Secular Song from 1600 to 1635', 342, 363–80.

in the arias, even if still barred in imperfect mensuration, and that a fluid alternation between various recitational and lyrical styles can already be found here. It is tempting to identify the singer 'Stefano', who sang the role of Anterote, as Stefano Landi. However, even if Landi and Domenico Mazzocchi did not know *Amor pudico* directly, they certainly were in touch with the musical techniques brought together in the surviving arias from this opera.

Epitome

❧

APPARENTLY Cardinal Montalto had studied music as a boy. His friend
Vincenzo Giustiniani said that he sang expressively and played the harpsichord.
It is not unlikely that young Alessandro attended the music school to which
Vincenzo was sent by his father and sang the repertoire that Giustiniani later
describes (Ch. 3). One of the leading schools in Rome, famous for training
solo singers, was across the street from the Giustiniani palace at the church of San
Luigi dei Francesi, where Ruggiero Giovannelli was *maestro di cappella*, 1583–
91, followed by Giovanni Bernardino Nanino, 1591–1608. In 1587, 17-year-old
Alessandro signed a letter to the harpsichordist Scipione Dentice 'as a brother'
(Ch. 2; Letter 1). These early experiences and friendships along with what must
have been an innate inclination and some degree of talent led the young cardinal to emphasize musical patronage, eventually more than any of his peers.

Montalto's desire to emulate Ferdinando de' Medici as patron of music
was undoubtedly conditioned by Ferdinando's decisive role in the election of
Montalto's great-uncle, Sixtus V, and by his continuing protection, friendship,
and political alliance with the Peretti family. Then, too, Ferdinando's cultivation
of the courtly art of elaboration upon *arie di stile recitativo, et cantativo* must have
resonated with Alessandro's own musical background and with such cultural
values as individuality, independence, free will, self-determination, effortless
mastery, and spontaneity, to which he seems to have been intuitively drawn. So,
after Ferdinando left the cardinalate to become Grand Duke of Tuscany in 1587,
Montalto maintained contact with Ferdinando's musicians, both those brought
from Rome to Florence—Vittoria Archilei, Onofrio Gualfreducci, Emilio de'
Cavalieri—and those already in Florence, particularly Giulio Caccini, *romano*, and
his daughter Francesca. Montalto, as a guest in Florence, witnessed several of the
earliest operas, in which some of his own singers participated.

But when Montalto began adding composers and singers of monody to his
own household, about 1607, they did not come from Florence, as he might have
wished, but largely from Rome and Naples. The same is true of the musicians

in the secondary and tertiary circles around him. This was apparently the out-
come of three factors: Montalto's temporary break with Ferdinando de' Medici
over the election of Pope Paul V, the concentration of the cardinal's ecclesiastical benefices and his brother's feuds in the Vice Realm of Naples, and, obviously,
Montalto's own location in Rome, with its extensive web of training institutions,
chapels, and patrons.

Cardinal Montalto may have tried to encourage musicians in his circles to pursue Florentine innovations—the design and description of *Amor pudico* suggests
that he did. But these singers and composers were also conditioned by traditions
and developments with which the Florentines had contact much earlier (Caccini)
or only indirectly (Peri, Gagliano). Among the ramifications, we find that the
monody repertoire preserved in sources stemming from Montalto's circles is
rich in elaboration of several types of strophic variation, the notated outgrowth
of well-developed and ramified kinds of improvisation based upon formulaic arias,
villanelle, and canzonette of various sorts. Both opposition and blending of various kinds and degrees of recitational and cantillational styles, on both large and
small scales, are especially characteristic of this repertoire, both in the strophic
variations and in solo madrigals. Giulio Caccini's type of arioso madrigal is
uncommon here. And although several species of recitative can be found in these
sources, none is identical with the kind Jacopo Peri used in his operas. The styles
of basso continuo writing, traceable back, perhaps, to the *rasgueado* accompaniment on the Spanish guitar practised in Naples, are also different from those of
Peri and Caccini. The ornamental passaggi in these works, some of the most difficult ever written, probably reflect the legendary abilities of Montalto's most
famous singer, Ippolita Recupito, but they also and not infrequently serve declamation and other aspects of text expression and provide one component of the
vivid contrasts that are notable in this music.

Montalto did not intend to propagate his composers' styles, if indeed he recognized them as distinctive. Instead, he hoarded their music, which is one reason
why we can trace the contents of several surviving manuscripts to his circles. But
the music was sometimes learnt by ear, as Cesare Marotta claimed, and at other
times transmitted in writing, even surreptitiously, to Marotta's correspondents.
Of course, Montalto's own musicians knew this repertoire well because they performed and heard it daily. Its features could then be disseminated and developed
by the younger musicians in the cardinal's household, like Giuseppe Giamberti
and Orazio Michi, and in his larger circles, such as Stefano Landi and Luigi
Rossi. These composers had, of course, other models to work from as well. But
Rossi composed several examples of what Marotta apparently would have called
a *Romanesca bastarda*, in which some stanzas of text are connected through variation and some are not, some in recitative and others in metrical aria style. The

earliest known examples of this procedure, by Marotta and Giovanni Domenico Puliaschi, come from Montalto's circles. Michi, Cardinal Montalto's most favoured musician in the end, eventually used recitational and cantillational styles in opposition in setting madrigals and single stanzas of canzonette in which the poetry contrasts verses with relatively prosaic diction with others suggestive of metrical rhythms. Here, again, the Montalto repertoire preserves early examples of the technique. Michi extended this approach to multi-strophic texts, in one case a text with more than one strophic pattern. In retrospect, then, we can say that the multipartite Roman chamber cantata had some roots in Roman and Neapolitan developments that did not depend exclusively on Florentine innovations.

It is more difficult to make the same claim for Roman opera. Recitational solo songs preserved among the Montalto sources may have been used in Cardinal Farnese's (originally Cardinal Montalto's?) 1596 production of *Il pastor fido*, but this is by no means certain. We have neither text nor music for Michele Peretti's pastorale of 1609, Montalto's pastorale of 1611, or his tragedy of Psyche from the same year. We know that Cesare Marotta composed recitatives in 1612 for Battista Guarini's intermedi based on episodes from Tasso's *Gerusalemme liberata*, but only arias survive. The same is true for *Amor pudico* (1614). But in the earliest surviving secular opera by a Roman composer, Stefano Landi's *La morte d'Orfeo* (1619), the recitative is, like much within the Montalto repertoire, more tempered by infusions of cantillational features with a bass more varied in pacing than is typical of the earliest Florentine and Mantuan music dramas. This sets the style for much Roman opera of the next two decades. The libretto structure of Landi's opera, 'five short tableaux, each with a nearly different set of characters, eighteen roles, none extensive',[1] and an intermedio built into the end of each act, resembles that of *Amor pudico*.

Cardinal Montalto's bones are now dust. His principal villa is demolished, his gardens a railway yard. His art collection and his library are dispersed. His wealth is gone and with it the lustre of his generosity. His family is extinct, his power dissolved. He is remembered only for art and for music.

---

[1] Margaret Murata, 'Morte d'Orfeo', *New Grove*, iii. 474.

Appendix A: Transcription of Letters

Editorial note: The following letters have been transcribed faithfully, without modernization of orthography. Some punctuations and capitalizations, which, in these manuscripts, are often subject to interpretation, have been chosen, at times, in order to render the meaning of these documents clearer to the modern reader. Italics have been used to identify letters added in expanding such abbreviations as do not use the period or colon and to identify titles of vocal works, as a convenience to the reader. The dates of letters nos. 16 and 75, written in Florence between 1 January and 25 March, have been transcribed as written, then corrected to modern style within square brackets. Addresses come from the backs of letters.

1. 10.i.1587   Cardinal Montalto to Scipione Dentice
I:Rasc, Confalonieri 48, fo. 141ᵛ; partially transcribed by Chater, 'Musical Patronage', 189

Al S.r Scipione Dentici

Io non so di haver havuto altra lettera di V.S. se non questa delli 3. del *presente*, et se ben tardi m'è però stato caro d'haver inteso il suo arrivo à salvam.to in Napoli, si come mi dispiace che hora si senta poco bene di salute. Così piaccia à Dio di risanarle presto. Io le proposi poi à Mons.r Ill.mo di Perugia per procurarle commodo et per il desiderio che havemo di vederla in questa Corte, dove s'io posso farle piacer' alcuno non mi sarà grave, che si vaglia di me. Et Idio le doni ogni contento. Di Roma il di X. di Gennaio 1587.

2. 18.iv.1587   Cardinal Montalto to Scipione Dentice
I:Rasv, Confalonieri 49, fo. 81ᵛ

Al S.r Scipione Dentice

Ill. Sig.re. Non solo non sento travaglio nel leggere le *lettere* di V.S. mà ne ricevo consolatione, et mi è accetto ogni officio, che mi venga dalla sua mano, sicome è questo, che ha fatto con la sua delli XI con la quale ho ricevuto le sue compositioni, che essendo suo parto non possono essere se non vaglessime. Così ne la ringratio, et le prego di Dio ogni contento. il dì 18. di Aprile 1587. Di V.S. come *fratello*

3. 4.vii.1587   Cardinal Montalto to Alfonso II d'Este, Duke of Ferrara
I:MOas, Cancelleria marchionale poi ducale estense, Sezione Estero, Carteggi con principi esteri, Busta 1405, B/149

Ser.mo S.r mio oss.mo

Se bene io potevo promettermi dalla benignità di V. Alt.za ogni gratia, et favore, per la devota servitù, che le porto. Tuttavia la demostratione, che l'è piacciuto di far' nella persona mia per la pensione, che mi si riserva in quella Chiesa di Ferrara, supera ogni merito mio, sè bene è conforme alla grandezza dell'animo suo. Spero nondimeno, che V. Alt.za conoscerà, ch'è impiegata in un suo ser.re che di volontà non cede ad altri, sè ben di forze è inferiore à molti. Et poi che per la mia debbolezza non la posso riconoscer' con altro vengo à renderlene quelle maggior gratie, ch'io devo et à pregar' la M.tà di Dio, che le doni all'incontro quella felicità, che desidera. Et le bacio le mani. Di Roma il di iiii di Luglio MDLXXXVII. Di V. Alt.za Ser.re affett.mo A. Cardinal Montalto

4. 2.i.1588   Cardinal Montalto to the Duchess of Torremaggiore
I:Rasv, Confalonieri 49, fo. 292; cited by Chater, 'Musical Patronage', 190

Alla Duchessa di Torremaggior'

Desiderando il Dottor Pompeo Stabile d'introdursi nella servitù di V. Ecc.za con animo di continuarla per qualche anno, et cognoscendo io l'ottime qualità sue, che lo fa degno d'esser amato et . . .

5. 28.vi.1588   Cardinal Montalto to Monsignor del Monte
I:Rasv, Confalonieri 50, fo. 207; transcribed in Chater, 'Luca Marenzio: New Documents, New Observations', 4–6

A Mons.r del Monte

Maestro Luca Marentio essendo persona di quelle virtuose qualità che V.S. deve sapere si rende da se stesso grato à ciascuno, et non ha bisogno d'alcuna raccomandatione, con tutto cio amandolo io molto per i meriti suoi ho voluto farle saper con questa mia che tutte le gratie demostrat.mi et tutto piu[?] che si compiacerà di fargli oltre che saranno ben collocate, io ne ricevero particolar contento, et ne sentiro molto gradito alli quali mi racc.o Di Roma il di 28. di Giugno 1588.

6. 12.xii.1588   Cardinal Montalto to the Duke of Savoy
I:Rasc, Confalonieri 50, fo. 426ᵛ; cited by Chater, 'Musical Patronage', 190

Al Duca di Savoia

Pompeo Stabile Napolitano gentilhuomo di honorate qualità et in particolar dipendenza da me onde desiderando egli hor di pigliar l'habito di qualche religione io lo ho essortato a procurar quella di S. Maurizio et Lazzaro, et introdurse nel serv.o di V. Alt.za . . .

7. 27.i.1589   Cardinal Montalto to Scipione Dentice
I:Rasv, Confalonieri 51, fo. 18ᵛ

Al S.r Scipione Dentice

Mentre V.S. era in Roma mi ricordo che vostro desiderio di fermarsi in questa Città nel servizio di Monsig.r Ill.o di Perugia il che per allora non soccedette, ultim.te tenendomi in proposito col Car.le l'ho trovato disposto à receverla con animo anco di darle luogo honorato appresso di se. Infino[?] ho voluto farglilo sapere, accio continuando nel medesimo desiderio se ne possa uscire à suo piacere. Così a me in particolar sarà caro per poterla godere, come molto desidero. et Idio la conservi . . . [?] il di 27 di Gennaio 1589

8. 18.viii.1590   Cardinal Montalto to the Nunzio of Naples
I:Rasv, Confalonieri 52, fo. 358ʳ

Al Nuntio di Napoli

Si trova apresso il S.r Duca di Traietto per quel che intendo una putta di sette anni, che per esser' instruitta nell'arte della musica la Duchessa di Bracciano mia sorella desidera molto di haverla qui seco per suo trattenimento, et la madre della detta putta se ne contenta, ma perche pare ch'il S.r Duca la lasci mal volentieri desidero che V.S. facerà ogni opera per che si contenti che mia sorella habbia questa sodisfatt.ne et potra spendere in cio nel nome mio dove sarà bisogno procurando che la figluola sia consegnata al S. Horatio Granucci mio Agente il qual tiene ordine dal S. Don Virginio mio cognato di riceverla et à V.S. mi racc.o. Di Roma il dì 18 d'Agosto 1590.

9. 18.viii.1590   Cardinal Montalto to his agent in Naples
I:Rasv, Confalonieri 52, fo. 353ᵛ

Al S. Hor.o Granucci

Scrivo à Monsig.r Nuntio pregandolo a far ogni opera perche quella putta che si trova apresso il S.r Duca di Traetto sia concessa alla Duchessa mia sorella, et si consegni à V.S. la quale potra solicitar questo neg.o procurando che quando p.a si mandi qua poi che la madre di essa se ne contenta e stia sana. Di Roma il dì XVIII di Agosto 1590.

10. 25.viii.1590   Cardinal Montalto to his agent in Naples
I:Rasv, Confalonieri 52, fo. 367ᵛ

Al Sig. Granucci

La Duchessa mia sorella si trova hora indisposta, et per quello non si serverà per adesso al S.r Duca et Duchessa di Traietto per quella putta musica.

11. 27.xii.1591   Cardinal Montalto to Scipione Dentice
I:Rasv, Confalonieri 52, fo. 131ᵛ; cited by Chater, 'Musical Patronage', 189

Al S.r Scipione Dentice

Non potessero ricever' dalla mano di V.S. cosa più grata di queste sue fatiche delle quali ha voluto farmi parte . . . Roma 27 dicembre 1591

12. 27.x.1593   Cardinal Montalto to Alfonso II d'Este, Duke of Ferrara
I:MOas, Cancelleria marchionale poi ducale estense, Sezione Estero, Carteggi con principi esteri, Busta 1405, B/149

Ser.mo S.r mio oss.mo

Quelli, che hanno cura d'esigere l'entrate dela mia Abbadia in Reggio, mi avvisano, che difficilm.te possono conseguire il mio diritto; per che ricorrendo ala giustitia non possono havere l'esecutione pronta contra li debitori allegandosi certo statuto dela città; per lo quale il rimedio esecutivo non è concesso salvo che alli Cittadini; restandone esclusi li chierici e li forestieri. Imperò vengo à pregare V. Alt.za che le piaccia commettere alli suoi giusdicenti nela Città, distretto, e Ducato di Reggio, che ove si tratterà al'avvenire de gli interessi miei per qualunque causa avanti di loro, habbino da precedere per giustitia,

secondo che s'usa per le cause de' propij cittadini, non ostanti il prefato statuto; il che
tanto più reputo di meritare appresso dela benignità di V. Alt.za per l'intenso desiderio
e divotione, che sarà in me sempre mai verso il ser.o di lei; à cui bacio le mani; e pregole
dal S.re Iddio ogni felicità. Di Roma alli 27. d'Ott.re 1593. Di V. Alt.za Affett.mo ser.re
A. Car*dinal* Montalto

13. 15.iv.1595   Cardinal Montalto to Alfonso II d'Este, Duke of Ferrara
I:MOas, Cancelleria marchionale poi ducale estense, Sezione Estero, Carteggi con principi esteri,
Busta 1405, B/149

Ser.mo Sig.re

La divotione, che è in me verso di V. Alt.za ricerca che io le habbia da communicare
quello, che passa intorno alli successi di casa mia; imperò dopò che si è con l'auttorità
di N. S.re concluso l'accasamento di Don Michele mio fratello con Donna Caterina
Gonzaga figlia del già Marchese Alfonso di Castelgiofredo, non hò voluto mancare di darne
per mezo di queste poche righe avviso al' Alt.za V.; la quale può tuttavia credere che insieme
con mio fratello riputerò sempre à particolariss.a gratia d'haver' à ricevere li suoi comandamenti. Con che le bacio per fine le mani; e pregole dal S.re Iddio ogni felicità. Di Roma
alli 15. d'Aprile 1595. Di V. Alt.za Affett.mo Ser.re A. Car*dinal* Montalto

14. 3.iv.1596   Girolamo Giglioli to Alfonso II d'Este, Duke of Ferrara
I:MOas, Cancelleria Ducale, Estero, Ambasciatori, Italia, Roma, Busta 155

Ho fatto l'uff.o col. S.r Car.le Montalto come V.A. mi comandò con l'Instru.e delli 23.
di Marzo, et le resi la lettera di lei, S.S. Ill.a dopo haverla humiliss.te ringratiata de gli
honori, che le piace compartirle, è passato a dire che le spiace delli sciagure di Mons.r
R.mo di costi, il qual si contenta di compacere, et d'aspettare, se bene malvolontieri la
sua ingrossar il debito, et ch'in questo mezzo pigliara li 1000 scudi, sperando che tosto
siano per esser' in termini. Dopo questo passò à dimandarmi del neg.o offrendosi pron-
tiss.o a ser.la conforme agli infiniti oblighi che tiene alla Ser.ma sua persona. Et uscì, ch'il
Papa le ne parlò ma cosi freddamente, che crede che non si caverà cosa buona da S.B.
alla quale non mancò però di dire à benef. di questa causa sino al segno, che però per li
Bolle: et sù questo mi dissi, che V.A. dovrebbe dimandare in questa congiuntura il S.r
Don Aless.ro Car.le perchè facilmente l'havrebbe. Io dopo havere ringratiato S. Ill.ma
di tutto, le disse, che non sapevo quali fossi la mente di S. A. S.ma [Summary in the margin:] Ciò e hab.a d.o à Montalto intorno alla sua pensione et la risposta

15. 18.v.1598   Cardinal Montalto to Cesare d'Este, Duke of Modena
I:MOas, Cancelleria marchionale poi ducale estense, Sezione Estero, Carteggi con principi esteri,
Busta 1405, B/149

Ser.mo S.r mio oss.mo

Il S.r Marchese Bentivoglio mi hà quì data la *lettera* di V. Alt.za delli 12. et insieme significata
si bene la benigna voluntà, che le piace continuarmi, che m'obliga d'haverle, come fò à
rendere le debite gratie, riserbandomi però di compir maggiorm.te in questa parte,
ovunque mi sarà da lei somministrato modo di poter con effetto sodisfare ala divotione
dell'animo mio verso il suo servitio. E perciò che nel soprapiù mi rapporto al medesimo
S.r Marchese, non mi stenderò più oltre con la *presente*, eccetto che per fine bacio à V.

Alt.za le mani, e prego il S.re Iddio che le conceda ogni felicità. Di Ferrara alli 18. di Maggio 1598. Di V. Alt.za Aff.mo ser.re A. Car*dinal* Montalto

16. 5.iii.1607 Giulio Caccini to Virginio Orsini
I:Rac, Archivio Orsini, Corrispondenza epistolare di Virginio II Orsini, II.C.Prot. XVI.166, n. 1, lettera 732

Ill.mo et Ecc.mo Sig.r mio Oss.mo
I miei gravi accidenti con tanta lassezza poi nel fine, hanno causato che non ho potuto ringraziare V.E. Ill.ma, come faccio hora con tutto l'affetto dell'animo, della benigniss.a offerta, che ci ha fatto della casa sua come già sa, che mi haveva dato l'ordine, per la nostra venuta à Roma, le mie fig.le ne erano tutte liete, e pareva loro mill'anni di venire, non tanto per ricevere, il favore, e grazia da V.E. Ill.ma ma per riveder lei particolarm.te sapendo certo insieme meco quanto sia l'hobbligo, che habbiamo tutti alla protezzione, che V.E. ha sempre tenuto della casa nostra, e di ciascheduno di noi in particolare che N. S.re ne la riconosca per noi. Per hora la nostra venuta costà si differirà ad altra occasione, per che havendo presentito di costà, che il S.r Card.le Montalto si era raffreddato in quello negozio, et havendognene per ciò dato motto con quattro righe, per sentirne la sua volontà, ho trovato non mi havendo risposto, esser vero, e quel, che mi preme più dubito haverlo disgustato, e persone la sua grazia, che se V.E. non ci aiuta e favorisce tutti, lei che conosce dentro la nostra humiltà per natura, e buona volontà ne saremo dolenti il tempo di nostra vita, e tutto lo riconosceremo per mia grazia e bontà di V.E. Ill.ma che recuperiamo questa grazia, non per altro se non per che tutti li siamo humiliss.i serv.i con che tutti facciamo debita riverenza, e ce la ricordiamo obbligatiss.mo che N. S.re preservi feliciss.ma. Di Firenze alli 5 di Marzo 1606 [1607] Di V.E. Ill.ma Servit.re Humiliss.mo e hobbligat.mo Giulio Caccini di Roma

17. 6.iii.1607 Michelangelo Buonarroti, il giovane, to Grand Duke Ferdinando dei Medici (draft)
I:Fl, Buonarroti 81, fo. 302^{r-v}

Conforme a che V.A. comanda ho cercato di intendere da M. Giulio Romano come sia passato sino a ora il negozio della Cecchina sua fig.la intorno all'andare a servire all'Ill.mo Card. Montalto e ne ho ritratto solo che egli stesso ne voleva scrivere a V.A. come io credo che ora mai abbia fatto. E volendo intendere del medesimo dal Sig.r Piero Guicciardini ho trovato che era in villa siche presi risoluzione di parlare col Sig.r Gualterrotto Guicciardini zio del Sig.r Abate Rucellai e da lui ho assai apertamente inteso che il negozio tra l'una parte e l'altra era al prese*nt*e assai raffreddato . . .

18. 28.vii.1607 Bernardo Bizzoni to Enzo Bentivoglio
I:FEas, Archivio Bentivoglio, Mazzo 9–41, fo. 255. (This letter is illegible in many places because the paper has been eroded by the ink.) Partially transcribed by Fabris, 'Frescobaldi e la musica in casa Bentivoglio', 67

Ill.mo S.r p.rone oss.mo
Io diedi conto a V.S. Ill.ma come delli denari delle cavalle pagati [sono] sessantadoi . . . da me hò . . . con il S.r Alessandro Piccinnini . . . infallibilmente Le mandarò le musiche

promesse tratano con occasione che il ser.mo Gran'Duca di Toscana per le nozze che si farano q.to carnavale à Fiorenza hà mandate à dimandare al S.r Card. Mont'Alto la S.ra Ippolita Musica celebre con il Marito, e tutto il conserto intiero di S.S. Ill.ma io à instanza di d.a Sig.a quale meritam.te canta con affetto sopra le molte opere del S.r Luzzascho . . . all'inclusa verà il s.r Luzzasco à vederla favorire le Sue opere passeggiate come à dar . . . l'opra sua per farsene honore a Fiorenza; io starò assicuro di questo favore, perciò che V.S. Ill.ma si vorrà interessare . . . impore con l'autorità sua; io lo farò pur sapere al S.r Card.le et al S.r Prencipe i quali mi assicurano gliene resteran con obbligo. . . . Dalli 28 di luglio 1607. Di V.S. Ill.ma Devotiss. S.re Bernardo Bizzoni

19. 15.viii.1607   Francesco Nappi to Enzo Bentivoglio
I:FEas, Archivio Bentivoglio, Mazzo 9–41, fo. 440^{r-v}

Ill.mo Sig.re p.rone oss.mo

Havendo l'Ill.mo S.re Card.le Borghese padrino gia fatto offitio con Mons.re Thes.re et il S.re Comiss.o della Camera per il serv.o di V.S. Ill.ma in modo che ella ne verrà compiaciuta; non mi e parso approposito di valermi delli fogli bianchi sottoscritti da lei per questi SS.ri. Ma perché io desidero servirla compitamente come devo non mancherò darne avviso a Aless.ro mio fratello per eseguirne quello che più sarà giudicato da lui conveniente per servire a V.S. Ill.ma alla quale ho voluto significare il rispetto che mi ha mosso cosi giudicare, et a non volere presentare la lettera per l'Ill.mo Montalto; giaché ella senz'altro molto e per ottenere l'intento suo.

L'historia che V.S. mi ha mandata mi e stata oltre modo cara, tanto più ch'all'inicio a chi l'ho presentata e stata cariss.ma onde non posso se non ringratiarnela in tutto l'animo, e quanto maggiore e stata la briga in procurarmela tanto più cresce l'obligo che le ne tengho.

Se del datio del Pescie l'Ill.mo S.re Card.le Borghese non ne havessi disposto a quest'hora a sua elettione V.S. Ill.ma potrebbe promettere sicuram.e di esserne servita da mio fratello et da me. Ma deve intervenire il comandam.o del S.re Card.le Padrone e forza l'ubbidire puntam.e onde essendoli nota per altro la prontezza dell'animo nostro et il desiderio di servirla mi basterà haverli accennato s'impedim.e senza stendermi (?) in altra giustificatione. Con chi facendoli riverenze li bacio con ogni affetto di core le mani ce me le racc.do in grazia. Di Roma li XV Agosto 1607. Di V.S. Ill.ma Aff.o s.o di cuore Franc.o Nappi

20. 22.viii.1607   Francesco Nappi to Enzo Bentivoglio
I:FEas, Archivio Bentivoglio, Mazzo 9–41, fo. 510^r

Ill.mo Sig.r mio oss.mo

Si puol V.S. assicurare che è tanto il desiderio et obligo che ho di servirla che non mancharo mai occasione che mi si ponghi d'effetuare q.to mio intenso desiderio tanto più per ogni raggione devo servirla in quello che tanto li preme e con tanta efficacia mi racomanda andare in vigilando accio resti servita nel negotio della valle d'agosta; e procuraro con ogni diligenza la soprait.e delle tratte venuta che vi[?] costa la relat.e dal Ill.mo S.r Card.le Legato. Non ho aviso del niuna[?] che sia giusto il quadro qual subbito mi sarà mandato e lo presentaro a nome di V.S. Ill.mo al S.r Card.le P.rone e l'acompagnarò con la lettera e con quelle megliori parole che sapero sel con l'opra parlarà per se stessa che e quadro di con la presente pero finisco con farli riverenza pregando da N. S. ogni conpito bene. Di Roma li 22 d'Agosto 1607. Di V.S. Ill.ma Aff.mo s.re di cuore Francesco Nappi

21. 22.viii.1607 Bernardo Bizzoni to Enzo Bentivoglio
I:FEas, Archivio Bentivoglio, Mazzo 9–41, fo. 512ʳ

Illmo Sig.r p.rone oss.mo

Ho havute alla posta le Musiche che V.S. Ill.ma s'è compiaciuta di mandarmi, e sono Ricercari senza parole antichi d'Adriano fatti solo per sonare, e furono lasciati dal n.ro ms. Geronimo Frescobaldi alla sua partenza per Fiandra con Mons.r mio al S. Luzzasco acciò me la mandasse. Ne bascio le mani à V.S. Ill.ma della cura s'hà preso per farmeli capitare. Il S. Luzzasco mi scrive che per la vecchiezza gli sono mancati li spiriti di Musica, e perciò fa scuse legitime alle q.le non si può replicare, che non potei favorire, e consolare la S.ra Hippolita, la quale con il suo Marito, S. Stelle (cosi faccio anch'io) resta satisfattis.a della bona volontà, di quel bono, santo e divino vecchio con tenere anch'obligo à V.S. Ill.ma come se l'havesse fatti q'lli doi canti da lei desiderati.

Il S. Pompeo Targone, et il Giulio Buratto suo cognato non si satiano per tutto, e con ogniuno di predicare le grandezze dell'Anima, et delle cortesie ricevute da V.S. Ill.ma, alla quale ne rendo anch'io grazie infinite si per questo, come per il saluto s'è degnata mandarmi per detti Sig.ri.

Sabbato penso mandarle un'Arietta di Musica, e procurare di seguitare tanto che n'azzecchi una che le dia un poco di gusto. Gran' crudeltà del S. Gio: Paolo poiche atesta di non mi rispondere mai alli saluti.

22. 25.viii.1607 Giovanni Benedetto Montesperelli to Enzo Bentivoglio
I:FEas, Archivio Bentivoglio, Mazzo 9–41, fo. 529ʳ⁻ᵛ

Ill.mo S.r mio oss.mo

Subito ricevuta la lettera di V.S. Ill.ma delli 18 del presente fui dal S.r Card.l p.rone e la diedi raguaglio del quadro già incominciato, et anco della tardanza seguita, lui stà con desiderio di crederle poiche da q.to gli hò detto stima che sarà in ogni perfettione, e ne ringratia infinitam.te V.S. Ill.ma. Da Mons.r Nappi intendo non sia arrivato per ancora in Ancona. Non mancherò di dirli a suo tempo q.to Lei mi ordina per poterlo presentare al p.rone conforme al desiderio di V.S. Ill.ma alla q.le per fine baccio le m. Della vale di Agosta non mancherò a suo tempo di raccordarla al s.r Card.le si come di gia hò co-minciato, e spero che senza fallo ne seguirà conforme desidera V.S. Ill.ma. . . . Di Roma li 25 di Ag.o 1607. Di V.S. Ill.ma Oblig.mo ser.re di cuore Gio: Benedetto Montesperelli

23. 26.viii.1607 Marc'Ant. Nappi to Enzo Bentivoglio
I:FEas, Archivio Bentivoglio, Mazzo 9–41, fo. 547ʳ⁻ᵛ

Ill.mo Sig.re mio, e p.rone coll.mo

Si sono riceute le due casse del quadro per l'Ill.mo s.r Card.e Borghese, e le salami per il s.r Targone, tutte ben cond.ne per conto si vede di fuori, e non manca sub.o far dilig.a per inviarle a Roma a Mons.r mio fratello acciò lui ne seguisse l'ord.e di V.S. Ill.ma. . . .

24. 28.viii.1607 Bernardo Bizzoni to Enzo Bentivoglio
I:FEas, Archivio Bentivoglio, Mazzo 9–41, fo. 535ʳ; partially transcribed by Fabris, 'Frescobaldi e la musica in casa Bentivoglio', 68

Ill.mo Sig.r p.rone oss.mo

Il S.r D. Hippolito Bolognese Musico ecc.te ch'altre volte stava con la bo: mem: del card. S. Quattro, et hora stà con il S.r Card. MontAlto, et è tenuto qui doppo il Sig.r Giuseppino, il p.o, m'hà dato l'incluso madrigale novo, e qui è tenuto m.to bello, perciò lo mando à V.S. Ill.ma; vero è che l'Arie qui di Roma riescono più a sentirle cantare, che à scriverle.

L'Antichità dell'Aria, e delle parole delle Romanesche ch'io le mandai non si può torre. L'altre imperfettioni l'hà levate il S. Gioseppino ch'è l'autore di q.lle con darmele scritte di mano sua, com'anco q.ll'Altra Aria che le mandai, che comincia, *Vezzosetta pastorella*; se V.S. Ill.ma non l'hà havute per p.a che può facilmente essere, e che habbia à caro à haverle, me lo scriva, ch'io subb.o La servirò con mandargliele; e tra tanto non mancarò anco di procacciarli q.ch'altra cosa nova come desiderosiss.o che son' di servirle. Et con pregarli dal Sig.re ogni bene, le faccio riverenza. Di Roma alli 28 d'Agosto 1607. Di V.S. Ill.ma Devotiss.o ser.e Bernardo Bizzoni

25. 24.iv.1610 Cardinal Montalto to Cardinal d'Este
I:MOas, Cancelleria, Estero, Carteggio di Principi, Italia, Roma, Busta 1405, fo. 150ʳ

Ill.mo R.mo Sig.r mio oss.mo

Essendo il Guarini, che mi hà data la *lettera* di V.S. Ill.ma persona di così buone, et honorate qualità, come ella scrive, merita per se stesso ogni aiuto, et io volontieri per questo rispetto, e per obedire à V.S. Ill.ma mi adoperarò à benefitio di esso, ovunque conosca potergli apportare giovam. In tanto mi raccomando quanto più posso nella *gratia* sua, e le bacio humiliss.e le mani. Di Roma alli 24 d'Aprile 1610. Di V.S. Ill.ma e R.ma A. Car*dinal* Montalto

26. 1.v.1610 Alfonso Verati to Guido Bentivoglio
I:FEas, Archivio Bentivoglio, Mazzo 9–53, fo. 201ʳ

Al Cav:re Bentivoglio chi dio guardi Ferrara

Ho ricevuta la litra di V.S. delli 23 del pasato alla quale ring.o V.S. infinitam:e del favore fatomi con il S:r Marchese, e pero mi andero tratenendo se dira la verita, quanto alli suoi vestiti vene uno finito l'altro se bartolomeo mi dispacera dui peci di casaola che tiene ancora sara presto finito ancor lui et subito non manchero inviarli.

L'ordinario pasato mandai per la posta la sua colana, et come sara gionta la si ricorda darne avisso, io non ho mai avuto nova se V.S. habbia ricevuti li colari che io diedi al ser:re del S:r Conte Manfredi come anco delle casse del Citarone et le chitare, la sua cagna sta beniss.mo et viene molto bella.

Dalle monache di santo ambrogio viene fata una grand:ma instanza per un ritrato che ano prestato à V.S. che non si ritrova, et le d:te lo vorebono avere perche dicono non esser il suo, et sono molto disgustate, et le SS:re mi ano deto che digratia, io scriva à V.S. se havese lasiato à qualche parte che si posia avere ne dia aviso à cio si posia restituirlo, qui non vie cossa di nuovo, inanti ieri vene qui alla musicha il SS. Card:le Bor*ghe*se, Caponi, et Leni dove canto ancora la S:ra Ipolita, et ebero grandis:mo gusto, come anco il S:r Enzo ne à ricevuto grand:mo favore dal S:r Card:le Montalto che mandò con me un suo à dire alla d:a S:ra Ipolita che ogni volta che il S:r Enzo la voleva che dovese subito venire à servirlo senza piu domandarse licenza à S.S. Ill:ma che tuta roma ne resta maraviliato, et per non aver altro à dire à V.S. per fine umilm:te li facio riverenza di Roma il di primo Magio 1610 Alfonso Verati

27. 8.x.1610 Cesare Marotta to Enzo Bentivoglio
I:FEas, Archivio Bentivoglio, Mazzo 9–55, fo. 86ʳ

Mi happare, come à miei familiari, darli aviso del nostro arrivo qui in Ferrara, et del felice viaggio che havemo hauto, con bona sanita de tutta la brigata, et in particolare della Sig.ra Catherina, quale per essere stata gravida, si è portata molto bene, et speramo havra felicis.mo parto. Io veramente ho sentito qualche poco di caldo, per essere venuto à cavallo, nulladimeno me la sono passato meglio che ho possuto, li allogiamenti poi sono stati dove boni, dove cattivi, et de tutti li danni hor ce ristoramo in casa propria. Poter di Dio poiche non havete hauto tanta descrittione per me scritta dal Guattaro mio scrivano quelli pochi versi detti di sopra, l'ho voluto scrivere io alle Illustrissime Signorie loro, accio imparino le creanze che devono usare con li familiari suoi aff:mi servi come siamo noi, de rallegrarci con queste bone nove, ma poiche V.S. non ha voluto ralegrarmi, mi sono rallegrato da me immaginandomi tutto il detto felice viaggio; à noi altri qui derelletti, abandonati, sconsolati, posti in oblio, che più non sent'io bussare dal cocchiero, per condurci in Piazza Nagona, onde mi si può cantare, *Ò tu che ne vai altiero*, non sentirai più bussare cocchiero, che certo, non so se vero ò falso mi parea, quando son privo di quello che havea, horsu lasciando da parti tutte queste belle cose, sul saldo la voglio pregare d'una gratia, et questa gratia cela dimando con tutto l'affetto del animo, con tutte le viscere del core, questa gratia mi sarà tanto cara, mi sara di tanto valore, mi sarà di tanta consolatione, mi rallegrerà di maniera, che sto per dire, che nel mondo non trovarei cosa che posse consolarmi, come questa gratia che li dimando, e Sig.r mio non mela negate, et questo ti prieo per pietate, la gratia che voglio, è che V.S. Ill.ma mi favorisca à volermi concedere tanta gratia, tanto favore, tanta cortesia, et lo resto lo dirò poi per l'altro procaccia, per adesso assieme con Ipolita mia li facemo sul saldo humilis:ma, profondis:ma svisceratis.ma inchinatis.ma riverentis.ma noi facemo anco alla Ill:ma Sig.ra Chaterina et Sig.ra Marchese [*sic*], et per fine restaremo pregando per la universale salute di sua casa, et N.S. vi conceda tanta sanità, quanta io ne vorrei per me di Roma il di 8 ottobre 1610. Di V.S. Ill.ma Aff.mo servo † Cav. Cesare Marotta accio il diavolo non si lo porti io fo questa †

28. 15.x.1610 Cesare Marotta to Enzo Bentivoglio
I:FEas, Archivio Bentivoglio, Mazzo 9–55, fo. 200ʳ

Ill.mo Sig.r mio

Non vorrei che mo che V.S. Ill.ma è in Ferrara, ingrossasse di modo la vista, et assieme il pensiero, che non conoscesse più li suoi servi, et sene scordasse à fatto, sicome fa di me, che pare che io non sia nel mondo, me favorisca dunque farmi conoscere, che ancora vive in V.S. Ill.ma il desiderio de farmi gratie, si come me ha fatto per il passato, et raccordarsi delle mie pretendenze, le quale veramente non merito respettivo à me, ma respettivo à chi me favorisce, ne posso essere degno, et perche so che m'intende, et che ne tiene particolare pensiero, non me stendo in altro, et questo per essere molto scarso di ceremonij havendo tutto lo scatolino consumato in una lettera qui alligata, diretta alla Sig.ra Chaterina mia Sig.ra quale si è raccordata favorirci darci aviso del viaggio gia fatto con bonis.ma sanità, et per fine li resto aff.mo servo, desiderosissimo de suoi comandamenti, et N.S. li conceda dal Cielo quanto desidera. di Roma li 15 ottobre 1610 Di V.S. Ill.ma Aff.mo et obligat:mo servo Cesare Marotta non me caro me favorisca de lettere di mano propria perche voglio poter la sera andare à dormire, et non stare à strologare

29. 20.x.1610   Cesare Marotta to Enzo Bentivoglio
I:FEas, Archivio Bentivoglio, Mazzo 9–55, fo. 287^r

Ill.mo Sig.r mio oss.mo,

Et tre con questa, vedremo alle quante lettere havrò risposta, forse la sottoscrittione è stata confusa, et non s'è inteso il mio nome, à questo anco remidiarò, e poter di Dio, ordinato allo Guattaro che me scriva due parolette, che li faori di mano propria non me ne curo, perche voglio la sera senza pensiero poter andare à letto, et non spendere tutto il mio in interpetri se la lettera della quale V.S. Ill.ma ha faorito ad Ippolita mia moglie, et sua serva, dice essere stata del meglio modo che sa, et che serà della mia, poiche so sicuro non havrà riguardo nesciuno, però hordini mi sia scritto, che non voglio stare ad impazzire con queste lettere di mano propria le lettere da mano propria per me le scriva à quel Principe della † et faccio il negotio habbia bon fine, et io mediante li Bentivoglio sia cav*aliere*. Io sono dato in tutto alla caccia con il mio archebuscio ch'è reuscito più lungo della cupola di S. Pietro, et certo me ne trovo assai bene, perche sibene perdo il sonno, acquisto sanità. L'altro giorno volendo andare col compotista di casa a caccia con le reti à lodole, et anco con li archibusci, oltra ci levassimo à 7 hore perche havevamo d'andare un pezzo lontano, Io geloso della mia acchinea, mi feci prestare un runzinetto maledetto ombroso, che quando fussimo alla salita di S.ta Maria à Maggiore, questo maledetto runzino se spagori del aria, et comingiò à fare il gran diavolo, di modo che io fu necessitato, ò per forza, ò per bona voglia andare di scena capiana terra, che stetti un'hora à non potermi movere, pure volli fare il bello humore in volere seguire la destinata caccia non curandomi del dolore, che non mi poteva movere, onde fu causa d'essere stato 4 giorni a letto. Hora questi sono li frutti della caccia, et poi pigliammo insino à 20 lodole, che importavano con la lepre che presi io la valuta di 15 baiocchi. Altro non ho che dirli qui se fanno apparecchi grandis.mi et superbis.mi per la canoniza.ne del beato Boromeo, quale sia quello preghi Iddio per noi. Alle Sig.re fo riverenze cento milla, con raccomandare alla Si.ra Caterina il negotio della +, et li raccordo il fido commisso, et per fine li fo riverenza raccordandola à comendarmi, et io prontis.mo in servirla di Roma li 20 ottobre 1610.

Di V.S. Ill.ma obliga.mo et aff.mo ser.re voglio che s'intenda Cesare Marotta

30. 27.x.1610   Alfonso Verati to Enzo Bentivoglio
I:FEas, Archivio Bentivoglio, Mazzo 9–55, fo. 431ʳ

Ill.mo Sig.r mio Sig.r et P.one oss.mo

Ieri sera Gionce il S.r Car.le Anibale Manfredi il qualle ho accom.to al melio sia potuto di alogiamento, per le spese del vito lui non vole per niuna maniera che seli faciano chi per questi dui giorni, del S.r Don Carlo non si e ancora sentito nuova alcuna. V.S. Ill.ma mi acusa di mandarmi una scatola per la S.r Ipolita ma io non ho ricevuto cossa alcuña. Il scrisi al Sig.r Principe Pereti per le caroce il qualli mi a risposto che io bacia le mani a V.S. Ill.ma. Per sua parte che se S.E. si ritrovera in Roma che lo servira molto volontieri delle caroce. Et si spera che sara in Roma senza alcun fallo et non me occorendo dirle altro con cio umilm.te a V.S. Ill.ma facio riverenza di Roma il di 27 ottob. 1610 Di V.S. Ill.ma Umiliss.mo et dev.mo ser.re Alfonso Verati

31. 10.xi.1610   Alfonso Verati to Enzo Bentivoglio
I:FEas, Archivio Bentivoglio, Mazzo 9–55+, fo. 608ʳ

Ill.mo Sig.r mio Sig.re et P.rone oss.mo

Ho ricevuta la litra di V.S. Ill.ma delli 3. stante et nel partic.re della scatola dela S.a Hipolita io avisai à V.S. Ill.ma la ricevuta et, che io haveva rechapitata, nel particolar della stella d'oro io ho inviata questa stimana per la condota non essendo stato meglio occhasione per mandarla la qualle V.S. Ill.ma dara ord.e era ricev.ta al arivo suo ben cond.ta et francha di porto, questi SS.r Ducha et Duchesa restano costi alegramente et sono molto ben visti, et regalati da questi S.ri Card.li et Prencipi et non vie nuova alcuna della sua partita, io non poso mandar linventario sino tanto che non sono partiti questi sig.ri poi che io non o tempo mancho di poter mangiare che sempre mi tragano occupato in suo serv.o et sub:ne *doppo* saranno partiti, io non manchero mandarlo, Mons.re Nappi non ancor venuto et non si aspeta sin à quatro o cinque giorni et al suo arrivo non manchero appresentarli le litre, et non ne occorrendo dir altro à V.S. Ill.ma per fine umilm.te li facio riverenza di Roma il di 10 novemb. 1610. Di V.S. Ill.ma Umiliss.mo et dev.mo ser.re Alfonso Verati

32. 12.xi.1610   Cesare Marotta to Enzo Bentivoglio
I:FEas, Archivio Bentivoglio, Mazzo 9–55, fo. 621ʳ; partially transcribed and translated by New-comb, 'Girolamo Frescobaldi, 1608–1615: A Documentary Study', 137–8

Ill.mo Sig.r mio oss.mo

Stevamo con grandis.mo martello, poiche conforme al solito non eravamo faoriti di sue lettere, onde caris.ma habiamo receuto quest'ultima ancorche brevissima sia stata, tutto per nostra mortificatione, pure l'andamo passando, ponendo in consideratione li fastidij et negotij che V.S. Ill.ma credemo che habbia, quali sono tanti che agiungendovi questo di scriverci alcuna volta, poco per queste cresceranno, ancorche ogni settimana ce faorisse. Haveressimo da dirli gran cose nove, ma cele raserbiamo à bocca, pure per non parere pultrone nel scrivere, ce ne dirrò qualche poche. La casa di V.S. Ill.ma è calamita di noi altri derelitti, et le pura[?] ce chiamato, et dove era la Sig.ra Chaterina, et Sig.ra Marchese nostre Sig.re dov'era il nostro protettore dico il Sig.re Enzo Bentivoglio, dove era la soavis.ma conversatione hieri sera giovedi da mezz'ora di notte sino alle 3 sonate. Conterò il tutto di ciò il nostro Sig.re Car.le diede mercodi da pranzo nella sua vigna al Sig.r Duca di Massa, suo fratello et altri di suoi Sig.ri et ne vado imaginando che questi Sig.ri facessero istanza di voler sentire Ippolita, et che di cio anco havea volontà la Sig.ra Duchessa. Il Sig.r Car.le finalmente ce diede ordine stessimo lesti per la detta sera, che ce havrebbe fatto chiamare, et feci per suo ordine li condure il mio Cimbalone. Fommo chiamati li, dove era quella Sig.ra veramente garbata, con tutti quelli altri Sig.ri et vi si incontrò anco il Sig.r Car.le Mellini. Ippolita al meglio modo possibile, cantò alcune cose, sibene con grandis.ma difficoltà, per essere lei gravida già di 6 mesi, et ha una gravidanza molto fastidiosa. V.S. Ill.ma come nòstro protettore ci faorirà incontrandosi con questi Sig.ri al loro ritorno far di mia moglie le scuse, che certo assicuro V.S. Ill.ma che quasi lei non può fiatare, et per consequenza non può cantare al suo solito. Quella Sig.ra fori di rigalare Ipolita d'una vergetta galantis.ma con alcuni diamanti, quale mia moglie recevi car.ma Il Sig.r Car.le nostro ci fa faori grandi, più del ordinario, et spesso ce regala di starne fasani, et altre galanterie, et questo stimamo assai, poiche con esse ce ho la sua bona gratia. In un'altra occasione secreta dove Ipolita cantò domesticamente, ponemmo fora *Se quel dolore*, quale lo dimandò S.S. Ill.ma dicendo esserli stato detto da V.S. Ill.ma et disse che li piaceva, hor vedete Sig.r mio quanta felicità, che agiungendovi la gratia della † credo sarò lo più felice huomo del mondo, et di questo negotio prego V.S. Ill.ma con tutte le viscere del core, poiche adesso venerebbe in un tempo molto opportuno per più rispetto, et perche credo me intenda non mi stendo in altro, solo restremo pregando il Sig.re li conceda sanità, con ogni contento, et à me la tanto desiata † di Roma li facemo humilis.ma riverenza questo di 12 novembre 1610. Di V.S. Ill.ma Aff.mo et humilis.mo servo Cesare Marotta, alias Ipolita de Recupito

33. 13.xi.1610   Vincentio Landinelli to Enzo Bentivoglio
I:FEas, Archivio Bentivoglio, Mazzo 9–55+, fos. 641–6 (degraded paper and largely illegible)

Ill.mo S.r P.ne Col.mo

Sono arrivati questa sera sul'Ave Maria li tre uccellini che V.S. Ill.ma ha mandati per la posta da Ferrara al S.r Car. Borghese dal quale son scernato[?] a punto ad uno o le sono sonate le due hore havendogli li . . . presentar . . . per il dubbio che ho havuto che non andassero a male quindi in casa dove e tanta girate. Il S. Car.le e queli cortiggiani quando li hanno veduti si sono molto spaventati per rispetto del becco. . . .

Giovedi mattina Il S. Prencipe Peretti fu con . . . Il S. Duca . . . dopo pranzo condusse lui et li fratelli per Roma a spatio, e hoggi sono andati a caccia, che sono rimasti alle due . . . li Ald.ni sono entrati . . . Giovedi sera ancor si fece la musica, e cantò alla presenza di S. Car.le Mont'Alto e di Melini chi . . . la S.ra Hippolita. Non poter dir altro. . . . Vincentio Landinelli

34. 13.xi.1610   Francesco Belfiore to Enzo Bentivoglio
I:FEas, Archivio Bentivoglio, Mazzo 9–55, fo. 633[r]; partially transcribed and translated by Newcomb, 'Girolamo Frescobaldi', 138, where the citation is incorrectly given as 'Mazza 53'

Ill.mo mio S.re e Padrone sing.mo

Questi SS.ri se ne stanno tuttavia attendendo avviso dell'arrivo della Galera à Civitavecchia sendo raguagliati della sua partita da Genova à 4 di questo. Vanno intanto pas-

sando il tempo con gusto, e sodisfattioni, poiche hieri andorno à caccia col S.r Principe
Savello, e tornorno con preda di cinque porci, e d'un caprio, et hoggi sono andati col
S.r Principe Peretti, ma non hanno amazzato che un cinghiale, e 'l primo feritore è stato
il S.r Co: Annibale. L'altra sera venne il S.r Card.e Montalto à visitare la S.ra Duchessa,
e questi altri SS.ri, e condì loro la gratia con far venire poco dopo la S.ra Hippolita à ren-
derli tutti stupidi col suo virtuoso talento. Confessò il S.r Duca, che fra gli altri mi pare
che habbi il gusto più delicato, e di più difficile contentatura, di non haver udita mai la
più soave, e più ben qualificata voce di questa, e tanto ch'ha detto su 'l saldo di non voler
sentire altra voce sola, per non perdere quel gusto che s'ha impresso di questa. . . .

35. 13.xi.1610   Alfonso Verati to Enzo Bentivoglio
I:FEas, Archivio Bentivoglio, Mazzo 9–55, fo. 639ʳ

Ill.mo Sig.r mio Sig.re et Pa.ne oss:mo

Ho ricevuta la litra di V.S. Ill.ma insieme con li bianchi, et ancor la scatola con la colana,
et l'orologio al quale o consignato in mani al Landinelli conforme mia comandato V.S.
Ill.ma. Per la partenza di questi SS:ri non vie ancor alcuna novella et sene stano costi alegramente favoriti molto da questi SS:ri Card.li, et Prencipi. Giovedi sera vene à visitar-
li il S:r Card:le Montalto, et vene la S:ra Hipolita, et la fece cantare, et si porto molto
bene per essere indissposta come elie, hoggi sono andati tutti alla cacia con il S:r Principe
Pereti, et sono tre ore di note, et non sono ancor tornati, et non poso darli ragualio della
cacia. Hora, e arivato batista con li grosi, et il S:r Landinelli gli a fato portar subito al
S:r Cardinale, et non so se potra V.S. Ill:ma aver risposta in tempo la S:ra Hipolita, et il
S:r Cesaro fano riverenza a V.S. Ill.ma come anco alle Ill:me SS:e Marchesa, et S:ra
Catarina, come ancor io facio il medemo di Roma il di 13 novembre 1610 Di V.S. Ill:ma
Umiliss:mo, et dev.mo ser.re Alfonso Verati

36. 13.xi.1610   Cardinal Montalto to Vincenzo Gonzaga, Duke of Mantua
I:MAas, Archivio Gonzaga, Busta 993, fos. 453ʳ–454ʳ

Ser.mo Sig.r mio oss.mo

La lettera che V. Alt.a si à compiaciuta scrivermi con l'occasione della venuta quà del
Monteverdi suo Maestro di Capella mi à capitata ultimam., et in risposta brevem.te le
dirò che non solo è persona di così buona qualità, e che tanto è grata all'Alt.za V., ma à
qualsivoglia altra, che tenga dipendenza da lei, procurarò sempre di mostrar con affetti
di somma benevolenza la molta stima, che ne faccio, et in tanto le baccio le mani di tutto
cuore. Di Roma alli 13 di Nov.re 1610. Il H.mo Serv. A. Card. Montalto

37. 17.xi.1610   Ercole Provinzale to Enzo Bentivoglio
I:FEas, Archivio Bentivoglio, Mazzo 9–55+, fo. 700ʳ⁻ᵛ; partially transcribed (with errors) and
translated by Newcomb, 'Girolamo Frescobaldi', 138, where the citation is incorrectly given
as 'Mazza 53, f. 700'

V.S. Ill:ma mi obliga troppo con la amorevolezza delle sue lettere. Giovedi dopo
pranzo lo Ill.mo S.r Car.le Borghese fu visto da me su il Corso in caroza et venere et
sabato dette udiencia all'imbasatori de Principi si che a fatto et fa tutte le atione da uno
come è per gracia di dio à una buona ciera come a N.S. . . .

Questa sera alla S.ra Ippolita fu a cantare nel palazzo di V.S. Ill.ma alla presenza di

Montalto et Mellini et il S.r D. Carlo, et il resto della famillia. Li sta da due ore di notte sina alle 4 et si porto bene cantò 5 canzone ma l'ultima fa stupenda nella spineta che sonava suo marito. Dicano che dopo sunò Allisandro che a questo non mi trovai presente se non quando canto la S.ra Ipolita. Devotissimo servitore Ercole Provinzale

38. 24.xi.1610 Vincenzo Landinelli to Enzo Bentivoglio
I:FEas, Archivio Bentivoglio, Mazzo 9–55+, fos. 779–82

Ill.mo S.e P.ne Colmo

Quanto maggiore sono state le difficoltà ŋela q.e dette Agente tanto maggior si scuopre il valore in V.S. Ill.m. . . .

Mandaro la *lette*ra che va a Don Carlo a . . . deve essere arrivato. Sono stato a salutare la S.ra Hippolita da parte di V.S. Ill.ma e le ho data la *lette*ra che le ha scrita la q*u*ale e stata carina. Lei e venuta tanto grossa che e una maraviglia e rauca in maniera che non può parlare non che cantare. . . . Divot.mo et oblig.mo ser.re Vincenzo Landinalli

39. 10.xii.1610 Cesare Marotta to Enzo Bentivoglio
I:FEas, Archivio Bentivoglio, Mazzo 9–55, fo. 923ʳ

Ill.mo Sig.r mio

Li tanti fastidij che V.S. Ill.ma tiene intorno alla bonificatione, sono quelli che me tengono legato le mani à non scriverli ogni giorno, et questo non per altro solo che me tenga in sua bona gratia, et per uno di suoi servi, poiche l'obligo che li devo è tale che s'io la servesse notte et giorno, et anco spendessi la vita, non mi parirebbe haver fatto nulla. Noi Dio gratia stamo bene, et alligrissimamente, poiche è pur per noi rasserenato quel cielo, che già era tutto tenebroso, et la rota della fortuna è alquanto voltata. Credo V.S. Ill.ma me intende. L'Ipolita sta bene sinhora per gratia del Sig.re et tutta via va crescendo la pansetta, et la ringratia della memoria che tiene di lei in scriverli di proprio pugno, et spessissimo la nominamo in occasione di gusto, et certo se adesso fusse in Roma havrebbe doppia consolatione, et il tutto non posso dire per lettera, ma lo raserbo à bocca piacendo al Sig.re. V.S. Ill.ma me farà faore passando per Bologna mandarmi 4 balle di sapone che mi è stato dimandato, et se troppo ardisco me perdoni, et ne incolpi la mia troppo sfacciatagine. Andamo credendo sia venuto il tempo del parto della Sig.ra Caterina, però stamo pregando il Sig.re la facci uscire in salvamento con un bello masculone. Don Gio: Jacomo [Maggi?] fa riverenza à V.S. Ill.ma et anco il Sig.r Don Pietro [Santolino da Fano], honorata et tutti di casa, et per fine resto servitoris.mo per servirla, con desiderio di vederla quanto prima, poiche ho tanto robba da dirli, che se non viene presto, io me imperò tanto che creperò; et facendo humilis.ma riverenza à V.S. Ill.ma fo fine pregandola dal Cielo ogni contento di Roma li 10 decembre 1610 Di V.S. Ill.ma Aff.mo servo † Cesare Marotta

40. 11.xii.1610 Francesco Belfiore to Enzo Bentivoglio
I:FEas, Archivio Bentivoglio, Mazzo 9–55, fo. 925ʳ

Il S.r Co: Annibale è stato questa sera per la prima volta à farsi conoscere da S.E. introdotto dal S.r Cav. Guarino, et hà mostrato di restar molto sodisfatto d'haver presa servitù con un tanto S.re. . . .

41. 2.iii.1611   Giovanni Giacomo Maggi to Cardinal Ferdinando Gonzaga
I:MAas, Archivio Gonzaga, Busta 998; transcribed with editorial emendations by Vogel, 'Marco da Gagliano', 562

Ill.mo et Rev.mo Sig.e P.ron mio oss.mo

Con questi dui righi vengo humilm.te à far' riverenza à V.S. Ill.ma e dirle anco che con l'occasione della pastorale che s'è fatta in casa q.o carnevale mi son servito del cimbalo che era in casa di V.S. Ill.ma quale hò trovato da un cimbalaro molto mal trattato perche havea cominciato à fare i piroli più grossi per far tenere l'accordio, ma la troppo gros- sezza hà fatto sfondare il cimbalo, et adesso tiene manco l'accordio di prima, lo tengo io in camera conservato al meglio che potrò sin'al ritorno di V.S. Ill.ma. Intanto le ricordo che vogli ordinare, e si facci fare un cimbalo buono in Firenze da Mastro Vincenzo Bolcione chi veram.te è valent'huomo in q.o esercitio et è questo che hà fatto il cimbalo della S.ra Ipolita e S.r Cesare che certo è riuscito il meglio cimbalo di Roma perchè hà gran voce, e se ci può cantar sop.a e cosi hà da essere quello di V.S. Ill.ma alla quale tutti unitam.te la S.ra Ipolita il S.r Cesare et io facemo riverenza baciamo le mani, e preghiamo presto e felice ritorno. Di Roma alli 2 di Marzo 1611. Di V.S. Ill.ma et R.ma Humiliss.mo ser.re
Gio. Jac.o Maggio

42. 18.iii.1611   Cesare Marotta to Enzo Bentivoglio
I:FEas, Archivio Bentivoglio, Mazzo 9–59, fo. 136ʳ

Ill.mo Sig.r mio oss.mo

Le gratie et faori che giornalmente da V.S. Ill.ma recevemo, sono tanti et tali che non potrei mai con lingua esplicarli, et se con altro non posso sodisfarne minima parte, almeno non cesserò pregare notte et giorno N.S. Iddio per la sua sanità, et de tutti di casa. habiamo receuto le anguille e cele goderemo per amore di V.S. Ill.ma assieme con il Sig.r nostro Gio: Jacomo [Maggi?], il quale fa riverenza à V.S. Ill.ma et alla sua venuta se è allestito uscirli al incontro con una superbis.ma Mula, più grande della cupola di S.to Pietro, alla quale calvaccata verrà anco la persona mia se però V.S. Ill.ma ne farà degno farmi avisato della giornata, quale sarà in breve, volendo sicome dice venire avanti le feste, quale sia insalvamento, et noi la stamo aspettando con grandis.mo desiderio, poiche stamo tutti come se venissimo di frascata; tanto più quanto per la disgratia succesa in casa mia; poiche Ippolita mia è stata molto male con febre, et la febre gagliardis.ma li venne 7 giorni prima del parto, et ogni giorno l'haveva, onde lei essendo stata si male, ha cagionato che la creatura habbia patita, et sia morta in utero, quale era femina, onde il parto era pericoloso, con tutto cio per Dio gratia, et della S.ma Vergine Maria, partorì presto, et con pochi dolori, et in ogni modo le restò la febre quale hora va interlasciando, et speramo in pochis.mi giorni serà del tutto ristorata. Il suo parto fù de martedi dui giorni prima della mettà di quatragesima, ho voluto del tutto dar aviso à V.S. Ill.ma perche lo ne senterà quello ne sentemo noi. Eramo tutti afflitti veramente per lei che steva male, ma hora stamo allegramente, perche speramo sia fuori di pericolo, et ce magnaremo le anguille allegramente; et perche lei adesso attende à magnare cappiri, et piccioni, le serbaremo la sua parte. Del negotio del che V.S. Ill.ma me faorisce è più approposit battere sula gratia libera, de che poi à bocca parlaremo alla lunga; li direi molte altre cose ma poiche

è per venire cossi di corto, le ruserbo alla venuta, intanto le restamo con infinitis.mo obligo.
Ippolita mia moglie li fa riverenza, desiderosis.ma di vederla, et per fine N.S. li conceda
ogni contento, et io li resto Aff.mo servo di Roma li 18 marzo 1611 Di V.S. Ill.ma Aff.mo
et oblig.mo se.re Cesare Marotta

43. 19.iii.1611   Alfonso Verati to Enzo Bentivoglio
I:FEas, Archivio Bentivoglio, Mazzo 9–59, fo. 168ʳ

Ill.mo Sig.r mio Sig.r et Pa.ne oss.mo

Ho ricevuta la litra di cambio mandatami dal Galanino per pagar il fito della cassa.
Ricevei ancor quella di V.S. Ill.ma deli 9 stante, et quanto al particolar della casa nostra
di fermarla conforme a quello mi comanda. Intanto staro atendendo aviso della buona
venuta di V.S. Ill:ma. La caseta del pesse sie trovata, et non o manchato subito farla ca-
pitar alla S:ra Ipolita insieme con le litre al S:r Cesare qualli ringratia V.S. Ill:ma del favor
fatoli. La d:ta S:ra Ipolita e stata molto male del suo parto, et ora comincia ad aver un
pocho di milioramento. Ieri io li mandai due mostre di vino per veder se li era cossa di
suo gusto come credo che sara per quello. Mi a riferito il suo ser:re et io gli o oferto che
sara la bota à sua instanza per ord:e di V.S. Ill:ma qualle per fine umilm:te facio riverenza
di Roma il di 19 marzo 1611 Di V.S. Ill.ma Umiliss.mo et dev.mo ser.re Alfonso Verati

44. 16.xi.1611   Cesare Marotta to Enzo Bentivoglio
I:FEas, Archivio Bentivoglio, Mazzo 9–62, fo. 167ʳ

Ill.mo Sig.r mio oss.mo

Doveva prima veramente fare mio debito con V.S. Ill.ma con farli riverenza, et ralle-
grarmi del figliolo maschio nato in bon'hora, et mio nuovo P.rone, ma non l'ho fatto,
dubitando che in quelli primi giorni non l'apportasse molestia, et anco che mie lettere
non fussero poste in oblio, per le furie delli negotij, ma hora che credo vadino tuttavia
mancando, ho voluto con questa farli riverenza, assieme con Ipolita mia moglie, et il
simile alla Sig.ra Marchesa, et Sig.ra Caterina, et tutti altri signori, rallegrandomi anco
dell'arrivo che costi ha fatto in buona saluta. Il mio negozio di Turino intendo camini
bene, il che aviso à V.S. Ill.ma perche sapendo quanto desidera favorirmi, so ne sentirà
particolar gusto, et del successo havrà ne avisaro à pieno, di qui non li do altro aviso, poiche
so di certo non mancano persone che minutamente l'avisano di ogni cosa, intanto la prico
à tenermi nella su bona gratia, et mandandomi le calzette nere di costì, poiche me disse
che si fanno si bone, et durano, io le receverò caris.me si perche mi verranno di sue mani,
come anco per essersi prolungato lo coroccio per alcuni mesi, et intanto resterò pregando
il Sig.re per ogni suo contento di Roma li 16 novembre 1611. Di V.S. Ill.ma Aff.mo Ser.re
Cesare Marotta

45. 8.xii.1611   Cesare Marotta to Enzo Bentivoglio
I:FEas, Archivio Bentivoglio, Mazzo 9–62, fo. 452ʳ

Ill.mo Sig.re mio oss.mo

Poiche V.S. Ill.ma favorisce tanto le cose mie, et in particolare quella ultima, onde fà instanza volerla, ce la manderò per quest'altro ordinario, poiche non ho possuto copiarla

adesso per alcune mie malangonie, cagionate da questa benedetta casa, quale ancora non si è hauta, et anco agravato da catarro con dolor di testa. Basta l'haverà senza altro per l'altro ordinario, si bene Ipolita era ordinata à non mandarla, sino che non venisse la scimiotta, quale credo sarebbe venuta. Se V.S. Ill.ma se ne fusse raccordato et risponderò anco à cinquecento lettere venutime di costì, et se questi congratulatorij meco sapessere che se paga 2 baiocchi per lettera di porto, credo havrebbero hauto riguardo à tanta spesa, si bene si rallegrano con me del cavalerato in erba, poiche sino adesso non si vede comparire principio de spedizione, onde prico V.S. Ill.ma come quello ha incomingiato à favorirmi, à volere anco fenire, de scrivere una lettera di suo pugno al Sig.r Ambasciatore di Savoia, acciò solleciti il negotio, et l'habbia per raccomandato, si bene in ogni occasione mi fa molti favori ecc.

Il Sig.r Domenico mi ha mostrato una lettera di V.S. Ill.ma et visto quanto dice intorno à quel negotio, et a me non pare troppo al proposito, et quello sarebbe l'ultimo rimedio, intanto e bisogno pensare altro ecc. Resto à V.S. Ill.ma suo servo di tutto core con farli humilis:ma riverenza assieme con Ipolita, et per fine N.S. li concedi ogni contento di Roma li 8 decembre 1611 Di V.S. Ill.ma Aff.mo S.re Il Cavalier Cesare Marotta

46. 14.xii.1611   Cesare Marotta to Caterina Bentivoglio
I:FEas, Archivio Bentivoglio, Mazzo 9–62, fo. 534ʳ

Ill.ma Sig.ra mia oss.ma

Prima di adesso ho fatto mio debito di ringraziare V.S. Ill.ma della lettera scrittami, rallegrandosi meco della gratia hauta dal Serenis.mo di Savoia, ma per dubio che non le sia venuta nelli mani, ardisco scriverli quest'altra, certificandola, che de tutto tengo anco particolar obligo à V.S. Ill.ma come quella che con tante lettere me ha in ciò favorita, ond'io li vivo il maggior servo obligato, che possi mai vivere nel mondo, à qualsivoglia persona, per qualsivoglia cagione, non vorrei se affligesse più per la morte di quel'Angelino, quale di continuo stà avanti al Sig.re Iddio à pregare per la sanità, et per ogni contento di V.S. Ill.ma; ma si consoli col volere suo, et col vedersi avanti l'altri suoi bell'Angiolini, alli quali N.S. conceda sanità. Ipolita mia li fa riverenza, et se li raccorda serva; il che facendo anco io fo fine pregandola dal Cielo ogni contento di Roma li 14 Xbre 1611 Di V.S. Ill.ma Aff.mo s.re Cesare Marotta

47. 14.xii.1611   Cesare Marotta to Enzo Bentivoglio
I:FEas, Archivio Bentivoglio, Mazzo 9–62, fo. 548ʳ

Ill.mo Sig.r mio oss.mo

Mando à V.S. Ill.ma l'aria che mi dimanda *Può ben fortuna* ecc. *Soavissimi lumi* non la mando, perche credo che l'habbia il Sig.r Antonio Guretta [= Goretti], che cela diedi quando fu qui, però caso che non l'havesse V.S. Ill.ma avisi che subbito la servirò con quello debito ch'io devo, et sempre li sarò l'istesso statoli per il passato, anzi ogni giorno più obligato, per li tante gratie che da lei giornalmente ricevo, del che tengo particolar pensiero. Ancora non è venuta la speditione di Savoia, et se V.S. Ill.ma non favorisce sollicitare con il Sig.r Ambasciatore, potrebbe andare alla lunga, et io con l'aspettativa potrei divenire paralitico. So che lo farà di suo proprio pugno, et con quella caldezza, con che sempre mi ha favorito, però non mi stendo in alto, solo stamo aspettando la scimiotta con queste sue, et suoi di Casa mi pare che troppo presto si siano rallegrati meco, però non ardisco rispondere à tutti. Solo per chiarirmi d'un dubio scrivo al Sig.r Manfredi m.ro del Sig.r Cornelio, et S. Aniballino. V.S. Ill.ma mi favorirà farcela capitare nelle mani, et procurarmi risposta, perche molto mi preme, et per fine li fo riverenza assieme con Ipolita mia et N.S. li conceda ogni contento di Roma li 14 Xbre 1611 Di V.S. Ill.ma Oblig.mo s.re Cesare Marotta

48. 21.i.1612   Vincenzo Landinelli to Enzo Bentivoglio
I:FEas, Archivio Bentivoglio, Mazzo 9–63 fo. 313; partially transcribed by Frederick Hammond, *Girolamo Frescobaldi* (Cambridge, Mass., 1983), 344

Ill.mo S.re et P.ron mio Col.mo

Hieri pregato condusse il S.r Amb.re di Fiandra con tre, o quattri altri ss.ri principalissimi fiamminghi à sentir sonare la Napolitana, et gli piaque in estremo, e volse sapere il nome, e cognome di lei, e del Marito, e lo noto sul libro, desiderando anco sentire la sig.ra Hippolita, ma perche il s.r Cesare si truova à letto per un poco di male ch'ha in una gamba, e gli conviene domandar licenza al s.r Cardinal Montalto non sarranno compiaciuti così presto, ho detto à questi ss.ri che in mantenendo questa Napolitana con fratello e sorelle importa a V.S. Ill.ma più di mille scudi all'anno, e spende altro tanto in mantenere altre simile virtuosi che cantano, e il Piccinino di Gironimo molto bene conosciuto da loro, accio che sono certificati che sorte di persona hanno per Nontio in Fiandra se bene non gli è parso nuovo; sapendo molto bene la qualità di questa Casa . . .

49. 8.ii.1612   Vincenzio Landinelli to Enzo Bentivoglio
I:FEas, Archivio Bentivoglio, Mazzo 9–63, fos. 503ʳ, 506ʳ

Ill.mo S.re et P.ron mio Col.mo

La Sig.ra Hippolita si truova in stato, che non puole venire in modo alcuno à Ferrara non ostante il desiderio grande ch'habbi di servire à V.S. Ill.ma insieme col Marito p.a perchè è gravida di due mesi la qual gravidanza gli da un fastidio straordinario 2.o il viaggio longo accompagnato con freddi, e facci con tanta incommodità 3.o et ultimo credo quando cessassero tutte queste difficoltà, il sapere, che Adrianella [Adriana Basile] del S.r Duca di Mantova deve intervenire in queste Feste faria risolverla à non venire, e veramente P.ron mio questi non sono tempi di scomodare le Donne oltre si aggionge, che il S.r Cesare non si sente à modo suo per conto d'una gamba, ò piede al quale si fece male e non poco con l'occasione dell'andata à Civitavecchia. Non hò potuto anco vedere il S.r Cavalier Guerino, il quale sebene è stato dalla d.a S.ra Hippolita, et gli habbi detto, che farà tutto quello che il S.r Card.l Montalto gli commandarà, con tutto ciò con me si è lasciata intendere di non poter venire per le cause d.e di sopra, sperando di havere a truovare scusa appresso la benignità di V.S. Ill.ma come quella che sa benissimo, che se potesse verria volando per darle questo gusto. Quanto alla S.ra Lucretia, et Marito si offeriscono pronti di ubidire sempre à i suoi commandamenti, non ostantte i medesimi impedimenti, che ritengono la S.ra Hippolita. Io non voglio dar legge à V.S. Ill.ma che mi è P.rone, et è prudentissima, ma le dico bene, che sarà più lodata da tutti se potrà far senza la Napolitana, et Marito, e per le spese e per altre cause molto ben note à lei, tanto più che il S.r Cardinal Vescovo non verrà altrimenti à far Carnevale à Ferrara, ma lo farà alla Madonna di Loreto, sebene il Cardinal Caetano hà fatto, e fa violenza, perche lo vadi à fare à Ravenna. Al qual Cardinal Leni hà fatto le sue raccomandationi, et supplicatolo conforme à quanto V.S. Ill.ma m'ha ordinato, mostrando che ella se era indotta à fare tornei, et altre Feste più per rispetto suo, che di qualsivogl'altra persona.

Al S.r Cardinal P.rone presentai hier mattina la sua *lettera* col Cartello, e mi disse che non era bene, ch'io facesse altr'istanza per queste Donne ne col S.r Cardinal Montalto ne con altri, e quanto al Cardinal Vescovo, che era ordine di N.S. che non venisse à Ferrara nei giorni carnevalitij, e che haverebbe letto con gusto il Cartello, del quale ho dato notitia anco al S.r Pignattelli.

Domattina in S. Agata à Monte Magnanapoli (poiche il Papa si ritrova à Montecavallo da hier mattina in qua) il S.r Cesare Marotti pigliarà la Croce di Savoia dalle mani del S.r Ambasciatore, e si truovaranno presenti à quest'attione li SS.ri Cardinali Borghese, Sezza, e Capponi con una comitiva grande de SS.ri e SS.re e ci sarà anco la S.ra Hippolita, attalche S.r mio se pensaste d'havere à trattare hora, che siamo intrati in queste dignità con persone ordinarie s'inganna. È ben vero, ch'ha comprata cara questa dignità, e questo è qualche pesa alla S.ra Hippolita, poiche gli costa fin'a quest'hora più di 300 scudi, ricconoscano quest'honorevolezza dalle mani di V.S Ill.ma. Si è aggiustato il negotio col S.r Roberto Primi, ma non e spedito perche vuole la ratificatione dell'Instrumento fatto da me come Pr.ore delli Mercanti senz'altra conditione, ma dall'altra parte esseguirà il tutto conforme al lor desiderio, e perche essi siano sicuri mandaranno la ratificatione in mano de chi vogliono, che non si farà cosa alcuna fin'a tanto quel tale non habbia veduto, e toccato con mano, che sia adempito ogni cosa à gusto loro, e di questo particolare ne do conto al S.r Dottor Cazzetta, e con quest'altro ordinario si mandaranno le scritture. Il male è che il Baccello si truova in secreta per lo schiaffo che diede in Banchi ad un sensale, e per questo si differirà la conclusione dell'altro negotio delli 200 luoghi de Monti per la Bonificatione. Questa causa è nel Tribunale di Mons.r Auditor della Camera, che la fa con molto rigore, e Dio voglia, che al Baccelli non costi buona somma di denari. Io non manco aiutarlo mediante il S.r Pignattello. La pena della bolla è di diece anni di Galea, e per questo anco come hò detto non si potranno haver i denari si presto, tanto più che i fr.elli del S.r Alessandro Nappi sono subintrati in luogo del S.r Marchese Bentivoglio i quali doveranno ratificare l'instrumento, la quale ratificatione mandarò al S.r Alessandro senz'altro sabbato prossimo.

Sono stato per presentare le l.re alla Prencipessa Peretti, et alla S.ra Costanza Ma[dre?] (cut off) e non hò potuto havendole trovate occupate, ci ritornarò domani.

Della Corte non hò che dir'altro à V.S. Ill.ma se non che questa mattina il S.r Cardinal Vescovo hà cominciate le sue vigite, e credo che in gr.a di V.S. Ill.ma compiacerà il Visdomini Cirugico, non ostante l'instanza del S.r Cardinal Pio per un'altro. Il Cardinal Mellini la saluta, e le raccomanda il negotio dei suoi grani. Bisogna tenerselo amico, perche dopo la caduta del Cardinal Nazzareto, è tenuto l'arcifanfano, ma più prudente, e Galanthuomo.

[new hand] Io farò di siccuro tutto quello potrò con la S.ra Hippolita, ma non credo riuscirà perche veramente i tempi sono cattivi, et ella non sta guari bene di sanità. Quanto alla Napolitana già ho scritto con le passate quell'occorre come sia astretta à lasciare la sorella non si potrà fare che non si scuopri ogni cosa, e la Charita vuole che si tenga celato q.to neg.o per l'amore di Dio se non per altro rispetto, et ancora non habbia di havere una vita infelice V.S. Ill.ma ci deve havere qualche consideratione. In oltre si sà che la S.ra Catterina è afflittiss.a per questa gente e però non è bene ne merita di ricevere maggior disgusto . . .

50. 18.ii.1612   Vincenzio Landinelli to Enzo Bentivoglio
I:FEas, Archivio Bentivoglio, Mazzo 9–63, fos. 646ʳ–647ʳ. The paper is in bad condition with many holes

Illmo S.re et P.rone oss.mo

Il Cavalier Guarino et io habbiamo usati tutti gl'artifitij possibili per indurre il S.r Cardinal Montalto a dar licenza alla S.ra Hippolita, che possa venire a Ferrara con l'occasione di queste feste, e mai è stato possibile cavargli altro di 'bocca, se non che desidera fare servitio à V.S. Ill.ma in ogni tempo, et in tutte le occasioni, ma quanto al venir d.a Hippolita non gli pare stagione à propposito ma con tutto ciò se ella voleva venire . . . all'arbietro suo, sapendo benissimo, che ella non porra un piede . . . all'uscio senza l'espresso suo commandamento . . . lei con dispiacer grande e del S.r Cavaliere, e . . . quel vero servitore che li sono havendo veduto ch'ha . . . staffetta a porta, e che a scritte *lettere* tanto effecaci per haver . . . hò fatto tutto quello hò saputo, e potuto, acciò ottenghi l'intento suo, e dal S.r Cavalier sod.o e da me è stato replicato, e triplicato al Med.o S. Cardinal per Dio grati, propponendo la devota servitù di V.S. Ill.ma et molte altre ragione farlo acconsentire, ma tutte invano. Habbiamo concluso (?) che sia stato tanto . . . per non aprir la strada ad altri Cavalieri di dimandarla e potria anco essere, che . . . S.ra Hippolita ritrovandosi gravida, et iĺ Marito poco sano per rispetto della sua gamba non habbino fatto offitio contrario, se bene con me hanno mostrato gran prontezza a talche V.S. Ill.ma intende, habbi patienza per questa volta, e facci senza la d.a Hippolita, poiche questo non è negotio, che dependa dalla volontà di lei, e del Marito perche in questo caso sa ben certo che sebene fusse deluviato non che piovuto, e che . . . havuta la pancia più grossa d'un tamburo et una gamba rotta, gl'haveria bisognato che fussero venuti, e questo e quanto m'occorre dire intorno a q.to particolare, per il quale sono stato tutt'hoggi in sino due hore di notte occupato. . . .

Patrone mio cosi il S. Cav.re Guarini come la S.ra Hippolita con il Cav.re suo marito fanno fede quanto io mi sia affaticato per che V.S. Ill.ma havesse questo gusto, ma si è toccata maggior . . . del S.r Car.l Mont'Alto di qu*es*ti S. si hanno imaginata. Di Roma li 18 di febraro 1612. Di V.S. Ill.ma Divot.mo et oblig.ma ser.re Vincentio Landinelli

51. 18.ii.1612   Alfonso Verati to Enzo Bentivoglio
I:FEas, Archivio Bentivoglio, Mazzo 9–63, fo. 634ʳ

Ill:mo Sig.r mio Sig.r et P*a*drone Col.mo

Ho ricevuta la litra di V.S. Ill:ma deli 14 del corente quale io non o manchato di andar à trovar il S:r Cesar Marota per pigliar ord:e conforme à quello mi comanda V.S. Ill:ma, et mi a risposto che lui era prontiss.mo per venire ma che non aveva ancora avuto ord:e nisuno dal S:r Card:e Montalto, et era di gia un ora di note, pero io non manchero di solicitar quanto sarà posibile il partire se verano altro non so dire à V.S. Ill:ma sopra questo particolare con che per fine umilm.te li facio riverenza di Roma il di 18 febraro 1612. Di V.S. Ill.ma umiliss.mo, et dev.mo ser.re Alfonso Verati

52. 18.ii.1612 Cesare Marotta to Enzo Bentivoglio
I:FEas, Archivio Bentivoglio, Mazzo 278, fo. 315ʳ. I have this transcription through the kindness of Dinko Fabris. It will also appear in his forthcoming book on the artistic patronage of the Bentivoglio family

Ill.mo sig.or mio oss.mo
Questa mattina, sabbato, dal sig.or Landinelli ho receuto il piego di V.S. Ill.ma, et sono stato tutt'oggi aspettando che il sig.or Car.le mio sig.re dovesse darmi alcuno ordine circa il nostro venire costì per servirla, et è già un'hora di notte, et non vedo novità alcuna. Ho voluto con tutto ciò scriverli queste poche parole, per non usare mala creanza, assicurandola che tenermo particolar memoria di servirla, sicome vedrà venendo l'ordine del padrone, senza il quale non posso, ne devo disporre di me in cosa alcuna della persona mia, sicome benissimo V.S. Ill.mo potrà considerare. Et per fine li fo humilissima riverenza assieme con Ipolita mia, pregandola da Cielo ogni contento. Di Roma li 18. febraro 1612. Aff.mo se.re Il Cavalier Don Cesare Marotta

53. 22.ii.1612 Alfonso Verati to Enzo Bentivoglio
I:FEas, Archivio Bentivoglio, Mazzo 9–63, fo. 683ʳ

Ill.mo Sig.r mio Sig.re et P*adro*ne coll.mo
Hoggi mi è capitato un plicho che va diritivo à un Capitano Gioseppe Girardi, et il soprascrito della sopra coperta era indirizato à me, et mi pare la mano del secretario di V.S. Ill.ma, et il sigilo di V.S. Ill.ma cosi, o cerchato di trovar d:to Cap:no, et non so trovar persona che mene sapia dar noticia chi si sia pero non manchero far praticha di trovarlo se sara posibille, della venuta della S:ra Hipolita credo V.S. Ill:ma à saputo oggni cossa del S:r Landinelli, et altro non me occorendo dir à V.S. Ill:ma per fine umilm:te li facio riverenza di Roma il di 22 febraro 1612. Di V.S. Ill:ma umiliss.mo, et dev.mo ser.re Alfonso Verati

54. 10.iii.1612 Vincenzo Landinelli to Enzo Bentivoglio
I:FEas, Archivio Bentivoglio, Mazzo 9–64, fos. 88ʳ–89ʳ

Ill.mo S.e P.ne Col.mo
Io sepi Giovedi mattina dal S.re Car.l p.ne quanto V.S. Ill.ma mi haveva scritto intorno al Sig.r Neapolitano, e lo fece ridere e poi mi fece chiamare in Camera, e mi domandò ch'io dovessi scriverle come gli era venuta voglia dell'Adriana e si stava col Duca di Mantova, e però pregasse V. S. Ill.ma da parte sua, e si facesse ogn'opera perchè venisse à stare con lui che l'haveria trattata nella maniera che tratta il S. Car.l Mont'Alto l'Ippolita oltra alla certa speranza, che le poteva dare . . .

55. 16.v.1612   Cesare Marotta to Enzo Bentivoglio
I:MOe, Autografoteca Campori, s.v. 'Cesare Marotta'

Ill.mo Sig.r mio oss.mo

Due di V.S. Ill.ma ho ricevuto adesso, e non prima, e però prima di adesso non ho risposto, ne questo mi ha impedito ch'io non habbia cercato servirla al meglio ch'io ho saputo, di già haverà ricevuto 4. intermedij fattomi fare in nome di V.S. Ill.ma dal Sig.r Ca.re Guarini, e se non fussero di suo gusto scusi la brevità del tempo, et anco il mio poco sapere, et acetti solo da me una prontiss.ma volontà ch'io tengo di servirla, ho inteso siano reusciti corti, questo non è mio defetto, starò aspettando il Sig.r Ca.re Guarini vi faccia l'agiunta, et poi subbito la servirò, intanto potrà fare imparare cotesti, poiche l'essersevi ben cantati, et ben consertati compariranno tanto più, et quello che ha cura consertarli, è bisogna sia prattico in cotesta maniera di musica ricitativa; Ipolita mia li fa riverenza, et seli raccorda serva, sicome anco alla Sig.ra Caterina, Sig.ra Marchesa, et tutti di Casa, et io per fine li vivo l'istesso obbigatis.mo servo di Roma li 16. Magio 1612 Di V.S. Ill.ma Aff.mo se.re Il Ca.re Cesare Marotta

56. 5.vi.1612   Cesare Marotta to Enzo Bentivoglio
I:FEas, Archivio Bentivoglio, Mazzo 9–65, fo. 578^r

Ill.mo Sig.r mio oss.mo

Io sono stato male, e stò ancora poco bene, però sono rimasto farli riverenza al mio solito, hora con la presente non solo li fo riverenza, ma ancora caldissimamente la ringratio delle 2 para di calzette mandatemi, et delli salami, quali sono venuti à tempo che à punto stamo svogliati, io indisposto, e mia moglie dubbiosa de pregnatura, quale ha anco ricevuto li guanti, e li godera in nome di V.S. Ill.ma. Io cercai subito servirla delli intermedij al meglio che ci ho saputo. Ho inteso alcuni siano riusciti corti, questo non è mio deffetto, et è cosa rimediabile con facilità. Intanto me comandi dove mi cognosce bono, che sempre mi troverà prontis.mo in servirla, e per fine li fo humilis:ma riverenza assieme con Ipolita mia, et N.S. li conceda ogni contento di Roma li 5 Giugno 1612 Di V.S. Ill.ma Aff.mo se.re Il Cavalier Marotta

57. 1.ix.1612   Cesare Marotta to Enzo Bentivoglio
I:FEas, Archivio Bentivoglio, Mazzo 9–67, fo. 11^r

Ill.mo Sig.r mio oss.mo

Poter del Mondo. Quanti ritiramenti, quant'intonature, quanti negotij; sarebbe tanto gran cosa il dire alle volte al secretario che scrivesse due paroline, per confirmatione della servitù che tengo appreso V.S. Ill.ma che mi priva del maggior contento che posso havere in questo mondo, che non l'essere comandato da chi ho tanto riceuto gratie, è favori. Dhe per pietà al meno, pria ch'io mi venghi meno, socorretemi con qualche vostra amorevole lettera, acciò possa conoscere, ch'io sia l'istesso, che sempre li sono stato. E se fia ver l'aita, non mi negate vita, io non so che dire, sono tanto contento, tanto allegro, tanto allegrissimo, per la prossima venuta del S. Enzo, che non posso parlare approposito, però venghi presto, allegramente, e di buona sanità, intanto li fo riverenza con tutt'il core, cossi facendo alla mia S.ra Caterina, et à tutti li gatti di cotesta casa, et N.S. li conceda ogni contento di Roma il p.o di settembre 1612 Di V.S. Ill.ma Aff.mo se.re il Ca.re D. Cesare Marotta

58. 20.ix.1612 Ippolita Recupito Marotta to Caterina Bentivoglio
I:FEas, Archivio Bentivoglio, Mazzo 9–67, fo. 387ʳ

Ill.ma Sig.ra mia oss.ma

Vorrei pure che V.S. Ill.ma se degnasse alle volte farmi degna de suoi commandamenti, tanto più quanto che sa benis.mo l'obblighi che li tengo, e s'io del continuo non li scrivo, fo per non fastidirla, et hora prendo sicurtà, mossa dalla passione ch'io sento, per esserli lontana, che se non moro, spero pure in Dio un giorno haverla à rivedere, et servirla. Il disgusto ch'io intesi della cascata del Sig.r Aniballino, fu contrapisato dal haver inteso sia guarito, è credami ch'io n'intesi quella istessa passione che ne sentiva V.S. Ill.ma professando io esserli serva di tanto debito alla mia Sig.ra Marchesa me li raccordo serva con farli riverenza, il che fa anco mio marito, al Sig.r Corachio, Sig.r Aniballino, Sig.ra Sabelluccia, et tutti di casa basciamo le mani, e per fine con restarli serva, et mio marito servo fo fine pregandola dal Cielo ogni contento di Roma li 20 settembre 1612 Di V.S. Ill.ma Aff.ma se.va Ipolita Recupito Marotta, moglie del Cavalier Marotta.

59. 20.ix.1612 Cesare Marotta to Enzo Bentivoglio
I:FEas, Archivio Bentivoglio, Mazzo 9–67, fo. 389ʳ

Ill.mo Sig.r mio oss.mo

Con ragione V.S. Ill.ma si può lamentare di me ch'io non habbia risposto ad alcune sue, poiche veramente non ho risposto, et il difetto non è cagionato da me, ne da mia negligenza, poiche non havrei mai usato termine di si mala creanza, ma il mancamento è venuto da questi della posta, che non mi hanno dato le lettere, et hieri à casa passando per la posta, mi chiamaro, et mi dettero due vecchie fatte di luglio, di V.S. Ill.ma et un'altra fatta di fresco in risposta d'una mia, però non m'abbia per mal creato, che per Dio, e per S.to Francesco cossi passa il fatto. Con grandis.mo desiderio stò aspettando la sua venuta, è sapendo la giornata verrò ad incontrarlo insino à Bagnaia, venendo di quella strada, ò verrò altrove, e tanto più verrò volentieri, quanto sentendo l'odore di quelli pretiosi salami, che fate gran torto all'affectione che li porto à non portarne una soma, et tutti darli à me, perche almeno io li so magniare, e non ci è pericolo, che li lascia marcire, et à fe di Cav.re che solo uno vi ho, et non vedo l'hora passino queste 4 tempora per mangiarmelo per la dolce memoria del mio caro S.r Enzo, tanto garbato tanto gentile, tanto amorevole, e più garbatis.mo più gentilis.mo più amorevolis.mo se porta una barca di salami. Ipolita mia li vive l'istessa serva affe.ma che sempre li è stata, et anco lei lo stà aspettando con grandis.mo desiderio per poterla servire. In tanto la prico à tenerci nella sua solita bona gratia, e per fine li facemo riverenza con tutt'il core di Roma li 20 settembre 1612 Di V.S. Ill.ma Aff.mo se.re il Cav.re Cesare Marotta

60. 11.x.1612　Cesare Marotta to Enzo Bentivogliò
I:FEas, Archivio Bentivoglio, Mazzo 9–68, fo. 147^r

Ill.mo Sig.r mio

Questa casa dove io sto l'è tanto dolorosa, tanto humida, tanto sogetta à falegniami, che
però io sono andato cercando mutarla, e già ne haveva trovato una molto approposito,
è stava à Santo Andrea della Valle, con tutto ciò non ho volsuto partirmi da questa, dove
stò con tanti incomodi come ho detto, è questo non per altro, e non ad altro fine che
per stare più vicino a V.S. Ill.ma, et acciò habbia più occasione d'essere da lei comandato,
havendo già destinato io d'havere à magniare più salami, più pollastri, più animelle, più
piccioni, più vitelle in casa vostra che in càsa mia, onde volentieri farò il comandamento che mi da di eligermi nel palazzo preso uno appartamento per la mia persona,
però venghino pure allegramente è presto che del tutto saremo d'accordo. Il suo secretario in mio nome la priegherà d'un favore per me, de trovarmi costì uno cagno per lo
schioppo che entri all'acqua, et che sia buono, che costì se ne fa professione, ma che sia
troppo grande, che non vorrei che magnasse la mia parte del pane, ma faremo à mezzo,
cio è una pagniotta per uno, e per fine li fo riverenza con tutti di mia casa di Roma li 11
ottobre 1612 Di V.S. Ill.ma Aff.mo se.re il Cav.re D. Cesare Marotta

61. 3.xi.1612　Cesare Marotta to Enzo Bentivoglio
I:FEas, Archivio Bentivoglio, Mazzo 9–68, fo. 431^r

Ill.mo Sig.r mio oss.mo

S'io fusse pregnio già sarei scoginto per tanto aspettare questa venuta di V.S. Ill.ma da
me tanto bramata, e poter di Dio che s'aspetta che venghino li diluvij la neve, li giacci, le
tempeste, le procelle le turbidis.me tramontane, vanno pur per Roma le calde arroste, si
sente pur gridare spaccia cammini, se vedono salciccie, tordi, caprij, piccioni d'Agliande,
Ruffulatti, finiscono li vini vecchi, incomingiano li raspati, si sente gridare carboni carboni, le Pell*icc*ie, li manichotti, le zimarre, scarpe à 3 sole, et altre cose simile. Se vedono
andare in volta, il fiume va grosso, le legna vanno incarenno, tutti questi sono segni
chiari che siamo molto viccini al S.r Inverno, pero mi sarebbe, che essendo V.S. Ill.ma
più dolce più souave, che non è tra la stagione la primavera, ò Autunno, che dovesse venire
prima del Inverno, ne porti la Cagna, ò Cagno, et che sia perfettis.mo e che magni poco.
Li fo humilis.ma riverenza di Roma li 3 9bre 1612 Di V.S. Ill.ma Aff.mo se.re il S.
Cav.re Marotta

62. 10.xi.1612　Cesare Marotta to Enzo Bentivoglio
I:FEas, Archivio Bentivoglio, Mazzo 9–68, fo. 500^r

Ill.mo Sig.r mio oss.mo

Poiche e risoluta non volersi partire di costì, prima che io mi svogli del suo favore, per
non tenerla più a tedio ho voluto il tutto eseguire; onde prico V.S. Ill.ma quanto posso
à favorirmi di raccomandare Pietro Santolino da Fano, al presente Gover.re di Cervia,
alla Communità di Ferrara, accio voglia eligerlo per uno luogo nella Rota di detta
Città per il futuro quinquennio, dovendosi à maggio prossimo far l'electione di quelli

Auditori. Di questo prico V.S. Ill.ma quanto posso, poiche questo tale Pietro è fr.ello
d'uno officiale de bravi di nostra casa, e del tutto prico à darmine risposta. Qui la stemo
aspettando con grandis.mo desiderio, però non si faccia tanto desiderare, e per fine li vivo
l'istesso di sempre, e N.S. li conceda ogni contento. Di Roma li 10 9bre 1612 Di V.S.
Ill.ma Aff.mo se.re il Cav.re D. Cesare Marotta

63. 30.iii.1613   Jacopo Cicognini to Enzo Bentivoglio
I:MOe, Autogr. Campori, s.v. 'Jacopo Cicognini'

Mando l'Adone à V.S. Ill.ma havendolo fatto copiare diligentissamente, et per esser favola
destinata per le prime nozze delle Ser.me Principesse di Toscana suplico V.S. Ill.ma che
ad alc.o non ne conceda copia. Et si come da lei mi fu ordinato, l'ho consegnato al Sig.r
Tomaso Baccelli, il quale ha pagato al copista venti giuli. Per lettere del S.r Merlini scritte
al Sig.r Gio. B.a Arpini mi ha ordinato per parte di V.S. Ill.ma che li deva mandare
l'Andromeda quale farò copiare, et quanto p.a la consegnerò al med.mo Sig.r Baccelli
che sarà altrettanta spesa se pero V.S. Ill.ma non comanderà in contrario. Intanto atten-
derò qualche suo comandamento reputandomi favorissimo qual'ora sarò degno di
potere servire. Ho hauto ottima speranza dall'Ill.mo et R.mo S.r Card.e Borghese di dover
sortire con buon governo. Starò à vedere quello seguirà et à suo tempo ne darò sonto à
V.S. Ill.ma alla q.lo fo le r.me rever.ze di Roma il dì 30 di Marzo 1613. Di V.S. Ill.ma
dev.mo ser.e Jac.o Cicognini

64. 4.v.1613   Francesca Caccini to Virginio Orsini
I:Rac, Archivio Orsini, Corrispondenza epistolare di Virginio II Orsini, II.C.Prot. XXIII.123,
n. 2, lettera 233

Ill.mo et Ecc.mo Sig.r mio Col.mo

Poiché non potei alla mia partita ringraziare in voce V.E. Ill.ma dei regali, di quali oltre
a tant'altre grazie da me ricevute in Casa sua, ella per render più infinito il numero degli
obblighi miei, si compiacque onorarmi, mi è parso mio debito ringraziarla adesso, il che
io fo con ogni umiltà, e con tutto l'affetto dell'animo, offrendole prontissim.te ogni occasione nella quale ella conosce che io la possa servire; per ch'io vivo sempre con questo
particolar desiderio di riconoscere con la mia servitù gli infiniti benefizi che da V.E. ho
ricevuto, e continuamente ricevo. Subito ch'io fui in Firenze andai a far riverenza alle
Sig. e sue fig.le le quali si rallegrorno assai, nell'aver nuove di V.E.; stanno beniss.mo e
mi hanno comandato, che per loro io le faccia riverenza e sono restate molto soddis-
fatte di alcune inform.ni che à l'una diedi di Roma et all'altra di Francia. Feci appresso
tutte le altre visite che ella mi comandò e tutte queste S.re ... S. M.a Vittoria ringraziano
V.E. della memoria che ella si degna tener di loro e se le ricordano umilm.te ser.vi; prossimo si farà il ballo nel quale io intervengo si che ... [entire line illegible] le occupazioni
potrò servire a V.E. Ill.ma de quei due Madrigali che le promiso per quelle Sig.re e per
più non la tediare insieme con mio marito le fo um.a riverenza pregandola da N.S. ogni
vero bene. Di Firenze alli 4 di Maggio 1613 Di. V.E. Ill.ma Umiliss.ma Serva Franc.ca
Cacc.ni nei Signor.ni

65. 11.v.1613 Francesca Caccini to Virginio Orsini
I:Rac, Archivio Orsini, Corrispondenza epistolare di Virginio II Orsini, II.C.Prot. XXV.126, n. 5, lettera 858

Ill.mo et Ecc.mo Sig.r mio Padrone Oss.mo

Mando à V.E. Ill.ma i due madrigali che già le sono in obbligo, non so se saraño di suo intero gusto, se bene in procurarlo non ho mancato di usarci ogni diligentia come farò sempre in tutte l'occasioni ch'ella mi porgerà di poterla servire, nelle quali mi troverà pront.ma conforme a gl'infiniti obblighi che le tengo. Prego V.E., che mi voglia far grazia di baciar le mani alla S.ra Cammilla, con tutte quell'altre Sig.re, et essendo sbrigata da tutto quello ch'io dovea operare per servizio de i Ser.mi Padroni in queste nozze aspetto con sommo desiderio di poter venire a servire a V.E. Ill.ma e con farle umil.ma riverenza insieme con mio marito prego N.S. per ogni sua vera felicità. Di Firenze alli 11 di Maggio 1613 Di V.E. Ill.ma Umil.ma et Obbligat.ma Serva Franc.ca Caccini Signor.ni

66. 29.vi.1613 Ippolito Macchiavelli to Ferdinando Gonzaga, Duke of Mantua
I:MAas, Archivio Gonzaga, Busta 1005, at the date

Ser.mo mio Sig.r Clementiss.o

Se l'A.V.S. potesse cosi vedere l'intimo dell'animo mio come io mi prometto che benignam.te si compiacerà di vedere questa mia pena di humiliss.a devota riverenza, sò mi conoscerebbe per quello per cui in vera devot.ne et osservanza hò sempre desiderato di notificarmele: ma ciò non può essere, et io non hò parole da bene esprimere q.to mio cosi devoto affetto. M'inchino dunque à V.A.S. supplicandola che si come in altri tempi si è degnata di gradire la mia devota servitù così hora si compiaccia non havere a sdegno l'affetto, con che me le raccommando in gradire, et di credere che in ogni mia operatione, et in ogni tempo procurarò di rendere testimoniaza al mondo de gli oblighi che le tengo, et all'A.V. del desid.rio che hò di poterla servire. Il S.r Paolo sà l'animo mio, e la devota osservanza ch'io porto à V.A.S. egli potrà farne fede, et attestare la riverenza, con che faccio q.to uff.o al quale ponendo fine per non più lungam.te à V.A.S. et le prego dal S.r Iddio la vita, et felicità che ella desidera. Di Roma à li 29 Giugno 1613. Di V. A. Ser.ma Humiliss.o et devottiss. Ser. Hippolito Macchiavelli

67. 13.vii.1613 Cesare Marotta to Enzo Bentivoglio
I:FEas, Archivio Bentivoglio, Mazzo 9–70, fo. 564ʳ

Ill.mo Sig.r mio oss.mo

V.S. Ill.ma mi fa troppi favori à degniarsi scrivermi di suo proprio pugnio, onde la prico à non farmi queste gratie, perche in questi tempi caldi mi confiarei tanto, che portarei pericolo di crepare, maggiormente adesso che sto godendo li salami da V.S. Ill.ma mandatomi, de quali neli rendo infinitissime gratie. Del particolare che mi scrive de incaminare adesso la nostra venuta costì, io ne lascio la cura à lei che à huomo che sa negotiare più de tutti gl'homini del mondo, ben vero à me parebbe che l'avanzare tempo, non sarebbe se non bene. Ho invidia del buon tempo che attende à pigliarsi in villa, et godere il fresco, che non posso dire cossi io, poiche qui la stagione va calda, e piacesse à Dio ch'io havesse fortuna anco costi poterla servire. Non si manca di attendere alla

Sig.ra Francesca, et à punto oggi l'ho finito il sonetto, et credo quando lo possederà non li dispiacerà. Per alcuni pochi giorni non li darò opera nova, volendo procurare che dica bene questo, appresso anderò agiustandoli quelle due mie opere che malamente cantava. Basta V.S. Ill.ma s'assicuri che non mancherò di diligenza, et fatica, del che spero ne vedrà l'esperienza. Qui stamo tutti bene, e con l'istessa prontezza di servirla, con che fo fine facendoli riverenza unitamente con la sig.ra Caterina, et tutti di casa di Roma li 13 luglio 1613. Di V.S. Ill.ma Aff.mo ser.re il Cav.re Marotta

68. 27.vii.1613   Cesare Marotta to Enzo Bentivoglio
I:FEas, Archivio Bentivoglio, Mazzo 9–70, fo. 709ʳ

Ill.mo sig.r mio

Sarà bisognio ch'io mandi à V.S. Ill.ma una fede del parrocchiano autenticata, per farli credere che io non manco attendere alla S. Francesca, et che ci vo ogni giorno, ecetto solo quando ho da servire il mio Sig.re Car.le et questo è poche volte, anzi le dico che io tralascio alla Sig.ra Anna Maria, che stò li 15 giorni à non andarci, per servire V.S. Ill.ma et in ciò solo mi dispiace che non voglia crederlo, parendomi che faccia torto à questa mia diligenza, et insieme al desiderio che tengo di servirla, con tutto ciò il tutto attribuisco alla mia mala fortuna, come quella che non vuole ch'io habbia tanta consolatione, d'essere vera questa mia buona voluntà ecc. Credo che sarà tarda in comprare il Palazzo di Riario, sicome ne scrive, dicendosi buplicamente [*sic*] per Roma, haverlo comprato il S. Antonio Manfroni. Lunedì sarà concistoro, et io mi sono insogniato non so che del nostro S. Nuntio di Fiandra, che se la fortuna vorrà farmi dire la verità, sarà causa ch'io mi privi de 6 botte per brugiare si bene spero mi potrebbono essere pagati assai care, con che bascio à V.S. Ill.ma le mani con tutti di casa di Roma li 27 luglio 1613. Di V.S. Ill.ma aff.mo se.re il Ca.re Marotta

69. 7.ix.1613   Cesare Marotta to Enzo Bentivoglio
I:FEas, Archivio Bentivoglio, Mazzo 9–71, fo. 374ʳ

Ill.mo sig.r mio oss.mo

Ho inteso consolatione infinita che V.S. Ill.ma doppo l'indispositione, sia ritornata nella sua pristina sanità, e N.S. Iddio lo custodisca in essa. Starò aspettando il comandamento per potere venire à servirla, e di ciò ho visto quanto V.S. Ill.ma scrive. Non manco attendere alla S.a Francesca quanto posso, e sto vicino à fenirle quel altra arietta, intanto sia sicuris.ma che ho particolar gusto di servirla, e vorrei essere tanto più bono, quanto che mi fa ogni giorno più favori. Alla Sig.ra Marchesa, alla Sig.ra Caterina, et tutti fo riverenza, sicome fa anco mia moglie, et la m.to Ill.re Sig.ra Cecchina Marotta, quale già incomincia à cantare e per fine resterò pregando il Sig.re per ogni contento di V.S. Ill.ma di Roma di 7 settembre 1613. Di V.S. Ill.ma aff.mo s.re il Cav.re D. Cesare Marotta

70. 25.ix.1613   Cesare Marotta to Enzo Bentivoglio
I:FEas, Archivio Bentivoglio, Mazzo 9–71, fo. 544ʳ

Ill.mo sig.r mio oss.mo

Francesco di V.S. Ill.ma è stato da me à mostrarmi una sua, à lui scritta è si e doluto meco, argomentando per essa, che appresso V.S. Ill.ma li sia stato fatto male officio. Io

in veritate non posso ne devo dire altro, solo che detto Francesco è desiderosissimo
d'imparare, e da molti che l'han visto, ho inteso dire che del continuo sia andato da
Don Ipolito [Macchiavelli], e che da lui mai è rimasto prendere lettione. Io di novo l'ho
inteso cantare, e mi pare che habbia fatto profitto, si come V.S. Ill.ma costì sentirà
ponendo però in consideratione il poco tempo che hà imparato, è l'havere mutato anco
m.ri, l'haverà qualche cosa nociuto. Mi sono offerto nel suo ritorno mostrarli io alcuna
cosa, dandomi ad intendere che non butterò à fatto il tempo, e questo si per servire V.S.
Ill.a come anco per il gran desiderio che esso tiene d'imparare. A punto dui giorni sono
l'ho fatto una arietta, però molto, è molto difficile, e mi dispiace per la brevità del tempo
non potercela mostrare come vorrei. Potrà di essa in tanto sentire l'abozzo, che al suo
ritorno poi, m'offero farcela dire di meglior modo. Mi dispiace non potere anc'io essere
costi per poterla servire, e maggiormente in questa occasione della venuta della Sig.ra
Francesca che essendo lei tanto principiante, sarebbe necessario havere app*resso* di lei il
suo m.ro, che il sonarli bene, importa la mettà del cantare, e per contrario il sonarcele
male. Le due opere che l'ha imparato ce l'ho date scritte, à fine costi se li possano rac-
cordare, dandomi ad intendere che se anderà scordando alcuna cosa, spero che V.S. Ill.ma
l'haverà compassione, si per essere principiante, come anco sapendo quanto sia difficile
questo cantare solo. Le due arie che mi dimanda, non li mando, perche so che non le
possono servire, che quando potessero servire pur le mandarei, ancorche il darle fora è
mio grandis.mo pregiuditio. Me le rasserbo à farcele godere qui di presenza, con che li
fo humilis.ma riverenza, assieme con Ipolita mia, di Roma li 25 settembre 1613. Di V.S.
Ill.ma Aff.mo se.re il Cav.re Cesare Marotta

71. 1.x.1613   Cesare Marotta to Girolamo Fioretti
I:FEas, Archivio Bentivoglio, Mazzo 9–71, fo. 591ʳ

M.to Ill.re Sig. mio,

Viene costi la Sig.ra Francesca, sicome V.S. sa, et mi dispiace che quelle cose che canta,
non li possieda tanto, quanto vorrei, acciò il Sig. Enzo restasse più sodisfatto, con tutto
ciò credo si haverà riguardo al poco tempo che ha imparato, che essendo questo cantar
solo mistiero tanto difficoltoso, seli concede lunghezza di tempo. Non dico di mesi, ma
di anni. Credo però che detta S.ra Francesca darà qualche sodisfattione, se pure costi se
conserterando con alcuno che li soni bene quelle opere quale tutte li ho date scritte giuste
nel modo che ce l'ha imparate, et scordandosi per l'intervalo alcuna cosa, ce li potrà rac-
cordare, con vederle scritte.

Ancorche il Comendatore di S.to Spirito desse ferma intentione al Sig.r Enzo di concedere la gratia al Archidiacono mio parente et darli l'Abbito, si come V.S. benis.mo sa
et doppo haver superato tutte quelle difficoltà che detto Comendatore desiderava, non
ha voluto in ogni modo spedirlo. Desiderava che lui fondasse un Priorato, esso lo fundò,
et fece le scritture giuste nel modo altre volte fatte in Napoli, et per l'istesso notaro per
prendere detto Abito, e le copie di detta fondatione, l'ho haute [cut off] et presentatele
al detto Comendatore, hanno in ciò non [cut off] che difficoltà, et il diffetto di queste
difficoltà, credo venghino più dal secretario della detta Religione, che dal Comendatore,
con tutto ciò il Comendatore è il p.rone di farlo, et può farlo, et deve farlo, se non per

altro, almeno per la promessa fatta al sig.r Enzo. Hora per finirla, ò dentro, ò fuora, vorrei chel il Sig.r Enzo scrivesse una lettera caldissima, e con alcune parole di suo pugnio al detto Comendatore, dicendolo che havendoli dato parola ferma di fare questa gratia à Don Gio: Domenico de Rentijs, voglia à sua istanza ultimarla, tanto più quanto che detto Gio: Dom.co ha fatto quelle prove, et fede che si desiderava, et già si sono presentate a detto Comendatore. Si desiderava anco che detto Gio: Dom.co si trovasse in Napoli uno di detto ordine che l'accettasse per suo compagnio; et questo lo trovò, et hebbe quello istesso che detto Comendatore li disse, ma questo non ha volsuto admetterlo dicendo, che questo Compagnio ha poco loco, et poche intrate, che non può acettare altri in sua compagnia, onde per superare questa difficoltà, il Comendatore me disse, che questo detto Don Gio: Do.co fondasse un Priorato, il quale come ho detto lo fondò nel istesso modo che altri sono stati fondati, con l'istessa rendita, à ciò anco ha trovato difficoltà, et per dirla sono stracco di andare più à S.to Spirito, di modo che V.S. che credo farà la lettera. Potrà andare toccando questo trascorso, et dirli che se in ciò trova alcuna difficoltà, deve superarla per amore del Sig.r Enzo, et per l'intentione adesso data, che se non vi fusse alcuna difficoltà non sarebbe gratia, et non occorreva il favore del Sig.r Enzo. Questa lettera V.S. me la mandi con una diretta al Sig.r Landinelli, poiche vorrei che il detto Landinelli cela portasse, et lo parlasse anco à bocca da parte del Sig.r Enzo, dimodo V.S. procurò la lettera al Comendatore, et anco al Sig.r Vicenzo Landinelli, et fatine un piego, et mandatimele, che io andero poi à portarle al Landinelli, et anderemo assieme dal Comendatore, potrà mandarle per sicura strada. Il Sig.r Car.le lunedi prossimo passato andò à Bagniaia, dove anderò ancora io, et tutta la mia casa, comandando cossi il Sig.r Car.le et stò aspettando mi rimandi la carrozza; li staremo da 15 giorni, però potrà avisare à chi manderà queste lettere, che non le diano se non in mani mie, et s'io fusse fuor di Roma che aspetti il mio ritorno. Altro non ho che dirli, io li vivo l'istesso di sempre, con che li bascio le mani di tutto core di Roma questo di p.o ottobre 1613. Di V.S. Ill.ma aff.mo s.re il Ca.re Marotta

72. 17.xii.1613   Cesare Marotta to Enzo Bentivoglio
I:FEas, Archivio Bentivoglio, Mazzo 9–72, fo. 287ʳ

Ill.mo Sig.r mio

Mando le musiche che mi ha comandato facesse, et ancorche stia tanto occupato, havendo à comporre tanti intermezzi per queste nozze del Sig.r Principe, nulla dimeno ho lasciato ogni cosa da parte per servirla, tanto più facendomene tanta fretta. Venerdi sera 13 del presente mese mi furo date le parole con il piego de V.S. Ill.ma dal S.r Ercole Provenzale, et oggi martedi mattina ho finito il tutto, et ancorche l'habbia fatto tanto al improviso, credo però non doveranno à fatto dispiacerli, pregandola però à dare ordine siano bene consertate, et ben cantate, che altrimenti le sarebbono di noia, et à me si farebbe torto. Vado credendo che per le gran nevi fatte in quelle parte di Fiandra, habbino causato che à quest'hora non siano anco giunti quelle collara, de quali dette ordine già un'anno fa dovessero venire, che s'io non mi fusse trovvato provisto d'altri collari, di certo ne anderei senza, et l'istesso impedimento è avenuto al portatore della Pistola di costì à me già promesami, che s'io non havesse hauto altre armi da difendermi, à quest'ora sarei già cenere. Almeno se fusse degniato darmi aviso se la Francesca si porta bene, è se quelle opere da me imparatele con tante fatiche, et stenti, sono di suo gusto, et se cele raccorda, et se le canta bene ò male, poiche non vorrei il tuto fusse buttato al vento. Intanto meli raccordo servo, et Ipolita con tutti di casa li fanno riverenza, con che di Roma ne fo fine questo di 17 Decembre 1613. Di V.S. Ill.ma Aff.mo s.re il Cav.re D. Cesare Marotta

73. 1.i.1614   Cesare Marotta to Enzo Bentivoglio
I:FEas, Archivio Bentivoglio, Mazzo 9–73, fo. 3ʳ

Ill.mo Sig.r mio

Vedo che V.S. Ill.ma è troppo partiale delle cose mie, onde le favorisce troppo. Io in quelle mandatole cercai la brevità, à fine non venissero à tedio. Hora che mi comanda ch'io facci l'agiunta in quel fine, l'ho fatta subbito, che havendo oggi mercore sul mezzo giorno ricevuto dal Provinzale la sua à gratis.ma tanto à me più grata, quanto mi fa degno di suoi comandamenti. Ho cercato oggi istesso servirla per l'occasione che si rappresenta della partenza della Posta, è questa giunta l'ho fatto alla cieca, non havendo copia di quelle musiche mandate, che era necessario haverle, per servirme delli sogetti. Con tutto ciò ho fatto al meglio possibile, onde la prico accettarle, et con esse il mio bono animo, quale sempre starà prontis.mo in servirla. E con questa occasione le mando le bone feste, che se V.S. Ill.ma me l'havesse mandato à me, io sarei stato in obligo mandarle la mangia che cossi s'usa qui. Intanto li fo riverenza assieme con mia moglie, facendo l'istesso alla Sig.ra Caterina, et Sig.ra Marchesa, et N. S. assieme li conserva lungo tempo di roma il primo gennaro 1614. Di V.S. Ill.ma aff.mo s.re il Cav.re Cesare Marotta

74. 3.iii.1614   Cesare Marotta to Enzo Bentivoglio
I:FEas, Archivio Bentivoglio, Mazzo 9–73, fo. 427ʳ

Ill.mo Sig.r mio oss.mo

Mando à V.S. Ill.ma la romanesca che mi comanda, ancorche mi la reserbava in mostrarla io alla Sig.ra Francesca, accio la sentisse da essa nel modo che desidererei fusse cantata, poiche vado argomentando che il mostrarla non sia facile à chi non ha bene la pratica di essa, che si bene è romanesca, nulladimeno io la chiamo romanesca bastarda, poiche in molti loci deve andare cantata con affetto, et in altri con tenute di voci, accenti, et altre diligenze, quale non si possono scrivere, ma vogliono la viva voce. Io assai fo quando obedisco li padroni. La prego si bene à non darli fora, perche non l'ho presentata, et mai ho voluto darla, ancorche mille richieste ne habbia hauto. Le parole delli nostri tramezzi qui fatti, non li mando perche V.S. Ill.ma à quest'hora li havrà riceuti dal S.r Provinzale. Le musiche di esse non le posso mandare, poiche subbito fenito la festa il S.r Card.le padrone volse il mio libro delle musiche, e non so à che fine. Forse lo facesse perche io non desse fuora alcune arie di essi tramezzi fatte da me, le quale hebbero fortuna di piacere universalmente, onde mi furno chieste da molte, et molte persone, anzi alcuni principij di esse mi erano rubbati, mentre erano cantate, che destramente alcuni musici curiosi nel sentirle le scrivevano, ma difficilmente potevano rubbarle intieramente, onde forse, il Sig.r Car.le per questo volse il mio libro, si che me scusi si hora come hora non posso di ciò servirla. Del honore fatto al sonetto *Donna bella, et crudele*, ne ringratio V.S. Ill.ma ma mi pare uno honore mozzo, poiche nella discrittione dice che questo sonetto era adornato di molti assaggi, et che fu il sigillo della festa, et che piacque tanto al populo, e poi dice che fu composto à Roma, e non dice da Chi, di modo che Roma si deve ringratiare V.S. Ill.ma et non io, poiche io in ciò non sono nominato à cosa alcuna, et nell'altre discrittione fatte in simile occasioni, ho visto ponere li nomi di chi ha composto le parole, et le musiche, à fine si sappia per il mondo, alla fine di cio io non mi ne curo, poiche in affetto io non ho questa albascia, ma dico quello che si usa, et cossi si deve fare, si come vedrà in questa discrittione nostra che si sta stampando. Io non l'ho letta, ne anco inteso parlarni, ma credo certo che in essa si nomineranno alcune parti principali. Ho inteso del S.r Geronimo che V.S. Ill.ma in breve anderà à Venetia. N.S. li dia buon viaggio, et in quella città si raccordi di me, di mia moglie, et della mia Pupa, ciò è à chi un pettino, à chi un' scopettino, à chi un poco di fettuccia, per memoria di questa andata, con che resto à V.S. Ill.ma servo di tutto core. alla Sig.ra Caterina Sig.ra Marchesa, et Signorini, et tutti fo riverenza unitamente con Ippolita mia, la quale se li raccorda serva, et per fine N.S. li conceda ogni contento di Roma li 3 Marzo 1614. Di V.S. Ill.ma Aff.mo et humilis.mo s.re il Cav.re Marotta

75. 14.iii.1614 Cesare Marotta to Enzo Bentivoglio
I:FEas, Archivio Bentivoglio, Mazzo 9–73, fo. 579ʳ

Ill.mo Sig.r mio oss.mo

Fatta Pasqua tengo animo assieme con mia moglie fare il viaggio della S.ma Madonna dello Reto [i.e. di Loreto], e perche V.S. Ill.ma me disse che risolvendomi di far detto viaggio celo dovesse avisare, non ho voluto mancare obedirla. Vado anco argomentando che sarebbe facil cosa con questa occasione haver anco licenza di arrivare costi per alcuni pochi giorni, ma come che da me non posso scoprirmi, mi parebbe, che piacendo cossi à V.S. Ill.ma di scrivere di novo al p.rone dicendoli che havendo presentito che noi volemo fare questo viaggio, con tal occasione S.S. si degnasse comandarci che ad istanza di V.S. Ill.ma dovessimo arrivare costì, ma la lettera per fare affetto vol essere calda, accio il padrone conosca che li preme questo. Li può anco accennare che adesso sono fenite qui le feste, per il che non ci è da fare nulla, che tanto più facilita la gratia. Questa lettera la vorrei presentare io al padrone, acciò dicendomi cosa alcuna, potesse con bel modo facilitare il venire, et anco vorrei una lettera diretta à me, dicendomi ch'io deggia presentare questa inclusa al padrone, con ordinarmi anco che à bocca li dicesse in nome di V.S. Ill.ma alcuna cosa sopra di ciò, et la lettera à me diretta vorebbe essere anco caldis.ma perche io con quella occasione la farei leggere al padrone, in fine adesso è il tempo ch'io esequisca questo mio desiderio, et insieme far conoscere à V.S. Ill.ma quanto io desideri servirla, che per fine li resto servo, et l'istesso Ipolita mia moglie, di Roma li 14 Marzo 1614. Di V.S. Ill.ma aff.mo s.re il Ca.re Marotta

76. 22.iii.1614 Francesca Caccini to Virginio Orsini
I:Rac, Archivio Orsini, Corrispondenza epistolare di Virginio II Orsini, II.C.Prot. XXIV.125, n. 1, lettera 164

Ill.mo et Ecc.mo Sig.re Padron mio sempre Oss.mo

Dalla Sig.ra Maria Cavalc.ti ho inteso come V.E. Ill.ma mi comanda, che io le scriva qual volontà io habbia di ritornare a Roma, onde per obbedire al suo comand.to et insieme

soddisfare al continuo desid.o, che ho di poter servire a V.E. non posso intorno à ciò
dirle se non, che da lei maggior grazia, et onore non potrei ricevere oltre à gli altri
infiniti, che ho ricevuto, ch'ella m'intercedesse licentia da' miei Ser.mi *Padroni*, di
venire a passare la prossima state à Roma, che per meno tempo non mi pare di dovere
mettermi in tal viaggio, perché invece di poter servire a V.E. altro non potrei fare che
noiarla, et incomodarla si come altra volta mi avvenne. Se havrò tanta buona fortuna
che ciò possa seguire io spero che magg.re occasione havrò di poterla servire di quella
che hebbi l'Ano passato per certi nuovi studij che ho fatto, i quali io non debbo ardire,
ne ardisco pensare, che per lor proprio merito possano darli gusto ma si bene credo che
almeno non li habbiano a dispiacere per la novità, che sempre suol dilettare, aspetterò
dunque con quel magg.r desid.o ch'io possa che segua l'effetto di quanto per sua bontà,
et amorevolezza ella mi promette per la l.ra della S.ra Maria, e vivendo sempre de-
sideros.ma di riconoscere co' la mia servitù quant'io sono obbligata a V.E. Ill.ma insieme
con mio marito le fo um.ma river.za con pregarle da N.S. le buone feste, et il fine
de' suoi desid.ri. Di Firenze alli 22 Marzo 1613 [1614] Di V.E..Ill.ma Umiliss.ma
obblig.ma Serva Franc.ca Cacc.ni Signor.ni

77. 5.iv.1614   Cesare Marotta to Enzo Bentivoglio
I:FEas, Archivio Bentivoglio, Mazzo 9–73, fo. 58^r

Ill.mo Sig.r mio oss.mo

Nel istesso tempo che io recevi la lettera della Sig.ra Marchesa diretta al Sig.r Car.le venne
giungendo qui il S. Guglielmo, onde rappresentandomi quella occasione, fece da esso
rappresentare la detta lettera al Sig.r Car.le et li feci dire che era venuto qui per alcuni
negotij, onde la Sig.ra Marchesa mi ha comandato che io desse questa lettera à V.S. Ill.ma
et ch'io in suo nome li raccomandasse questo negotio, et anco ho ordine dal Sig.r Enzo
che io deggio trattenermi sino alla partita della Sig.ra Ippolita, à fine vedi seco ad accom-
pagnarla. Il Sig.r Car.le li rispose amorevolis.te et li disse queste parole, io non ho altro
desiderio che di servire questi Sig.ri et quanto a me io sono contentis.mo che venghino
à servire questi Sig.ri però disponete la voluntà loro, che io sono pronto. La mattina seguente
io andai dal Sig.r Car.le et li disse che io haveva hauto lettere dà V.S. Ill.ma et dalla Sig.ra
Marchesa, dove me dicono che hanno fatto ufficio con V.S. Ill.ma acciò se contenti, che
con questa occasione di andare alla S.ma Casa dello Reto [i.e. di Loreto], arrivi con mia
moglie sino à Ferrara. Il Sig.r Car.le rispose io quanto à me ho gusto che andiate, et
vi do licenza che andiate, in ogni modo quando siete alla Madonna in quattro giorni
arriverete à Ferrara, et haverete strada boni.ma sempre piana. Io risposi che tutto questo
stava bene, ma che io havrei fatto quello che S.S. Ill.ma comandava, mi riplicò l'istesso,
sempre con amorevolezza grande, ma che il comandarmi ch'io venesse, non voleva, perche
altre volte da altri Sig.ri haveva hauto simili richiesti, et che non ha voluto comandare
ch'io vadi, onde però non vuole ne anco ad esso comandarmelo, siche stando cossi il negotio e facilitato assai, hora sono di parere, si come anco mi è stato consigliato, che V.S.
Ill.ma ò la istessa Sig.ra Marchesa riscrivesse al detto Sig.r Car.le et li può dire che da quel
mio huomo che ha presentato à V.S. Ill.ma la mia lettera ho inteso con quanta affectione mi vuole favorire della Sig.ra Ippolita, ma perche dal Cav.re suo marito, ne meno

dalla detta Sig.ra Ippolita ricevo risposta sicura della loro venuta, prego dunque di novo V.S. Ill.ma à raccordarsi di farsi chiamare il detto Cav.re et darli ordine che voglino venire, et questa lettera vuole essere come si deve, cioè calda, et sarebbe bene farla presentare dal Sig.r Landinelli, ma prima che la presenti parlare con me, che à bocca li dirò alcuni particolari. Questo tutto lo fo perche non vorrei fusse posto in consideratione al Sig.r Car.le, che il venire costi sia mia voluntà, et intanto che venghi questa lettera ci staremo ponendo in ordine, et mia moglie vuole purgarsi un poco, che per li cibbi di quadragesima si sente un poco aggravata di stomaco, et in tanto anco si anderà fermando il tempo, che qui è stravagantis.mo, et ogni giorno piove. Io non rispondo alla Sig.ra Marchesa, che per avere un poco di scesa in un'occhio non posso troppo scrivere, in intanto mi raserbo à bocca molte facetie con che li fo riverenza di Roma li 5 aprile 1614. Di V.S. Ill.ma aff.mo s.re il Cav. M.ta [postscript:] Vorrei che questa lettera fusse stracciata quando sarà letta.

78. 8.vii.1614   Cesare d'Este, Duke of Modena, to Cardinal Montalto
I:MOas, Marchionale poi Ducale Estense, Estero, Carteggio di Principi e Signore, Italia, Roma, Busta 150 (draft of a letter)

Al Card.le Montalto

Piero, e Giovanni Guttierez raccommandatimi da V.S. Ill.ma col mezo della sua gratissima lettera sono stati da me veduti volentieri e non solo nel fermarsi quì ma nel partire anche. Hanno provato di quanta autorità sia presso di me ogni ufficio fatto da lei la qual mente non cessa mai di favorirmi con vere mostrationi di cordiale affetto. Mi va tuttavia accresciuto il desiderio e l'obligo di dimostrarli con vivi efetti la prontissima mia volontà di servirle sempre. Ringratiando dunque V.S. Ill.ma della presente occ.ne la supplico à porgermi delle maggiori e con tutto l'assicuro . . .

79. 9.vii.1614   Cardinal Montalto to Cesare d'Este, Duke of Modena
I:MOas, Marchionale poi Ducale Estense, Estero, Carteggio di Principi e Signore, Italia, Roma, Busta 150

S.r Prencipe di Modona

L'Hippolita musica è stata favorita più di quello ch'ella stessa havesse mai potuto disiderare, essendosi V. Alt.za, e cotesti altri Ser.mi miei SS.ri compiacciuti d'ascoltare il suo canto, il quale hò cariss.o, che sia stato loro dilettevole, come à me è singolarm.te accetto l'humaniss.o offitio che V. Alt.za in quest'occasione si è degnata far meco, confermandomi tuttavia maggiorm.te nella certezza, ch'io tengo, che la mia servitù sia da lei aggradita, e la ne rendo infinite gratie, con baciarle le mani. Di Roma alli 9. di Luglio 1614. Di V. Alt.za Hum.mo ser. A. Car. Montalto

80. 22.x.1614   Jacopo Cicognini to Ferdinando Gonzaga, Duke of Mantua
I:MAas, Archivio Gonzaga, Busta 1006, no. 716

Ser.mo mio Sig.re et Padrone Col.mo

Trovomi in Roma, et benchè da molti venga sollevata la mia cond.ne, non per questo ad alc.o mi sono già mai obligato di servire, anzi dopo il festino, che io composi per il Sig.r Principe Peretti me ne andai in Governo ne la Città di Segni, dove son stato sin al presente, e di nuovo vengo trattenuto dal Sig.r Duca di Bracciano, mà alla fine sarà forza tornare alla Patria poiche troppo gran pegno vi ho lasciato: Desideravo una volta avanti io deponesse quei studi, che si mi dilettano, et dicessi a Dio a' quei virtuosi esercitij nelli quali V.A.S. sà, che io ho qualche talento, venirmene un Carnevale a farle hum.a rever.za, et in segno della mia continuata devotione, et osservanza presentarle quel opere, che son pur dal universale desiderate alla luce, et non poche di numero, et sarebbe mia somma fortuna, e felicità, il poter in quel tempo, che io mi fermasse non esser ser.re inutile del A.V.S. tanto più, che havendo nuove fatiche, e già finito me assicuro che ella non si sdegnerebbe di riguardarle con occhio benigno et se io sarò fatto degno di un minimo cenno obedirò V.A.S., alla q.le hum.te inchinandomi prego da N.S. lunga vita, et continuate gratie. Da Roma il di 22 di ott.re 1614. Di V.A. Ser.ma devo.mo et oblig.mo ser.re Jacopo Cicognini

81. 18.iv.1615   Enzo Bentivoglio to Antonio Goretti
I:FEbca, Autografo 3112

Ill.mo Sig.r

Averà V.S. qui congionta una lettera dirittiva al P. J. Giorgio Capp.no in virtù della quale sarà consegnato a' mendicanti il vecchio Munistero, contentandomi io, che si riserba la celebrazione dello strumento alla mia venuta a Ferrara. Intanto V.S. si compiacerà di attendere alle musiche della Comedia; che io di quà non mi dimenticherò di procurar dell'opere da cantare in diverse maniere, e le manderò in mano di V.S. per darle questo gusto; poiche io sò, che niuno mai ha preteso di darle cosa alcuna di musica per grazia; e l'aria che ultim.e imparava Francesca io non l'ho mai avuta dal Cav.re, sicome ne anche il seg.rio, che perciò non poteva lasciarla, oltreche, si può dire, che la Francesca, ancora non la sapesse in alcuna parte, e lasciando di entrare in altro, a V.S. mi offero, di cuore. Di Roma li 18. Aprile 1615 Enzo Ben.o

82. 25.iv.1615   Enzo Bentivoglio to Antonio Goretti
I:FEbca, Autografo 3113

Ill.mo Sig.re

Mi giova di sperare, che a quest'ora coteste due Donne debbano aver' apprese perfettam.e tutte l'opere da recitarsi per Intramezzi della Tragedia; onde V.S. potrebbe cominciare à provar con tutti gli altri, invitandogli per mia parte, ed assicurandogli, che gli resterò doppiam.te ubbligato, se al mio ritorno troverò, che per loro diligenza, e sollecitudine sieno gl'Intramezzi in ordinanza tale, che possino subito rappresentarsi; estraord.te, non si dimenticando ancora di far'essercitare a Francesca l'opere scritte nel suo libro, quali vorrei, ch'imparasse a sonar con l'Istrum.to, e V.S. mi farà part.re piacere di affaticarseci; Intanto me le offero, di cuore. Di Roma li 25 Aprile 1615 E. Bent.o

83. 27.iv.1615   Enzo Bentivoglio to Antonio Goretti
I:FEbca, Autografo 3114

Ill.mo Sig.re

Ringrazio V.S. tanto del buon aug.rio, che mi ha fatta della san.ma quanto degli avvisi, che mi ha dato intorno al negozio degli Restagni[?], ed in ciò raccomando a V.S. la spedi-

zione. Mi sarà a cuore il S.r Aless.ro, e nel part.re delle sue provig.ni li provverò ogni
vantaggio. E a V.S. per fine mi offero, di cuore di Roma li 27 Aprile 1615 Enzo Bent.o

84. 30.iv.1614 Cesare Marotta to Enzo Bentivoglio
I:FEas, Archivio Bentivoglio, Mazza 74, fo. 376. I have this transcription through the kindness
of Dinko Fabris. It will also appear in his forthcoming book on the artistic patronage of the
Bentivoglio family

Ill.mo sig.r mio oss.mo
Qui non è piovuto ma è diluviato ogni giorno, onde non ho prima possuto risolvermi
di partire. Oggi a punto il tempo ha lasciato di piovere onde vado vedendo voglia
accomodarsi; son' però risoluto partire domenica, o lunedì che saranno 4 del mese di
Maggio. Però V.S. Ill.ma potrà inviare subbito la carrozza, acciò la troviamo alla S.ma
Casa; con che li raccordo che io sono religioso, et vengo da religiosissimo, et non farò
poco condurmi con la mia brigata sino a Loreto: voglio inferire che con la carozza
mandi biada per li cavalli per li cocchieri et per noi altri, altrimenti per la strada ci
magnaremo li cavalli. Questi sig.ri Angonitani fanno istanza che ci vogliamo fermare
alcuni giorni in Angona; io per dirla vorrei venire a dirittura, che questo mese che il
sig.r Car.le mi dà licenza, Io vorrei tutto spendere in servire V.S. Ill.ma. Mi parebbe
dunque che per li cocchieri mi scrivesse una lettera comandandomi espressamente che
subbito voglia partirmi di Angona eseguire il viaggio, acciò se mi facessero istanza, posso
mostrare detta lettera, et venirmene subbito costì. Intanto assieme con mia moglie li
facemo riverenza, cossì anco alla sig.ra marchesa, sig.ra Caterina et a tutti di casa, et
N. S. li conceda ogni contento, et lunga vita. Di V.S. Ill.ma Aff.mo se.re il Cav.re
Cesare Marotta

85. 16.v.1615 Enzo Bentivoglio to Antonio Goretti
I:FEbca, Autografo 3115

Ill.mo Sig.re
Averò caro d'intendere, che gli Mendicanti abbiano preso il posesso del vecchio con-
vento de P. P. Cappuccini; ed insieme, che gli quattro Dottori a' quali fu rimesso il negozio
de Restagni abbiano fatto la loro relatione; ed in questo negozio raccomando a V.S. la
sollecitudine.

Cotesta andata della Comp.a della Morte a Loreto averò disturbato assai l'ordine de'
miei Intramezzi; V.S. procuri, che almeno le Donne sappiano ben cantare le sue parti;
e che Francesca continui d'imparare a sonare le aeri, che canta. E per fine saluto V.S. di
cuore. Di Roma li 16 Maggio 1615 Di V.S. Enzo Bent.o

86. 30.v.1615 Enzo Bentivoglio to Antonio Goretti
I:FEbca, Autografo 3116

Ill.mo Sig.re
Delle pretenzioni de P.ri Cappuccini, se ne potrà trattare al mio ritorno a Ferrara.
Intanto V.S. potrà pensare al modo di aggiustare questa differenza.

Quanto a gl'Intramezzi; hora che sono ritornati gli Cantori da Loreto V.S. haverà magg.e

commodo, di attenderci; sicome la prego a voler fare; raccomandole part.re coteste due
Donne; aggiungendole nel part.re della Francesca, che mi sarà di part.re sodisfatt.ne che
V.S. procuri di superare con la diligenza, e sollecitudine sua, la poca voglia, ch'ella hà
d'imparare. E per fine saluto V.S. di cuore. Di Roma li 30. Maggio 1615 di V.S. E. Bent.o
[postscript:] V.S. Facia studiar le Donne e Fran.ca di Cimbalo

87. 8.vi.1615   Girolamo Fioretti to Enzo Bentivoglio
I:FEas, Archivio Bentivoglio, Mazzo 9–80, fos. 9ʳ and 12ʳ; partially transcribed by Hammond,
Girolamo Frescobaldi, 341

Ill.mo Sig.r mio Sig.re e p.rone col.mo

Scrivo a V.S. Ill.ma la quì annessa nel part.re del memoriale degli Interessati nella
bonif.ne di Lugo, acciò occorrendo posso mostrarla ad alcuno di cotesti Sig.ri, che premono nel neg.re nel quale io mi adoprerò con ogni diligenza, e sollecitudine regolan-
domi sempre col parere del S. Landinelli.

Quanto a Baldassarre riscossi le lettere del S. Cav.re Marotta, e del S. Nanini, e le
diedi ad ambidoi, perche nissuno di questi Sig.ri và mai alla posta per lettere. Continuano
d'insegnargli sicome continuano in dolersi del diffetto dell'Intonatione al quale sti-
mano di non poter quasi rimediare, giudicando che ciò proceda, che il putto sia di
maggior'età di quello è stato detto a V.S. Ill.ma, e che per conseguenza gli habbia da
durar poco la voce. M'hanno però imposto, che io scriva a V.S. Ill.ma che loro presto
se ne chiariranno, e che l'assicuri, che da essi non si manca di far ogni opra, perche lei
conosca che le sono veri, e divotissimi servitori. Il S.r Cav.re ha fornito d'insegnarli il
sonetto, sebene tuttavia attende a farglilo esercitare per ridurlo totalmente a perfettione;
et intanto và componendo un aria nuova per insegnarglila. Il S.r Nanini anch'esso continua d'insegnargli con ogni diligenza, e rende gratie a V.S. Ill.ma del honore, che gli ha
fatto con la sua lettera, et oltre le solite lettioni che da a Baldassarre di cantare, e comporre gl'insegna anche à sonare sù la parte, havendogli io avvisato, che V.S. Ill.ma di questo
haverebbe gusto part.re. Farò anche l'uffizio col S.r Frescobaldi, sicome hò fatto con
la S.a Ippolita, la quale mi dice, che V.S. Ill.ma conoscerà da gli effetti, che lei l'haverà
servita. V.S. Ill.ma nel resto non dubiti, che il Putto sia per isviarsi perche io me ne piglio
part.re pensiero, richiedendo così il debito, che tengo di ubbidire ad ogni suo cenno.
Mi raccomando per fine nella sua benigna protett.ne, e con inchinarmele riverentiss.te
prego Dio N. S.re che le conceda ogni grandezza. Di Roma li 8 Giugno 1615. Di V.S.
Ill.ma Humil.mo et dev.mo se.re perpetuo Girolamo Fioretti. [postscript:] Del Castrato
darò avviso a V.S. Ill.ma col seg.te ord.rio e ne caverò la risolut.ne come farò della
tratta del S. Marchese Villa.

88. 8.vi.1615   Girolamo Fioretti to Enzo Bentivoglio
I:FEas, Archivio Bentivoglio, Mazzo 9–80, fo. 10ʳ

Ill.mo Sig.re mio Sig.re e p.ron col.mo

Conforme all'ordine di V.S. Ill.ma e 'l parere del S.r Landinelli portai al S.r Card.le Millino
il memoriale sottoscritto dalli Interessati nella bonific.ne di Lugo, accompagnandolo

con quelle parole, ch'io stimai opportune per indurre S.S.a Ill.ma a pigliar la protettione di questo negotio. Mi ascoltò benignam.e e doppo haver letto il mem.e mi disse,
che dovessi lasciarmi credenza dei giorni, e che intanto confermassi a V.S. Ill.ma il continuato desiderio, che tiene di servirlo in tutte le cose. Tornerò da S.S. Ill.ma dimani,
per ricevere i suoi comandi in questo part.re; conchè à V.S. Ill.ma per fine humilmente
m'inchino aug.li felicissimi, e prosperi avvenim.ti. Di Roma li 8 Giugno 1615. Di V.S.
Ill.ma Humiliss.mo e Div.mo s.re perpetuo Girolamo Fioretti

89. 13.vi.1615 Girolamo Fioretti to Enzo Bentivoglio
I:FEas, Archivio Bentivoglio, Mazzo 9–80, fos. 25ʳ–26ʳ

Ill.mo Sig.r mio Sig.re e p.ron col.mo
Sarà V.S. Ill.ma già arrivata à Ferrara, e come voglio sperare, con buona salute onde io
vengo a farle humile riverenza, con raccomandarmi nella sua protett.ne. Nel resto,
perche credo, che possa esser di gusto à V.S. Ill.ma, non lascierò di raguagliarla con ogni
ord.rio del proffitto di Baldassarre, il quale continua di andare à pigliar lettione dal S.r
Nanini, accompagnandolo sempre il Ghenizzi, sicome fà quando và à scuola di sonare
dal S.r Girolamo. Il S.r Cav.re Marotta hà risoluto di darli lettione tre, e quattro volte al
giorno, ma però poco per volta; havendo così giudicato, che sia bene, per non confonderlo
nell'apprendere, ma tanto il S.r Nanini, quanto il med.o S. Cav.re dicono, che pecca assaissimo nell'Intonare; al che però cercheranno di rimediare con ogni lor potere.

Diedi gli dieci scudi alla S.ra Hippolita, la quale ne rende a V.S. Ill.ma infinite grazie,
e se le ricorda serva obbligatissima.

Il negozio della licenza per il S.r Battista Muzzarelli, il S.r Card.le Millino l'ha rimesso
al S.r Bongiovanni, ne se ne piglierà risoluzione fintanto, ch'esso S.r Bong.ni non haverà
riferito al S.r Card.le il suo parere. Io lo sollecierò à far quanto prima la detta relazione.

Quanto alla grazia del S.r Bellerofonte Castaldi raccomandato dal S.r Ferrante, credo
che molto difficilm.te potrà ottenersi, essendo negozio spettante all'Inquisizione, nella
quale dove si tratta di graziare, e mitigare pene à condennati, non se ne vede mai il fine,
tanto mi ha detto il S.r D. Giacomo del S.r Card.le Millino, che è informatiss.o di simili negozi.

N. Sig.re tornò Venerdi mattina da Frascati, fermandosi poi alla stanza di Monte
Cavallo, ed hoggi ha fatto Cappella in S.ta Maria Magg.re dove anche dimattina assi-
sterà alla Messa. Il S.r Landinelli mi hà detto questa sera di tener' ordine da V.S. Ill.ma di
parlare al S.r Ottavio Catalano sopra il part.re di quel giovane; ma perche non conosce
il S.r Catalano, siamo rimasti di parlargli insieme, aggiungendo à V.S. Ill.ma, che quel
giovane è mio grand.mo amico, onde credo, che le mie parole valeranno qualche cosa à
disponerlo à venire, massime per l'informazione, ch'io potrò darli di cotesti paesi, dove
io sono stato de gli anni intieri. Io mi adoprerò in questa, ed in ogni altra cosa, dove si
tratterà di ser.re a V.S. Ill.ma con quella diligenza, e fedeltà, che lei puole argomentare dall'infinita mia divozione, e dagli obblighi, che tengo a lei, et all'Ill.ma sua casa, alla
quale prego Dio N. S.re, che conceda eterna felicità, e grandezza, et a V.S. Ill.ma per
fine humiliss.te m'inchino. Di Roma li 13 Giugno 1615. Di V.S. Ill.ma Humiliss.o e
Divot.mo ser.re Girolamo Fioretti

90. 20.vi.1615 Girolamo Fioretti to Enzo Bentivoglio
I:FEas, Archivio Bentivoglio, Mazzo 9–80, fos. 45, 48, 46, 47

Ill.mo Sig.re mio S.re e p.rone col.mo

Il S.re Card.le Millino hà ordinato al suo Agente d'Imola, che debba concedere al S.r Battista Muzzarelli la licenza, che desidera, mentre pero non vi concorra difficoltà, come il S.r Battista pone nel memoriale, che in tutti i casi il S.r Card.le ne dovrebbe esser'avvisato.

Quanto à Cesare castrato di S. Giovanni, egli diede la negativa al S.r Ottavio Catalano, sebene esso S.r Catalano disse poi al S.r Landinelli, che il giovane havea detto di volerci pensare; tuttavia il S.r Cav.re Marotta risolse, che gli ne dovessimo parlare insieme, sicome habbiamo fatto, ma però senza proffitto alcuno, ancorache da noi gli fosse d.o, che niuno più di V.S. Ill.ma poteva aiutarlo à conseguire il luogo in Cappella dove egli aspira, e che pensasse bene à disgustare il S.r Catalano, che gli ha chiesto quasi per gratia, che si contentasse di venire al ser.zo di V.S. Ill.ma, mostrandoli com'è molto obbligato ad esso S.r Catalano, e che ne poteva sperare nuovi benefizij, oltre gli avantaggi, che haverebbe conseguiti da V.S. Ill.ma di favori, e regali, e di mille altre cose. Io gli dissi anche di esser rimasto in Roma per commandam. di V.S. Ill.ma, solo per trattar seco questo negozio, perche lei sapeva, che tra noi passava strettiss.a amicizia, e che perciò haveva giudicato, ch'egli più facilm.te si fosse indotto à venire à Ferrara, dove saressimo stati allegram.te di Camerata, e con tale occasione lo raguagliai di mille gusti, che haverebbe havuto in coteste bande, anteponendoli sempre, che haverebbe fatto maggior guadagno costì, che in Roma. Finalm.te ne il S.r Cav.re, ne io potemmo cavargli altra risposta di bocca, se non che era risolutissimo di non volersi partire di Roma, e che si maravigliava di noi, che l'andavamo persuadendo à far il contrario. Io lo lasciai dicendo di non voler accettare questa esclusiva, e che il S.r Cav.re haverebbe scritto à V.S. Ill.ma ch'egli ci voleva pensare, sicome haveva detto al S.r Catalano, sebene egli negò subito, e confirmò di haver data ad esso ancora la negativa. Il S.r Cav.re mi hà ordinato, che scriva a V.S. Ill.ma tutto questo, che passa, con aggiungerle, che tiene per certo che il giovane non si vorrà partire di Roma; ed io lo credo perche tengo informazione, che egli vive, come si suol dire, alla carlona, praticando con certi personaggi, che sono tutti dati in preda alla cupidia, et alle lascivie, anzi ch'esso stesso hà confessato al S.r Cav.re, et a me di esser innamorato in una giovane in maniera, che non gli pare di vivere quando stà un'hora lontano da lei. Consideri mò V.S. Ill.ma à che è ridotto l'Amore, che viene strapazzato fino da Castrati. Per concluderla si è risoluto di fargli parlare nuovam.e dal S. Catalano, stimando che il S.r Landinelli non sia troppo buon mezzo in queste materie, perche, come V.S. Ill.ma sà benissimo, egli hà cercato molte volte di divertire l'animo di lei da tali spese, quali egli stima, che siano gittate nel mare. Intanto staremo attendendo i commandi di V.S. Ill.ma supplicandola à credere, che si sia fatto ogni sforzo, acciò restasse servita in questo particolare, sicome richiedeva l'obbligo, che noi tenemo d'ubbidirla con ogni fedeltà, e diligenza.

Questa mattina ho condotto Baldassarre dal S.r Camillo medico, acciò l'ordinasse qualche rimedio per la rogna, la quale hà cominciato a tornarli, e particolarm.e nelle mani, ed al S.r Cav.re dispiace grandem.e. Hà risoluto, che se gli debba dare il siero per X giorni, e poi si ricondura da lui, che ordinerà un'altro medicamento, come si farà subito. Nel resto continua di andare dal Nanini ogni giorno, dove io mi trovo ogni mattina, e gli dà due buon'hore lettione dispensandone una in farlo cantare, ed intonar bene, e l'altra in farlo attendere allo studio del Contrapunto alla mente e Composit.ne che però l'hò provisto di dui altri libri, che gli erano necessari. Il S.r Cav.re continua di farlo cantare più volte il giorno, sicome accennai a V.S. Ill.ma. Va similmente à pigliar lettione dal S.r Girolamo Frescobaldi ogni giorno alle 16 hore. In questo particolare vuole il mio debito che avvertisca a V.S. Ill.ma, che il Ragazzo è stato male avvezzato per l'innanzi, e mi accorgo, che quando puole ci fà stare il Cav.re. Perciò io crederei, che V.S. Ill.ma risolvesse bene, mentre ordinasse al Ghenizzi con una lettera come si deve, che l'accompagni, quando và a pigliar lettione; ma di ciò la supplico à non farmene autore perche al S. Cav.re potrebbe forse dispiacere; ma l'obbligo mio verso V.S. Ill.ma non richiede altrimenti.

Il memoriale sottoscritto da gli part.ri Interessati nella Bonific.ne di Lugo è in mia mano; l'avviso a V.S. Ill.ma, acciò commandi quello io ne debbia fare, e se vuole, che lo consegni al S.r Landinelli.

Se V.S. Ill.ma, come mi promise, ed io ne la sup.o si degnerà d'impiegarmi in negozi suoi propri, e de' suoi amici, mi farà grazia, ed honor specialiss.o ed io la servirò conforme all'obbligo mio; poiche sicome le dissi qui in Roma, non hò pensiero di applicarmi à nuova servitù. Prego per fine Dio bened., che conceda a V.S. Ill.ma feliciss.a fine di tutti i suoi pensieri, mentre io humilm.te me l'inchino, con raccomand.le in protettione Di Roma li 20 Giugno 1615. Di V.S. Ill.ma Humiliss.mo e Devo.mo se.re Girolamo Fioretti

91. 20.vi.1615   Cesare Marotta to Enzo Bentivoglio
I:FEas, Archivio Bentivoglio, Mazzo 9–80, fo. 49ʳ

Ho detto il Sig.r Geronimo che dovesse dar conto à V.S. Ill.ma di quel habbiamo trattato con il Castrato, il quale non vuol venire in modo alcuno et l'habbiamo detto tanto io et il Sig.re Geronimo che haveriamo convertito un sasso, con tutto ciò non mancaremo di parlarli di nuovo insieme con il S. Ottavio Catalano, et faremo tutto il possibile acciò V.S. Ill.ma resti servita. Non ho trattato di ciò con il S. Landinelli si perche ha mill'altri negotij per la testa, come ancora havendo conosciuto che lui non inchina che V.S. Ill.ma faccia di queste opere. Del ragazzo non voglio per hora dirli altro, volendolo procurare ancora per alcuni altri giorni, e poi darò aviso à V.S. Ill.ma tanto circo l'imparare, quanto al suo modo di vivere, io non mancherò fare ogni forzo, et diligenza per servirla sicome farà anco Ipolita mia moglie, quando parrà il putto essere in termine, et che sarà ben guarito della rogna, con che bascio à V.S. Ill.ma humilmente le mani di Roma li 20 Giugno 1615. Di V.S. Ill.ma Humil.mo ser.re il Cav.re Cesare Marotta

92. 8.vii.1615   Girolamo Fioretti to Enzo Bentivoglio
I:FEas, Archivio Bentivoglio, Mazzo 9–80, fos. 236ʳ–238ʳ

Ill.mo Sig.re mio Sig.re e p.ron cols.mo

Dall'annessa lettera V.S. Ill.ma intenderà quello habbia risposto il Com.rio della Cam.ra, sopra la tratta per il S.r Marchese Villa. Potrà V.S. Ill.ma per se medesima argomentare, che non vuol far'il Ser.zio, senza ch'io sti à dirle altro sopra questo part.re.

Di Baldassarre poi posso dirle, che non ha più rogna alle mani havendoglile fatte lavare con un saponetto, che in due, o tre volte l'ha risanato; starà hora alla dispos.ne della S.ra Hippolita l'insegnarli di sonare la Chitarra; ed io non mancherò di ricordarle qual sia il gusto di V.S. Ill.ma in questa parte. Intanto potrà dar lei quell'ordine, che le parrà acciò Baldassarre habbia una Chitarra da poter istudiare, non havendo la S.ra Hipp:ta Chitarra da prestargli. Io ancora gli insegnarò quel poco, che ne sò perche possi ad una occasione cantare anche le musiche, che egli saprà all'Italiana. Nel resto và continuando gli soliti studi ed io l'ho raccomandato di nuovo al S.r Cav.re, et al S.r Nanini, come anche al S.r Frescobaldi, il quale dice, che gl'insegnerà à sonare sù la parte come V.S. Ill.ma commanda; sebene il S.r Nanini ancora gli fa esercitare questo medesimo studio, havendonelo io pregato per parte di V.S. Ill.ma alla quale il S.re Landinelli ha scritto veram.te con troppa amplific.ne dicendole, che il Putto haveva mutato voce, e che non imparava cosa alcuna, ma come quello che non è di questa professione, e per conseguenza non intende i termini di essa, merita di esser' iscusato, massime non havendo altro fine, se non che V.S. Ill.ma non facesse questa spesa senza poterne ritrarre alcun gusto; al che noi ancora habbiamo havuto part.re riguardo, e perciò le habbiamo scritto il parer nostro, acciò ella non possa mai restare mal sodisfatta della nostra servitù. Ora si attende ad insegnarli, et ad esortarlo à non disordinare con le mani, poiche il far disordini in altra maniera non gli sarà permesso per la diligente cura, che se ne tiene. Ma veram.e questi sig.ri stanno fermi nel loro primo proposito parendogli, che il mancam.to dell'intonat.ne non possi esser diffetto naturale. Si attenderà, come ho detto à sollecitare di farlo studiare, ed il S.r Cav.re hà dato principio ad insegnarli l'ottava *Non havete à temer ch'in forma nova*, opera da davero bella continuando insieme di fargli esercitare il sonetto, che hà fornito d'imparare, acciò se lo metta à memoria per cantarlo, e sonarlo senza libro quando bisognarà. Il padre di questo ragazzo stà moribondo, e per quanto mi dicono questa volta al sicuro non la scapperà.

Di Gioseppino ancora ne haveremo per pochi giorni, essendo diventato pazzo del tutto, e mangia, e dorme pochissimo. Delle pazzie, che fa se ne potrebbono formar libri, ma il tutto consiste nella sua miseria.

Domenica mattina si fece nella Chiesa della Minerva l'abiuraz.ne di tre condennati dall'Inquisiz.ne. Il Primo era un Prete di qui del ben morire detto il P. Aniello, la 2.a una donna detta la Beata Sor Giulia; Questa era Siciliana, ma il Prete anzi detto Napolit.no com'era il terzo, ch'era Dottore eloquentissimo; Tuttatre insieme queste persone havevano cominciato a fondare una nuova setta, che per opinione teneva che gli peccati della carne, e part.te gli stupri delle Vergini, non solo non fossero peccati, ma atti puri, preparatorij alla Communione; Onde la buona Suor Giulia havia con poca difficoltà sedotto un numero incredibile di huomini, e Donne, quali faceva congregare in sua casa, entrandone per due porte separatam.te, e quivi doppo haver fatto un sermone intorno al lor primo proposito, lei chinandosi si alzava i panni con una grand.ma veneratione, e mostrava le parti vergognose assistendovi come doi ministri del sacrif.o il Prete, et il Dott.r sudetto, et in spetie di adoratione a quelle parti infami, dicevano, che all'homo si apriva la porta del Cielo, e mille altri concetti vituperosissimi; Si faceva poi avanti il buon'Aniello, et armata manu usava seco carnalm.te fintanto, ch'era stanco in maniera, che bisognava moverlo sopra il letto, mostrandolo à figlioli, e figlie spirituali e dandogli ad intendere, che se n'era gito in estasi, come anche la Suor Giulia, la quale pretendendo di esser magg.re e la prima di tutte le Donne sante, che fossero state grate a Dio et honorate di doni principalissimi, teneva le loro imagini in quella camera infame come per suo trofeo, et . . . [?] l'altre parole horrende, che diceva a quelle beate imagini, à quella di S.ta Caterina da Siena in ispetie diceva, . . . [?] passava il tempo nei piaceri della carne, che lei non era arrivata a conseguire una minima parte delle dolcezze celestiali, e de' secreti di Dio, com'era avvenuto à lei, et à suoi consorti, ne quali si verificava quel detto dell'Evangelio, dove dice Vobis datum est nosse misteria Regni Dei. Queste, e simili infamie ammetteva Suor Giulia, et tutti gli figlioli sp.li i quali serrandosi all'oscuro in Cong.ne si congiungevano carnalm.te ad honore della B. S. Giulia, la quale per tutto Napoli era tenuta Santissima. Sarebbe lungo il dire l'altre forfanterie del Prete, e di quell'altro Dottore, non essendo stato sufficiente lo spatio di tre hore a leggere i loro Processi pieni di tutte quelle infamie, che si possino imaginare. Per penitenza pn.le gli fu dato il carcere perpetuo, con orationi, e digiuni. Si trovarono à questa abiuratione 21 de primi Card.li, e vi fù anche il S. Card.le Borghese, strapazzati tutti dalla moltitud.ne del popolo in maniera che gli svizzeri non erano sufficienti à diffendergli dal tumulto. Vi furono anche in un palco con le Gelosie alcune Sig.e principalissime, le quali, assicuro V.S. Ill.ma, che sentirono di bellissime cose, perche, come ho detto, in quei processi vi era d'omnis generis musicorum, et erano letti dà un Cantore di N. S.re tanto bene, e distintam.te, e con voce cosi sonora, che ne pur una sola parola se ne poteva male intendere. Hora per tutta Roma non si parla di altro, e veram.te ci voleva qualche altra novità, poiche della Guerra non se ne parlava più, dicendosi, che la Pace gia era confermata. Queste abiurationi hanno tenuto così impedito in continue Cong.ni il S. Cav.re Millini, che non hò potuto haver udienza per la risposta del memoriale, che lasciai a V.S. Ill.ma da presentare a N. S.re, ma non passeranno dei giorni, ch'io ne haverò cavato il netto, e col seg.te ordinario ne darò conto a V.S. Ill.ma.

Il S.r Nanini la supp.ca à favorirlo d'intendere da cotesti Ecc.mi Sig.ri Medici de' quali ella si serve, che rimedio sarebbe buono per il male, che egli prova di debolezza di stomaco, e di vertigini, et honorarlo poi della ricetta, overo di qualche ceroto raro.

Quanto al Castrato io ho fatto ogni sforzo per ridurlo alla voglia di V.S. Ill.ma ma la cosa è disperata, poiche sta in superbia tale questa bestia, che se fosse il primo huomo del mondo non dovrebbe dire l'impertinenze, che dice, se lui non conosce la sua ventura suo danno, et al fine non è in lui altro di buono, che quella poca voce accompagnata da mille vitij, che al sicuro V.S. Ill.ma in processo di poco tempo ne sarebbe rimasta disgustata, e poi per quello che lei se ne vuol servire hà tanto bisogno di maestro, quanto ogni altro, che canti costì; perche è avvezzo à cantare i Kirie eleison alla disperata, senza curarsi di altra politia. Vedrò di trovare Piperno o altri, e lo manderò subito, assicurandolo, che il partito, che lei propone sarà accettato da ogni altro, benche valent'huomo, fuori che da questa carogna che de' 12 mesi dell'anno, ne sta 13 pieno di poltroneria di rogna, e non si diletta di cosa alcuna.

Supplico V.S. Ill.ma à farmi gratia, che occorrendole di scrivere al S.re Card. Leni, et al S.r Abbate Pignattelli si compiaceria di raccomandarmegli nel modo, che lei sa fare quando vuole da dovero favorire, mandando le lettere in mia mano, che le presenterò io medesimo; con che facendo a V.S. Ill.ma hum.ma riverenza resto aug.le il colmo di ogni vera grandezza. Di Roma li 8 di luglio 1615. Di V.S. Ill.ma Hum.mo e Div.mo Se.re perpetuo Girolamo Fioretti

93. 18.vii.1615   Girolamo Fioretti to Enzo Bentivoglio
I:FEas, Archivio Bentivoglio, Mazzo 9–80, fo. 268ʳ

Ill.mo Sig.re mio Sig.re e p.rone col.mo

Hò fatto prattica per trovare a V.S. Ill.ma un Contralto, e me ne sono stati proposti molti, alcuni de' quali, che sarebbono assai sufficienti non vogliono partirsi di Roma, altri non gli hò stimati à proposito, fuori che uno il quale serve in seminario, et è da forma, ed il S:r Nanini mi dice ch'è buon suggetto, ma io à questo non hò potuto parlare, ma dimani che sarà Domenica andero à sentirlo al Giesù, e con iscusa di visitare quel m.ro di Cappella, ch'è mio amico, gli parlerò, e procurerò di ridurlo al volere di V.S. Ill.ma. Mi è stato proposto ancora un giovane, che veramente hà assai buona voce, e sarebbe à proposito per cantare in Comedia, ma perche hà un braccio solo non hò voluto parlargli, oltreche non sò se volesse partirsi di Roma, sebene io crederei di disporvelo. Se à V.S. Ill.ma non dasse fastidio questo suo mancam.to, lui nel resto è bon giovane, ben costumato di bella presenza, hà dispositione, e come hò detto bella voce. Scrive ancora con la mano sinistra benissimo, e guadagna buoni di in copiare cose di musica, et altro. Starò attendendo il command.o di V.S. Ill.ma ed intanto parlerò à quello del seminario, et anderò intendendo di qualch'un'altro ancora. Piperno non vuol partirsi di Roma, e tanto più quanto si trova in maliss.mo termine essendo pieno, come si suol dire, di cacio, et ovi, fin à gli occhi, che a pena può reggersi in piedi, e pare, che gli cominci à mancare la voce; e si vide, che haverà poca vita, perche gli disordini che ha fatti sono stati troppo grandi.

Baldassarre è stato due giorni senza pigliar lett.ne essendo stato a casa sua per l'occasione della morte del Padre. Hora ripiglierà gli soliti studij, e dimani conforme al solito anderà à cantare alla Chiesa nuova.

Quì abbiamo un caldo più, che grand.mo con che a V.S. Ill.ma riverentem.te m'inchino et aug.ro felicissimo adempim.to d'ogni suo pensiero. Di Roma li 18 luglio 1615. Di V.S. Ill.ma Hum.mo e Div.mo ser. perpetuo G.mo Fioretti

94. 22.vii.1615   Girolamo Fioretti to Enzo Bentivoglio
I:FEas, Archivio Bentivoglio, Mazzo 9–80, fos. 280ʳ–282ʳ

Ill.mo S.re mio S.re e p.ron col.mo

Come scrissi a V.S. Ill.ma con le passate di voler fare, hò sentiti molti contralti, per scieglierne uno à prop.to per suo ser.zio, ma vedendo finalm.te, che nissuno mi sodisfaceva mi risolsi di dare nuovo assalto à Cesare, sicome ho fatto hoggi assalendolo all'improviso con questo stratagema di tener nuovo ordine da V.S. Ill.ma di pregarlo perche non vuole andare a ser.la che almeno si voglia contentare di farle servitio di cantare in questa occ.ne della Comedia, che vuol fare fra pochi giorni, per il qual'effetto V.S. Ill.ma prometteva di regalarlo in maniera che se ne sarebbe contentato, e che gli haverebbe pagate le spese delli viaggi. A questo mi diede ancora la solita negativa dicendo di non voler partirsi di Roma ne per poco ne per assai tempo. Il che inteso da me, soggionsi quasi risentitam.te che tenevo ordine espresso mentre egli non voleva venir d'accordo, che havessi a far ricorso all'Abbate Pignattelli, il quale oltre l'autorità, ch'ha sopra di lui come Canonico di S. Giovanni, gli l'haverebbe fatto commandare anche dal S.r Card.le Borghese e così V.S. Ill.ma haverebbe havuto il suo intento, senza havesse alcun obbligo à lui. Queste parole gli fecero metter il cervello à partito, onde si risolse di voler promettere, che per questa occasione sarebbe venuto, purche io gli facessi haver licenza dal Capitolo sicome io subito gli promisi di fare anzi di più, che dal Capitolo med.o l'haverei fatto assicurare, che al suo ritorno gli haverebbe havuto il med.o luogo in quella Cappella, che tiene al *presente*. Sopragiunse il S.r Ottavio Catalano, il quale havevo prima informato di quello che volevo negotiare, e promesse à Cesare che al suo ritorno, mentre non fossi stato subito provisto, egli l'haverebbe tenuto in casa à sue spese, e volse, ch'io gli promettessi di fargli dare quello haverebbe guadagnato in [quella] Cappella, fintanto, che si fosse accomodato. Io mi contentai di consentire, sapendo che V.S. Ill.ma quando l'haverà costì non lo lascierà più partire, ed in tutti i casi il Sig.r Pignattelli ad instanza di V.S. Ill.ma lo farebbe subito provedere. Restammo poi di parlarne con un Canonico d.o il S.r Rodolfini il quale tiene protettione grand.ma di Cesare, e sono più che fratelli, e basta. Andammo à trovarlo di compagnia e lo pregammo à voler anch'esso concorrere à dar questo gusto a V.S. Ill.ma aggiungendogli quanto mi pareva necess.rio dirle che lei è tanto amata dal S.r Card. Borghese, truandole della sua grandezza, e di molti altri part.ri. Egli ci fece alcune obbiettioni, le quali io rifiutai destram.te, ma non potei già superare la difficoltà, ch'egli propose, dicendo, che per quello, che à lui toccava, non consigliava, ne voleva in modo alcuno, che si partisse di Roma, prima che fosse passato il sol leone. Io gli replicai quanto potei, adducendoli l'esempio del Cav. Marotta, ch'era venuto di costà a Roma; ma finalm.te non valse alcuna ragione, poiche il neg.zio non si potè concludere in altra maniera, se non che si dava parola, che Cesare sarebbe venuto a se.re V.S. Ill.ma per l'occ.ne della Comedia, e che si metterebbe in viaggio alla prima acqua di Agosto. Così restammo in appuntamento; ed io hò usato questo tiro per inviarglielo costà, parendomi di non poter trovar miglior strada per ser.la. Resta hora, ch'ella scriva una lettera al S.r Abbate Pignattelli in mia credenza per questo negotio acciò possi haver la licenza, e con tal'occasione la sup.co à caldam.te raccomandarmegli, però come suo ser.re che in altra maniera non potendo, essendomi necessario se voglio ser.re a V.S. Ill.ma qui in Roma, come voglio fare sempre, e trattare qualche suo negotio, ch'io habbia dipendenza dal S.r Abbate per tutto quello che potesse occorrere. Similm.te potrà scrivere (e questo è de essentia) una lettera al S.r Mario Rodolfini, che è quel Canonico di sopra nominato, dicendole di haver inteso da me la sua prontezza ecc. e che lo prega à voler ridurre il neg.o à fine; e l'ingrandisca, perche qui consiste il punto. Gli potra dar titolo di M.to Ill.re perche è di buona casata. Al S.r Catalano potrà anche scrivere nel med.o suggetto; et à questo ancora V.S. Ill.ma resti servita per sua benignità di raccomandarmi pur anche come suo ser.re perche nella musica può farmi molti servigi rilevanti, de quali V.S. Ill.ma a Dio piacendo haverà qualche gusto, e procurerò di darlene saggio in persona di Baldassarre il quale continua d'imparare; e per esso si farà la musica passaggiata alle parole

O solenne Vitt.a, havend'io riscossa, e presentata la lettera al S.r Marotta. Starò attendendo, che V.S. Ill.ma mi mandi queste tre lettere, ed intanto la supplico ad iscusarmi se non è rimasta in cio servita come vorrebbe, assicurandola che non si è potuto far di vantaggio. Le fò hum.ma riv.za Di Roma il giorno di S.ta M.a Maddalena 1615. Hum.mo e Div.mo se.re perpetuo Gir.mo Fioretti

[postscript:] Questa lettera è mal scritta, essendomi convenuto scriverla in una bottega per la gran pioggia che mi ha colto fuori di casa. Resti perciò servita d'iscusarmene. Il S.r Gio: Domenico [Puliaschi] Cantore è ammalato di febre.

95. 29.vii.1615   Girolamo Fioretti to Enzo Bentivoglio
I:FEas, Archivio Bentivoglio, Mazzo 9–80, fo. 346ʳ

Ill.mo S.re mio Sig.re e p.ron col.mo

Il S.r Cav.re Marotta hà posto in musica il madrigale *O solenne Vittoria* havendolo adornato di passaggi proportionati alla capacità di Baldassarre, al quale di già hà cominciato ad insegnarlo, accio volendo V.S. Ill.ma, come gli hà scritto, servirsene nella Comedia possa ad ogni suo cenno farlo venire a Ferrara. Il S.r Nanini anch'esso non lascia d'insegnarli con ogni diligenza, sebene con poca speranza di profitto, non cessando nel Putto il natio difetto della mala intonatione, anzi che più tosto si và augumentando, onde ne teme la mutatione della voce. Questi doi virtuosi si disperano, che gli sia capitato alle mani soggetto così poco habile à fargli honore appresso di V.S. Ill.ma, alla quale, mi hanno ordinato, ch'io debba dare parte di questo loro disgusto, con assicurarla, che da essi non si manca di usare ogni studio, accio V.S. Ill.ma rimanga servita conforme all'obbligo, e disid.o che ne tengono. Io non manco di far'animo à tutti doi, avertendogli, che V.S. Ill.ma resterà appagata della loro pronta volontà di ser.la, e che non gli mancharanno altre occasioni di mostrarle, quanto essi le sieno divoti, e veri servitori.

Nel part.re del Contralto starò attendendo la commissione di V.S. Ill.ma rimettendomi a quanto sopra di cio lungam.te le scrissi con le passate.

Questa mattina hò visitato il S.r Gio. Domenico [Puliaschi] Cantore, il quale hà acquistato assai di miglioramento, e mi hà pregato à volerlo ricordare a V.S. Ill.ma ser.re di vera divotione.

È morto Michele cavallerizzo, che cavalcava al Coliseo. La Sig.ra Formicina dama bellissima si ritrova fuori di Roma con suo marito ambiduo spediti da medici; talche in cambio di trovar il fresco, che andavano cercando, havranno trovato la morte.

Gli Sig.ri Aldobrandini tuttavia sono ritenuti in Castello Sant'Angelo.

Questi giorni à dietro si è fatta monaca convertita con sua madre quella bella spagnuolina, che habitava dirimpetto à S. Giacomo de gl'Incurabili. Haveva mobili di molto valore, e fra l'altre cose cento vesti superbissime, senza l'Argenteria, e gioie, che ascendevano à grossa somma.

Quì proviamo caldi eccessivi, e senza refrigerio di buoni melloni, poiche l'acque, che sono piovute, e che quasi ogni giorno piovono, gli hanno rovinati; oltre che cagionano un caldo noiosissimo; con che, a V.S. Ill.ma riverentem.te inchinandomi, le auguro per fine felicissima riuscita d'ogni suo pensiero. Di Roma li 29 di luglio 1615. Di V.S. Ill.ma Hum.mo e Div.mo S.re perpetuo Girolamo Fioretti

96. 12.viii.1615   Girolamo Fioretti to Enzo Bentivoglio
I:FEas, Archivio Bentivoglio, Mazzo 9–80, fo. 492ʳ

Ill.mo Sig.re mio Sig.re e p.ron col.mo

Cesare Castrato è andato col Rodolfini à Tivoli per la festa, che la si è fatta di S. Lorenzo; subito che intenderò che sia tornato presenterò la lettera al S.r Abbate Pignatelli, accio gli parli, et ottenga quanto V.S. Ill.ma disidera. Al S.r Catalani ho resa la lettera ad esso dirittiva, si ricorda se.re a V.S. Ill.ma dicendo che la servirà con ogni prontezza.

Quanto a Baldassarre non hò che dirle di nuovo. Continua ne gli soliti studj e ne soliti diffetti. Dove più V.S. Ill.ma mi commanda, che io l'avvisi quando sarà tempo di mandarlo costà, io credo, che potrà farlo venire in compagnia di Cesare se pur verrà, overo di Giovanni del S.r Ferrante, stimando che nella Comedia voglia servirsi di lui ancora per sonare il chitarrone, stanteche lo sona sicuro su la parte, ed ha buona orecchia, e buon giuditio in seguitare quei, che cantano. Hò salutato poi il Sig. Cav.re Marotta, ed il S.r Nanini conforme all'ordine di V.S. Ill.ma quali le fanno hum.ma riverenza, assicurandola che loro fanno ogni sforzo, perche Baldassarre faccia profitto, in maniera che V.S. Ill.ma possi riconoscere in esso qualche effetto della divotione, che à lei professano.

Di nuovo habbiamo la morte del P.re del S.re Card. Borghese, fu condotto alla sepoltura hiersera con pompa e comitiva superbiss.a. È morto ancora ms. Nicola hoste di Porta Settimiana, ch'era quel compare del S.r Landinelli, che dava quel buon vino a V.S. Ill.ma alla quale io per fine hum.te m'inchino, pregando Dio N. S.re che le conceda feliciss.mo adempim.to di cio che desidera. Di Roma li XII di Agosto 1615. Di V.S. Ill.ma Hum.mo e Div.mo S.re perpetuo Girolamo Fioretti.

[postscript:] Il S.r Francesco castrato del S.r Card. P.rone si ricorda a V.S. Ill.ma divotissimo se.re, e la sup.ca à comandarlo. Mi farà V.S. Ill.ma gratia singolare di rispondere in maniera che gli possi mostrar la lettera come hò fatto al S.r Gio: Dom.co [Puliaschi] acciò apparisca, che io gli fo il servigio.

97. 22.viii.1615   Girolamo Fioretti to Enzo Bentivoglio
I:FEas, Archivio Bentivoglio, Mazzo 9–80, fos. 580ʳ–582ʳ

Ill.mo S.re mio S.re e p.ron col.mo

Subito ricevuta la lettera di V.S. Ill.ma portai al S.r Cav.re Marotta le parole delle furie, ch'in essa erano incluse, esponendogli qual sarebbe stato il suo gusto, et informandolo appieno delle musiche, che doppo precedere, e seguire alle dette parole, acciò non le facessi di qualche tuono, che riuscisse difficile da inserirlo nell'altre musiche. Mi rispose con la solita prontezza, che haverebbe servita V.S. Ill.ma ma che prima bisognava, che si liberasse da alcune musiche, che havea principiato per il S.r Duca di S:to Gemini, e di alcun'altre, de' quali vuol servirsi per suo gusto in una barchetta il giorno festivo di S. Bartolomeo; Basta che V.S. Ill.ma resterà servita compitam.te.

Dove poi V.S. Ill.ma mi commanda, che debba dirle il mio parere circa il far venire a Ferrara il Ghenizzi, e Baldassarre, io credo, che sarà boniss.a rissoluzione, massime volendosene ella servire nella Comedia, perche, trattando di Baldassarre, io diffido, che sia per acquistar più di quello, che hà fatto, poiche quel diffetto dell'Intonazione mette in disperazione tutti quelli, che gl'insegnano, in maniera, che io non hò ardito di por mano ad insegnargli cosa alcuna, tuttoche ne havessi estremo disiderio, per esercitarmi in servire à V.S. Ill.ma. Il S.r Cav.re fin qui gli hà insegnato un sonetto, l'aria *Non havet'à temer ch'in forma nova*, il mad.le *O solenne Vitt.ria* ed hora gli fa esercitare una Romanesca, con le parole *O quante volte in van cor mio ti chiamo*. Il S.r Nanini gli hà insegnato doi mottetti passaggiati; oltre al dargli lezzione di contrapunto, in iscritto, et alla mente, et insegnargli a sonare i med.i mottetti.

Quanto à i dinari, che V.S. Ill.ma vuol sapere, che bisognano per Giovanni, il S.r Cav.re mi dice, che a settembre entrerà ne' quattro mesi della spesa, che importeranno scudi 24 oltre dui altri scudi che prestò al med.o Giovanni finquando venne a Roma l'anno passato, quale dice, che consumò nel viaggio; oltre di ciò mi dice esso Giovanni, che hà pegni à gl'Ebrei per la somma di scudi sette, overo otto, se ben mi ricordo, aggiungendomi di haverlo detto a V.S. Ill.ma ancora qui in Roma; che del resto lui non ha altro intrigo, e che ad ogni cenno di lei, si metterà subito in viaggio; io hò detto ad ambidoi, che si preparino, e che esercitino le opere che loro sono state insegnate, perche al sicuro V.S. Ill.ma con la risposta della p.nte mi manderà l'ord.ne d'inviargli à Ferrara, se bene io credo che non potranno partir prima che a mezzo settembre, non tanto per il caldo, che perche Baldassarre non havrà prima imparata, e la romanesca, ed il madrigale col duo delle Furie. Starò perciò attendendo i commandi di V.S. Ill.ma, ed intanto solleciterò il Cav:re a far la musica à quelle parole, acciò Baldassarre possa subito cominciar'ad apprenderle, che se V.S. Ill.ma pur commandasse che partissero subito, non ha rispetto alcuno, che possi vietargli la subita esecuzione del suo comandam.to.

Intesi poi ch'era tornato in Roma Cesare Castrato, onde hieri mattina presentai al S.r Abbate Pignatelli la l.ra di V.S. Ill.ma informandolo pienam.te del suo disiderio. Si dimostrò pront.mo di far l'uffizio, e che Domenica, che sarà dimani gli havrebbe parlato, ma che dubitava, che per esser questo giovane molto dato al buon tempo, difficilm.te si sarebbe ridotto a partirsi di Roma per dimorarvi lungo spazio tempo, perche ad un disviato, e così malvolonteroso come lui sarebbe parso lungo tempo lo spazio di sei soli mesi. Tornerò per la risposta, e dimattina presenterò ancor'io la lettera al S.r Rodolfini, acciò sia più disposto à compiacere il S.r Abbate, ancorche io sia sicurissimo, che per l'amicizia stretta che ha con Cesare difficilm.te consentirà, che sia assente lungo tempo da Roma. Al S.r Catalani già hò resa la sua lettera, ed ha promesso di favorir'il negozio, e me insieme in tutto quello, che potrà, il che sicome lo riconosco dall'efficace racc.ne di V.S. Ill.ma così le ne rendo con ogni humiltà quelle grazie, che posso magg.ri e perche non devo lasciar di dar parte a V.S. Ill.ma come à mio primo, e p.nte Sig.re delle mie deliberazioni, humilm.te le significo, come il S.r Co. Annibale Manfredi, non havendo persona che gli servisse nello scrivere, et essendosi rissoluto di non durar più tanta fatica di scriver'ogni cosa da se stesso, per fuggire quel continuo incommodo del dettare tutte le lettere; hà preso me al suo ser.zio sebene son poco buono à cosa alcuna. E perche V.S. Ill.ma mi comandò che in questi parti.ri io facessi ricapito del S.r Landinelli, ne parlai prima seco, e mi disse che accettassi il partito, perche V.S. Ill.ma ne sarebbe rimasta gustata in tutto, e per tutto, e che questa era boniss.a occasione per me,

per il disiderio, che tengo d'imparare. Io ricevero per gr.a specialiss.a che V.S. Ill.ma si
degni di certificarmi del suo gusto volendo io sempre servirla, et ubbidirla non meno,
che ogn'altro suo ser.re, che stia appresso alla sua persona. Sebene io tengo per certo,
che lei non possa esserne se non gustata sapendo quanto il S.r Conte le sia amico, e che
tanto più volentieri mi hà preso al suo servizio, quanto son stato ser.re di V.S. Ill.ma.

Nel resto quì habbiamo di nuovo la morte del quartogenito del S.r D. Virg.o Orsini
d.o D. Carlo, quale l'Ambas.r di Francia haveva addottato cosi per figliolo. Il suo male
è stato di varoli.

Il S.r Duca di S.to Gemini hà rissoluto di ritirarsi con tutta la famiglia à M.te Libretto
sua terra, per dove partirà in termine, di poche settimane, ed il suo palazzo di Pasquino
si affitterà, che per quanto intendo ci metteranno la locanda, non trovandosi fin hora,
chi habbia pensiero di pigliarlo.

Per Roma si dice publicam.te che Mons.r Nunzio di Fiandra ha ottenuta licenza da
N. S.re, e che in suo luogo sia destinato Mons.r Vitelliano Visconti. Io non m'estendo
in dare a V.S. Ill.ma avviso alcuno di quello che succede qui alla corte, sapendo, che dal
S.r Landinelli glie ne sono partecipati i più riconditi, e nuovi; e qui finendo a V.S. Ill.ma
hum.te m'inchino, aug.le il colmo di ogni somma grandezza. Di Roma li 22 d'Agosto
1615. Di V.S. Ill.ma Hum.mo e Divot.mo s.re perpetuo G.mo Fioretti

98. 29.viii.1615   Pompeo Lasco to Enzo Bentivoglio
I:FEas, Archivio Bentivoglio, Mazzo 9–80, fo. 616ʳ

Ill.mo Si.re p.ron mio Colend.mo
Grand.mo contento hò ric.to dalla l.ra de 15 del cor.te che V.S. Ill.ma si è degnata scrivermi con la buona nuova che mi da della sua salute, la qual preggio più che ogn'altra
cosa del mondo, e del raguaglio dell'apportam.ti del maestro Giovanni, e non sono
punto in dubbio della sua amorevolezza ch'essa non sia per farci usare ogni diligenza
possibile che rieschi virtuoso, e da qualche cosa, che stando sotto la sua servitù, e protettione, non se ne può sperare se non benef.o et honore, e circa la voce che mi dice, si
sia mutata da alcuni giorni in quà, questo io l'ho à buon segno, perche non farà più altra
mutatione, e bisogna, che il suo maestro lo facci cantar'alto quanto più può, e spesso,
attalche se assuefacci in quello, e non è da dubitar punto che facci altra mutatione poiche
quanto haveva da fare l'ha già fatto. Del resto rendo infinitiss.e grazie à V.S. Ill.ma della
buona protettione che ne tiene, et io resto obligato à pregar sua D. M.tà per la salute sua,
con che facendoli hum.ma river.a li auguro ogni magg.r contento, e felicità. Di Roma
li 29 d'agosto 1615. Di V.S. Ill.ma Oblig.mo et aff.mo se.re Pompeo Lasco

99. 29.viii.1615   Girolamo Fioretti to Enzo Bentivoglio
I:FEas, Archivio Bentivoglio, Mazzo 9–80, fos. 620ʳ–621ʳ

Ill.mo S.re mio S.re e p.ron col.mo
Mi è capitato con quest'ord.rio il piego inviatomi da V.S. Ill.ma, e subito in esecuz.ne
di quanto ella mi ordinava, presentai al Ghenizzi la lettera à lui dirittiva con la parte di
Rinaldo, dicendogli, che si preparasse per venire a Ferrara, perchè disegnavo d'inviarlo
la matt.na seguente conforme all'ordine, che ne tenevo. Dissi il med.mo a Baldassarre

dandone parte al S.r Cav.r Marotta, il quale appunto in quell'hora stava copiando le musiche delle Furie, e mi rispose, che bisognava ben eseguire il command.to di V.S. Ill.ma, ma che insieme si poteva anche haver riguardo al suo buon servigio, e che però il suo parere sarebbe stato, che si fossero trattenuti doi, ò tre giorni, accioche in questo tempo, benche breviss.mo, Baldassarre potesse almeno imparare il modo di cantar le musiche delle furie, perche il Ghenizzi gli l'havrebbe poi insegnate di tutto punto parte nel viaggio, e parte a Ferrara. Io dunque conoscendo, che veramente il buon ser.zio di V.S. Ill.ma richiedeva il far à questa maniera massime, che oltre di ciò il Ghenizzi, e Baldassarre impugnavano gagliard.te dicendo di non potersi preparare in 24 hore. Fui portato à consentire, che si dovessero trattenere per tutto questo mese, havendomi essi promesso che sarebbeno all'ordine per partire il primo di Settembre, sicome dovrano fare senza fallo alcuno, ed il S.r Provenzali gli provederà delle cose necess.rie per il viaggio, se bene anch'egli concorreva meco nella risoluzione di mandargli subito, ma per le cagioni sud.e siamo stati sforzati à cedere. Il Ghenizzi attende ad imparare la parte di Rinaldo, e Baldassarre à fornire d'apprendere la Romanesca *O quante volte invan* ecc. quale sarebbe rimasta imperfetta.

Quanto à Cesare Castrato il negotio è spedito, poiche ne l'autorità del S.r Abbate Pignattelli, ne l'esortazioni del S.r Catalani, ne le mie preghiere sono state sufficienti à disporlo a promettere di voler ser.re a V.S. Ill.ma per sei mesi, ma à tutti hà risposto con egual impertinenza, havendo sempre in bocca un'assoluta negativa, la quale disgustò oltre modo il S.r Abbate che gli trattava di questo neg.zio con ogni termine di cortesia, offerendosi per rispetto di lei ad esser suo perpetuo protettore, ma nulla è valso, poiche, come il S.r Abbate disse da principio, si è troppo dato in preda al buon tempo, per non dire à i vitij de' quali abbonda in maniera, che dopo essersi licenziato da questo parlamento, ritornò in choro, perche se gli parlò à S. Gio:, sbuffando, e dicendo, che se V.S. Ill.ma haveva gusto di lui, voleva, che venisse ella medesima à Roma. Consideri hora per se stessa il rimanente, e quanto sarebbe continuato nel suo ser.zio, aggiungendosi à questo, che oltre che putisce, per le tre fontanelle che hà, in modo che non se gli può avvicinare, è di così cattiva memoria, che non imparerebbe à mente dieci versi in un'anno; e qui lo sappiamo tutti per l'esperienza, che n'habbiamo fatta in diverse occasioni.

Nel resto qui non c'è cosa, che si possa dar'à V.S. Ill.ma per nuova, eccetto che la partita del S.r Co: Camillo Sassoni, del Perondelli, del Dott.r Nigrelli e del Dott.r Ridolfo Lorenzi, gli quali si sono inviati costà per la via di Loreto, e sono partiti questa notte alle 6 hore. E con tal fine à V.S. Ill.ma riv.te m'inchino, aug.la in perpetuo felicissima. Di Roma di 29 d'Agosto 1615. Di V.S. Ill.ma Hum.mo e Div.mo S.re perpetuo Girolamo Fioretti

100. 2.ix.1615   Cesare Marotta to Enzo Bentivoglio
I:FEas, Archivio Bentivoglio, Mazzo 81, fo. 16. I have this transcription through the kindness of Dinko Fabris. It will also appear in his forthcoming book on the artistic patronage of the Bentivoglio family

Ill.mo sig.r mio e padrone oss.mo
Con l'occasione della venuta costì de Baldesarro et il Ghenizzi, vengo con la presente a farli riverenza, raccordandomeli servo. Le parole da V.S. Ill.ma mandatime sono state

da me poste in musica nel meglior modo che ho saputo, et ho cercato obedirla con adornarle d'alcuni passaggi. Potrà farle bene imparare da detto Baldessarro, poiché per la brevità del tempo non ho possuto, conforme il mio dovere, farcele cantare di tutto punto, sicome anco l'altre cose che l'ho imparato: et di ciò non mi stendo in altro, che V.S. Ill.ma come sig.re di singular giuditio, so ponerà in consideratione che in si poco tempo in questa professione della musica non si può far meracoli. Intanto acetti da me il vivo desiderio che tengo di servirla. Unitamente con Ipolita mia moglie ci rallegramo del figlio maschio a V.S. Ill.ma nato, e piaccia al Sig.re concederli sempre ogni compita esaltatione. E per fine li facemo riverenza sicome anco alla sig.ra e sig.ra Marchesa, di Roma li 2 settembre, 1615 Di V.S. Ill.ma oblig.mo se.re Il Ca.re Cesare Marotta

101. 21.x.1615   Girolamo Fioretti to Enzo Bentivoglio
I:FEas, Archivio Bentivoglio, Mazzo 9–81, fo. 540ʳ

Ill.mo S.re mio S.re e p.ron col.mo
Sono a Frascati col S.r Ambas.re venutoci con l'Ill.mo Pio; onde non posso eseguire per hora il comand.to di V.S. Ill.ma, se non con la solita mia pronta volontà di ubbidirla. Al mio ritorno a Roma supplicherò il S.r Card.le Giust.no per il S.r D. Manfredo, e procurerò di trovarle à V.S. Ill.ma il Soprano. Intanto con una grand.ma fretta humiliss.te me l'inchino, riserbandomi à scriverle più diffusam.te col seg.te ord.rio. Di Frascati di 21 ott.re 1615. Di V.S. Ill.ma alla quale accuso la ricevuta della l.ra diretta al Cap.no Mattamora. Humil.mo e Div.mo D.re perpetuo Girolamo Fioretti

102. 4.xii.1615   Cesare Marotta to Enzo Bentivoglio
I:FEas, Archivio Bentivoglio, Mazzo 9–82, fos. 459ʳ–460ʳ

Ill.mo Sig.r mio oss.mo
Vengo con la presente à dare à V.S. Ill.ma conto, della figlia femina che Ipolita mia moglie ha partorito, et il tutto Dio gratia con buona salute di ambi dui, è si bene è femina, nulla dimeno à me è car.ma come cosa che mi viene dal voler divino, tanto più confidandomi nella servitù ch'io tengo d'alcuni miei sig.ri et particolarmente da V.S. Ill.ma. Mi viene occasione contra ogni mio volere di fastidirla d'una gratia che hora qui li dimando.

Questi giorni à dietro in una vigna dove fui condotto d'alcuni miei amici, come si suol dire per stare allegramente, e per occasione di sonare vi portai la spinettina del nostro Car.le delle corde d'oro, ivi sentendono dire quelli lavoranti, che quelle corde fussero d'oro, uno credo di essi celatamente le strappò tutte, del che prometto à V.S. Ill.ma haver riceuto disgusto grande, che se fusse stata mia non me ne sarei curato, ma essendo cosa del p.rone, mi ha parso voler rimediare à questo inconveniente, senza farsi motto al detto p.rone, con volere solamente fastidirne V.S. Ill.ma, e perche in questa città non vi è persona che sappij tirare queste corde d'oro, in tal caso ho scritto in Firenze al istesso che è solito fare tutte l'altre poste già in opra in più spinette, et à quest'hora sono già tirate, et m'importa haverle presto per potere ponere in ordine questa detta spinetta, prima che il Sig.r Car.le ne sappi nulla; credevo à quest'hora potermi valere delli frutti della

mia pentione, per potere sodisfare à questo debito, ma ancora non mi è capitato danaro
alcuno, et in tal caso ho pensato fastidire V.S. Ill.ma pregandola quanto posso à favorirmi
voler rimettere in Firenze scudi venti, quali siano pagati in mano del Sig.re Cavaliere
Giugni, guardarobba maggiore di quella Altezza, che Sua Sig.ria saprà che farne, et V.S.
Ill.ma non perdirà nulla, poiche il Sig.r Ferrante mi è debitore di detta somma, et li scriverò
li rimetta à V.S. Ill.ma so che anco il detto Sig.r Ferrante mi farria il favore, ma come
cosa che mi preme la prestezza, ho voluto prendere strada di dare à V.S. Ill.ma questo
incomodo, assicurandola che ce ne restarò con obligo singolare, et si à sorte non fusse
degno ricevere questo favore, havrò caro esserne avisato, per potere rimediare per altra
strada, poiche sicome ho detto di sopra mi preme il presto, so che mi havrà per escusato
se in ciò prendo troppo sicurtà, aggiungendo questo obligo à tanti altri infiniti che li
devo. Ipolita mia li fa riverenza, et se li raccorda serva, l'istesso alla Sig.ra Caterina, et
Sig.ra Marchesa, il che facendo anco io fo fine con pregarli dal Cielo ogni compita
felicità, di Roma li 4 Decembre 1615. Di V.S. Ill.ma oblig.mo se.re il Cav.re Cesare
Marotta

103. 31.xii.1615   Cesare Marotta to Enzo Bentivoglio
I:FEas, Archivio Bentivoglio, Mazzo 9–82, fo. 684ʳ

Ill.mo Sig.r mio e p.ron oss.mo

Può essere che il Sig.r Angelo Fiorenzola cognato del Sig.r Cav.re Giugni, quale stava
qui in Roma secretario del S. Duca Gio: Antonio, si scordasse dar conto al detto Giugni
di questa rimessa, poiche io, quando mi occorse di far fare le dette corde, ne parlai al detto
Sig.r Angelo come quello che mi hà fatto fare dell'altre, et mi rispose ch'io dovesse far
pagare al detto Giugni la valuta, che esso havrebbe hauto pensiero di farmi fare le corde;
può essere ancora che il detto Sig. Angelo con la speranza che haveva d'in giorno in giorno
di partirsi alla volta di Firenze, et questo con l'aspettativa della nuova promotione fatta,
essendo già molto tempo fa il detto Sig. Angelo fatto secretario del Sig.r Car.le de
Medici, si serbasse questo negotio à bocca con il Giugni, et cossi credo sarà stato. Le corde
sono già fatte, et le sto aspettando. V.S. Ill.ma potrà di nuovo favorirmi, se pare farà bisogno, dare nuovo ordine, che sia pagata la summa ò in mano del Giugni, ò vero in mano
del detto Sig.r Angelo Fiorenzola à fine si possa rimborsare della spesa fatta, ò pure si meglio
li paresse, et per meno briga et più sicurezza, farmili pagare qui in Roma, poiche il detto
S. Angelo si stà aspettando di hora qui, sicome mi scrive, et seco dovrà portare le corde,
et io ce li darò di mano propria non potrà dolersi di me, havendo visto che li danari si
sariano già pagati in Firenze, che lui mi havesse dato conto al Giugni sicome rimanes-
simo, et à V.S. Ill.ma chiamo perdono di tanto incomodo che li do, che il tutto fo spinto
dalla troppo sua amorevolezza verso me, et casa mia.

Desidero intendere come si porta il Ghenizzi, et Baldissarro, et intanto V.S. Ill.ma veda
si mi conosce bono in servirla, che ogni giorno mi troverà più pronto. Mia moglie li fa
riverenza, cossi anco alla Sig.ra et Sig.ra Marchesa, et io per fine me l'inchino con augu-
rarli dal Cielo ogni esaltatione. Di Roma li 31 Decembre 1615. Di V.S. Ill.ma oblig.mo
se.re il Cav.re Cesare Marotta

104. 6.i.1616 Cesare Marotta to Enzo Bentivoglio
I:FEas, Archivio Bentivoglio, Mazzo 9–83, fo. 65ʳ

Ill.mo Sig.r mio oss.mo

Con un'altra mia lettera ringratiai V.S. Ill.ma del ordine che haveva dato in Firenze, acciò fussero pagati quelli danari in mano del Cav.re Giugni, et se il negotio non hebbe buono esito lo cagionò il Sig.r Angelo Fiorenzuola, quale doveva, secondo l'appontamento tra noi preso, dar di ciò conto al detto Cav.re Giugni, del tutto ho avisato a lungo V.S. Ill.ma perche le corde sono già fatte, havendone hauto cura il detto Angelo Fiorenzuola, pregava, sicome anco di novo prego a volere fare rimettere in mano del Sig.r Angelo Fiorenzola la detta summa di scudi venti, o anco per maggior sicurezza, et meno incomodo, dare ordine che questi danari siano pagati in Roma nelle mie mani, poiche ho hauto fermo aviso, che il detto Sig.r Angelo sia di breve ritorno qui, anzi si stà aspettando da giorno in giorno, et io potrò darceli in mano propria, però non intendo agravare il suo gusto. Faccia V.S. Ill.ma quel che più l'aggrada. Il suo cimbalo se ritrova dove sono tutte l'altre sue robbe nella casa alla Longara, et è ben custodito, et stà ben conditionato. Non occorre di farlo venire in casa mia, perche feci ponere in ordine quel ch'io haveva, del quale si servi Baldesarro per studiare in quel tempo che si fermò qui. Ho sentito particolar gusto per haver inteso che costì stanno allegramente ponendo alla via la Comedia, et altre feste. In fine dove è il Sig.r Enzo non vi può essere ne otio, ne malinconia. N.S. lo facci vivere mill'anni con ogni contento. Ipolita mia li fa cento riverenze sicome anco alla Sig.ra et Sig.ra Marchesa, et tutti di Casa. et io per fine me l'offero al solito, ciò è obligatis.mo se.re di Roma li 6 gennaro 1616. Di V.S. Ill.ma devo.mo et oblig.mo se.re il Cav.re Cesare Marotta

105. 20.i.1616 Girolamo Fioretti to Enzo Bentivoglio
I:FEas, Archivio Bentivoglio, Mazzo 9–83, fo. 141ʳ

Ill.mo Sig.r mio Sig.r P.ron col.mo

Prima che mi giungesse il comand.to di V.S. Ill.ma, io havea persuaso il padre di quel putto, di cui le scrisse il S.r Catalani, et havea ridotto il negotio à tal segno, ch'ella si sarebbe potuta contentare, e della sufficienza del putto, e del partito, col quale io havrei fatteglieile havere. Ma perche prima di venire à conclusion nissuna, io giudicai, che per ogni rispetto fosse bene saper l'età del putto, et haverne fede autentica, se ne dimandò al padre, il quale con la maggior semplicità, che si possa imaginare, rispose incontinente, che era nelli 15 anni, cosa che ha fatto stupir il S.r Catalani, e me ancora, poiche dalla piccola statura di lui, e dall'altezza della sua voce, argomentavamo, che non dovesse passar gli dodici anni. Siamo dunque rimasti delusi della speranza, che havevamo concepita di poter servire V.S. Ill.ma cosi di presente in questo part.e, onde se n'è maggiorm.te accresciuto in noi il desiderio, e siamo disposti di cercar tutta Roma per trovar un soggetto habile ad imparare, ma però, che di già habbia buoni principi, perche sappiamo bene, che à V.S. Ill.ma piace di essere servita con prestezza. Si assicuri dunque, che, per quanto potrà dipendere dalle nostre forze, non passerà Pasqua, ch'ella sarà proveduta di un soprano, et io particolar.te ci haverò quella premura, che per tanti rispetti si deve.

Il libro, datomi dal S.r Francesco, fù da me consegnato al S.r Perendelli; onde a quest'hora V.S. Ill.ma l'havrà ricevuto.

Io hebbi solam.te hieri sera le lettere, e però hoggi solo hò potuto cominciar à servirla, e sebene è stato un tempo cattiviss.mo, tuttavia son'andato cercando il Cap.no Mattamoros, come potrà certificarle il S. Cav.r Marotta, à cui hò dato lettera, che à lui era indirizzata. Dimattina farò la stessa diligenza, e se intenderò, che non si trovi in Roma, gl'invierò la lettera a Napoli per la staffetta, che dovrà partire dimani doppo il pranzo.

Il S.r Ambasciatore è col S.r Card.l Cattaneo alle caccie di Cisterna, dove se ne stanno con una nobiliss.a conversazione: subito che sia ritornato gli dirò quanto V.S. Ill.ma si è compiaciuta di ordinarmi.

Hieri mattina fui à pranzo con il S.r Landinelli, ed in quel tempo gli fù resa una relazione della Tragedia di V.S. Ill.ma, inviatagli dal S.r Sufanni, il quale scrive in una sua lettera, ch'è la più miracolosa cosa, che habbia mai veduta. Io ne certificai il S.r Vinc.o, e nel leggere la relazione gli andai rappresentando suttiliss.te i moti, e le qualità delle macchine, il quale ne resto meravigliato, e perche fù interrotto, riserbammo di finirla di leggere con mig.re commodità. Non voglio lasciar di dirle, che facessimo un numero infinito di brindisi alla sanità di V.S. Ill.ma, e di Mons. Ill.mo suo fratello, et alla perpetua felicità di tutta la sua casa.

Supplico V.S. Ill.ma a farmi grazia di honorarmi di alcuna delle d.e relazioni acciò possa consolare il desiderio, e la brama, che n'hanno molti sig.ri di qualità, poiche la fama porta le lodi di quest'opera fin alle stelle; et io ancora vorrei pur almeno con il leggerla mitigare il disgusto, che hò havuto di non potermi trovare a goderla presenzial.te. V.S. Ill.ma resti servita di honorarmi continuam.te de' suoi comandi, sicura di non potermi dar maggior segno, ch'io le viva in grazia. E lo fò hum.ma riv.za. Di Roma li 20 di Gennaio 1616. Di V.S. Ill.ma la quale, piacendole di honorarmi delle relazioni, potrà dar ordine, che mi sieno inviate sotto coperta del S. Ambas.re. Io non prometto di amplificarle, mentre le leggerò ad alcuno, perche la condizione loro è tale, che per se stessa si rende ammirabile à tutti. Umiliss.mo e Div.mo S.re perpetuo Girolamo Fioretti

106. 27.ii.1616   Cesare Marotta to Enzo Bentivoglio
I:FEas, Archivio Bentivoglio, Mazzo 9–83, fo. 408^{r-v}

Ill.mo Sig.re mio oss.mo
Vengo con questa à fare riverenza à V.S. Ill.ma et insieme darli la buona quatragesima. Fin qui è corso il grido delle feste costi fatte questo Carnevale da V.S. Ill.ma si della tragedia come anco delle barriere, giostre, et altre allegrezze. Infine il Sig.r Enzo è quello che tiene allegra tutta la Città. N.S. sia quello ogni giorno più lo felicite. L'essere bello importa molto, et ni havemo l'esperienza del S. Siverino già scalco di V.S. Ill.ma che con la sua bellezza ha invaghito una Dama di modo tale, che essendoli in quel tempo morto il marito, ancorche combattuta fusse da varij amanti, volse per sua elettione, come quello che tra loro portava il vanto delle bellezze, prendere per suo sposo il detto Siverino, con dote di 12 millia scudi contanti, et altri finimenti di Casa, onde se ne vive

allegramente con Carrozza, servi, serve, donne di compagno, et altri ministri di Casa.
Con altre mie pregai V.S. Ill.ma a favorirmi di dare di nove ordine in Firenze, acciò fussero
pagati quelli venti scudi in mano del S. Cav.re Giugni, ò vero in mano del S. Agnolo
Firenzuoli, e perche non ni aviso alcuno, la supplico à degnarsi darmene l'ultima
resolutione à fine possa prendere altro partito non pacendomi ne anco il dovere ch'io
debba tante volte fastidire V.S. Ill.ma per questa causa, alla quale io et Ipolita mia ci
raccordamo servi, cosi anco alla Sig.ra et tutti di Casa, da Roma questo di 27 febraro
1616. Di V.S. Ill.mo Oblig.mo se.re Il Cav.re Cesare Marotta

107. 4.iii.1616   Cesare Marotta to Enzo Bentivoglio
I:FEas, Archivio Bentivoglio, Mazzo 9–83, fo. 453ʳ

Ill.mo Sig.re mio oss.mo

È stata da me la madre di Baldesarro e mi ha pregato ch'io scrivesse à V.S. Ill.ma racco-
mandandoli la sua persona, ritrovandosi in stato di necessità con famiglia, senza alcuno
agiuto, et che di già in nome di V.S. Ill.ma li fu promesso soccorso, il tutto l'ho voluto
significarli, per l'istanza da lei fattami, non intentendo di volere agravare, il volere, et gusto
di V.S. Ill.ma. Più volte ho fatto istanza à V.S. Ill.ma di volere sapere l'ultima certezza,
che in Firenza si è dato nuovo ordine che si paghino quelli venti scudi et perche non
ritengo aviso di novo ce ne prego. Dal Sig.r Ferrante ho riceuto à punto hier mattino
scudi dieci m.ta per mano del Sig.r Vicenzo Landinelli, si che almeno V.S. Ill.ma si contenti far pagare in Firenze li rimanenti scudi dieci in mano del S. Angelo Firensuoli, ò
vero per più sicurezza farmeli pagare qui à me, poiche il detto S. Angelo si stà aspettando qui d'in giorno in giorno, et potrò darceli io di propria mano, con che li do
humilis.ma riverenza, di Roma li 4 marzo 1616. Di V.S. Ill.ma Se.re obl.mo il Ca.re Cesare
Marotta

108. 18.vi.1616   Cesare Marotta to Enzo Bentivoglio
I:FEas, Archivio Bentivoglio, Mazzo 9–84, fo. 657ʳ

Ill.mo Sig.r mio oss.mo

Ringratio infinitam.te V.S. Ill.ma della buona voluntà che ha hauto di mandarmi li
salami, ma delli salami non la posso ringratiare poiche non l'ho riceuto, et il Cocchiero
che costì venne, dice che non li è stato consignato cosa alcuna. Ben vero dice che un' di
Casa di V.S. Ill.ma circa tre hore di notte andò all'hosteria dove detto Cocchiero era
allogiato, et perche trovò serrate le porte mentre tutti erano andati à letto, si posse à bussare, et il detto cocchiero intese, et si affacciò alla finestra, et conoscendo che era di Casa
di V.S. Ill.ma chiamò l'hoste che aprisse, disse che haveva seco uno canestrino diretto à
me. Li disse che dovesse lasciarlo al hoste, che sarebbe stato suo pensiero portarmelo, et
esso non volse lasciarlo, et celo ritornò in dietro. La mattina che doveva partire detto
Cocchiero, dice che venne à Casa di V.S. Ill.ma per ritrovare questo huomo che haveva
questo canestrino, ne mai fu possibile il ritrovarlo, siche io non ho riceuto li salami.
Con questo fo fine facendoli riverenza assieme con Ipolita mia moglie. Di Roma li 18
giugno 1616 Di V.S. Ill.ma aff.mo se.re il Cav.re Cesare Marotta

109. 11.vii.1616   Ercole Provinzale to Enzo Bentivoglio
I:FEas, Archivio Bentivoglio, Mazzo 9–80, fo. 206ʳ

Ill:mo S.re mio S.re et Patr.e Coll.mo

Il S.re Landinello a ristitouitto tutte le robe che ebe di ordine di V.S. Ill.ma da due cantemplore[?] in fora per metere in fresco il vino io li o ristitouitto la ricevuta che mi fece di dette robe io non manco e non mancaro di fare meter stese a l'aria tutti li pani ma in particolare il cochio a cio si conservano per questi caldi. Monsu di Vandomo che veneva per ambasiattore straordinario per il Re di Franza non vera piu sino a ottobre. Si dice per cosa certa che Francia e Spagna fano instancia a N.S. per che faccia Cardinalli et si tiene che alla piu longa si farano alle tempre del autuno. Dopo esser statto infinitte volte dal Racana[?] et averli parlatto il S.re Landinelli alcune volte Aniballo ci e statto pur ancora lui molte volte a tutte a dato sempre speranza di volerlo provedere ma ultimamente si e ristretto a dire che non vole mutare officialli per questi caldi e qui e andatto secondo me a finire il negocio ma l'andatto sia idio bisogna fare ogni cosa per il mellio se bene a me come dise a V.S. Ill.ma faceva uno gran solevamento et a V.S. Ill.ma con ogni riverencia li bacio le mane di roma il di 11 lulie 1616 [first written '1615', then altered to '1616']. Di V.S. Ill.ma Devottiss.mo et Umilliss.mo ser.e Ercole Provinzalle.

[Postscript:] Il S.re Girolimo in tutti li modi voria mandare uno contralto a V.S. Ill.ma. Io non mancaro di stare in pratica acio V.S. Ill.ma abi il suo intento. Iosepino e morte cioue il musico.

110. 24.v.1618   Girolamo Fioretti to Enzo Bentivoglio
I:FEas, Archivio Bentivoglio, Mazzo 9–109, fos. 654ʳ–655ʳ

Ill.mo Sig.r mio Sig.r P.ron col.mo

La mia malattia havrà facilm.te dato occasione a V.S. Ill.ma di formar qualche concetto in pregiudizio della divotis.a et impermutabile servitù mia, la quale toltone questo unico impedimento, non incontrerà mai cosa, che possa essere atta à disturbarle il corso della mia ubbidienza verso i suoi comand.ti. Mons.r Nappi, che può esser testimonio del mio male, può insieme far fede del disgusto, ch'io hò havuto, mentre vedevo di non poter servire V.S. Ill.ma di quegli avvisi, che mi haveva richiesto, con quella celerità, che dovevo, e che userò sempre nell'ubbedire à suoi cenni. La supplico dunque à scusar la mia necessità, et a far prova della mia divozione in altre occorrenze. Quanto al part.re de musici, le dirò brievem.te, che qui in Roma pochi ve ne sono di habilità proporzionata al bisogno del Ser.mo di Parma; tuttavia i più à proposito saranno per Soprani i seguenti. Il S.r Francesco Severo musico di cappella e ser.re attuale del S.r Card.e Borghese P.rone. Il S.r Lorenzo Marrobino musico di cappella similm.te, e che hà voce gagliardiss.a. Ambidue sono Castrati. Per Contralti il S.r Ferdinando musico di cappella, che sebene hà un solo braccio, tuttavia ne tiene uno di ferro, con che opera, che non si conosce il suo difetto in molte azioni; e sarebbe ottimo, perche hà voce gagliardiss.a et ingegno. D. Pietro Antonio Bolognese musico del Card.le Montalto, ed è quegli, che servì à V.S. Ill.ma nel Torneo per Mercurio. Per Tenori il S.r Gio: Dominico Puliaschi

Musico di N.Sre e ser.re attuale del Card.e P.rone. Egli canta ancora in Baritono mirabilm.te. Di Tenori, che habbiano voci gagliarde ve ne sono, ma non potrieno haver grazia à servire nello stile recitativo come li sud.ti. Per Basso ci è uno d.o S.r Gio: Parino musico di N. S.re, che hà voce gagliardiss.a. Morì Melchiorre, che per recitare in scena era esquisitiss.mo. Non propongo à V.S. Ill.ma la Sig.ra Ippolita ne Cleria di Camilluccia, perche lo stimo uno sproposito. Le dico bene, che se mi accennerà, che personaggi habbia S.A. S.ma bisogno di far rapresentare, io vedrò di trovar, ò per meglio dire, di proporre qualch'un'altro conforme al bisogno. Sebene qui in Roma l'Ill.mo S.r Card.le Farnese ad un suo cenno havrà persone, che troppo meglio di me sapranno dare questa informazione, la quale hò scritta à V.S. Ill.ma più per ubbidirla, che per credenza, ch'io habbia, ch'ella possa restarne soddisfatta, perche ben conosco la mia inhabilità in tutte le cose, ma particolar.te in queste di musica, com'è ben persuaso à cotesti SS.ri musici di Fer.a. A V.S. Ill.ma m'inchino humilis.te e le auguro ogni grandezza. Di Roma di 24 di maggio 1618. Di V.S. Ill.ma Um.mo e Div.mo Se.re Girolamo Fioretti

III. 4.ii.1620 Cesare Marotta to Enzo Bentivoglio
I:FEas, Archivio Bentivoglio, Mazzo 134, fo. 71ʳ. I have the following transcribed excerpt through the kindness of Dinko Fabris. It will also appear in his forthcoming book on the artistic patronage of the Bentivoglio family.

Ho tardato fin hora in fare riverenza a V.S. Ill.ma assieme con Ipolita mia consorte, mentre mi sono andato credendo che fusse occupata nelle negotij, havendo anco preso sicurta che V.S. Ill.ma sia certissima del ossequio, et obligo che li tengo, vengo pero hora a sodisfare a questo mio debito, pregandole a tener memoria di me, et della detta mia consorte, mentre li vivemo tanto svisceratissimi servitori raccordandole con questa occasione di fare quello officio che V.S. Ill.ma sa con il Sig. Giovani Torfanini padrone della casa dove abito, et perche di cio a pieno ne fu da noi informato a voce, mi parebbe superfluo in replicarcelo, solo li raccordo a farmi degno di suoi comandi. Ipolita mia, ed io facemo riverenza alla sig.ra Marchesa, desiderosissimi di rivederla, cossi anco al sig.r Cornelio, et tutti signorini, et per fine restaro pregando il sig.re Iddio per la sanita vi V.S. Ill.ma et ogni contento. Di Roma a li 4 febraro 1620. Di V.S. Ill.ma Aff.mo et oblig.mo ser.re il Cav.re Cesare Marotta

112. 15.ix.1624 Ippolita Recupito to Enzo Bentivoglio
I:FEas, Archivio Bentivoglio, Mazzo 183, fo. 86ʳ. I have the following transcribed excerpt through the kindness of Dinko Fabris. It will also appear in his forthcoming book on the artistic patronage of the Bentivoglio family

La viva sertu, che tengo con V.E., causata dalla sua benignita, e magnificenza, mi rende certa e sicura d'ogni grazia appresso lei. Mentre ella fu qui, e discorrendole io del negozio della casa dove al presente abito, e dove molte volte V.E. si e degnata favorirmi, che e di un tal Gio: Torfanino bolognese; e perche io ora mi ritrovo avere assegnamento di 20 luoghi de monti, avendo il cavaliere mio marito fatto esito della vigna contro mio volere, pero vorrei rinvestirli in casa. E se ella si ricorda, mi disse ch'averia dato a questo tale tanti beni stabili sul Bolognese, e presone tanti luoghi de monti. Avendone gia l'occasione per le mani, quando a V.E. sia commodo, io lo ricevero per favore singularissimo, e numeraro ancor gusto tra l'altri favori e grazie ricevute da V.E., alla quale facendo umilissima riverenza, come anco alla S.ra marchesa, fo fine baciando ad ambe le mani . . .

Appendix B: Inventories with Concordances of Music Sources

The following inventories with concordances are intended to accompany the text in Chapter 5. The first three paragraphs in that chapter provide the context and key to the selection and ordering of these inventories.

Names of composers and poets are given here as found in the sources; supplementary elements and names not found in the sources are enclosed in square brackets. Under the heading *type*, the musical form or genre is given first, followed by the poetic form of the text in parentheses. Concordances are designated using standard RISM sigla.

The following manuscripts were searched for concordances:

A:Kr, MS L81

B:Bc, MS Littera S. no. 16662; MS Littera S. no. 16663; MS 704

B:Br, Codex II 275 D

CS:Pnm, II.La.2

GB:Lbm, Add. 30491; Add. 31440; Add. 36877; Egerton 2971; Royal App. 55

GB:Ob, Tenbury MS 1018; Tenbury MS 1019

GB:Och, Mus. 8781, 879, 880

I:Baf, Ms. 1424

I:Bas, Ms. IV 86/746a

I:Bc, CC.225; Q140; Q27.4; Q49

I:Bu, MS 646 VI

I:BR, Franchi Collection, MS without signature

I:Fc, MS Barbera

I:Fn, Banco rari 238; Landau Musica 2; Magl. XIX.23; Magl. XIX.24; Magl. XIX.25; Magl. XIX.30; Magl. XIX.66; Magl. XIX.109; Magl. XIX.115; Magl. XIX.138; Magl. XIX.168; Cl. VII, 1222 bis

I:MOe, Ital. 1384.αK.6.31; Mus. C 311; Mus. E 318; Mus. F 1526; Mus. F 1527; Mus. G 52: Mus. G 239

I:Nc, MS 7664

I:Rc, MS 2466

I:Rcas, MS 2472; MS 2490

I:Rn, Ms. mus. 56

I:Ru, Ms. mus. 279

I:Rvat, Chigi Q.IV.8

I:Vc, Torrefranca 250

PL:Kj, MS *olim* 40153; MS *olim* 40591

US:BE, Music MS 757

US:PHu, MS Ital. 57

Concordances with printed sources were sought through the indexes of Emil Vogel, Alfred Einstein, François Lesure, and Claudio Sartori (eds.), *Bibliografia della musica italiana vocale profana pubblicata dal 1500 al 1700*, 3 vols. (new edn., Pomezia, 1977), for prints of single composers; and Emil Vogel and Alfred Einstein, *Bibliothek der gedruckten weltlichen Vocalmusik Italiens aus den Jahren 1500–1700* (rev. edn., Hildesheim, 1962), for printed anthologies.

Table 1   359

TABLE 1. Inventory with Concordances of I:Vc, Torrefranca 250

Folios	Incipit	Composer	Poet	Type	Concordances
1–4	Ama pur ninfa gradita	Don Ipolito [Macchiavelli]		strophic variations (canzonetta)	I:Ru, MS 279, fo. 69^{r-v}
4^v–8^v	Dolce auretta	D. Ipolito [Macchiavelli]		strophic variations (canzonetta)	
9–10^v	Ochi meco piangete			composite (canzonetta)	
11–12^v	Questi spirti gentil di te ragionano	[Pellegrino Mutij]	[Jacopo Cicognini]	strophic variations (terza rima)	Amor pudico, hora quarta, Pellegrino Mutij GB:Lbm, Add. 36877, fo. 118^r I:Bc, Q140, fos. 1^r–3^r
13–14^v	Porto celato il mio nobil pensiero			strophic variations (canzonetta)	
15–16^v	Ahi dispietato Amor come consenti		[Bernardo Tasso]	strophic variations (ottava rima)	
17–21	Venuto pur quel lagrimabil giorno	Don Ipolito [Macchiavelli]		strophic variations (ottava rima)	I:Ru, MS 279, fos. 1^r–8^v, Don Hipolito
21^v–25	Somiglia foglia a cui fa guerra il vento			strophic variations (sonetto)	
25^v–29	Solingo augello che piangendo vai	D. Ipolito [Macchiavelli]	[Pietro Bembo]	strophic variations (sonetto)	
29^v–34	Amorosa Licori	Giuseppino [Cenci]		dialogue	I:Baf, MS 1424, fos. 35^v–42^r, Giuseppino I:Ru, MS 279, fos. 37^v–44^v Il maggio fiorito (1623), 20–8
34^v–37	Quando il ciel vago s'infiora	Don Ipolito [Macchiavelli]	[Battista Guarini]	strophic variations (canzonetta)	Intermedi (1616), 27
37^v–41	Dhe Filli vita mia se mai ti punsero	Don Ipolito [Macchiavelli]		strophic variations (canzonetta)	
41^v–45	Perche non togli o Clori i pesci al fiume	Giuseppino [Cenci]		dialogue	I:Baf, MS 1424, fos. 42^v–46^r, Giuseppino

Table 1. Cont'd

Folios	Incipit	Composer	Poet	Type	Concordances
45^v–48	*In che misero punto hor qui mi mena*	[Ottavio Catalani]	[Torquato Tasso]	double strophic variations (ottava rima)	*Ghirlanda amorosa* (1621), Paolo Quagliati 'Lamento cantato dalla Sig.a Olimpia Saponara nella comedia del Ill.mo Sig.r Cardinal Savelli' *Gerusalemme liberata*, XIX. 105–8 I:Bc, CC.225, fos. 20^v–24^r I:Ru, MS 279, fos. 70^r–74^v, Ottavio Cattalano
48^v–51	*Io che l'età solea viver nel fango*	Giuseppino [Cenci]	[Giovanni della Casa]	strophic variations (sonetto)	I:Baf, MS 1424, fos. 29^v–32^r, Giuseppino [Cenci]
51^v–53	*Dolcissime pupille ond'io mi vivo*		[Battista Guarini]	strophic variations (canzonetta)	I:Baf, MS 1424, fos. 16^v–19^r
53^v–56	*Anima bella che nel sen ten stai*	Gioseppino [Cenci]	[Jacopo Cicognini]	strophic variations (sonetto)	*Amor pudico*, hora quarta; the libretto implies that this music was by 'Pietro Ciamoricone dell'Illustriss. Borghese' I:Baf, MS 1424, fos. 5^v–9^r I:MOe, Mus. E 318, fos. 7^v–9^r I:Ru, MS 279, fos. 17^r–20^v
56^v–62	*Ochi belli occhi rei*			recitative	I:Bc, CC.225, fos. 6^v–11^v
62^v–66	*Dunque Clorida mia per questi prati*	Giuseppino [Cenci]		strophic variations (canzonetta)	I:Baf, MS 1424, fos. 1^v–5^r, Giuseppino [Cenci]
66^v–70^v	*Lasciatemi morire*	[Claudio] Monteverdi	[Ottavio Rinuccini]	recitative	Claudio Monteverdi, *L'Arianna* (1608) GB:Lbm, Add. 30491, fos. 39^r–42^r, [Claudio] Monte Verdi As 'Lamento della Maddalena sopra quel d'Ariadna con nuova aggiunta di C.E.' in I:Bu, Mus MS 646, VI, fos. 1^r–6^v

Table 1 361

71–73v	Dove, dove ten fuggi anima bella	[Cesare] Marotti	strophic variations (canzonetta)	I:Fn, Banco Rari 238, pp. 18–32 I:MOe, Mus. G. 239, pp. 1–9, [Claudio] Monteverdi Il maggio fiorito (1623) Lamento d'Arianna del Signor Claudio Monteverde (1623) Claudio Monteverdi, Il sesto libro de madrigali (Venice: Amadino, 1614) As 'Jam moriar mi fili', in Claudio Monteverdi, Selva morale e spirituale (1640)
73v–75	O durezze amarissime d'amore	[Cesare] Marotti	strophic variations (ottava rima)	Intermedi (1616), 19
75v–77	Suavissimi lumi al cui splendore	[Cesare] Marotti	strophic variations (canzonetta)	Mentioned in Marotta's letter of 14.x.1611 I:Baf, MS 1424, fos. 48v–50r I:MOe, Mus. E 318, fos. 5v–6v
77v–79	Vita della mia vita egl'e pur vero	D. Ipolito [Macchiavelli] [Bernardo Tasso]	strophic variations (ottava rima)	US:PHu, MS Ital. 57, fos. 16v–17v A setting with similar music is ascribed to 'Gioseppe Cenci' in Le risonanti sfere (1629)
79v–80 bis	Io pur deggio partire	Ipolito [Macchiavelli]	strophic variations (canzonetta)	
80 bisv–81	Io piango tu non torni il duol non sciema		madrigal	I:Bc, CC.225, fo. 12r–v
81v–82	Io vorrei pur morir cosi mi preme		madrigal	I:Bc, CC.225, fos. 13r–14r
82v–83	Dunque da me ten fuggi ho mio tesoro		madrigal	
83v–84	Alma afflitta che fai	[Giovanni Battista Marino]	madrigal	I:Bc, CC.225, fos. 14v–16r
84v–85	Temer donna non dei	[Giovanni Battista Marino]	duet (madrigal)	I:Bc, CC.225, fos. 18v–20r

TABLE 1. Cont'd

Folios	Incipit	Composer	Poet	Type	Concordances
85ᵛ–86	O quanto sei gentile car' augellino		[Battista Guarini]	madrigal	I:Bc, CC.225, fos. 16ᵛ–18ʳ I:Bc, Q140, fos. 10ᶜ–11ᵛ
86ᵛ–87	Donna per acquetar vostro desire		[Bartolomeo Gottifredi]	madrigal	US:PHu, MS Ital. 57, fos. 1ᵛ–2ʳ The text is 'Non m'è grave il morire', by Bartolomeo Gottifredi with the first two lines reversed.
87ᵛ–88	Deh dolc'anima mia	Giuseppino [Cenci]	[Battista Guarini]	madrigal	Il pastor fido, III. iii GB: Lbm, Add. 36877, fo. 37ᵛ
89–89ᵛ	Amiam Fillide amiam ah non rispondi		[Battista Guarini]	madrigal (two parts)	
90ᵛ–91	Quel augellin che canta		[Battista Guarini]	madrigal	Il pastor fido, I. i
91ᵛ–92	Dolcissimo usignolo		[Battista Guarini]	madrigal (three parts)	
92ᵛ–93	O Filli, o Filli queste voci estreme			madrigal	
93ᵛ–94	Tu torni anima mia			madrigal	
94ᵛ–95	Doppo un lungo sospiro			madrigal (two parts)	
95ᵛ–96ᵛ	Se 'n così grav' e dolorosi accenti	[Abundio Antonelli]		strophic variations (sonetto, missing part 4)	Robletti, Raccolta de varii concerti musicali (1621), Abundio Antonelli, complete
97–97ᵛ	Ch'io t'ami et ami più della mia vita	[Raffaello Rontani]	[Battista Guarini]	recitative	Il pastor fido, III. iii Raffaello Rontani, Le varie musiche . . . libro primo (1614)
98–98ᵛ	Son questi miei sospir messaggi ardenti			strophic variations (terza rima)	
99–99ᵛ	Non credete ch'io v'ami ahi lasso e ch'io	[Raffaello Rontani]		recitative (sonetto)	Raffaello Rontani, Le varie musiche . . . libro terzo (1619)
100–101	Tu godi il sol ch'agli occhi miei s'asconde	[Raffaello Rontani]	[Battista Guarini]	recitative (sonetto)	Raffaello Rontani, Le varie musiche . . . libro terzo (1619)

101^{v}–102	*O tu che fra le selve occulta vivi*		[Bernardo Tasso]	madrigal with echo	
102^{v}–103	*Ecco solinga e delle selve amica*	[Marco da Gagliano]		madrigal with echo	Pietro Benedetti, *Musiche . . . libro secondo* (1613), Marco da Gagliano
103^{v}–105^{v}	*O dell'ombrosa notte amati orrori*	[Cesare Marotta]		composite strophic variations (terza rima)	I:Bc, CC.225, fos. 1^{r}–5^{r} GB:Lbm, Add. 36877, fo. 108^{r-v} Attribution established by similarity to *Suavissimi lumi*, mentioned in Cesare Marotta's letter of 14.x.1611.
106–107^{v}	*Che più giova mirar occh'infelici*	[Cesare] Marotti		strophic variations (ottava rima)	Intermedi (1616), 36

TABLE 2. Inventory with Concordances of I:Bc, CC.225

Folios	Incipit	Composer	Poet	Type	Concordances
1–5	*O dell'ombrosa notte amati orori*	[Cesare Marotta]		composite strophic variations (terza rima)	I:Vc, Torrefranca 250, fos. 103ᵛ–105ᵛ; GB:Lbm, Add. 36877, fo. 108ʳ⁻ᵛ; Attribution established by similarity to *Suavissimi lumi*, mentioned in Cesare Marotta's letter of 14.x.1611.
5ᵛ–11ᵛ	*Occhi belli occhi rei*			recitative	I:Vc, Torrefranca 250, fos. 56ᵛ–62ʳ
12–12ᵛ	*Io vorrei pur morir così mi preme*			madrigal	I:Vc, Torrefranca 250, fos. 81ʳ–82ʳ
13–14	*Dunque da me ten fuggi ho mio thesoro*			madrigal	I:Vc, Torrefranca 250, fos. 82ᵛ–83ʳ
14ᵛ–16	*Alma afflitta che fai*		[Giovanni Battista Marino]	madrigal	I:Vc, Torrefranca 250, fos. 83ᵛ–84ʳ
16–18	*O quanto sei gentile car'augellino*		[Battista Guarini]	madrigal	I:Bc, Q140, fos. 10ᵛ–11ʳ; I:Vc, Torrefranca 250, fos. 85ᵛ–86ʳ
18ᵛ–20	*Temer donna non dei*		[Giovanni Battista Marino]	duet (madrigal)	I:Vc, Torrefranca 250, fos. 84ᵛ–85ʳ
20ᵛ–24	*In che misero punto hor qui me mena*	[Ottavio Cattalani]	[Torquato Tasso]	double strophic variations (ottava rima)	'Lamento di Ermenia cantato nella commedia di Savelli' *Gerusalemme liberata*, XIX. 105, 3; I:Ru, MS 279, fos. 70ʳ–74ᵛ, Ottavio Catalani; I:Vc, Torrefranca 250, fos. 45ᵛ–48ʳ
24ᵛ–27	*Leggiadri occhi sereni*	[Giuseppe Cenci]		strophic variations (canzonetta)	GB:Lbm, Add. 36877, fos. 110ʳ–111ʳ; I:Baf, MS 1424, fos. 9ᵛ–13ʳ, Giuseppino [Cenci]; I:Fn, Cl. VII, 1222 bis, fo. 26ᵛ; I:MOe, Mus. E 318, fos. 12ʳ–13ᵛ; US:PHu, MS Ital. 57, fos. 22ᵛ–24ʳ; *Concerti amorosi* (1623), 46–7
29–30	*Occhi stelle fatali*			strophic (canzonetta)	GB:Lbm, Add. 36877, fo. 109ʳ⁻ᵛ; GB:Ob, Tenbury MS 1019, fo. 4ʳ; I:Fn, Magl. XIX.66, fo. 25ᵛ

Table 2

365

Folio	Incipit	Composer	Author	Form	Source
30v–31	Occhi piangete			strophic (canzonetta)	I:Fn, Magl. XIX.24, fos. 15v–16r
31v–32	Voi partite sdegniose	[Raffaello Rontani]		strophic (canzonetta)	I:Rsc, A.Ms.247, fo. 17v Concerti amorosi (1623), 10 Raffaello Rontani, Le varie musiche (1618)
32v–33	Dhe mirate luci ingrate	[Giovanni Domenico Puliaschi]	[Ottavio Rinuccini]	strophic (canzonetta)	Ghirlandetta amorosa (1621), [Giovanni] Domenico Puliasca
33v–34	D'una guancia alma e redente			strophic (canzonetta)	
34v–35	Ho pur d'or il crin anc'io			strophic (canzonetta)	
35v–36	Questa bell' Amor			strophic (canzonetta)	
36v–37	Mie speranze lusinghiere			strophic (canzonetta)	
37v–38	Arsi et ardo per voi ma nel ardore			strophic (terna rima)	
38v–39	Felic'era il mio core			strophic (canzonetta)	
39v–40	Dhe vieni Clori			strophic (canzonetta)	
40v–41	Aure placide volanti			strophic (canzonetta)	
41v–42	Care treccie aura stami			strophic (canzonetta)	
42v–43	Falsi sospiri			strophic (canzonetta)	
43v–44	Se pietad'in voi non trovasi			strophic (canzonetta)	
44v–45	Bella Clori non fuggire			strophic (canzonetta)	I:Fn, Cl. VII, 1222 bis, fos. 58v–59r Concerti amorosi (1623), 9
45v–46	S'alcun vi giura cortes' amante			strophic (canzonetta)	Concerti amorosi (1623), 3
46v–47	Ferma, ferma non percotere			strophic (canzonetta)	Concerti amorosi (1623), 34–5
47v–48	Amar donna superba			strophic (canzonetta)	
48v–49	O di raggi e di fiammelle	[Francesco Severi]	['Incolto', Accademico Immaturo]	strophic (canzonetta)	Vezzosetti fiori (1622), 5, Francesco Severi
49v–50	Dhe girate / Luci amate		[Isabella Andreini]	strophic (canzonetta)	US:PHu, MS Ital. 57, fos. 26v–27r
50–51	Chi d'Amor piag'e sospira			strophic (canzonetta)	I:Bc, Q140, fos. 12
51v–52	Rompa lo sdegno le dure catene			strophic (canzonetta)	I:Fn, Cl. VII, 1222 bis, fos. 25v–26r Concerti amorosi (1623), 38–9

Table 2. Cont'd

Folios	Incipit	Composer	Poet	Type	Concordances
52ᵛ–53	Voi mi dite ch'io non v'ami	[Ottavio Catalani]	[Baldo Cataneo]	strophic (canzonetta)	I:Fn, Cl. VII, 1222 bis, fo. 19ʳ⁻ᵛ Robletti, Racolta de varii concerti musicali (1620), Ottavio Catalani Concerti amorosi (1623), 17
53ᵛ–54	Ove ne vai pastor così doglioso			strophic (dialogue)	
54ᵛ–55	Io so che trovasi			strophic (canzonetta)	I:Rsc, A.Ms.247, fo. 15ʳ
55ᵛ–56	Più non sento del tuo dardo			strophic (canzonetta)	GB:Lbm, Add. 31440, fos. 7ʳ–8ʳ
56ᵛ–58	Bella e vaga Filli vezzosa			strophic (canzonetta)	

Table 3

367

TABLE 3. Inventory with Concordances of I:Baf, MS 1424

Folios	Incipit	Composer	Poet	Type	Concordances
1ᵛ–5	*Dunque Clorida mia per questi prati*	Giuseppino [Cenci]		strophic variations (canzonetta)	I:Vc, Torrefranca 250, fos. 62ᵛ–66ʳ, Giuseppino [Cenci]
5ᵛ–9	*Anima bella che nel sen te stai*	Giuseppino [Cenci]	[Jacopo Cicognini]	strophic variations (sonetto)	*Amor pudico*, hora quarta. The libretto implies that this music was by 'Pietro Ciamoricone dell'Illustriss. Borghese' I:MOe, Mus. E 318, fos. 7ᵛ–9ʳ I:Ru, MS 279, fos. 17ʳ–20ᵛ I:Vc, Torrefranca 250, fos. 53ᵛ–56ʳ, Gioseppino [Cenci]
9ᵛ–13	*Leggiadri occhi sereni*	Giuseppino [Cenci]		strophic variations (canzonetta)	GB:Lbm, Add. 36877, fos. 110ᵛ–111ʳ I:Bc, CC.225, fos. 24ᵛ–27ʳ I:MOe, Mus. E 318, fos. 12ʳ–13ᵛ I:Fn, Cl. VII, 1222 bis, fo. 26ᵛ US:PHu, MS Ital. 57, fos. 22ᵛ–24ʳ *Concerti amorosi* (1623), 46–7
14ᵛ–16	*A sì duri lamenti*			strophic variations (canzonetta)	I:Ru, MS 279, fos. 20ᵛ–24ʳ I:Bc, Q140, fo. 12ᵛ, one strophe only and syllabic
16ᵛ–19	*Dolcissime pupille ond'io mi vivo*			strophic variations (canzonetta)	I:Vc, Torrefranca 250, fos. 51ᵛ–53ʳ
19ᵛ–22	*Voi pur mi promettesti occhi sereni*			strophic variations (canzonetta)	
22ᵛ–26	*Ben fuggirsi vedran la nev'e 'l gielo*			·strophic variations (canzonetta)	
26ᵛ–29	*Questa ch'el cor mi fura*	Stefano Landi		strophic variations (canzonetta)	Stefano Landi, *Arie* (1620)
29ᵛ–32	*Io che l'età solea viver nel fango*	Giuseppino [Cenci]	[Giovanni della Casa]	strophic variations (sonetto)	I:Vc, Torrefranca 250, fos. 48ᵛ–51ʳ, Giuseppino [Cenci]
32ᵛ–35	*Felice che discior tra fiamme ardenti*	[Stefano Landi]		strophic variations (canzonetta)	Stefano Landi, *Arie* (1620)

TABLE 3. Cont'd

Folios	Incipit	Composer	Poet	Type	Concordances
35ᵛ–42	*Amorosa Licori*	Giuseppino [Cenci]		dialogue	I:Ru, MS 279, fos. 37ᵛ–44ʳ I:Vc, Torrefranca 250, fos. 29ᵛ–34ʳ, Giuseppino [Cenci] *Il maggio fiorito* (1623), 7–8
42ᵛ–46	*Perche non togli o Clori i pesci al fiume*	Giuseppino [Cenci]		dialogue	I:Vc, Torrefranca 250, fos. 41ᵛ–45ʳ, Giuseppino [Cenci] *Ghirlandetta amorosa* (1621), Paolo Quagliati
46ᵛ–48	*Può ben fortuna far ch'io m'allontani*	[Cesare Marotta]		strophic variations (canzonetta)	Mentioned in Marotta's letter of 14.x.1611
48ᵛ–50	*Suavissimi lumi al cui splendore*	[Cesare Marotta]		strophic variations (canzonetta)	Mentioned in Marotta's letter of 14.x.1611 I:MOe, Mus. E 318, fos. 5ᵛ–6ᵛ I:Vc, Torrefranca 250, fos. 75ᵛ–77ʳ, [Cesare] Marotti
50ᵛ–53	*Se 'l dolce sguardo di costei m'ancide*	Giuseppino [Cenci]		strophic variations (sonetto, missing part 4)	
53ᵛ	*Eaurilla mia quando m'accese* (incomplete)			strophic (canzonetta)	GB:Lbm, Add. 36877, fo. 104ʳ–ᵛ I:Fn, Cl. VII, 1222 bis, fo. 69ʳ

Table 4

369

TABLE 4. Inventory with Concordances of I:Ru, MS 279

Folios	Incipit	Composer	Poet	Type	Concordances
1–8ᵛ	*Venuto è pur quel lagrimabil giorno*	Don Hipolito [Macchiaveli]		strophic variations (ottava rima)	I:Vc, Torrefranca 250, fos. 17ᵛ–21ʳ, Don Ipolito [Macchiavelli]
9–16ᵛ	*Udite Amanti udite*		[Andrea Salvadori]	recitative	
17–20ᵛ	*Anima bella che nel sen ti stai*	[Giuseppe Cenci]	[Jacopo Cicognini]	strophic variations (sonetto)	*Amor pudico*, hora quarta; the libretto implies that this music was by 'Pietro Ciamoricone dell'Illustriss. Borghese' I:Baf, MS 1424, fos. 5ᵛ–9ʳ, Giuseppino [Cenci] I:MOe, Mus. E 318, fos. 7ᵛ–9ʳ I:Vc, Torrefranca 250, fos. 53ᵛ–56ʳ, Gioseppino [Cenci]
20ᵛ–24	*A si duri lamenti*			strophic variations (canzonetta)	I:Baf, MS 1424, fos. 14ᵛ–16ᵛ I:Bc, Q140, fo. 12ᵛ, one strophe only and syllabic
24ᵛ–31	*Tu parti anima mia*			recitative with some variations (canzonetta)	I:Fn, Magl. XIX.23, fos. 18ᵛ–21ᵛ, incomplete
33–36ᵛ	*Infelice colui che s'innamora*			strophic variations (canzonetta)	I:Fc, Barbera, fos. 77ᵛ–78ᵛ
37	*Dov'e Fillide mia dove risplende*				Last folio only
37ᵛ–44ᵛ	*Amorosa Licori*	[Giuseppe Cenci]		dialogue	First part is missing I:Baf, MS 1424, fos. 35ᵛ–42ʳ, Giuseppino [Cenci] I:Vc, Torrefranca 250, fos. 29ᵛ–34ʳ, Giuseppino [Cenci] *Il maggio fiorito* (1623), 20–8
45–48	*Chi vuol veder il sole*	Gio[vanni] Domenico [Puliaschi]		strophic variations (canzonetta)	Giovanni Domenico Puliaschi, *Gemma musicale* (1618)
48ᵛ–52ᵛ	*Tu dormi e 'l dolce sonno*	[Cesare] Marotti		strophic variations (canzonetta)	GB:Lbm, Add. 30491, fos. 42ᵛ–43ᵛ, Jacopo Peri

TABLE 4. Cont'd

Folios	Incipit	Composer	Poet	Type	Concordances
53v–56	Amor io ben sapea	Stefano Landi		strophic variations (canzonetta)	CS:Pnm, II.I.a.2, fos. 50r–52r, Jacopo Peri I:Fc, Barbera, fo. 31r–v
56v–60v	Dhe mira egli canto spuntar la rosa	Belardino Nanino	[Torquato Tasso]	strophic variations (ottava rima)	Francesco Mannelli, Ciacone et arie (1629), Stefano Landi, lost Gerusalemme liberata, XVI. 14 and 15
61–68v	Pascomi di sospir languendo e debile	Fra[ncesca] Caccini	[Michelanglo Buonarroti, Jr.]	dialogue	Il Passatempo (1614)
69–69v	[Ama pur ninfa gradita]	[Ippolito Macchiavelli]		strophic variations (canzonetta, missing the first three parts)	I:Vc, Torrefranca 250, fos. 1r–4r, Ipolito [Macchiavelli]
70–74v	In che misero punto hor qui me mena	Otavio Cattalano	[Torquato Tasso]	double strophic variations (ottava rima)	Gerusalemme liberata, XIX. 105, 3 I:Bc, CC.225, fos. 20v–24r I:Vc, Torrefranca 250, fos. 45v–48r
77–80v	Io v'amo anima mia	Stefano Landi	[Anibale Pocaterra]	duet (madrigal)	Francesco Mannelli, Ciacone e arie (1629), Stefano Landi, missing
81–90	Questa bella guerriera	Stefano Landi		duet (madrigal)	
90v–96v	Superbo te ne vai legno fugace	Stefano Landi		duet (madrigal)	
96v–100v	Se non è cosa in terra	Stefano Landi		duet (madrigal)	

Table 5

371

TABLE 5. Inventory with Concordances of US:PHu, MS Ital. 57

Folios	Incipit	Composer	Poet	Type	Concordances
1	Ah fuggite fuggite				
1^v–2	Donna, per acquetar vostro desire		[Bartolomeo Gottifredi]	madrigal	I:Vc, Torrefranca 250, fos. 86^v–87^r The text is 'Non m'è grave il morire' by Bartolomeo Gottifredi with the first two lines reversed.
2^v–3	Care lagrime mie		[Livio Celiano]	madrigal	
3^v–5^v	Pace non trovo, e non ho da far guerra		[Francesco Petrarca]	strophic variations (sonetto)	
6^v–8	Pargoletta vezzosa e ridente			duet (canzonetta)	I:Fn, Magl. XIX.25, fos. 14^v–16^r I:Fn, Cl. VII, 1222 bis, fos. 22^v–23^r Concerti amorosi (1623), 28–9
8^v–9	Se non hai di ferro il core			duet (canzonetta)	I:Fn, Cl. VII, 1222 bis, fo. 27^{r-v} Concerti amorosi (1623), 48–9, for solo voice
9^v–10^v	Ahi com'a un vago sol cortese giro	[Giuseppino Cenci]	[Battista Guarini]	madrigal	Pietro Maria Marsolo, Secondo libro dei madrigali (1614), Giuseppino [Cenci]
11–12	Crud'Amarilli, che col non'ancora		[Battista Guarini]	madrigal	Il pastor fido, I. ii
12^v–13	Vorrei baciarti, o Filli		[Giovanni Battista Marino]	madrigal	
13^v–14	Ecco che pur al fine			strophic (canzonetta)	I:Bc, Q140, fo. 11^v Scherzi amorosi (2/1620), 18–19
14^v–15^v	Amarilli crudel, e ria			duet (canzonetta)	
16	Tempo ben fu			strophic (canzonetta)	
16^v–17^v	Vita de la mia vita egl'è pur vero	[Ippolito Macchiavelli or Giuseppino Cenci]	[Bernardo Tasso]	strophic variations (ottava rima)	I:Vc, Torrefranca 250, fos. 77^v–79^r, Don Ipolito [Macchiavelli] A setting with similar music is

TABLE 5. Cont'd

Folios	Incipit	Composer	Poet	Type	Concordances
18	*Vaga e lucente*		['Finco', Accademico Trasformato]	strophic (canzonetta, only one strophe given)	ascribed to 'Gioseppe Cenci' in *Le risonanti sfere* (1629) I:Bc, Q140, fo. 23^r
18^v–20	*O voi ch'intorno al lagrimoso canto*			strophic variations (ottava rima)	I: Fn, Cl. VII, 1222 bis, fo. 28^v *Concerti amorosi* (1623), 42–5
20^v–21	*O leggiadri occhi belli, occhi miei cari*			duet (canzonetta)	I:Fn, B.R. 238, fos. 4^r–5^r
21^v–22	*Ecco Lidia mia bella*		[Baldo Cataneo]	duet (canzonetta)	I:Fn, Cl. VII, 1222 bis, fo. 23^{r-v} I:Fn, Magl. XIX.25, fos. 26^v–27^r *Concerti amorosi* (1623), 30–1, for solo voice
22^v–24	*Leggiadri occhi sereni*	[Giuseppino Cenci]		strophic variations (canzonetta)	GB:Lbm, Add. 36877, fos. 110^v–111^r I:Baf, MS 1424, fos. 9^v–13^r, Giuseppino [Cenci] I:Bc, CC.225, fos. 24^v–27^r I:Fn, Cl. VII, 1222 bis, fo. 26^v I:MOe, Mus. E 318, fos. 12^r–13^v *Concerti amorosi* (1623), 46–7
24^v–25^v	*Questa piaga mi sia sempre nel core*			strophic variations (ottava rima)	I:MOe, Mus. F 1527, fos. 25^r–26^r
25^v–26	*Piu non amo piu non ardo*	[Giuseppino Cenci]		duet (canzonetta)	*Raccolta de varii concerti musicali* (1621), Giuseppe Cenci. Begins the same as *Più non amo* in I:Bc, Q140, fo. 41^r
26^v–27	*Dhe girate/Luci amate*		[Isabella Andreini]	strophic (canzonetta)	I:Bc, CC.225, fos. 49^v–50^r
27^v–28^v	*La mia Filli crudel spesso mi fugge*			duet (canzonetta)	I:Fn, Cl. VII, 1222 bis, fo. 95^r

Table 6

373

TABLE 6. Inventory with Concordances of I:MOe, Mus. E 318

Folios	Incipit	Composer	Poet	Type	Concordances
2	*Lilla, Lilla giovineta*			duet (canzonetta)	
2ᵛ–3ᵛ	*O dolcissimi sguardi*			duet (canzonetta)	
4	*Pastorella che si bella*			duet (canzonetta)	I:Bc, Q140, fo. 35ᵛ
4ᵛ–5	*In qual parte del mondo havrò ricetto*			strophic variations (ottava rima)	
5ᵛ–6ᵛ	*Suavissimi lumi al cui splendore*	[Cesare Marotta]		strophic variations (canzonetta)	Mentioned in Marotta's letter of 14.x.1611 I:Baf, MS 1424, fos. 48ᵛ–50ᶠ I:Vc, Torrefranca 250, fos. 75ᵛ–77ᶠ, [Cesare] Marotti
7ᵛ–9	*Anima bella che nel sen ten stai*	[Giuseppino Cenci]	[Jacopo Cicognini]	strophic variations (sonetto)	*Amore pudica, hora quarta*; the libretto implies that this music was by 'Pietro Ciamoricone dell'Illustriss. Borghese' I:Baf, MS 1424, fos. 5ᵛ–9ᶠ I:Ru, MS 279, fos. 17ᶠ–20ᵛ I:Vc, Torrefranca 250, fos. 53ᵛ–56ᶠ, Gioseppino [Cenci]
9ᵛ	*Questa tener angioletta*	[Ippolito Macchiavelli or Orazio Michi?]		strophic variations (canzonetta)	I:Fn, Magl. XIX.23, fos. 15ᵛ–17ᶠ, D.H.M. [=Don Hipplito Macchiavelli or Don Horatio Michi?]
11ᵛ–13	*Leggiadri occhi sereni*	[Giuseppino Cenci]		strophic variations (canzonetta)	GB:Lbm, Add. 36877, fos. 110ᵛ–111ᶠ I:Baf, MS 1424, fos. 9ᵛ–13ᶠ, Giuseppino [Cenci] I:Bc, CC.225, fos. 24ᵛ–27ᶠ I:Fn, Cl. VII, 1222 bis, fo. 26ᵛ US:PHu, MS Ital. 57, fos. 22ᵛ–24ᶠ *Concerti amorosi* (1623), 46–7

TABLE 7. Inventory with Concordances of I:Bc, Q140

Folios	Incipit	Composer	Poet	Type	Concordances
1–3	Questi spirti gentili di te ragionano	[Pelegrino Mutij]	[Jacopo Cicognini]	strophic variations (terza rima)	Amor pudico, hora quarta, Pellegrino Mutij GB:Lbm, Add. 36877, fo. 118ʳ I:Vc, Torrefranca 250, fos. 11ᵛ–12ᵛ
3ᵛ	Altro non e 'l mio cor			strophic (canzonetta, one strophe only)	GB:Lbm, Add. 36877, fos 22ᵛ–24ʳ I:Fn, Cl. VII, 1222 bis, fos. 73ᵛ–74ʳ Affetti amorosi (1618), 15
4	Lasso perche mi fuggi		[Battista Guarini]	madrigal	
6	Ben è ver, ch'ei pargoleggia		[Gabriello Chiabrera]	strophic (canzonetta, one strophe only)	
7–9	La gloria di colui, che 'l tutto muove	[Giovanni Domenico Puliaschi]	[Jacopo Cicognini]	composite strophic variations (terza rima)	Amor pudico, hora quarta, [Giovanni] Domenico Puliaschi
10–11	O come sei gentile		[Battista Guarini]	madrigal	I:Bc, CC.225, fos. 16ʳ–18ʳ I:Vc, Torrefranca 250, fos. 85ᵛ–86ʳ US:PHu, MS Ital. 57, fos. 13ᵛ–14ʳ
11ᵛ	Ecco che pur al fine			strophic (canzonetta, one strophe only)	
12	Rompa lo sdegno le dure catene			strophic (canzonetta, one strophe only)	I:Bc, CC.225, fos. 51ᵛ–52ʳ I:Fn, Cl. VII, 1222 bis, fos. 25ᵛ–26ʳ Concerti amorosi (1623), 38–9
12ᵛ	A si duri lamenti			strophic (canzonetta, one strophe only)	I:Baf, MS 1424, fos. 14ᵛ–16ᵛ, strophic variations I:Ru, MS 279, fos. 20ᵛ–24ʳ, strophic variations
12ᵛ–14ᵛ	Vidi ondegiar questi infecondi campi			strophic variations (sonetto)	
15	Con un dolent' oime			strophic (canzonetta, one strophe only)	I:Fn, Cl. VII, 1222 bis, fos. 84ᵛ–85ʳ
15ᵛ	Ecco la luce ch'a noi conduce		[Gabriello Chiabrera]	strophic (canzonetta, one strophe only)	

Table 7

375

16	*Perche mi fuggi*		strophic (canzonetta, one strophe only)	
17–17ᵛ	*Vezzosett'e bella Clori*		strophic (canzonetta, one strophe only)	
18–18ᵛ	*La mia Clori vezzosa*		strophic (canzonetta, one strophe only)	GB:Lbm, Add. 36877, fos. 39ᵛ–40ᵛ; *Affetti amorosi* (1618), 24–5
19	*Da queste selve, e questi alpestri monti*		strophic (canzonetta, one strophe only)	*Concerti amorosi* (1623), 1
19ᵛ–22	*La furiera de bei lampi*		duet (canzonetta)	
22ᵛ, 25	*Perche sei bella*		duet (canzonetta)	
23	*Vag'e lucente*	['Finco', Accademico Trasformato]	strophic (canzonetta, one strophe only)	Incomplete; US:PHu, MS Ital. 57, fo. 18ʳ
23ᵛ–24	*Gioite meco*		duet (canzonetta)	
25	*Quella bell'amor che sospirar mi fa*		strophic (canzonetta, one strophe only)	I:Fc, Barbera, fo. 64ʳ; I:Fc, Barbera, fo. 138ʳ; I:Fn, MS Cl. VII, 1222 bis, fo. 82ʳ; *Affetti amorosi* (1618), 9
26	*Arsi un temp'e l'ardore*		strophic (canzonetta, one strophe only)	
26ᵛ–28ᵛ	*Destar potess'io pur in quel bel seno*		strophic variations (ottava rima)	
29	*Giovinetta vezzosa*		strophic (canzonetta, one strophe only)	
30–31ᵛ	*Ecco Silvio colei che 'n odio tanto*	[Battista Guarini]	recitative	*Il pastor fido*, IV. ix
32–33ᵛ	*Per te mi struggo sol, sol per te moro*		strophic variations (ottava rima)	
34–34ᵛ	*Dovro dunque morire*	[Giulio Caccini]	madrigal	Giulio Caccini, *Le nuove musiche* (1602); B:Bc, MS 704, fo. 45ʳ; GB:Ob, Tenbury MS 1018, fo. 39ᵛ
35	*Fuggon i giorni*		duet (canzonetta)	

Table 7. Cont'd

Folios	Incipit	Composer	Poet	Type	Concordances
35ᵛ	*Pastorella che si bella*			strophic (canzonetta, one strophe given)	I:MOe, Mus. E 318, fo. 4ʳ
36	*Dhe soprite colorite*			strophic (canzonetta, one strophe given)	
36ᵛ	*Aure belle aure vezzose*			strophic (canzonetta, one strophe given)	I:Fc, Barbera, fos. 19ᵛ–20ʳ
37ᵛ–38	*Ecco la primavera*			duet (canzonetta)	GB:Lbm, Add. 36877, fos. 89ᵛ–90ʳ
38ᵛ	*Filli gentile perche fug'ogn'hora*	[Filippo Piccinini]		strophic (canzonetta, one strophe given)	Enrico Radesca, *Il quarto libro delle canzonette* (1610), Filippo Piccinini, 'Volta per ballare'
39ᵛ	*Bona sera mastro Taddeo*			strophic (canzonetta, one strophe given)	
40ᵛ	*Splendete sereni*			strophic (canzonetta, one strophe given)	GB:Lbm, Add. 36877, fo. 59ʳ⁻ᵛ; I:Fn, Cl. VII, 1222 bis, fos. 70ᵛ–71ʳ *Affetti amorosi* (1618), 17
41	*Più non amo più non ardo*	[Giuseppino Cenci?]		strophic (canzonetta, one strophe given)	Begins the same as *Più non amo* in *Raccolta de varii concerti musicali* (1621), p. 20, by Giuseppe Cenci, and in US:PHu, MS Ital. 57, fos. 25ᵛ–26ʳ

Table 8

TABLE 8. Inventory with Concordances of I:Rsc, A.Ms. 247

Folios	Incipit	Composer	Poet	Type	Concordances
14	*Vostro fui, vostro sono*			strophic (canzonetta)	
14	*Lungo tempo si dissi io*			strophic (canzonetta)	
14ᵛ	*Per torbido mare*	Marc'Antonio Pasqualini or Orazio Michi?		strophic (canzonetta)	I:Rvat, Barb. lat. 4151, fos. 46ᵛ–48ʳ
15	*Io so che trovasi*			strophic (canzonetta)	I:Bc, CC.225, fos. 54ᵛ–55ʳ
16	*Maggio ritorna*			strophic (canzonetta)	
16ᵛ	*Chi vuole aconciare*			strophic (canzonetta)	
17ᵛ	*Stelle homicide*			strophic (canzonetta)	
17ᵛ	*Voi partite sdegnose*			strophic (canzonetta)	GB:Lbm, Add. 36877, fo. 123ʳ⁻ᵛ I:Bc, CC.225, fos. 31ᵛ–32ʳ I:Fn, Cl. VII, 1222 bis, fos. 59ᵛ–60ʳ I:Fn, Magl. XIX.24, fos. 15ᵛ–16ʳ *Concerti amorosi* (1623), 10
18	*Pastorella ove t'ascondi*			strophic (canzonetta)	
18	*O bellissimi cappelli*			strophic (canzonetta)	
18ᵛ	*Dolci sospiri*			strophic (canzonetta)	
19ᵛ	*Stanch'alle membra ne porgeva riposo*			strophic (canzonetta)	
19ᵛ	*Immaginar non posso*			strophic (canzonetta)	
20	*Usa ver ove, crudel, qual più severo*			strophic (canzonetta)	
20	*Deh, perche ciel non odi i miei lamenti*			strophic (canzonetta)	
20ᵛ	*Piansi ben mio, la pena, il grave ardore*			strophic (canzonetta)	

Table 9. Inventory with Concordances of *Concerti amorosi* (1623)

Folios	Incipit	Composer	Poet	Type	Concordances
1	*Trà queste selve*			strophic (canzonetta)	I:Bc, Q140, fo. 19^r
2	*Non è mercede di pura fede*			strophic (canzonetta)	I:Fn, Magl. XIX.24, fos. 25^v–26^r I:Fn, Cl. VII, 1222 bis, fo. 32^v
3^v	*S'alcun vi giura cortesi amanti*			strophic (canzonetta)	I:Bc, CC.225, fos. 45^v–46^v I:Fn, Cl. VII, 1222 bis, 50^v–51
4	*Eco l'alma mia*			strophic (canzonetta)	GB:Lbm, Add. 36877, fos. 120^v–121^r
5	*Perche mi fugite o crudele*			strophic (canzonetta)	I:Fn, Cl. VII, 1222 bis, fo. 59^v
6–7^v	*Misero amante io vivo*			strophic (canzonetta)	I:Fn, Cl. VII, 1222 bis, fos. 47^v–48^r
8^v	*Tu non hai provato amore*			strophic (canzonetta)	I:Fn, Cl. VII, 1222 bis, fos. 32^v–35^r
9^v	*Bella Clori non fuggire*			strophic (canzonetta)	I:Bc, CC.225, fos. 44^v–45^r I:Fn, Cl. VII, 1222 bis, fos. 54^v–55^r
10	*Vôi partite sdegnose*			strophic (canzonetta)	GB:Lbm, Add. 36877, fo. 123^{r-v} I:Bc, CC.225, fos. 31^v–32^r I:Fn, Cl. VII, 1222 bis, fos. 59^v–60^r I:Fn, Magl. XIX.24, fos. 15^v–16^r I:Rsc, 247, fo. 17^v
11	*Non più con mest'accenti*			strophic (canzonetta)	GB:Lbm, Add. 36877, fos. 142^v–143^r I:Fn, Cl. VII, 1222 bis, fo. 56^{r-v}
12^v	*Poiche la crud'è fera*			strophic (canzonetta)	I:Fn, Cl. VII, 1222 bis, fo. 62^r
13^v	*Se tu nieghi ò ria beltà*			strophic (canzonetta)	I:Fn, Cl. VII, 1222 bis, fo. 48^v
14^v	*Ahi che morir mi sent'o tu*			strophic (canzonetta)	GB:Lbm, Add. 36877, fo. 21^{r-v} I:Fn, Cl. VII, 1222 bis, fo. 49^r
15	*Crudel ove ne vai*			strophic (canzonetta)	I:Fn, Cl. VII, 1222 bis, fos. 49^v–50^v
16	*Crudel così tradirmi*			strophic (canzonetta)	I:Fn, Cl. VII, 1222 bis, fo. 19^r
17^v	*Vôi mi dite ch'io non v'ami*	[Ottavio Catalani]	[Baldo Cataneo]	strophic (canzonetta)	I:Bc, CC.225, fos. 52^v–53^r I:Fn, Cl. VII, 1222 bis, fo. 15^{r-v} Robletti, *Raccolta de varie concerti musicali* (1620),

Table 9

Ottavio Catalani
Concerti amorosi (1623), 17

Folio	Title	Attribution	Form	Source
18–19^v	*Donzelletta lascivetta*		strophic (canzonetta)	I:Fn, Cl. VII, 1222 bis, fos. 19^v–20^r
20–21^v	*Vezzose pastorelle*		strophic (canzonetta)	I:Fc, Barbera, fos. 130^r–131^r; I:Fn, Cl. VII, 1222 bis, fo. 20^{r-v}
22^v	*Amarillide mia crudel*		strophic (canzonetta)	I:Fn, Cl. VII, 1222 bis, fos. 20^v–21^r
23^v	*S'Amor'è cieco non può 'l vero scorgere*		strophic (canzonetta)	I:Fn, Cl. VII, 1222 bis, fo. 21^r
24^v	*Se rivolg'in me serene*		strophic (canzonetta)	I:Fn, Cl. VII, 1222 bis, fo. 21^{r-v}
25^v	*Ochi belli saette d'amore*		strophic (canzonetta)	
26–27^v	*Pianget'ochi piangete*		strophic (canzonetta)	I:Fn, Cl. VII, 1222 bis, fo. 22^{r-v}
28–29^v	*Pargoletta vezzosa e ridente*		strophic (canzonetta)	I:Fn, Magl. XIX.25, fos. 14^v–16^r; I:Fn, Cl. VII, 1222 bis, fos. 22^v–23^r; US:PHu, MS Ital. 57, fos. 6^v–8^r
30–31^v	*Ecco Lidia mia bella*	[Baldo Cataneo]	strophic (canzonetta)	I:Fn, Magl. XIX.25, fos. 26^v–27^r; I:Fn, Cl. VII, 1222 bis, fo. 23^{r-v}; US:PHu, MS Ital. 57, fos. 21^v–22^r
32^v	*Gia t'è noto crudel c'hormai io mortò*		strophic (canzonetta)	I:Fn, Cl. VII, 1222 bis, fos. 23^v–24^r
33^v	*Io vorrei pur fuggir*		strophic (canzonetta)	I:Fn, Magl. XIX.24, fos. 39^v–40^r; I:Fn, Cl. VII, 1222 bis, fo. 24^r
34–35^v	*Ferma ferma non percottere*		strophic (canzonetta)	I:Bc, CC.225, fos. 46^v–47^r; I:Fn, Cl. VII, 1222 bis, fos. 24^v–25^r
36–37^v	*Hora s'à tanti*		strophic (canzonetta)	
38–39^v	*Rompa lo sdegno le dure catene*		strophic (canzonetta)	I:Bc, CC.225, fos. 51^v–52^r; I:Bc, Q140, fo. 12^r; I:Fn, Cl. VII, 1222 bis, fos. 25^v–26^r
40–41^v	*Amarillide deh vieni*	[Gabriello Chiabrera]	strophic (canzonetta)	B:Bc, MS 704, fos. 209^r–212^r; I:Fn, Cl. VII, 1222 bis, fo. 26^{r-v}; I:Fn, Magl. XIX.25, fos. 17^v–19^r
42–45^v	*O voi ch'intorno al lagrimoso canto*		strophic variations (ottava rima)	

TABLE 9. Cont'd

Folios	Incipit	Composer	Poet	Type	Concordances
48–49[v]	Se non hai di ferro il core			strophic (canzonetta)	I:Fn, Cl. VII, 1222 bis, fo. 27[r–v] US:PHu, MS Ital. 57, fos. 8[v]–9[r]
50–51[v]	Pupilette vezzosette			strophic (canzonetta)	
52–53[v]	Quanto più cruda sete			strophic (canzonetta)	I:Fn, Cl. VII, 1222 bis, fo. 28[r]
54–55[v]	O fiamma del mio cor luce amorosa			strophic variations (ottava rima)	

Table 10   381

TABLE 10. Inventory with Concordances of *Affetti amorosi* (1618)

Pages	Incipit	Composer	Poet	Type	Concordances
2–3	*Leggiadri occhi belli occhi miei cari*			strophic (canzonetta)	GB:Lbm, Add. 36877, fos. 110^v–111^r
4–5	*Più non hò non hò cor io*			strophic (canzonetta)	GB:Lbm, Add. 36877, fos. 122^v–123^r
6–7	*Lauretta mia quando m'accese*			strophic (canzonetta)	
8	*Amor il mio tormento e la mia pena*			strophic (sonetto)	I:Fn, Cl. VII, 1222 bis, fo. 72^r
9	*Quella bella amor*			strophic (canzonetta)	I:Bc, Q140, fo. 25^r I:Fc, Barbera, fo. 64^r I:Fc, Barbera, fo. 138^r I:Fn, Cl. VII, 1222 bis, fo. 82^r
10	*Dolce, e soave io mi credea*			strophic (canzonetta)	I:Fn, Cl. VII, 1222 bis, fo. 72^v
11	*Angioletta tropp'in fretta*			strophic (canzonetta)	I:Fn, Cl. VII, 1222 bis, fo. 42^{r-v}
12	*Passò l'ardore, e vivo in festa e 'n gioco*			strophic (canzonetta)	I:Fn, Cl. VII, 1222 bis, fo. 42^v
13	*Se terrena baltà passa e non dura*			strophic (ottava rima)	I:Fn, Cl. VII, 1222 bis, fo. 73^r
14	*Vaghi amanti che bramate*			strophic (canzonetta)	I:Fn, Cl. VII, 1222 bis, fos. 69^r–70^r
15	*Altro non è il mio cor*			strophic (canzonetta)	I:Bc, Q140, fo. 3^v I:Fn, Cl. VII, 1222 bis, fos. 73^v–74^r GB:Lbm, Add. 36877, fos. 22^r–24^r
16	*Splendete, splendete serene serene*			strophic (canzonetta)	GB:Lbm, Add. 36877, fo. 59^{r-v} I:Bc, Q140, fo. 40^v I:Fn, Cl. VII, 1222 bis, fos. 70^v–71^r
17	*O Clorida già che s'adornano*			strophic (canzonetta)	GB:Lbm, Add. 36877, fo. 31^v
18–19	*O begl'occhi, o belle chiome*			strophic (canzonetta)	I:Fn, Cl. VII, 1222 bis, fos. 64^v–65^r GB:Lbm, Add. 36877, fos. 6^r–7^r
20–1	*Bella Filli crudele*			strophic (canzonetta)	I:Fn, Cl. VII, 1222 bis, fos. 74^v–75^r GB:Lbm, Add. 36877, fos. 16^v–17^r GB:Lbm, Add. 31440, fos. 31^v–32^r
22–3	*Pargoletta vezzosa*			strophic (canzonetta)	
24–5	*La mia Clori amorosa*			strophic (canzonetta)	I:Fn, Cl. VII, 1222 bis, fo. 76^{r-v} I:Bc, Q140, fo. 18^{r-v}

TABLE 10. Cont'd

Pages	Incipit	Composer	Poet	Type	Concordances
26–7	Pargoletta che non sai			strophic (canzonetta)	I:Fn, Cl. VII, 1222 bis, fo. 77^{r-v}
28–9	O dolc'aura o dolci venti			strophic (canzonetta)	I:Fn, Cl. VII, 1222 bis, fos. 87^r–88^r / GB:Lbm, Add. 36877, fos. 91^v–92^r
30–1	Deh Filli vientene	[J. H. Kapsberger]		strophic (canzonetta)	GB:Lbm, Add 36877, fo. 116^{r-v} / I:Fn, Cl. VII, 1222 bis, fos. 89^v–90^r / J. H. Kapsberger, *Secondo libro di villanelle* (1619), 8
32–3	E viver e morire			strophic (canzonetta)	
34–5	Stelle ridente e liete			strophic (canzonetta)	
36–7	Lusinghiero infido amore			strophic (canzonetta)	I:Fn, Cl. VII, 1222 bis, fos. 90^v–91^r
38	O begl'occhi ò chiare stelle			strophic (canzonetta)	I:Fn, Cl. VII, 1222 bis, fo. 91^v
39	Bella mia questo mio core			strophic (canzonetta)	I:Fn, Cl. VII, 1222 bis, fo. 92^r
40	Dov'io credea le mie speranze havere			strophic (canzonetta)	I:Fn, Cl. VII, 1222 bis, fo. 68^r
41–2	Dunque il mio fido amore			strophic (canzonetta)	I:Fn, Cl. VII, 1222 bis, fo. 43^r
42–3	Amar donna superba			strophic (canzonetta)	I:Fn, Cl. VII, 1222 bis, fo. 43^v
44	Amar ingrato amante			strophic (canzonetta)	I:Fn, Cl. VII, 1222 bis, fo. 44^r
46	Mi parto e nel partir ti dico amore			strophic (canzonetta)	I:Fn, Cl. VII, 1222 bis, fo. 44^v
47	Non ardu chiu non ardo com'ardia			strophic (canzonetta)	I:Fn, Cl. VII, 1222 bis, fo. 45^r
48	Si ben mustru di fora tutu y elu			strophic (romance)	I:Fn, Cl. VII, 1222 bis, fo. 45^v
49	Ingrata disleali ed incostanti			strophic (romance)	I:Fn, Cl. VII, 1222 bis, fo. 45^r
50–1	Ay que contento			strophic (romance)	I:Fn, Cl. VII, 1222 bis, fo. 45^v
52–3	Vuestra bellezza señora			strophic (romance)	

Table 11

383

TABLE 11. Inventory with Concordances of *Scherzi amorosi* (2/1620)

Pages	Incipit	Composer	Poet	Type	Concordances
1	*Filli vezzosa*			strophic (canzonetta)	I:Fn, Cl. VII, 1222 bis, fos. 45ᵛ–46ʳ
2	*Tirinto mio tu mi feristi*			strophic (canzonetta)	I:Fn, Cl. VII, 1222 bis, fo. 84ʳ
3	*Se per voi e 'l cor di cenere*			strophic (canzonetta)	
4	*Eurilla, ò core ò vita*			strophic (canzonetta)	I:Fn, Cl. VII, 1222 bis, fos. 47ʳ–48ʳ
5	*Amor che degg'io far*			strophic (canzonetta)	I:Fc, Barbera, fo. 140ʳ; I:Fn, Cl. VII, 1222 bis, fo. 48ʳ⁻ᵛ
6	*Donna ingrata senz'amore*			strophic (canzonetta)	I:Fn, Cl. VII, 1222 bis, fos. 48ᵛ–49ʳ
7	*O mio core novello*			strophic (canzonetta)	
8	*Hor che gli augelli cantando volano*	[Jacopo Peri]		strophic (canzonetta)	Jacopo Peri, *Le varie musiche* (2nd edn., 1619), 2–3; I:Fn, Cl. VII, 1222 bis, fo. 50ʳ⁻ᵛ
9	*Godi pur col novo amante*			strophic (canzonetta)	I:Fn, Cl. VII, 1222 bis, fo. 55ʳ
10	*Amerai tù mio core*			strophic (canzonetta)	I:Fn, Cl. VII, 1222 bis, fos. 28ᵛ–29ʳ
12	*Torna torna ostinato core*			strophic (canzonetta)	I:Fn, Cl. VII, 1222 bis, fo. 30ʳ⁻ᵛ; With words 'Fuggi, fuggi dolente core': *Scherzi amorosi* (1622), 13; GB:Lbm, Add 36877, fos. 111ᵛ–112ʳ; and I:Fn, Cl. VII, 1222 bis, fos. 62ᵛ–63ʳ
14	*Perche taci cor mio*			strophic (canzonetta)	I:Fn, Cl. VII, 1222 bis, fos. 30ᵛ–31ʳ
16	*Amor diletto*			strophic (canzonetta)	I:Fn, Cl. VII, 1222 bis, fos. 31ᵛ–32ʳ
17	*Hor godete d'Amore ò donne amanti*			strophic (canzonetta)	I:Fn, Cl. VII, 1222 bis, fo. 32ʳ⁻ᵛ
18	*Ohime che far degg'io*			strophic (canzonetta)	Alt. text *Ecco che pur al fine*: I:Bc, Q140, fo 11ᵛ; US: PHu, MS Ital. 57, fos. 13ᵛ–14ʳ
20	*Non vuoi ch'io t'ami*			strophic (canzonetta)	I:Fn, Cl. VII, 1222 bis, fos. 33ᵛ–34ʳ
21	*Giovinetta vezzosa*			strophic (canzonetta)	
22	*Per gioia del mio cor*			strophic (canzonetta)	I:Fn, Cl. VII, 1222 bis, fos. 34ᵛ–35ʳ
23	*Gioite, gioite*	[J. H. Kapsberger]		strophic (canzonetta)	Kapsberger, *Libro secondo di villanelle* (1619), 17

Table II. Cont'd

Pages	Incipit	Composer	Poet	Type	Concordances
24	*Alma mia dove ten vai*			strophic (canzonetta)	I:Fn, Cl. VII, 1222 bis, fo. 59^{r-v} I:Fc, Barbera, fo. 7^r GB:Lbm, Add. 36877, fos. 105^v–106^v
25	*Non partais mi*			strophic (canzonetta)	
26	*Tres ninnas me dan enosos*			strophic (canzonetta)	
27	*De mis tormentos y enosos*			strophic (canzonetta)	
28–9	*Quien menoscabas mis benes?*			strophic (canzonetta)	
30	*Suspiri miei che d'avra in hura siti*			strophic (canzonetta)	

Table 12

385

TABLE 12. Inventory with Concordances of *Ghirlandetta amorosa* (1621)

Order in the partbooks	Incipit	Composer	Poet	Type	Concordances
1	*Tutte le vist'homai son fatte accorte*	Fabio Costantini		sectional (canzonetta)	I:Fn, Magl. XIX.24, fos. 33ᵛ–34ʳ
2	*Alla gloria alli honori*	Girolamo Frescobaldi		strophic variations (canzonetta)	
3	*Deh scoprite colorite*	Alessandro Costantini		strophic (canzonetta)	
4	*Ecco nata or or la rosa*	Alessandro Costantini		strophic (canzonetta)	
5	*Mentre che Febo con suoi raggi d'oro*	Pelegrino Mutij		duet (canzonetta)	
6	*O della vita mia, vita, e sostegno*	Fabio Costantini		strophic variation duet (sesta rima)	
7	*Non dormo no, non sognio*	Giovanni Francesco Anerio		sectional (sonetto)	*Il maggio fiorito* (1623), 8–9
8	*Dove io credea le mie speranze vere*	Cecchina di Fiorenza [Francesca Caccini]		strophic (canzonetta)	I:Fn, Cl. VII, 1222 bis, fo. 68ʳ Francesca Caccini, *Il primo libro delle musiche* (1618)
9	*Splendor de gli'occhi miei*	Alessandro Costantini		strophic (canzonetta)	*Giardino musicale* (1621), 7, Alessandro Costantini
10	*Aure vaghe, aure gioconde*	Alessandro Costantini		strophic (canzonetta)	
11	*Deh mirate luce ingrate*	[Giovanni] Domenico Puliasca [Puliaschi]		strophic (canzonetta)	I:Bc, CC.225, fos. 32ᵛ–33ʳ
12	*Vaghe ninfe, e pastori*	Fabio Costantini		strophic (canzonetta)	
13	*Dolce augellin se forse per conforto*	Fabio Costantini		duet (madrigal)	I:Fn, Cl. VII, 1222 bis, fos. 31ᵛ–32ʳ
14	*Gioisce l'aria il ciel*			sectional duet (sonetto)	I:Fn, Cl. VII, 1222 bis, fo. 32ʳ–ᵛ
15	*Si me dolc'il torment'e 'l pianger gioco*	Theofilo Gargari	[Jacopo Sannazzaro, *Arcadia*, II]	duet (madrigal)	

TABLE 12. Cont'd

Order in the partbooks	Incipit	Composer	Poet	Type	Concordances
16	Così vol mia ventura over mio fallo	Theofilo Gargari		duet (madrigal)	
17	O cor sempre dolente	Giovanni Bernardino Nanini		duet (madrigal)	
18	Se la doglia el martire	Alessandro Costantini	[Giambattista Marino]	duet (madrigal)	
19	Donna mentre vi miro	Alessandro Costantini	[Battista Guarini]	duet (madrigal)	
20	Non porta ghiaccio Aprile	Fabio Costantini	[Antonio Pocaterra]	duet (madrigal)	
21	Riede primavera	Fabio Costantini	[Giambattista Marino]	duet (canzonetta)	
22	Ecco ch'all'apparire	Fabio Costantini	[Francesco Maria Turigii]	dialogue	
23	Perche non togli, ò Clori	Paolo Quagliati		dialogue	I:Vc, Torrefranca 250, fos. 41^{v}–45^{r}, Giuseppino [Cenci] I:Baf, MS 1424, fos. 42^{v}–46^{r}, Giuseppino [Cenci]
24	S'ardo il mondo com'io	Fabio Costantini		dialogue	
25	Giacea pensolo Aminta	Alessandro Costantini		madrigal a 3	
26	Ninfe, Ninfe venite	Fabio Costantini	[Francesco Maria Turigii]	madrigal a 3	
27	Lieti amanti	Iacomo Benincasa	[Jacopo Sannazzaro, Arcadia, VI]	canzonetta a 3	
28	Amor tu parti io sent'al tuo partire	Alessandro Costantini		concerted madrigal	
29–30	Voi pur da me partiste	Alessandro Costantini		concerted madrigal a 4	

Table 13 387

TABLE 13. Inventory with Concordances of *Giardino musicale di varii eccellenti autori* (1621)

Pages	Incipit	Composer	Poet	Type	Concordances
3–6	*Liete, verdi, fiorite, e fresche valli*	Ottavio Catalani		cantata (sonetto)	
7	*Splendor degli occhi miei*	Alessandro Costantini		strophic (canzonetta)	*Ghirlandetta amorosa* (1621), 11, Alessandro Costantini
8–10	*O bell'occhi che guerrieri*	Girolamo Frescobaldi		strophic variations (canzonetta)	
11	*Vivrò frà miei tormenti e le mie pene*	Giovanni Boschetto Boschetti		strophic variations (quarta rima)	
12	*Negatemi crudele*	Ottavio Catalani		strophic (canzonetta)	I:Fn, Cl. VII, 1222 bis, fo. 154ʳ
13	*In van lusinghi in van prometti, e giuri*	Stefano Landi		strophic (canzonetta)	
14–15	*Quel rosignol ch'in si soavi accenti*	Raffael Rontani		strophic variations (sonetto)	
16	*Armilla ingrata*	Giovanni Boschetto Boschetti		strophic (canzonetta)	
17	*Ferma ferma hai non percotere*	Francesco Cerasolo		strophic (canzonetta)	
18–19	*Al dolce mormorar*	Abundio Antonelli		duet (canzonetta)	*L'aurata cintia armonica* (1622), 25–7, Abundio Antonelli
20	*Piangete occhi piangete*	Raffaelle Rontani		strophic (canzonetta)	I:Fn, Cl. VII, 1222 bis, fo. 22ʳ⁻ᵛ *Concerti amorosi* (1623), 26–7
21	*Cara dolce amorosetta*	Alessandro Costantini		duet (canzonetta)	
22	*La mia leggiadra Filli*	Francesco Cerasolo		duet (canzonetta)	
23	*Quand'il ciel mi fè soggetto*	Giovanni Boschetto Boschetti		strophic (canzonetta)	*L'aurata cintia armonica* (1623), 31–2, [Giovanni] Boschetto

TABLE 14. Inventory with Concordances of *Raccolta de varii concerti musicali* (1621)

Pages	Incipit	Composer	Poet	Type	Concordances
3–4	*Disse costei e gl'occhi su le gote*	Giovanni Bernardino Nanini		strophic (sonetto)	
5	*Chi mirar desia bellezza*	Raffael Rontani		strophic (canzonetta)	
6	*Voi mi dite ch'io non c'ami*	Ottavio Catalano	[Baldo Cataneo]	strophic (canzonetta)	I:Bc, CC.225, fos. 52^v–53^r, [Ottavio Catalani] *Concerti amorosi* (1623), 17
7	*Cor mio se questa sera*	Ottavio Catalano		strophic (canzonetta)	GB:Lbm, Add. 31440, fos. 12^v–13^r
8–10	*Se perche à voi tolga e più non v'ami*	Giuseppe Cenci		strophic variations (terza rima)	
10	*Ite dolenti miei sospiri*	Pellegrino Mutij		strophic (canzonetta)	
12	*Bella Filli io son ferito*			strophic (canzonetta)	
12–14	*Se così gravi e dolorosi accenti*	Abundio Antonelli		strophic variations (sonetto)	I:Vc, Torrefranca 250, fos. 95^v–96^v
14	*O rosetta che rosetta*	Abundio Antonelli		strophic (canzonetta)	
15	*Leggiadra rosa*	Stefano Landi		strophic (canzonetta)	
16	*Voi voi rubaste il core*	Domenico Mazzocchi		strophic (canzonetta)	
17	*Fuggi fuggi dolente mio core*	Don Hipolito Macchiavelli		strophic (canzonetta)	
18	*Filli da tuoi bei sguardi*	Domenico Mazzocchi		duet (canzonetta)	
19	*Quanto più miro la vaga mia stella*	Raffael Rontani		duet (canzonetta)	US:PHu, MS Ital. 57, fos. 25^v–26^r.
20	*Più non amo più non ardo iniquo amore*	Giuseppe Cenci		duet (canzonetta)	Begins the same as I:Bc, Q140, fo. 41^r

Table 15

389

TABLE 15. Inventory with Concordances of *L'aurata cintia armonica* (1622)

Pages	Incipit	Composer	Poet	Type	Concordances
3–4	*O felici guerrieri, che ricetto*	Fabio Costantini		strophic (ottava rima)	
5–6	*Fiammeggiante del ciel fulgida*	Fabio Costantini		dialogue	
7	*Per pianto la mia carne si distilla*	Teofilo Gargarij	[Jacopo Sannazzaro, *Arcadia*, II]	madrigal	
8	*Hor pensat'al mio mal qual'esser deve*	Teofilo Gargarij	[Jacopo Sannazzaro, *Arcadia*, II]	madrigal	
9–11	*La mia Clori vezzosa*	Pellegrino Mutij		duet (canzonetta)	
12–14	*Ricciutella pargoletta*	[Giovanni Boschetto] Boschetti		strophic (canzonetta)	GB:Lbm, Add. 36877, fos. 98^v–99^v
14–15	*Lascivette Pastorelle*	[Giovanni Boschetto] Boschetti		strophic (canzonetta)	
16–17	*Pastorelle vagh'e belle*	Giovanni Francesco Anerio		strophic (canzonetta)	
18–19	*Care lacrime mie*	Alessandro Costantini		madrigal	
19–24	*Mentre sorge l'aurora*	[Ferdinando] Grappuccioli		strophic (canzonetta)	*Vezzosetti fiori* (1622), 22–4, Ferdinando Grappuccioli
25–7	*Al dolce mormorar*	Abundio Antonelli		strophic (canzonetta)	*Giardino musicale* (1621), 18–19, Abundio Antonelli
28–30	*Pargoletta son'io*	Alessandro Costantini		dialogue	*Vezzosetti fiori* (1622), 15–17, Alessandro Costantini
31–2	*Quand'il ciel mi se soggetto*	[Giovanni] Boschetto		strophic (canzonetta)	*Giardino musicale* (1621), 23, Giovanni Boschetto Boschetti
33	*O bella Clori*	Fabio Costantini		dialogue	
34	*Era l'anima mia*	Girolamo Frescobaldi	[Battista Guarini]	duet (madrigal)	
35–7	*Cruda Amarilli, che col nom'ancora*	Alessandro Costantini	[Battista Guarini]	duet (madrigal)	
38	*Ch'io t'ami, e t'ami più della mia vita*	Alessandro Costantini	[Battista Guarini]	duet (madrigal)	
39	*Col fior de fiori in mano*	Fabio Costantini		duet (madrigal)	
40–3	*La mia leggiadr'e vaga pastorella*	Fabio Costantini	[Claudio Achillini]	canzonetta a 4	

TABLE 16. Inventory with Concordances of *Vezzosetti fiori di varii eccellenti autori* (1622)

Pages	Incipit	Composer	Poet	Type	Concordances
3	*Vedi l'alba ò bella Clori*	Giovanni Antonio Todini		strophic (canzonetta)	
4	*Se perch'io viva in pianti è mi consumi*	Giovanni Antonio Todini		strophic (canzonetta)	
5	*O di raggi e di fiamelle*	Francesco Severi		strophic (canzonetta)	I:Bc, CC.225, fos. 48ᵛ–49ʳ
6	*Non si può soffrir oime*	Giovanni Giacomo Porro		strophic (canzonetta)	
7	*Bel crin d'oro*	Gregorio Veneri		strophic (canzonetta)	
8–9	*Deh mira egli cantò spuntar la rosa*	Enrico Torscianello	[Torquato Tasso]	strophic variations (ottava rima)	
10	*Non voglio amare*	Nicolò Borboni		strophic (canzonetta)	
11	*Io vo cercando un core*	Antonio Granata		strophic (canzonetta)	
12–13	*Dhe se giusta pietà mosse già mai*	Francesco Pesce		strophic variations (ottava rima)	
14	*Vivi contenta chore*	Pietro Paolo Sabbatini		strophic (canzonetta)	
15–17	*Pargoletta son'io*	Alessandro Constantini		dialogue	*L'aurata cintia armonica* (1623), 28–30, Alessandro Costantini
18	*Le vostre chiome amate*	Nicolò Borboni		duet (canzonetta)	
19	*Vaghi rai de cigli ardenti*	Pelegrino Mutii		duet (canzonetta)	*Il maggio fiorito* (1623), 14
20–1	*Mille scherzi, e canti belli*	Pelegrino Mutii		duet (canzonetta)	GB:Lbm, Add. 36877, fo. 95ʳ⁻ᵛ
22–4	*Mentre sorge l'Aurora*	Ferdinando Grappuccioli		duet (canzonetta)	*L'aurata cintia armonica* (1623), 19–24, Grappuccio

Table 17   391

TABLE 17. Inventory with Concordances of *Il maggio fiorito* (1623)

Pages	Incipit	Composer	Poet	Type	Concordances
4	*Guida Pastor il gregge*			madrigal	
5–8	*Lasciatemi morire*	[Claudio Monteverdi]	[Ottavio Rinuccini]	recitative	Claudio Monteverdi, *L'Arianna* (1608) I:Vc, Torrefranca 250, fos. 66ʳ–70ᵛ GB:Lbm, Add. 30491, fos. 39ʳ–42ʳ, [Claudio] Monte Verdi As 'Lamento della Maddalena sopra quel d'Ariadna con nuova aggiunta di C.E.' in I:Bu, Mus MS 646, VI, fos. 1ᵛ–6ʳ I:Fn, B. R. 238, pp. 18–32 I:MOe, Mus. G 239, pp. 1–9, [Claudio] Monteverdi *Lamento d'Arianna* del Signor Claudio Monteverde (1623) Claudio Monteverdi, *Il sesto libro de madrigali* (Venice: Amadino, 1614) As 'Jam moriar mi fili', in Claudio Monteverdi, *Selva morale e spirituale* (1640)
6	*Zeffiretti lusinghieri*			strophic (canzonetta)	GB:Lbm, Add. 36877, fos. 125ᵛ–126ʳ; GB: Lbm, Add. 31440, fos. 32ᵛ–33ʳ; I:MOe, Mus. G239, fos. 54ʳ–55ʳ; Marsolo, *Secondo libro dei madrigali a quattro voci* (1614), Giulio Caccini
7	*Ochi soli d'amore*	[Giulio Caccini]		madrigal	I:MOe, Mus. G 239, fos. 54ʳ–55ʳ GB:Lbm, Add. 31440, fos. 32ᵛ–33ʳ
7	*Vezzosett'hor che l'Aurora si discopr'à te*			strophic (canzonetta)	
7–8	*Amarilli io mi parto*	[Giulio Caccini]		madrigal	*L'allegre notti di Fiorenza* (Venice: Gardano, 1608), 17–18, Giulio Caccini
8–9	*Non dormo nò, non sogno*			recitative	
9–10	*Poich'ò perso 'l mio ben*			madrigal	

TABLE 17. Cont'd

Pages	Incipit	Composer	Poet	Type	Concordances
10	*Feritevi ferite/viperei mordaci*			madrigal	
11	*Unico mio tesoro*			strophic (canzonetta)	
12	*Lungi allegrezza*			madrigal	
13	*Pastorelle vagh'è belle*	[Giovanni Francesco Anerio]		duet (canzonetta)	*L'aurata cintia armonica* (1623), 16–17, Giovanni Francesco Anerio
14	*Mille scherzi, e canti belli*	[Pelegrino Mutii]		One strophe (canzonetta)	*Vezzosetti fiori* (1622), 20–1, Pelegrino Mutii GB:Lbm, Add. 36877, fo. 95[r–v]
15–16	*Spiega la vela nocchiero*			One strophe (canzonetta) dialogue	
16–19	*Ecco Maggio pastori*			one strophe (canzonetta) dialogue	
19	*Donna io vorrei dir molto*				
20–8	*Amorosa Licori*	[Giuseppe Cenci]		dialogue	I:Vc, Torrefranca 250, fos. 29[v]–34[r], Giuseppino I:Ru, MS 279, fos. 37[v]–44[v] I:Baf, MS 1424, fos. 35[v]–42[r], Giuseppino

Table 18

393

TABLE 18. Inventory with Concordances of Giuseppe Giamberti, *Poesie diverse poste in musica* (1623)

Pages	Incipit	Composer	Poet	Type	Concordances
3–4	*Gioisco quando il mio bel sol rimiro*	Giuseppe Giamberti		sectional (ottava rima)	
5–8	*Ne lungo exilio mai donna mi mosse*	Giuseppe Giamberti		strophic variations (sonetto)	
9–12	*Per cercar terra ignota e pelegrina*	Giovanni Bernardino Nanino		strophic variations (sonetto)	
13–15	*O sguardo incauto ladro*	Giuseppe Giamberti		madrigal	
16–18	*Ove lasso ne fuggo*	Giuseppe Giamberti		strophic variations (ottava rima)	
19	*Cinto ho l'alma si forte*	Giuseppe Giamberti		strophic (canzonetta)	
20	*Se pietade in voi non trovasi*	Giuseppe Giamberti		strophic (canzonetta)	
21	*Tu sei pur bella pur tu sei*	Giuseppe Giamberti		strophic (canzonetta)	
22	*O mia felice vita*	Giuseppe Giamberti		strophic (canzonetta)	
23	*Più non t'amo e non t'adoro*	Giuseppe Giamberti		strophic (canzonetta)	
24	*Luci belle luci ingrate*	Giuseppe Giamberti		strophic (canzonetta)	
25	*Bell'e vezzosa Fili amorosa*	Giuseppe Giamberti		strophic (canzonetta)	
26	*Sono intricato*	Giuseppe Giamberti		strophic (canzonetta)	
27–33	*Ecco l'alma staggione*	Giuseppe Giamberti		dialogue	
34–5	*Com'è breve il sereno del giorno*	Giuseppe Giamberti		duet (canzonetta)	
36–7	*In questo duro scoglio*	Giuseppe Giamberti		trio (canzonetta)	
38–9	*Piaga dolce d'amore*	Paolo Agostini		madrigal *a 3*	

TABLE 19. Inventory with Concordances of GB:Lbm, Add. 36877

Folios	Incipit	Composer	Poet	Type	Concordances
2–2^v	Chi mi sente cantar per certo dice	[Simone Radesca]		strophic (canzonetta)	I:Bc, Q27.4, fo. 192, [Simone] Radesca I:MOe, Mus. C 311 (Bottegari), fo. 9^r, Bottegari
2^v–3^v	Un di soletto ridd'il diletto	[Girolamo Montesardo]		strophic (canzonetta)	L'allegre notti di Fiorenza (1608), 4, Girolamo Montesardo I:MOe, Mus. F 1527, fo. 28^r I:Fc, Barbera, fo. 146^r
3^v–4	Mentre pomposa, tu ne stai rosa			strophic (canzonetta)	I:Fn, Cl. VII, 1222 bis, fo. 87^r
4^v–5	Mira quel pesce mira			strophic (canzonetta)	
5–6	Vezzosett'e care pupillette ardenti			strophic (canzonetta)	
6–7	Oh begl'occhi, oh belle chiome			strophic (canzonetta)	I:Fn, Cl. VII, 1222 bis, fos. 64^v–65^r Affetti amorosi (1618), 18–19
7–8^v	Ardi pure felice oh mio core			strophic (canzonetta)	
8^v–9	Oh tu ch'a tutt'hore dimori vicina			strophic (canzonetta)	I:Fn, Magl. XIX.66, fo. 85^v B:Bc, MS 704, fos. 189^v–190^r
9–9^v	Il Gelsomino, che in bel giardino			strophic (canzonetta)	
9^v–10	Hor ch'esce fuor l'Aurora			strophic (canzonetta)	
10^v–11^v	O quando farò ritorno			strophic (canzonetta)	
12–12^v	Alle gioie alle gioie pastore			strophic (canzonetta)	I:Fc, Barbera, fos. 104^r–105^r GB:Lbm, Add. 31440, fos. 20^v–21^r
13–13^v	In questa verde riva			strophic (canzonetta)	
14–14^v	Voi mi date martire, per farmi morire			strophic (canzonetta)	I:Fn, Magl. XIX.25, fos. 12^v–13^r
14^v	Per che ten fuggi oh Fillide			strophic (canzonetta)	I:Fn, Magl. XIX.66, fos. 20^v–22^r B:Bc, MS 704, fos. 89^v–92^r
15	Quando miro il vago volto			dialogue	

Table 19

395

Folio	Incipit	Composer	Form	Sources
16ᵛ–17	Bella Filli crudele		strophic (canzonetta)	I:Fn, Cl. VII, 1222 bis, fos. 74ᵛ–75ʳ / GB:Lbm, Add. 31440, fos. 31ᵛ–32ʳ
17ᵛ–18	Alla caccia, alla caccia, alla caccia pastori	[J. H. Kapsberger]	strophic (canzonetta)	I:Fn, Cl. VII, 1222 bis, fo. 92ᵛ / GB:Lbm, Add. 31440, fos. 69ᵛ–70ʳ / J. H. Kapsberger, Libro primo di villanelle (1610)
18ᵛ	Oh bocca amorosa, oh grate parole	[Girolamo Montesardo]	strophic (canzonetta)	L'allegre notti di Fiorenza (1608), 26, Girolamo Montesardo
19–19ᵛ	Press'a un fonte stan'assito		strophic (canzonetta)	
20–20ᵛ	Vezzosette e bella		strophic (canzonetta)	
21–21ᵛ	Ahi che morir mi sento		strophic (canzonetta)	I:Fn, Cl. VII, 1222 bis, fo. 53ʳ / Concerti amorosi (1623), 14
22–22ᵛ	Più che mai vagh'e bella	[Gemignano Capilupi]	strophic (canzonetta)	I:Fn, Magl. XIX.25, fos. 29ᵛ–30ʳ / Canzonette à tre voci di Horatio Vecchi, et di Gemignano Capi Lupi de Modona (1597)
22–24ᵛ	Altro non è 'l mio cor		strophic (canzonetta)	I:Fn, Cl. VII, 1222 bis, fos. 73ᵛ–74ʳ / I:Bc, Q140, fo. 3ᵛ / Affetti amorosi (1618), 15
24–24ᵛ	Crudel che fai, che più non miro		strophic (canzonetta)	
25	Vaghi augelletti, che nei boschetti		strophic (canzonetta)	
25	Partomi donn'e teco lass'il core		strophic (canzonetta)	
26–26ᵛ	La vit'alberga dov'è bellezza		strophic (canzonetta)	
26ᵛ–27	Crudel signora, tu vuoi ch'io mora		strophic (canzonetta)	GB:Lbm, Add. 31440, fos. 29ᵛ–30ʳ
27	Viva fiamm'amorosa		strophic (canzonetta)	
28–28ᵛ	Amorosette ninfa		strophic (canzonetta)	
28–29ᵛ	Chi veder un sol desia		strophic (canzonetta)	
29ᵛ–30	Ochi strali amorosi		strophic (canzonetta)	
30ᵛ–31	Per i monti, e per le valli		strophic (canzonetta)	
31ᵛ	Oh Clorida gia che s'adornano		strophic (canzonetta)	I:Fn, Cl. VII, 1222 bis, fos. 82ᵛ–83ʳ

TABLE 19. Cont'd

Folios	Incipit	Composer	Poet	Type	Concordances
32–32ᵛ	Hor ch'a noi rimena	[Francesco Rasi]		strophic (canzonetta)	Francesco Rasi, *Vaghezze di musica* (1608)
33	Crudel' tu vuoi, ch'io mora, ecco ch'io moro			strophic (canzonetta)	
33ᵛ–34	Non ha 'l ciel cotanti lumi	[Giulio Caccini]	[Ottavio Rinuccini]	strophic (canzonetta)	B:Bc, MS 704, fos. 79ᵛ–80ʳ; I:Fc, Barbera, fos. 21ᵛ–22ʳ; I:Fn, Magl. XIX.30; Giulio Caccini, *Nuove musiche e nuova maniera di scriverle* (1614)
34–34ᵛ	Ghirland', e fiori di dolci odori			strophic (canzonetta)	
35–35ᵛ	Ninfe vezzose, vagh'amorose			strophic (canzonetta)	
36	Occhi un tempo mia vita	[Giuseppino Cenci]		madrigal	I:Bc, Q27.4, fo. 124ʳ, Giuseppino [Cenci]
36ᵛ	Dolce mio crudel			madrigal	
37	Oh' dolc'anima mia dunqu'e pur vero			madrigal	GB:Lbm, Add. 31440, fos. 39ᵛ–40ʳ
37ᵛ	Deh dolce anima mia	[Giuseppino Cenci]	[Battista Guarini]	madrigal	*Il pastor fido*, III. iii; I:Vc, Torrefranca 250, fos. 87ᵛ–88ᵛ
38	Parlo, miser', ò taccio?		[Battista Guarini]	madrigal	
38ᵛ	Oh bella si ma fera			madrigal	
39–40ᵛ	La mia Clori vezzosa			strophic (canzonetta)	I:Bc, Q140, fo. 18ʳ⁻ᵛ; I:Fn, Cl. VII, 1222 bis, fo. 76ʳ⁻ᵛ
41–41ᵛ	Vorria saper da voi sarij dottori			strophic (canzonetta)	
41ᵛ–42	Se per voi s'ard'e si more	[J. H. Kapsberger]		strophic (canzonetta)	J. H. Kapsberger, *Libro primo di villanelle* (1610)
42–42ᵛ	Stavasi assisa Clori			strophic (canzonetta)	
43–43ᵛ	Oh leggiadr' occhi, bell'occhi miei cari			strophic (canzonetta)	US:PHu, MS Ital. 57, fos. 20ᵛ–21ʳ; I:Fn, Cl. VII, 1222 bis, fos. 40ᵛ–41ʳ; I:Fn, B.R. 238, fos. 4ʳ–5ʳ

Table 19   397

Folios	Incipit	Composer	Poet	Form	Source
44ᵛ–45ᵛ	*Fiorite valli, campastr'amine*	[J. H. Kapsberger]		strophic (canzonetta)	J. H. Kapsberger, *Libro primo di villanelle* (1610)
46–46ᵛ	*Tu segui oh bell'Aminta*			strophic (canzonetta)	
47	*S'hai maior' mal che 'l morir, que'l morire*			strophic (romance)	
47ᵛ–48	*Mas ventura fuora*			strophic (romance)	
48–49	*Dama ni flacca ni gorda*			strophic (romance)	
49ᵛ–50	*Quien quiere entrar co migo e nel bareo*			strophic (romance)	
50–51	*Ay como las esperanzas*			strophic (romance)	
51ᵛ–52	*Vuestros ochos dama*			strophic (romance)	
52ᵛ–53	*Sennora mij fe os en pegno*			strophic (romance)	
53–53ᵛ	*Con esperanzas espero*			strophic (romance)	
54	*Fue a cazza la negna*			strophic (romance)	
54ᵛ–56ᵛ	*Donde ira sin dineros el hombre*			strophic (romance)	
57–57ᵛ	*Menina formosa*			strophic (romance)	
58–59	*Ho lloreis segnora*			strophic (romance)	
59–59ᵛ	*Splendete splendede serene serene*			strophic (canzonetta)	I:Fn, Cl. VII, 1222 bis, fos. 70ᵛ–71ʳ; I:Bc, Q140, fo. 40ᵛ; *Affetti amorosi* (1618), 17
60	*Fanciulletta ritrosetta*			strophic (canzonetta)	I:Fc, Barbera, fos. 128ᵛ–129ʳ
60ᵛ	*Fuggi fuggi dal petto mio*			strophic (canzonetta)	
61–61ᵛ	*Che farò dolce mia vita*			strophic (canzonetta)	
61ᵛ–62	*Per che non mi mirate*			strophic (canzonetta)	
62ᵛ–63ᵛ	*Madre mi vò far frate*			strophic (canzonetta)	
64–65	*Ardi, ardi cor' mio*	[Giulio Caccini]	[Ottavio Rinuccini]	strophic (canzonetta)	B:Bc, MS 704, fos. 77ʳ–78ʳ; I:Fn, Magl. XIX.66, fo. 62ᵛ; Giulio Caccini, *Le nuove musiche* (1602)
65ᵛ–66ᵛ	*Ciaschun' che passa qui*			strophic (canzonetta)	
67–68	*Qui fu che mi ferì*			strophic (canzonetta)	I:Fn, Magl. XIX.24, fos. 23ᵛ–24ʳ

TABLE 19. Cont'd

Folios	Incipit	Composer	Poet	Type	Concordances
68ᵛ–69ᵛ	Clori mia bella			strophic (canzonetta)	
70–71	Oh che bel stare			strophic (canzonetta)	
71ᵛ–72	Alle danze alle danze vezzose			strophic (canzonetta)	
72ᵛ–73ᵛ	Chi vuol fusa, cuchiar' e cuchiarelle			strophic (canzonetta)	
74–74ᵛ	Apr'il suo verde seno			strophic (canzonetta)	
74ᵛ–75	Per che non cred'al mio pianto			strophic (canzonetta)	
75ᵛ–76ᵛ	Alma, che scorgi tu			strophic (canzonetta)	
77–78	Con un' dolente ahime			strophic (canzonetta)	
78ᵛ–79ᵛ	Su l'herbe verd'e tenere			strophic (canzonetta)	
80–80ᵛ	Soccor' Amore, al fier' ardore			strophic (canzonetta)	
80ᵛ–81ᵛ	Oh che dolce languire			strophic (canzonetta)	
81ᵛ–82ᵛ	Bella Fillide star, non possono			strophic (canzonetta)	
83ᵛ	Oh solitario, et à me grato monte			strophic (canzonetta)	
84–84ᵛ	Amorosa pupilletta			strophic (canzonetta)	
85–85ᵛ	Semplicetta farfalletta			strophic (canzonetta)	
86–86ᵛ	Ecco Clori mia bella			strophic (canzonetta)	
87	Anima del cor mio			strophic (canzonetta)	I:Fn, Cl. VII, 1222 bis, fo. 123ᵛ
87ᵛ–88	Scoprit'à me sere			strophic (canzonetta)	
88ᵛ–89	Da che voi mi lassasti io vi lassai			strophic (canzonetta)	
89ᵛ–90	Ecco la primavera			strophic (canzonetta)	I:Bc, Q140, fos. 37ᵛ–38ʳ
90ᵛ–91	Oh piagge oh menti oh fiumi			strophic (canzonetta)	I:Fn, Cl. VII, 1222 bis, fos. 87ᵛ–88ᵛ
91ᵛ–92	Oh dolce Aur', oh dolci venti			strophic (canzonetta)	Affetti amorosi (1618), 28–9
92ᵛ–93ᵛ	Oh ben sparsi sospiri			strophic (canzonetta)	

Table 19

399

Folio	Incipit	Author	Form	Sources
93v–94	Fuggi crudele, fugg'infedele		strophic (canzonetta)	
94v–95	Questa bell' Amor'		strophic (canzonetta)	I:Bc, CC.225, fos. 35v–36r; I:Fc, Barbera, fo. 138r
95–95v	Mille scherzi, e canti belli	[Pellegrino Mutii]	strophic (canzonetta)	Il maggio fiorito (1623), 14 Vezzetti fiori (1622), 20–1, Pellegrino Mutii
96	Chi vive amando, chi vive amando		strophic (canzonetta)	
96v–97	Deh ridete, deh ridet'homai che 'l riso		strophic (canzonetta)	
97–97v	Ecco è pur giunt' oh Clori		strophic (canzonetta)	
98–98v	Questa bella Amor'		strophic (canzonetta)	I:Fc, Barbera, fo. 64r; I:Bc, CC.225, fos. 35v–36r
98v–99	Ricciutella pargoletta	[Giovanni Boschetto Boschetti]	strophic (canzonetta)	L'aurata cintia (1622), 12–14, [Giovanni Boschetto] Boschetti
99v–100	Filli serena, del cor catena		strophic (canzonetta)	
100v–101	Oh quanto tu sei bella		strophic (canzonetta)	
101–101v	Caminad sospiros adonde soleris		strophic (romance)	
102–102v	Abreme essos ochos bella, bella morena		strophic (romance)	
102v–103	Con el aire que corre Orillas del mar		strophic variations (villancico)	
103v–104	Senor Boticario guarde su haja hum hum		strophic (romance)	
104–104v	Eurilla mia quando m'aceso		strophic (canzonetta)	I:Fn, Cl.VII, 1222 bis, fo. 69r; I:Baf, MS 1424, fo. 53v
105–105v	Ecco riede, ecco soggiorna	[Giovanni Francesco Anerio]	strophic (canzonetta)	G. F. Anerio, Selva armonica (1617)
105v–106v	Alma mia dove ten' vai	[Ottavio Rinuccini]	strophic (canzonetta)	I:Fc, Barbera, fo. 7r; I:Fn, Cl. VII, 1222 bis, fo. 59r–v; Affetti amorosi (1618), 24
106v–107	La sul mattin' d'aprile		strophic (canzonetta)	
107v–108	Non vo piu cantar d'amore		strophic (canzonetta)	

TABLE 19. Cont'd

Folios	Incipit	Composer	Poet	Type	Concordances
108ᵛ–108ᵛ	Oh dell'ombrosa notte amati orrori	[Cesare Marotta]		strophic variations, modified (terza rima)	I:Vc, Torrefranca 250, fos. 103ᵛ–105ᵛ, Cesare Marotta I:Bc, CC.225, fos. 1ʳ–5ʳ
109–109ᵛ	Occhi stelle fatali			strophic (canzonetta)	I:Bc, CC.225, fos. 29ᵛ–30ʳ I:Fn, Magl. XIX.66, fo. 25ᵛ GB:Ob, Tenbury MS 1019, fo. 4ʳ
109ᵛ–110	Dormend'hiersera, pareami morire				
110ᵛ–111	Leggiadr'occhi sereni	[Giuseppino Cenci]		strophic (canzonetta)	US:PHu, MS Ital. 57, fos. 22ᵛ–24ʳ I:MOe, Mus. E 318, fos. 12²–13ᵛ I:Bc, CC.225, fos. 24ᵛ–27 I:Baf, MS 1424, fos. 9ᵛ–13ʳ, Giuseppino [Cenci] I:Fn, Cl. VII, 1222 bis, fo. 26ᵛ
111ᵛ–112	Fuggi, fuggi dolente core			strophic (canzonetta)	I:Fn, Cl. VII, 1222 bis, fos. 62ᵛ–63ʳ I:Fn, B.R. 238, fos. 8ᵛ–9ʳ Scherzi amorosi (1622), 13 With words Torna torna ostinato core: I:Fn, Cl. VII, 1222 bis, fo. 30ʳ⁻ᵛ; Scherzi amorosi (2/1620), 12
112ᵛ–113	Fuggi 'l verno dai dolori			strophic (canzonetta)	
113ᵛ	Vorria morire sol per uscire			strophic (canzonetta)	
114–114ᵛ	Occhi belli, occhi sereni			strophic (canzonetta)	
114ᵛ–115	Deh vieni oh Clori a' i dolci amori			strophic (canzonetta)	
115ᵛ–116	Capelli d'oro d'Amor tesoro			strophic (canzonetta)	
116ᵛ–116ᵛ	Deh Filli vientene	[J. H. Kapsberger]		strophic (canzonetta)	I:Fn, Cl. VII, 1222 bis, fos. 89ᵛ–90ʳ Affetti amorosi (1618), 30–1 J. H. Kapsberger, Libro secondo di villanelle (1619), 8
117–117ᵛ	Ecco l'alba, ecco l'aurora			strophic (canzonetta)	
118	Questi spirti gentil di te ragionano	[Pellegrino Mutij]	[Jacopo Cicognini]	strophic variations (terza rima)	Amor pudico (1614), Pellegrino Mutij

Table 19

401

118^v	*Lacrimosa pietà, e le piu consolami*		strophic (canzonetta)	I:Vc, Torrefranca 250, fos. 11^r–12^v
119–119^v	*Oh dolci sguardi*		strophic (canzonetta)	I:Bc, Q140, fos. 1^r–3^r
119^v	*Piangon 'al pianger mio le fere e i sassi*	[Octavio Rinuccini]	strophic variations (ottava rima)	Intermedi, 1616, 47
120–120^v	*Amarilli mio bene*		strophic (canzonetta)	
120^v–121	*Ecco l'alma mia bella*		strophic (canzonetta)	*Concerti amorosi* (1623), 4
121^v–122	*Ombrosa boscora*		strophic (canzonetta)	
122^v–123	*Più non hò piu non ho cor io*		strophic (canzonetta)	I:Fn, Cl. VII, 1222 bis, fo. 41^r–v; *Affetti amorosi* (1618), 4–5
123–123^v	*Voi partite sdegnose*		strophic (canzonetta)	I:Fn, Cl. VII, 1222 bis, fos. 59^v–60^r; I:Fn, Magl. XIX.24, fos. 15^v–16^r; *Concerti amorosi* (1623), 10; I:Bc, CC.225, fos. 31^v–32^r
123^v–124	*Stanca del mio penar fortun' homai*		strophic (canzonetta)	
124^v	*Caldi sospiri ch'uscite dal core*	[Raffaello Rontani]	strophic (canzonetta)	I:Fn, Cl. VII, 1222 bis, fo. 81^v; I:Fn, Magl. XIX.24, fos. 28^v–29^r; Raffaello Rontani, *Le varie musiche … libro primo* (1614)
125–125^v	*Voi mi fuggite, e schernite*		strophic (canzonetta)	
125^v–126^r	*Zeffiretti lusinghieri*		strophic (canzonetta)	*Il maggio fiorito* (1623), 6
127–128	*Occhi belli, occhi sdegnosi*		cantata	
128^v–129	*Sento piu cruda, piu crud' e piu rigida*		strophic (canzonetta)	
129^v	*Se vedessi le piaghe, ch'io porto nel cor*		strophic (canzonetta)	I:Fn, Magl. XIX.24, fos. 35^r–36^r; I:Fn, Cl. VII, 1222 bis, fo. 65^v; I:Fn, Cl. VII, 1222 bis, fo. 148^v
130–130^v	*Sento lo strale che m'ha piagato*	[Francesco Petratti]	strophic (canzonetta)	Petratti, *Il primo libro d'arie* (1620)
131^v	*E sanat'il mio core*		strophic (canzonetta)	
132–132^v	*Piena di bellezze, tu mi fai morire*		strophic (canzonetta)	I:MOe, Mus. G 239, fos. 42^r–43^r, B. C.; I:Fn, Cl. VII, 1222 bis, fo. 58^r–v

TABLE 19. Cont'd

Folios	Incipit	Composer	Poet	Type	Concordances
133–134	Non ha sott'il ciel			strophic (canzonetta)	
134–134^v	Son tanti, e lo sapete			strophic (canzonetta)	
135–135^v	Si dolce è'l tormento ch'in seno mi stà	[Francesco Petratti]		strophic (canzonetta)	Petratti, Il primo libro d'arie (1620)
135^v–136	Ancidetemi pur lumi vezzosi			strophic (canzonetta)	
136^v–137	Quand'io dico, ch'io v'adoro			strophic (canzonetta)	
137^v–138^v	Amar' chi m'odia			strophic (canzonetta)	
139–139^v	Vorrei, vorrei, signora mia bella			strophic (canzonetta)	
140–140^v	Clori apparve si bell'a gl'occhi miei			strophic (canzonetta)	
140^v	Per creder' troppo a parolett'e sguardi			strophic (canzonetta)	
141–142	Partirò vita mia			strophic (canzonetta)	
142–142^v	Io vo cercando colei ch'adoro			strophic (canzonetta)	
142^v–143	Non piu con mesti accenti			strophic (canzonetta)	I:Fn, Cl. VII, 1222 bis, fo. 60^{r-v} Concerti amorosi (1623), 11
143^v	Se Dio, che tutto puo, ne puo, ne vale			[strophic variations?] (sonetto)	
144	Sig.r simile a me le membra havesti			[strophic variations?] (sonetto)	
144^v	Non più romor, cane rabbidi, non più			[strophic variations?] (sonetto)	
145^v–146	Amore tu vuoi ch'io lacrimi			[strophic variations?] (sonetto)	
146	Anna mia, se dell'Anno havete il nome			[strophic variations?] (sonetto)	

Table 20   403

TABLE 20. Inventory with Concordances of I: Fn, CI, VII, 1222 bis

Folios	Incipit	Composer	Poet	Type	Concordances
19	Crudel così rea di mi			madrigal	Concerti amorosi (1623), fo. 16ʳ
19–19ᵛ	Voi mi dite che sò non se ami	[Ottavio Catalani]		strophic (canzonetta)	Raccolta de varii concerti musicali (1620), Ottavio Catalani; Concerti amorosi (1623), fo. 17ʳ
19ᵛ–20	Donzelletta lascivetta, sorgi sorgi dalle piume			strophic (canzonetta)	Concerti amorosi (1623), fos. 18ᵛ–19ʳ
20–20ᵛ	Vezzose pastorelle			strophic (canzonetta)	I:Fc, Barbera, fos. 130ʳ–131ʳ; Concerti amorosi (1623), fos. 20ᵛ–21ʳ
20ᵛ–21	Amarillide mia crudel			strophic (canzonetta)	Concerti amorosi (1623), fo. 22ʳ
21	S'amor è cieco non puo 'l vero scorgere			one strophe (canzonetta)	Concerti amorosi (1623), fo. 23ʳ
21–21ᵛ	Se rivolggi in me serene			strophic (canzonetta)	Concerti amorosi (1623), fo. 21ʳ⁻ᵛ
22–22ᵛ	Piangete occhi piangete	[Raffaello Rontani]		strophic (canzonetta)	Concerti amorosi (1623), fos. 26ᵛ–27ʳ; Giardino musicale (1621), 20, Raffaelle Rontani
22ᵛ–23	Pargoletta vezzosa e ridente			strophic (canzonetta)	I:Fn, Magl. XIX.25, fos. 14ᵛ–16ᵛ; US:PHu, MS Ital. 57, fos. 6ᵛ–8ʳ; Concerti amorosi (1623), fos. 28ᵛ–29ʳ
23–23ᵛ	Ecco Lidia mia bella			strophic (canzonetta)	I:Fn, Magl. XIX.25, fos. 26ᵛ–27ʳ; US:PHu, MS Ital. 57, fos. 21ᵛ–22ʳ; Concerti amorosi (1623), fos. 30ᵛ–31ʳ
23ᵛ–24	Già c'è noto crudel ch'omai son morto			strophic (canzonetta)	Concerti amorosi (1623), fo. 32ʳ
24	Io vorrei pur fuggir			strophic (canzonetta)	I:Fn, Magl. XIX.24, fos. 39ᵛ–40ʳ; Concerti amorosi (1623), fo. 33ʳ
24ᵛ–25	Ferma ferma non percotere			strophic (canzonetta)	I:Bc, CC.225, fos. 46ᵛ–47ʳ; Concerti amorosi (1623), fos. 34ᵛ–35ʳ
25–25ᵛ	Hora s'amanti			strophic (canzonetta)	

Table 20. Cont'd

Folios	Incipit	Composer	Poet	Type	Concordances
25v–26	Rompa la sdegnio le dure catene			strophic (canzonetta)	I:Bc, CC.225, fos. 51v–52r; I:Bc, Q140, fo. 12r; Concerti amorosi (1623), fos. 38v–39r
26–26v	Amarillide deh vieni		[Gabriello Chiabrera]	strophic (canzonetta)	B:Bc, MS 704, fos. 209r–212r; I:Fn, Magl. XIX.25, fos. 17v–19r; Concerti amorosi (1623), fos. 40r–41r
26v	Leggiadri ochi serene	[Giuseppino Cenci]		strophic (canzonetta)	GB:Lbm, Add. 36877, fos. 110v–111r; I:Baf, MS 1424, fos. 9r–13r, Giuseppino [Cenci]; I:Bc, CC.225, fos. 24r–27r; I:MOe, Mus. E 318, fos. 12r–13v; US:PHu, MS Ital. 57, fos. 22v–24r; Concerti amorosi (1623), fos. 46r–47r
27–27v	Se non hai di ferro il core			strophic (canzonetta)	US:PHu, MS Ital. 57, fos. 8v–9r; Concerti amorosi (1623), fos. 48v–49r
27v	Pupillette vezzosette			strophic (canzonetta)	GB:Lbm, Add. 36877, fos. 5r–6r; Concerti amorosi (1623), fos. 56r–57r
28	Quanto più cruda sete			strophic (canzonetta)	Concerti amorosi (1623), fos. 52r–53r
28v	O voi ch'intorno al lacremoso canto			strophic variations (canzonetta)	US:PHu, MS Ital. 57, fos. 18v–20r; Concerti amorosi (1623), fos. 42r–45r
28v–29	Amerai tu mio core			strophic (canzonetta)	Scherzi amorosi (2/1620), 10
29v–30	Ecco sorgon gl'albori			strophic (canzonetta)	
30–30v	Torna torna ostinato core			strophic (canzonetta)	Scherzi amorosi (2/1620), 12; With words 'Fuggi, fuggi dolente core': GB:Lbm, Add. 36877, fos. 111v–112r; I:Fn, Cl. VII, 1222 bis, fos. 62v–63r
30v–31	Perche taci cor mio			strophic (canzonetta)	Scherzi amorosi (2/1620), 14
31–31v	Io son la Primavera			strophic (canzonetta)	

Table 20 405

Folio	Incipit	Form	Source
31ᵛ–32	*Amor diletto*	strophic (canzonetta)	*Scherzi amorosi* (2/1620), 16
32–32ᵛ	*Hor godete d'amor ò donna amata*	strophic (canzonetta)	*Scherzi amorosi* (2/1620), 17
33ᵛ–34	*Non vuoi ch'io t'ami*	strophic (canzonetta)	*Scherzi amorosi* (2/1620), 20
34–34ᵛ	*Giovinetta vezzosetta*	strophic (canzonetta)	I:Bc, Q140, fo. 29ʳ
34ᵛ–35	*Per gioia del mio cor*	strophic (canzonetta)	*Scherzi amorosi* (2/1620), 22
35–35ᵛ	*Gioite gioite*	strophic (canzonetta)	*Scherzi amorosi* (2/1620), 23
35ᵛ–36	*Sospiri miei che d'ona in hora chiti*	strophic (canzonetta)	*Concerti amorosi* (1623), fo. 2ʳ; I:Fn, Magl. XIX.24, fos. 25ᵛ–26ʳ
36ᵛ	*Non è mercede di pura fede*	strophic (canzonetta)	*Concerti amorosi* (1623), fo. 8ʳ
36ᵛ–37	*Tu non hai provato amore*	strophic (canzonetta)	
37–37ᵛ	*Donne poi che il mio corno*	strophic (canzonetta)	
38	*Bella si mia troppo altera*	strophic (canzonetta)	
38ᵛ–39	*Son tanti e lo sapete*	strophic (canzonetta)	
39–39ᵛ	*Mai mai è*	strophic (canzonetta)	
39ᵛ–40	*Una vecchia sdentata e bavosa*	strophic (canzonetta)	
40–40ᵛ	*A te sola conviene*	strophic (canzonetta)	
40ᵛ–41	*O leggiadri occhi belli occhi miei cari*	strophic (canzonetta)	I:Fn, B.R. 238, fos. 4ᵛ–5ʳ; US:PHu, MS Ital. 57, fos. 20ᵛ–21ʳ; GB:Lbm, Add. 36877, fo. 43ʳ⁻ᵛ
41–41ᵛ	*Più non ho no ho cor io*	strophic (canzonetta)	GB:Lbm, Add. 36877, fos. 122ᵛ–123ʳ
42–42ᵛ	*Angioletta troppo infretta*	strophic (canzonetta)	*Affetti amorosi* (1618), 11
42ᵛ	*Lasso l'ardore a vivo in fest'e in gioco*	strophic (canzonetta)	*Affetti amorosi* (1618), 12
43	*Dunque il mio fido amore*	strophic (canzonetta)	*Affetti amorosi* (1618), 41–2
43ᵛ	*Amar donna superba*	strophic (canzonetta)	*Affetti amorosi* (1618), 42–3
44	*Amar ingrato amante*	strophic (canzonetta)	*Affetti amorosi* (1618), 44
44ᵛ	*Che parto e nel partir ti dico amore*	strophic (canzonetta)	*Affetti amorosi* (1618), 46
45	*Si ben mostro di fora tuttu retu*	strophic (canzonetta)	*Affetti amorosi* (1618), 48
45	*Non ardu chiu non andu com'ardere*	strophic (canzonetta)	*Affetti amorosi* (1618), 47

TABLE 20. Cont'd

Folios	Incipit	Composer	Poet	Type	Concordances
45^v	Ingrata desleale ed incostante			strophic (canzonetta)	Affetti amorosi (1618), 49
45^v–46	Filli vezzosa			strophic (canzonetta)	Scherzi amorosi (2/1620), 1
46^v	Sol per voi ho 'l cor di cenere			strophic (canzonetta)	
47–48	Eurilla, ò core, ò vita			strophic (canzonetta)	Scherzi amorosi (2/1620), 4
48–48^v	Amor che degg'io far			strophic (canzonetta)	I:Fc, Barbera, fo. 146^v / Scherzi amorosi (2/1620), 5
48^v–49	Donna ingrata son l'amore			strophic (canzonetta)	Scherzi amorosi (2/1620), 6
49–50	O mio core che non vezzo			strophic (canzonetta)	Scherzi amorosi (2/1620), 7
50–50^v	Hor che gli augelli cantando volano	[Jacopo Peri]		strophic (canzonetta)	Scherzi amorosi (2/1620), 8 / Peri, Le varie musiche (2nd edn, 1619)
50^v–51	S'Alcun vi giura cortes'amanti			strophic (canzonetta)	I:Bc, CC.225, fos. 45^v–46^r / Concerti amorosi (1623), fos. 3^r
51^v	Ecco l'alma la mirabella			strophic (canzonetta)	
51^v–52	Misero amante io vivo			strophic (canzonetta)	Concerti amorosi (1623), fos. 6^r–7^r
52^v	Se tu nieghi ò ria belva à miei preghi la pietà			strophic (canzonetta)	Concerti amorosi (1623), fo. 13^r
53	Ahi che morir mi sento e tu chete			strophic (canzonetta)	GB:Lbm, Add. 36877, fo. 21^{r-v} / Concerti amorosi (1623), fo. 14^v
53^v–54^v	Crudele ove ne vai			strophic (canzonetta)	Concerti amorosi (1623), fo. 15^r
55	Godi pur col nuovo amante			strophic (canzonetta)	Scherzi amorosi (2/1620), 9
55^v–56	Io per voi piango e sospiro			strophic (canzonetta)	
56^v–57	Com'in ciel balen			strophic (canzonetta)	
57–57^v	Che mi val che tu m'amai			strophic (canzonetta)	
57^v–58	Per dolc sguardi e parolett'accorte			strophic (canzonetta)	
58–58^v	Piena di beltade tu mi fai languire			strophic (canzonetta)	GB:Lbm, Add. 36877, fo. 132^v / I:MOe, Mus. G 239, fos. 42^v–43^r, B. C.

Table 20

407

58ᵛ–59	*Bella Clori non fuggire*		strophic (canzonetta)	I:Bc, CC.225, fos. 44ᵛ–45ʳ; *Concerti amorosi* (1623), fo. 9ʳ
59–59ᵛ	*Alma mia dove ten stai*	[Ottavio Rinuccini]	strophic (canzonetta)	I:Fc, Barbera, fo. 7ʳ; GB:Lbm, Add. 36877, fos. 105ᵛ–106ᵛ; *Scherzi amorosi* (2/1620), 24
59ᵛ–60	*Voi partite sdegnose*	[Raffaello Rontani]	strophic (canzonetta)	I:Fn, Magl. XIX.24, fos. 15ᵛ–16ʳ; GB:Lbm, Add. 36877, fo. 123ʳ⁻ᵛ; *Concerti amorosi* (1623), fo. 10ʳ; I:Bc, CC.225, fos. 31ᵛ–32ʳ, [Raffaelle Rontani]
60–60ᵛ	*Non più con mesti'accenti*		strophic (canzonetta)	*Concerti amorosi* (1623), fo. 11ʳ; GB:Lbm, Add. 36877, fos. 142ᵛ–143ʳ
60ᵛ–61	*Hai pur mentito dhi mentitrice*		strophic (canzonetta)	
61–61ᵛ	*Piu vere per morire*		strophic (canzonetta)	
62	*Occhi belli chetta d'aprire*		strophic (canzonetta)	
62ᵛ–62ᵛ	*Io parto del tuo viso o mia tesona*		strophic (canzonetta)	
62ᵛ–63	*Fuggi fuggi dolente core*		strophic (canzonetta)	I:Fn, B.R. 238, fos. 8ᵛ–9ʳ; GB:Lbm, Add. 36877, fos. 111ᵛ–112ʳ; *Scherzi amorosi* (2/1620), 13; With words 'Torna, torna ostinato core': I:Fn, Cl. VII, 1222 bis, fo. 30ʳ⁻ᵛ; *Scherzi amorosi* (2/1620), 12
63–63ᵛ	*Che mi val che tu m'ami*		strophic (canzonetta)	
63ᵛ	*Perche mi fuggite crudele*		strophic (canzonetta)	*Concerti amorosi* (1623), fo. 5ʳ
64–64ᵛ	*La bella Dorinda con l'oche in lampagna sen va*		strophic (canzonetta)	
64ᵛ–65	*Belli occhi o belle chiome*		strophic (canzonetta)	GB:Lbm, Add. 36877, fos. 6ʳ–7ʳ; *Affetti amorosi* (1618), 18–19
65ᵛ	*Se vedeste le piaghe ch'io porto nel cor*		strophic (canzonetta)	I:Fn, Magl. XIX.24, fos. 35ᵛ–36ʳ; GB:Lbm, Add. 36877, fo. 129ᵛ
66	*Poiche la cruda e fera*		strophic (canzonetta)	*Concerti amorosi* (1623), fo. 12ʳ
66ᵛ–67	*Fra queste selve*		strophic (canzonetta)	

Table 20. Cont'd

Folios	Incipit	Composer	Poet	Type	Concordances
67–67^v	Stelle ardenti e liete			strophic (canzonetta)	
68	Dove io credea le mie speranze havere	[Francesca Caccini]		strophic (canzonetta)	Affetti amorosi (1618), 40
68^v	Folgorate Saettate			strophic (canzonetta)	
69	Eurilla mia quando m'avese			strophic (canzonetta)	I:Baf, MS 1424. fo. 53^v; GB:Lbm, Add. 36877. fo. 104^{r-v}
69^v–70	Vaghi amanti che bramate			strophic (canzonetta)	Affetti amorosi (1618), 14
70^v–71	Splendete splendete			strophic (canzonetta)	GB:Lbm, Add. 36877. fo. 59^{r-v}; I:Bc, Q140, fo. 40^v; Affetti amorosi (1618), 16
71^v	Crudel tu vuoi partire			strophic (canzonetta)	I:Fc, Barbera, fo. 4^r
72	Amor il mio tormento e la mia fede			strophic (canzonetta)	Affetti amorosi (1618), 8
72^v	Dolce e soave io mi credea morire d'amore			strophic (canzonetta)	Affetti amorosi (1618), 10
73	Se terrena beltà passa si non duca			strophic (ottava rima)	Affetti amorosi (1618), 13
73^v–74	Altro non è il mio cor			strophic (canzonetta)	GB:Lbm, Add. 36877. fos. 22^r–24; I:Bc, Q140, fo. 3^v; Affetti amorosi (1618), 15
74^v–75	Bella Filli crudele se bramate che mora			strophic (canzonetta)	GB:Lbm, Add. 31440. fos. 31^v–32^r; GB:Lbm, Add. 36877. fos. 16^v–17^r; Affetti amorosi (1618), 20–1
75^v–76	Pargoletta vezzosa pargoletta amorosa			strophic (canzonetta)	I:Fn, Magl. XIX.25, fos. 14^v–16^r; US:PHu, MS Ital. 57, fos. 6^v–8^r; Concerti amorosi (1623), fos. 28^r–29^r
76–76^v	La mia Clori amorosa			strophic (canzonetta)	I:Bc, Q140, fo. 18^v; Affetti amorosi (1618), 24–5
77–77^v	Pargoletta che non sai			strophic (canzonetta)	Affetti amorosi (1618), 26–7

Table 20

409

78–80^v	O grata cucina		strophic (canzonetta)	GB:Lbm, Add. 36877, fo. 124^v
80^v–81	O stelle omicide		strophic (canzonetta)	I:Bc, Q140, fo. 25^r
81^v	Caldi sospiri ch'uscite dal core		strophic (canzonetta)	I:Fc, Barbera, fo. 64^r
82	Quella bella amor		strophic (canzonetta)	I:Fc, Barbera, fo. 138^r *Affetti amorosi* (1618), 9
82^v–83	O Clorida gia che l'adornano		strophic (canzonetta)	GB:Lbm, Add. 36877, fo. 31^r
83–83^v	O crude veglie		strophic (canzonetta)	
84	Tirinto mio tu mi feresti		strophic (canzonetta)	*Scherzi amorosi* (2/1622), 2
84^v–85	Con un dolente ohime		strophic (canzonetta)	
85^v–86^v	Accorta lusinghiera lieta		strophic (canzonetta)	
87	Mentre pomposa te ne stai rosa		strophic (canzonetta)	GB:Lbm, Add. 36877, fos. 3^v–4^r
87^v–88	O dolci aure o dolci venti		strophic (canzonetta)	GB:Lbm, Add. 36877, fos. 91^r–92^r *Affetti amorosi* (1618), 28–9
88^v–89	Vzzosetta pastorella		strophic (canzonetta)	
89^v–90	Dhe Filli vientene	[J. H. Kapsberger]	strophic (canzonetta)	GB:Lbm, Add. 36877, fo. 116^v *Affetti amorosi* (1618), 30–1 J. H. Kapsberger, *Secondo libro di villanelle* (1619), 8
90^v–91	Lusinghiero infido amore		strophic (canzonetta)	*Affetti amorosi* (1618), 36–7
91^v	O begl'occhi o chiare stelle		strophic (canzonetta)	*Affetti amorosi* (1618), 38
92	Bella mia questo mio core		strophic (canzonetta)	*Affetti amorosi* (1618), 39
92^v	Alla caccia alla caccia pastori	[J. H. Kapsberger]	strophic (canzonetta)	GB:Lbm, Add. 36877, fos. 17^v–18^r GB:Lbm, Add. 31440, fos. 69^r–70^r J. H. Kapsberger, *Libro primo di villanelle* (1610)
93–93^v	Io mi parto mi parto mia vita		strophic (canzonetta)	
94	Quanti duoli e quanti affanni		strophic (canzonetta)	
94^v	Crudel tu vuoi ch'io moia		strophic (canzonetta)	
95	La mia Filli crudel spesso mi fuggi		strophic (canzonetta)	GB:Lbm, Add. 36877, fos. 26^r–27^r
95^v	Venita dallo splendor della luce		strophic (canzonetta)	US:PHu, MS Ital. 57, fos. 27^v–28^v

TABLE 20. Cont'd

Folios	Incipit	Composer	Poet	Type	Concordances
96	*Se m'ami io t'amo e sempre io t'amarò*			strophic (canzonetta)	
96v	*Non si veda del mio fiato*			strophic (canzonetta)	
97	*Figlio dormi dormi figlio*			strophic (canzonetta)	
97v–98	*T'amerò vita mia*			strophic (canzonetta)	
98v	*Quel core quel core crudel*			strophic (canzonetta)	
99	*Quest'ingrata ch'ogn'hora mi fugge*			strophic (canzonetta)	
99v	*Amore poiche non giovano*			strophic (canzonetta)	I:Fn, Magl. XIX.24, fos. 32^v–33^r
100	*Lacrimate mi tutti*			strophic (canzonetta)	
100v	*Rimanti in pace ormai dolce mia vita*			strophic (canzonetta)	
101–101v	*Aure placide e volanti*			strophic (canzonetta)	I:Bc, CC.225, fos. 40^v–41^r GB:Lbm, Add. 3440, fos. 6^v–7^r
102–103v	*Son prontissimo sempre à voler far*			dialogue	
104–104v	*O ritrosetta crudele*			strophic (canzonetta)	
105	*Donna superba che farai tu*			strophic (canzonetta)	
105v	*Voi partite, ò mio sole*		[Francesco Balducci]	strophic (canzonetta)	
106–106v	*Perfidissima ingrata, ò nemica amore*			strophic (canzonetta)	
106v	*Manda amor entusfadiga*			strophic (canzonetta)	
107–108	*D'una donna empia, e crudele*			strophic (canzonetta)	
108–108v	*Non più parole*			strophic (canzonetta)	
108v	*Un sospiretto sol un amoroso sguardo*			strophic (canzonetta)	

Table 20   411

			GB:Lbm, Add. 36877, fo. 87ʳ
109	Sempre dunque credetti	strophic (canzonetta)	
109ᵛ–110	Mi sento piagato	strophic (canzonetta)	
110	Io piango e cerco un V. ch'in dolce foco	[strophic variations?] (sonetto)	
110ᵛ–111	Lingua perfida, e crudele	strophic (canzonetta)	
111ᵛ	Ladra benche m'alletti	strophic (canzonetta)	
112	Ho il cor ferito, e morirò	strophic (canzonetta)	
112ᵛ	Promettesti crudele di dare aita	strophic (canzonetta)	
113	La mia ninfa vezzosetta	strophic (canzonetta)	
113ᵛ	Amor tu mi tormenti	strophic (canzonetta)	
114	Così va così va	strophic (canzonetta)	
114ᵛ	Cate sta pur di fora	strophic (canzonetta)	
115–115ᵛ	Se d'etate ò bella donna	strophic (canzonetta)	
116	La vaga mia Clori ch'odiavami ognhor	strophic (canzonetta)	
116ᵛ	La mia Filli la cruda Filli	strophic (canzonetta)	
116ᵛ–117	Ochi che sette	strophic (canzonetta)	
118–118ᵛ	Tu sei donna il danno	strophic (canzonetta)	
119	Perche dunque o mio bene	strophic (canzonetta)	
119ᵛ–121	Han bel tempo le puttane	strophic (canzonetta)	
121	Dori bramandomi e fuggemi bacciami	strophic (canzonetta)	
121ᵛ	Stò perta mio bene	strophic (canzonetta)	
122	Con la mia donna amor se congiurato	strophic (canzonetta)	
122ᵛ	Ove ten fuggi infretta	strophic (canzonetta)	
123	Ochi ch'io tanto adoro	strophic (canzonetta)	
123ᵛ	Anima del cor mio	strophic (canzonetta)	
124	Se mi pensate son le nostre vie	strophic (canzonetta)	

Table 20. Cont'd

Folios	Incipit	Composer	Poet	Type	Concordances
124ᵛ	Non tante serenate			strophic (canzonetta)	
125	Se pensi ch'io t'ami,			strophic (canzonetta)	
125ᵛ	Amorosa pargoletta			strophic (canzonetta)	
126	Dhe voltate tal volta le luci serene			strophic (canzonetta)	
126ᵛ	Non me ne curo a fè			strophic (canzonetta)	
127	T'amerò più che mai			strophic (canzonetta)	
127ᵛ	Tu m'allandoni cruda			strophic (canzonetta)	
128	Passar'il mondo Tina			strophic (canzonetta)	
129	Gia pretosa al mio duol			strophic (canzonetta)	
130ᵛ–134	Sospirate o fidi amori			strophic (canzonetta)	
134ᵛ–135	Venite al mormorio			strophic (canzonetta)	
135ᵛ–137ᵛ	Zerbiai gioioe			strophic (canzonetta)	
138–139ᵛ	Dal ponte, e dai marmi			strophic (canzonetta)	
140–141ᵛ	Donne vaghe e gentili			strophic (canzonetta)	
142–143	Quand'io penso talhora			strophic (canzonetta)	
143ᵛ–144ᵛ	Fanno l'zerbino			strophic (canzonetta)	
144–146ᵛ	Ve venuto un riso			strophic (canzonetta)	
147	Ho questo renuntiato			strophic (canzonetta)	
147ᵛ	Non ti creder giammai d'essermi grata			strophic (canzonetta)	
148	Se pietad'in voi non trovasi			strophic (canzonetta)	I:Bc, CC.225, fos. 43ᵛ–44ʳ
148ᵛ	Se vedesti lega piaghe ch'io porto nel cor			strophic (canzonetta)	GB:Lbm, Add. 36877, fo. 129ᵛ I:Fn, Magl. XIX.24, fos. 35ᵛ–36ʳ
149–150	Cruda voglia empia cor pietata sorte			strophic (canzonetta)	

Table 20

413

150v–151v	Sospiroso notte e giorno		strophic (canzonetta)	
152–152v	Non ci voglio più pentare		strophic (canzonetta)	
153–153v	D'una guancia alm'e ridente	[Ottavio Rinuccini]	strophic (canzonetta)	I:Bc, CC.225, fos. 33v–34r
154	Negatemi crudel		strophic (canzonetta)	Giardino musicale (1621), 12, Ottavio Catalani
154v	Vorrei sapere quali son chiuguai[?]	[Ottavio Catalani]	[strophic variations?] (ottava rima)	
154v	Misero, et infelice à cui si crede		[strophic variations?] (ottava rima)	
155	Li misteri d'amore ogn'un non sa		strophic (canzonetta)	
155v	Amor lasciami stare		strophic (canzonetta)	
156–156v	Caccia su, e ghigna		strophic (canzonetta)	
157	Parla parla mio core		strophic (canzonetta)	

BIBLIOGRAPHY

ABERT, ANNA AMALIE, 'Tasso, Guarini e l'opera', *Nuova rivista musicale italiana*, 4 (1970), 827–40.

ABROMSON, MORTON COLP, *Painting in Rome during the Papacy of Clement VIII (1592–1605): A Documented Study* (New York, 1981).

ACUTIS, CESARE, *Cancioneros musicali spagnoli in Italia (1585–1635)* (Pisa, 1971).

ADEMOLLO, ALESSANDRO, *La bell'Adriana ed altre virtuose del suo tempo alla corte di Mantova* (Città di Castello, 1888).

AGO, RENATA, *Carriere e clientele nella Roma barocca* (Rome, 1990).

ALALEONE, DOMENICO, *Storia dell'oratorio musicale in Italia* (Milan, 1945).

ALDRICH, PUTNAM, *Rhythm in Seventeenth-Century Italian Monody* (London, 1966).

ALEGAMBE, PHILIPPE, *Bibliotheca scriptorum Societatis Iesu* (Antwerp: Meursius, 1643).

AMAT, JOAN CARLOS, *Guitarra española de cinco órdenes la qual enseña de templar y tañer rasgado* (2nd edn., Lérida: Lorenço, 1627).

AMBROS, AUGUST WILHELM, *Geschichte der Musik*, iv, 3rd edn., ed. Hugo Leichtentritt (Leipzig, 1909).

ANNIBALDI, CLAUDIO, 'Il mecenate "politico": Ancora sul patronato musicale del Cardinale Pietro Aldobrandini (*ca.* 1570–1621)', *Studi musicali*, 16 (1987), 33–93; 17 (1988), 101–78.

ANTOLINI, BIANCA MARIA, 'Cantanti e letterati a Roma nella prima metà del Seicento: Alcune osservazioni', in Della Seta and Piperno (eds.), *In cantu et in sermone*, 347–62.

ANTONELLI, GIUSEPPE, *Indice dei manoscritti della Civica Biblioteca di Ferrara, Parte prima* (Ferrara, 1884).

APFEL, ERNST, 'Rhythmisch-metrische und andere Beobachtungen an Ostinatobässen', *Archiv für Musikwissenschaft*, 33 (1976), 48–53.

AVELLINI, LUISA, 'Tra Umoristi e Gelati: L'accademia romana e la cultura emiliana del primo e del pieno Seicento', *Studi seicenteschi*, 23 (1982), 109–37.

BAGLIONE, GIOVANNI, *Le vite de' pittori, scultori ed architetti dal Pontificato di Gregorio XIII. sino à tutto quello d'Urbano Ottavo* (2nd edn., Rome: Manelsi, 1649).

BANCHIERI, ADRIANO, *Cartella musicale nel canto figurato fermo et contrapunto* (3rd edn., Venice: Vincenti, 1614).

BANK, J. A., *Tactus, Tempo and Notation in Mensural Music from the 13th to the 17th Century* (Amsterdam, 1972).

BARASSI, ELENA FERRARI, 'La villanella napoletana nell testimonianza di un letterato', *Nuova rivista musicale italiana*, 2 (1968), 164–87.

BARBIERI, PATRIZIO, 'Ancora sugli organi di S. Lorenzo in Damaso, Roma—Con un elenco di organisti e maestri di cappella dal sec. XV al XIX', *Amici dell'organo*, 2 (1985), 91–9.

BARON, JOHN H., 'Monody: A Study in Terminology', *Musical Quarterly*, 54 (1968), 462–74.

BARON, JOHN H., 'Secular Spanish Solo Song in Non-Spanish Sources, 1559–1640', *Journal of the American Musicological Society*, 30 (1977), 20–42.

BECHERINI, BIANCA, 'La musica nelle "sacre rappresentazioni" fiorentine', *Rivista musicale italiana*, 53 (1951), 193–241.

—— 'Un canta in panca fiorentino: Antonio di Guido', *Rivista musicale italiana*, 50 (1948), 241–7.

BENTIVOGLIO, GUIDO, *Memorie e lettere*, ed. Costantino Panigada (Scrittori d'Italia, 150; Bari, 1934).

BERMUDO, JUAN, *Comiença el libro llamado declaracion de instrumentos musicales* (Ossuna: Juan de Leon, 1555).

BERNER, SAMUEL, 'The Florentine Patriciate in the Transition from Republic to *Principato*, 1530–1609', *Studies in Medieval and Renaissance History*, 9 (1972), 203–46.

—— 'Florentine Political Thought in the Late Cinquecento', *Il pensiero politico*, 3 (1970), 177–99.

—— 'Florentine Society in the Late Sixteenth and Early Seventeenth Centuries', *Studies in the Renaissance*, 18 (1971), 203–46.

BERSELLI, ALDO (ed.), *Storia della Emilia Romagna* (Bologna, 1977).

BERTINI, GIOVANNI MARIA, ACUTIS, C., and AVILA, P. L., *La romanza spagnola in Italia* (Turin, 1970).

BESWICH, DELBERT MEACHAM, 'The Problem of Tonality in Seventeenth-Century Music' (Ph.D. diss., University of North Carolina, 1950).

BIANCONI, LORENZO, *Music in the Seventeenth Century*, trans. David Bryant (Cambridge, 1987).

BLUNT, ANTHONY, *Guide to Baroque Rome* (New York, 1982).

BONGI, SALVATORE, *Discorso sulla musica dei suoi tempi di Vincenzo Giustiniani Marchese di Bassano* (Lucca, 1878).

—— *Inventario del R. Archivio di Stato in Lucca* (Lucca, 1888).

BONORA, ALFREDO, and GIANI, EMILIO, *Catalogo delle opere musicali . . . città di Bologna: R. Accademia Filarmonica—Collezione privata Ambrosini—Archivio e Museo di S. Petronio* (Parma, 1914–39).

BORSI, STEFANO, *Roma di Sisto V: La Pianta di Antonio Tempesta, 1593* (Rome, 1986).

BORSOOK, EVE, 'Art and Politics at the Medici Court', *Mitteilungen des Kunsthistorischen Institutes in Florenz*, 12, 13, and 14 (1965, 1967, 1969).

BOTTARI, M. GIOVANNI, *Raccolta di lettere sulla pittura, scultura ed architettura scritte da' più celebri personaggi dei secoli XV, XVI e XVII*, vi (Milan, 1822).

BOVICELLI, GIOVANNI BATTISTA, *Regole passaggi di musica, madrigali e motetti passeggiati* (Venice, 1594; facs. edn., Kassel, 1957).

BOYER, FERDINAND, 'Les Orsini et les musiciens d'Italie au début du XVIIᵉ siècle', in *Mélanges de philologie, d'histoire et de littérature offerts à Henri Hauvette* (Paris, 1934), 301–10.

BRAINARD, PAUL, 'Proportional Notation in the Music of Schütz and His Contemporaries', *Current Musicology*, 50 (1992), 21–47.

BRICCIO, GIOVANNI, *Il pianto, et la mestitia dell'alma città di Roma, per la morte dell'Illustriss.*

et Reverendiss. Sig. Alessandro Peretti Cardinal Montalto, Vescovo Albanense, Vicecancellario, Summator Papae, & Protettore di Polonia (Rome: Grignani, 1623).

BROWN, HOWARD MAYER, 'Emulation, Competition, and Homage: Imitation and Theories of Imitation in the Renaissance', *Journal of the American Musicological Society*, 35 (1982), 1–48.

—— 'The Geography of Florentine Monody: Caccini at Home and Abroad', *Early Music*, 9 (1981), 147–68.

—— *Instrumental Music Printed before 1600: A Bibliography* (Cambridge, Mass., 1965).

—— 'Petrarch in Naples: Notes on the Formation of Giaches de Wert's Style', in Richard Charteris (ed.), *Essays on Italian Music in the Cinquecento* (Sydney, 1990), 16–50.

—— 'Psyche's Lament: Some Music for the Medici Wedding in 1656', in Laurence Berman (ed.), *Words and Music: The Scholar's View: A Medley of Problems and Solutions Compiled in Honor of A. Tillman Merritt by Sundry Hands* (Cambridge, Mass., 1972), 1–27.

—— 'Vincenzo Galilei in Rome: His First Book of Lute Music (1563) and its Cultural Context', in Victor Coelho (ed.), *Music and Science in the Age of Galileo* (The University of Western Ontario Series in Philosophy of Science, 51; Dordrecht, 1992), 153–84.

BUKOFZER, MANFRED, *Music in the Baroque Era from Monteverdi to Bach* (New York, 1947).

BURKE, PETER, 'Conspicuous Consumption in Early Modern Italy', in his *Historical Anthropology of Early Modern Italy* (Cambridge, 1987).

—— *The Historical Anthropology of Early Modern Italy* (Cambridge, 1987).

CAIMO, POMPEO, *De calido innato libri tres* (Venice: Piutus, 1626).

—— *De nobilitate* (Udine: Schiratti, 1634).

—— *Dell'ingegno humano de' suoi segni, della sua differenza negli huomini, e nelle donne, e del suo buono indirizzo* (Venice: Brogrollo, 1629).

—— *Parallelo politico delle republiche antiche e moderne* (Padua: Tozzi, 1627).

CALUORI, ELEANOR, *The Cantatas of Luigi Rossi: Analysis and Thematic Index* (Ann Arbor, 1981).

CAMETTI, ALBERTO, 'Chi era "l'Hippolita"', cantatrice del cardinal di Montalto', *Sammelbände der Internationalen Musikgesellschaft*, 15 (1913–14), 111–23.

—— 'La scuola dei *pueri cantus* di S. Luigi dei francesi in Roma e i suoi principali allievi (1591–1623): Gregorio, Comenico e Bartolomeo Allegri, Antonio Cifra, Orazio Benevoli', *Rivista musicale italiana*, 22 (1915), 593–641.

—— 'Orazio Michi "dell'Arpa," virtuoso e compositore di musica della prima metà del Seicento', *Rivista musicale italiana*, 21 (1914), 203–71.

Cancionero musical de la Casa de Medinaceli (Siglo XVI), i: *Polifonía Profana*, ed. Miguel Querol Gavaldá (Monumentos de la Música Española, 8; Barcelona, 1949).

CARDAMONE, DONNA G., *The canzone villanesca alla napolitana and Related Forms, 1537–1570*, 2 vols. (Ann Arbor, 1981).

—— 'Madrigali a Tre et Arie Napolitane: A Typographical and Repertorial Study', *Journal of the American Musicological Society*, 35 (1982), 436–81.

CARDAMONE, DONNA G., 'The Prince of Salerno and the Dynamics of Oral Transmission in Songs of Political Exile', *Acta musicologica*, 67 (1995), 77–108.

CARDELLA, LORENZO, *Memorie storiche de' cardinali della santa romana chiesa* (Rome, 1793).

CARTER, TIM, '"An Air New and Grateful to the Ear": The Concept of *Aria* in Late Renaissance and Early Baroque Italy', *Music Analysis*, 12 (1993), 127–45.

—— 'Caccini's *Amarilli, mia bella*: Some Questions (and a Few Answers)', *Journal of the Royal Musical Association*, 113 (1988), 250–73.

—— 'A Florentine Wedding of 1608', *Acta musicologica*, 55 (1983), 89–107.

—— 'Giulio Caccini (1551–1618): New Facts, New Music', *Studi musicali*, 16 (1987), 13–32.

—— *Jacopo Peri, 1561–1633: His Life and Works* (New York, 1989).

—— 'Intriguing Laments: Sigismondo d'India, Claudio Monteverdi, and Dido *alla parmigiana* (1628)', *Journal of the American Musicological Society*, 49 (1996), 32–69.

—— *Music in Late Renaissance and Early Baroque Italy* (London, 1992).

—— 'On the Composition and Performance of Caccini's *Le nuove musiche* (1602)', *Early Music*, 12 (1984), 208–17.

CASIMIRI, RAFFAELE, *Cantori, maestri, organisti della Cappella Lateranense negli atti capitolari (sec. XV–XVII)*, ed. Laura Callegari [Hill] (Biblioteca di 'Quadrivium', Note d'Archivio: Bibliografia, biografia e storia, 6; Bologna, 1984).

—— '"Disciplina musicae" e "mastri di cappella" dopo il Concilio di Trento nei maggiori istituti ecclesiastici di Roma: Seminario Romano, Collegio Germanico, Collegio Inglese (Sec. XVI–XVII)', *Note d'archivio per la storia musicale*, 12 (1935), 1–26, 73–81; 15 (1938), 1–14, 49–64, 97–112, 145–56, 225–47.

CAVALLINI, IVANO, 'Sugli improvvisatori del Cinque-Seicento: Persistenze, nuovi repertori e qualche riconoscimento', *Recercare*, 1 (1989), 24–40.

CAVAZZINI, PATRIZIA, 'New Documents for Cardinal Alessandro Peretti Montalto's Frescoes at Bagnaia', *Burlington Magazine*, 135 (1993), 316–27.

CECCHI, PAOLO, 'Le "Cantade a voce sola" (1633) di Giovanni Felice Sances', *Rassegna veneta di studi musicali*, 5–6 (1989–90), 137–80.

CECI, GIUSEPPE, 'I feudatari napoletani alla fine del sec. XVI', *Archivio storico per le provincie napoletane*, 24 (1899), 122–38.

CELANI, ENRICO, 'I cantori della cappella pontificia nei secoli XVI–XVIII', *Rivista musicale italiana*, 14 (1907), 764–75.

—— *Una pagina di feudalismo: La signoria dei Peretti-Savelli-Sforza-Cesarini sulla contea di Celano e baronia di Pescina (1591–1806)* (Città di Castello, 1893).

CERRETO, SCIPIONE, *Della prattica musica vocale, et strumentale* (Naples: Carlino, 1601).

—— *Dell'arbore musicale* (Naples: Sottile, 1608).

CHAFE, ERIC, *Monteverdi's Tonal Language* (New York, 1992).

CHAMBERS, D. S., 'The Economic Predicament of Renaissance Cardinals', *Studies in Medieval and Renaissance History*, iii, ed. William M. Bowsky (Lincoln, Nebr., 1966), 289–311.

CHATER, JAMES, 'Luca Marenzio: New Documents, New Observations', *Music & Letters*, 64 (1983), 2–11.

—— 'Musical Patronage in Rome at the Turn of the Seventeenth Century: The Case of Cardinal Montalto', *Studi musicali*, 16 (1987), 179–227.

CLEMENTI, FILIPPO, *Il carnevale romano nelle cronache contemporanee* (Rome, 1899).

COCHRANE, ERIC, *Florence in the Forgotten Centuries, 1527–1800: A History of Florence and the Florentines in the Age of the Grand Dukes* (Chicago, 1973).

COELHO, VICTOR ANAND, 'The Manuscript Sources of Seventeenth-Century Italian Lute Music: A "Catalogue Raisonné"' (Ph.D. diss., University of California at Los Angeles, 1989).

—— 'G. G. Kapsberger in Rome, 1604–1645: New Biographical Data', *Journal of the Lute Society*, 16 (1983), 103–33.

—— *Manuscript Sources of Seventeenth-Century Italian Lute Music* (New York, 1993).

COFFIN, DAVID R., *The Villa in the Life of Renaissance Rome* (Princeton, 1979).

CONNORS, JOSEPH, and RICE, LOUISE (eds.), *Specchio di Roma Barocca: Una guida inedita del XVII secolo* (Rome, 1991).

COOK, SUSAN C., and LaMAY, THOMASIN K., *Virtuose in Italy, 1600–1640: A Reference Guide* (New York, 1984).

CORTESI, PAOLO, *De Cardinalatu* (Rome, 1510).

CRESCIMBENI, GIOVANNI MARIA, *L'istoria della basilica diaconale collegiata, e parrocchiale di S. Maria in Cosmedin di Roma* (Rome, 1715).

CRINÒ, ANNA MIRA, 'Virtuose di canto e poeti a Roma e a Firenze nella prima meta del Seicento', *Studi secenteschi*, 1 (1960), 175–93.

CROPPER, ELIZABETH, PERINI, GIOVANNA, and SOLINA, FRANCESCO (eds.), *Documentary Culture: Florence and Rome from Grand Duke Ferdinand I to Pope Alexander VII* (Bologna, 1992).

CULLEY, THOMAS D., *Jesuits and Music*, i: *A Study of the Musicians Connected with the German College in Rome during the 17th Century and of their Activities in Northern Europe* (Sources and Studies for the History of the Jesuits, 2; Rome, 1970).

D'ANCONA, ALESSANDRO, *Origini del teatro italiano* (Turin, 1891).

DeFORD, RUTH IRENE, 'The Evolution of Rhythmic Style in Italian Secular Music of the Late Sixteenth Century', *Studi musicali*, 10 (1981), 43–74.

—— 'Musical Relationships between the Italian Madrigal and Light Genres in the Sixteenth Century', *Musica disciplina*, 39 (1985), 107–68.

—— 'Ruggiero Giovannelli and the Madrigal in Rome, 1572–1599' (Ph.D. diss., Harvard University, 1975).

DELLA SETA, FABRIZIO and PIPERNO, FRANCO (eds.), *In cantu et in sermone: For Nino Pirrotta on his 80th Birthday* (Italian Medieval and Renaissance Studies of the University of Western Australia, 2; Florence, 1989).

DELUMEAU, JEAN, *Vie économique et sociale de Rome dans la secon de moitié du XVIe siècle*, 2 vols. (Paris, 1957).

DEVOTO, DANIEL, 'Encore sur "la" sarabande', *Revue de musicologie*, 50 (1964), 189–96.

DONI, GIOVANNI BATTISTA, *Annotazioni sopra il compendio de' generi e de' modi della musica* (Rome: Fei, 1640).

—— *Compendio del trattato de' generi e de' modi della musica* (Rome, 1635).

DONI, GIOVANNI BATTISTA, 'Discorso sopra la perfettione delle melodie', in his *Compendio del trattato de' generi*.

DONINGTON, GLORIA ROSE, 'The Cantatas of Carissimi' (Ph.D. diss., Yale University, 1959).

—— 'The Cantatas of Giacomo Carissimi', *Musical Quarterly*, 48 (1962), 204–15.

—— 'The Italian Cantata of the Baroque Period', in Wolf Arlt (ed.), *Gattungen der Musik in Einzeldarstellungen: Gedenkschrift Leo Schrade* (Bern, 1973), i. 655–77; repr. in *Garland Library of the History of Western Music*, ed. Rosand, *Seventeenth Century*, 241–63.

D'ONOFRIO, CESARE, 'Una grande scomparsa: Villa Montalto, la più vasta esistita entro le mura', *Capitolium*, 45/2–3 (1970), 59–63.

—— *Roma nel Seicento* (Florence, 1969).

EINSTEIN, ALFRED, 'Die Aria di Ruggiero', *Sammelbände der Internationalen Musikgesellschaft*, 13 (1911–12), 446–7.

—— *The Italian Madrigal*, trans. Alexander H. Krappe, Roger H. Sessions, and Oliver Strunk (Princeton, 1949).

—— 'Der stile nuovo auf dem Gebiet der profanen Kammermusik', in Guido Adler, *Handbuch der Musikgeschichte* (Frankfurt am Main, 1924), 370–85.

ERIG, RICHARD, and GUTMANN, VERONIKA (eds.), *Italienische Diminutionen: Die zwischen 1553 und 1638 mehrmals bearbeiteten Sätze* (Prattica musicale, 1; Zürich, 1979).

FABBRI, MARIO, GARBERO ZORZI, ELVIRA, and PETRIOLI TOFANI, ANNAMARIA, *Il luogo teatrale a Firenze: Spettacolo e musica nella Firenze medicea* (Documenti e restituzioni, 1; Milan, 1975).

FABBRI, PAOLO, POMPILIO, ANGELO, and VASSALLI, ANTONIO, 'Frescobaldi e le raccolte con composizioni a voce sola del primo Seicento', in *Girolamo Frescobaldi nel IV centenario della nascita*, ed. Durante and Fabris, 233–80.

FABRIS, DINKO, *Andrea Falconieri napoletano: Un liutista-compositore del seicento* (Rome, 1987).

—— 'L'arpa napoletana, simbolismo estetico-sonoro di uno strumento musicale del primo Seicento', in Franco Fanizza (ed.), *Modernità e coscienza estetica* (Publicazioni della Cattedra di Estetica; Naples, 1986), 211–62.

—— 'Frescobaldi e la musica in casa Bentivoglio', in *Girolamo Frescobaldi nel IV centenario della nascita*, ed. Durante and Fabris, 63–85.

FAGIOLO DELL'ARCO, MAURIZIO, *L'effimero barocco: Strutture della festa nella Roma del '600*, 2 vols. (Rome, 1977–8).

FALDI, ITALO, RÖTTGEN, HERWARTH, et al., *Il cavalier d'Arpino: Roma—Palazzo Venezia, giugno–luglio, 1973* (Rome, 1973).

FAVARA, ALBERTO, *Corpus di musiche popolari siciliane*, ed. Ottavio Tiby (Accademia di Scienze Lettere e Arti di Palermo, Supplemento agli Atti, 4; Palermo, 1957).

FELLERER, KARL GUSTAV, 'Monodie und Diminutionsmodelle', *Sborník prací filosofické fakulty Brněnské university*, Ročník 14, *Rada uměnovědná* (Brno, 1965), 79–85.

FENLON, IAIN, 'Preparations for a Princess: Florence 1588–89', in Della Seta and Piperno (eds.), *In cantu et in sermone*, 259–81.

FERAND, ERNEST T., *Die Improvisation in der Musik* (Zürich, 1938).

—— 'Improvised Vocal Counterpoint in the Late Renaissance and Early Baroque', *Annales musicologiques*, 4 (1956), 129–74.

—— ' "Sodaine and Unexpected" Music in the Renaissance', *Musical Quarterly*, 37 (1951), 10–27.

FERRETTI, M., and PASQUALI, M., 'Cronostassi critica dei legati, vicelegati e governatori di Bologna dal sec. XVI al XVII', *Atti e memorie della Deputazione di Storia Patria per le Provincie di Romagna*, NS 23 (1972), 117–301.

FILINGERIO, PLACIDO, *In funere Alexandri Peretti Card. Montalti oratio habita Romae in Templo S. Andreae Cleric. Regular. ab eodem Cardinali aedificato* (Rome: Mascardi, 1623).

FIORAVANTI BARALDI, ANNA MARIA, 'Pier Francesco Battistelli e l'impresa bentivolesca di Gualtieri in un carteggio', in *Frescobaldi e il suo tempo nel quarto centenario della nascita* (Venice, 1983), 161–72.

FORBES, JAMES, 'The Nonliturgical Vocal Music of Johannes Hieronymus Kapsberger (1580–1651)' (Ph.D. diss., University of North Carolina, 1977).

FORTUNE, NIGEL, 'A Florentine Manuscript and its Place in Italian Song', *Acta musicologica*, 23 (1951), 124–36.

—— 'Italian Secular Monody from 1600 to 1635: An Introductory Survey', *Musical Quarterly*, 39 (1953), 171–95; repr. in *Garland Library*, ed. Rosand, *Seventeenth Century*, 47–71.

—— 'Italian Secular Song from 1600 to 1635: The Origins and Development of Accompanied Monody' (Ph.D. diss., Gonville and Caius College, Cambridge, 1953).

—— 'Italian 17th-Century Singing', *Music & Letters*, 35 (1954), 206–19; repr. in *Garland Library*, ed. Rosand, *Seventeenth Century*, 72–85.

—— 'Solo Song and Cantata', in *The Age of Humanism, 1540–1630*, ed. Gerald Abraham (New Oxford History of Music, 5; Oxford, 1968), 125–217.

FRANCHI, SAVERIO, *Drammaturgia romana: Repertorio bibliografico cronologico dei testi drammatici pubblicati a Roma e nel Lazio, Secolo XVII* (Rome, 1988).

FREY, HERMANN-WALTHER, 'Das Diarium der Sixtinischen Sängerkapelle in Rom für das Jahr 1594', *Analecta musicologica*, 14 (1974), 455–505.

FUCILLA, JOSEPH, ' "Cupid and the Bee": Addenda', *Publications of the Modern Language Association*, 58 (1943), 575–9.

GAETA BERTELÀ, GIOVANNA, and PETRIOLI TOFANI, ANNAMARIA, *Feste e apparati medicei da Cosimo I a Cosimo II* (Florence, 1969).

GALLUZZI, RIGUCCIO, *Istoria del Granducato di Toscana sotto il governo della casa Medici*, 7 vols. (Cambiagi, 1781; 2nd edn., Livorno, 1820–1).

GANDOLFI, RICCARDO, 'Lettere inedite scritte da musicisti e letterati appartenenti alla seconda metà del secolo XVI, estratte dal R. Archivio di Stato in Firenze', *Rivista musicale italiana*, 20 (1913), 527–54.

The Garland Library of the History of Western Music, ed. Ellen Rosand, v: *Baroque Music*, i: *Seventeenth Century* (New York, 1985).

GASPARI, GAETANO, *Catalogo della biblioteca del Liceo Musicale di Bologna*, 5 vols. (Bologna, 1890–1943).

GELLNER, E., 'Patrons and Clients', in E. Gellner and J. Waterbury (eds.), *Patrons and Clients in Mediterranean Societies* (London, 1977), 1–20.

GHISI, FEDERICO, 'An Early Seventeenth Century Manuscript with Unpublished Monodic Music by Peri, Giulio Romano and Marco da Gagliano', *Acta musicologica*, 20 (1948), 46–60.

GHISLANZONI, ALBERTO, *Luigi Rossi (Aloysius de Rubeis): Biografia e analisi delle composizioni* (Milan, 1954).

GIANTURCO, CAROLYN, 'Nuove considerazioni su *il tedio del recitativo* delle prime opere romane', *Rivista italiana di musicologia*, 18 (1982), 212–39.

GILIBERTI, VINCENZIO, *Montalto: Orazione . . . nel funerale d'Alessandro Peretti Cardinal Montalto Vicecancelliero di S. Chiesa* (Rome: Mascardi, 1623).

Girolamo Frescobaldi nel IV centenario della nascita: Atti del convegno internazionale di studi (Ferrara, 9–14 settembre 1983), ed. Sergio Durante and Dinko Fabris (Quaderni della Rivista italiana di musicologia, 10; Florence, 1986).

GIUSTINIANI, VINCENZO, *Discorso sopra la musica* [1628], in Angelo Solerti, *Le origini del melodramma: Testimonianze dei contemporanei* (Turin, 1903), 98–128; trans. Carol MacClintock (American Institute of Musicology, Musicological Studies and Documents, 9; Rome, 1962), 63–80.

GNOLI, DOMENICO, *Vittoria Accoramboni: Storia del secolo XVI* (Florence, 1870).

GODT, IRVING, 'A Monteverdi Source Reappears: The "Grilanda" of F. M. Fucci', *Music & Letters*, 60 (1979), 429–39.

GOFFMAN, ERVING, *The Presentation of Self in Everyday Life* (rev. edn., New York, 1959).

GOMBOSI, OTTO, 'Italia, patria del basso ostinato', *Rassegna musicale*, 7 (1934), 14–25.

GRAFTON, ANTHONY (ed.), *Rome Reborn: The Vatican Library and Renaissance Culture* (Washington, 1993).

GREENLEE, ROBERT, '*Dispositione di voce*: Passage to Florid Singing', *Early Music*, 15 (1987), 47–55.

GUNDERSHEIMER, WERNER L., 'Patronage in the Renaissance: An Exploratory Approach', in G. F. Lytle and S. Orgel (eds.), *Patronage in the Renaissance* (Princeton, 1981), 3–23.

HAAR, JAMES, 'Arie per cantar stanze ariostesche', in Maria Antonella Balsano (ed.), *L'Ariosto, la musica, i musicisti* (Florence, 1981), 31–46.

—— *Essays on Italian Poetry and Music in the Renaissance, 1350–1600* (Berkeley and Los Angeles, 1986).

—— 'The "Madrigale arioso": A Mid-Century Development in the Cinquecento Madrigal', *Studi musicali*, 12 (1983), 203–19.

HALE, J. R., *Florence and the Medici: The Pattern of Control* (Plymouth, 1977).

HALL, MONICA J. L., 'The "Guitarra española" of Joan Carlos Amat', *Early Music*, 6 (1978), 362–73.

HALL, STEWART, 'The Toad in the Garden: Thatcherism among the Theorists', in Cary Nelson and Lawrence Grossberg (eds.), *Marxism and the Interpretation of Culture* (Urbana, Ill., 1988), 35–57.

HAMMOND, FREDERICK, *Girolamo Frescobaldi* (Cambridge, Mass., 1983).

—— *Music & Spectacle in Baroque Rome: Barberini Patronage under Urban VIII* (New Haven, 1994).

HANNING, BARBARA RUSSANO, *Of Poetry and Music's Power: Humanism and the Creation of Opera* (Studies in Musicology, 13; Ann Arbor, 1980).

HARTMANN, ARNOLD, Jr., 'Battista Guarini and *Il Pastor Fido*', *Musical Quarterly*, 39 (1953), 415–25.

HASKELL, FRANCIS, *Patrons and Painter: A Study in the Relations between Italian Art and Society in the Age of the Baroque* (New York, 1971).

HATHAWAY, BAXTER, *The Age of Criticism: The Late Renaissance in Italy* (Westport, Conn., 1962).

HERRICK, MARVIN T., *Tragicomedy: Its Origin and Development in Italy, France, and England* (Urbana, Ill., 1962).

HILL, JOHN WALTER, 'Florence: Musical Spectacle and Drama, 1570–1650', in Curtis Price (ed.), *The Early Baroque Era from the Late 16th Century to the 1660s* (Music and Society, ed. Stanley Sadie; New York, 1993), 121–45.

—— 'Frescobaldi's *Arie* and the Musical Circle around Cardinal Montalto', in Alexander Silbiger (ed.), *Frescobaldi Studies* (Durham, NC, 1987), 157–94; also in Italian as 'Le *Arie* di Frescobaldi e la cerchia musicale del cardinal Montalto', in *Girolamo Frescobaldi*, ed. Durante and Fabris, 215–32.

—— 'Guarini's Last Stage Work', in *Atti del XIV Congresso della Società Internazionale di Musicologia: Trasmissione e recezione delle forme di cultura musicale*, iii: *Free Papers* (Turin, 1990), 131–54.

—— 'Pellegrino Mutij e la nascente monodia in Polonia', *Quadrivium*, NS 1 (1990), 7–18.

—— 'Realized Continuo Accompaniments from Florence, c. 1600', *Early Music*, 11 (1983), 194–208.

—— 'Training a Singer for *Musica Recitativa* in Early Seventeenth-Century Italy: The Case of Baldassare', in Siegfried Gmeinwieser, David Hiley, and Jörg Riedlbauer (eds.), *Musicologica Humana: Festschrift for Warren and Ursula Kirkendale* (Florence, 1994), 345–57.

HITCHCOCK, H. Wiley, 'Caccini's "Other" *Nuove musiche*', *Journal of the American Musicological Society*, 27 (1974), 438–60.

—— 'Vocal Ornamentation in Caccini's *Nuove Musiche*', *Musical Quarterly*, 56 (1970), 389–404.

HOLZER, ROBERT RAU, 'Music and Poetry in Seventeenth-Century Rome: Settings of the Canzonetta and Cantata Texts of Francesco Balducci, Domenico Benigni, Francesco Melosio, and Antonio Abati' (Ph.D. diss., University of Pennsylvania, 1990).

—— ' "Sono d'altro garbo . . . le canzonette che si cantano oggi": Pietro della Valle on Music and Modernity in the Seventeenth Century', *Studi musicali*, 20 (1991), 253–306.

HORSLEY, IMOGENE, 'Monteverdi's Use of Borrowed Material in "Sfogava con le stelle" ', *Music & Letters*, 59 (1978), 316–28.

HUDSON, RICHARD, 'The Concept of Mode in Italian Guitar Music during the First Half of the 17th Century', *Acta musicologica*, 42 (1970), 163–83.

—— *The Folia, the Saraband, the Passacaglia, and the Chaconne*, ii: *The Saraband* (Musicological Studies and Documents, 35; Neuhausen-Stuttgart, 1982).

HUTTON, JAMES, 'Cupid and the Bee', *Publications of the Modern Language Association*, 56 (1941), 1036–58.

JACKSON, ROLAND (ed.), *Neapolitan Keyboard Composers, circa 1600* (Corpus of Early Keyboard Music, 24; Rome, 1967).

JOHNSON, MARGARET F., 'Agazzari's *Eumelio*, a "Dramma Pastorale" ', *Musical Quarterly*, 57 (1971), 491–505.

JOYCE, JOHN JOSEPH, 'The Monodies of Sigismondo d'India' (Ph.D. diss., Tulane University, 1975).

KAST, PAUL, 'Biographische Notizen zu römischen Musikern des 17. Jahrhunderts', *Analecta musicologica*, 1 (1963), 38–69.

KASTNER, MACARIO SANTIAGO, *Antonio und Hernando de Cabezón: Eine Chronik dargestellt am Leben zweier Generationen von Organisten* (Tutzing, 1977).

KIRKENDALE, WARREN, *L'Aria di Fiorenza, id est il Ballo del Gran Duca* (Florence, 1972).

—— *The Court Musicians in Florence during the Principate of the Medici with a Reconstruction of the Artistic Establishment* (Historiae musicae cultores biblioteca, 61; Florence, 1993).

—— 'Zur Biographie des ersten Orfeo, Francesco Rasi', in *Claudio Monteverdi: Festschrift Reinhold Hammerstein zum 70. Geburtstag* (Laaber, 1986), 297–335.

LARSON, KEITH AUSTIN, 'Condizione sociale dei musicisti e dei loro committenti nella Napoli del Cinque e Seicento', in Lorenzo Bianconi and Renato Bossa (eds.), *Musica e cultura a Napoli dal XV al XIX secolo* (Quaderni della Rivista italiana di musicologia, 9; Florence, 1983), 61–77.

—— 'The Unaccompanied Madrigal in Naples from 1536 to 1654' (Ph.D. diss., Harvard University, 1985).

LAVIN, IRVING, 'Bernini's Bust of Cardinal Montalto', *Burlington Magazine*, 127 (1985), 32–8.

LAZZARO-BRUNO, CLAUDIA, 'The Villa Lante at Bagnaia' (Ph.D. diss., Princeton University, 1974).

LEDBETTER, STEVEN, 'Luca Marenzio: New Biographical Findings' (Ph.D. diss., New York University, 1971).

LEOPOLD, SILKE, 'Chiabrera und die Monodie: Die Entwicklung der Arie', *Studi musicali*, 10 (1981), 75–106.

—— *Stefano Landi: Beiträge zur Biographie—Untersuchungen zur weltlichen und geistlichen Vokalmusik* (Hamburger Beiträge zur Musikwissenschaft, 17; Hamburg, 1976).

LEVIN, HARRY, *The Myth of the Golden Age in the Renaissance* (Bloomington, Ind., 1969).

LIONNET, JEAN, 'André Maugars: Risposta data a un curioso sul sentimento della musica d'Italia', *Nuova rivista musicale à italiana*, 19 (1985), 681–705.

—— 'Quelques aspects de la vie musicale à Saint-Louis-des-Français de Giovanni Bernardino Nanino à Alessandro Melani (1591–1698)', in *Les Fondations nationales dans la Rome pontificale* (Collection de l'école française de Rome, 52; Rome, 1981), 333–75.

—— 'The Borghese Family and Music during the First Half of the Seventeenth Century', *Music & Letters*, 74 (1993), 519–29.

LIPPMANN, FRIEDRICH, 'Giovanni de Macque fra Roma e Napoli: Nuovi documenti', *Rivista italiana di musicologia*, 13 (1978), 243–79.

Litta, Pompeo, *Famiglie celebri italiane*, seconda serie, ii (Naples, 1913).

MacClintock, Carol (ed.), *The Bottegari Lutebook* (The Wellesley Edition, 8; Wellesley, 1965).

—— *Giaches de Wert (1535–1596): Life and Works* (Musicological Studies and Documents, 17; [Rome], 1966).

Madonna, Maria Luisa (ed.), *Roma di Sisto V: Le arti e la cultura* (Rome, 1993).

Mamone, Sara, *Il teatro nella Firenze medicea* (Problemi di storia dello spettacolo, 9; Milan, 1981).

Marcon, Giulio, Maddalo, Silvia, and Marcolini, Giuliana, 'Per una storia dell'esodo del patrimonio artistico ferrarese a Roma', in *Frescobaldi e il suo tempo nel quarto centenario della nascita* (Venice, 1983), 93–112.

Marsolo, Pietro Maria, *Madrigali a quattro voci sulle monodie di Giulio Caccini e d'altri autori, e altre opere*, ed. Lorenzo Bianconi (Musiche rinascimentali siciliane, 4; Rome, 1973).

Martini, Giovanni Battista, *Storia della musica*, i (Bologna: Volpe, 1757).

Masciotta, Giambattista, *Il Molise dalle origini ai nostri giorni*, iii: *Il circondario d'Isernia* (Cava dei Tirreni, 1952).

Masera, Maria Giovanni, 'Alcune lettere inedite di Francesca Caccini', *Rassegna musicale*, 4 (1940), 173–82.

Massimo, Camillo Vittorio Emanuele, *Notizie istoriche della Villa Massimo alle Terme Diocleziane* (Rome, 1836).

Maze, Nancy Cole, 'Tenbury Ms 1018: A Key to Caccini's Art of Embellishment', *Journal of the American Musicological Society*, 9 (1956), 61–3.

Mersenne, Marin, *Harmonie universelle* (Paris, 1636–7).

Miehling, Klaus, *Das Tempo in der Musik von Barock und Vorklassik: Die Antwort der Quellen auf ein umstrittenes Thema* (Wilhelmshaven, 1993).

Mirollo, James, *The Poet of the Marvelous: Giambattista Marino* (New York, 1965).

Molho, Anthony, 'Patronage and the State in Early Modern Italy', in Antoni Maczak (ed.), *Klientelsysteme im Europa der frühen Neuzeit* (Munich, 1988), 233–42.

Molinari, Cesare, *Le nozze degli dèi: Un saggio sul grande spettacolo italiano nel Seicento* (Rome, 1968).

Montella, Giovanni Domenico, *Il settimo libro de' madrigali a cinque voci*, ed. Iole Di Gregorio (Musiche del rinascimento italiano, 1; Florence, 1990).

Monteverdi, Claudio, *Lettere, dediche, e prefazioni*, ed. Domenico de' Paoli (Rome, 1973).

Morelli, Arnaldo, *Catalogo del fondo musicale della Biblioteca Nazionale Centrale Vittorio Emanuele II di Roma* (Rome, 1989).

—— *Il tempio armonico: Musica nell'oratorio dei Filippini in Roma (1575–1705)* = *Analecta musicologica*, 27 (Laaber, 1991).

Moroni, Gaetano, *Dizionario di erudizione storico-ecclesiastica*, 103 vols. (Venice, 1840–61).

Murata, Margaret, 'La cantata romana fra mecenatismo e collezionismo', in Claudio Annibaldi (ed.), *La musica e il mondo: Mecenatismo e committenza musicale in Italia tra Quattro e Settecento* (Bologna, 1993), 253–66.

MURATA, MARGARET, 'Classical Tragedy in the History of Early Opera in Rome', *Early Music History*, 4 (1984), 101–34.

—— *Operas for the Papal Court, 1631–1668* (Ann Arbor, 1981).

—— 'The Recitative Soliloquy', *Journal of the American Musicological Society*, 32 (1979), 45–73.

NAGLER, ALOIS MARIA, *Theatre Festivals of the Medici, 1539–1637* (New Haven, 1964).

NETTL, PAUL, 'Über ein handschriftliches Sammelwerk von Gesängen italienischer Früh-monodie', *Zeitschrift für Musikwissenschaft*, 2 (1919–20), 83–93.

NEWCOMB, ANTHONY, 'Girolamo Frescobaldi, 1608–1615: A Documentary Study in which Information also Appears Concerning Giulio and Settimia Caccini, the Brothers Piccinini, Stefano Landi, and Ippolita Recupito', *Annales musicologiques*, 7 (1964–77), 111–58.

—— *The Madrigal at Ferrara, 1579–1597* (Princeton, 1980).

NORBERG-SCHULZ, CHRISTIAN, *Meaning in Western Architecture* (New York, 1980).

NUTTER, DAVID, 'Gli "altri intermezzi" del Guarini in una descrizione del 1587', *Studi e problemi di critica testuale*, 30 (1985), 51–64.

ORBAAN, J. A. F., *Documenti sul barocco in Roma* (Rome, 1920).

—— 'La Roma di Sisto V negli *avvisi*', *Archivio della R. Società Romana di storia patria*, 33 (1910), 277–312.

O'REGAN, NOEL, *Institutional Patronage in Post-Tridentine Rome: Music at Santissima Trinità dei Pellegrini 1550–1650* (Royal Musical Association Monographs, 7; London, 1996).

ORTIZ, DIEGO, *Trattado de glosas sobre clausulas y otros generos de puntos en la musica de violones* (Rome: Dorico, 1553).

OSSI, MASSIMO, 'Claudio Monteverdi's *Ordine novo, bello et gustevole*: The Canzonetta as Dramatic Module and Formal Archetype', *Journal of the American Musicological Society*, 45 (1992), 261–304.

OSTHOFF, WOLFGANG, *Theatergesang und darstellende Musik in der italienischen Renaissance (15. und 16. Jahrhundert)* (Tutzing, 1969).

PALISCA, CLAUDE V., 'The Alterati of Florence, Pioneers in the Theory of Dramatic Music', in *New Looks at Italian Opera: Essays in Honor of Donald J. Grout* (Ithaca, NY, 1968), 9–38; repr. in Palisca, *Studies in the History of Italian Music and Music Theory*, 408–31.

—— 'The "Camerata Fiorentina": A Reappraisal', *Studi musicali*, 1 (1972), 203–36; repr. in *The Garland Library of the History of Western Music*, ed. Ellen Rosand, xi: *Opera*, i: *Up to Mozart* (New York, 1985), 45–80.

—— 'The First Performance of "Euridice"', in *Queens College Twenty-fifth Anniversary Festschrift (1937–1962)* (Flushing, NY, 1964), 1–23; repr. in Palisca, *Studies*, 432–51.

—— 'Peri and the Theory of Recitative', *Studies in Music*, 15 (1981), 51–61; repr. in Palisca, *Studies*, 452–66.

—— *Studies in the History of Italian Music and Music Theory* (Oxford, 1994).

—— 'Vincenzo Galilei and Some Links between "Pseudo-Monody" and Monody', *Musical Quarterly*, 46 (1960), 344–60; repr. in Palisca, *Studies*, 346–63.

—— 'Vincenzo Galilei's Arrangements for Voice and Lute', in Gustave Reese and

Robert J. Snow (eds.), *Essays in Musicology in Honor of Dragan Plamenac on His 70th Birthday* (Pittsburgh, 1969), 207–32; repr. in Palisca, *Studies*, 364–88.

PANNELLA, LINA, 'Caccini, Francesca', *Dizionario biografico degli italiani*, 16 (Rome, 1973), 19–23.

PARADISO, ROMOLO, *Copia d'una lettera del Sig. Romolo Paradiso con quale dà avviso dell'apparato, e grandezza, con che si è rappresentato il festino dell'Eccellentiss. Sig. Principe Peretti* (Rome: Girolamo Discepolo, 1614).

PARISI, SUSAN, 'Ducal Patronage of Music in Mantua, 1587–1627: An Archival Study' (Ph.D. diss., University of Illinois, 1989).

PASTOR, LUDWIG VON, *Geschichte der Päpste seit dem Ausgang des Mittelalters*, 40 vols. (Freiburg im Breisgau, 1886–9).

—— *The History of the Popes from the Close of the Middle Ages*, trans. Dom Ernest Fraf *et al.*, 40 vols. (London, 1923–53).

PIRROTTA, NINO, 'New Glimpses of an Unwritten Tradition', in Laurence Berman (ed.), *Words and Music: The Scholar's View* (Cambridge, Mass., 1972), 271–91.

—— 'Temperaments and Tendencies in the Florentine Camerata', *Musical Quarterly*, 40 (1954), 169–89.

—— and POVOLEDO, ELENA, *Li due Orfei: Da Poliziano a Monteverdi* (Turin, 1969; 2nd edn., 1975); English trans. as *Music and Theatre from Poliziano to Monteverdi*, trans. Karen Eales (Cambridge Studies in Music; Cambridge, 1982).

PISTOLESI, FRANCESCO (ed.), *La prima biografia autentica di Papa Sisto V scritta dall'Anonimo della Biblioteca Ferraioli di Roma* (Montalto, 1925).

PLAYFORD, JOHN, *Introduction to the Skill of Musick* (rev. edn., London, 1694).

PORTER, WILLIAM VERNON, 'A Central Source of Early Monody: Brussels, Conservatory 704', *Studi musicali*, 12 (1983), 239–79; 13 (1984), 139–67.

—— 'The Origins of the Baroque Solo Song: A Study of Italian Manuscripts and Prints from 1590–1610' (Ph.D. diss., Yale University, 1962).

PRUNIÈRES, HENRI, 'The Italian Cantata of the XVII Century', *Music & Letters*, 7 (1926), 38–48, 120–32.

—— 'Notes sur la vie de Luigi Rossi', *Sammelbände der Internationalen Musikgesellschaft*, 12 (1910–11), 12–16.

QUAST, MATTHIAS, *Die Villa Montalto in Rom: Entstehung und Gestalt im Cinquecento* (Tuduv-Studien, Reihe Kunstgeschichte, 45; Munich, 1991).

RACEK, JAN, 'Die italienische begleitete Monodie und das Problem der Entwicklung der italienischen Solokantate', in *Liber amicorum Charles van den Borren* (Antwerp, 1964), 166–91.

—— *Stilprobleme der italienischen Monodie: Ein Beitrag zur Geschichte des einstimmigen Barockliedes* (Opera Universitatis Purkynianae Brunensis Facultas Philosophica, 103; Prague, 1965).

RATTI, NICOLA, *Della famiglia Sforza* (Rome: Il Salamoni, 1794).

REINER, STUART, 'Preparations in Parma—1618, 1627–28', *Music Review*, 25 (1964), 273–301.

—— 'La Vag'Angioletta (and Others)', *Analecta musicologica*, 14 (1974), 26–87.

RIEMANN, HUGO, 'Der "Basso ostinato" und die Anfänge der Kantate', *Sammelbände der Internationalen Musikgesellschaft*, 13 (1911–12), 531–43.

Romances y letras a tres vozes, ed. Miguel Querol Gavaldá (Monumentos de la música española, 18; Barcelona, 1956).

ROSE, GLORIA, *see* Donington, Gloria Rose.

ROSSI, FRANCO, *I manoscritti del Fondo Torrefranca del Conservatorio Benedetto Marcello: Catalogo per autori* (Historiae musicae cultores, 45; Florence, 1986).

ROSSI, VITTORIO, *Battista Guarini ed Il pastor fido: Studio biografico-critico* (Turin, 1886).

ROTONDI, JOSEPH EMILIO, 'Literary and Musical Aspects of Roman Opera, 1600–1650' (Ph.D. diss., University of Pennsylvania, 1959).

RÖTTGEN, HERWARTH (ed.), *Il Cavalier d'Arpino: Roma, Palazzo Venezia, giugno–luglio 1973* (Rome, 1973).

SALERNO, LUIGI, 'The Picture Gallery of Vincenzo Giustiniani', *Burlington Magazine*, 102 (1960), 21–7, 93–106, 135–48.

SALVADORI, ANDREA, *Le poesie* (Rome: Ercole, 1668).

SCHIAVO, ARMANDO, *Il Palazzo della Cancellaria* (Rome 1964).

SCHLEIER, ERICH, 'Ancora su Antonio Caracci e il ciclo di Alessandro Magno per il cardinal Montalto', *Paragone—Arte*, 32/381 (Nov. 1981), 10–25.

—— 'Domenichino, Lanfranco, Albani, and Cardinal Montalto's Alexander Cycle', *Art Bulletin*, 50 (1968), 188–93.

—— 'Le "storie di Alessandro Magno" del Cardinale Montalto', *Arte illustrata*, 5 (1972), 310–20.

SCHMIDL, CARLO, *Dizionario universale dei musicisti* (Milan, 1937).

SCHMITZ, EUGEN, *Geschichte der Kantate und des geistliche Konzerts*, i: *Geschichte der weltlichen Solokantate* (2nd edn., Leipzig, 1955).

SOLERTI, ANGELO, 'Laura Guidiccioni ed Emilio de' Cavalieri (i primi tentativi del melodramma)', *Rivista musicale italiana*, 9 (1902), 797–829.

—— *Musica, ballo e drammatica alla corte medicea dal 1600 al 1637* (Florence, 1905).

—— *Le origini del melodramma: Testimonianze dei contemporanei* (Turin, 1903).

SOUTHORN, JANET, *Power and Display in the Seventeenth Century: The Arts and their Patrons in Modena and Ferrara* (Cambridge, 1988).

SPEZZAFERRO, LUIGI, 'La cultura del cardinal Del Monte e il primo tempo del Caravaggio', *Storia dell'arte*, 9–10 (1971), 57–92.

SPOHR, HELGA, 'Studien zur italienischen Tanzkomposition um 1600' (Ph.D. diss., Albert-Ludwigs-Universität zu Freiburg im Breisgau, 1956).

STEIN, LOUISE K., 'Accompaniment and Continuo in Spanish Baroque Music', in *España en la música de occidente: Actas del congresso internacionale* (Madrid, 1987), ii. 357–70.

—— *Songs of Mortals, Dialogues of the Gods: Music and Theatre in Seventeenth-Century Spain* (Oxford, 1993).

STERNFELD, FREDERICK, 'The First Printed Opera Libretto', *Music & Letters*, 59 (1978), 121–38.

STRONG, ROY, *Art and Power: Renaissance Festivals, 1450–1650* (Berkeley and Los Angeles, 1984).

TAGLIAVINI, LUIGI FERDINANDO, 'Il Ballo di Mantova, ovvero "Fuggi, fuggi da questo cielo," ovvero "Cecilia," ovvero . . .', in Bernhard Hangartner and Urs Fischer (eds.), *Max Lütolf zum 60. Geburtstag: Festschrift* (Basle, 1994), 135–75.

TESTI, FLAVIO, *La musica italiana nel Seicento*, 2 vols. (Milan, 1970–2).

TOESCA, ILARIA, 'Note sulla storia del Palazzo Giustiniani a San Luigi dei Francesci', *Bollettino d'arte*, 42 (1957), 296–308.

TOMLINSON, GARY, *Monteverdi and the End of the Renaissance* (Oxford, 1987).

TOPPI, NICOLÒ, *Biblioteca napoletana* (Naples: Bulifon, 1678).

TORREFRANCA, FAUSTO, 'Il lamento di Erminia di Claudio Monteverdi', *Inedito: Quaderno musicale*, 2 (1944), 31–42; supplement, 1–8.

TREND, JOHN BRANDE, *The Music of Spanish History to 1600* (London, 1926).

TYLER, JAMES, *The Early Guitar: A History and Handbook* (Early Music Series, 4; Oxford, 1980).

UGHI, LUIGI, *Dizionario storico degli uomini illustri ferraresi* (Ferrara, 1804).

VALTIERI, SIMONETTA, *La basilica di S. Lorenzo in Damaso nel Palazzo della Cancellaria a Roma attraverso il suo archivio ritenuto scomparso* (Rome, 1984).

VOGEL, EMIL, 'Marco da Gagliano: Zur Geschichte des florentiner Musiklebens von 1570–1650', *Vierteljahrsschrift für Musikwissenschaft*, 5 (1889), 396–442, 509–68.

VOLPE, CARLO, 'Altre notizie per la storia di Alessandro del cardinal Montalto', *Paragone—Arte*, 28/333 (Nov. 1977), 3–7, 93–5.

WADDY, PATRICIA, *Seventeenth-Century Roman Palaces: Use and the Art of the Plan* (New York, 1990).

WALKER, D. P. (ed.), *Les Fêtes du mariage de Ferdinand de Médicis et de Christine de Lorraine*, i: *Musique des intermèdes de 'La Pellegrina'* (Paris, 1963).

WAŹBIŃSKI, ZYGMUNT, *Il cardinale Francesco Maria Del Monte, 1549–1626* (Florence, 1994).

WEIL-GARRIS, KATHLEEN, and D'AMICO, JOHN F., 'The Renaissance Cardinal's Ideal Palace: A Chapter from Cortesi's De Cardinalatu', *Memoirs of the American Academy in Rome*, 35: *Studies in Italian Art History*, 1: *Studies in Italian Art and Architecture, 15th through 18th Centuries*, ed. Henry A. Millon (Rome, 1980), 45–123.

WEISSMAN, RONALD, 'Taking Patronage Seriously: Mediterranean Values and Renaissance Society', in F. W. Kent and Patricia Simons (eds.), *Patronage, Art, and Society in Renaissance Italy* (Oxford, 1987), 25–45.

WHENHAM, JOHN, *Duet and Dialogue in the Age of Monteverdi* (Ann Arbor, 1982).

WILLIAMSON, EDWARD, *Bernardo Tasso* (Rome, 1951).

WILLIER, STEPHEN, 'Rhythmic Variants in Early Manuscript Versions of Caccini's Monodies', *Journal of the American Musicological Society*, 36 (1983), 481–97.

ZACOUR, NORMAN P., and HIRSCH, RUDOLF, *Catalog of the Manuscripts in the Libraries of the University of Pennsylvania to 1800* (Philadelphia, 1965).

ZORZI, LUDOVICO, 'Introduzione', in Mario Fabbri *et al.*, *Il luogo teatrale a Firenze*.

—— *Il potere e lo spazio: La scena del principe* (Florence, 1980).

—— *Il teatro e la città* (Turin, 1977).

INDEX OF COMPOSITIONS

GENERAL INDEX